THE LIMITS OF ANCIENT BIOGRAPHY

THE LIMITS OF ANCIENT BIOGRAPHY

Editors

Brian McGing

and

Judith Mossman

Contributors

Ewen Bowie, Richard Burridge, John Dillon, Mark Edwards,
Sean Freyne, Noreen Humble, Elizabeth Irwin, Jason König,
Andrew Mayes, Brian McGing, John Moles, Judith Mossman,
Christopher Pelling, Alexia Petsalis-Diomidis,
Zuleika Rodgers, Keith Sidwell, Simon Swain, Justin Taylor,
Michael Trapp, Tim Whitmarsh, Alexei Zadorojnyi

The Classical Press of Wales

First published in 2006 by
The Classical Press of Wales
15 Rosehill Terrace, Swansea SA1 6JN
Tel: +44 (0)1792 458397
Fax: +44 (0)1792 464067
www.classicalpressofwales.co.uk

Distributor in the United States of America:
The David Brown Book Co.
PO Box 511, Oakville, CT 06779
Tel: +1 (860) 945–9329
Fax: +1 (860) 945–9468

ISBN 1–905125–12–7

A catalogue record for this book is available from the British Library

Typeset by Ernest and Andrew Buckley, Clunton, Shropshire
Printed and bound in the UK by Gomer Press, Llandysul, Ceredigion, Wales

---

The Classical Press of Wales, an independent venture, was founded in 1993, initially to support the work of classicists and ancient historians in Wales and their collaborators from further afield. More recently it has published work initiated by scholars internationally. While retaining a special loyalty to Wales and the Celtic countries, the Press welcomes scholarly contributions from all parts of the world.

The symbol of the Press is the Red Kite. This bird, once widespread in Britain, was reduced by 1905 to some five individuals confined to a small area known as 'The Desert of Wales' – the upper Tywi valley. Geneticists report that the stock was saved from terminal inbreeding by the arrival of one stray female bird from Germany. After much careful protection, the Red Kite now thrives – in Wales and beyond.

CONTENTS

PREFACE

This volume had its genesis in a biography workshop organized (splendidly) by Judith Mossman, and held at All Hallows College, Dublin in September 2001. The workshop itself took place under the aegis, and with the financial support, of the Programme for Mediterranean and Near Eastern Studies at Trinity College Dublin, a joint research project of the Schools of Classics and of Hebrew, Biblical and Theological Studies (latterly renamed Religions and Theology). Started in 1999, the project seeks to study diverse aspects of the cultural encounter in the ancient world between east and west. We acknowledge with gratitude the generous funding received under the Irish government's Programme for Research in Third Level Institutions, efficiently administered by the Higher Education Authority. Our title echoes that of C.S. Kraus (ed.) *The Limits of Historiography* (Leiden 1999). We hope the editor of that excellent volume will regard our imitation of her title as a form of flattery rather than of competition.

B. McG.

INTRODUCTION

Brian McGing and *Judith Mossman*

'There are three rules for writing biography, but unfortunately no one knows what they are.' This attractive, but somewhat suspect, 'quotation'[1] does illustrate well just how slippery the term 'biography' is. And a quick look at the shelves of a modern bookshop – interestingly in the history, not biography, section – turns up two examples very much on the frontiers of the land we probably think of as biography: P. Ackroyd, *London. The biography* (London 2000) and P. Lamont, *The Rise of the Indian Rope Trick. The biography of a legend* (London 2004). Neither author offers any justification for using the term biography: in his introduction, Ackroyd compares London to a body, which seems to be his reason for calling it a biography (if it is alive, you can write a biography of it?), but Lamont actually says he is writing history.[2] Clearly, the word 'biography' in a title sells, and not just in the publicity shots that masquerade as biographies of film, football or pop stars. A random selection from a catalogue search reveals the following biographical subjects: a country church, a germ, a nation, a silver fox, a tree, a Victorian village, bric-à-brac, the constitution of the United States, the English language.[3] In many cases use of the term is purely meretricious (or, more kindly, metaphorical) and means little more than 'the story of'; and the story does not even need to have come to an end. But the suggestion that the biographical form and techniques used to analyse and present the life of a person might profitably be transferred to tell the story of something other than a person, can lead in interesting literary directions. Virginia Woolf's perfectly structured biography of Elizabeth Browning's dog, Flush, is a brilliant parody of Lytton Strachey's biographical style.[4] Stretching the genre considerably further is Mark Kurlansky's study, *Cod. A biography of the fish that changed the world* (New York 1997). While it would be easy to argue that this is not really a biography at all, the author does consciously exploit biographical techniques and conventions, and there is a strong sense of moving from birth through life to the death (to all intents and purposes) of the cod industry. The same biographical movement, although perhaps more artificially constructed, is to be found in Jack Miles, *God. A biography* (New York 1995), which is a study of the literary figure of God as presented in the Hebrew Bible. In order to have God moving from action to speech to silence (a sort of death) Miles has to use the Hebrew Bible rather than the Old Testament (which has the prophets at the end rather than in the middle). Although the attempt to present God as moving from vigorous creator to a sort of silent and eternal old age is perhaps not entirely successful, this is something close to a biography in its examination of the deeds, character and personality of God.

If the genre-bending, and indeed genre-busting, world of modern writing takes us beyond the limits of what we usually think of as biography, what exactly biography was in the ancient world, and how it was written, are equally slippery concepts and equally subject to challenge: not least because of the methodological difficulty of using genre-theory to discuss ancient prose writing which is not oratory.[5] Of course that has not prevented people from trying to define ancient biography, to trace its origins, or indeed to identify texts which challenge the notional boundaries of their supposed genre. Many of these attempts have been very fruitful, but some have suffered from the adoption of too strict a notion of what a genre might be or mean; even some recent work has tended to view exceptional texts as 'bad' examples of biography, or perhaps as 'not' biography.[6] We need a more sophisticated approach than that, and yet the alternative gambit of stating that it does not matter or that there is no real genre of ancient biography will hardly do either: some ancient biographers, after all, were very clear indeed that they were writing not history but lives,[7] and it is evidently constructive to try to discern when and where texts are innovating, renewing and playing with expectations of their readers, which are inevitably partly influenced by generic character-istics.[8] Edwards has suggested that it may be preferable not to strive to define a genre of biography, but to think instead in terms of 'the biographical' and recognize it not as a genre but as a trait present in a variety of texts.[9] Yet when a reader begins a text which is entitled 'A Life of...' he or she inevitably has some generically-inspired expectations which are more precise than a concept of 'the biographical' alone conveys. Edwards' cautionary note was welcome, but may be too cautious, as Pelling argues, using the approach of Dubrow, who sees the reader approaching the text with a question which is then provision-ally answered:[10] what if this work is a biography? Then probably it will begin somewhere near the birth of the subject and end somewhere near his or her death, and will include information about his or her actions and characteristics – but perhaps this text will be interestingly different... Recent work on the concept of genre, while it recognizes generic essentialism to some degree, lays more emphasis on generic experimentation, the power of texts simultaneously to react to and to reinvent genres; this is surely right, and seems an approach particularly suited to the complexities of a 'messy' genre like biography.[11]

Whatever can or cannot be said about the genre of ancient biography, one thing is clear: as Momigliano showed, it was not called *biographia*.[12] Ancient biographers wrote *bioi*, lives. This nomenclature perhaps suggests that, although no definition can possibly embrace the full variety even of those ancient biographical texts which survive, leave alone those lost to us, Momigliano's basic working definition may nonetheless be useful, a benign piece of vestigial essentialism: 'an account of the life of a man from birth to death is what I call biography.'[13] His further contention that 'nobody nowadays is likely to doubt that biography is some kind of history', may raise rather more questions than it solves, though it must be admitted that it is clear that ancient biographers frequently did define themselves against history.[14] But Momigliano's extraordinarily wide-ranging attempt to trace the origins of biography quite rightly covers far more influences than just historical writing, with the result that his work, in conveying a sense of biography as fluid and versatile, has stood the test of time extremely well, even though he never does succeed in explaining why the ancients separated biography so firmly from history, in their protestations if not in their literary presentation.[15] And if for Momigliano ancient views of the genre are inexplicable, at least he notwithstanding takes them into account, always a wise proceeding. It may well be perfectly proper to project some modern categories back onto ancient texts and create categories such as 'political biography', as Geiger argues for,[16] as long as this does not lead us to criticize ancient texts for not living up to generic expectations they were never trying to fulfil; but if ancient writers of lives wished to distinguish themselves from writers of history there must be a reason for it. Strachey, in drawing a distinction between 'strictly biographical' and 'historical' points of view, remarks: 'human beings are too important to be treated as mere symptoms of the past. They have a value which is independent of any temporal processes – which is eternal, and must be felt for its own sake.' The telling of the individual's story, it is implied, the description of the individual, both call for different skills from the writing of history and allow for, even demand, a greater variation in form. But the argument cannot really run: 'people are different, therefore biographies are different in form to accommodate different lives', since it is clearly possible to write lives of the same subject which vary wildly in form. A case in point would be Plutarch's and Suetonius' *Lives* of Julius Caesar, which are very differently organized as well as very different in outlook.

Leo, indeed, famously divided biography into two types, the Plutarchean and the Suetonian,[17] the former being characterized by a straightforward chronological approach and the latter by a combination of chronology with a more thematic description of the subject. This distinction now seems much too neat, partly thanks to the discovery of other forms of biography, such as Satyrus' *Life of Euripides*, written in dialogue, but even though we may accept that Leo's use of this distinction and his account of the origins of the different types of biography were flawed, it remains useful to acknowledge that biographies even of the same individual can look very different from one another and so bring out very different facets of an individual.[18] To return to the relationship of biography and history: perhaps the real reason ancient authors made the distinction so firmly was to allow themselves freer rein, to head off criticism that information they wished to include in what they wrote was inappropriate; perhaps the problem really lay in the primacy of the Thucydidean definition of history (as against the more open Herodotean model with its happy mixture of chronology and description of individuals and nations)[19] and not in biography at all. Perhaps, to use an analogy from poetry, biography must inevitably define itself against history just as comedy must define itself against tragedy.

It may also be interesting to ask, as Swain among others does, whether there are particular historical contexts which are particularly conducive to the production of biography.[20] This is an approach which works well for late antiquity, but sometimes in relation to other societies simply founders: why on earth *isn't* fifth-century Athens teeming with political biography? The question is a recurring one: Francis Bacon, as Momigliano recorded,[21] was puzzled at the comparative paucity of biography in his own day (*The Advancement of Learning* [1605], II.ii.10): 'For lives, I do find it strange that these times have so little esteemed the virtues of the times, as that the writing of lives should be no more frequent. For although there be not many sovereign princes or absolute commanders, and that states are most collected into monarchies, yet are there many worthy personages that deserve better than dispersed report or barren elogies'; and this was echoed closely three hundred years later by Lytton Strachey: 'the art of biography seems to have fallen on evil times in England... With us, the most delicate and humane of all the branches of the art of writing has been relegated to the journeymen of letters; we do not reflect that it is perhaps as difficult to write a good life as to live one.'[22] Clearly neither an abundance of good subjects nor an abundance of good writers guarantees the production of good (or any) biography; we are thrown back on explanations involving the interests of other kinds of thinkers such as Theophrastus or Freud; or forced to look for more indirect motives for writing biography than the commemoration of famous men, such as nostalgia for the past, or polemic, or, as with the English Puritan biographies and autobiographies from the early seventeenth century, the promulgation of religion.

We have included essays on autobiography in this volume, because the autobiography[23] seems the most obvious way in which writers have toyed with the genre of biography – since, among other differences, the writing of an autobiography necessarily contracts the describable boundaries of the subject's life, and the parameters of the work, though they may begin at birth, must find a form of closure other than death.[24] Again, some have been uncomfortable with the notion of a genre of autobiography, and have preferred the concept of 'the autobiographical', especially in relation to works such as the *Anabasis*, and Caesar's *Commentarii*.

Braund remarks: 'whichever model or metaphor we use, genre always involves a balance between consistency and innovation, framework and deviation. That is why a study of genre is always concerned with boundaries. And that means that the richest texts for generic studies are not the supposed archetypes (though these we also need) but those which explore the boundaries...'[25] This volume seeks to examine some of the frontiers of ancient biography – the methodology and themes of works that are themselves on the border with, or sliding towards, other genres, or indeed of canonical biographies in their relationship with neighbouring genres, such as history or letter- and travel-writing. In pursuing this subject we also aimed to introduce some inter-cultural considerations, particularly between the Judaeo-Christian and Graeco-Roman worlds.

We start in Biblical times. ANDREW MAYES journeys widely over the Near East in his study of possible biographical models for certain parts of the Old Testament. Egyptian tomb inscriptions, with their obituaries of the deceased, bear a close resemblance to aspects of Nehemiah's memoirs; but it is in the story of the rise of David, generally seen as historical work of the highest order, that the Old Testament comes closest to biography (or to biostructuring, perhaps?).[26] This is an ideological story composed for a king who usurped the throne and needed justification for his seizure of power. An interesting parallel with thirteenth-century Hittite historiography is examined, and the mixture of myth, saga and biographical material that might have gone into the account of David's rise to power; but Mayes does not believe the story derives from anything that could be formally identified as a biography of David. If he searches for biography in history, LIZ IRWIN moves in the other direction, from biography to history: she is concerned with the inter-play of poetry, biography and history in the *Lives of the Poets*. Starting from the widespread assumption that the biographical traditions surrounding poets cannot be trusted because they derive from their own works, she sets the story of Solon's poem *Salamis*, and his association with Odysseus' behaviour in *Iliad* 2, in the wider context of the political exploitation of poetry by politicians in the Greek archaic age.

In the past, New Testament scholars and classical scholars have rarely had much to do with each other. Discussion of the genres of the Gospels, however, has led them recently into much closer dialogue. The view that the Gospels belong to the genre of Greek biography, while not universally accepted, has at least led most scholars to think that this is a fruitful line of investigation. Our section on 'Holy Lives' opens with this debate, and with a restatement by RICHARD BURRIDGE of his influential arguments in support of the Gospels as Greek biography. (He also discusses some of the consequences of this position.) The case he argues requires what is for some people too rigidly formal and anachronistic an understanding of genre, and MARK EDWARDS enunciates these serious reservations. SEAN FREYNE provides a clear summary of where the debate stands and the direction in which he thinks it might profitably go. He concentrates on Mark's Gospel and assesses in some detail two major approaches: that of Vernon Robbins, who emphasizes socio-rhetorical analysis rather then shared literary features, and makes considerable comparative play with Xenophon's *Memorabilia*; and that of Mary Anne Tolbert, who analyses authorial audience rather then genre in itself, and believes that the ancient novel provides the closest literary correspondence to Mark and the most direct access to his audience. Freyne himself proposes a sort of inter-textual reading that does not require a classificatory understanding of genre. *Luke-Acts* presents a very particular challenge to genre scholars, as it is generally thought to be a two-part, but single, work, the Gospel part of which looks something like biography, and the *Acts* part of which can convincingly be seen as history. JUSTIN TAYLOR re-examines the subject, starting with the thesis of Charles Talbert that Diogenes Laertius' *Lives and Opinions of Eminent Philosophers* provides a later, but the best, example of the sort of model that lay behind the work. In contrast to many, Taylor believes that this remains a fruitful hypothesis. Even if you think that *Acts* resembles most closely Hellenistic historiography, it contains notable biographical elements about Peter and Paul. Taylor regards the importance of their biographies in *Acts* as a way of emphasizing the unity of Jesus' succession.

JOHN MOLES moves from the genre of the Gospels to the intellectual context of early Christianity; and particularly to the controversial topic of Cynic influence. This is another area in which New Testament scholars and classicists have gone about their own business without much reference to each other, a gap Moles seeks to bridge. If the Cynic model is accepted – and Moles is inclined to accept it – it has important consequences for the whole literary representation of Jesus and early Christianity.

Philo of Alexandria is one of the great representatives of the intellectual encounter between Judaism and Hellenism. His *Life of Moses* has inhabited for a long time a shadowy world between Jewish literature and Greek. It was written in Greek, claims to be a biography, and conforms closely to the formal requirements of the genre, but, perhaps out of oversight rather than conscious decision, has never been admitted by classicists into the canon of Graeco-Roman biography, where it certainly belongs. BRIAN McGING observes the ways in which Philo manipulates the Old Testament sources to present a sanitized and Hellenized, or at least less Hebraic, Moses to what must be a wider than purely Jewish audience. Philostratus' reputation as a Greek biographer is more secure, although, as EWEN BOWIE observes, features of his eight-book *Life of Apollonius* perhaps bring it closer to romance than biography. Bowie's main concern is to examine the manner in which the sophists of Philostratus' *Lives of the Sophists*, characterized very much in terms of lust, anger, grief, youthfulness, are assimilated with the heroes of Homeric epic; and to a lesser extent, how Philostratus' dialogue *Heroicus* employs a sort of biographical 'portrait gallery format' in its depiction of Greek and Trojan heroes. JOHN DILLON takes us into the world of late antique biography, and to the borders between hagiography and biography. These later lives of holy men, he argues, are not necessarily about idealized archetypes or rhetorical convention. Eusebius and Porphyry, for instance, are not composing lives to exemplify the ideal of the holy man. Marinus' *Life of Proclus*, on the other hand, is hagiography, and 'hagiography written by a rather dull dog'. Damascius' *Life of Isidore* is a more complicated mixture.

Josephus' short work, appended to the *Antiquities*, and known as the *Life*, is the first complete extant example of an autobiography we have in Graeco-Roman literature, and forms a useful introduction to the sometimes complicated strands that go to make up literary self-portraits. ZULEIKA RODGERS outlines the many and conflicting cross-currents that went into Josephus' portrayal of himself, and studies in particular how his opponent, Justus of Tiberias, might have influenced the way he chose to represent himself in the *Vita*. How and why Aelius Aristides chose to represent himself in his work the *Sacred Tales*, is the subject of ALEXIA PETSALIS-DIOMIDIS' article. Although it is often seen as a thinly-disguised autobiography, she argues that the autobiographical elements make better sense in the context of praise of Asclepius through the personal testimony of the author; Aristides' emphasis on himself and his body has to do with Asclepian votive offerings rather than with self-absorption. The text is religious in intent and effect. Aristides' authorship is presented as an experiential and transformational process, linked closely with pilgrimage. One of the notable features of Lucian's works that appear to be, in some sense, biographies – *Demonax*, *Alexander the False Prophet* and *On the Death of Peregrinus* – is the extent to which Lucian himself is implicated in them in autobiographical mode, a mode which many scholars have regarded as providing an accurate picture of his real life. KEITH SIDWELL and NOREEN HUMBLE treat this evidence with much greater caution in their study of Lucian's *Dream*. This short work, in which he describes how he came to choose his career, is shot through with literary reminiscences. Sidwell and Humble examine what these reminiscences might contribute to the meaning of the work. 'In the end', they conclude, 'autobiography is only an ideology of the self', the more cleverly constructed, the more difficult to deconstruct. JASON KÖNIG continues this theme with his close reading of *On the Death of Peregrinus*. He argues that Lucian seeks to convey the theatricality – and difficulty in controlling this theatricality – of all biographical and autobiographical representation; the intertwining throughout the work of non-Christian and Christian biographical material, including a number of striking parallels with the crucifixion narratives of the Gospels, contributes to the same effect. Central to his case is his analysis of the relationship between Christian and non-Christian narrative, which he sees on the whole as a world of intertext, rather than of direct allusion.

Just as Julius Caesar's career broke physical and figurative boundaries, and changed the rules of his world, so too, argues CHRISTOPHER PELLING, those who wrote about him were forced to change the rules of writing and break, or bend, the genres in which they were composing. This article is about genre, in particular the subtle generic inter-play between history and biography in what Plutarch, Appian and Dio have to say on Caesar. The 'biostructuring' of Dio's imperial books can also be perceived in his coverage of Caesar, but his history has not quite turned into biography: 'there is a wider historical vision here'. So too Appian's treatment of Caesarian times has certainly pushed history to the very frontier with biography, but perhaps not quite over it. And in the reverse direction, Plutarch's *Caesar* defies, to a certain extent, the generic expectations of biography raised by his famous statement at the beginning of the *Alexander*, that he is writing not history, but *Lives*. Another genre on the frontiers of biography is travel and geographical writing, as Momigliano pointed out: indeed he identified travel writing as a particularly early form of biography or autobiography.[27] This is the subject of JUDITH MOSSMAN's contribution, which discusses the use of travel anecdotes in historical writing and in Plutarch, especially in the *Alexander*. Anecdotes of all kinds can be seen as the building blocks of biography, and Mossman seeks to discern whether there is a significant difference in the use of travel anecdotes in Plutarch from that in the extant Alexander-histories; in fact it seems that writing about travel transcends genre. Perhaps this is not particularly surprising since, as Braund notes, travel imagery is often used by ancient authors to make programmatic literary statements and can itself be a metaphor for generic innovation.[28]

One of the most controversial biographies in classical literature is Tacitus' *Agricola*. As TIM WHITMARSH points out, an earlier generation could not even agree that it was a biography, sloping, as it does, towards encomium, funeral oratory, ethnography and history. With the more fluid interpretations of genre now current, this is less problematic than the meaning of the work. How are we to read this ideologically committed, but rhetorically ambiguous, text? It is, as Whitmarsh says, 'a discomforting, challenging read; a text that seems to promise a guide to virtuous life under the principate, but stages instead the disturbing compromises involved in pursuing such a life'.

Letters are often an ingredient in biographical constructions – one thinks easily of the imperial letters in Suetonius' *Lives* – and MIKE TRAPP analyses their various functions in biography. He also investigates the ways in which they can be more actively biographical and autobiographical, especially when issued as collections, when they can become, in themselves, a sort of biography: those of Cicero, or St Paul, for instance. Slightly different are the pseudepigraphic letters, where 'the collective impression of the whole set is part of the plan from the outset'. In this connection Trapp takes the example of the *Epistles* of Chion of Heraclea, which, although usually regarded as an 'epistolary novel' or 'philosophical novel in letters', he is prepared to call an 'epistolary biography'. If extratextual letters can provide the raw material for biography, ALEXEI ZADOROJNYI looks at intratextual letters, as a theme in biographical writing, and examines the role played by literacy in the presentation of Roman emperors, and particularly the relationship between literacy and the portrayal of tyranny.

Our journey along the frontiers of biography started with the Old Testament in Egypt and the Near East, and SIMON SWAIN brings us back there at the end, to the very different world of late antiquity and classical Islam. His study is centred on the figure of Galen, along with Hippokrates one of the two medical superstars of the ancient world. In the Graeco-Roman tradition doctors scarcely generated a biographical literature, but Swain argues that biographical material about Galen did exist and that the history of medicine ascribed to John the Grammarian drew on it. Galen's reputation grew steadily, but he was nowhere more appreciated than amongst the elite of Muslim society, who produced an extensive biographical literature on him, of which Swain analyses some of the most striking features. Galen's transmission to the Islamic world represents a cultural exchange of exceptional importance.

We hope that by juxtaposing essays on works from different traditions, different times, and with different forms, we may at least have succeeded in illustrating the variety of ancient biography. It is highly unlikely that we shall have been able to define it, explain it, or pin down its extraordinary nature; but we hope that we shall have contributed to a growing tendency to take ancient biographies seriously, to read and study them more widely and more on their own terms, and to appreciate and understand them better. Like North in his preface to Plutarch's *Lives*, 'we wish you all the profit of the book'.

Notes

[1] 'Meryle Secret paraphrasing Somerset Maugham', apparently, according to Backscheider 1999, 163.

[2] On the relationship between biography and history, see further below. For ancient parallels for extending the concept of biography to cover the concept of a place or nation see the βίος Ἑλλάδος of Dicaearchus and Varro's *vita populi Romani*.

[3] Gifford 1999; Karlen 2000; Maude 1970; Seton 1915; Jackson 1979; Cobbold 1977; Cooke 1998; Mitchell 1964; Millward 1989.

[4] Woolf 1933.

[5] See Russell 1981, 148–58, Geiger 1985, 12–13; it is significant that the excellent article of Conte and Most on *genre* in OCD^3 discusses poetry throughout.

[6] So Dihle 1998, 121, though he acknowledges the difficulties of defining the genre, nonetheless rules that Isocrates' *Evagoras* does not really count as biography; and Goulet 1998, 219 evolves a three dimensional schema involving a notional ideal biography in relation to which (non-existent) text he can plot actual texts as 'déformations', or 'contaminations' (230) of this Platonic Form of a biography. See Pelling 2001, 273–6.

[7] Plutarch *Alex.* 1.1, Nepos *Praef. Pelop.* 1.1, on which see Geiger 1985, 21–2. The opening of Suetonius' *Lives of the Caesars* is lost. As Barchiesi urges (in Harrison 2001, 163), we should not regard ancient views on literary matters as mere curiosities.

[8] So it is surely meant to be felt that Plutarch's *Antony* continues for so long after Antony's demise (see Pelling in Roberts et al. 1997, 228–50). And see further below on autobiography.

[9] Edwards, in Edwards and Swain 1997, 228–34.

[10] Pelling in Kraus 1999, 328–30, quoting Dubrow 1982, 106–7.

[11] See e.g. Barchiesi in Harrison 2001, 142–63; he must also be right that 'some degree of vestigial essentialism is unavoidable in all critical positions about genre' (154). For texts constantly redefining the existing system of literary genres see 162–3.

[12] Momigliano 1993, 12.

[13] Momigliano 1993, 11.

[14] The obvious example is once again Plut. *Alex.* 1.1. More recently, Lytton Strachey's preface also describes his biographical endeavour against the background of historical writing: 'the history of the Victorian Age will never be written: we know too much about it... It is not by the direct method of a scrupulous narration that the explorer of the past can hope to depict that singular epoch. If he is wise, he will adopt a subtler strategy... He will row out over that great ocean of material, and lower down into it, here and there, a little bucket, which will bring up to the light of day some characteristic specimen, from those far depths, to be examined with a careful curiosity. Guided by these considerations... I have attempted, through the medium of biography, to present some Victorian visions to the modern eye.' This to some extent acts out Carlyle's remark in 'On History' (1838): 'History is the essence of innumerable biographies'.

[15] 1993, 6. He wisely eschews the desire to create a genealogy for biography of the kind Weinreich produced for the novel (quoted by Barchiesi in Harrison 2001, 147).

[16] Geiger 1985, 9–29; he stresses political biography's close relationship to history on 23.

[17] Leo 1901.

[18] It also remains a useful distinction to think with in terms of later biography.

[19] Not everyone is happy with Homeyer's (1962) tracing of the origins of biography

to Herodotus; but if one thinks in terms of affinities rather than origins then Herodotus indeed seems to have more biographic tendencies than Thucydides (so much less given to anecdote), despite passages like the 'potted' biographies of Pausanias and Themistocles in book I and what might almost be called the 'biostructuring' of much of the rest of the work (the term is Pelling's: see Pelling in Edwards and Swain 1997, 117–18).

[20] Swain in Edwards and Swain 1997, 1–37; see also Momigliano 1993, e.g. 33–8, 44–5, and 121, though it actually seems very odd to remark (38) that 'for Athens we can say that the cultural background as a whole did not favour the prominence of biography or autobiography'.

[21] Momigliano 1993, 45.

[22] The last clause echoes Carlyle's *Essay* on Jean Paul Friedrich Richter (1838): 'A well-written Life is almost as rare as a well-spent one.'

[23] See Momigliano 1993, 14–15 for the term.

[24] Modern novelists can play with this genre just as they can with biography: Charles Dickens plays skilfully with the autobiographical form in *David Copperfield* (1849–50), incorporating genuinely autobiographical elements into the self-conscious 'autobiography' of someone else, and pointing this up in the highly artful opening: under the chapter heading *I am born* the opening sentence runs: 'Whether I shall turn out to be the hero of my own life, or whether that station will be held by anybody else, these pages must show.'

[25] Braund in Harrison 2001, 141.

[26] See further in n. 19 above.

[27] See Momigliano 1993, 28–30 on Skylax of Caryanda.

[28] Braund in Harrison 2001, 140; she mentions this in the context of metaphors of genre culled from mapping. See e.g. Sen. *Ep.* 33.11 and indeed Barchiesi in Harrison 2001, 162: 'we still don't have a comprehensive account of imagery *about* genre, a map of generic ideology and iconology which should be able to cross, and criss-cross, the border between programmatic *écriture* and ancient criticism, between praxis and theory.' As Barchiesi himself points out, the metaphors with which genre is described are not innocent.

Bibliography

Backscheider, P.R.
  1999   *Reflections on Biography*, Oxford.
Cobbold, R.
  1977   *The Biography of a Victorian Village: Richard Cobbold's account of Wortham, Suffolk 1860*, London.
Cooke, M.
  1998   *The Biography of Bric-à-Brac: Investigating the process of consumption in Brighton's second-hand book markets*, Brighton.
Dihle, A.
  1998   'Zur antiken Biographie', in *Entretiens Hardt* 44, 119–46.
Edwards, M.J. and Swain, S. (eds.)
  1997   *Portraits: Biographical representation in the Greek and Latin literature of the Roman Empire*, Oxford.

Brian McGing and Judith Mossman

Geiger, J.
1985   *Cornelius Nepos and Ancient Political Biography*, Stuttgart.
Gifford, H.
1999   *The Biography of a Country Church: Berwick St John*, Berwick St John.
Goulet, R.
1998   'Histoire et Mystère. Les Vies de philosophes de l'antiquité tardive', in *Entretiens Hardt* 44, 217–65.
Harrison, S.J. (ed.)
2001   *Texts, Ideas, and the Classics: Scholarship, theory and classical literature*, Oxford.
Homeyer, H.
1962   'Zu den Anfängen der griechischen Biographie', *Philologus* 106, 75–85.
Jackson, J.P.
1979   *The Biography of a Tree*, London.
Karlen, A.
2000   *The Biography of a Germ*, London.
Kraus, C.S. (ed.)
1999   *The Limits of Historiography: Genre and narrative in historical texts*, Leiden.
Leo, F.
1901   *Die griechisch-römische Biographie nach ihrer literarischer Form*, Leipzig.
Maude, A.
1970   *Biography of a Nation: A short history of Britain*, London.
Millward, C.M.
1989   *A Biography of the English Language*, London.
Mitchell, B.
1964   *A Biography of the Constitution of the United States*, Oxford.
Momigliano, A.
1993   *The Development of Greek Biography*, Harvard.
Pelling, C.
2001   Review of *Entretiens Hardt* 44, *CR* 51.2, 273–6.
Roberts, D.H., Dunn, F.M. and Fowler, D. (eds.)
1997   *Classical Closure: Reading the end in Greek and Latin literature*, Princeton.
Russell, D.A.
1981   *Criticism in Antiquity*, London.
Seton, E.T.
1915   *The Biography of a Silver Fox*, London.

1

BIOGRAPHY IN THE ANCIENT WORLD: THE STORY OF THE RISE OF DAVID

Andrew D.H. Mayes

I

A strictly formal approach to the subject of biographical or autobiographical writing in the Old Testament would yield meagre enough results. Prophets occasionally make autobiographical statements in the interests of providing a setting for a revelation of the divine will (e.g. Hos. 3.1–3; Amos 7.10–17; Is. 8.1–4), and a large section of Jeremiah (chaps. 26–45) has been understood as a biography composed by his scribe Baruch, but in none of these cases is the term 'biography' or 'autobiography' justified. All of this material has its focus on the oracle, the preaching, and has a function of validating or legitimizing either the oracle or the prophet, rather than that of providing anything remotely like an account of the life of the prophet. In some cases, the nature of the material is that of prophetic legend, portraying the prophet as 'a bearer of a divine power, as bearer of a divine word, and as the instrument through whom Yahweh worked his will'.[1] While they may supply some biographical information, in the form of recording occasional words and deeds of the prophet, the purpose of these legends is not that of providing a history of the prophet.

It is only very much later, in the time of the post-exilic Nehemiah, that one encounters a literary form which has a strong affinity with an existing biographical tradition, in this case ultimately deriving from Egypt.[2] This tradition, which goes back to the Egyptian Old Kingdom, is constituted by tomb inscriptions of high officials, designed to promote the worthiness of the individual in the face of judgment after death. Reciting historical events and recording significant achievements of the individual in the service of the king, these inscriptions in form antedate and prepare the way for the development of the Egyptian royal commemorative inscriptions and Egyptian historiography; as *apologia* for lives well lived in the service of Maat, these tomb biographies also lead to the expansive catalogues of virtues finding their deposit in wisdom instructions. Tomb biographies are thus fundamental to

1

the development of Egyptian literature, and in themselves were an enduring form from the Old Kingdom to the Late Period.

In the Late Period, that is from the 22nd dynasty to the Roman period in Egypt, which covers the late monarchic, exilic and post-exilic periods in Judah, the biographies have a strong didactic tone, presenting the life of the individual as an example of piety and good conduct.[3] It is with these Late Period biographies that the Memoirs of Nehemiah (Neh. 1.1–7.7; 12.27–13.31) provide a close formal parallel.[4] The Egyptian biographies, following a short introduction, begin with the statement 'He says', followed by first person narrative; so Neh. 1.1 begins with the heading 'The words of Nehemiah, the son of Hacaliah', and continues with a first person narrative. In both cases, the subject is a high court official. In both contexts, the official has both religious and social-ethical concerns: both the restoration and renewal of buildings and religious institutions, and the protection of the weak, are the responsibilities discharged by the official. In both cases, the task undertaken is done in the service of the God, involving a divine appointment and commission. It is clear that at least by the time of Nehemiah the Egyptian biographical tradition was exercising a cultural influence in Palestine, to the extent that the Nehemiah Memoirs may be argued to be based on an Egyptian prototype.[5] The prototype is a votive inscription, set up in a temple or tomb, in which the subject presents himself as an example to his fellow-men and as justified before the gods. The Nehemiah Memoirs, while not perhaps so clearly didactic, share many of the characteristics of the Egyptian texts. So Nehemiah presents his life work as his justification before God: 'Remember for my good, O my God, all that I have done for this people' (Neh. 5.19); ' Remember me, O my God, concerning this, and wipe not out my good deeds that I have done for the house of my God and for his service' (Neh. 13.14; cf. also Neh. 13.22, 31).

II

It has been noted, however, that 'Ancient Egyptian culture never produced true "biographies" – that is, non-fictional life-stories and character studies adopting the third person, as was the case in ancient Greece and Rome... The primary intent (of Egyptian autobiographies) was to secure the maintenance of the funerary cult. In later periods autobiographies, especially those of priests, temple administrators, and religious persons, were also linked to the gods' cults and enjoyed circulation in the temples'.[6] Maybe this is rather naive about the non-fictional status of later classical biography, but this observation, together with the point that (Egyptian) autobiographies are not a fixed form but rather 'compositions that consist of different elements embedded into a common framework',[7] does provide a pretext for extending our review of Old Testament materials in order to incorporate elements of the Old Testament historiographic tradition that lie somewhere between biography and historiography. What I mean is that Old Testament historiography, as represented especially by the so-called deuteronomistic history in Deuteronomy–2 Kings, in part comprises materials which at least at first glance have some claim to the designation 'biography', and that this claim is not to be denied even if at second glance it is clear that the nature of this material as non-fictional cannot easily be upheld at every point. The text I consider here extends from 1 Samuel 16 to 2 Samuel 5 and deals with the rise of David to be king.[8]

Following Samuel's rejection of Saul as king (1 Sam. 15), the prophet is commanded by God to go to Jesse the Bethlehemite where he will find among Jesse's sons the one who is to be Saul's successor. Seven of Jesse's sons are paraded before Samuel, all to be rejected, until finally the youngest, David, is summoned from his job as shepherd. 'Now he was ruddy, and had beautiful eyes, and was handsome. And the Lord said (to Samuel) "Arise, anoint him; for this is he" ' (1 Sam. 16.12). David subsequently came to Saul's attention in two ways: first, as a skilled musician, he is summoned to Saul's court to relieve the king's black moods of depression ('Whenever the evil spirit from God was upon Saul, David took the lyre and played it with his hand; so Saul was refreshed, and was well, and the evil spirit departed from him' [1 Sam. 16.23]); secondly, in the confrontation between Israel and the Philistines, David slew the Philistine champion Goliath, and 'when the Philistines heard that their champion was dead they fled' (1 Sam. 17.51). 'Whose son is this youth?' enquired Saul, again leading to David's being brought to the court of Saul, without, in either case, Saul's being aware of David's destiny as signified by Samuel.

David's success over Goliath may have saved Israel but it also in the end destroyed David's relationship with Saul. 'Saul has slain his thousands', sang the women of Israel, 'but David his ten thousands' (1 Sam. 18.7). Saul's jealous attempts on David's life led to David's flight from Saul. Through his friendship with Saul's son Jonathan, he tried unsuccessfully to maintain safe contact with Saul, but was forced to take refuge in the wilderness of Judah, there to live as an outlaw at the head of a band of disaffected men while making a living through offering protection to wealthy farmers in the area. Saul's continuing persecution eventually forced David to hire himself out to the Philistines, a position which he used, however, to gain favour with the inhabitants of the cities of Judah, all the while deceiving the Philistine king Achish into thinking that he was making himself 'utterly abhorred by his people Israel; therefore he shall be my servant always' (1 Sam. 27.12).

Inevitably, Israel and the Philistines met in battle. David was banished from the scene by the Philistines, and the story confirms his distance from that fateful encounter by putting David in the far south fighting the Amalekites, while Israel under Saul met the Philistines in battle at Aphek. Saul and three of his sons, including Jonathan, were killed. David subsequently went up to Judah, and was there made king over the house of Judah, while Ishbaal, a surviving son of Saul, was made king over Israel by Abner the commander of Saul's army. The long war of attrition between the house of Saul and the house of David culminated in Abner's betrayal of his master, Abner's death at the hand of Joab, David's army commander, and the murder of Ishbaal. 'So all the elders of Israel came to the king at Hebron; and King David made a covenant with them at Hebron before the Lord, and they anointed David king over Israel'(2 Sam. 5.3). David's subsequent capture of Jerusalem and defeat of the Philistines consolidated his position as king.

Even this bare outline suggests that the story has to do with something more than an account of a series of events. Rather, it has a legitimizing purpose,[9] and it is this which gives it its biographical tone. The story is not only about the rise of David; it is also about the fall of Saul. The rise of one and decline of the other are steady and relentless. Yahweh has taken his spirit from Saul and sent him an evil spirit (1 Sam. 16.14), whereas he is 'with David' (1 Sam. 16.18; 17.37; 18.12, 14, 28; 20.13; 2 Sam. 5.10); he sends a positive answer to David's enquiries (1 Sam. 23.2, 4, 9 ff.; 30.7 ff.; 2 Sam. 2.1; 5.19, 23) but gives no answer to Saul (1 Sam. 28.6). Saul, Jonathan and others realize what the situation is, and regularly give expression to it before David (1 Sam. 18.8; 24.20 f.; 26.25 [Saul]; 20.13 ff.; 23.15 ff. [Jonathan]; 25.30 [Abigail]; 2 Sam. 3.9 ff.,18 [Abner]; 5.1–2 [Israel]). David's position is put in an even more positive light by the tendency of the story to remove from him any possible guilt for his own actions, particularly in relation to any involvement in the deaths of Saul, Jonathan, Ishbaal and Abner. David's going over to the Philistines, an act hardly to be expected of Israel's future king, was a measure of the severity of Saul's persecution (1 Sam. 26.19), but even while in that position he covertly protected Israel by defeating another traditional enemy, the Amalekites (1 Sam. 27.8 ff.). David, the divinely-led legitimate successor to Saul, is innocent of any responsibility for Saul's downfall. At the height of Saul's persecution of him, at a point where in fact David had Saul in his power, he said to a supporter Abishai, 'Do not destroy him; for who can put forth his hand against the Lord's anointed and be guiltless?...As the Lord lives, the Lord will smite him; or his day will come to die; or he shall go down into battle and perish' (1 Sam. 26.9 f.). The story is concerned throughout to emphasize David's loyalty to his master (1 Sam. 24.7, 9, 11; 26.17 ff. etc.). Despite Saul's repeated attempts on his life David does not react, and was free of any association with the events leading to the deaths of

Saul, Jonathan, Ishbaal and Abner. He had not taken part in the Philistine battle against Israel, having been rejected from participation by the Philistines themselves; in fact, at the time of Saul's death on Mt Gilboa, David, though in the service of the Philistines, was far away, three days' journey from the scene of the battle (1 Sam. 30.1; 2 Sam. 1.2). Saul's death was prophesied by Samuel's ghost (1 Sam. 28.19), and in the end he killed himself (1 Sam. 31.4). The messenger who thought he brought good news to David and himself claimed to have killed Saul, was put to death: 'And David said to him, "Your blood be upon your head, for your own mouth has testified against you saying 'I have killed the Lord's anointed'"'. Subsequently, it is only by Yahweh's express direction that David made a move towards becoming king (2 Sam. 2.1 ff.). Similarly, in relation to the deaths of Abner and Ishbaal, the story makes clear that David is innocent (2 Sam. 3.19–27; 4.2–7), and those who are guilty are cursed (2 Sam. 3.28 f., 39) or punished (2 Sam. 4.12). The burial and mourning rites are properly carried out, and in the end 'all the people took notice of it, and it pleased them, as everything that the king did pleased all the people' (2 Sam. 3.36).

The blatantly ideological nature of this account does not, of course, necessarily disqualify it as a piece of history writing or indeed as an example of biography. In fact, this character of the account is the basis of a comparison that has been made[10] between the story and a genre of Hittite historiography represented by the thirteenth century Apology of Hattusilis III. This apology, like the story of David's rise, has been seen as composed for a king who has usurped the throne and is intended to justify his seizure of power. So, as in the David story, reference is made to early military success as a trusted commander of the royal predecessor, as well as to popular support, innocence in all dealings with his predecessor, the favour of the deity, and accession to the throne without any plotting on his part. This character of the David story, confirmed by comparison with the Hittite text, could be held to suggest that the story of David's rise goes back to a biographical type of document written in Judah during the reign of David and aimed at northern supporters of the house of Saul who questioned the legitimacy of David's rule.[11]

III

An appreciation of how the story of David's rise has been widely understood in Old Testament scholarship requires some consideration of the broad framework customarily employed by scholars of Old Testament literary history. This involves not only a view of the abstract development of literary form, but also, and essentially, an understanding of the historical and sociological contexts within which the forms of Israelite literature have undergone this development. The fundamental work on this was done by Hermann Gunkel and Hugo Gressmann, at the end of the nineteenth century and beginning of the twentieth century, with the most significant supplementary study being carried out by Gerhard von Rad and Martin Noth in the middle of the last century. Old Testament scholarship still widely operates in the light of their results.

Gunkel and Gressmann developed their theory on Old Testament literary types in relation to commentary work on Genesis,[12] where contemporary critical Old Testament scholarship had long concluded that historical writing was not to be found. Genesis is argued to be a collection of sagas, the saga being a literary type which can be distinguished from historical writing by a number of criteria: sagas are transmitted orally, history is written; sagas deal with private and domestic affairs, history with public and political events; sagas draw on tradition and imagination, history on witnesses and records; sagas freely relate the miraculous and improbable, history deals with the possible and the probable; sagas are intended to entertain and inspire, history to inform. But if sagas can be distinguished from history, so also different kinds of sagas should be demarcated. In particular, the mythical sagas of Gen. 1–11 should be distinguished from the patriarchal sagas of Gen. 12–50, while both types should be distinguished from the hero sagas, this last category forming a transition from the saga type to historical writing.

All sagas are now preserved in written form, of course, but these often contain mythical motifs which allow original non-Israelite myths lying behind the present Israelite mythical sagas to be discerned. Sagas, which were originally brief, have also been joined together into saga chains, and in some cases, as with the Joseph story, given narrative elaboration into a novella. The saga is thus not a static entity. Apart from its own intrinsic development, there stands behind it the myth, and, in its later development, history writing.

In the transition to history writing the hero saga is crucial.[13] This type deals with individuals prominent in the community, figures such as Moses, Joshua, Gideon, Samson, Saul and David. Gunkel also referred to them as historical sagas in order to indicate that they are to do with actual persons, places and events; but they differ from history writing in that they, like sagas in general, incorporate the miraculous and improbable. Such historical sagas are on the way to history writing, and the latter indeed took over from historical sagas much of the technique of saga narration, including the creation of suspense, repetition and the pairing of heroes. However, history writing deals with the more recent past, and with public figures, kings and princes, telling of how things actually were, so excluding the miraculous, while sagas deal with the more distant past, the patriarchs or the heroes of the conquest and period of the judges. Moreover, history writing, even if its techniques draw on the sagas, comes to form part of historical works which incorporate historical documents such as king lists, royal annals, inscriptions and chronicles.

The rise of history writing presupposes the rise of the state. The earliest example of history writing is the story of Abimelech in Judges 9 when the first attempt was made to establish a monarchy, but history flourished with the rise of the monarchy under Saul and David, with the finest example being the story of the revolt of Absalom in 2 Sam. 13 (15)–20. It is this aspect of Gunkel's form-critical work, the social, historical and political setting of the literary type of history writing, that has been worked on especially by von Rad and Noth.[14] For both, following Gunkel, history writing begins with the monarchy. Although it is Israel's faith, providing the notion of divine sovereignty and purpose in history, which allowed for the production of historical writing, it was the political state, and especially the Solomonic enlightenment, which introduced a flood of secular ideas into Israel, and so made possible the production of such works as the Succession Narrative in 2 Sam. 9–20; 1 Kings 1–2, where divine activity is a hidden force guiding the outcome of events in the political realm. So the saga provided the technique, recent political events and personalities provided the subject matter, faith provided the notion of purpose and meaning, and the state in the form of the Solomonic enlightenment provided the overall intellectual context within which historical writing arose in the early Israelite monarchy. The Story of David's Rise and the Succession Narrative, which immediately follows in 2 Samuel, are thus seen as historical works of the highest order.

IV

We are not here concerned with the issue of historicity, although the assumption behind this scheme is in fact that historical writing is generally historically reliable; and so it is noticeable that histories of Israel written by Old Testament scholars have in the past tended to be confident in using Old Testament material, such as the Story of the Rise of David and the Succession Narrative, in reconstructing a reliable history of Israel from the time of the foundation of the monarchy.

Our main concern is with the Story of the Rise of David as a possible biography. What has been said so far might suggest the conclusion that this Story is biography, that it comes from the time of David, and that it forms part of that more general literary development which resulted in the rise of history writing from the older stages of production of myths and sagas. Such a conclusion would fit with our general expectation, encouraged also by the Egyptian material referred to earlier, that biography represents an early literary form which belongs in the context of the development of historiography.[15] Some details support this. Much of the material in the Story takes the form of hero sagas, or historical sagas, which have great individuals and events as their subject, and which, as a type, belong to an early stage and form the transition to historical writing.[16] The combination of such saga material with more directly historical record – such as David's position as captain of a thousand in the service of Saul (1 Sam. 18.18) or David's activities as a leader of a mercenary band in the wilderness (1 Sam. 25), or as a Habiru leader, a mercenary who hired himself out to the Philistines (1 Sam. 27 f.)[17] – points to the desire to create a sanitized picture of David which, however distortive of reality, could still be legitimately classified as biography.

Caution, however, is needed. The parallel with the Hittite text, the Apology of Hattusilis III, while very suggestive, cannot be determinative of the genre of 1 Sam. 16 – 2 Sam. 5. Even with regard to the Hittite text there are difficulties, its classification as an autobiography being based on little more than the use of the first person style.[18] But even if it should be so classified, and though the parallel with the account of the rise of David may be close, the conclusion does not follow that this story is a Davidic biography. In the first place, it is clear from, for example, the extensive influence from ancient Near Eastern legal and treaty texts on the deuteronomistic literature of the Old Testament, that biblical writers made creative use of a variety of established genres for particular literary purposes not directly related to the original setting and purpose of the genre. Secondly, the Story of David's Rise is also a story about the downfall of Saul. The connection with Saul is not just one in which knowledge of Saul as Israel's first king is the general background presupposed in an otherwise independent Story of the Rise of David. Rather, there are literary and thematic connections between the Story of the Rise of David and earlier material on Saul,[19] and indeed probably also with 2 Samuel 7, lying outside the traditional boundaries of the Story of the Rise of David. In other words, the Story of David's Rise was never anything other than part of a much more extensive literary work, even though it makes use of independent earlier material. Thirdly, the purpose of this story is not simply to justify David's taking the throne from Saul. Insofar as it has that purpose, that should be seen as an element in the narratorial skill of the implied author of the material, leading his implied readers towards an expectation of the situation as it is going to develop.[20] But over and above that purpose, the story also intends to justify monarchy as such. The inviolability of the Lord's anointed is a significant basic theme of the story. It thus functions as a strong defence of the institution of the Davidic dynastic monarchy over and above the concern to legitimate David in particular over against Saul. In this light, the story is hardly to be separated from the wider context of the deuteronomistic history which, at least in its first edition, was strongly focused on the centrality of the Davidic dynasty for the welfare of Israel.[21]

Although the history of origins of the deuteronomistic history is very much disputed territory, it is most probable that it went through at least two editions, and that the first of these was pre-exilic and associated with the centralizing and reforming movement of the Judean king Josiah in the mid-seventh century. It is often noted that Josiah is presented in 2 Kings 22–3 as David *redivivus*; not least of the elements contributing to this is his purification of Jerusalem and its temple, and the associated centralization of the kingdom on its capital. The correspondence is much more comprehensive: the historical presentation of Josiah, a time when the new boy king replaced the evil Manasseh in the context of division over the kingship within Israel, and led his people to independence from their erstwhile Assyrian enemies, has its prototype in the presented history of David, the new boy king who replaced the evil Saul in the context of division over the kingship within Israel, and with the backing of his people led them to independence from the Philistines. 2 Kings 22.2 makes the comparison explicit: '(Josiah) did what was right in the eyes of the Lord, and walked in all the way of David his father, and he did not turn aside to the right hand or to the left.' From this perspective the Story of the Rise of David must be classified not in the first instance as biography of David, but rather as an integral element of a more comprehensive historiography serving as the ideological foundation for the reign of Josiah.

There may well be older biographical-type material, in the sense of historical record, present here. Its separation from its present context, however, is difficult and uncertain. By analogy with other contemporary ancient Near Eastern states it is not at all unlikely that Israelite commemorative inscriptions existed,[22] and such may in part at least have been the source of information used by the later (deuteronomistic) writers, but such inscriptions have not been preserved.[23] Moreover, there is a good case to be made for taking some of the information provided by the Story as deriving from official annals: this would be true especially of short notes, perhaps particularly those which stand in some tension with the interpretative context within which they are now to be found.[24] Furthermore, there are stories here, both the clear hero-type saga such as that of David and Goliath, and the narrative of David's activities as a *habiru* leader in the southern wilderness, which either in their form or in the moral ambiguity of their content, can hardly be claimed to be the invention of the deuteronomistic historian. However, none of this information can very credibly be claimed to derive from an existing composition which formally constituted a biography of David, whether or not we measure this according to Egyptian prototypes. It is first in the historiographic work of the deuteronomist that this existing information has been collated into a narrative presentation which, in constructing a picture of David, presents an ideal-type figure to serve as propaganda for a later descendant.

Notes

[1] Cf. March 1974, 173–4, with reference to the Elijah-Elisha legends.

[2] On the following see especially Van Seters 1983, 181–7; Gnirs 2001, 184–9. For a useful collection of relevant texts, with introductions see Lichtheim 1975–80, especially 1975, 3–12.

[3] Cf. the Late Period biographies in Lichtheim 1980, 13–65.

[4] Cf. von Rad 1964, 176–87; Van Seters 1983, 186–7. Von Rad refers in particular to Otto 1954.

[5] Von Rad, while noting certain differences between the Egyptian material and the Nehemiah Memoirs (for example, the latter are not so didactic or directly addressed to the reader in the manner of the Egyptian material), points to one inscription in particular ('The Statue Inscription of Peftuaneith', in Lichtheim 1980, 33–6) as providing a remarkably close parallel to the Nehemiah Memoirs. This particular inscription derives from the late Saite period, when native Egyptian rule was replaced by a Persian administration under Cambyses and Darius I.

[6] Gnirs 2001, 185.

[7] Gnirs, *ibid.*

[8] The so-called Succession Narrative in 2 Samuel 9–20; 1 Kings 1–2 also has much biographical-type content. Its focus, however, is more closely on the dynasty of David than on the individual David. The background and purpose of the work is now a matter of wide debate (for a review of some discussion, see Gottwald 1985, 317–8; Van Seters 1983, 277–91), and it is very unlikely that it can any longer be easily accepted as 'the oldest specimen of ancient Israelite historical writing' (von Rad, 1966, 176), from the hand of a member of the royal court in the time of Solomon.

[9] On this reading of the Story of David's Rise, see especially Crüsemann 1978; also Rendtorff 1971, 428–39; Smith 1951, 167–9; Brettler 1995, 97–111.

[10] Cf. P. Kyle McCarter 1980, 27–30.

[11] Cf. also Gottwald 1985, 315–6.

[12] For studies of the work of Gunkel and Gressmann see especially J.A. Wilcoxen 1974, 58–79; Van Seters 1983, 209–13. I have maintained the word 'saga' for the German *Sage*, following Wilcoxen, rather than using the term 'legend' (as Van Seters). In order to avoid confusion (in which respect Van Seters is not wholly successful in his criticism of Gunkel and Gressmann), it is better to reserve the term 'legend' for the context (of holy men) to which Gunkel restricted it, cf. Wilcoxen 1974, 78 f.

[13] Cf. Wilcoxen 1974, 73 f.

[14] Von Rad 1966, 166–204; Noth 1958, 1498–1504.

[15] It should be noted that Noth, *ibid.*, regarded the Story of David's Rise as historical writing, and the genre of biography as an offshoot of historical writing in some respects anticipated in early prophetic legends and prophetic vision reports. The ancient Near Eastern evidence, however, would scarcely support this as a general conclusion as far as form is concerned.

[16] So especially the story of the choice of David by Samuel in 1 Samuel 16, and the Goliath story in 1 Samuel 17.

[17] On this type of historical record, which the author of the Story of the Rise of David has set in a new interpretative context, see especially Rendtorff 1971.

[18] Cf. Van Seters 1983, 118–21, who prefers to see the text as an edict in which Hattusilis is not justifying his right to rule but rather is giving the reasons why the goddess

Ishtar should receive particular honour. Note that the so-called Egyptian biographies also relate strongly to the maintenance of the cults of the gods; cf. Gnirs 2001, 185. For a critical discussion of Van Seters at this point cf. Younger 1990, 29–30.

[19] Cf. 1 Sam. 19.18–24 with 1 Sam. 10.10–12. On the wider literary connections, see especially Van Seters 1983, 264–71.

[20] The literary theory referred to is now widely seen as significant for Old Testament study; for an application of it to a different context, cf. Mayes 2001.

[21] Whether or not there was a pre-deuteronomistic Saul-David story is a matter of dispute. In any case, it is highly unlikely that such a story, which would come under the heading of *belles lettres*, would have originated in the early monarchic period. The reign of Solomon cannot with any justification be described as an 'enlightenment' period in Israel. The use of writing at this early stage in state formation would have had strictly utilitarian purposes, and not those presupposed by works such as the Story of the Rise of David and the Succession Narrative; cf. Redford 1992, 303–4.

[22] Cf. Van Seters 1983, 191–5, 298–9.

[23] Perhaps 2 Sam. 18.18 records the existence of such a commemorative inscription.

[24] One might refer, for example, to 1 Sam. 18.7, where the song of the women scarcely suits the context in which David has killed only Goliath, or 1 Sam. 18.13, where David's being made commander of a thousand is hardly to be understood against the background of Saul's jealousy and desire to remove David from his presence. On this, see particularly Rendtorff 1971.

Bibliography

Brettler, M.Z.
   1995   *The Creation of History in Ancient Israel*, London.
Crüsemann, F.
   1978   *Der Widerstand gegen das Königtum*, Neukirchen.
Gnirs, A.M.
   2001   'Biographies', in Redford (ed.) *The Oxford Encyclopedia of Ancient Egypt*, vol. I, 184–9.
Gottwald, N.K.
   1985   *The Hebrew Bible: A socio-literary introduction*, Philadelphia.
Hayes, J.H. (ed.)
   1974   *Old Testament Form Criticism*, San Antonio.
Lichtheim, M.
   1975–80   *Ancient Egyptian Literature*, vols. I–III, Berkeley and Los Angeles.
McCarter, P. Kyle
   1980   *1 Samuel*, Anchor Bible 8, New York.
March, W.E.
   1974   'Prophecy', in Hayes (ed.) *Old Testament Form Criticism*, San Antonio, 141–77.
Mayes, A.D.H.
   2001   'Deuteronomistic royal ideology in Judges 17–21', *Biblical Interpretation* 9, 3, 241–58.
Noth, M.
   1958   'Geschichtsschreibung im Alten Testament', *Die Religion in Geschichte und*

*Gegenwart*³, II, Tübingen, 1498–1504.

Otto, E.
1954   *Die biographischen Inschriften der ägyptischen Spätzeit*, Leiden.
Redford, D.B.
1992   *Egypt, Canaan and Israel in Ancient Times*, Princeton.
Redford, D.B. (ed.)
2001   *The Oxford Encyclopedia of Ancient Egypt*, Oxford.
Rendtorff, R.
1971   'Beobachtungen zur altisraelitischen Geschichtsschreibung anhand der Geschichte vom Aufstieg Davids', in H.W. Wolff (ed.) *Probleme biblischer Theologie: Gerhard von Rad zum 70.Geburtstag*, Munich, 428–39.
Smith, M.
1951   'The so-called "Biography of David" in the Books of Samuel and Kings', *Harvard Theological Review* 44, 167–9.
Van Seters, J.
1983   *In Search of History: Historiography in the ancient world and the origins of biblical history*, New Haven.
von Rad, G.
1964   'Die Nehemia-Denkschrift', *Zeitschrift für die alttestamentliche Wissenschaft* 76, 176–87.
1966   'The beginning of historical writing in ancient Israel', in *The Problem of the Hexateuch and Other Essays*, Edinburgh, 166–204.
Wilcoxen, J.A.
1974   'Narrative', in Hayes (ed.) *Old Testament Form Criticism*, 57–98.
Younger, K.L.
1990   *Ancient Conquest Accounts: A study in ancient near eastern and biblical history writing*, in Journal for the Study of the Old Testament, Supplement Series 98, Sheffield.

2

THE BIOGRAPHIES OF POETS: THE CASE OF SOLON[1]

Elizabeth Irwin

The 'I' of early Greek poetry and its role in the creation of poets' biographies have been relatively settled topics in recent years. After the flurry of excitement aroused by the Cologne Epode, scholarship now seems to bask in the afterglow of a near consensus on two issues. Most would certainly think twice before reading the 'I' of the early Greek poets autobiographically, and the line championed by Mary Lefkowitz on the unreliability of the biographical traditions of poets as inventions based on the poets' own poetry has become an orthodoxy.[2]

It would of course be wrong to deny the important corrective this recognition provided. But I hope to complicate the now clichéd approach to the poets' biographies by looking at the issues raised by another archaic poet, namely Solon. Solon was, strangely, if not indeed perversely, neglected in these formative debates on the generic quality of the poet's 'I'. Not that I would suggest conspiracy. Certainly the new fragments of Archilochus and his rather pointed 'I' did make him the obvious battleground for separating the 'I' of the poetry from that of the poet and for appreciating the role of the poetic 'I' in generating the biographical traditional. And yet, Archilochus does seem to have been a convenient fall-guy: in Archilochus' case sacrificing the autobiographical 'I' had remarkably little consequence for the writing of history,[3] and actually rescued scholars of moral rectitude from believing a beloved poet to be a 'schwerer Psychopath'.[4]

What would have happened, though, had the literary critics turned their attention to a figure like Solon? Far fewer, especially among historians, would have taken the results with equanimity. Unlike the situation with Archilochus, there is far too much history at stake to dismiss out of hand the 'I' of his poetry. Lefkowitz indeed becomes contradictory when she turns to Solon. Although she generally argues, on the one hand, that the biographical tradition cannot be trusted because it derives from the poet's own work, she then says in the case of Solon, 'If more of Solon's poetry survived we could distinguish with more confidence between the *real* events in his life and the accretions of tradition'.[5] Implicit in this contradiction is the further questionable assumption that poetry can ever be treated as straightforward historical documents.

Moreover Solon, himself, raises a category unexplored by Lefkowitz. It is clear that Solon's poetry influenced his manner of reception. But given the awareness of the power of poetry to preserve *kleos*, there remains the possibility that a poet could be actively involved in his or her own reception. For instance, was Solon remembered as he was simply because later generations created and placed him within certain narrative patterns, or did he in his poetry, and perhaps actions in the political sphere, exploit a *topos* already available to him? With Solon the question becomes all the more pointed because in the case of the *nomothetic* poet controlling reception would certainly be politically construed.

In what follows I will focus on a prominent story from the poetry and biographical tradition of Solon, the performance of Solon's *Salamis*, in order to examine the problems of interpretation besetting poets' biographies and to raise some more general issues about the genre of biography. Plutarch records the most extended version of this well-known and often repeated story:

ἐπεὶ δὲ μακρόν τινα καὶ δυσχερῆ πόλεμον οἱ ἐν ἄστει περὶ τῆς Σαλαμινίων νήσου Μεγαρεῦσι πολεμοῦντες ἐξέκαμον, καὶ νόμον ἔθεντο μήτε γράψαι τινὰ μήτ' εἰπεῖν αὖθις ὡς χρὴ τὴν πόλιν ἀντιποιεῖσθαι τῆς Σαλαμῖνος, ἢ θανάτῳ ζημιοῦσθαι, βαρέως φέρων τὴν ἀδοξίαν ὁ Σόλων, καὶ τῶν νέων ὁρῶν πολλοὺς δεομένους ἀρχῆς ἐπὶ τὸν πόλεμον, αὐτοὺς δὲ μὴ θαρροῦντας ἄρξασθαι διὰ τὸν νόμον, ἐσκήψατο μὲν ἔκστασιν τῶν λογισμῶν, καὶ λόγος εἰς τὴν πόλιν ἐκ τῆς οἰκίας διεδόθη παρακινητικῶς ἔχειν αὐτόν· ἐλεγεῖα δὲ κρύφα συνθεὶς καὶ μελετήσας ὥστε λέγειν ἀπὸ στόματος, ἐξεπήδησεν εἰς τὴν ἀγορὰν ἄφνω, πιλίδιον περιθέμενος. ὄχλου δὲ πολλοῦ συνδραμόντος, ἀναβὰς ἐπὶ τὸν τοῦ κήρυκος λίθον, ἐν ᾠδῇ διεξῆλθε τὴν ἐλεγείαν ἧς ἐστιν ἀρχή·

αὐτὸς κῆρυξ ἦλθον ἀφ' ἱμερτῆς Σαλαμῖνος,
κόσμον ἐπέων ᾠδὴν ἀντ' ἀγορῆς θέμενος.

τοῦτο τὸ ποίημα Σαλαμὶς ἐπιγέγραπται καὶ στίχων ἑκατόν ἐστι, χαριέντως πάνυ πεποιημένων. τότε δ' ᾀσθέντος αὐτοῦ, καὶ τῶν φίλων τοῦ Σόλωνος ἀρξαμένων ἐπαινεῖν, μάλιστα δὲ τοῦ Πεισιστράτου τοῖς πολίταις ἐγκελευομένου καὶ παρορμῶντος πείθεσθαι τῷ λέγοντι, λύσαντες τὸν νόμον αὖθις ἥπτοντο τοῦ πολέμου, προστησάμενοι τὸν Σόλωνα.

Once when the Athenians were tired out with a war they were waging against the Megarians for the island of Salamis, they made a law that no one in future, on the pain of death, should move in writing or orally that the city take up its contention for Salamis. Solon could not endure the disgrace of this, and when he saw that many of the young men wanted steps taken to bring on the war, but did not dare to take those steps themselves on account of the law, he pretended to be out of his head, and a report was given out to the city by his family that he showed signs of madness. He then secretly composed some elegiac verses, and after rehearsing them so that he could say them by rote, he sallied out into the market place of a sudden with a *pilidion* on his head. After a large crowd had collected there, he got upon the herald's stone and recited the poem which begins:

> Behold in me a herald come from lovely Salamis,
> With a song in ordered verse instead of a harangue.

This poem is entitled *Salamis*, and contains a hundred very graceful verses. When Solon had sung it, his friends began to praise him, and Peisistratus in particular urged and incited the citizens to obey his words. They therefore repealed the law and renewed the war, putting Solon in command of it.

(Loeb translation, Perrin)[6]

Despite being a favourite of the ancients, most scholars today would credit this story with little historical value. When the story does receive attention, that attention is almost entirely reduced to debates regarding the performance of archaic elegy. Scholars ask whether this testimony proves that elegy was performed in public contexts such as the agora, or whether the story merely arose from the poem itself, an example of sympotic role-playing.[7]

In what follows I will attempt to do a little more with this story. I shall argue, first, that an analysis of the logic and of elements of the story demonstrates an ancient reading of Solonian poetics through a connection of his poetic stance with the figure of Odysseus, and second, that this identification of Solon's poetic stance may have relevance for understanding his politics. This will seem in some ways an old-fashioned piece, smacking of the somewhat dubious exercise of detecting the kernel of historical truth in the obviously embellished tradition. But I will not be advocating a return to a period of naïve belief in the biographical tradition. Instead, I want to use this story to focus on the problems involved in handling the detailed stories of the biographies of poets, to occupy a Solonian middle ground between approaches either gullible or dismissive in their approach to these rich stories. I will ask: what are these stories good for? what can they tell us about both poet and poetry? and can they, ultimately, have any historical value?

Three methodological points enable an assay upon that interpretive middle ground, and are crucial for approaching this historically very suspect material. First, one can engage with the details of the biographical tradition without passing judgment on their historicity. Studies that identify the common τόποι within traditional narratives, the legends surrounding wise man, lawgiver or poet, are of course valuable, but they do not eliminate the need to deal with the specific elements and logic of the individual narratives.[8] After all, the relationship between the generic pattern and its individual proponents, evolving as it does over time, is hardly likely to be unidirectional.

Moreover, the tendency to smooth over differences, to identify similarity at the expense of detail, generates a dangerously circular argument. After all, poets did have lives.[9]

Second, the biographical traditions of poets can contain important and often early evidence for the reception of both the poets and their poetry precisely because these traditions are derived largely from their poetry (often lost to us).[10] Moreover, we cannot and ought not to exclude the possibility that the poet may have been not only proactive, but even occasionally successful, in influencing his own reception through his poetry. The fragments of Solon's poetry are replete with attempts to manipulate the reception of its 'I'.[11]

Finally, in those cases where it seems as arbitrary to accept as to reject events in the biographical tradition, one should try to pursue the consequences of both positions. This is a difficult strategy, but runs less risk of imposing upon antiquity our criteria of plausibility. I will try to maintain this dual perspective in what follows.[12]

In relation to the *Salamis* story, these general points suggest the following lines of interpretation. First, 'disbelief' in the first performance of the *Salamis* and the generic quality of the story does not sanction neglect of its details. After all, as scholars we must admit that we would prefer to have this story than not, and also that the reasons governing the inclusion of its details are indeed worth exploring. And moreover, Solon's role in attempting to control reception needs to be recognized. Second, while the most extended versions of this account are late and themselves likely to have been constructed in large part from the poem itself, their creation and preservation nevertheless indicate important elements about how audiences heard Solon's poetry: that is, on the Lefkowitz model, the story is worth analysing in detail because at the very least it reveals crucial aspects of ancient reception of Solon's *Salamis*, reception that may well go back to a very early date. Finally, as scholarly debate swings back and forth on the historicity of the first performance – an essentially irresolvable debate – it seems prudent to explore the consequences of both possibilities. Even without actual performance in the agora, the poetic stance may still be deemed to be political. So, though contradictory on her own terms, Lefkowitz is no doubt right that if we had more of Solon's poetry we would know more about the history of archaic Athens, but perhaps not in quite the way she expected.

Solon and Odysseus

Before that question of real or fiction can even be broached, it is important to understand the logic of the story itself. To begin, the story manifestly centres on the issue of Solon's stance. It's an elaborate one: a feigned madman assuming the role of a herald haranguing his audience in elegiacs, the fusion of a poetic and a political stance. And we as scholars have responded implicitly to the focus of the text on stance when we debate whether the stance is actual or fictional. But there is more to Solon's poetic stance than meets the eye. Several kinds of evidence suggest that an *Odyssean* stance lies behind Solon's performance of the *Salamis* and moreover that this connection with Odysseus serves to illuminate aspects of Solonian poetics, if not also Solonian politics.[13]

A scholion to *Iliad* 2.183, relying on the authority of Aristotle, provides an explicit connection between Solon's behaviour and a Homeric portrayal of Odysseus:

ἀπὸ δὲ χλαῖναν βάλε· ἀπρεπὲς εἶναι δοκεῖ τὴν χλαῖναν ἀποβαλόντα μονοχίτωνα θεῖν τὸν Ὀδυσσέα διὰ τοῦ στρατοπέδου, καὶ μάλιστα οἷος Ὀδυσσεὺς εἶναι ὑπείληπται. φησὶ δ᾽ Ἀριστοτέλης, ἵνα διὰ τοῦτο θαυμάζων ὁ ὄχλος ἐπιστρέφηται, καὶ ἐξικνῆται ἡ φωνὴ ὡς ἐπὶ μεῖζονα ἄλλου ἄλλοθεν συνιόντος, οἷον καὶ Σόλων λέγεται πεποιηκέναι, ὅτε συνῆγε τὸν ὄχλον περὶ Σαλαμῖνος.[14]

He threw off his *chlaina*: it seems to be inappropriate for Odysseus to run through the camp wearing only his *chiton*, having cast off his *chlaina*, and most of all inappropriate for someone of the sort Odysseus is supposed to be. But Aristotle says that he did it so that the crowd might turn back in amazement and his voice might reach a greater area and people would gather from all directions as also Solon is said to have done, when he was gathering the crowd on account of Salamis.

Beyond a connection of Solon's manner of exhortation and Odysseus', there is further thematic overlap between *Iliad* 2 and the *Salamis*. Shame is an important ingredient in both accounts: responding to Athena's reproach, Odysseus exhorts the Achaeans to remain (*Il.* 2.166 ff., esp. ll. 190–1), while Solon in frs. 2–3 exhorts his audience to thrust away the shame of losing Salamis.[15] At the very least, this passage demonstrates an ancient reading of the Salamis tradition that associated the stance of Solon with that of Odysseus in Book 2. It may, however, be the case that Solon's poem was proactive in creating this reception, whether or not an actual performance in the agora also influenced it.

The connection does not seem to rest merely on the identification of analogous behaviour between the lawgiver and the hero. In what follows I will show how a crucial detail of the *Salamis* story points to the same identification. Obscure in itself, the *pilidion* Solon dons before running into the agora functions to evoke the figure of Odysseus. Moreover, not only is the *pilidion* among our earliest attested elements in this story, it is also as we shall see a detail that can epitomize the entire narrative.[16]

The earliest connection of the *pilidion* with Solon occurs in a fourth-century incident of political mud-slinging.[17] Representations of Solon are the currency of this vehement exchange between Demosthenes and Aeschines: Aeschines claims to be a veritable Solon of modesty: unlike the antics of his opponent Timarchus, Aeschines carries himself as Solon, speaking with his hand in his cloak just as one can see Solon do in the famous statue in Salamis.[18] Demosthenes in turn seizes on Aeschines' Solonian self-fashioning. He retaliates by criticizing Aeschines' behaviour during the embassy to Philip, likening it to Solon's behaviour over Salamis:[19]

οὐ λέγειν εἴσω τὴν χεῖρ' ἔχοντ', Αἰσχίνη, δεῖ, οὔ, ἀλλὰ πρεσβεύειν εἴσω τὴν χεῖρ' ἔχοντα. σὺ δ' ἐκεῖ προτείνας καὶ ὑποσχὼν καὶ καταισχύνας τούτους ἐνθάδε σεμνολογεῖ, καὶ λογάρια δύστηνα μελετήσας καὶ φωνασκήσας οὐκ οἴει δίκην δώσειν τηλικούτων καὶ τοσούτων ἀδικημάτων, κἂν πιλίδιον λαβὼν ἐπὶ τὴν κεφαλὴν περινοστῇς καὶ ἐμοὶ λοιδορῇ. (19.255)

You should keep your hand inside, Aeschines, not when making a speech; no, you should keep it inside when going on an embassy. When you were in Macedonia, you stretched it out and held it open and were a disgrace to Athens; but here you pontificate, and because you've rehearsed some wretched phrases and trained your voice do you think you won't be punished for all these terrible crimes, if you put a felt cap on your head and walk around and criticize me?[20]

Demosthenes' reference to the *pilidion* turns Aeschines' Solonian stance against him. Solon becomes less the figure of old-fashioned restraint than the clever politician, donning a costume in which he contrives to speak with impunity.

So our earliest reference employs this detail as evocative of the larger story of Solon and *Salamis*, but what is the significance of the *pilidion* in the Salamis incident? While some have argued that the associations of this hat are with sickness, analysis of the occurrences of this rare word shows that the *pilidion* is almost invariably associated with travel,[21] and the traveler's cap is certainly an appropriate accoutrement for Solon who assumes the stance of the herald returning from Salamis as it would also be for Aeschines returning from his embassy. Travel is of course suggestive of Odysseus and the verb περινοστέω in the Demosthenes passage may well be evoking another aspect of an Odyssean persona.[22]

But associations with travel would not be sufficient to connect Solon with Odysseus, nor would it exhaust this detail's significance. More important is its connection with impunity, a clue which leads us to Aristophanes' *Acharnians*. In a famous Euripidean parody Dicaeopolis asks for the costume of Telephus in which to make his defence:

κἀκεῖνά μοι δὸς τἀκόλουθα τῶν ῥακῶν,

τὸ πιλίδιον περὶ τὴν κεφαλὴν τὸ Μύσιον
δεῖ γάρ με δόξαι πτωχὸν εἶναι τήμερον.
εἶναι μὲν ὅσπερ εἰμί, φαίνεσθαι δὲ μή.[23]

Give to me the props that go with the rags, the little Mysian felt cap for my head, 'For today I must seem to be a beggar, to be the very man who I am and yet appear not so.'

Some scholars have argued that Aristophanes is drawing on the *Salamis* story for his depiction here of Dicaeopolis with *pilidion* seeking to speak with impunity. It seems true that Solon lurks behind the Telephus stance of Dicaeopolis, but it is Euripides' *Telephus* that helps us to understand what lies behind Solon's stance itself.

The text and its scholia emphasize that an important element of the Aristophanic scene is Euripides' own depiction of Telephus, a depiction that importantly includes the *pilidion*.[24] Commenting on current performance practice, one agitated scholiast to the *Acharnian* lines rails, πρὸς τοὺς νῦν ὑποκριτὰς, ὅτι χωρὶς πίλου εἰσάγουσι τὸν Τήλεφον. τὸ δὲ τοῦ Τηλέφου πιλίδιον, τὸ νῦν λεγόμενον καμαλαύκιον, 'This is of relevance to the actors today because they bring Telephus on stage without a *pilos*. The *pilidion* of Telephus, what we call today the *kamalaukion*.' Another scholion tells us that lines 440–1 in fact repeat two lines from Euripides' *Telephus*,[25] and scholars are in agreement that parody of the *Telephus* is a pervasive feature of the *Acharnians*.[26]

The *Acharnians* and its scholia introduce two new lines of investigation, both of which lead toward Odysseus: Euripides' portrayal of Telephus and the substitution in the scholion of πῖλος for πιλίδιον. To begin with the first, it is certain that Euripides' Telephus owes much to Odysseus.[27] *Fr.* 715 of the *Telephus* explicitly draws a connection between Telephus and Odysseus: οὖ τ' ἄρ' Ὀδυσσεύς ἐστιν αἰμύλος μόνος | χρεία διδάσκει, κ' ἂν βραδύς τις ᾖ, σοφόν, 'Odysseus is not unrivalled as a wheedler, so it seems. Need teaches a man to be clever, even one who is slow to learn.' Moreover, Telephus resembles Odysseus not only in his rhetorical skill, but also in the action of Euripides' drama: Telephus' appearance disguised as a beggar is likely to have been shaped by portrayals of Odysseus in the *Odyssey* and the *Cypria*.[28] The scholia to the *Clouds* imply that Euripides was the originator of Telephus' appearance as a beggar, and further describe how the poet placed Telephus as a beggar with a leather wallet at the door of Agamemnon, a role evoking Odyssean depictions of Odysseus.[29] Euripides no doubt employed an irony involving temporality: Odysseus, in ignorance of future events, faces a character behaving as he himself will later be forced to do. As a scholion to Aelius Aristides suggests, the play surely took advantage of the rich dramatic possibilities of pitting two rhetorically gifted characters against one another, and having the master speaker, Odysseus, meet his match.[30] So Odysseus lurks behind Euripides' *Telephus*.

Second, the substitution in the scholion of πῖλος for *pilidion* opens up connections to an overwhelming number of literary and artistic representations of Odysseus wearing a πῖλος or πιλίον, a more common diminutive than πιλίδιον.[31] The scholia display their understanding of the process of this association. The word πῖλος appears only once in Homer, in the *Doloneia*, where Odysseus dons a πῖλος from which according to the scholia to these lines (10.265) ζωγράφοι καὶ πλάσται πιλίον ἐπέθεσαν τῷ Ὀδυσσεῖ, 'the artists placed a *pilion* on Odysseus'. The feature is so strongly attached to Odysseus that it elicits two frequent contrary reactions: either an assertion that the wearing of a πῖλος was actually not distinctive despite its singular mention in the *Iliad* or an identification of the first artist to pick up on this singularity, usually Apollodorus.[32] This claim, however, for a late fifth-century origin does not upset the possible associations of Solon's πιλίδιον with Odysseus' πῖλος or πιλίον. While there may have been some new popularity in this feature of Odysseus or more exclusivity in its usage, numerous representations of Odysseus exist from the late seventh to mid-fifth century in which he already wears a πῖλος.[33]

So the detail of the *pilidion* in the Salamis narrative evokes Odysseus and complements the recognition of similarity between Solon and Odysseus seen in the Aristotle fragment. But how is this identification relevant to Solon?

One might say that a tradition connecting Solon with Odysseus provides a reading of Solon's poetry. It is certainly the case that Solon's poetry is infused with Odyssean-style material. Solon 4W is famously so. Its first lines have long invited comparison with general themes and specific passages of the *Odyssey*.[34] This thematic resonance might lead one to conclude that an Odyssean stance in the *Salamis* story reflects a more general association by ancient readers of Solon's poetic stance with one in accord with the *Odyssey* and its chief character; here one might add that traditions of Solon's travels and Solon's own poem, 19W, regarding a trip to Cyprus would be worth exploring in this context.[35]

And yet, to argue for this thematic reading of Solon's poetry based on the *pilidion* would be premature. For the *pilidion* needs to be appreciated within its narrative context, a context of martial exhortation. For actually the entirety of the Salamis story renders a more nuanced reading of Solon's style of exhortation elegy, and from there may be implied a political stance. We therefore turn now to examine Solonian-style martial exhortation.

Odyssean poetics

Solon's *Salamis* is a contribution to the well-known type of elegy, martial *paraenesis*. Polyaenus calls the poem Ἀρήϊα ᾄσματα ('songs of Ares') with which Solon ἤγειρεν Ἀθηναίους ἐπὶ τὴν μάχην, 'roused the Athenians to battle' (1.20.1). 'Let us go to Salamis to fight for a lovely island and push away bitter disgrace': this stirring command of fr. 3 places the *Salamis* firmly in the tradition best known from the poetry of Tyrtaeus and Callinus.[36] And yet, at the level of ancient reception the political dimension of this exhortation of Solon is articulated far differently from, for instance, that of Tyrtaeus. While Lycurgus (*In Leocr.* 107) may recall how the early Spartans placed such a high value on Tyrtaeus, making a law that his poetry be recited on campaign, νομίζοντες οὕτως ἂν αὐτοὺς μάλιστα πρὸ τῆς πατρίδος ἐθέλειν ἀποθνήσκειν ('considering that thus would they be most willing to die on behalf of their fatherland'),[37] Solon's elegiac exhortations find themselves embedded in an elaborate ancient account of a very different nature, and in particular one involving cunning. Such differences at the level of ancient reception raise the question what Solon may have done with this genre.

And once again the story brings us back to Odysseus. We saw the explicit connection made in antiquity between the martial exhortation of Solon and that of the Iliadic Odysseus. Such a connection with heroic epic exhortation is certainly not unusual for elegy. On the contrary, a heroic stance seems implicit in the epicizing language of martial exhortation elegy. For Solon to assume the role of the Iliadic Odysseus in his *Salamis* may be seen as part and parcel of exhortation elegy and Solon's stance would display a similar relationship to the Odysseus of *Iliad* 2 as scholars have argued to exist between the exhortations of other elegiac poets and those of Iliadic heroes.[38]

So in this respect Solon's brand of martial exhortation would feature aspects of generic continuity. The *Salamis* belongs to martial *paraenesis*, and the ancient accounts recalling Solon's part in this affair do suggest certain elements characteristic of martial exhortation elegy. Typical elements of sympotic elegy are present in the event as recorded by Plutarch. Plutarch says first that the νέοι were intent on war, and attributes to Solon the noble motivation of finding it difficult to bear the ἀδοξία of losing Salamis; later he speaks of the instrumentality of Solon's φίλοι in inciting the πολῖται to war. Νέοι (significantly the addressees of Tyrtaean exhortation) and φίλοι belong to sectional language (particularly in contrast to the civic grouping, πολῖται), and name the typical participants in the symposium.[39]

And yet, here is where the story of the biographical tradition introduces an important reading. Accounts of the poem's alleged *al fresco* performance suggest generic discontinuity. The performance of the *Salamis* in the agora, whether derived from the poem or actual, provides a contrast to the typical performance context of elegy, and it is clear that this feature of the story was both crucial and considered unusual. The story in fact localizes the insanity in the agora, that is, in the performance context of the poem.[40] Diogenes

Laertius is telling in this regard. He omits the detail of the *pilidion*, saying rather that Solon rushed into the agora garlanded (1.46). The garland and recitation of poetry are the typical elements of the symposium.[41] Performance of this exhortation elegy in the agora then suggests a travesty of performance context. In using the term ὄχλος for the target of this exhortation, the fragment of Aristotle further emphasizes, in somewhat derogatory fashion, the general audience of this exhortation, not the *philoi* of the symposium. Taken together, the story surrounding the *Salamis* portrays Solon as participating in martial exhortation elegy, replete with heroic self-fashioning, but at the same time portrays him as transgressing the boundaries of its appropriate context and audience, literally or metaphorically, using, moreover, a figure such as Odysseus who may not have been typical for aristocratic appropriation.[42] This story therefore provides a valuable reading of Solonian martial elegy. Moreover, this is where poetics begins to shade into politics.

Solon's feigned madness and the detail of the law deserve some attention. Although the earliest allusion to the *pilidion*, that of Demosthenes, does not explicitly mention the feigning of madness (though it may be implicit in the impunity which Demosthenes seems to suggest the *pilidion* brings), this may still be an early element, and it is therefore worth exploring this feature in connection with Solon's stance as Odysseus. Odysseus is above all the character *par excellence* of assumed roles, including the feigning of madness. Odysseus' use of this pretence to avoid the Trojan War was told as early as the *Cypria*, according to Proclus, and seems to have remained a popular theme, as one of Sophocles' titles, Ὀδυσσεὺς μαινόμενος, suggests. If the associations of Solon with Odysseus were not only made by some of his readers and audiences,[43] but were actually encouraged by Solon through the 92 missing lines of the *Salamis* and possibly also through his actions, then it would be possible to see the rich potential for exploitation offered by this role. One might wonder whether an Odysseus-stance along the lines described by Agamemnon in Aeschylus' play of the same name was being drawn upon: μόνος δ᾽ Ὀδυσσεύς, ὅσπερ οὐχ ἑκὼν ἔπλει | ζευχθεὶς ἕτοιμος ἦν ἐμοὶ σειραφόρος ('Odysseus alone, the very man who did not sail of his own accord, when once in harness proved to me a ready tracehorse', 841–2). Odysseus was the character reluctant to go to war, but when there was no choice, he became the most reliable and committed to its completion. Such a position fits well the comparison of Solon with the Odysseus of *Iliad* 2 quoted above. In terms of a political position, the stance of a reluctant warrior, rather than war-monger, would be a valuable one for convincing an otherwise unwilling citizen body and for courting the largest possible political audience.

The law prohibiting speech about the loss of Salamis may also have significance. As an element of the narrative, this detail explains why Solon assumed such a stance, why he simply *could not* directly address the people. But the impunity desired from this poetic or dramatic role may actually be interpreted as relating to the ambitions of a particular political stance. This assumed poetic role may function as a strategy simultaneously to push an aim that could be construed as private or sectional without compromising a relationship, already developed or inchoate, to the δῆμος.[44] Such ambiguities in this position – a transgressor of sympotic norms, yet advocating war – would help to explain how Solon came to be accepted as νομοθέτης. But if one finds this getting all too historical and personal, quite apart from the politics implicit in inciting renewed war over Salamis, the detail of the law introduces the notion of transgression and in this respect may be read more generally as a critical evaluation of the content and function of Solonian elegy. It represents Solon as transgressor, extending the boundaries of sympotic elegy, either through content or through the implied audience addressed within his poetry, or both.

So as a reading of Solonian martial elegy the *Salamis* story conveys transgression, both legal, a broken law, and social, madness and deception, and the site of this transgression is significantly the agora. Whether the public audience was literal or belongs to the fiction created in the poem is in this respect unimportant; after the alleged first performance the matter is almost entirely academic.

Conclusion

I conclude here, but this is in many respects just a beginning. Although the *Salamis* story is only a tradition, with so many traditions of good and wise lawgiver informing our approach to Solon's poetry it is important to see where cracks emerge, where the biographical tradition allows us to read against its own dominant narrative in order to gain a fresh view of Solon and his poetry. A closer reading of the *Salamis* story encourages two directions to pursue, the purely poetic and the political. To follow the poetic, this story and a closer reading of it lead to a greater appreciation of Solon's elegiac stance. One may further pursue his Odyssean stance and examine how it relates to the choices and alignments to epic performed by his fellow elegists.[45] More importantly, one may pursue how Solon's other poetry bears out this characterization of him as the transgressive sympotic poet. For instance, the prominence and quality of the treatment of the *dēmos* in his elegy is exceptional among extant elegists, as the example of the transgressive formulation of giving epic *geras* to the *dēmos* in fr. 5.[46]

This is the poetic direction, but particularly with the issue of the *dēmos*, we slide quickly into the political. One might here begin to explore the associations of Odysseus as a political stance in the archaic period, suggested

by the story of Solon's confrontation of Peisistratos: οὐ καλῶς, ὦ παῖ
Ἱπποκράτους, ὑποκρίνῃ τὸν Ὁμηρικὸν Ὀδυσσέα· ταὐτὰ γὰρ ποιεῖς τοὺς
πολίτας παρακρουόμενος, οἷς ἐκεῖνος τοὺς πολεμίους ἐξηπάτησεν αἰκισάμενος
ἑαυτόν, 'Not nobly, son of Hippocrates, do you play the Homeric Odysseus;
for by that same ploy do you mislead your fellow citizens by which he
deceived his enemies when he disfigured himself' (Plut. *Solon* 30, cf. D.L.
1.60). And, perhaps more importantly, we may recognize the plausible link
between Solon and other poetic political operators among his contemporaries. Solonian elegy may have been influenced by, if it did not also (almost)
entirely belong to, a body of poetry produced by other archaic political
figures. Solon's political day job may make him seem a special case among
early Greek poets, but ancient testimony suggests that his poetic inclina-
tions were characteristic of other exceptional, and even tyrannical, archaic
political figures, such as Periander and Pittacus, whose fragments sadly do
not survive, probably because they did not write for cities with quite so
exceptional a future.[47]

Against the wider context of archaic political exploitation of poetry, *pace*
Lefkowitz, more of Solon's poetry would not necessarily tell us anything
more specific about land tenure in Attica or the nature of the *Boulē*, but
it could tell us quite a lot about political posturing in the archaic period,
a historical phenomenon in itself.

Notes

[1] A version of this article now appears in Irwin 2005, 102–53 and cf. 2006, 40–4.

[2] Lefkowitz 1976 and 1981. For an earlier treatment of the subject see Fairweather
1974. For a recent survey with bibliography see Irwin 1998.

[3] This is demonstrated by the cheerful, if ironic, Forrest 1982, 255: 'For, it is now very
properly insisted, the words of a lyric poet must not be taken too literally, must certainly
not be taken autobiographically. It is no longer permitted to say 'Archilochus was an
aristocrat, but a bastard aristocrat', 'Archilochus rejected the accepted code of military
honour by boasting that he had thrown away his shield in battle to save his own skin',
'Archilochus loved to dance when drunk' and so on. Rather we must say that society now
recognized the existence of and could sing about drunken bastard shield-throwers. That
takes away a bit of the spice, but the fact remains and is important.'

[4] Merkelbach 1974, 113. Archilochus even gave the ancients pause, see famously
Critias' censure (Ael. *VH* 10.13).

[5] Lefkowitz 1981, 47–8 (italics are mine).

[6] Plut. *Sol.* 8 Ziegler. The remaining fragments are preserved in D.L. 1.47 (2–3). For
the sources see Martina 1968, 122–30. For a full discussion of the Salamis affair see
Linforth 1919, 249–64; French 1957; Hopper 1961, 208–17; Piccirelli 1978; Rhodes
1981, 199–200 and 224; Taylor 1997, 21–47; Noussia 1999, 61–72, and 2001, 223–33
and Mülke 2002, 73–88.

[7] Performance in the agora: West 1974, Tedeschi 1982. Biographical fiction derived from the poetry: Lefkowitz 1981, Bowie 1986. The tide does seem to be turning: Stehle 1997, 61–3 at least entertains the possibility of the performance of Solon's elegiacs in the agora, while, most recently, Kurke 1999, 26, n. 64 *contra* Bowie is 'inclined to put more stock in the traditions about their performance'.

[8] See, for example, Szegedy-Maszak 1978 and Martin 1993.

[9] A related point is that narrative patterns are not just something imposed upon figures after they live; they can be self-imposed, consciously and unconsciously, and thereby inform the way people within a culture organize and understand their own lives. That something smacks of a *topos* does not exclude the possibility of its having happened: that stars are said to marry and divorce frequently does not mean that Elizabeth Taylor did not (the same man twice!). Given that this is the case, it becomes more fruitful to consider how and why individuals end up living their cultural narratives, as well as to investigate the evolving dialogue between these two entities.

[10] See Graziosi 2002 who develops this approach with the life of Homer.

[11] See for instance 4a, 5, 10, 19, 32, 34, 36, 37W, etc.

[12] As admirably done by Stehle 1997, 61–3.

[13] Vox 1984, 17–48 and Noussia 2001, 228–9 have also identified an Odyssean stance in the Salamis story, but with different emphasis.

[14] Arist. fr. 3.143 Rose from Porphyr. Ὅμηρ. ζητήμ. It is uncertain from the phrasing whether the last clauses should be attributed to Aristotle.

[15] Diogenes' account (1.46) is even more similar to *Iliad* 2 (50–2, 184, 442–4) in that Solon, although mad, has a herald with him to recite his poem. Robertson 1998, 301 sees military associations, calling this a 'muster under arms'.

[16] As Kurke and Dougherty 1993, 6, argue, despite being late, narratives such as this one surrounding Solon's *Salamis* can sometimes retain 'metaphors or systems of signification that correspond to archaic ones' which will be particularly visible in those details that are 'anomalous or obscure within the text in which they are embedded.'

[17] Demosthenes 19.255. The emendation of Plut. *Sol.* 8 to πιλίδιον by Bryan is on the strength of Demosthenes. The manuscripts of Plutarch preserve πλινθίον and πιλίον for Solon's cap. See Mastrocinque 1984, 31, n. 15; Facelière 1947, 237.

[18] *Against Timarchus* 25–7. Aeschines' unflattering description of Timarchus (ῥίψας θοἰμάτιον γυμνὸς ἐπαγκρατίαζεν ἐν τῇ ἐκκλησία, 'And having thrown off his cloak he practised his gymnastics naked in the assembly', 26) in terms similar to the scholion discussed above may suggest that Aeschines' own appropriation of the lawgiver was initiated by Timarchus' first attempting to adopt a (different) Solonian stance.

[19] Against the scholarly consensus, the most recent commentator on this speech, MacDowell 2000, 311, feels the connection with Solon is not explicit enough.

[20] MacDowell's text and translation 2000, 164–5.

[21] The word is rare in Greek literature, appearing once in each of four classical authors (Dem. 19.255, Ar. *Acharnians* 439, Antiphanes 33K [Ath. 12.544f], Plato *Rep.* 406d), in scholia to these passages, twice in Plutarch (Plut. *Moralia* 1127b and *Sol.* 8), and in the Suda. Facelière's view (1947) 247 that in Solon's story the πιλίδιον evokes illness (cf. *RE* s.v. πῖλος 1332) is based on a misinterpretation of the sources, as Lowry 1991, 162–75 has demonstrated. For other scholars who recognize the association of this cap with travel see Else 1965, 40; West 1974, 12; Facelière 1947, 238 and Lucian, *Anacharsis* 16 where πῖλος appears humorously in a conversation between Anacharsis and Solon.

²² And also, interestingly, the Solonian persona, first attested in his own poetry, 19W.

²³ *Acharnians* 438–41. Mastrocinque 1984 actually argues that Dicaeopolis' stance in the *Acharnians* is modelled upon Solon's Salamis story.

²⁴ See Foley 1988, 41, n. 31, who mentions two vases which depict Telephus with a πῖλος (a Campanian bell krater in Naples, 350–325 BC, and an Attic *pelike* 350–325 BC, *ARV2* 1473), thus confirming 'the strong association of the cap with the role'. See also Taplin 1992, 37–8 and *LIMC* s.v. 'Agamemnon'.

²⁵ Eur. *Telephus* fr. 698. *Telephus* fragments are from Collard 1995. See the schol. Ar. *Ach.* ad loc.

²⁶ Foley 1988 and Heath 1987.

²⁷ See Collard et al. 1995, 19, 23–4 and Jouan 1966, 251.

²⁸ In addition to returning to Ithaca in disguise, Odysseus also enters Troy with this ploy: *Od.* 4.242–64; Procl. l. 224–7 Sev. and Eur. *Hecuba* 239–50. Another connection with narratives involving Odysseus is the threat to the baby Orestes evoking Palamedes' threat to the baby Telemachus recounted in the *Cypria*, see Procl. *Chrest.* 119–21 Sev.

²⁹ Tzetzes ad *Nubes* 920a: οἷον πτωχὸν Εὐριπίδης συσκευάζει τὸν Τήλεφον στρατηγὸν ὄντα Μυσίας μετὰ πηριδίου ἐλθόντα προσαίτην εἰς τὴν Ἑλλάδα καὶ τῆς Ἀγαμέμνονος αὐλῆς μόλις ποτὲ πυλωρὸν γεγονότα· δι' ὃν καὶ κωμῳδεῖται, 'Just as Euripides equips Telephus, a military leader of Mysia, as a beggar with a leather wallet coming to Greece and finally ending up an attendant at the door of Agamemnon. On account of this he is parodied in comedy.' For Odysseus as a beggar at the door, *Od.* 17.239, 356–63, 412–3, 466–7; cf. also 17.221 and Collard 1995: 23–4. For mention of his wallet see 17.197 (=18.108), 357, 411, 466–7.

³⁰ Euripides is certainly the poet spoken of in the scholion on Ael. Arist. 2.59 Behrs (p. 16, 14 Jebb [vol. 2]): τις τῶν ποιητῶν εἰσάγει τὸν Τήλεφον ἐλέγχοντα τὸν Ὀδυσσέα ἐκ τῶν αὐτοῦ λόγων, οὓς πρὸς τὸν Τήλεφον εἶπε, 'Some one of the poets brings Telephus on stage censuring Odysseus with the words that Odysseus spoke to Telephus.'

³¹ Ancient testimony for Odysseus and the πῖλος: Lucian, *De Saltatione* 83.14 tells of an actor playing Odysseus who was struck so hard on the head by his Ajax that he would have died were it not that he was wearing his πῖλος. See also schol. *Il.* 10.265a, Eustathius *Comm. ad Il.* ad loc., Lucian *Menippus* 8.3, Soranus *Vita Hippocratis* 12.2. For the πιλίον and Odysseus, see schol. *Il.* 10.265a, Plut. *Cato Major* 9.3.8, Polyb. *Historiae* 35.6.4.3. For visual representations of Odysseus in his πῖλος see *LIMC* s.v. 'Odysseus.' For modern acknowledgement of the link between πῖλος and Odysseus see Burkert 1983, 133. While Brommer's caution 1983, 110–11, that the πῖλος is neither an entirely exclusive nor constant attribute of Odysseus in the archaic period is justified, his narrow approach leaves no room for an archaic development of the typology which later became exclusive, and moreover privileges too much the literary sources giving a late fifth-century date. At any rate, his identification of the πέτασος as the most frequent headgear in archaic visual representations of Odysseus may lend further support to Solon's Odyssean role. If those scholars who argue from fr. 1 (Freeman 1926, 171 n. 2 followed by Flacelière 1947, 247) that Solon was originally depicted as wearing a πέτασος are correct, the replacement of the πέτασος with the πῖλος may confirm an early identification of Solon's role with Odysseus: it is possible to argue that as the πῖλος became exclusively characteristic of Odysseus by the end of the fifth century, its popularity exerted influence on the hat of the Salamis tradition, *despite* the poem's actual reference to heralding.

32 Schol. *Il.* 10.265. Eustathius (ad loc.) reflects this pattern of reaction: ἰστέον δὲ καὶ ὅτι πάσῃ μέν περικεφαλαίᾳ κατὰ τοὺς παλαιοὺς συμβέβηκε πῖλον ἔχειν ἐντός. οἱ δὲ νεώτεροι ὡς ἴδιόν τι ἀκούσαντες ἐνταῦθα τὸ τοῦ πίλου ἔπεισαν τοὺς ζωγράφους πιλίον περιτιθέναι τῷ Ὀδυσσεῖ. καὶ τοῦτο πρῶτος, φασίν, ἐποίησεν Ἀπολλόδωρος ὁ σκιαγράφος, 'Let it be known that according to the ancients it was normal to have a *pilos* in every helmet. But the *neoteroi*, having heard the bit about the *pilos* as something unique, persuaded the painters to place a *pilion* on Odysseus and the first to do this, they say, was Apollodorus.' But Apollodorus does not have a unanimous claim: both Pliny *NH* 35.108 and Serv. Verg. A. 2.44 attribute this innovation to Nicomachus.

33 Earliest is the bronze relief from Olympia (*c.* 620 [Olympia B 3600]). Certainly if the πιλίδιον of Euripides' *Telephus* was influenced by Odysseus, this would indicate a consciousness of this attribute's associations with Odysseus predating even Apollodorus.

34 Compare Solon 4W. 1–10 with *Odyssey* 1.32–43, 18.138–42. For discussion see Nestle 1942, 113–39; Jaeger 1966, 83–4; Adkins 1985, 114–15. See also, most recently, Noussia 2001, Mülke 2002 ad loc. and Irwin 2005, 113–34.

35 Gallo 1976, and Irwin 1999a, and 1999b, 95–7.

36 ἴομεν ἐς Σαλαμῖνα μαχησόμενοι περὶ νήσου | ἱμετῆς χαλεπόν τ' αἶσχος ἀπωσόμενοι.

37 For discussion of this passage see Bowie 1990; tempered by Kurke 1999, 26, n. 64.

38 Examples of overlap between epic and elegiac exhortation: Callinus 1W and *Iliad* 12. 310–28 (Sarpedon), 13.95–124 (Poseidon), 15. 494–9 (Hector). Tyrtaeus 11.11–14 and *Il.* 5.529–32 (Agam.) = 15.561–4 (Aias); cf. 11. 29–34 and *Il.* 13.130–5, 16.215–7. See Latacz 1977; Krischer 1979; Fowler 1987, 30–2; Singor 1995; cf. Eust. 385 ad *Iliad* 3.39 ff.

39 Compare the speech of Athenagoras in Thuc. 6.38–9 for the dichotomy of reluctant citizen body and aristocratic νέοι eager for war.

40 As Lowry 1991, 168, observes, the several versions localize the insanity in the agora, no doubt due at least in part to the phrase ἀντ' ἀγορῆς ('instead of a speech') in fr. 1. For this phrase see Noussia 1999, 63 and 69; 2001, 226 and 231, and Mülke 2002, 74–5 and 81–2.

41 The assumption of roles is a feature of sympotic poetry and behaviour. See, for example, Theogn. 257–60, 579–80, 861–4, Alc. 10 LP, Anacreon 40 (385P) and Bowie 1986, 16–20.

42 See Pucci 1997, 53–5, and Rose 1975 and 1992, chap. 2.

43 Consider the scholion to *Il.* 17.265 describing Solon as μιμησάμενον τὴν Ὁμήρου ποίησιν ἐν ἅπασιν, 'Solon imitated the poetry of Homer in all respects', and also D.L. 1.57, μᾶλλον οὖν Σόλων Ὅμηρον ἐφώτισεν ἢ Πεισίστρατος, 'Solon did more to illuminate Homer than Peisistratus'. For comment on the latter passage see Piccirilli 1975, 29–36.

44 On the problems of reconstructing Athenian internal politics around this affair see Hopper 1961, 208–17. For further discussion see Irwin 2005, 146 n. 93.

45 Irwin 2005, chs. 4–5.

46 On *geras* to the *dēmos*: Anhalt 1993, 100–1; Irwin 1999b, 149–54; Noussia 2001, 268–9; Mülke 2002, 184; Irwin 2005, 230–44. For elegiac representations of the *dēmos* see Archilochus 14W, Tyrtaeus 4W.5, Callinus 1W.16, Theognis 233, 847, 947–8, etc. On the subject of Solon's transgressive elegy see now Irwin 2006.

[47] See D.L. 1.78 (Pittacus), 97 (Periander) (and see Stephan. Schol. ad Arist. Rhet. 1375b31). Gentili and Prato 1985, 14–45, include Pittacus and Periander in their edition of the elegian poets. That Lobo of Argos may well be Diogenes' source for the poetic output of these figures ought not to undermine the testimony; see now Farinelli 2000. For poetic tyrants, compare also the poetic activities of Solon's fellow countryman and tyrant, Hipparchus; see Ford 1985, 88–95. On Solon and tyranny see Irwin 2005, chs. 7–8.

Bibliography

Adkins, A.W.H.
  1985   *Poetic Craft in the Early Greek Elegists*, Chicago.
Anhalt, E.K.
  1993   *Solon, the Singer*, Lanham.
Bowie, E.L.
  1986   'Early Greek elegy, symposium and public festival', *JHS* 106, 13–35.
  1990   '*Miles Ludens*? The problem of martial exhortation in early Greek elegy', in Murray, *Sympotica*, 221–9.
Brommer, F.
  1983   *Odysseus in der Antiken Kunst*, Darmstadt.
Collard, C. et al.
  1995   *Selected Fragmentary Plays: Euripides*, Warminster.
Crielaard, J.
  1995   *Homeric Questions*, Amsterdam, 183–200.
Dougherty, C. and Kurke, L. (eds.)
  1993   *Cultural Poetics in Archaic Greece: Cult, performance, politics*, Cambridge.
Else, G.
  1965   *The Origin and Early Form of Greek Tragedy*, Cambridge, Mass.
Fairweather, J.
  1974   'Fiction in the biographies of ancient writers', *Ancient Society* 5, 234–55.
Farinelli, C.
  2000   'Lobone di Argo ovvero la psiosi moderna del falso antico', *Aion* 22, 367–79.
Flacelière, R.
  1947   'Le bonnet de Solon', *REA* 49, 235–47.
Foley, H.
  1988   'Tragedy and politics in Aristophanes' *Acharnians*', *JHS* 108, 33–47.
Ford, A.
  1985   'The seal of Theognis: The politics of authorship in archaic Greece', in G. Nagy and T. Figueira, *Theognis of Megara: Poetry and the polis*, Baltimore, 82–95.
Forrest, W.G.
  1982   'Euboea and the islands', *Cambridge Ancient History* 3.3, Cambridge.
Fowler, R.
  1987   *The Nature of Early Greek Lyric: Three preliminary studies*, Toronto.
Freeman, K.
  1926   *The Life and Work of Solon*, London.

French, A.
   1957   'Solon and the Megarian question', *JHS* 77, 238–64.
Gallo, I.
   1976   'Solone a Soli', *QUCC* 21, 29–36.
Gentili, B. and Prato, C.
   1985   *Poetarum Elegiacorum Testimonia et Fragmenta*, vol. II, Leipzig.
Graziosi, B.
   2002   *Inventing Homer: The reception of epic*, Cambridge.
Heath, M.
   1987   'Euripides' *Telephus*', *CQ* 37, 272–80.
Hopper, R.
   1961   'Plain, shore and hill in early Athens', *ABSA* 56, 189–21.
Irwin, E.
   1988   'Biography, fiction and the Archilochean *ainos*', *JHS* 118, 177–83.
   1999   'Solecising in Solon's colony', *BICS* 43, 187–93.
   2005   *Solon and Early Greek Poetry: The politics of exhortation*, Cambridge.
   2006   'The transgressive elegy of Solon?', in J. Blok and A. Lardinois, *Solon of Athens: New historical and philological approaches*, Leiden, 36–78.
Jaeger, W.
   1966   'Solon's *Eunomia*', in *Five Essays*, Montreal, 75–99.
Jouan, F.
   1966   *Euripides et les légendes des chants cypriens*, Paris.
Krischer, T.
   1979   'Die Elegie des Kallinos', *Hermes* 107, 385–9.
Kurke, L.
   1999   *Coins, Bodies, Games and Gold*, Princeton.
Latacz, J.
   1979   *Kampfparänese, Kampfdarstellung und Kampfwirklichkeit in der* Ilias*, bei Kallinos und Tyrtaios*, Munich.
Lefkowitz, M.
   1976   'Fictions in literary biography: the new poem and the Archilochus legend', *Arethusa* 9, 181–9.
   1981   *The Lives of the Greek Poets,* London.
Linforth, I.
   1919   *Solon the Athenian*, Berkeley.
Lowry, E.
   1991   *Thersites: A study in comic shame*, New York.
MacDowell, D.M.
   2000   *Demosthenes. On the false embassy*, Oxford.
Martin, R.
   1993   'The seven sages as performers of wisdom', in Dougherty and Kurke (eds.) *Cultural Poetics in Archaic Greece*, 108–30.
Martina, A.
   1968   *Solon*, Rome.
Mastrocinque, A.
   1984   'Gli stracci de Telefo et il capello di Solone', *SIFC* 77, 25–34.

Mülke, C.
   2002   *Solons Politische Elegien und Iamben* (*Fr.* 1–13; 32–7 West). *Einleitung, Text, Übersetzung, Kommentar*, Leipzig.
Murray, O.
   1990   *Sympotica*, Oxford.
Nestle, W.
   1942   'Odyssee-Interpretationen II', *Hermes* 77, 113–39.
Noussia, M.
   1999   *A Commentary on Solon's Poems*, London.
   2001   *Solone. Frammenti dell' opera poetica*, Milan.
Piccirilli, L.
   1975   Megarika. *Testimonianze e Frammenti*, Pisa.
   1978   'Solone e la guerra per Salamina', *ASNP* 8, 1–13.
Pucci, P.
   1997   *The Song of the Sirens. Essays on Homer*, Lanham, Md.
Rhodes, P.J.
   1981   *A Commentary on the Aristotelian* Athenaion Politeia, Oxford.
Robertson, N.
   1998   'The city center of archaic Athens', *Hesperia* 67, 283–302.
Rose, P.
   1975   'Class ambivalence in the *Odyssey*', *Historia* 24, 129–49.
   1992   *Sons of the Gods, Children of the Earth: Ideology and literary form in ancient Greece*, Ithaca and London.
Singor, H.W.
   1995   '*Eni Protoisi Machesthai*', in Crielaard, *Homeric Questions*, 183–200.
Slings, S.
   1990   'The I in personal archaic lyric: an introduction', in S. Slings (ed.) *The Poet's I in Archaic Greek Lyric*, Amsterdam, 1–30.
Stehle, E.
   1997   *Performance and Gender in Ancient Greece*, Princeton.
Szegedy-Maszak, A.
   1978   'Legends of the Greek lawgivers', *GRBS* 19, 199–209.
Taylor, M.C.
   1997   *Salamis and the Salaminioi. The history of an unofficial Athenian demos*, Amsterdam.
Tedeschi, G.
   1982   'Solone e lo spazio della comunicazione elegiaca', *QUCC* n.s. 10, 33–46.
Van Wees, H.
   1992   *Status Warriors. War, violence, and society in Homer and history*, Amsterdam.
Vox, O.
   1984   *Solone autoritratto*, Padua.

3

READING THE GOSPELS AS BIOGRAPHY

Richard A. Burridge

1. The Gospels as a form of ancient biography[1]

A proper understanding of genre is central to the interpretation of any communication. Communication theory looks at the three main aspects of transmitter, message and receiver. In written works, this becomes author, text and audience or reader. Immediately the importance of discerning the kind of communication is clear. Both sender and receiver must use the same language and so correct interpretation depends on a correct identification of the genre. One does not listen to a fairy story in the same way as to a news broadcast. Thus genre is a key convention guiding both composition and interpretation. Genre forms a 'contract' or agreement, often unspoken or unwritten, or even unconscious, between author and reader, by which the author writes according to a set of expectations and conventions and we interpret the work using the same conventions. Genre is identified through a wide range of 'generic features' which may be signalled in advance, or embedded in a work's formal, structural composition and content. Taken together, such features communicate the 'family resemblance' of a work – its genre.

Therefore, before we can read the Gospels we have to discover what kind of books they might be. Differing understandings of their genre will have differing implications for their interpretation. For much of the ancient and mediaeval periods, the Gospels were interpreted on several levels: the literal, allegorical, moral and anagogical or mystical readings. The Reformers rejected all readings except for the literal, and on this basis the Gospels were interpreted as history – the stories of Jesus, even biographies. This led to their being used as a basis for the production of romantic 'Lives' such as Ernest Renan's *Life of Jesus* (1863). However, during the nineteenth century biographies began to explain the character of a person by considering his or her upbringing, formative years, schooling, psychological development and so on. The Gospels began to look unlike such biographies.

During the 1920s, scholars like Karl Ludwig Schmidt and Rudolf Bultmann rejected any notion that the Gospels were biographies: the Gospels have no interest in Jesus' human personality, appearance or character, nor do

31

they tell us anything about the rest of his life, other than his brief public ministry and an extended concentration on his death. Instead, the Gospels were seen as popular folk literature, collections of stories handed down orally. Far from being biographies, the Gospels were described as 'unique' forms of literature.[2] Furthermore, the development of form-critical approaches to the Gospels meant that they were no longer interpreted as whole narratives. Instead, they concentrated on each individual *pericope*, or section, and the focus for interpretation moved more to the passage's *Sitz im Leben* in the early church.

Redaction criticism concentrated on each Gospel's theological interests and the development of theories about the communities which produced them. Once the Gospels were seen as a type of 'community' documents, then their interpretation focused on the development of the communities within which and for which they were produced.[3] However, redaction critics also saw the writers of the Gospels as theologians, and the development of new literary approaches to the Gospels viewed them as conscious literary artists. This reopened the question of the genre of the Gospels and their place within the context of first-century literature, with scholars like Talbert and Aune beginning to treat the Gospels as biographies.[4]

A generic comparison of a group of different works from different authors will illustrate the nature of any genre. I undertook this exercise with ten examples of ancient biography: Isocrates' *Evagoras*, Xenophon's *Agesilaus*, Satyrus' *Euripides*, Nepos' *Atticus*, Philo's *Moses*, Tacitus' *Agricola*, Plutarch's *Cato Minor*, Suetonius' *Lives of the Caesars*, Lucian's *Demonax* and Philostratus' *Apollonius of Tyana*. This is a diverse group deliberately chosen to include the origins of biography in fourth-century BC rhetorical encomia through to third-century AD forerunners of the novel and hagiography. These form a diverse and flexible genre, yet still one with a recognizable family resemblance in both form and content. Many of them were known as 'lives', βίοι or *vitae*; the word 'biography' itself does not appear until the fifth-century work of Damascius, preserved in the ninth-century writer Photius. Bultmann's statement that the Gospels are not biography was a result of comparing them with modern examples and ideas of biography. This is a category error; when using the word 'biography' of both the Gospels and ancient 'Lives', we must avoid modern connotations, and compare them with one another to ascertain their shared generic features.

From the formal or structural perspective, ancient *Lives* are written in continuous prose narrative, between 10,000 and 20,000 words in length – the amount on a typical scroll of about 30–35 feet in length. Unlike modern biographies, Graeco-Roman lives do not cover a person's whole life in chronological sequence, and have little psychological analysis of the subject's character. They may begin with a brief mention of the hero's ancestry, family or city, his birth and an occasional anecdote about his upbringing; but usually the narrative moves rapidly on to his public debut later in life. Accounts of generals, politicians or statesmen are more chronologically ordered, recounting their great deeds and virtues, while lives of philosophers, writers or thinkers tend to be more anecdotal, arranged topically around collections of material to display their ideas and teachings. While the author may claim to provide information about his subject, often his underlying aims may include apologetic, polemic or didactic. Many ancient biographies cover the subject's death in great detail, since here he reveals his true character, gives his definitive teaching or does his greatest deed. Finally, detailed analysis of the verbal structure of ancient biographies reveals another generic feature. While most narratives have a wide variety of subjects, it is characteristic of biography that attention stays focused on one particular person with a quarter to a third of the verbs dominated by the subject, while another 15 per cent to 30 per cent occur in sayings, speeches or quotations from the person.

Like other ancient biographies, the Gospels are continuous prose narratives of the length of a single scroll, composed of stories, anecdotes, sayings and speeches. Their concentration on Jesus' public ministry from his baptism to death, and on his teaching and great deeds is not very different from the content of other ancient biographies. Similarly, the amount of space given to the last week of Jesus' life, his death and the resurrection reflects that given to the subject's death and subsequent events in works by Plutarch, Tacitus, Nepos and Philostratus. Verbal analysis demonstrates that Jesus is the subject of a quarter of the verbs in Mark's Gospel, with a further fifth spoken by him in his teaching and parables.[5] About half of the verbs in the other Gospels either have Jesus as the subject or are on his lips: like other ancient biographies, Jesus' deeds and words are of vital importance for the evangelists' portraits of Jesus. Therefore these marked similarities of form and content demonstrate that the Gospels have the generic features of ancient biographies and must be interpreted in that light.

Although this view is still contested, it is fair to say that it has won wide acceptance,[6] and is increasingly establishing itself as a starting assumption in, for instance, Biblical dictionaries and reference books, Gospel commentaries and wider interpretative studies.[7] If we view the Gospels as a form of ancient biography, however, the question arises of how this affects the way we read them. I will spend the rest of this article discussing some of the issues that have emerged from this genre hypothesis. These include the Christological consequences of the Gospels' focus upon Jesus, their sociological setting and their relationship to Jewish writings as well as to Graeco-Roman literature.

2. Reading the Gospels as Christological narrative

If the Gospels are a form of ancient biography, we must study them with the same biographical concentration upon their subject, to see the particular way each portrays an understanding of Jesus. The Gospels are nothing less than Christology in narrative form.

One implication of the biographical hypothesis is that the Gospels are about a person, more than theological ideas. Therefore the hermeneutical key for understanding them is not to be found in presumed problems in their hypothetical communities, but rather in their Christology. Every passage must be interpreted in the light of the biographical genre of the whole: what this story tells us about the author's understanding of Jesus. This Christological approach can be illustrated easily by considering the notorious problem of Mark's depiction of the disciples as lacking in faith. Despite the suggestion that the disciples are given the secret (μυστήριον) of the Kingdom of God (4.11), they fail to understand, and Jesus gets increasingly frustrated with them especially in the three boat scenes (4.40–1; 6.50–2; 8.14–21); James and John want the best seats in heaven (10.35–45), while they all fail to understand the Passion predictions (8.32–3; 9.32; 10.32–41). Eventually, they fall asleep in Gethsemane and desert Jesus, leaving Judas to betray him and Peter to deny him (14.37–50, 66–72). Not only scholars find this picture rather harsh; even Matthew and Luke 'improve' it, so that Matthew turns Mark's 'no faith' (Mk. 4.40) into 'men of little faith' (Matt. 8.26), while in Luke the disciples ask Jesus, 'increase our faith' (Lk. 17.5).

Form- and redaction-critical approaches seek to solve this problem by relating it to certain groups in the early church. Thus, Weeden's account is actually entitled *Mark: Traditions in conflict*; he sees the slow-witted disciples as standing for other leaders, particularly those with a *theios anēr* Christology to whom Mark is opposed.[8] Quite apart from the fact that there are problems over the concept of *theios anēr*, such an approach does not do justice to the positive material about the disciples in Mark: Jesus continues to explain things to them (e.g. 7.17–23; 8.34–8; 10.23–31; 11.20–5; 13); he has pity on their exhausted sleep (14.38); and Peter has at least followed Jesus into danger after the others fled, as he promised (14.29). If the disciples represent the wrong leaders, why does Jesus promise to meet them in Galilee (14.28; 16.7)?

Once we read the Gospels through the genre of ancient biography, then the Christological key can be used to interpret such passages. The point of each passage is not to tell us about the disciples, but about the biography's subject – namely, Jesus of Nazareth – in this case, that he is someone who is hard to understand and tough to follow. Given both the positive and the negative aspects of the disciples' portrayal, the readers should not be surprised if they find discipleship difficult; yet it is such struggling disciples whom Jesus calls and teaches, despite the difficulties. Thus, reading the Gospels in their biographical genre has immediate benefit for their interpretation.

Traditional form-critical approaches to the Gospels saw them as a collection of individual *pericopae*, separated or 'cut off' (περικόπτω) from their contexts, strung together like beads on a string with little overall coherence. Redaction critics looked at the evangelists' theological treatment of each story, thus bringing back the author, while narrative critics have redirected our attention back to the story as a whole. Studies such as those by Rhoads and Michie on Mark, Kingsbury on Matthew, Tannehill on Luke-Acts and Culpepper on John have analysed the plot lines throughout each Gospel, looking at how the characters develop, how repetition and reference back or forward in the narrative can lead to irony, and how the main themes are resolved in a climax.[9] Unfortunately, narrative critics did not grapple with the issue of genre in their initial studies until recently. Thus Rhoads says 'genre criticism is increasingly important for narrative analysis'.[10] Similarly, Culpepper admits that his 'discussion of plot in *Anatomy of the Fourth Gospel* does not adequately relate it to the issue of the genre of the Gospel or its structure'; therefore he proceeds to summarize the biographical hypothesis, noting that 'the conclusion that John is biography has fuelled several significant analyses of its plot', and he applies his recognition that 'the Gospel of John, therefore, is an ancient biography in dramatic form' to his account of John.[11]

The biographical genre for the Gospels takes this another step forward, leading us to expect the depiction of one person, the subject, as understood by another person, the author, leading up to the climax of the subject's death. Instead of a form-critical approach to the Gospels as Passion narratives preceded by disjointed *pericopae* strung together, biographical-narratological readings show how each evangelist traces his various themes through the Gospel to be resolved at the Passion.

In my *Four Gospels, One Jesus?* I attempted to provide such a biographical narrative reading of each Gospel, using the traditional images found in books like the Book of Kells in Trinity College, Dublin.[12] Thus Mark depicts Jesus like a lion who appears almost from nowhere (1.9), who then rushes around, being misunderstood by everybody, including his family and friends and the authorities (3.19–35). The descriptions of Jesus as an enigmatic wonder-worker who binds people to secrecy, the eschatological prophet who will suffer and die in Jerusalem as both Son of God and Son of Man, are held together in complementary tension in a biographical narrative, rather than as deriving from different historical traditions. Jesus finds Jerusalem and the Temple as barren as the fig-tree and prophesies their same destruction (11–13). He suffers and dies alone in dark desolation: 'my God, my God, why have you forsaken me?' (15.34) as the Passion brings to a climax all Mark's themes. Even the ending is full of enigma, fear and awe (16.1–8).

In Matthew, however, we have Jesus' Jewish background, genealogy and birth (1–2). He is another Moses, who teaches from mountains (5.1) and fulfils the law and the prophets, giving his teaching in five great blocks like the Pentateuch (5–7, 10, 13, 18, 24–5). Unfortunately, this brings him into conflict with the leaders of Israel. In the Passion, the cry of abandonment is answered by an earthquake as *everyone* realizes this was truly the Son of God (27.51–4, cf. Mk. 15.39). Finally, the Resurrection continues with further divine earthquakes and a new Israel on a mountain commissioned to go to the Gentiles (28.1–20).[13] Again, the climax resolves all the themes of the Gospel.

Luke begins with a Greek periodic Preface (Lk. 1.1–4) and sets Jesus within the history of both Israel and contemporary Roman rule (Lk. 1.5–80; 2.1; 3.1). Jesus is concerned for the poor, the lost, outcasts, women, Samaritans and Gentiles. He is also the man of prayer (11.1–4). At the Passion he cares for women (23.27–31) and prays for the soldiers and the penitent thief (23.34, 43), committing himself in trust to his Father (23.46). After the resurrection, history looks forward from Israel's past to the world's future (24.44–7). The Gospel ends as it began 'in Jerusalem with great joy, in the Temple blessing God' (24.51–2, cf. 1.5–23). Such a clear balanced biographical narrative reflects a single author and purpose.

John begins, in the beginning, with God (Jn. 1.1–18). Jesus is constantly centre stage and he is characterized as the author interweaves 'signs' and discourse, revealing the effect of meditation and theological reflection upon the person of Jesus. Opposition from 'the Jews' develops through the first half (2–12); at the climax, Jesus gathers his disciples, washes their feet and explains what will happen (13–17). The 'hour of glory' is also the Passion: throughout Jesus is serenely in control, directing events (19.11), organizing his mother and disciples (19.26–7), fulfilling scripture (19.28) until finally 'it is accomplished' (19.30). After the resurrection he appears as he wishes to comfort Mary (20.14), challenge Thomas (20.26) and restore Peter (21.15–19). Once again, we have a clear portrait through the ministry of Jesus culminating in his death and resurrection.

These four individual accounts, each concerned with the resolution of their particular themes, were composed by four writers, each portraying a particular view of Jesus in the manner of ancient biography. The fact that the fathers chose to keep four separate accounts in the canon, despite the problems of plurality and possible conflict,[14] demonstrates that they recognized these works as coherent single accounts of Jesus – and therefore they need to be read in that way today.

3. Reading the Gospels in their social setting

(a) *Communities or audiences*

New Testament scholars often assume that the Gospels were written within the context of a community and produced specifically for that community. In fact, these are two separate issues, since it is possible for a work to be written within one group, but aimed at people outside that community, or conversely, to be directed at a community by an individual writing from outside it. A volume edited by Richard Bauckham entitled *The Gospels for all Christians: Rethinking the Gospel audiences*, provides a critique of such community approaches. If the Gospels are a form of Graeco-Roman biography, we should consider whether Lives functioned in such a community-based way in the ancient world.[15]

One parallel may be the philosophical schools of the fourth and third centuries BC. Various βίοι of philosophers date from this period, although since the works themselves are not preserved, we cannot be sure how fully they fit the genre.[16] However, they are still written for a wider audience – to attract people outside the author's own group.

Closer in time to the Gospels, we have the sequence of 'Cato literature': from Cicero's panegyric, the *Cato*, Caesar's reply the *Anti-Cato* and a succession of works by Brutus, Hirtius, Augustus and Thrasea Paetus as 'Catonism' became 'an ideological hallmark of the Early Principate'.[17] However, this was more of a sequence of Lives than a 'school' or 'Cato community'. Something similar happens in Tacitus' *Agricola*; it may have been written after Domitian's fall as a political apology for people like Tacitus and Agricola who worked with evil emperors (42.4).[18] Thus while the book is written within one group (Tacitus and his family) it is aimed at others involved in Roman politics; in biographies, it is the portrait of the subject which matters more than the readership.

This should make us hesitate about hypothetical 'Matthean' or 'Johannine' communities without further specific evidence. Interpreting the Gospels as βίοι provides a critique of too much community-based sociological analysis of the Gospel audiences. More recently, scholars have moved away from reconstructing the evangelists' communities to what Mary Ann Beavis describes as a 'more general audience of early Christian missionary teaching/preaching'.[19] Reading the Gospels as βίοι confirms that this development is more helpful than imagined communities.

(b) *Social function*

Genre can sometimes be a clue to both the social context and the function for which a work was composed – as, for example, encomia were delivered on certain specific social occasions. The problem with the biographical hypothesis for the Gospels is that there were a variety of functions for ancient βίοι, and different lives appear to have been used in different ways – for praise and blame (Xenophon's *Agesilaus*), but also for exemplary, moral purposes (Plutarch), for didactic or information (Satyrus), to preserve the memory of a great man (Tacitus' *Agricola*) or even, in the case of Lucian or Philostratus, simply to entertain.[20] Therefore, putting the Gospels into this genre does not automatically answer all our questions about purpose and social function within a community setting.

However, one possible setting for the Gospel communities arises from the social functions of apologetic and polemic, as was the case with early βίοι in the philosophical schools through to the later debate between Christians and Pagans at the end of the third and early fourth centuries AD with lives like Porphyry's *Plotinus* and Eusebius' *Origen*.[21] This function also suggests a wider audience for 'social legitimation' whereby an author seeks to explain or justify the position taken by himself or his social grouping, as in the lives of Cato or the *Agricola*. Graham Stanton has declared that 'this is precisely the social function I envisage for Matthew's βίος of Jesus' and he goes on to argue for a wider audience than just one single 'Matthean community'.[22] Similarly in Luke-Acts, we have the constant declaration of the 'innocence' of Jesus (by Pilate 23.4, 14–15, 22 and also in Luke's redaction of the centurion in 23.47), and this is then repeated frequently of the early church leaders such as Peter and Paul in Acts. This implies that the author envisaged a wider public, aiming to legitimate the church in the eyes of contemporary society. Thus the social functions of apologetic and polemic suggest that the Gospels, like other βίοι, are written for wider audiences than just single communities.

(c) *Social setting of delivery and publication*
It is often assumed that the Gospels were read in church, either in worship (hence the various lectionary hypotheses) or for instruction (hence sugges-tions about manuals of teaching).[23] This takes us straight into questions about the production and publication of ancient texts and the extent to which people were able to read them. Reading aloud was one of the main ways of 'publication' in the ancient world, often as entertainment after dinner. To this extent we can see a 'communal setting' (rather than the tighter defini-tion of a sectarian community) as a frequent feature of ancient literature. The *Agricola* contains many *sententiae*, pithy little maxims which conclude each section with a rhetorical flourish – allowing a 'pause for applause'. Similarly, the style of Lucian's *Demonax* lends itself to oral delivery, with space for audience reaction (even laughter?) after each anecdote.

One of the reasons for the division of ancient works into 'books' is that one scroll is about the amount which can be delivered in one 'sitting'. The average length of a book of Herodotus or Thucydides is about 20,000 words, which would take around two hours to read. After the Alexandrian library reforms, an average 30–35 feet scroll would contain 10,000 to 25,000 words – exactly the range into which both the Gospels and many ancient βίοι fall.[24] We are so used to hearing the Gospels in lectionary use in small sections of twelve to twenty verses or studying individual *pericopae* that we forget that the entire text can be read out aloud in a couple of hours. It is significant that Alec McCowen's dramatic solo rendition of Mark's Gospel (in the King James' Version) has been an evening's entertainment on stage on both sides of the Atlantic; the video recording of his performance runs for only 105 minutes in total.[25] Christopher Bryan's *A Preface to Mark* provides an interesting study of that Gospel as a Hellenistic life designed to be read aloud.[26]

Consideration of how βίοι, like those of Tacitus and Lucian, were read aloud or performed can benefit Gospel studies, illuminating how they may have been read, not just in one community, but in many different groups in many lands. Thus viewing the Gospels as ancient biographies can liberate us from the circularity of deducing the communities from the text and then interpreting the text in light of these (deduced) communities. Instead, this generic comparison provides external evidence of social groupings and levels in which βίοι functioned.

4. Gospel genre and the absence of Rabbinic biography

Several scholars have drawn attention to the absence of any proper comparison of the Gospels with Jewish literature. Work has concentrated on Graeco-Roman biography because this was the genre increasingly being proposed for the Gospels. If we accept arguments, however, for a generic relationship of the Gospels with Graeco-Roman biography, the question of why the evangelists used this genre and not a Jewish one still needs to be faced (see Burridge 2000).

(a) *The absence of Rabbinic biography*

First, we must note that it is very common to compare individual *pericopae* in the Gospels with rabbinic material. Thus, Rabbi Michael Hilton and Fr Gordian Marshall OP in *The Gospels and Rabbinic Judaism: A study guide* compare Jesus' sayings with rabbinic sources. The Great Commandment, (Mark 12.28–34 and the parallels in Matt. 22.34–40 and Luke 10.25–8) is compared with a *Sifra* passage from Rabbi Akiba on Lev. 19.18, Genesis Rabba 24.7 (on Gen. 5.1) and the famous story from the Babylonian Talmud, *Shabbat* 31A, of the different reactions from Shammai and Hillel when asked to teach the whole law to a Gentile enquirer standing on one leg: Shammai chased the questioner away, while Hillel repeated the Golden Rule as the sum of the whole Torah, with the rest as commentary, but still to be learned. Hilton concludes that 'Jesus at his most "rabbinic" engaged in lively debate and answering some of the same questions as the rabbis'.[27]

An international symposium on Hillel and Jesus held in Jerusalem in June 1992, devotes some 170 pages to comparisons of their sayings.[28] Philip Alexander notes that 'the overriding feeling is one of astonishment at the convergence of the two traditions'.[29] Alexander has written extensively on such rabbinic writings, and how New Testament scholars should use this material.[30] He collected together some rabbinic stories to compare 'Rabbinic biography and the Biography of Jesus', concluding, 'there are parallels to the individual pericopae, and at this level similarities are very strong. In terms of form, function, setting and motif, the Rabbinic anecdotes are very close to the Gospel pericopae, and there can be little doubt that both belong to the same broad Palestinian Jewish tradition of story-telling.'[31]

Since Bultmann and other form-critics saw the Gospels as strung together like beads on a string, we might expect rabbinic stories to form similar accounts of Hillel, Shammai or others. Yet, this is precisely what we do *not* find, much to everybody's surprise. Thus Philip Alexander concludes his study of 'Rabbinic biography and the biography of Jesus' as follows: 'there are no Rabbinic parallels to the Gospels as such. This is by far the most important single conclusion to emerge from this paper... There is not a trace of an ancient biography of any of the Sages... This is a profound enigma.'[32]

Jacob Neusner has devoted much study to this question. In 1984, in his *In Search of Talmudic Biography*, he states that 'there is no composition of tales and stories into a sustained biography'.[33] He followed this with an analysis of *Why No Gospels in Talmudic Judaism?* The stories about sages were never compiled into biographical narratives or Gospels: they are 'the compositions no one made'.[34] In *The Incarnation of God* again he stresses: 'While the two Talmuds present stories about sages, neither one contains anything we might call a "gospel" of a sage or even a chapter of a gospel. There is no sustained biography of any sage.'[35] Finally, he answered the claim of similarities between the Gospels and Jewish material with *Are there really Tannaitic Parallels to the Gospels?*[36]

In the symposium on *Jesus and Hillel*, Gottstein notes the 'basic differences between the nature of Talmudic literature and the nature of the Gospels. We have no Talmudic Gospel of any Rabbi.' He continues, 'the present discussion assumes Gospel writing to be a form of biography', and concludes, 'one could therefore ask why we do not have any instances of rabbinic biography'.[37]

(b) *Possible literary reasons for this absence*

Most rabbinic material consists of anecdotes, which are more about a rabbi's teaching than his actions. Many of the stories are dialogue which leads up to actual saying, with any narrative at the start to set the scene. Thus the rabbinic material is more like Q or Gospel of Thomas, i.e. it has the genre of sayings, *logia*, more than biographical narrative. Philip Alexander says that the rabbinic stories have an 'intensely oral character…against the more prosy "written" style of the Gospels'. They are 'extremely compressed, allusive, witty, dramatic and learned'; more like bits from a play to be performed than a text to be read, intended for oral circulation, not in written form.[38] In *The Incarnation of God*, Neusner applies a 'taxonomy of narrative' to the material and finds 'five species of the genus narrative'.[39] The problem with this is that 'narrative' is neither a genus nor a genre in itself according to most literary theory of genres, and his five 'species' are not clearly identified as subgenres.

However, the basic point is clear, that the rabbinic anecdotes are directed more towards sayings than actions. This would not prevent their being compiled into an ancient biography. Lucian's *Demonax* has a brief preface and account of the philosopher's life, followed by a large number of anecdotes all strung together, each composed mainly of dialogue leading up to a pronouncement or decision by the great sage – yet it is still called a 'life', βίος. In fact, the *Demonax* is more loosely structured with less integration of teaching and activity than even Mark's Gospel.[40]

Thus although the rabbinic material is more anecdotal than are the Gospels and some ancient lives, it still contains enough biographical elements (through sage stories, narratives, precedents and death scenes) to enable an editor to compile a 'life of Hillel' or whoever. Such an account would have been recognisable as ancient biography and have looked like the *Demonax*. Literary and generic reasons alone are therefore not sufficient to explain this curious absence of rabbinic biography.

(c) *Theological reasons – the Christological focus*

Biography directs the audience's attention to the life and character of the subject. The decision to write a biographical account of Jesus has important Christological implications. Equally, the failure to write, or even compile from the anecdotes, any biographies of the rabbis also has significant implications.

Neusner argues that this is a reflection of the fact that the individual sages are not the centre of attention. '*Sage-stories turn out not to tell about sages at all; they are stories about the Torah personified. Sage-stories cannot yield a gospel because they are not about sages anyway. They are about the Torah…* The Gospel does just the opposite, with its focus on the uniqueness of the hero.'[41] Alexander makes the same point: 'The obvious answer is that neither Eliezer nor any other Sage held in Rabbinic Judaism the central position that Jesus held in early Christianity. The centre of Rabbinic Judaism was Torah; the centre of Christianity was the person of Jesus, and the existence of the Gospels is, in itself, a testimony to this fact.'[42] Similarly Rabbi Michael Hilton says: 'The Gospels can thus be regarded as a kind of commentary on Jesus' life, in much the same way as the Rabbis comment on biblical texts'.[43] Similarly, Gottstein in comparing Jesus and Hillel stresses that 'Gospel writing would be the product of the particular religious understanding of the messianic, and therefore salvific, activity of Jesus. The lack of Gospels in rabbinic literature would then be a less significant issue, since no salvific claim is attached to any particular Rabbi.'[44]

Thus the literary shift from unconnected anecdotes about Jesus, which resemble rabbinic material, to composing them together in the genre of an ancient biography is making an enormous Christological claim. Rabbinic biography is not possible, because no rabbi is unique and each is only important as he represents the Torah, which holds the central place. To write a biography is to replace the Torah by putting a human person in the centre of the stage. The literary genre makes a major theological shift which becomes an explicit Christological claim – that Jesus of Nazareth is Torah embodied.[45]

5. Reading the Gospels' biographical narrative in ethical debate

The final area to which we want to apply the biographical genre of the Gospels concerns New Testament ethics. The biographical-narrative approach to the Gospels reminds us that the Gospels are not just collections of Jesus' teachings. Such documents did exist, such as the Gospel of Thomas, or later Gnostic Gospels, which were just sayings and had no narrative about Jesus' life, actions – or even his death. It is probable that Q, if it existed as a document, was a similar collection of sayings; the narrative context of the Q sayings is usually supplied by Luke or Matthew – and there is no Q material in the Passion narratives. Many approaches to the ethics of Jesus treat the canonical Gospels as though they were like these collections of sayings and just concentrate on his teaching and words. Central to all ancient biography is that the picture of the subject is built up through both their words *and* their deeds. So to find the heart of Jesus' ethic we need to consider both his ethical teaching *and* his actual practice. This leads to the question of the relation of Jesus' ethical teaching (often strict and rigorous) to his pastoral practice (so open and accepting that it offends religious and moral authorities).

The first thing to note is the Gospels are ancient biographies, not primarily ethical texts (as, say, Aristotle's *Nicomachean Ethics*), nor is Jesus portrayed as just a moral teacher, despite so many people's estimation of him as such. Jesus' ethical teaching is not a separate and discrete set of maxims, but is part of his proclamation of the kingdom of God. It is primarily intended to elicit a response from his hearers to live as disciples within the community of others who also respond and follow. In his appeal for the eschatological restoration of the people of God, Jesus intensified the demands of the Law with his rigorous ethic of renunciation and self-denial in the major human experiences of money, sex, power, violence, and so forth while at the same time his central stress on love and forgiveness opened the community to the very people who had moral difficulties in these areas. Hence he was regularly accused of being 'a glutton and a drunkard, a friend of tax collectors and sinners' (Matt. 11.19, Luke 7.34).[46]

Ancient biographies held together both words and deeds in portraying their central subject. Many were written explicitly to give an example to others to emulate: Xenophon composed his *Agesilaus* to provide an example (παράδειγμα) for others to follow to become better people (ἀνδραγαθίαν ἀσκεῖν, 10.2). Equally, Plutarch aims to provide examples so that by imitating (μίμησις) the virtues and avoiding the vices described, the reader can improve his own moral character (*Pericles* 1; *Aem. Paul.* 1). Equally in the Gospels, the readers are exhorted to follow Jesus' example in accepting and welcoming others (Mark 1.17; Luke 6.36). Paul also stresses the theme of imitation: 'be imitators of me, as I am of Christ' (1 Cor. 11.1; Phil. 3.17; 1 Thess. 1.6), following the 'example to imitate' (τύπον μιμεῖσθαι) (2 Thess. 3.7, 9).[47] Therefore, as befits a biographical narrative, we must confront this paradox between Jesus' teaching and his activity and behaviour.

In studying Jesus' ethics, therefore, it is not enough just to outline the main points of his teaching. Both the biographical genre of the Gospels and the ancient idea of imitation suggest that such study must be earthed in his practical example, both of calling people to repentance and discipleship – but also his open pastoral acceptance of sinners. All too often those who apply New Testament ethics to today end up doing one or the other: that is, teaching a rigorist ethic with strenuous demands which seems condemnatory and alienates people from the church – or having an open acceptance of sinners and being accused of having no ethics at all! Thus even here, the biographical genre of the Gospels has significant implications for today.[48]

Notes

[1] This section is a summary of my revised PhD thesis, originally published as *What are the Gospels? A comparison with Graeco-Roman biography*, SNTS MS 70 (Cambridge 1992, paperback 1995); a revised and updated edition was published by Eerdmans in 2004.

[2] Bultmann 1972, 371–4.

[3] See for example, Kee 1977, for Mark's community; Balch 1991 for Matthew's; Esler 1987 for Luke's; Brown 1979, on the Johannine community.

[4] Talbert 1978a; Aune 1988.

[5] See my analysis charts of verbal subjects in *What are the Gospels?*, App. I, 261–74.

[6] For the response of New Testament scholars, see, for instance, Neyrey 1993, 361–3; Tuckett 1993, 74–5; Stibbe 1993, 380–1; Papaphilippopoulos 1994, 420–1; Porter 1993, 113; Ellis 1993, 56; Clark 1992, 334; Müller 1993, 514–15; Mountford, 1993, 24; Alexander 1994, 73–6/84–6. Classical reaction from Brenk 1994; Duff 1996, 265–6.

[7] Reference books: Tannehill 1995, 68–70; Tuckett 1995, 71–86; Pelling 1996, 241–2; Wansbrough 2001, 1001–2; commentaries: Garland 1993, 5–9; Bryan 1993, vii, 27–30; Witherington III 2001, 1–9; Witherington III 1998, 2–39; wider studies: Wright 1992, 373, 381, 390, 391, 411–12; Wright 1996, 112–13; Frickenschmidt 1997; Hurtado 2003, 279 (see esp. n. 45) and 281–2. Perhaps the most trenchant criticism has come from Edwards 1997, but see also Collins 1995, who argues that the Gospels are more like historical monographs than biographies; and Wills 1997, and Vines 2002, who favour a relationship with the early novel.

[8] Weeden 1971.

[9] Rhoads and Michie 1982; Kingsbury 1988; Tannehill 1986 and 1990; Culpepper 1983. See also Stibbe 1992; Powell 1990 and 1993.

[10] Rhoads 1999, 275.

[11] Culpepper 1997, 188–99; quotations from pp. 189, 192, 198.

[12] Burridge, 1994, 2005.

[13] For a good comparison of Matthew with Mark, see Houlden 1987.

[14] For the four-fold canon and plurality, see Skeat 1992, 194–9, and Cullmann 1956, 37–54, translated from the original German article in *TZ*, i (1945), 23–42; see also Burridge 1994, 25–7, 164–79.

[15] Burridge 1998, 113–45; for responses to this volume as a whole, see Esler 1998, 235–48, and Bauckham's reply, 249–53, and Sim 2001, 3–27.

[16] See Wehrli 1967–9, for the fragments; for further discussion of the schools, see Momigliano 1971, 66–79; and for a comparison of Hellenistic school biographies with Acts, see Alexander 1993.

[17] Geiger 1979, 48–72, quotation from 48.

[18] See Furneaux 1898, 10–15; also Dorey 1969, 1–18; Syme 1958, vol. 1, 26–9, 125–31.

[19] Beavis 1989, 171; see also Tolbert 1989; see esp. 59–79 and 303–6.

[20] For a fuller list of the functions of βίοι, see Burridge 1992, 149–52 and 185–8; also, Talbert 1978b, 1620–3.

[21] See Cox 1983, especially 135.

[22] Stanton 1994, 9–23, quotation from 10; see also Stanton 1992, 70, also 104–7 and 378–9 for more on legitimation, and 232–55 for the use of Matthew in early Christian-Jewish polemic and apologetic.

[23] For worship, see Goulder 1978; see also Beavis 1989, for a comprehensive discussion of proposals for Mark's audience in terms of worship, 46–50, and teaching, 50–66.

[24] Scrolls tended to be 8–12 inches high and 30–35 feet long; columns were 2–4 inches wide, with 18–25 letters per line and 35–45 lines per column; see Kenyon and Roberts 1970, 172–5; on the relative lengths of different genres, see Burridge 1992, 118–19.

[25] The video of Alec McCowen's solo performance of St Mark's Gospel is produced by Arthur Cantor Films, 2112 Broadway, Suite 400, New York, NY 10023.

[26] Bryan 1993.

[27] Hilton and Marshall 1988, 34.

[28] Charlesworth and Johns 1997.

[29] Alexander 1997, 363–88; quotation from 388.

[30] See for example, Alexander 1983, 237–46.

[31] Alexander 1984, 19–50; quotation from 42.

[32] Alexander 1984, 40.

[33] Neusner 1984, 2.

[34] Neusner 1988, 33–8.

[35] Neusner 1988, 213.

[36] Neusner 1993.

[37] Goshen Gottstein 1997, 31–55; quotations from 34–5.

[38] Alexander 1984, 42.

[39] Neusner 1988, 214.

[40] See my discussion of the *Demonax* in Burridge 1992, 166, 170–1.

[41] Neusner 1988, 52–3; his italics.

[42] Alexander 1984, 41.

[43] Hilton and Marshall 1988, 13.

[44] Goshen Gottstein, 1997, 35

[45] Schoneveld 1990, 77–93.

[46] See Sanders 1985, 206, 283, 323 for the accusation that Jesus allowed the 'wicked' into the kingdom.

[47] See McGrath 1991, 289–98; McGrath compares this with Luther's idea of 'being conformed to Christ' and Calvin's being 'incorporated into Christ' (296).

[48] These last few paragraphs are a summary of part of a major research project on *New Testament Ethics Today* upon which I have been working over recent years, to be published by Eerdmans in 2007 as *Imitating Jesus: An inclusive approach to New Testament ethics*.

Bibliography

Alexander, L.C.A.

1993   'Acts and ancient intellectual biography', in B.W. Winter and A.C. Clarke (eds.) *The Book of Acts in its First Century Setting*, vol. 1 of *The Book of Acts in its Ancient Literary Setting*, Grand Rapids.

1994   Review of Burridge 1992 in *Evangelical Quarterly* 66, 73–6, also reprinted in *European Journal of Theology* 3.1, 1994, 84–6.

Alexander, P.S.

1983   'Rabbinic Judaism and the New Testament', *ZNW* 74, 237–46.

1984   'Rabbinic biography and the biography of Jesus: a survey of the evidence', in C.M. Tuckett (ed.) *Synoptic Studies: The Ampleforth conferences of 1982 and 1983*, JSNT SS 7, Sheffield, 19–50.

1997   'Jesus and the Golden Rule', in Charlesworth and Johns (eds.) *Hillel and Jesus*, 363–88.

Aune, D.E.
  1988   *The New Testament in its Literary Environment*, Cambridge.
Balch, D.L. (ed.)
  1991   *Social History of the Matthean Community*, Minneapolis.
Beavis, Mary Ann
  1989   *Mark's Audience: The literary and social setting of Mark 4.11–12*, JSNTSS 33, Sheffield.
Brenk, Fred
  1994   Review of Burridge 1992 in *Gnomon* (66).
Brown, R.E.
  1979   *The Community of the Beloved Disciple*, London.
Bryan, C.
  1993   *A Preface to Mark: Notes on the Gospel in its literary and cultural settings*, Oxford.
Bultmann, R.
  1972   *The History of the Synoptic Tradition*, Oxford.
Burridge, R.A.
  1992   *What are the Gospels? A comparison with Graeco-Roman biography*, SNTS MS 70, Cambridge. Revised and updated edn, Grand Rapids 2004.
  1994   *Four Gospels, One Jesus? A symbolic reading*, Grand Rapids and London. Revised and updated edn, 2005.
  1998   'About people, by people, for people: Gospel genre and audiences', in R. Bauckham (ed.) *The Gospels for all Christians: Rethinking the Gospel audiences*, Grand Rapids, 113–45.
  2000   'Gospel genre, christological controversy and the absence of rabbinic biography: some implications of the biographical hypothesis', in D.G. Horrell and C.M. Tuckett (eds.) *Christology, Controversy and Community: New Testament essays in honour of David Catchpole*, Leiden.
  2007   *Imitating Jesus: An inclusive approach to New Testament ethics*, Grand Rapids.
Camp, G.
  2002   'Woe to you hypocrites! Law and leaders in the Gospel of Matthew', PhD thesis, University of Sheffield, 64–5.
Charlesworth, J.H. and Johns, L.L. (eds.)
  1997   *Hillel and Jesus: Comparative studies of two major religious leaders*, Minneapolis.
Clark, N.
  1992   Review of Burridge 1992 in *Expository Times*, August, 334.
Collins, A.Y.
  1995   'Genre and the Gospels', *JR* 75.2, 239–46.
Cox, P.
  1983   *Biography in Late Antiquity: A quest for the Holy Man*, California.
Cullmann, O.
  1956   'The plurality of the Gospels as a theological problem in antiquity', in A.J.B. Higgins (ed.) *The Early Church: Studies in early Christian history and theology*, Philadelphia. Transl. from the orig. German article in *TZ* i, 23–42.

Culpepper, R.A.
    1983   *Anatomy of the Fourth Gospel: A study in literary design*, Philadelphia.
    1997   'The plot of John's story of Jesus', in J.D. Kingsbury (ed.) *Gospel Interpretation: Narrative-Critical and Social-Scientific Approaches*, Harrisburg.

Dorey, T.A.
    1969   'Agricola' and 'Domitian', in *Tacitus*, London.

Duff, T.
    1996   Review of Burridge 1992 in *The Classical Review*, n.s. XLVI.2, 265–6.

Edwards, M.J.
    1997   'Biography and the biographic', in M.J. Edwards and S. Swain (eds.) *Portraits: Biographical representation in the Greek and Latin literature of the Roman Empire*, Oxford, 227–36.

Ellis, E.E.
    1993   Review of Burridge 1992 in *Southwestern Journal of Theology*, 36.1, 56.

Esler, P.F.
    1987   *Community and Gospel in Luke-Acts*, SNTS MS 57, Cambridge.
    1998   'Community and Gospel in early Christianity: A response to Richard Bauckham's *Gospels for all Christians*, *Scottish Journal of Theology* 51.2, 235–48.

Frickenschmidt, D.
    1997   *Evangelium als Biographie: Die vier Evangelien im Rahmen antiker Erzählkunst*, Tübingen.

Furneaux, H.
    1898   *Cornelii Taciti*, Vita Agricolae, Oxford.

Garland, D.E.
    1993   *Reading Matthew: A literary and theological commentary on the first Gospel*, London.

Geiger, J.
    1979   'Munatius Rufus and Thrasea Paetus on Cato the Younger', *Athenaeum* 57, 48–72.

Goshen Gottstein, A.
    1997   'Jesus and Hillel: Are comparisons possible?', in Charlesworth and Johns (eds.) *Hillel and Jesus*, 31–55.

Goulder, M.
    1978   *The Evangelist's Calendar: A lectionary explanation of the development of scripture*, London.

Hilton, Rabbi M. and Marshall, Fr G., OP
    1988   *The Gospels and Rabbinic Judaism: A study guide*, London.

Houlden, J.L.
    1987   *Backward into Light: The passion and resurrection of Jesus according to Matthew and Mark*, London.

Hurtado, L.
    2003   *Lord Jesus Christ: Devotion to Jesus in earliest Christianity*, Grand Rapids.

Kee, H.C.
    1977   *The Community of the New Age*, Philadelphia.

Kenyon, F.G. and Roberts, C.H.
    1970   'Books, Greek and Latin', *The Oxford Classical Dictionary*, 2nd edn, Oxford.

Kingsbury, J.D.
   1988   *Matthew as Story*, 2nd edn, Philadelphia. First edn. 1986.
McGrath, A.
   1991   'In what way can Jesus be a moral example for Christians?', *Journal of the Evangelical Theological Society* 34, 289–98.
Momigliano, A.
   1971   *The Development of Greek Biography*, Harvard.
Mountford, B.
   1993   Review of Burridge 1992 in *Theological Book Review* 5.3 (June) 24.
Müller, U.B.
   1993   Review of Burridge 1992 in *Theologische Literaturzeitung* 118.6, 514–15.
Neusner, J.
   1984   *In Search of Talmudic Biography: The problem of the attributed saying*, Brown Judaic Studies 70, Chicago.
   1988a   *The Incarnation of God: The character of divinity in formative Judaism*, Philadelphia.
   1988b   *Why No Gospels in Talmudic Judaism?*, Atlanta.
   1993   *Are there really Tannaitic Parallels to the Gospels? A refutation of Morton Smith*, South Florida Studies in the history of Judaism, no. 80.
Neyrey, J.
   1993   Review of Burridge 1992 in *CBQ* (April) 361–3.
Papaphilippopoulos, R.
   1994   Review of Burridge 1992 in *Scottish Journal of Theology* 47.3, 420–1.
Pelling, C.B.R.
   1996   'Biography, Greek', *The Oxford Classical Dictionary*, Oxford, 241–2.
   1999   'Epilogue', in C. Kraus (ed.) *The Limits of Historiography*, Leiden, 325–60.
Porter, S.E.
   1993   Review of Burridge 1992 in *JSNT* 59 (Sept), 113.
Powell, M.A.
   1990   *What is Narrative Criticism? A new approach to the Bible*, Minneapolis. London 1993.
Rhoads, D.
   1999   'Narrative criticism: practice and prospects', in D. Rhoads and K. Syreeni (eds.) *Characterization in the Gospels: Reconceiving narrative criticism*, JSNT SS 184, Sheffield.
Rhoads, D. and Michie, D.
   1982   *Mark as Story: An introduction to the narrative of a Gospel*, Philadelphia.
Sanders, E.P.
   1985   *Jesus and Judaism*, London.
Schoneveld, J.
   1990   'Torah in the flesh: a new reading of the prologue of the Gospel of John as a contribution to a christology without anti-semitism', in M. Lowe (ed.) *The New Testament and Christian-Jewish Dialogue: Studies in honor of David Flusser*, Emmanuel 24/25, Jerusalem, 77–93.
Sim, D.C.
   2001   'The Gospels for all Christians? A response to Richard Bauckham', *JSNT* 84, 3–27.

Skeat, T.C.
  1992   'Irenaeus and the four-fold Gospel canon', *Nov T* 34.2, 194–9.
Stanton, G.N.
  1992   *A Gospel for a New People: Studies in Matthew*, Edinburgh.
  1994   'Revisiting Matthew's communities', in E.H. Loverington (ed.) *SBL Seminar Papers*, Atlanta.
Stibbe, M.W.G.,
  1992   *John as Storyteller: Narrative criticism and the Fourth Gospel*, SNTSMS 73, Cambridge.
  1993   Review of Burridge 1992 in *Biblical Interpretation* 1,3, 380–1.
Syme, R.
  1958   *Tacitus*, Oxford.
Talbert, C.H.
  1978a   *What is a Gospel? The genre of the canonical Gospels*, London.
  1978b   'Biographies of philosophers and rulers as instruments of religious propaganda in Mediterranean antiquity', *ANRW* II.16.2, 1620–3.
Tannehill, R.C.
  1986 and 1990   *The Narrative Unity of Luke-Acts: A literary interpretation*, 2 vols., Philadelphia and Minneapolis.
  1995   'The Gospels and narrative literature', *The New Interpreter's Bible*, vol. VIII, Nashville, 68–70.
Tolbert, M.A.
  1989   *Sowing the Gospel: Mark's world in literary-historical perspective*, Minneapolis.
Tuckett, C.M.
  1993   Review of Burridge 1992 in *Theology* XCVI No. 769, 74–5.
  1995   'Jesus and the Gospels', *NIB* VIII, Nashville, 71–86.
Vines, M.E.
  2002   *The Problem of the Markan Genre: The Gospel of Mark and the Jewish novel*, Atlanta.
Wansbrough, H.
  2001   'The four Gospels in synopsis', in J. Barton and J. Muddiman (eds.) *The Oxford Bible Commentary*, Oxford, 1001–2.
Weeden, T.J.
  1971   *Mark: Traditions in conflict*, Philadelphia.
Wehrli, F.
  1967–9 *Die Schule des Aristoteles*, 10 vols., Basel.
Wills, L.M.
  1997   *The Quest of the Historical Gospel: Mark, John and the origins of the Gospel genre*, London.
Witherington III, B.
  1998   *The Acts of the Apostles: A socio-rhetorical commentary*, Grand Rapids.
  2001   *The Gospel of Mark: A socio-rhetorical commentary*, Grand Rapids.
Wright, N.T.
  1992   *Christian Origins and the Question of God*: vol. 1, *The New Testament and the People of God*, London.
  1996   *Christian Origins and the Question of God*: vol. 2, *Jesus and the Victory of God*, London.

49

4

GOSPEL AND GENRE: SOME RESERVATIONS

Mark Edwards

During the last few decades it has become almost a dogma in some quarters that every work of Greek or Latin literature was written in conformity with certain rigid precepts, known to the audience of the time but obscure to us, and that therefore the initial task for a critic of the Gospels is to assign them to a genre and learn its rules.[1] The study of genre is often treated as a branch of rhetoric, and I should say at once, to forestall misunderstanding, that it is no part of my purpose to disparage the application of rhetorical terms and categories to the earliest Christian writings. It is possible that the world had never seen the like of Jesus, it is possible that converts to the infant church were seduced as much by the novelty of its doctrines as by any *praeparatio evangelica*; it would not have been possible, even for men inspired by God, to win the ear of multitudes had they written a form of Greek that was entirely new in idiom and style. Commentators from the patristic era to the present have acknowledged that the New Testament teems with literary devices;[2] only in recent years has it been customary to argue that the authors must have acquired these arts at school.[3] To prove that they had enjoyed such an education, we should need to do more than demonstrate the presence in their writings of such figures as anaphora, hyperbole, asyndeton or litotes; such terms, like those of grammar, merely codify the practices in which most competent speakers of a language will engage before they have learned to give a name to them. Furthermore, a writer may deploy all the tropes and yet fail to be eloquent, just as one may fail to speak fluent English while observing all the written laws of orthography and syntax. On one page of a modern tabloid newspaper, for instance, one could find a higher incidence of apostrophe, paronomasia or alliteration than in the collected works of Gibbon, Newman or Macaulay; that is one of many indications that these authors, unlike the editors and readers of the *Sun*, have mastered writing as a craft.

We ought not to treat the injunctions of the rhetorical handbooks as though they were legal formulae, susceptible of any interpretation that can be reconciled with the lexicographic meaning of the words. The handbooks functioned only as ancillaries to the practice of composition, which consisted for the most part in the imitation of acknowledged classics. The counsels of the teacher were interpretable only when they were set alongside the works whose merits they were designed to illustrate; success was judged by likeness to the model, not by a bald fidelity to the rule. Whatever Procrustean measures may be adopted to harmonize the idiosyncrasies of the New Testament with the ideals of professional teachers, it remains true that there is nothing which reminds us less of a speech by Dio Chrysostom or Aelius Aristides than the entreaties, expostulations and invectives of St Paul. No generation of scholars before our own has been so ready to write of Paul as though his letters were intended for the eyes of Menander Rhetor or Quintilian; no generation in the past four centuries has been so ignorant of the great exemplars which the readers of Quintilian and Menander were expected to have by heart.

We have no choice but to follow practice rather than prescription when we come to the question of genre. Whatever this term means in current English, it has no equivalent in the ancient manuals, the majority of which, at a time when the rich more commonly made a profession of speaking than of writing, were designed to impart the skills of public oratory. They do supply an arsenal of terms for the discrimination of literary types, but when modern scholars employ these instruments some see genres where others see motifs. Discord in nomenclature is more frequent in the criticism of prose than in that of poetry: poetry was circumscribed by metres which remained unchanged for centuries, and when, as in Greek tragedy and its Latin imitations, strict prosody was allied to conventions which determined diction, tone and choice of subject, we need not doubt that the later authors were conscious heirs to a literary form. Of the early masters we cannot speak with certainty, as the form was being invented in their hands, and we identify the common genre of Aeschylus, Euripides, Ezekiel, Accius, Seneca and the *Christus Patiens*, not by matching each of them with some Aristotelian definition, but by tracing a perspicuous history of imitation, or by noting that when later authors quote them they describe the source as a tragedy or the work of a tragic poet. Where both these factors are wanting – and that is generally the case when we attempt to classify prose – we are left to deduce the genre from our vulnerable perceptions of dependence and affinity between the surviving texts.

The elasticity of the resultant structures is apparent to every connoisseur of recent work on the so-called 'ancient novel'; we should not assume, however, that the most notorious problems are the only ones, and if we followed the usage of the ancients, there would occasionally be little more consensus in the taxonomy of verse. It was not true even in Roman times that the verse-form was dictated by the subject, so that wars were always chanted in hexameters or love in elegiacs; the possible themes for epic that are contemplated by Virgil in the third book of the *Georgics*, for example, were handled by contemporary poets in elegiacs, and Parthenius, when he dedicated his amoretti to Cornelius Gallus, implied that they would admit of versification in either metre.[4] No one disputes that Virgil emulates Homer in the *Aeneid*, and that both were epic poets; but does it follow, because he imitates Hesiod, Aratus and Lucretius in the *Georgics*, that all four were exponents of a single genre, distinct from epic even though it was also written in verses of six feet? We speak today of scientific or didactic poetry, but to the Greeks all hexameter was *epos*. Lucretius asked to be measured against Ennius, and Hesiod's *Theogony*, which is certainly an epic, has much in common with his *Works and Days*. Homer and Empedocles both wielded the hexameter in narrative, and if no one had seen fit to call the latter an epic poet, why would Aristotle insist that he was not?

If the boundaries of epic remain protean, that is partly because there is no Greek poem that styles itself an epos; on the other hand, instances of *bios* in the rubric to a prose narrative are legion. Such writings satisfy the definition of biography, if by this we mean no more than a relation of the chief events in a person's life, including some account of his work and character. For the most part, however, they cannot vie in length with modern specimens of the genre, and the best of them, unlike the lucubrations of our own day, bear the marks of polished compilation rather than research. Plutarch and Diogenes Laertius would have passed in the Victorian era as masters of the biographical essay; the *bioi* which escort the works of poets and philosophers in some manuscripts are in modern parlance biographical prefaces, not biographies. The longer works, which naturally command the lion's share of recent study, seldom carry the title *bios*. Philostratus rehearsed 'the things in honour of (or concerning) Apollonius of Tyana', while Iamblichus introduced his philosophic encyclopaedia, not with a *Life of Pythagoras*, but with a treatise *On the Pythagorean Life*. There is more historical matter to be gleaned from panegyrics, among which most would reckon the *Evagoras* of Isocrates, and perhaps, if we are to judge by similarity of nomenclature, the *Proclus, or On Happiness*, of Marinus. If we hesitate to count Xenophon's *Reminiscences of Socrates* as a biography,[5] it will not be on account of its length, which is nothing compared with that of the *Apollonius*, nor on account of its title, as there are other biographical exercises which are not *bioi*: the reason will be rather that it offers us a series of discrete conversations rather than a continuous account of the subject's life.

It is most unlikely that Xenophon was purposely eschewing the *bios* for a different genre when he composed his *Reminiscences*. For one thing, we shall be at a loss to name another specimen of this genre if, as is usual, we attach the labels *bios* or biography to the *Proclus* of Marinus and to Porphyry's essay *On the Life of Plotinus and the Arrangement of his Works*. Whether or not we ought to call them by an appellation that they do not bear in the manuscripts, these works are clearly biographies in the modern sense; the reticence and selectivity which they share with Xenophon bespeak not the pursuit of a common literary form but a similarity of motive in the authors. All three, as philosophers in the midst of chattering rivals, wished to prove that they had been not merely associates but intimates of great masters, the aura of whose friendship would outshine the reputation of their more assiduous pupils. For the rest, these memoirs are as different as it is possible for three accounts of the recent dead to be. Only in Marinus, for example, is the narrative framed by the birth and death of the subject; Xenophon supplies no dates, while Porphyry, who assigns a year to most events with extraordinary precision, seems determined not to recount them in the order of their occurrence. Words are the stuff of memory in Xenophon, but the aphorisms of Porphyry and Proclus are embedded in the anecdotes of their admiring pupils, as though the text, to borrow a metaphor from their own philosophy, were the ostreaceous tenement of an audible but incorporeal soul. Xenophon's work, as we observed above, is no biography and no *bios*; but if we banish it to a class of one, we must concede that there is at least one ancient book without a genre after all.

Biologists have learned to group organisms into phyla, orders, genera and species not by enumerating superficial likenesses, but by working out the process by which one set of limbs or organs has evolved into another, to which it may not bear any obvious resemblance.[6] In the same way it may be that the study of ancient literature has more to learn from histories of imitation and influence than from a simple physiognomy of genres. Xenophon's depiction of his master is germane to our present subject, the genealogy of the Gospels, for at least three reasons. First, it is the work of a contemporary and disciple, as one canonical Gospel and a number of apocryphal testimonies claim to be. Secondly, it was written not to humour the curiosity of an otherwise disinterested public, but to reverse a fatal prejudice and to propagate the teachings of a martyr. Thirdly, it bears in Greek the title *Apomnemoneumata*, and Justin Martyr avails himself of the same rare term in a passage which conveyed the first intimation to the pagans that the Church possessed any written souvenir of the work of Christ.[7] The womb of the Gospels, according to the theory which has retained its popularity throughout the twentieth century, was also a catalogue of more or less isolated sayings, interspersed perhaps with shreds of narrative, but only later prefixed to a continuous account of the Saviour's ministry in Jerusalem, which culminated in his arrest and passion. To trace the vermiculations of the 'Marcan sayings-source', or of the hypothetical document called Q in modern scholarship, is a task beyond my powers, and (I suspect) beyond the patience of the reader; the discovery of the Coptic *Gospel of Thomas* in 1945 is, if nothing else, a proof that such collections were in use.

Papias, the John Aubrey of the Church in the second century, gives the following information, on which scholars of our own day have begun to look more kindly than their tutors:

> [Mark] accompanied Peter, who tailored his instruction to what was needful, but without aiming at an orderly rehearsal of the Lord's sayings. Therefore Mark did not err at all when he wrote down some things according to his own memory. In one thing indeed he was specially careful – not to omit anything that he had heard or to introduce any falsehood into his statements... Matthew compiled the logia in the Hebrew tongue, and each interpreted them to the best of his ability. Eusebius, *Ecclesiastical History* 3.39

Papias foreshadows the higher criticism of a later epoch in deriving the tradition from two sources – one a written narrative which cannot have differed much from the extant Gospel of Mark, and one a group of apophthegms which he ascribes to Matthew. The latter was evidently not coterminous with the Gospel that now bears the name of Matthew, but Papias, as I would read him, indicates his knowledge of at least two other documents, more ample than the sayings source, when he adds that 'each' (ἕκαστος) had interpreted the Aramaic utterances according to his capacity. This politic remark explains itself when we consider how differently the same words of Jesus are attested in parallel verses of Matthew, Thomas, Mark and Luke. An apologetic note is heard again when Papias says that Mark wrote down what he heard from Peter, but without regard to order. Such a reservation would have been unnecessary had there been no other record whose chronology he believed to be superior to Mark's; and since neither Luke nor Matthew contradicts Mark in their arrangement of material, all the evidence suggests that the favoured Gospel is one that now stands fourth in our New Testament, and is there attributed to a certain John.

As I have already intimated, John is the evangelist who most resembles Xenophon – first because he professes to write from autopsy, and secondly because he makes Christ speak not only in isolated sallies, but in colloquies with a single interlocutor, whose questions guide his tongue. Martin Hengel is the most illustrious of the modern commentators who believe that in this Gospel we have the memoirs of a witness;[8] the radical theologian John Robinson, public enemy of the orthodox in his lifetime, proved almost too conservative for his friends in his posthumous volume on *The Priority of John*.[9] Yet whether it is the work of John the Apostle, of John the Elder, of another John unknown to us or (as many think) of a 'Johannine community', this

Gospel is not composed in the classical manner, for it follows a meandering course which appears at times to have crossed the river Lethe. One cannot construct a journal of Christ's movements from the Johannine accounts of his three or four visits to Jerusalem; and no one who had learned Greek from good masters would have veered between the second person singular and the second person plural as Jesus does in a private talk with Nicodemus, compounding the solecism with a prophecy – 'the Son of Man shall be lifted up' – which is lost on Nicodemus in chapter 3, yet overheard and answered by a crowd of other Jews in chapter 12. Whether these anomalies be evidence of an arcane design or of no design, they may help to explain why there have been so many theories about the genesis of the Gospel and so few attempts to identify its genre; one suspects that the work of John, like that of Xenophon, is not so much a specimen as a species in itself.

For the literary botanist, on the other hand, the criticism of Mark in recent years has been a veritable Eden, in which some have even exercised the privilege of inventing names which God vouchsafed to Adam. It is generally, although not universally, agreed that Mark's is the earliest of the three synoptic Gospels, and does not depend on that of John for the handful of sayings and anecdotes that they have in common. Hence it is also widely held that, whatever Sibylline leaves of written history may have come to hand along with the oral testimonies, the author of this narrative (or its prototype) was the first who made use of writing to perpetuate a whole body of traditions. Since no one writes exactly as he speaks, this enterprise will have entailed the adoption of idioms, rhythms and constructive artifices that were not to be encountered in the forum; as we have noted above, however, literary devices can exist without literary taste or training. Benjamin Jowett, liberal theologian and translator of Plato for the nineteenth century, declared that there are only two good sentences of Greek in the whole New Testament, and did not attribute either of them to Mark.[10] Collectively at least, we possess more Greek than the Victorians, and the papyrologists tell us that the prose of the apostolic writers, far removed as it is from the polished *koine* of the period, is not a demotic *patois*, but the tongue of lawyers, notaries and other men of business.[11] Then as now, it was evidently possible for a man to be proficient in his calling, yet narrow in his vocabulary, fallible in grammar and deaf to style.

The Evangelists, of course, possess a natural gift for pathos and a turn of phrase that providence has denied to merchant bankers; but that only makes it all the more improbable that their work would bear the marks of a formal schooling when they have not acquired the purity of diction which was a *pons asinorum* for any aspirant to a career in rhetoric. That is our gain as readers, since (as De Quincey pointed out[12]) the dullest prose is that of the partially educated; but as scholars we are in the position of a meteorologist who goes to a distant latitude and discovers that the signs which he is accustomed to consult are either missing or present only to deceive. The remedy is a candid observation of phenomena, which might reveal (for example) that some pagan book, perused without instruction, had left its trace in the Gospels; all too often, however, it appears that modern authors who have tried to impose a genre on the Gospels have been forced to deny the phenomena, or at least to apply low standards in distinguishing the salient from the banal.

Thus the four 'common motifs' adduced in Christopher Bryan's recent *Preface to Mark*[13] do not suffice, in my opinion, to characterize the Gospel as a *bios*; rather they remind us, when we weigh their insufficiency against the tact and learning of the author, that the keenest eye sees only what the intellect is willing to perceive:

1. In the opening verse of Mark – 'the gospel of Jesus Christ, the son of God' – Bryan detects a vestige of a regular trait in Greek and Latin lives – the glorification of the hero through his birth and ancestry. But even if this were true, what would it prove? The fallacy which adorns a man with the merits and achievements of his forefathers is almost universal in human society, and if we compare the first ten chapters of an Icelandic saga with the typical prologue of a Greek biography, we find ourselves confirming the proverbial shortness of the Greek memory. As for birth, that too is the common lot, and it requires a certain hardihood to place it anywhere in a biography but at the inception of the main narrative. What is remarkable in the Gospel of Mark is not that it begins by styling Christ the Son of God – if indeed it does, for not all manuscripts contain this reading – but that it says no more in any manuscript. Pagan accounts of Heracles, Pythagoras, Alexander and Apollonius of Tyana all record the names of their putative human fathers, even when they inform us that the true father was a god. Mark, on the other hand, has nothing to say of the time or place of Christ's nativity, and fails to provide him with the patronymic that was demanded by both Greek and Jewish custom. Even in chapter 6, where Christ's detractors ask how one of such low origins can presume to work a miracle, their epithets for him are 'carpenter' and 'son of Mary', not, as in the thirteenth chapter of Matthew, 'son of a carpenter'. Either Mark was ignorant of this honorific convention, or – since that is not very probable in a student of the Old Testament – he avoided it, for reasons which are not hard to divine.

2. The second motif that Bryan finds to be typical of biography among the Greeks and Romans is that it gives some account of the hero's education. He admits that Mark is silent on the education of Jesus, but directs us to a parallel in the anonymous (and obscure) *Life of Secundus* which he has already cited

to prove that ancient lives do not always record the origins of the hero. This is artful casuistry, but taxonomy is a science, and must therefore derive its data from the most ubiquitous and transmissible properties of a species. One does not conclude that birds are mammals because the platypus lays eggs.

3. The third motif which, according to Bryan, reveals the generic character of the Gospel is that it celebrates the deeds of the protagonist. So does the *Odyssey*, so do the *Ramayana*, the *Tain*, the *Heimskringla* of Snorri Sturluson, *David Copperfield* and the book of Jeremiah; even Bryan concedes that this is an element which 'naturally' appears in all commemorative literature, and it goes without saying that if there had been no deeds there would be no life.

4. More interesting is Bryan's fourth stipulation that the *bios* ought to end with the subject's death; for this is indeed a hallmark of the works that a modern reader would call biographies, in contrast, say, to Xenophon's *Reminiscences*, the *Anabasis* of Arrian and the Acts of the Apostles. Yet here Bryan seems inclined to qualify, rather than (as elsewhere) to embellish, the similarities between the Gospel of Mark and pagan lives, alleging that the canons of the genre would forbid such an ignominious dénouement as a death by crucifixion. But in fact it was never the duty of biographers to bring a life to a decorous termination: the lives of Cicero, Antony and Crassus end ingloriously in Plutarch; the deaths of Roman Emperors are as squalid as their careers in Suetonius and the *Historia Augusta*; every chapter in Lucian's tale of the death of Peregrinus is a satire; Diogenes Laertius records that Zeno committed suicide after stubbing his toe and that Chrysippus perished laughing at his own joke. The author of a posthumous memoir might be obliged to vindicate a death that seemed ridiculous or culpable to others: thus Porphyry dwells defiantly on the last illness of Plotinus, which estranged him from his friends and prompted gloating among astrologers, while Nepos admires the voluntary departure of his friend Atticus from the world, though a Roman less disposed to melancholy might have deemed it an act of cowardice. The death of Christ in Mark is of course unusual, as Bryan observes, in being succeeded by the Resurrection – or more exactly, by the annunciation of it. It is also, as Bryan does not observe, unusually prominent in the story, since the sequence of events that leads to the trial and execution of Christ commences in the ninth of sixteen chapters. No pagan biographical work could reasonably be described as a passion narrative with a prologue, unless the Platonic *Phaedo* (which admittedly is not devoid of biographical touches) is to be counted as an instalment in a life of Socrates.

Of Bryan's four criteria, therefore, the first two are not met by Mark, the third is nugatory and to say that the fourth is met would be as if one said that Everest has the dimensions of a hill or that *Remembrance of Things Past* is not too short to be called a novel. The great American scholar Morton Smith took more account of the singularities of the Gospel when he postulated, rather than discovered, an ancient class of aretalogies, or recitations of heroic deeds.[14] A sovereign example of this genre would be Aristotle's sparse list of Pythagorean miracles, which certainly bears comparison with portions of the Gospels; there is also, however, a sovereign objection to the theory in that the original shape of Aristotle's work *On the Pythagoreans* remains obscure, and if we discount the late concatenations of poetic myths in digests such as that of Apollodorus, such a paratactic summary of legends surrounding a single man is difficult to parallel in Greek or Latin prose. As Howard Clark Kee has demonstrated and every Christian preacher used to know, the 'mighty works' or *dunameis* of Mark's hero are prefigured in the Biblical accounts of Moses, Elijah and Elisha;[15] a pagan monograph like Lucian's *Demonax* might furnish a richer catalogue of sayings, but like any pagan memoir that aspired to respectability, it is free of miracles. Anyone who cites Philostratus' life of Apollonius as an instance of the genre proposed by Smith should be forced to read every one of its laboured speeches, and to count up all the occasions when the sage either disdains to work a miracle or exposes the natural cause of a phenomenon that bewitches the minds of others. As for the term 'aretalogy', this generally denotes in classical usage a list of titles and prerogatives pertaining to a god.

It is none the less a laudable corollary of Smith's thesis that it does not misrepresent the Gospel of Mark as a commonplace Greek biography. It has undergone a strange inversion in some modern writing, which maintains that Mark composed his Gospel, not as an aretalogy, but as an antidote to that genre, or at least to false cult of the θεῖος ἀνήρ, who is widely supposed to have been the idol of popular devotion and of literary romance.[16] On this view, Mark's object was to substitute a theology of the Cross for a theology of glory, to admonish us that the victory of the good consists in suffering, and the self-denying lowliness of man reveals the majesty of God. While I am inclined to think that this is good theology, I cannot persuade myself that is the theology of Mark. If he was acquainted with the expression θεῖος ἀνήρ, he will have known the typical bearer of it was not a thaumaturge, but a man endowed by the gods with such sagacity that he needed no instruction in the virtues. That is the primary sense of the term from Plato to Philostratus, whose life of Apollonius was written expressly to counteract the notion that Apollonius was a γόης – the name applied by educated Hellenes to the counterfeit philosopher who overawes the mob by his real or simulated ability to repeal the laws of nature. It is Mark himself who fills his book with miracles, more abundantly than any surviving pagan text, and when on three occasions the disciples are said not to understand Jesus, it is never implied that the lesson which they fail to understand is the one that modern interpreters read into the Gospel. When they see him walking on the water, they mistake him for a spirit because they 'considered not the miracle of the loaves' (6.52). When he chides them later for lack of understanding, it is after he has reminded them of two miraculous feedings (8.21). When he enjoins them not to tell anyone about the Transfiguration 'until the Son of Man be risen from the dead', it is not the title Son of Man that perplexes them, but the prophecy of his rising (9.10). In short they perceive well enough that he is a man, but not how great a man he is.

Mark could not have written a conventional life of such an unconventional figure as Jesus. This is not to deny that Jesus shared a host of features with other characters in history and legend, and not only – to reiterate a point that I made earlier in this paper – in the history and legend of the Greeks. A thoroughgoing census of the affinities between Jesus and the household names of classical culture – few of them by any definition θεῖοι ἄνδρες – was performed by Arnold Toynbee as an appendix to the sixth volume of his *Study of History*.[17] Neglected by New Testament scholars, this survey can be read with profit by anyone less learned than the author – that is, by anyone at all. Nevertheless, the 87 traits in Toynbee's catalogue do not constitute a paradigm since Christ is the only man who exhibits all of them, and even then not in any single Gospel. Toynbee, who was writing as a historian, not as a literary critic, had no interest in establishing a genre for the Gospels: he quotes all four without discrimination or attention to the context, and is even more eclectic in his exploitation of the pagan sources. Whatever may be true of Julius Caesar, the Christ who has left his mark on the world is the Christ of the Evangelists, and the Gospels cannot be used as raw materials for an independent study of his life.

Let me end with another reservation. I do not maintain, with Jowett, that the study of classical literature is of no use in construing or interpreting the New Testament. Language is a continuum, and while we cannot assume that every writer of ancient Greek will have been governed by the precedent and authority of great masters, we can assume that whatever was tolerable in learned prose was also tolerable in Greek of any standard. Here, as elsewhere, bad scholarship has been busy, and repairs must be executed by good scholarship. Discussion of the completeness of Mark's Gospel has been bedevilled, for example, by the assertion that Greek writers never end a book with γάρ; in 1972 Peter Van der Horst produced an example of such an ending from a famous work, the *Enneads* of Plotinus, which had escaped attention chiefly because so few had cared to search.[18] Again, it is sometimes wrongly said that Gospels are anomalous because the author is not named in the proem; a nodding acquaintance with Plato, Plutarch, Lucian or Porphyry (to take a few names at random) would have undeceived the victims of this error. It may be that in the same way an inquiry into ancient theories of genre would shed light upon the practices and motives of the apostolic writers; it may be that for our own purposes we have the right to assign their works to genres that they themselves did not acknowledge. But first we must have a purpose – labelling an artefact is frequently the beginning, not the end, of an inquiry into its function, and the labelling of genres is as much a constructive as a detective enterprise – and secondly we shall accomplish nothing if we squeeze bold inferences from frail hypotheses or browbeat one another with selective information before we have honestly endeavoured to gather all the materials needed for the task.

Notes

[1] For erudite criticism of this vogue, see Reiser 1999, 1–24.

[2] See Fairweather 1994, 1–22.

[3] The bellwether of the movement is Betz 1974.

[4] Lightfoot 1999, 308.

[5] As Richard Burridge 1992, 128 ff., does. Burridge's book is one of the most empirical and incisive of modern studies on this topic, yet it seems to me that his choice of specimen *bioi* has determined his conclusions, and if genre is defined by the 'expectations' of the audience, we may reasonably doubt whether *any* writing that was not described as a *bios* in antiquity was designed to arouse the same expectation as those which bore this title.

[6] See further Foucault 1970, 268–79.

[7] Heard 1954, 122–9 suggests that Justin echoes Papias' reference to Mark's exercise of memory (see below); Barnard 1997, 181–2 replies that Justin never mentions Papias, but alludes to the *Memorabilia* of Xenophon at *2 Apology* 11.

[8] Hengel 1985.

[9] Robinson 1985.

[10] Jowett 1860, 396, referring to Luke 1.1 and Acts 1.1.

[11] See Gamble 1995.

[12] De Quincey 1897, 148–50.

[13] Bryan 1993, 50–3.

[14] Smith 1971, 174–99.

[15] Kee 1973, 402–22.

[16] The seminal work is Bieler 1935–6.

[17] Toynbee 1979, 377–476.

[18] Van der Horst 1972.

Bibliography

Barnard, L.W.
    1997   *St Justin Martyr: The first and second Apologies*, New York.
Betz, H.D.
    1974   *Galatians*, Philadelphia.

Bieler, L.
1935–6   ΘΕΙΟΣ ΑΝΗΡ: *Das Bild des 'gottlichen Menschen' in Spätantike und Frühchristentum,* 2 vols., Vienna.
Bryan, C.
1993   *A Preface to Mark*, Cambridge.
Burridge, R.
1992   *What are the Gospels?*, Cambridge.
De Quincey, T.
1897   'Style', in D. Masson (ed.) *Collected Writings*, London, 148–50.
Fairweather, J.
1994   'The Epistle to the Galatians and classical rhetoric', part 1, *Tyndale Bulletin* 45, 1–22.
Foucault, M.
1970   *The Order of Things*, New York.
Gamble, H.
1995   *Books and Readers in the Early Church*, New Haven and London.
Heard, R.G.
1954   'Apomnemoneumata in Papias, Justin and Irenaeus', *New Testament Studies* 1, 122–9.
Hengel, M.
1985   *The Johannine Question*, transl. J. Bowden, London.
Jowett, B.
1860   'The interpretation of Scripture', in *Essays and Reviews*, London.
Kee, H.C.
1973   'Aretalogy and Gospel', *Journal of Biblical Literature* 92, 402–22.
Reiser, M.
1999   'Die Stellung der Evangelien in der antiken Literatur', *Zeitschrift für Neutestamentliche Wissenschaft* 90, 1–24.
Robinson, J.A.T.
1985   *The Priority of John*, London.
Smith, M.
1971   'Prolegomena to aretalogies: Divine men, the Gospels and Jesus', *Journal of Biblical Literature* 90, 174–99.
Toynbee, A.
1979   *A Study of History* VI, Oxford and New York.
Van der Horst, P.
1972   'Can a book end with γάρ?', *Journal of Theological Studies* 23.

5

MARK'S GOSPEL AND ANCIENT BIOGRAPHY

Sean Freyne

A review of the last century and a half of critical scholarship of the Gospels suggests that the question of their relationship to other genres, especially that of ancient *Bioi*, has not frequently been discussed. This is quite surprising when it is recalled that in the same period the issue of a 'Life' of the historical Jesus has rarely been off the scholarly agenda. There are several reasons for this neglect, not least the enormous influence that Rudolph Bultmann has had on the field of New Testament scholarship throughout a major part of the last century. At the end of his pioneering work, *The History of the Synoptic Tradition* (original German edition 1928) – a work in which ironically he compares the pre-gospel units, with various parallels from Graeco-Roman literature – he rejects any such comparisons for the completed Gospels. These would merely show how different the Gospels are, according to Bultmann. However, this does not mean that their authors developed a separate genre, something which would have entailed a history of such writing, subsequently. That process was curtailed because of the early canonization of the fourfold Gospel. As a result, the Synoptics are, in Bultmann's view, mere receptacles for the oral tradition.[1] Redaction criticism was to change this minimalist view of the Gospel authorship, but even then the emphasis was more on the distinctive theological rather than literary character of these works. True, occasional comparisons had been made between the Gospels and ancient *Bioi*, during the heyday of form and redaction criticism, but it was only with the turn to literary, as distinct from historical, criticism in the 1980s that the question received any serious and sustained discussion.[2]

Even then the guild of New Testament scholars was not altogether convinced. Thus, David Aune's severe criticism of Charles Talbert's *What is a Gospel? The genre of the Synoptic Gospels* (1977) would have spoken for many insofar as they reflected on the issue at all. Amos Wilder, the Harvard poet and New Testament scholar, wrote as follows about the Gospels, while adopting a thoroughly informed literary approach to the Bible:

All the literary forms of the New Testament, even those that seem to have a Christian background, fall definitely outside the categories of formal literature, as practised in the world of culture of that time... The gospel form is the only wholly new genre created by the Church, and the author Mark receives the credit for it. Yet this anonymous work is in large degree a group project... As a type of composition it is not like ancient biography or tragedy. Dibelius has shown how different it is from narratives, perhaps superficially similar, of the fate of the hero or of the life and death of a saint or a martyr. Yet all such accounts were written with an appeal to sentiment, with sharper portraiture or with fuller biographical details. Mark represents a divine transaction whose import involves heaven and earth, and even the scenes of the passion are recounted with a corresponding austerity. The Gospel action is not so much a history as a ritual re-enactment or mimesis. The believer did not hear it as a record of the past.[3]

Talbert had challenged Bultmann's claim about the futility of any comparison of the Gospels with contemporary secular literature. He proposed that ancient *Bioi* functioned similarly to the Gospels, (a) by employing a mythic pattern in dealing with their subject; (b) by functioning in a quasi-cultic manner in preserving the religious or ethical values of a group of devotees of the subject of the work; and (c) by defending the world-affirming attitude of the early Christians – the necessary precondition for producing any biography – an attitude, which it had been claimed, the early Christian eschatological outlook precluded. Among several alleged failures to deal adequately with the data, Talbert drew Aune's ire by his typology of ancient didactic Lives into five different functional specializations. According to Aune this typology is not based on formal features of the works in question, but is neatly contrived to give a desired result in terms of the functions of the different Gospels.[4] More recent discussion of Talbert's work by Richard Burridge and Dirk Frickenschmidt, while sharing Aune's criticism of Talbert's control of the ancient sources and his too rigid categorization of different works to suit his typology, are, nevertheless more appreciative of his achievement in refocusing the question of gospel genre in the context of ancient biography, thereby giving new impetus to the debate. [5]

The studies of Burridge (1992) and Frickenschmidt (1997) do make considerable advances on previous discussion. The former operates with a more flexible and nuanced understanding of genre, and the latter, with traditional German thoroughness, examines the typical features of more than 140 ancient writings which can be classified as biographical. While following somewhat separate lines of inquiry they both agree that the Gospels do indeed have a 'family resemblance' with ancient biography. Burridge highlights both internal and external features of certain chosen works as criteria for determining the gospel genre, foremost of which is the amount of space allocated to a single character. This is measured by the frequency with which this person is the subject of verbs, in contrast to the minimal space that is given to the actions of other characters in the narrative. In this concentration on the main character there are standard *topoi* that recur – birth, ancestry, education, deeds, virtues, death – and the treatment of these will vary according to the different type of biography – philosophical or political for example – that is being produced. Frickenschmidt believes that, despite his more sophisticated theoretical approach, Burridge has not adequately dealt with these themes. He posits what he describes as a 'basis-biographie', that underlies all ancient biography, comprising an *arche*, or beginning, an *akme*, or middle, and the *telos* or concluding account of the death and vindication of the subject. This brief, tripartite outline was developed, he claims, in the context either of history-writing or encomium, but it provided plenty of opportunity for development in various directions in all three parts, something that Frickenschmidt illustrates amply from his data basis of 142 biographical works consulted.

In the context of such a wide canvass, both in terms of a more flexible notion of the genre and its multifaceted application in ancient biographic literature, there can be little doubt that the Gospels may indeed also be included within a list of ancient biographies. However, such a generalized conclusion is only helpful if it illuminates aspects of individual works that otherwise would not have been noted or properly evaluated. In a word, the proof of every pudding is in the eating. In this brief communication I propose to examine two discussions of Mark that draw on very different kinds of ancient narrative material in order to make my own suggestion as to how this discussion might progress more fruitfully.

Mark and Xenophon's *Memorabilia*

Vernon K. Robbins was trained as a classicist and has developed a special interest in the socio-rhetorical character of ancient literature. By this he means the social impact of a work in terms of expectations and impulses to action that different rhetorical devices give rise to in different social and cultural contexts. He is, therefore, less interested in discerning formal similarities between different writings, the style of analysis favoured by most previous discussions of the Gospels' genre. Instead, he focuses on the impact that the manipulation of and experimentation with conventional forms are likely to make, attending, therefore, as much to the reception as to the production of a work. In his 1984 study, *Jesus the Teacher. A socio-rhetorical study of Mark,* Robbins applies these insights to the study of a gospel, by examining its socio-rhetorical strategies, which, he claims, must be interpreted in the light of both Graeco-Roman and Jewish/Israelite practices. Xenophon's *Memorabilia* provides the best analogue to Mark from the Graeco-Roman point of view, since it is our oldest and most complete example of the *Bios* of a disciple-gathering teacher, which is the dominating feature of the first Gospel also. [6]

Even though Mark is described as the *Apomnemoneumata tou Petrou* by Papias in the early second century CE, thereby consciously categorizing it with Xenophon's work, the two differ considerably in other respects. Not merely are they stylistically far apart, but the role which the narrator plays in each is quite different. Xenophon, as the real author, retains his full identity, commenting in his own name on Socrates' deeds and words, explaining his reasons for choosing different kinds of material and describing his friendship with the main character. Mark, on the other hand, employs an anonymous narrator who often merges with the ideal reader for all practical purposes, except for very occasional side comments.[7] In addition, Xenophon integrates lengthy Socratic dialogues with accounts of Socrates' deeds, whereas Mark treats the reader to a series of episodes, depicting the deeds of Jesus, giving very little of the main character's dialogue, despite insisting that there is a connection between the two (cf. Mk 1.27; 6.3).

Despite these telling differences in style, form and narration, Robbins insists that both works are concerned with presenting their main characters as examples of wisdom and authority in their dealings with those around them. Thus, Xenophon's declaration that 'all teachers show their disciples how they themselves do what they teach, and lead them on by speech...' (*Mem.* 1.2, 17), could equally apply to the Jesus-figure in Mark. In order to achieve the desired effect Xenophon utilizes a repertoire of phrases that he repeats with minor variations following a definite three-stage pattern throughout the work. The stages are as follows: the teacher does what he teaches others; the teacher interacts with others to impart the system of thought and action that he embodies, and the teacher transmits this system to the next generation. In Mark also we find a similar strategy of repetition operative, both in terms of the overall structure (Mk 6.31–45; 8.1–10 and Mk 8.31–10.45), and within individual scenes (Mk 4.2–10; 12.2–8; 14.32–8 and 66–72).[8] Unlike Socrates, however, Jesus speaks not about his own person, but rather about 'the gospel', or 'kingdom of God', (1.14f.; 3.22) as the reference point for his actions, thereby emphasizing the fact that the source of his wisdom is not personal, in contrast to the Greek tradition.[9] Robbins attributes this contrast to Mark's indebtedness to the Jewish prophetic tradition, as illustrated by the oft-repeated formula in the Hebrew Bible, 'the word of the Lord came to me...' Significantly, however, despite sharing the conception of total dependence on God that underlies it, the formula itself does not occur in Mark, because of his adaptation to the Graeco-Roman cultural codes in his presentation of Jesus. Instead, the authority for his words and deeds is repeatedly being questioned as he moves from place to place, generating a sense of mysterious presence and a veiled identity which he seeks to communicate to his chosen disciples privately.[10]

Having established this shared pattern and its rhetorical intention in both works on the basis of the repetitive *topoi* in each, Robbins then proceeds to a more detailed examination of the three phases of the relationship between teacher and disciples – the initial encounter, the intermediate stage of the learning process, and the final farewell and death. We may briefly outline his treatment of each stage, noting how it combines elements of the Jewish prophetic tradition with the rhetorical style of the Graeco-Roman biographical genre.

(i) In the initial phase the call of Jesus to his disciples parallels the call of God in the Israelite tradition to Abraham, Moses and the prophets. In both cases it is unconditional, immediate and direct. However, because it lacks any divine sanction if this call is rejected, Jesus appears to be acting autonomously as in the Greek Socratic tradition, summoning others to join him and share his life-style. There is no scene in which Jesus, as a teacher of wisdom, is told by God what to do or say. Instead, 'he takes over the functions of Yahweh, with Yahweh's sanction, but without detailed directions.' The God of Israel is present in the Markan story but he never instructs Jesus during his adult life. 'Thus, a basic dimension of the messianic nature of Jesus' activity in Mark arises from his adaptation of the autonomous nature of the teacher in the Graeco-Roman tradition, and the subsequent importation of this into the Jewish tradition in which God has been the dominant autonomous figure.'[11]

(ii) The second phase of the cycle has to do with the teaching and learning relationship between master and pupils. Here again, Robbins finds elements of both traditions in the Markan account, 'which takes elements of the Jewish prophetic tradition into the intellectual environment engaged in the dynamics of Greek *paideia*.'[12] It is highly significant that, in contrast to the Israelite covenantal system, there is no sanction, at least in the present of the reader, for refusal to obey the system being imparted, though such obedience is both anticipated and expected. For this reason Robbins regards as unconvincing some recent trends which suggest that the disciples in Mark are portrayed as heretical figures.[13] The Greek tradition of *paideia*, which the author is following, does not envisage a test of allegiance, but rather shares a presumption that the encounter with the teacher is beneficial, even if the system of thought and action cannot be fully fathomed by the disciples.

(iii) The final phase is that of farewell and departure of the teacher. Here again, Robbins argues for a fusion of the two traditions. The farewell speech is common to both and prepares the disciples for the absence of the teacher. A temple discourse became a widespread literary form in Graeco-Roman literature in which matters of deep significance to the teacher and the followers were discussed. The death of the martyred prophet and the suffering just one was greatly valued in the Jewish setting, whereas the tradition of a just king dying 'so that they might rescue their subjects through their own blood' (1 Clement 55.1–5), had become a recognized *topos* in the Graeco-Roman context of the first century. That may explain the fact that it is only in the trial and crucifixion scene that Jesus is given the title 'king of the Jews' in the Markan narrative.[14]

Mark and popular romance

Robbins' proposal presumes a sophisticated fusion of Graeco-Roman rhetorical forms and themes with Israelite or Jewish perspectives on the teacher-disciple tradition. Such an achievement presupposes a relatively high level of acquaintance with Graeco-Roman literary practices by both the author and readers of the Gospel at an early stage of Christian self-understanding. For this rhetoric to have been effective in social terms, as Robbins would have it, there is the presumption that the early Christian recipients of the Gospel would have seen themselves as a scholastic community aspiring to the higher level of Greek *paideia*. This assumption has been challenged by Mary Ann Tolbert's comparison of Mark with popular Hellenistic novels, a small number of which has survived. Her project is to discuss the genre of Mark in the context of establishing the authorial audience and its expectations in approaching the text. In her view, attempts to read the Gospel as aretalogy, *bios* or *memorabilia* fail because they are too narrowly focused and do not take sufficient account of all aspects of Mark's text.[15]

Even more significant in Tolbert's view is the fact that Mark's Gospel does not display the same linguistic skill and literary acumen as the works with which it has traditionally been compared. At this level she relies on Marius Reiser's detailed study of the Alexander Romance, which combines a paratactic and repetitive style of narration with popular folkloristic motifs and colouring, aspects that are common to Mark.[16] Her proposal to discuss the authorial audience (not the genre per se) is based on her belief that as a literary type Mark corresponds best to the ancient novel, especially Xenophon of Ephesus' *Anthia and Habrocomes*, in terms of the kind of audience that each presumes.[17] This suggestion would correspond well with what we know from elsewhere about the social background and educational level of the earliest Christians. 'Christian converts come from an expanding urban class of artisans, traders, administrators of middle rank and freed slaves,' she writes, and speculation about the audience of the ancient novel points to the same group.[18] Such audiences reflect the ethos of travel, erosion of elitist aristocratic values and the wider diffusion of literacy at a certain level within Graeco-Roman society by the first century CE.

Tolbert freely recognizes that the extant ancient novels differ considerably from Mark in terms of their romantic plots and the popular entertainment which they offered through stories of violence, adventure and travel. However, in her view there is a distinct possibility that the extant erotic romances are only one sub-group of a larger cluster of ancient novels which would include such 'biographic' works as Xenophon's *Cyropaedia*, *The Alexander Romance* and Philostratus' *Life of Apollonius*. However, that hypothesis is not essential to the case she seeks to argue, namely, that through these extant works we have the most immediate and direct access to the audience of ancient popular literature, and therefore also to the audience of Mark.[19]

Does reading it within this context illuminate Mark's narrative? Three aspects suggest themselves for special attention, namely, the plot, characterization and overall structure of the work. Structurally, popular novels combine a historiographic form with epic and dramatic content, and as such may be described as 'mixed genres', lacking the clean-cut lines of classical types. While they use historical characters, locations and events, these features can be deceptive, according to Tolbert. They are more stereotypical than actual and are concerned with a generalized verisimilitude rather than with an actual representation of reality. The journey motif borrowed from the epic tradition functions to give a kind of unity to discrete episodes. The opening encounter, the turning point and the recognition scene lend dramatic features to the whole, as do the individual episodes with their brief dialogues between various characters, interspersed with narratorial comment on the events occurring.

However, it is in the characterization and the plot that one can see the similarities between the popular novels and the Gospels most clearly. The plots in the novels are totally predictable, if somewhat more complex, because of the two characters who go their separate ways before being re-united in the end. A Homeric trait is the shared divine and human agency, and the outcome is lacking in any surprise. The attention is not on what will happen, but on how it will come about. Likewise the characterization is flat and essentially illustrative of principles rather than representative of individual human response to actual situations. Nor is there any concern with psychological development or growth through the plot, even when the fortunes of individuals may have changed.

Having thus established to her satisfaction the similarities between Mark and popular Graeco-Roman novels, especially with regard to audience expectation in terms of introductions, summaries, anticipations and plot summaries, Tolbert proceeds to a more detailed examination of the Markan structure and rhetoric. Here, aspects of situational (as distinct from verbal) irony – coming close to parody, as in the bread section (Mk 6–8) – correspond to scenes in both Chariton and Xenophon. The role of third

level narration is also significant in each, in particular, the functional correspondence between the parables of the Sower (Mk 4.2–10) and that of the
Vineyard (Mk 12.1–10), and the role of oracles in Xenophon's work. Each
parable is situated strategically within the overall plot, one at an early stage
once the reader has been familiarized with various initial reactions to Jesus,
and the other just before the dénouement in Jerusalem. Both are transpar-
ently allegorical in terms of the plot and its outcome, displaying the general
principles which organize the whole story. Tolbert's analysis in the major part
of her study is an attempt to establish this link between these parables and
the subsequent narration of events and episodes in accordance with what
might be expected from the typical audience of such a work.

Some concluding reflections

Neither Robbins' nor Tolbert's study can be categorized as an exploration of
genre per se. The former's emphasis on socio-rhetorical analysis means that
he is more concerned with the persuasive impact of the work's repetitive and
progressive patterns in terms of performance, rather than with identifying
shared formal literary features of various works. Xenophon's *Memorabilia*
provides him with a basic template of the disciple-gathering teacher style
of biography, and this is exploited in a reading exercise that takes account
of cultural variants of the wisdom teacher/philosopher type of biography.
Likewise, Tolbert is more concerned with authorial audience than with
genre, consideration of which merely helps her to uncover expectations and
attitudes shared by readers of popular literature in antiquity. Even Frickenschmidt's study, for all its wide-ranging search for shared motifs and topics,
fails to convince as a genre study in the strict sense. In his desire to classify
the Gospels within the general category of ancient Lives, he draws on
aspects of many different works, but without being able to narrow down the
comparison to a single work, or even sub-type. For him the uniqueness of
Mark (against Bultmann and other German scholars) consists in its 'highly
pregnant elaboration of the conventional and widely diffused family of literature that is ancient Biography, against the History of Religions background
of ancient Judaism'. This formulation of how his project relates to Mark
seems to me to be not dissimilar in the end to that of Robbins and Tolbert;
all three are engaged in an exercise of intertextual reading, even though each
has made different choices from the available field: as disciple-gathering
biography (Robbins), popular novels (Tolbert) or the complete family of
extant biography from Graeco-Roman antiquity (Frickenschmidt).

Lest I be accused of explaining the *ignotum* (biographic genre) per
ignotius (intertextuality), let me explain the sense in which I am using
this 'trendy' term. Intertextuality differs from comparative literature in

that it does not seek to establish genetic links or direct, causal influences between writings. Rather, it applies to texts the insight from the semiotics of language, namely, that all texts, whether consciously or otherwise, share in the discursive practices of all other texts, 'the Book of Culture'. As *parole* is to *langue*, so individual texts are to all other texts, a specific actualization of the possibilities for meaningful discourse that are offered through all previous texts. This insight has important repercussions for the way in which we view both the author and the reader. Authorial agency is no longer a matter of complete autonomy or simple imitation of previous works. A writer is always also a reader, a 'digester' and re-arranger of texts and experiences, in order to form his/her own text. But this presupposes an active reader who enters into dialogue with the author through the medium of the text, but interacting with it on the basis of the textual possibilities that s/he can bring to the reading process.[20] Thus, in Roland Barthes' words, 'the I that approaches the text (as reader) is itself already a plurality of other texts, of infinite or lost codes.'

In order to bring some semblance of order into what would otherwise be a chaotic situation, the structuralist literary critic, Jonathan Culler, has suggested that it should be possible to retain this broad and indeterminate meaning of intertextuality, without re-introducing source and redaction criticism under another name.[21] This can be achieved by adopting from linguistics the notion of presuppositions, both logical and pragmatic, and applying these in literary studies. In linguistics logical presuppositions mean that every assertion inevitably implies other assertions and their opposites, even when these are not explicitly articulated. Recognition of this phenomenon in the study of literature would inevitably assist in delimiting the discursive practices that a given text employs, and at the same time would preclude the need to consider certain other types of discourse that are *a priori* excluded. Pragmatic presuppositions, on the other hand, refer to the various rhetorical strategies that are brought into play by special kinds of discourse, on the analogy of speech-act theory in linguistics which highlights the performative function of language. These strategies are based on the relationship between a work and the situation it seeks to address. Thus, we are able to infer certain situations on the basis of the choices that are made, in that a work is pragmatically, that is rhetorically, related to a whole series of other works through the employment of conventions which constitute a genre, broadly defined. As applied to the study of literature, acknowledgment of that fact will inevitably clarify and define the discursive practices that a given text is engaged in. The concern should not be to name other works of the same genre, so defined, for comparative purposes, but rather to attend to the conventions that underline the discursive space occupied by a particular work and identify how these are employed in this specific instance in order to achieve a certain result. Thus far Culler, with apologies for this potted account of his proposal.

On reflection Culler's description of what from his perspective is involved in an inter-textual reading seems to describe rather well the work of both Robbins and Tolbert. By focusing on the disciple-gathering teacher style of ancient biography as represented by the *Memorabilia*, Robbins has defined the field for an inter-textual reading of the Gospel rather narrowly, in that other possibilities such as apocalyptic writings are necessarily excluded (logical presupposition). At the same time his concern with the socio-rhetorical implications of the work reflects a real concern with its pragmatic presuppositions, even if one is not always convinced by the similarities in the patterns he proposes from the prophetic and Jewish tradition. The logical presupposition of Tolbert's concentration on popular literature would seem to be biased against history writing as providing a suitable inter-text for reading Mark, whereas her concern with the audience expectation of ancient romances is a very clear example of what Culler describes as the pragmatic presuppositions of the discursive practices of Mark.

This would seem to imply that genre study is not an end in itself but serves a useful, if limited, role in understanding the process of communication that takes place between author and reader through the medium of a text. As conducted in the past in New Testament studies at least, the quest for the genre of the Gospels has been based too much on a classificatory under-standing of genre, thereby treating texts as objective artefacts, independently of their production and reception. Recent theoretical discussion of genre, as reflected in the work of David Tracy for instance, stresses the role of imagi-nation in the communication of an experience through the exploitation of generic conventions in order to produce a structured, meaningful whole.[22] Thus, while it may be possible to speak of particular genres as ideal types, there are as many variations possible as there are authors who wish to convey their experiences and have chosen a variety of discursive practices in order to communicate these. Acquaintance with as wide a range of such practices as are appropriate and available for any given culture or context will clearly be important for the modern reader also. It is only by attending to the distortions as well as the similarities that it will be possible to discern the creativity and conventionality of Mark, Plutarch, or indeed any other ancient biographer, and for judgements on these we need to be 'well-read'!

Notes
[1] Bultmann 1968, 373 f. For a critique of Bultmann's claim that the Gospels did not

generate a history of narratives about Jesus cf. Cancik 1984, 85–114, especially 91 f., who claims that in the period 50–400 CE as many as fifty works dealing with the deeds and words of Jesus can be documented and ascribed to a genre based on the Gospels.

² Cf. Kee 1977, 14–29 for a discussion of suggestions regarding the literary antecedents of Mark. Also Beardslee 1970, for a more general discussion.

³ Wilder 1971, 28.

⁴ Aune 1981, 9–60, especially 40–2.

⁵ Burridge 1992, 84–6; Frickenschmidt 1997, 50–3.

⁶ Robbins does not confine himself in his discussion solely to a comparison of these two works, but ranges over a representative sample of both traditions dealing with the teacher-disciple relationship, of which the Socratic model continued to be the dominant one in the Graeco-Roman realm. Cf. Diogenes Laertius' (*c.* 200–250 CE) account of the initial meeting between Xenophon and Socrates in his *Lives of Eminent Philosophers* (2, 48).

⁷ For a perceptive account of the narrator in Mark cf. Fowler 1991.

⁸ This feature has been well exposed by Perrin 1972, one of the early exponents of Redaction Criticism of the Gospels, with regard to the threefold prediction of the passion, and the call to disciples also to lose their lives (Mk 8.31–10.45).

⁹ This contrast is in line with the difference in emphasis between Jewish and Greek biography as outlined by Frickenschmidt 1996: the former stresses the subject's closeness to God, whereas the latter highlights the personal virtues of the main character in line with Greek views of the good life (263–6).

¹⁰ Robbins 1984, 72, notes 67 and 76 for details from the *Memorabilia* and the Gospel.

¹¹ Robbins 1984, 119.

¹² Ibid., 167.

¹³ Cf. several essays in Telford (ed.) 1995, especially Weeden, 89–104.

¹⁴ Robbins 1984, 171–96.

¹⁵ Tolbert 1989, 55–9.

¹⁶ Reiser 1984, 131–64.

¹⁷ On the 'orality' of the ancient novel cf. Hägg 1994, 47–81.

¹⁸ Tolbert 1989, 61 f., relying mainly on the study of Hägg 1983, 81–109. For a more recent discussion of the readership of the ancient novel cf. Bowie 1996, 87–106. For a discussion of the social status of the first Christians cf. Theissen 1982; Malherbe 1977; Meeks 1983.

¹⁹ Tolbert 1989, 65–70.

²⁰ For succinct but clear statements of contemporary approaches to intertextuality, cf. the essays by Delorme and van Wolde 1989, 35–42 and 43–50.

²¹ Culler 1981, especially 100–18.

²² Tracy 1981, 127–30, especially 129.

Bibliography

Aune, D.E.

1981   'The problem of the genre of the Gospels: A critique of C.H. Talbert's *What is a Gospel?*', in France and Wenham (eds.) *Gospel Perspectives*, 9–60.

Beardslee, W.A.
1970   *Literary Criticism of the New Testament*, Philadelphia.

Bowie, E.
1996   'The ancient reader of the Greek novel', in Schmeling (ed.) *The Novel in the Ancient World*, 87–106.

Bultmann, R.
1968   *The History of the Synoptic Tradition*, English translation, Oxford.

Burridge, R.
1992   *What are the Gospels?*, SNTSMS 70, Cambridge.

Cancik, H. (ed.)
1984   *Markus-Philologie*, WUNT 33, Tübingen.

Clark Kee, H.
1977   *Community of the New Age. Studies in Mark's Gospel*, Philadelphia.

Culler, J.
1981   *The Pursuit of Signs: Semiotics, literature, deconstruction*, London.

Delorme, J.
1989   'Intertextualities about Mark', in Draisma (ed.) *Intertextuality in Biblical Writings*, 35–42.

Draisma, S. (ed.)
1989   *Intertextuality in Biblical Writings. Essays in honour of Bas van Iersel*, Kampen.

Eriksen, R. (ed.)
1994   *Contexts of Pre-Novel Narrative: The European tradition*, Berlin.

Fowler, R.M.
1991   *Let the Reader Understand. Reader-response criticism in the Gospel of Mark*, Minneapolis.

France, R.T. and Wenham, D. (eds.)
1981   *Gospel Perspectives. Studies of history and tradition in the four Gospels*, Sheffield.

Frickenschmidt, D.
1997   *Evangelium als Biographie. Die Vier Evangelien im Rahmen antiker Erzähl-kunst*, Tübingen.

Hägg, T.
1983   *The Novel in Antiquity*, Oxford.
1994   'Orality, literacy and the "readership" of the Greek novel', in Eriksen (ed.) *Contexts of Pre-Novel Narrative*, 47–81.

Malherbe, A.
1977   *Social Aspects of Early Christianity*, Baton Rouge and London.

Meeks, W.
1983   *The First Urban Christians*, New Haven and London.

Perrin, N.
1972   *What is Redaction Criticism?*, Philadelphia.

Reiser, M.
1984   'Der Alexanderroman und das Markusevangelium', in Cancik (ed.) *Markus-Philologie*, 131–64.

Robbins, V.
1984   *Jesus the Teacher. A socio-rhetorical study of Mark*, Philadelphia.

Schmeling, G. (ed.)

1996   *The Novel in the Ancient World*, Leiden.

Talbert, C.

1977   *What is a Gospel?*, Philadelphia.

Telford, W.R. (ed.)

1985   *The Interpretation of Mark*, 2nd edn, Edinburgh.

Theissen, G.

1982   *The Social Setting of Pauline Christianity. Essays on Corinth*, Edinburgh.

Tolbert, M.A.

1989   *Sowing the Gospel. Mark's Gospel in literary-historical perspective*, Minnea-
        polis.

Tracy, D.

1981   *The Analogical Imagination. Christian theology of pluralism*, London.

van Walde, E.

1989   'Trendy intertextuality?', in Draisma (ed.) *Intertextuality in Biblical Writings*,
        43–50.

Weeden, T.J.

1985   'The heresy that necessitated Mark's Gospel', in Telford (ed.) *The Interpreta-
        tion of Mark*, 89–104.

Wilder, A.

1971   *Early Christian Rhetoric: The language of the Gospel*, Cambridge, Mass.

6

THE ACTS OF THE APOSTLES AS BIOGRAPHY

Justin Taylor

A good hypothesis is not necessarily one that is right, but rather, one that is fruitful. This could be the case with regard to the hypothesis of Charles H. Talbert concerning the literary genre of the two New Testament writings attributed to Luke, the Third Gospel and the Acts of the Apostles.[1] The Talbert hypothesis provides an answer to a question that did not really arise until the twentieth century. In 1927, in a book that has become a classic,[2] *The Making of Luke-Acts*, Henry J. Cadbury argued that the Gospel and the Book of Acts formed originally a single literary work, written in two parts. These two parts, volumes, let us say, only became separated when Luke's Gospel was placed as the third in the collection of the four Gospels. This opinion has gradually come to be accepted by just about everyone, and the hyphen thus introduced between 'Luke' and 'Acts' in the title of Cadbury's book is now taken for granted.

But there is a problem. If Luke-Acts was in fact conceived and produced as a single book, what then was the literary genre of that book? The question, as I have said, was new. For until then, the Gospel could be regarded as belonging to one literary genre – biography, let us say – and the Book of Acts to another – history, for the sake of the argument. Now Luke-Acts as perceived by Cadbury seems to be a hybrid. Where else in literature do we find an example of a two-part work, of which each part belongs to a different literary genre? It was precisely this difficulty that Talbert set out to meet.[3] He argued that the two-part work dedicated to Theophilus (cf. Luke 1.3 and Acts 1.1) fits reasonably well a pattern known from certain of the *Lives and Opinions of Eminent Philosophers* written by Diogenes Laertius in the third century AD. According to this pattern, a life of the founder (A) was followed by information concerning his successors (B) then, in a number of cases, also by compendia of his teachings (C). The purpose of the second element was especially to indicate the true succession from the founder.

This A+B+C pattern is followed by Diogenes Laertius in his *Lives* of *Aristippus* (Life: 2.65–84; Pupils: 2.85–6; Summary of opinions of the Cyrenaic school: 2.86–104); of *Plato* (Life: 3.1–45; Disciples: 3.46–7;

Doctrine: 3.47–109); of *Zeno* (Life: 7.1–35; Successors and other disciples: 7.36–8; Doctrine: 7.38–160); of *Pythagoras* (Life: 8.1–44; Succession: 8.45–6; Teachings: 8.48–50); and of *Epicurus* (Life: 10.1–21; Successors and other disciples: 10.22–8; Views: 10.29–154). It is true that these are only five out of a total of 182 *Lives*. On the other hand, they are among the most significant, as concerning founders of acknowledged schools. It should further be observed that a good number of Diogenes' *Lives*, such as that of Socrates, include also the names of disciples and successors of philosophers – so Talbert's A+B. Not only that, but the *Lives* are not infrequently arranged so that those of disciples follow those of their masters. A good case in point is Book V, which begins with the *Life* of Aristotle. There follows that of Theophrastus, who is expressly described as Aristotle's most outstanding pupil and as his successor in the school. Afterwards comes Theophrastus' successor Strato, then his successor Lyco. A source frequently cited by Diogenes was the *Successions* of Sotion: the title suggests the contemporary interest in the subject. That it interested also the Jewish world, is indicated by the well known Rabbinic tractate *Pirke Aboth*.

Talbert anticipates the obvious objection that a literary pattern found in a writer of the third century can hardly be attributed without further ado to a writer 200 years earlier. He provides evidence that the A+B pattern – founder followed by successors – was in use in *Lives* of philosophers written before the Christian era, even if no complete example survives. A notable instance would seem to be the *Life* of Aristotle by Hermippus, written in the third century BC.[4] Talbert admits, however, that, in the examples provided by Diogenes Laertius, the B element usually amounts to no more than lists of pupils or successors, and falls far short of the developed narratives of Acts. It is also clear – as Loveday Alexander points out – that the developed narratives characteristic of Acts are quite different from the series of anecdotes of which Diogenes' *Lives* are largely composed.[5] Still, he claims that '(t)he most likely option for explaining these similarities between Laertius' *Lives* and Luke-Acts would seem to be the hypothesis of their dependence upon a *common pattern* used in depicting lives of philosophers'.[6]

Luke's choice of such a pattern would mean, of course, that he identifies Jesus as the founder of a philosophical school. Such a characterization need not surprise us. For the ancients, a philosopher was usually closer to a religious than to an academic figure in the modern sense. The great philosophers could even be regarded as in some sense divine, at least by their disciples and adherents. These latter were typically organized as a sort of 'church'. Indeed Luke does not hesitate to describe the group of Jesus' disciples in Jerusalem in terms that would have reminded his readers of the Pythagoreans (cf. Acts 2.44–5; 4.32–5). According to Talbert,[7] Luke's purpose in Acts was to establish who are the true successors of Jesus: namely, the Twelve with Peter at their head, and Paul.

Talbert's hypothesis has been much discussed, but has largely failed to convince. David E. Aune perhaps dismisses it too summarily.[8] In a collective volume on American Acts criticism, Mikeal C. Parsons and Joseph B. Tyson do Talbert the honour of placing him alongside Henry Cadbury and John Knox as an important American contributor to the study of Acts.[9] In that volume, Parsons himself, J. Bradley Chance and David P. Moessner discuss Talbert's views, and Talbert has the right of reply. More recently, Talbert has further explained and defended his hypothesis on the genre of Luke-Acts,[10] and especially the point of establishing the true succession from Jesus.[11]

The most fundamental criticism would come from those (at the moment, few) who do not accept that 'Luke-Acts' is in fact conceived as a work in two parts and would regard Acts not as the continuation of the Gospel but rather as its sequel. The most searching re-examination of the issue has come from Mikeal C. Parsons and Richard I. Pervo.[12] These authors do not challenge the authorial unity of the two books: they are undoubtedly written by the same person. But they argue that their undisputed canonical *dis*unity cannot be lightly dismissed: the simple fact is, that Luke is not followed by Acts in any manuscript or ancient list of New Testament books.[13] Further, they point out the difficulties in establishing the generic, narrative and theological unity of Luke and Acts that should follow from the Cadbury hypothesis. This debate has, of course, important consequences for Talbert. For, if the contentious hyphen be removed, it is no longer necessary to look for a single literary genre that would embrace both 'Luke and Acts'.

My object is not, however, to discuss the Talbert hypothesis as such. Rather, I want to show that it remains a fruitful hypothesis, whether or not one accepts the underlying premise, namely the opinion expressed by Cadbury more than 75 years ago.

First, then, let us suppose that Luke-Acts must be regarded as a single work in two parts, and that we are looking consequently for literary prec-edents or at least analogies for its apparently hybrid genre. Support for the prior hypothesis – that Luke-Acts is a single work – comes from the literary analyses of the Acts of the Apostles published in 1990 by Marie-Emile Boismard and Arnaud Lamouille, of the Ecole Biblique in Jerusalem.[14] According to these authors, the process that led to the Book of Acts as we know it was one of successive redactions involving several authors and a final reviser. For the first part of Acts, chapters 1–12, together with chapter 15, the earliest text, at the origin of the process of redaction, was a 'Petrine Document'. This was a true continuation of an earlier form of the Gospel. In other words, according to these authors, there was once a single text in which a life of Jesus was continued with an account of his followers after the resurrection. This second part, which followed on the first without any break, showed the disciples in Jerusalem grouped around Peter. It told of their way of life, their witness to the resurrection through healing and preaching, the first expansion of the new faith outside Jerusalem and notably in Samaria, the conversion of the first Gentile (the centurion Cornelius); it ended with Peter's divinely aided escape from 'Herod's' prison.

It seems to me that there are interesting analogies between this reconstructed 'Petrine Document' and Iamblichus' *Pythagorean* (way of) *Life*. In the latter, there are not only compendia of Pythagoras' teaching, under several headings, but also detailed descriptions of the way of life led by his disciples, as well as numerous narratives concerning his followers even after his death. On the other hand, all is encompassed within the literary framework of a 'Life of Pythagoras', whose departure from the scene comes near the end of the work. In that final respect, of course, there is a notable formal difference between Iamblichus' work and the 'Petrine Document'. Nevertheless, the Life of Jesus continued in the 'Petrine Document' could well be thought of as a sort of *De Christiana Vita*, by analogy with Iamblichus' *De Pythagorica Vita*.

Of course, we are dealing with a hypothetical and reconstructed text, on the one hand, and, on the other, with a really existing text which, however, was written some two centuries after the other is supposed to have been produced. The latter difficulty is of the same order as that encountered by Talbert in comparing Luke-Acts with the *Lives* of Diogenes Laertius. It can be met by the same evidence suggesting the use, well before Luke, of the A+B pattern in writing the lives of founders of philosophical schools; that is, the inclusion in them of information concerning the followers.

On the other hand, if Acts is taken by itself – so, not regarded as Part II of a work in two volumes – it conforms well enough to the pattern of Hellenistic historiography. At least, that is my belief, in which I am not alone, although some scholars, notably Richard I. Pervo,[15] have argued that it should be regarded rather as a work of fiction. The Gospel of Luke, for its part, conforms to the pattern of ancient biography.[16] Now, even if we do not class Acts as biography, the book features some notable biographical elements. It is my purpose in this second part to explore them. Let us recall that a Graeco-Roman biography usually, though not invariably, begins with the birth, early upbringing and education of the subject, often includes a moral portrait and anecdotes illustrative of character, as well as a narrative of events in the person's life, and concludes with the death of the subject.[17]

First, let us consider the case of Peter. The treatment of Peter in Acts follows that in the Gospel, and is thus an important narrative and – I believe

– intentional link between the two texts. In Luke's Gospel Peter is the best rounded character after Jesus. He is named as 'Peter' or 'Simon Peter' 21 times, to which should be added nine occasions where he is called 'Simon'. This is roughly about the same number of mentions – both absolutely and in proportion to the length of the Gospel – as in Matthew (respectively 23 and two). Mark's 20 occurrences of the name 'Peter' or 'Simon Peter' and five of the name 'Simon' constitute a higher proportion in this shorter Gospel. It is in John's Gospel, however, that 'Peter' or 'Simon Peter' is named most frequently – 34 times – with five occurrences of 'Simon' referring to him.

From the Third Gospel we already know many biographical details about Peter. We are told nothing about his birth, parenthood or upbringing. He comes on stage without introduction and under the name of Simon shortly after the beginning of Jesus' public ministry (Luke 4.38 f.) The place is Capernaum, and we learn that he has a mother-in-law, and so a wife. Not long afterwards (5.1–11), we learn that Simon is a fisherman on the lake of Gennesareth, that he has a second name Peter, and that he has partners called James and John, sons of Zebedee. Jesus rewards the use of his boat with a wondrous catch of fish, and the episode ends with Simon and his partners abandoning their trade and following Jesus. It is not, however, until somewhat later that Jesus calls Simon, whom he names Peter – without explanation, and eleven others including Peter's brother Andrew and his former partners James and John, to be his 'apostles' (6.12–16). It is Peter who declares that Jesus is 'the Christ of God' (9.20) and who, with John and James, witnesses the raising to life of Jairus' daughter (8.51–6) and Jesus' transfiguration (9.28–36). On two occasions Peter asks a question that expresses his surprise at Jesus' teaching (12.41 and 18.28).

It is in the Passion narrative that Peter features most frequently. Jesus sends him with John to prepare the Passover (22.8–13). At the Last Supper, Jesus foretells a moment of testing for 'Simon', but adds that he has prayed for him, that his faith might not fail and bids him, when he has 'turned again', to strengthen his brethren. Peter protests his readiness to go with Jesus to prison and death, to which Jesus replies by predicting that he will deny him three times before cockcrow (22.31–4). After Jesus' arrest, Peter follows 'at a distance' right to the high priest's house. In one of the most dramatic scenes in the Gospel, he denies three times that he knows Jesus; the cock crows, 'And the Lord turned and looked at Peter'; Peter remembers Jesus' prediction and goes out and weeps bitterly (22.54–62). Ironically, it is another Simon – of Cyrene – who helps Jesus carry his cross to the place of execution (23.26). In a verse that is not read in all texts (24.12), Peter, on hearing the women tell of an empty tomb and angels, 'rose and ran to the tomb; stooping and looking in, he saw the linen cloths by themselves; and he went home wondering at what had happened.' The two disciples return from Emmaus with news of how they recognized Jesus 'in the breaking of the bread', only to be told, 'The Lord has risen indeed and has appeared to Simon!' (24.34f.). Luke provides us with no 'moral portrait' of Simon Peter, but by the end of the Gospel we feel we know him well.

The figure of Peter dominates the first part of Acts, though not to the exclusion of other important characters, notably Stephen, Philip and Saul. In Acts chaps. 1–12 plus 15, 'Peter' or 'Simon Peter' is named 56 times, to which we should probably add James' reference to 'Symeon' in 15.14. On the other hand, he does not really develop in the course of the narrative. Here we recall that ancient biographers did not show the same interest that we do in the development of their subject's character, but tended to treat the person as a finished product.[18] Peter in Acts is simply and massively the leader of the group. He takes the initiative in replacing Judas (Acts 1.15–26), explains to the crowd the meaning of the event of Pentecost and invites the first converts (2.14–41). With John, who is, however, something of a 'lay' figure, he raises up the man lame from birth, who was begging at the Beautiful Gate of the Temple, and tells the crowd that gathers that this wonder has been worked by faith in the name of Jesus raised from the dead by God (3.1–26). He is arrested but uses his appearance before the authorities to testify to the resurrection (4.1–22). Peter's word of power brings death to Ananias and Sapphira (5.1–11), but even his shadow can heal the sick (5.15). He is the spokesman for the apostles before the council (5.29). Once again with John he goes to Samaria, confers the Holy Spirit on those who had been baptized following the preaching and miracles of Philip and rebukes Simon Magus (8.14–25). When attention returns to Peter, he has left Jerusalem for Lydda and Jaffa, where he heals a paralyzed man and brings a dead woman back to life (9.32–43). He is the protagonist in a central episode in the book, when a Roman centurion and his household at Caesarea receive the Holy Spirit and are baptized without first undergoing circumcision (10.1–11.18). The account in Acts 12 of Peter's escape from prison undoubtedly has overtones of his death and resurrection. Indeed, it has even been interpreted as a coded narrative of Peter's death in Jerusalem at the hands of Agrippa I.[19] In any case, he leaves the scene for 'another place', apparently making room in Jerusalem for James (12.17). His surprising reappearance at the Assembly of Jerusalem (15.7–11) is perhaps best explained by taking this episode as originally the continuation of the narrative concerning Cornelius.

The other dominant character of Acts is, of course, Paul. His biography is even more important for the content of the second part of the book than is that of Peter for the first. He enters on the scene in Acts under the name of Saul, as a 'young man' who is a bystander at the stoning of Stephen, a deed of which he is said to approve (Acts 7.58 and 8.1). Later in the book (22.3) we learn from a speech by Paul that he is a Jew born in Tarsus in Cilicia, brought up in Jerusalem[20] and educated 'at the feet of' the rabbi Gamaliel (I). This threefold sequence – 'I was born (γεγεννημένος)...brought up (ἀνατεθραμμένος)...educated (πεπαιδευμένος)' – is found also in autobiographical statements by Arrian and by Ovid.[21] Incidentally, close attention to this passage should have prevented biographers and commentators of Paul from inserting the usual excursus upon the Greek rhetorical education he would have received at Tarsus, since he was not 'educated' there but in Jerusalem. We further learn from Paul in Acts that he is a citizen of Tarsus but also a Roman citizen (21.39 and 22.25, also 16.37).

Returning to the order of Acts, Saul is depicted briefly but vividly as a persecutor of the Church (8.3). He is still 'breathing threats and murder against the disciples of the Lord' in Acts 9.1 and sets off for Damascus, under the authority of the high priest, to arrest and bring to Jerusalem any followers of the Way he might find there. Then comes the well-known story of his conversion (9.3–19). Paul himself retells this event twice in Acts (22.3–21 and 26.2–18), with interesting variations of the narrative. In Damascus Saul proclaims to the Jews that Jesus is the Son of God. There is a plot to kill him, and the disciples have to get him out of the city by lowering him over the wall in a basket. He comes to Jerusalem, where the disciples' mistrust of the former persecutor is overcome by the patronage of Barnabas. A dispute with 'the Hellenists' brings threats to his life, and the disciples bundle him off to Caesarea for Tarsus (9.19–30). 'So,' comments the narrator (9.31), 'the Church throughout all Judea and Galilee and Samaria had peace and was built up.' The account in Acts has points both of convergence with and of divergence from those given by Paul in his letters (cf. Gal. 1.13–24; Phil. 2.5–6; 2 Cor. 11.32–3); it is not our purpose here to discuss them.[22] A little later in Acts, Barnabas brings Saul to Antioch, where – in turbulent circumstances, it seems – 'the disciples were for the first time called *Christiani*' (11.25–6). Then both take relief from the disciples in Damascus to the brethren in Jerusalem and eventually return with John Mark (11.29–30 and 12.25).

From chap. 13 onwards, the Acts of the Apostles become, to all intents and purposes, the Acts of Paul. Still called Saul and apparently subordinate to Barnabas, he goes to Cyprus, where the Roman proconsul Sergius Paulus can be identified at least approximately (13.1–12). At Paphos we learn that Saul is 'also called Paul' (13.9). No explanation is offered for the second name, and commentators have variously tried to supply one. They then cross to Pamphylia, and the party suddenly becomes 'Paul and his companions' (13.13). Barnabas continues to be named from time to time, but mostly in a secondary capacity. After their journey through Pamphylia, Pisidia, Phrygia, Lycaonia and back to the coast, the missionaries return to Antioch (13.14–14.28). It is from there that Paul and Barnabas go once more to Jerusalem for the decisive Assembly of Acts 15. Here again there are questions of reconciliation with Paul in Gal. 2.1–14. The following chapters (16.1–18.22) recount Paul's 'Second Missionary Journey', essentially in Macedonia (Philippi and Thessalonica) and Achaia (Athens and Corinth). In Corinth, his appearance before the proconsul Gallio provides one of the few absolute chronological markers in Acts, AD 51.[23] The 'Third Missionary Journey', essentially to Ephesus, takes up Acts 18.23–21.16, when Paul comes once again to Jerusalem. There he is the centre of a riot in the Temple, is taken into Roman custody, sent to Caesarea, where he appears before two Roman procurators, Felix and Festus as well as king Agrippa II and his sister Berenice, appeals to Caesar and leaves for Rome (21.17–26.32). There, after sea-storm and shipwreck on Malta, he arrives and is allowed to live, under guard, in private lodgings (27.1–28.31). The book ends with Paul 'preaching the kingdom of God and teaching about the Lord Jesus Christ quite openly and unhindered'.

It is possible to construct a reasonably detailed biography of Paul from the information given in Acts. The narrative includes several memorable episodes, such as Paul before the Areopagus in Athens and the silversmiths' riot in Ephesus, as well as the storm at sea, which would be equally at home in historiography or biography – or in fiction. There are also anecdotes, such as those concerning Eutychus in 20.7–12 or Paul's nephew in 23.16–22, which belong rather to the genre of biography than of historiography. Luke gives no formal moral portrait, but, as with Peter in the Gospel and Acts, Paul comes across in his own words and actions as a living, credible person. The farewell speech to the Elders of Ephesus (20.17–35) functions as a retrospective view of his ministry, as a spiritual testament and also as a self-justification on laying down office. As is notorious, Acts ends before Paul's trial in Rome. Thus, in one sense, the reader is left hanging, and the narrative does not include Paul's death, as a biography normally would. There are almost as many theories about why the book ends where it does as there are commentators. On the other hand, there are hints throughout chapters 20 and 21 that Paul is going to his death. All the same, the conclusion of Acts indicates that Luke's primary purpose is not 'to present a life of Paul but to emphasize the worldwide proclamation of the Pauline gospel'.[24]

In sum, although the Book of Acts cannot be regarded as a biography of Peter and Paul, it does contain important biographical elements concerning them. Indeed, if you abstracted the Pauline material from Acts – no difficult task – and reconstructed it as an independent text, I think you might be able to argue successfully that what you would then have would be a 'Life of Paul'. Conversely, without that material, there would not be much left of Acts from chapter 9 onwards.

An interesting feature of Luke's technique in Acts, is the effect of melding together the figures of Peter and Paul. A number of parallels are implicitly drawn. Peter heals a lame man in Jerusalem (3.7), so does Paul at Lystra (14.10). Peter restores a dead person to life (9.41), so does Paul (20.12). Their figures are even identified. Paul is the Apostle of the Gentiles, but it is Peter who receives the first Gentile convert. Most interestingly, at the Assembly of Jerusalem, Peter is given a speech which could well be drawn from the text of one of Paul's letters (15.7–11). The result is that we read Peter and Paul as forming a closely united pair – which is not necessarily the impression gained from Paul in Gal. 2.11–14.

That brings me to my last point. The element of establishing the true succession from the founder – the point of B, according to Talbert's schema – is also present in Acts. There is no doubt from the first part of the work that the group around Peter is to be seen as the continuation of Jesus' own disciples. There is, however, a problem about James and the group around him, which even Luke is obliged to acknowledge. Peter must give an account to James of his dealings with Cornelius. But then he disappears, only to reappear at the 'Council of Jerusalem' where he and James are in agreement. After that James is the sole leader of Jesus' followers in Jerusalem, but many questions are left hanging in the air. An even greater problem occurs with Paul. As we have seen, Luke makes every effort – despite Paul himself – to associate him with the Jerusalem apostles. Paul is there with James at the Assembly of Jerusalem. Later in the book, Paul follows James' advice. So they also agree.

The issue implicit in this is the canon of the New Testament – first, of the canon in the sense of a 'rule', then in that of a 'list'. The canon in the sense of a 'rule' is the agreement of Peter and Paul, who are represented as together the true successors of Jesus. But their agreement does not exclude James and it includes also John (who is frequently seen with Peter in the early chapters of Acts, as in Luke). It is on the basis of this 'rule' that the 'list' or canon of authoritative books of the New Testament is finally drawn up. It corresponds to those who 'shook hands' at Jerusalem according to Gal. 2.9: on the one hand James, Cephas and John, on the other hand Paul and his companions. So, in the New Testament, the Gospels represent Peter and also John, while the Epistles bring together Paul, James, and once again Peter and John. The Book of Acts forms the hinge on which the whole collection swings. The significance of this 'canon' is easily seen when it is compared with the one implicit in the Pseudo-Clementine literature. There Peter and James agree, and Paul is excluded.

The Christianity of the New Testament, centred on Peter and Paul, has for many centuries been regarded as the sole heir of Jesus. It is certainly the sole surviving heir. In the first and second centuries, however, there were rivals in the field. For want of a better term we must call them 'Jewish Christians'. Their claims to be the true successors of Jesus might have seemed at the time to be even stronger than those of New Testament Christianity. The two Lucan works – whether or not they be regarded as strictly a single work in two parts – are arguing a thesis about who are the heirs of Jesus.

I hope thus to have shown that the Talbert hypothesis on the literary genre of what he took to be the two-part work Luke-Acts retains its interest and fruitfulness. In any case, it serves to highlight the importance of the biographical elements in the Acts of the Apostles.

Notes

[1] On the literary genre of Luke's Gospel and Acts, see Burridge 1977b. For general questions of introduction, with bibliography, to both New Testament writings, see Brown 1997, 225–332.

[2] Cadbury 1927.

[3] Talbert 1974, especially 125–40.

[4] Talbert 1974, 130–1; cf. also 133.

[5] Alexander 2005, 7.

[6] Talbert 1974, 135 – italics the author's.

[7] Talbert 1974, 135.

[8] Aune 1987, 78–9.

[9] Parsons and Tyson 1992.

[10] Talbert 1996.

[11] Talbert 1998.

[12] Parsons and Pervo 1993.

[13] These do not always give the canonical order of Matthew, Mark, Luke, John. Two ancient texts (Codex Bezae and Codex Washingtonensis) have Matthew, John, Luke, Mark. But so far no list gives an order, e.g. Matthew, John, Mark, Luke, that would place Luke and Acts in immediate sequence.

[14] Boismard and Lamouille 1990.

[15] Pervo 1987.

[16] Thus Burridge 1992, and summarily 1997b, 513.

[17] See Burridge 1997a.

[18] See Talbert 1974, 128.

[19] e.g. by Robinson 1945, and by Smaltz 1952.

[20] The Greek ἐν τῇ πόλει ταύτῃ could grammatically refer either to Tarsus, just mentioned, or to Jersualem, where Paul is speaking. It is usually taken to be the latter, but, even if Tarsus is meant, it refers to Paul's early upbringing and not to his formal education.

[21] See Conzelmann 1987, 186.

[22] For such discussions, which have not produced a consensus, see commentaries on

Acts or the Pauline Letters, which refer also to more specialized treatments.

²³ See Murphy-O'Connor 1990, 138–60.

²⁴ Aune 1974, 118. Similarly Burridge 1997b, 523.

Bibliography

Alexander, L.C.A.

2005   *Acts in its Ancient Literary Context: A classicist looks at the Acts of the Apostles*, Library of New Testament Studies, London and New York.

Aune, D.E.

1987   *The New Testament in its Literary Environment*, Library of Early Christianity 8, Philadelphia.

Boismard, M.-E. and Lamouille, A.

1987   *Les Actes des deux Apôtres*, vols. I–III, Études Bibliques, n.s. 12–14, Paris.

Brown, R.E.

1996   *An Introduction to the New Testament*, The Anchor Bible Reference Library, New York.

Burridge, R.A.

1977a   'Biography', in Porter, *Handbook of Classical Rhetoric in the Hellenistic Period*, 371–91.

1977b   'The Gospels and Acts', in Porter, *Handbook of Classical Rhetoric in the Hellenistic Period*, 507–32.

1992   *What Are the Gospels? A comparison with Graeco-Roman biography*, SNTS Monograph Series 70, Cambridge.

Cadbury, H.J.

1927   *The Making of Luke-Acts*, New York.

Chance, J.B.

1992   'Talbert's new perspectives on Luke-Acts: The ABC's of ancient lives', in Parsons and Tyson (eds.) *Cadbury, Knox and Talbert*, 181–201.

Conzelmann, H.

1987   *Acts of the Apostles* (Hermeneia; ET of *Die Apostelgeschichte*, 2nd revised edn, 1972), Philadelphia.

Moessner, D.P.

1992   'Re-reading Talbert's "Luke": the bios of "balance" or the bias of history?', in Parsons and Tyson (eds.) *Cadbury, Knox and Talbert*, 203–28.

Murphy-O'Connor, J.

1990   *St Paul's Corinth: Texts and archaeology*, 2nd edn revised and enlarged, Collegeville, Minn.

Parsons, M.C.

1992   'Reading Talbert: new perspectives on Luke and Acts 4', in Parsons and Tyson (eds.) *Cadbury, Knox and Talbert*, 133–79.

Parsons, M.C. and Pervo, R.I.

1993   *Rethinking the Unity of Luke and Acts*, Minneapolis.

Parsons, M.C. and Tyson, J.B. (eds.)

1992a   *Cadbury, Knox and Talbert: American contributions to the study of Acts*, SBL Centennial Publications 18, Atlanta.

Pervo, R.I.
   1987   *Profit with Delight: The literary genre of the Acts of the Apostles*, Philadelphia.
Porter, S.E.
   1977   *Handbook of Classical Rhetoric in the Hellenistic Period, 330 BC–AD 400*, Leiden.
Robinson, D.F.
   1945   'Where and when did Peter die?', *Journal of Biblical Literature* 64, 255–67.
Smaltz, W.M.
   1952   'Did Peter die in Jerusalem?', *Journal of Biblical Literature* 71, 211–16.
Talbert, C.H.
   1974   *Literary Patterns, Theological Themes and the Genre of Luke-Acts*, SBL Monograph Series 20, Missoula.
   1992   'Reading Chance, Moessner and Parsons', in Parsons and Tyson (eds.) *Cadbury, Knox and Talbert*, 224–40.
   1996   'The Acts of the Apostles: monograph or "bios"?', in Ben Witherington III (ed.) *History, Literature and Society in the Book of Acts*, Cambridge, 58–72.
Talbert, C.H. and Stepp, P.L.
   1998   'Succession in Mediterranean antiquity, Part I: The Lukan milieu'; 'Part II: Luke-Acts', in SBL 1998 Seminar Papers, Part I, 148–68; Part II, 169–79.

7

CYNIC INFLUENCE UPON FIRST-CENTURY JUDAISM AND EARLY CHRISTIANITY?

John Moles

Scholarship that moves within the interfaces between different subject areas and different disciplines is often exciting, as well as being personally energizing for scholars who are at risk of becoming stale within their 'proper' fields. Such scholarship is also sometimes indispensable as a way of making progress in a particular area. But it has obvious dangers. Few scholars possess equal competence on both sides of any given interface, and the validity of any such interface may itself be in question ('did "a" really come into contact with "b"?'), as also the validity of one or other of its constituent elements ('was "b" of any real importance?').

For Christian and Jewish scholars the study of the historical Jesus and of the New Testament involves another kind of interface and one that is even more hazardous: that between scholarship and religious belief. Many such scholars are involved both in academic or scholarly and in religious or confessional spheres, and they struggle – with varying degrees of success or, indeed, of resolve – to maintain the necessary critical distances between these different types of activities.[1] Scholarly engagement with this kind of material should entail both a preliminary acknowledgement of interest and, in the analysis of the material itself, studious suppression of the 'personal voice'.[2] This does not mean that personal judgements about questions of quality or value are not ultimately appropriate.[3]

This paper treats claims, made particularly over the last few decades (though anticipated already in the late nineteenth and early twentieth centuries),[4] that Greek Cynicism influenced both the representation and the reality both of first-century Judaism (of the kind exemplified by Jesus and his followers and by Paul) and of early Christianity.[5] As it happens, these same decades have seen a renaissance of research on Cynicism by classicists.[6] But, while there has been some scholarly traffic between the two groupings and some slight overlap of personnel, by and large the classicists have ignored this parallel movement in New Testament studies.

This Cynic-Jewish-Christian interface is sufficiently exciting, and, if it is valid, it brings new material and new scholarship into a field heavily over-worked and heavily over-subscribed. But it is of course highly problematic. Not only does it raise in an acute form the controversial general question of the extent of classical influence upon the world of the New Testament[7] but its stakes for believing Christians are high. Thus if Jesus turned out to be a Cynic who made no real divine claims and for whom no such claims were made by his closest followers in the period immediately after his death, the doctrine of the Incarnation could be rescued only by such a radically 'Liberal' formulation as that of John Dominic Crossan, controversial New Testament scholar, former Roman Catholic priest, and still (at least in his own estima-tion) a Christian: 'to media or audience questions insisting, "Yes, yes, but was he *really* divine?", I answer again and again that, for the first as for the twenty-first century, Jesus was and is divine for those who experience in him *the* manifestation of God'.[8] Again, a Cynic Jesus could be – and, indeed, has been – invoked by those who claim Jesus as a radical social reformer in (alleged) contrast to the (allegedly) bourgeoisifying tendencies of Paul, tendencies which rapidly came to dominate early Christianity.[9] From this point of view, a sentiment such as 'it is easier for a camel to go through the eye of a needle than for a rich man to enter the kingdom of God' (Mark 10.25) would be taken at face value and the consequences for contemporary Christianity would be challenging indeed.

But not only is there a question about the validity of the interface, there is even a question about the validity of the Cynic constituent itself. For the status of Cynicism – philosophy or way of life? – has been debated since antiquity,[10] and further, within the most recent classical scholarship, a pro-found divide seems to be opening up between those for whom the Cynics are genuine Socratics who articulate serious philosophical beliefs through their admitted public exhibitionism[11] and those for whom Cynic 'performance' and 'rhetoric' seem effectively to be the beginning and end of the Cynics' significance.[12]

Who, then, is competent to assess this Cynic-Christian interface? The model has been extensively discussed by more 'orthodox' New Testament scholars and largely rejected by them.[13] But its exponents have not been routed: they are nothing if not dogged, and the debate itself has been nothing if not repetitive. Furthermore, some of the model's most uncompromising opponents seem disturbingly ignorant about Cynicism. For example, Tom Wright's answer to the question (put to him at the Durham New Testament Seminar in 1996) 'what about the Cynic model?' was: 'its proponents have never been able to produce any good parallels for the Kingdom'.[14] And some curious cultural allusions in some of these responses bespeak defensiveness and anxiety and a consequent failure to maintain due scholarly detachment.[15] Equally, however, the use of the Cynic material made by some of the model's exponents seems quite cavalier.

Ideally, then, this interface should be assessed by a person who is equally expert in Cynicism and in New Testament and in related studies and who is completely objective in the contemplation of Judaism and Christianity. Naturally, no such person exists.

The present paper is written by someone who has made some contribution to the renaissance of classical scholarship on Cynicism and who thus hopes from that side to introduce into this debate some suitably Cynic rigour; who is committed to the view that the Cynics were serious moralists and that they were important and influential; who (as will be obvious) has no professional competence in New Testament studies; who is an assiduously practising and intermittently (in some sense) believing Anglican; who in this scholarly context admits to a certain fideistic anxiety but seeks conscientiously to suppress it; and who, nevertheless, thinks that questions of value cannot ultimately be excluded.

The 'Cynic model' is associated with scholars such as Malberbe, Thiessen, Downing, Mack, Crossan, Kloppenborg, Vaage and Seeley,[16] Mack and Crossan being prominent members of the famous – or notorious – American 'Jesus seminar'.[17] The model is applied in different ways and in different areas; these different applications can be regarded alternatively as free-standing or as constituting a cumulative case for general Cynic influence upon early Christianity and the sort of Judaism from which it sprang, back to, and including, Jesus himself. Downing is the leading exponent of this cumulative case: he is also the scholar who puts the Cynic case in its strongest form: that is: not all Cynics were Christians but all Christians were Cynics – more or less, or at least there was a recognized family relationship. This notion of the family is important to Downing, because it allows for diversity within a basic similarity. Even as restricted to Jesus, however, the model admits a considerable range: from a fully-fledged more-or-less secular Cynic, to a Cynic with a strong religious slant, to a Jewish rabbi more or less influenced by Cynicism, to a figure who need not actually have been influenced by Cynicism but for whom a Cynic model happens to provide the best ancient analogy.[18]

This paper is less concerned with the model's different forms than with the fundamental prior question of whether it has anything to be said for it at all. Part I will try to establish the historical constraints on such a general model – in rather the same way as, a generation ago, A.E. Harvey tried to establish the historical constraints on the reconstruction of the historical Jesus.[19] Part II will survey the evidence adduced in favour of the model and Part III will attempt some conclusions.

John Moles

I. Problems about Cynicism and their methodological and practical implications for the Cynic model

Space restrictions impose an appropriate dogmatism, though one that seeks to incorporate the methodological rigour absent from many modern reconstructions of Cynicism.[20]

1.1 *Was Cynicism a more or less uniform philosophy/way of life?*

To be sure, some simple distinctions are needed: between Cynicism as lived, Cynicism as written, Cynicism as appropriated by other philosophies and Cynicism as itself influenced by other philosophies. Within Cynicism as lived, one needs to distinguish – in adaptation of Lovejoy-Boas terminology[21] – between 'hard' Cynics (rigorous followers of Diogenes) and 'soft' Cynics (those who compromised with existing social or political structures, e.g. by marrying or engaging in political life – such as Demonax).[22] Beyond these distinctions, however, one should not go. Both advocates of the Cynic model such as Downing and opponents of it such as Betz and Wright greatly exaggerate Cynicism's diversity. Advocates do this because they want to make the model as capacious as possible, so that practically any manifestations of Greek popular philosophy can be labelled 'Cynic'. Opponents do this because they want to undermine the very notion of 'a Cynic model'. Thus Tom Wright: 'who were the Cynics? The answers are always fuzzy, since it was of the essence of the movement that its adherents sat loose to formal structures. Everybody's definition, in the ancient as in the modern world, would carry some problematic aspects'.[23] On the contrary, what is striking about Cynicism is how little it changes over its 1000-year history or from place to place.[24] Why should it? Diogenes had solved all the problems of life.[25]

The belief in great Cynic diversity stems from two errors. The first is a misconception of the idea of the individual. A Cynic is an individual in the sense that he claims complete self-sufficiency and rejects the values of society at large. He is not an individual in the sense that he can embody any way of life that he chooses. The second is a misconception of the notion of (in Wright's words) 'sitting loose to formal structures'. This notion is often taken to imply that Cynicism's doctrinal base was flexible and indeterminate, but, while it is true that Cynicism's doctrines are few and simple and that they necessarily involve the rejection of all the doctrinal baggage of conventional philosophy, they nevertheless are internally coherent and they underpin the way of life.[26]

1.2 *The range of source material and the problem of Stoic texts*

Why should it matter if Downing et al. cast their source net too widely? While such scholars are sometimes wrong to categorize their comparative material as 'Cynic', might it be reasonable to talk of the influence on Jesus of 'Greek popular philosophy', abandoning the specific term 'Cynic', while maintaining the broad insight? But terminological exactitude does matter, for two reasons: first, Cynic positions are pretty distinctive and Downing et al. trade considerably on this distinctiveness; secondly, most scholars would find it implausible to posit the availability to Jesus of Greek philosophical material that goes beyond Cynicism.[27]

Stoic writers pose a particular problem: writers such as Seneca, Dio Chrysostom and Epictetus are freely raided by Downing et al. for Cynic material.[28] Yet the legitimacy of this procedure varies: some Stoic contexts are essentially Cynic contexts (since Stoicism was born from Cynicism and Stoic ethics were greatly influenced by Cynic ethics); others are completely opposed to Cynicism.[29] Downing et al. often fail to make this vital context distinction. Use of Epictetus' *On Cynicism* (3.22) is particularly difficult. Epictetus offers a bowdlerized, Stoicized, and highly religious Cynic:[30] a gift to Downing et al., because you can then claim that there were real-life Cynics who did not urinate, defecate, masturbate and fornicate in public (all characteristic Cynic activities),[31] and who also asserted a close personal relationship with God. But Epictetus' Cynic is a theoretical construct: there never were such Cynics, not even Epictetus himself. Yet it is a construct largely derived from Cynic realities: use of the *On Cynicism* is not wrong per se but it must be discriminating.

1.3 *Cynic literary forms*
Neither is appeal to *Cynic* literary material unproblematic. Three literary forms are crucial.

The first is 'diatribe', a form much canvassed in New Testament scholarship[32] but one whose boundaries and whose very existence have been fiercely debated in classical scholarship. It is certainly untenable to view diatribe as a tight literary genre with a whole series of formal elements; but classicists' obsessing over whether 'diatribe' exists has been equally unhelpful. We should agree that there was indeed a form called diatribe, that it describes the oral lecture, either in its original form or in a literary mimesis, and that it is particularly used of the popular sermon, itself particularly associated with, though not restricted to, the Cynics, who indeed probably invented it.[33]

The second literary form is the Cynics' collections of *chreiai*,[34] collections which could function as building-blocks of full biographies, as, for example, in Diogenes Laertius' *Lives of the Philosophers*.[35]

The third form, hypothetically, is 'Cynic biography', a form to which we shall return.[36]

1.4 *Cynics and religion*
As we have seen, Epictetus' *On Cynicism* makes the Cynic a strongly religious

figure and Epictetus' conception of the Cynic as a divine messenger from God has been much invoked by exponents of the Cynic model. This raises the whole vexed question of Cynics and religion.[37]

In ancient philosophy generally, the inclusion of the wise man within the category of the 'holy man' is very widespread. Cynics, too, use such religious language extensively: they represent themselves as 'god-like', 'friends of the gods', 'sons of Zeus', etc.[38] What does such language mean? Certainly, it means that, if you are a Cynic, you can have the happiness, freedom, etc. traditionally attributed to the gods. But many distinguished scholars of Cynicism, including, recently, Marie-Odile Goulet-Cazé, have argued that Cynics generally were agnostic or even atheist.

Now it is true that Cynics ridicule conventional religion and that religion cannot be important to a Cynic: he has all his happiness and freedom (a freedom which includes freedom from superstition) right now. Nevertheless, appeal to the example of the gods obviously carries less force if you do not believe in them,[39] and there is strong reason to suppose that the gods were factored in to Diogenes' *cosmopolis*.[40] Gods *plural* – what about God singular? From Homer onwards, classical polytheism always carries the potentiality of monotheism, and within Cynicism the conception of the Cynic as a divine messenger from god seems to go back to Onesicritus in *c.* 320 BCE , probably back to Crates and perhaps even to Diogenes himself.[41]

Could a Cynic put God *singular* at the head of the universe? Ought he not to put Nature there?[42] Yet there are substantially Cynic texts which come close to equating nature with the divine principle that interpenetrates the cosmos.[43] These texts are Stoic-influenced, but the move they make is not a big one: Diogenes himself invoked 'right reason' as a cosmic principle,[44] and his anti-Prometheus myth[45] argued a fundamentally benign natural order as established by Zeus. Nevertheless, on balance it must be said that Cynicism's religious language has more to do with validation of the Cynic's philosophical role than with religious thought in any strong sense.

1.5 *Cynics and other people*

Also controversial within classical scholarship on Cynicism is the extent to which Cynics have positive concern for others. How far are such things as Jesus' having disciples, his practice of 'commensality' and his moral concern for others compatible with Cynic ideas? The answer is that they are broadly compatible. Although the Cynic is independent and self-sufficient, he has a philanthropic concern for others:[46] he tries to convert them, he attracts followers or disciples,[47] and he has some conception of a Cynic community.[48]

1.6 *The Cynic way of life*

As adherents of a primitivist conception of nature, Cynics are themselves poor, advocate poverty and associate with the poor and the socially marginalized;[49] they wander,[50] and they promote and practise a basic economic egalitarianism.[51] All this, too, is broadly compatible with Jesus' way of life, though Jesus and his followers stop short of the outright begging that is one of the Cynics' trademarks. Even more alien to the celibate Jesus and his followers is that most distinctive of Cynic trademarks: the public performance of all natural functions, though it is interesting to note that such behaviour does find parallels in some stories in the Talmud.[52]

1.7 *Cynics and politics*[53]

'Hard' Cynics reject all political institutions as unnatural and espouse anarchy. This does not make them political activists in any conventional sense: they need only a minimal level of subsistence and they reject armed conflict. There is no room here for 'Jesus the Zealot' (that is, leader of a patriotic, anti-Roman, revolutionary movement).[54] What, then, of 'Cynic kingship'? The concept was absorbed by conventional kingship ideology but its original point is to disavow conventional kingship in favour of Cynic kingship, which, as it were, flips the categories and is thus simply a metaphor for the Cynic way of life (with a range of easily derivable implications: self-mastery, total freedom to do as one likes, rejection of worldly power and pomp, etc.). So a 'hard' Cynic could certainly say 'the kingdom of god is at hand' or 'within you',[55] meaning that you – you yourself – can attain the perfect god-like state here and now. Such a Cynic interpretation underpins Crossan's single biggest idea about Jesus' ministry: that of 'the brokerless kingdom of god'.[56] This, of course, is not necessarily to say that Jesus' kingdom *is* the Cynic kingdom: but it is to say that a Cynic could speak in those terms. On the other hand, a 'hard' Cynic should certainly not say: 'Render to Caesar the things that are Caesar's' (Mark 12.17). But a 'soft' Cynic could say that, and indeed, in their respective relations with Antigonus Gonatas and Trajan, Bion of Borysthenes and Dio Chrysostom effectively did so.[57]

1.8 *Cynics and eastern wisdom*

Were there ever any real links, or overlap, between Cynics and eastern holy men, especially Jewish ones? Most scholars now discount eastern influence on Cynicism in favour of general resemblance (one ascetic type looks pretty much like another). Nevertheless, because of its elevation of Nature over Culture and its general iconoclasm, Cynicism is constitutionally welcoming to 'alien wisdom';[58] some leading Cynics came from the East; the legend of Diogenes was early contaminated by lore about the Indian gymnosophists;[59]

the Cynic Oenomaus of Gadara (*floruit* 120 CE) is identifiable with the Jewish philosopher Abnimos of the Talmud,[60] and the great Jewish philosopher Philo of Alexandria (*floruit* 20 CE) was expert in Cynicism as well as Stoicism.[61] So there is a *general* possibility of two-way traffic here.

1.9 *Hellenism in Jewish Palestine*

This hugely controversial question[62] is obviously of some relevance to the present enquiry. Was such Hellenization as there was limited to the city and upper-class? Yet this question is less important in relation to Cynicism, which, although sometimes practised by members of the elite who had lost, or abandoned, that status, was not in itself an elite activity.

1.10 *The general existence of practical Cynicism at the start of the first century* CE

Did practical Cynicism even exist at the time of Jesus' birth? (The question is framed in this way because, although the hypothesis that Jesus could have encountered Cynicism through the reading of Cynic texts is not theoretically falsifiable, few scholars would find it plausible.)[63] Such distinguished scholars of ancient philosophy as E. Zeller and J. Bernays maintained that Cynicism died out in the last two centuries BCE and that when it revived in the middle of the first century CE it had only been reborn out of Stoicism, and this view is still maintained by A.A. Long.[64] If such scholars are correct, that form of the Cynic model which claims direct Cynic influence is immediately vitiated, certainly as applied to Jesus and surely also as applied to Paul. Not only, however, do Malherbe's analyses prove Cynicism's vitality in Paul's lifetime in contexts which exclude 'rebirth from Stoicism' (as we shall see),[65] but the evidence on the classical side is also sufficient to validate this conclusion.[66]

1.11 *Could Jesus have encountered practical Cynicism?*

But the case of Paul, born in the city of Tarsus in Cilicia, fluent both in spoken and in written Greek, and internationally travelled, is not the same as that of Jesus of Nazareth. Could a Galilean villager have encountered practical Cynicism at the start of the first century CE ?

Nazareth is about four miles from the Hellenistic city Sepphoris (with which Jesus is not recorded to have had any contact) and about twenty miles from the Transjordan Greek city of Gadara. On the current majority view, archaeological analysis of Sepphoris at the relevant time makes it, despite the Hellenism of its refounder Herod Antipas, both racially and culturally a very Jewish city.[67] Could there have been Greek Cynics or Jewish Cynics there? If there were, how could Jesus have encountered them? What sort of contacts were there between the Galilean cities and villages?[68] As a carpenter's son, might Jesus have visited Sepphoris to help his father in its rebuilding?[69]

In apparent contrast to Sepphoris, Gadara produced the Cynic Menippus in the third century BCE , the Cynicizing poet Meleager in the 2nd/1st centuries BCE, and the Jewish Cynic Oenomaus towards the end of the first century CE. Might Gadara have had a Cynic community within Jesus' lifetime? If so, could he have come into contact with it? While Jesus visited the environs of Gadara during his ministry,[70] he began that ministry in the villages and countryside of Galilee and he is never recorded as having visited *poleis* in the full sense of that term, although he certainly visited the *chōrai* of such *poleis*.[71]

The question of 'village' and 'countryside' as opposed to 'city' in relation both to Jesus' upbringing and to his ministry is a difficult one. Might a useful distinction be drawn between attitude to cities (tension, even hostility, with practical consequences for Jesus' ministry: avoidance of *poleis* in the strict sense) and actual knowledge (whether as the result of the general commercial contacts that obtained between village and city, of hearsay, or of pre-ministry visits)? Agricultural and commercial contacts between Sepphoris and the surrounding villages are certain;[72] Jesus knew about city life, including Greek reclining at meals,[73] and he also knew something about pagan religion, both Greek and Roman.[74]

Might there also have been Cynics in the countryside of Galilee? Positive attestation of the phenomenon of 'country Cynics' in any cultural context is slight but not non-existent,[75] and there must have been such Cynics, because, although Cynics generally frequented the cities (in order both to beg and to maximize converts), they are fundamentally hostile to the city, *qua* contrary to nature, and they 'wander' from place to place, so must sometimes be found in the countryside. The existence of country Cynics, however, is obviously much less likely in contexts where there are no city Cynics, but the *chōrai* of *poleis* could afford a more plausible context.

To question 1.11, then, no final answer can be given. Those classicists (like the present writer) who believe in the widespread diffusion of Cynicism in the Hellenistic period, and who (again like the present writer) suspect that the much-touted 'decline' of Cynicism after the end of the third century BCE is more likely to reflect gaps in the evidence rather than any very substantial historical reality, will find it possible that the young Jesus could have encountered practical Cynicism, perhaps through pre-ministry visits to Sepphoris or Gadara or the latter's *chōra*. The notorious blank in Jesus' pre-ministry career makes one wonder if some of it was spent in travelling. John Dillon pleasantly sees Jesus' early career as similar to Socrates' in Plato's *Apology*, with Jesus searching for the truth – maybe visiting the Essenes, maybe the Gadarene Cynics – before striking out on his own.[76] Alternatively, of course, he may just have been working with his father. But even that would not provide a decisive

negative to the question. And, of course, if the evidence adduced in favour
of the Cynic model is sufficiently solid, it itself constitutes evidence for the
availability to Jesus of practical Cynicism.

1.12 *Could Jesus speak Greek?*
This, surely, is highly desirable, perhaps even indispensable, for the Cynic
model to work. Downing does not think it is indispensable, but it is not clear
how a Greek-less Jesus could have acquired the Cynic-like social *langue* which
Downing attributes to him. But in any case it is hard to believe that a first-
century Jew – even a Galilean – whose life and sayings are almost exclusively
recorded in Greek,[77] who is represented as talking directly to Romans and
to a Greek woman (Mark 7.26), two of whose disciples have Greek names
(Andrew and Philip), and who even *seems* to make bilingual Aramaic-Greek
puns could not speak (at least some) Greek.[78] Probably a majority of New
Testament and historical Jesus scholars now believe that Jesus could speak
Greek, though many of these shirk what seems the natural consequence:
namely, that Jesus must have had at least some knowledge of Greek culture.
But this he anyway seems to have had.[79]

II. Evidence adduced in favour of the Cynic model
The treatment here is anachronistic and designed to move progressively from
the certain to the controversial and thereby to provide some controls for
assessing the plausibility of the cumulative case.

2.1 *Cynic influence on Paul*
Following Bultmann, several modern scholars, including Malherbe, Hock,
Downing, Deming, have argued for various kinds of Cynic influence (alike
on style and rhetoric, on thought and – to some extent – on way of life)
upon Paul, though these scholars (Downing partially excepted) do not claim
Paul as actually Cynic.[80] Not all of the parallels adduced with Cynic diatribe
are convincing, but there are undoubtedly some convincing parallels, both
of thought and of sentence structure, between Paul and Antisthenes[81] and
Teles.[82] Malherbe also demonstrates Paul's frequent self-definition through,
and against, Cynic categories, and his analyses prove Pauline Christianity's
engagement both with Cynic ethics and with real-life contemporary Cynics.

All these findings are of interest in themselves, but they might help the
cumulative Cynic case: if a Jewish wandering rabbi and preacher, a follower
and imitator of Jesus, who began his ministry in the decade after Jesus' death,
comported himself in these ways, that might increase the possibility of the
wandering[83] rabbi and preacher Jesus coming into some similar category. In
any event, it is astonishing, and surely reprehensible, that these Cynic aspects

of Paul are entirely neglected in what might broadly be described as orthodox Christian treatments of Paul's theology.[84]

2.2 *Cynic influence on the Church fathers*
Downing, Dorival and others have analysed how the Christian fathers often proclaimed, and often disclaimed, a link between Christian virtue and Cynic virtue.[85] There are also the concrete cases of Peregrinus, recorded – with derision – by Lucian[86] and Maximus.[87] If Christian virtue aims to imitate Jesus and sometimes does so in Cynic mode, was Jesus himself rather Cynic?

2.3 *Cynic influence on pictorial representations of Jesus*
Some of the earliest pictorial representations of Jesus make him look like a Cynic.[88] Again the question: why?

2.4 *Cynic influence on the Gospels?*
The case for Cynic influence on the Gospels depends partly on the subject-matter, partly on formal considerations. That the Gospels are generically biographies, always the obvious reading, has been comprehensively argued by Burridge and Frickenschmidt, and the overall case is decisive.[89] Of course, as Christopher Pelling has repeatedly taught us, ancient biography is a very flexible genre. The Gospels surely also fall slightly more specifically into the category of the biography of the 'holy man' (not that dissimilar from Philostratus' *Life* of *Apollonius of Tyana*, Apollonius for that very reason becoming a pagan rival to Jesus).[90] The Gospels also contain much *chreia* material, with standard narrative patterns. In a general way, then, the Gospels have something of the flavour of Cynic biography (like the reconstructible early biographical treatments of Diogenes, Diogenes Laertius' Book 6,[91] or Lucian's *Demonax*).[92] This seems true also of Q, the hypothetical but (in the opinion of the present writer) certain second written source both of Matthew and of Luke (Mark being the first written source).[93] Does this light Cynic biographical flavouring say anything about the biographical hero?

The case for Jesus as Cynic in some sense (within, as we have seen, a considerable range) may invoke the individual items or the broad cumulative case already mentioned but within the New Testament it must depend on: (a) the general representation of Jesus' activities, teachings and styles of exposition; and (b) certain specific parallels.

(a) The former may be most economically presented in list form:
Jesus' 'wanderings' and 'homelessness',[94] high public profile, general low-life associations, including, strikingly, women and even women followers, 'free-loading' (not 'begging' in the strict sense), 'communism',[95] reversal/

subversion of normal hierarchies (the Sermon on the Mount), 'internation-alism',[96] elevation of poverty and criticism of wealth, elevation of physical endurance as a moral test, ideals of voluntary self-abasement and suffering, at least partial rejection of conventional political structures (for the Kingdom of God is certainly far more important than the Kingdom of Caesar),[97] attacks on money-lenders and big-wigs, attacks on at least some aspects of institutionalized religion, fast, often abusive and aggressive wit, aphorisms, appeals to nature and animals ('consider the lilies of the field', etc.), vigorous, colloquial, non- or anti-intellectual style of exposition and concomitant rejection of 'cleverness', general emphasis on practical, everyday virtue.

Naturally, not all scholars would agree with the inclusion – even for possible consideration – of all these elements. For example, Marshall claims that 'the strong presence of women among Jesus' followers has *no* Cynic precedent' (present writer's italics).[98] But the famous (and historical) case of the 'dog wedding' of Crates and Hipparchia, of Hipparchia's 'disciple-ship' of Crates and of their subsequent fully-shared public 'living together' instantiates the Cynic principle of total sexual equality, a principle laid down by Diogenes himself.[99] If, as the very fame of Hipparchia's example suggests, few women in practice braved the extreme physical and societal demands of the 'hard Cynic' way of life, the principle remains important, as does the fact that Diogenes' ideal *Politeia* explicitly embraced women.[100]

The above list also raises a simple but important methodological point. Individual 'Cynic' items are often contested on the ground that other evidence tells against them. But the force of such objections requires precise calibration. For example, Crossan and his followers regularly adduce as one of Jesus' Cynic attributes his alleged 'itineracy'.[101] The seemingly correct insist-ence of Dunn and other scholars that 'Jesus made his base' in Capernaum, where he had 'his home',[102] has *some* force against a 100 per cent *Jesus-Cynicus* model, yet even in this case its force is not absolute: Diogenes himself, the very type of the 'hard Cynic', who undoubtedly proclaimed his 'wander-ings' and 'homelessness' and did indeed *sometimes* 'wander',[103] *largely* based himself in Athens; nor were all Cynics '*hard*' Cynics. And the insistence has *no* force against the model which claims that even 'hard' Cynicism is (only) one of several influences upon Jesus, who, like Diogenes and other Cynics, undoubtedly *sometimes* represented himself as 'homeless'.

One should, then, allow this collection of items, or something like them, to be viable *possibilities*, but all one can really say about them is that, if one already knew that Jesus was a Cynic or was Cynic-influenced, most of this material would be Cynic or Cynic-influenced, but it does not itself prove the case or even establish much of a presumption in its favour.

(b) Most of Downing's 'parallels' are too generalized. Discussion is here restricted to five crucial cases adduced by Downing and others:

(i) 'Who is my mother, who are my brothers?' (Mark 3.21, 31–5; Matthew 12.46–50; Luke 8.19–21; from Q).[104] This rejection and 'redefinition' of the family has no Jewish parallels, but is paralleled in the Cynic doctrine 'the wise man is the kin of his peer' (D.L. 6.105): Cynics, who do not marry, have no use for the family (D.L. 6.72) and they redefine 'kinship' in moral/philosophical terms.

(ii) 'Leave the dead to bury their dead' (Matthew 8.21–2; Luke 9.59–60). This shocking dismissal of funeral rites is quite un-Jewish, but has Cynic parallels.[105]

(iii) 'You're not to carry a purse with you at all, nor a satchel, and don't wear sandals/Take nothing for your journey, no satchel, no bread, no money, no change of shirt, no sandals, no staff (Luke 10.4; Matthew 10.9–10; Mark 6.7–13; variations of detail; from Q).[106]

Advocates of the Cynic model such as Kloppenborg, Mack, Vaage and Downing take this as very Cynic. Thus Downing: 'if the first Christian missionaries obeyed instructions of [this] kind, they would have looked like a kind of Cynic, displaying a very obvious poverty...a raggedly cloaked and outspoken figure with no luggage and no money would not just have looked Cynic, he would obviously have wanted to'.[107] Crossan is more cautious, finding both Cynic and non-Cynic elements.[108] Opponents of the Cynic model naturally stress the latter.

How to arbitrate? The absence of shoes, bread and money (thereby entailing economic dependency on others) and the restriction to a single garment look Cynic; the exclusion of purse or satchel and staff looks un-Cynic, but pointedly so: in such exercises of self-definition you exclude the badges of groups to which you either are, or appear, close (characteristically, the man who says 'I'm not black' is not white but rather dark). Thus the mission passages seem to establish a recognition on the part of the New Testament of a certain resemblance between the disciples – and by extension Jesus – and the Cynics, a resemblance which Jesus himself is represented as acknowledging, though also as qualifying, taking the first Christians even farther down the ascetic road than the Cynics. These passages, which go back to Q, put the Cynic portrayal of Jesus very early; and they make Jesus himself aware of a certain kinship with the Cynics. From a reader-response point of view, also, the readerships both of Q and of the Gospels would surely have read these passages as, so to speak, 'modified Cynic'.

(iv) The temptation of Jesus (Matthew 4.8; Luke 4.5–6; Q): 'The Adversary [*diabolos*] took Jesus up into a very high mountain and showed him all the world's kingdoms and their splendour, and said, I will give you all these'.[109]

Since Downing seems to be right that 'there is no Jewish parallel for this offer',[110] he is surely then also right in sensing two Cynic parallels: (a) the meeting between great worldly king and Cynic philosopher where the king offers the philosopher anything he likes and the philosopher rejects the offer with contempt (Alexander and Diogenes, Caligula and Demetrius); and (b) the existential choice between two opposed concepts – whether Virtue and Vice/Pleasure (the choice of Heracles) or Kingship and Tyranny, a choice sometimes offered at the top of a mountain. If so, and if the temptation is historical in the sense that Jesus told his disciples of some such visionary experience, he was familiar with this sort of Cynic temptation material which he then absorbed into his Jewish religious thinking (of course, Cynics do not believe in the Devil).

(vi) The two-roads motif (Matthew 7.13–14; Luke 13.23–4; Q): 'Enter by the narrow gate. There's a wide gate and a broad pathway leading to destruction, and lots of people use them. But it's a constricted gate and it's a narrow path that leads to life, and there aren't many who use those at all'.[111]

This looks very Cynic: the road imagery, the contrast between the wide destructive road used by the many and the narrow, difficult, road used by the few that leads to salvation. In Cynic texts the two-roads motif is often conjoined with the Choice between Virtue and Vice *vel sim.* Now it is true that 'the two roads' motif is widespread in sapiential Jewish-Christian literature and is also found in the Qumran material, and that it is elsewhere used by Jesus himself ('I am the Way', etc. [John 14.6]). But it is not the bare motif that counts: it is the detailed way in which the motif is developed. It is also true that 'the two roads' motif is everywhere in classical literature, from Hesiod on, often with development very similar to Jesus' here,[112] but few scholars now claim that Jesus was familiar with classical literature.[113] Hence another simple methodological consideration: where there is a range of classical parallels, the Cynic ones must trump the others.

III. Conclusions

The facts that Paul was influenced by Cynicism and sometimes himself assumed an ambiguous Cynic role and that early Christians saw a parallel between Christian and Cynic asceticism are not decisive. It could be that, once Christianity expanded beyond Palestine to include Gentiles and progressively detached itself from its Jewish base and personnel, it had to package itself for the wider world and one of the already available, and not altogether unsuitable, packagings was Cynicism. One might compare Christian theology's appropriation of some aspects of Stoicism.[114] But there seems sufficient evidence within the New Testament and – behind the New Testament – in Q to show that the Greek-speaking Jesus and his disciples (who included

Greek speakers who had Greek names and who had contacts with Greeks) already saw some parallels between themselves and contemporary Cynics. In which case, the ambiguous Cynic colouring of Paul and later Christians does reflect something about Christianity from its origins. In which case also, that colouring acquires a certain evidential value in its own right: it represents *their* reading – not just *our* reading – of Jesus and the New Testament. Within the New Testament, if the detailed parallels are of sufficient weight, then the general representation of Jesus and his characteristic activities has also to be brought into the picture, and likewise the Gospels' lightly Cynic biographical character. So the present writer discerns Cynic influence on Jesus' way of life, social and political attitudes, general behaviour and manner of teaching. Jesus must have seen and heard Cynics: he knew what they looked like, he knew some of their characteristic stories and narrative patterns. Of course, he eschewed the characteristic shamelessness of hard Cynicism, but, Jew though he was, he was able – like the later Abnimos/Oenomaus – to see through this shamelessness to the Cynics' real virtues.

Any attempt to reconstruct the complexity of the historical Jesus obviously has to factor in the many non-Cynic elements whose existence should not remotely be denied. These include (even on Downing's highly elastic conception of Cynicism) miracles, eschatology and 'Christology'.[115] These are, of course, huge elements. To these should be added Jesus' strong *personal* sense of God and the strong religious piety. There are parallels for these latter elements in Stoics such as Epictetus and Musonius, as Downing stresses, Stoics who show clear Cynic influence in certain contexts. But not in these contexts, as has been argued above.[116] Unsurprisingly, all these non-Cynic elements focus on the strongly religious aspects of Jesus and raise the whole question of his situatedness within Jewish traditions. It is in these areas, then, that the Cynic model comes under intolerable strain. Conversely, however, the Cynic material seems sufficiently strong to challenge, even to undermine, the contention that Jesus is to be understood solely within Jewish traditions. Nor can this Cynic influence upon Jesus be sanitized within any model of a pre-existent Jewish form of Cynicism.

Jesus the Cynic *tout court*, then? Certainly not. Jesus the Cynic to some extent? Yes. The finding has large implications for the reconstruction of the historical Jesus, for the influence of Hellenism on first-century Judaism, for the history of the early Christian church, and for the necessary refashioning of contemporary Christianity.

IV. Tailpiece

Notwithstanding its immensely rich and varied *Nachleben*, most classicist scholars of ancient philosophy have a low opinion of Cynicism, largely because of Cynicism's very considerable theoretical inadequacies. But questions of quality or value cannot be brushed aside. From a modern perspective, we can see that, partly, though not wholly, because of those very theoretical inadequacies, Cynicism effortlessly attained some ethical positions that were qualitatively far superior to those of 'great' ancient philosophies such as Platonism, Aristotelianism and Stoicism. Long, for example, has written:

> [Diogenes'] ethical values took no account of social status and nationality, and this emphasizes the radical character of Diogenes' criticism of traditional attitudes. A study of Aristotle's painful defence of slavery in *Politics* Book I should make the point beyond doubt.[117]

Quite, and the insight cannot be exaggerated. Today, after decades of studious avoidance of such value judgements, due to embarrassment both over the ludicrously inflated claims that earlier generations made for the civilizing benefits of classical culture and over the horrors highlighted by rigorous scholarly analysis of such central institutions of that culture as the Roman games, there seems to be renewed interest among classicists in arguing the value and utility of ancient philosophy for modern people.[118]

In a rare and uncharacteristic expression of his 'personal voice', the present writer confesses that at a time of acute depression many years ago he derived great, indeed decisive, solace from ancient Cynicism: he was saved not by Jesus but by *Dio-genes* (wrong god, wrong son). Admirable, however, as Cynic ethics are, they are greatly surpassed by Christian ones. Yet the latter turn out to have been influenced by the former. No doubt of it, then, as in the first, so in the twenty-first, century AD, Christian Cynicism is the place to be. The broad consequences of this are sufficiently clear. I leave it to Christian theologians and ethicists to work out the details.

Classical scholars of ancient philosophy who are less impressed by Cynicism than I am but who happen also to be Christians face an even greater moral and intellectual challenge: of all the ancient pagan philosophies, Cynicism is the one most nearly endorsed by God.[119]

Acknowledgements
Versions of this paper under various titles were given at the 'Beyond Biography' conference in Dublin; at the New Testament Seminar in Durham (October 1998); at the *Hibernian Hellenists* in Maynooth (9th October 1998); at the New Testament Seminar in Sheffield (11th February 2002); and at the *Classical Association* in Durham (26th April 2002). My thanks to the respective organizers (Jimmy Dunn; Maureen Alden; Brian McGing and Judith Mossman [whose kindness beggars description]; Loveday Alexander; and Gordon Cockburn); to all those who made helpful comments on those occasions; to Gerald Downing for helpful phone conversations over the years; and to Loren Stuckenbruck for advice on linguistic matters and for scrutiny of the penultimate draft.

Notes

[1] Of course, some dispute such formulations, e.g. Wright 1996, xiv: 'it is enough to say that I come to this work as a practising historian and as a practising Christian, and that my experience of both worlds suggests – to put it no stronger – that neither of them need feel compromised by intimate association with the other'. But, equally of course, *nothing* in this *apologia* is uncontentious.

[2] A movement of that name within classical scholarship has been much savaged: Hanson, Heath and Thornton 2001.

[3] See p. 104 below.

[4] e.g. Zeller 1893; Wendland 1895; 1912; Geffken 1909; Bultmann 1910.

[5] Select references in n. 16 below; for the refinement – no necessary Cynic influence on Jesus but 'objective' affinity – see p. 91 and n. 18 below; 'early Christianity' is a prejudicial term, but convenient.

[6] Noteworthy contributions: Paquet 1975; Kindstrand 1976; Billerbeck 1978; 1979; 1991; Moles 1983a; 1993; 1995; 1996a; 2000; Giannantoni 1990 II (fragments); IV (critical discussions); Goulet and Goulet-Cazé 1993; Goulet-Cazé 1986; 1990; 1993; 1994; 1996; 2003; Branham 1993; 1996; Branham and Goulet-Cazé 1996; Navia 1996; 1998; Luck 1997; Fuentes Gonzalez 1998.

[7] For radical recent claims in favour of such influence cf. MacDonald 2000; 2003; Thiede 2004; Moles forthcoming b.

[8] Crossan 1995, 216.

[9] Cf. e.g. Downing 1987c; 1988a, ix–x; Ste Croix 1981, 433 (using different terminology).

[10] D.L. 6.103; cf. also p. 92 and n. 26 below.

[11] e.g. Kindstrand 1976; Goulet-Cazé 1986; 1993; 1994; 1996; Moles 1983a; 1993; 1995; 1996; 2000; Long 1996.

[12] Cf. the influential Branham 1993; 1996.

[13] e.g. Tuckett 1989; 1996, 368–91; Betz 1994; Robinson 1994, 1997; Eddy 1996; Wright 1996, 66–74; Aune 1997; Marshall 1997; Ebner 1998, 393–412; Brown 1999, 89, 822; Powell 1999, 68–73, 107; Maccoby 2003, 39–43; Dunn 2003a, 154, 298–300 and index, s.v. 'Jesus: Cynic influence on'; Freyne 2004, 14, 136–7. These 'rejections' in fact vary considerably both in intensity and focus: Dunn 2003a, for example, is far less dismissive than Wright 1996, while Maccoby 2003, 39 judges that [the Cynic model] 'does take account of certain authentic features presented in the Gospels'.

[14] See p. 95 below.

[15] Cf. e.g. Brown 1994, 677–78, with the response of Crossan 1995, 212 ff.; van Beeck 1994, 97, cf. Wright 1996, 44: '[Crossan as] a rather skeptical New Testament professor with the soul of a leprechaun'; Theissen and Merz 1998, 11 ('the "non-eschatological Jesus" seems to have more Californian than Galilean local colouring').

[16] e.g., and very variously: Malherbe 1970; 1980; 1983a; 1983b; 1984; 1987; 1989; 1992; Theissen 1978, 14–15; 1992, 43–4; Downing 1984; 1987a; 1987b; 1987c; 1988a 1988b; 1992; 1993; 1994; 1996; 1998a; 1998b; 2001; Mack 1988, 67–74, 179–92; 1993; 1997; 2001, 41–58; Crossan 1991, 72–88, 338–41; Kloppenborg 1987, 306–16, 326; 2000, 420–42; Vaage 1987; 1994; Seeley 1992; 1993; 1996.

[17] Descriptions (largely hostile) in Wright 1996, 29–35; Brown 1996, 820–4; Dunn 2003, 58–62; self-presentation: http://religion.rutgers.edu/jseminar/.

[18] e.g. Crossan 1994, 122; Kloppenborg 2000, 420–42.

[19] Harvey 1982.

[20] I here reiterate, sometimes closely, my own published views on Cynicism but 'key' crucial points and arguments. Proper reconstruction of Cynicism must establish a hierarchy of evidence, as e.g. von Fritz 1927; Höistad 1948, 5–21 (though weakened by mistaken rejection of the 'shameless' Diogenes); Goulet-Cazé 1986; 1994; Moles 1983a, 104; 1993; 1995; 1996a; 2000; Giannantoni 1990, IV. Such rigour is effectively abandoned by (e.g.) Branham 1993; 1996; Navia 1996; 1998; cf. also n. 99 below. Throughout, I ignore the Cynic letters, much adduced by Downing et al. and held important by Attridge 1976 and Malherbe 1977: since they are effectively impossible to date or contextualize, their utility is problematic.

[21] Lovejoy-Boas 1935, 9–11.

[22] Cf. Jones 1986, 90–8; Branham 1989, 57–63; Moles 1995, 156; 1997; whether or not Demonax the man is a Lucianic fiction (as e.g. Clay 1992, 3426, 3428), he represents a recognisable *type*.

[23] Wright 1996, 66.

[24] Cf. e.g. Dudley 1937, 207; Moles 1983a, 112 n. 73; Krueger 1996, 73, 92.

[25] Epicureanism is usefully parallel, that is, on the usual view that 'changes' introduced by Epicurus' followers and successors developed and refined Epicurus' original teachings in order to meet opponents' objections rather than radically to overhaul them.

[26] Crucial are Diogenes' appeal to *phusis* (D.L. 6.71) and his Kronos/Zeus/anti-Prometheus myth: D.L. 6.44; Str. 15.1.64 = Onesicritus fr. 17a; D. Chr. 6.25, cf. 8.33; Brown 1948, 149 n. 152; Moles 1983a, 116 n. 103; Martin 1997.

[27] See p. 102 below.

[28] The classification of Seneca and Epictetus as 'Stoic' is sure; Dio is more difficult: although heavily Plato-influenced (Trapp 2000), he was taught by the Stoic philosopher Musonius Rufus; he sometimes classes himself as 'Stoic' (e.g. 30.30); his most substantial works are Stoic (Russell 1992, 6); and this is no doubt his most appropriate general classification; still, Cynic influence on him is also considerable: Brancacci 2000; Moles forthcoming (a).

[29] On Stoicism's appropriation of Cynicism see e.g. Rist 1969, 54–80; Billerbeck 1978; Goulet-Cazé 2003 and n. 30 below.

[30] Dudley 1937, 190–8; Billerbeck 1978, 1–9; 1993, 321–3; 1996, 207–8; Goulet-Cazé 1990, 2773–6; Long 2002, 58–61; rather differently: Schofield 2004, 451–55.

[31] On this problem see p. 95 below.

[32] Huge bibliography, but cf. e.g. Bultmann 1910; Stowers 1981; Schmeller 1987; Malherbe 1992, 313–20.

[33] Moles 1996b.

[34] Cf. e.g. Hock and O'Neil 1986–2002; Kindstrand 1986.

[35] Cf. Goulet-Cazé 1992, 3978–90.

[36] p. 99 below.

[37] Goulet-Cazé 1993; 1996; Moles 1993, 113–14; 1995, 138 n. 27.

[38] A list of references in Moles 1993, 270; 1996a, 113–14.

[39] Epicureanism is again illuminatingly parallel (that is, on the orthodox and – I believe – correct view that the Epicureans believed in the gods).

[40] D.L. 6.72 with Moles 1995, 138, 142.

[41] Moles 1983a, 112 n. 73, 115; 1993, 270; 1996a, 113.

[42] That is, given the primacy of 'life according to nature' as a Cynic principle (n. 26 above).

[43] Moles 1983a, 118.

[44] D.L. 6.73, with Dudley 1937, 33; Moles 1983a, 114.

[45] Cf. n. 26 above.

[46] Cf. especially Kindstrand 1976, 61, 247; Moles 1983a, 112–14; 1996a, 114–15.

[47] Cf. e.g. D.L. 6.78–97.

[48] Clearly evidenced in Diogenes' *Politeia*: Moles 1995, 140–1.

[49] Good comment in Brenk 2000.

[50] Cf. e.g. D.L. 6.38 (Diogenes' famous tragic verses); Montiglio 2000, 99.

[51] Moles 1995, 137; 2000, 426.

[52] Maccoby 2003, 107–8.

[53] Moles 1993; 1995; 1996a; 2000.

[54] Both this view of the historical Jesus and the prior assumption of a coherent 'Zealot' movement are nowadays generally discredited: see e.g. Bammel and Moule 1984; Dunn 2003a, 272–3; Freyne 2004, 135–6.

[55] Extensive discussions of the Kingdom in Wright 1996, 198–472; Dunn 2003a, 390–487.

[56] Crossan 1991, 422.

[57] Moles 1995, 149–50, 155–6.

[58] Cf. e.g. Romm 1996; Martin 1996; note especially for our purposes Dio Chrysostom's 'praise of the Essenes' (Crosby 1951, 379), evidently written in Cynic 'alien wisdom' mode.

[59] Onesicritus fr. 17(a); D.L. 6.23 with Höistad 1948, 137.

[60] Hammerstaedt 1990, 2836–9.

[61] Wendland 1895; Dudley 1937, 186–7; Downing 1988a, 194.

[62] Neusner 1986; Hengel 1974; 1989; Levine 1998; Collins and Sterling 2001; Freyne 2004, 14; Thiede 2004, 13–32.

[63] *Pace* Mack 2001, 64: '[Jesus] may have read Meleager'. Thiede's very positive view of Jesus' Hellenic culture (n. 74 below) might also allow this.

[64] Moles 1983a, 120–23; Long 2002, 59.

[65] See p. 98 below.

[66] Moles 1983a, 120–3; Goulet-Cazé 1990, 2723; 1996, 13–14.

[67] Dunn 2003a, 299–300; for a different emphasis see Thiede 2004, 21; the dating of the theatre is important: Dunn 2003a, 299 n. 198; Thiede 2004, 131 n. 13.

[68] See e.g. Crossan 1991, 17–19 (Nazareth as 'satellite' of Sepphoris); Thiede 2004, 13–15; *contra* Freyne 2000, 195–6, 205–6; Dunn 2003a, 301–2 (both arguing 'tension' between city and village).

[69] A common hypothesis: e.g. Batey 1991, 70, 103; Theissen and Merz 1998, 165–6; Thiede 2004, 15 (following the tradition that 'carpenter' underestimates Joseph's status).

[70] Mark 5.1–20; Matthew 8.28–34; Luke 8.26–39, with the decisive arguments for Gadara of Thiede 2004, 44–7.

[71] Ste Croix 1981, 427–30; still more nuanced discussion in Dunn 2003a, 319–21.

[72] Dunn 2003a, 301.

[73] Dunn 2003a, 320.

[74] See the exciting discussions of Thiede 2004, 66–72 and Freyne 2004, 55–6; cf. also the very positive view of Jesus' acquaintance with Greek culture in Thiede 2004, 13–32, a view that allows little distinction between 'city' and 'village'.

75 Downing 1992, 82–3, 148–9.

76 So John Dillon in the discussion at the Dublin conference.

77 Two possible exceptions: (1) Papias as quoted by Euseb. *EH* 3.39.16 says that Matthew 'put together' the *logia* of Jesus in 'the Hebrew dialect'; but this is best interpreted as an Aramaic collection of *sayings*: Brown 1999, 210–11; Thiede 2004, 148 n. 39; (2) an Aramaic Q (cf. n. 93 below), sometimes hypothesized, is rendered unlikely by the closeness of the verbal parallels between Matthew and Luke: Dunn 2003a, 43.

78 Sevenster 1968, 3–21; Hengel 1974, 56–106; Meier 1991, 255–68; Porter 1994; Wright 1996, 147 and n. 3; Dunn 2003, 315; Thiede 2004, 12, 68–71; if, as many now believe, the *Letter of James* is authentically by Jerusalem James and Jerusalem James was Jesus' (full or half-) brother, the case is yet further strengthened.

79 See p. 97 and n. 74 above.

80 e.g. Malherbe as cited in n. 16 above; Downing 1988, 187–91 (with useful summaries of several of Malherbe's Pauline papers); 1998b; Barton 2003, 41–2; Deming 2004.

81 Funke 1970; Malherbe 1983b.

82 Two precise illustrations: Malherbe 1992, 315 (I Corinthians 7.27 ~ Teles 10.6 ff. Hense); Deming 2004, 157 (I Corinthians 7.21 ~ Teles 2.10.65–80 O'Neil).

83 On Jesus as 'wanderer' see p. 100 below.

84 e.g. Wright 1991; Dunn 1998.

85 Downing 1993; 1996; Dorival 1993.

86 See Jason König's paper in this volume.

87 Dudley 1937, 204–6.

88 Conceded even by Betz 1994, 461.

89 Burridge 1992; cf. also his restatement in this volume; Frickenschmidt 1997; Dunn 2003a, 184–6.

90 Bowersock 1994, 96–7, 109–11; the relationship is admittedly complicated by the fact that Philostratus is registering pagan anxiety about Christianity and seems sometimes even to imitate or 'trump' Gospel miracles: Thiede 2004, 37–8.

91 Kindstrand 1986; Goulet-Cazé 1992.

92 References in n. 22 above.

93 Most New Testament scholars accept Q's existence (disagreement characteristically centring on boundaries and orientation, especially as regards alleged Cynic elements); some treatments: Kloppenborg 1987; 1988; 1994; 1995; 2000; Brown 1999, 116–22; Dunn 2003a, 41–4, 147–60; Head and Williams 2003. Anyone trained in *Quellenforschung* in ancient historiography and biography would, I believe, regard Q's existence as certain, even though it is now rejected by Goodacre 2002 and Thiede 2004, 123 and 158 n. 6. The non-existence of Q would not destroy the present paper but would entail some modification. The significance of Q in this context is that it supports the case for a (partially) 'Cynic' Jesus in writing predating the Gospels (see p. 102 below). Neither does Dunn's distinction (2003a, 148–9) between 'oral q' and 'written Q' substantially affect this paper, provided 'oral q' also has Cynic elements.

94 'Foxes have holes, and birds of the air have nests, but the Son of Man has nowhere to lay his head' (Luke 9.57–8; Matthew 8.19–20).

95 John 12.6, 13.29, cf. Acts 2.44–5, 4.32–7, 5.1–11.

96 e.g. 'nowhere in Israel have I found faith like this' (Matthew 8.10); whether Jesus himself already envisaged a Gentile mission (Mark 13.10; Matthew 28.18–19; Acts 1.8) is of course hugely disputed: arguments in favour in e.g. Thiede 2004, 57; Freyne 2004, 111–13.

[97] Such implicit subversion of worldly power is becoming a major scholarly concern: cf. e.g. Wright 2003, 656; Thiede 2004, 66–8; Freyne 2004, 149.

[98] Marshall 1997, 60, cited approvingly by Dunn 2003a, 536 n. 231.

[99] D.L. 6.96–7 with Rist 1969, 60–2; Moles 1983b, 126–7; 1995, 139. Diogenes' principle: D.L. 6.72 (from his *Politeia*): such evidence overrides the *chreia* (and *graffito*) evidence too often taken by modern scholars as proving Diogenic misogyny (on the methodological point see n. 20 above).

[100] D.L. 6.72.

[101] e.g. Downing 1988a, vi, 43; Crossan 1991, 342–3; Crossan and Reed 2001, 125–8 (other references with polemical rejection in Dunn 2003a, 159 and n. 96).

[102] Dunn 2003a, 317.

[103] D.L. 6.38; Montiglio 2000, 99; D. Chr. 6.1–7.

[104] Downing 1988a, 126 (without the crucial D.L. 6.105); 'softening' interpretation of Jesus' saying in Dunn 2003a, 592–9, but the distinction between a '100% *Jesus-Cynicus* model' and a 'Cynic-influenced' model is again apposite.

[105] Downing 1988a, 44; cf. e.g. Diogenes' derisive dismissal of conventional funeral rites (D.L. 6.79); for a thoroughgoing hunt for parallels, both Jewish and Greek, for this saying of Jesus see Hengel 1981, 3–13, allowing Cynic parallels (5–6 and n. 11), though contextually denying them, but such a Cynic sentiment could underpin both Jesus' offensive rejection of Jewish religious custom and his sense of urgency (Dunn 2003a, 504–5), just as in Cynicism itself it ridicules both Greek religious custom and the inessential.

[106] Downing 1988a, 47.

[107] Downing 1988a, vi.

[108] Crossan 1991, 338–9.

[109] Downing 1988a, 15–16, 23.

[110] Dunn 2003a, 381 n. 193 hazards 'an echo of Moses on top of Pisgah looking over the Promised Land', but, if that is evoked, it is as a *contrast*.

[111] Downing 1988a, 76–8.

[112] As both Mike Trapp in Dublin and Peter Heslin in Durham insisted, against the present conclusion.

[113] Always excepting Thiede (n. 74 above).

[114] Or indeed Acts' appropriation of Dionysiac narrative patterns: Moles, forthcoming b.

[115] Downing 1988a, viii, 36.

[116] p. 94.

[117] Long 1974, 4; for similar claims cf. Moles 1983a, 119–20; 1995, 158; 2000, 434.

[118] e.g. Long 2002, 259, 271–2.

[119] This formulation is intended to allow: (a) for the fact that I am not arguing 'a 100% *Jesus-Cynicus* model'; and (b) for *all possible* responses to the problems of the Incarnation and of 'kenotic theology'.

Bibliography

Arnal, W.E. and Desjardins, M.
 1997   *Whose Historical Jesus?*, Waterloo.
Attridge, H.W.
 1976   *First Century Cynicism in the Epistles of Heraclitus*, Missoula.

Aune, D.E.
  1997   'Jesus and Cynics in first-century Palestine: some critical considerations', in Charlesworth and Johns (eds.) *Hillel and Jesus*, 176–92.
Bammel, E. and Moule, C.F.D. (eds.)
  1984   *Jesus and the Politics of his Day*, Cambridge.
Barton, S.C.
  2003   'Paul as missionary and pastor', in Dunn (ed.) *The Cambridge Companion to St Paul*, 34–48.
Batey, R.A.
  1991   *Jesus and the Forgotten City: New light on Sepphoris and the urban world of Jesus*, Grand Rapids.
Beeck, F.J. van,
  1994   'The quest of the Historical Jesus: origins, achievements, and the specter of diminishing returns', in J. Carlson and R.A. Ludwig (eds.) *Jesus and Faith: A conversation on the work of John Dominic Crossan*, Maryknoll, N.Y., 83–99.
Betz, H.D.
  1994   'Jesus and the Cynics: survey and analysis of a hypothesis', *JR* 74, 453–75.
Billerbeck, M.
  1978   *Vom Kynismus: Epiktet*, Leiden.
  1979   *Der Kyniker Demetrius*, Leiden.
  1991   *Die Kyniker in der moderne Forschung*, Amsterdam.
  1992   'The ideal Cynic from Epictetus to Julian', in Branham and Goulet-Cazé (eds.) *The Cynics*, 205–21.
  1993   'Le cynisme idéalisé d' Épictète à Julien', in Goulet and Goulet-Cazé (eds.) *Le cynisme et ses prolongements*, 319–38.
Bowersock, G.W.
  1992   'Cinismo e stoicismo nel libro VI (103–105) di Diogene Laerzio', *ANRW* 2.36.6, 4049–75.
  1994   *Fiction as History: Nero to Julian*, Berkeley, Los Angeles and London.
  2000   'Dio, Socrates, and Cynicism', in S. Swain (ed.) *Dio Chrysostom: Politics, letters, and philosophy*, Oxford 240–60.
Branham, R.B.
  1987   *Unruly Eloquence: Lucian and the comedy of traditions*, Cambridge, Mass.
  1993   'Diogenes' rhetoric and the invention of Cynicism', in Goulet and Goulet-Cazé (eds.) *Le cynisme et ses prolongements*, 445–74.
  1996   'Diogenes' rhetoric and the *Invention* of Cynicism', in Branham and Goulet-Cazé (eds.) *The Cynics*, 81–104.
Branham, R.B. and Goulet-Cazé, M.-O. (eds.)
  1996   *The Cynics: The Cynic movement in antiquity and its legacy*, Berkeley, Los Angeles and London.
Brenk, F.E.
  2000   'Dio on the simple and self-sufficient life', in Swain (ed.) *Dio Chrysostom: Politics, letters, and philosophy*, 261–78.
Brown, R.E.
  1994   *The Death of the Messiah: From Gethsemane to the grave. A commentary on the passion narratives in the four Gospels*, New York.

1999   *An Introduction to the New Testament*, New York, London, Toronto, Sydney and Auckland.

Brown, T.S.
1949   *Onesicritus: A study in Hellenistic historiography*, Berkeley.

Bultmann, R.
1910   *Der Stil der paulinischen Predigt und die kynisch-stoische Diatribe*, Göttingen.

Burridge, R.A.
1992   *What are the Gospels? A comparison with Graeco-Roman biography*, Cambridge.

Charlesworth, J.H. and Johns, L.L. (eds.)
1997   *Hillel and Jesus*, Minneapolis.

Chilton, B. and Evans, C.A. (eds.)
1994   *Studying the Historical Jesus: Evaluations of the state of current research*, Leiden.

Clay, D.
1992   'Lucian of Samosata: Four philosophical lives, Nigrinus, Demonax, Peregrinus, Alexsander Pseudomantis', *ANRW* 2.36.5, 3406–50.

Collins, J.J. and Sterling, G.E. (eds.)
2001   *Hellenism in the Land of Israel*, Notre Dame, Ind.

Crosby, H.L.
1951   *Dio Chrysostom* V, Cambridge, Mass., and London.

Crossan, J.D.
1991   *The Historical Jesus: The life of a Mediterranean Jewish peasant*, Edinburgh.
1994   *Jesus: A revolutionary biography*, San Francisco.
1995   *Who Killed Jesus?*, New York.

Crossan, J.D. and Reed, J.L.
2001   *Excavating Jesus: Beneath the stones, behind the texts*, London.

Dorival, G.
1993   'L'image des Cyniques chez les Pères grecs', in Goulet and Goulet-Cazé (eds.) *Le cynisme et ses prolongements*, 419–43.

Downing, F.G.
1984   'Cynics and Christians', *NTS* 30, 584–93.
1987a   'Interpretation and the "culture gap"', *SJT*, 161–71.
1987b   'The social contexts of Jesus the Teacher: construction or reconstruction', *NTS* 33, 439–51.
1987c   *Jesus and the Threat of Freedom*, London.
1988a   *Christ and the Cynics*, Sheffield.
1988b   'Quite like Q – A Genre for Q: the "Lives" of Cynic philosophers', *Biblica* 69.2, 196–225, revised version in Downing, *Cynics and Christian Origins*, 114–42.
1992   *Cynics and Christian Origins*, Edinburgh.
1993   'Cynics and Early Christianity', in Goulet and Goulet-Cazé (eds.) *Le cynisme et ses prolongements*, Paris, 281–304.
1994   'A genre for Q and a socio-cultural context for Q', *JSNT* 55, 3–26.
1996   'Word-processing in the ancient world', *JSNT* 64, 29–48.
1998a   'Deeper reflections on the Jewish Cynic Jesus', *JBL* 117.1, 97–104, reprinted

in *Making Sense in (and of) the first Christian Century, JSNTS* 197, 2000 122–133.

1998b   *Cynics, Paul and the Pauline Churches*, London and New York.

2001   'The Jewish Cynic Jesus', in M. Labahn and A. Schmidt (eds.) *Jesus, Mark and Q: The teaching of Jesus and its earliest records, JSNTS* 214, 184–214.

Dudley, D.R.

1937   *A History of Cynicism*, London.

Dunn, J.D.G.,

1998   *The Theology of Paul the Apostle*, Grand Rapids and Edinburgh.

2003a   *Jesus Remembered: Christianity in the making*, vol. 1, Grand Rapids and Cambridge.

Dunn, J.D.G. (ed.)

2003b   *The Cambridge Companion to St Paul*, Cambridge.

Ebner, M.

1998   *Jesus – ein Weisheitslehrer? Synoptische Weisheitslogien im Traditions-prozess*, Freiburg.

Eddy, P.R.

1996   'Jesus as Diogenes? Reflections on the Cynic Jesus thesis', *JBL* 115, 446–69.

Freyne, S.

2000   *Galilee and Gospel*, Tübingen.

2004   *Jesus a Jewish Galilean*, London and New York.

Fritz, K. von

1926   *Quellen-Untersuchungen zu Leben und Philosophie des Diogenes von Sinope, Philologus* Supplementband 18.2, Leipzig.

Fuentes-Gonzalez, P.P.

1998   *Les diatribes de Télès*, Paris.

Funke, H.

1970   'Antisthenes bei Paulus', *Hermes* 98, 459–71.

Geffken, J.

1909   *Kynika und Verwandtes*, Heidelberg.

Giannantoni, G.

1990   *Socratis et Socraticorum Reliquiae*, Naples.

Goulet, R. (ed.)

1994   *Dictionnaire des philosophes antiques II*, Paris.

Goulet, R. and Goulet-Cazé, M.-O. (eds.)

1993   *Le cynisme et ses prolongements*, Paris.

Goulet-Cazé, M.-O.

1986   *L'ascèse cynique: un commentaire sur Diogène Laërce VI, 70–1*, Paris.

1990   'Le cynisme à l'époque imperiale', *ANRW* 2.36.4, 2720–833.

1992   'Le livre VI de Diogène Laërce: analyse de sa structure et réflexions méthodologiques', *ANRW* 2.36.6, 3880–4048.

1993   'Les premiers cyniques et la religion', in Goulet and Goulet-Cazé (eds.) *Le cynisme et ses prolongements*, 117–58.

1994   'Cratès de Thèbes' and 'Diogène de Sinope', in Goulet (ed.) *Dictionnaire des philosophes antiques II*, 496–500 and 812–20.

1996   'Religion and the early Cynics', in Branham and Goulet-Cazé (eds.) *The Cynics*, 47–80.

2003   *Les* Kynika *du stoïcisme*, Wiesbaden.

Griffin, M.T.

1993   'Le mouvement cynique et les Romains: attraction et répulsion', in Goulet and Goulet-Cazé (eds.) *Le cynisme et ses prolongements*, 241–58.

1996   'Cynicism and the Romans: attraction and repulsion', in Branham and Goulet-Cazé (eds.) *The Cynics*, 190–204.

Hammerstaedt, J.

1990   'Oinomaos von Gadara', *ANRW* 2.36.4, 2834–65.

Hanson, V.D., Heath, J. and Thornton, B.S.

2001   *Bonfire of the Humanities: Rescuing the Classics in an impoverished age*, Wilmington.

Harvey, A.E.

1982   *Jesus and the Constraints of History*, London.

Head, P. and Williams, P.J.

2003   'Q Review', *Tyndale Bulletin* 54.1, 119–44.

Hengel, M.

1974   *Judaism and Hellenism: Studies in their encounter in Palestine during the early Hellenistic period*, London.

1981   *The Charismatic Leader and His Followers*, Edinburgh.

1989   *The 'Hellenization' of Judaea in the First Century after Christ*, London.

Hock, R.F.

1980   *The Social Context of Paul's Ministry: Tentmaking and apostleship*, Philadelphia.

Hock, R.F. and O'Neil, E.N.

1986–2002   *The Chreia in Ancient Rhetoric*, Atlanta.

Höistad, R.

1948   *Cynic Hero and Cynic King*, Uppsala.

Jones, C.P.

1986   *Culture and Society in Lucian*, Cambridge, Mass.

Kindstrand, J.F.

1976   *Bion of Borysthenes*, Uppsala.

1986   'Diogenes Laertius and the "chreia" tradition', *Elenchos* 71/72, 214–43.

Kloppenborg, J.S.

1987   *The Formation of Q: Trajectories in ancient wisdom collections*, Philadelphia.

1988   *Q Parallels: Synopsis, critical notes, and concordance*, Polebridge.

Kloppenborg, J.S. (ed.)

1994   *The Shape of Q: Signal essays on the Sayings Gospel*, Minneapolis.

1995   *Conflict and Invention: Literary, rhetorical and social studies in the Sayings Gospel Q*, Valley Forge.

2000   *Excavating Q: The history and setting of the Sayings Gospel*, Minneapolis.

Krueger, D.

1996   *Symeon the Holy Fool: Leontius' Life and the late antique city*, Berkeley, Los Angeles and London.

Laks, A. and Schofield, M. (eds.)

1995   *Justice and Generosity*, Cambridge.

Levine, L.I.

1998   *Judaism and Hellenism in Antiquity, Conflict or Confluence?*, Peabody, Mass.

Long, A.A.
  1974   *Hellenistic Philosophy*, London.
  1996   'The Socratic tradition: Diogenes, Crates, and Hellenistic ethics', in Branham and Goulet-Cazé (eds.) *The Cynics*, 28–46.
  2002   *Epictetus*, Oxford.
Lovejoy, A.O. and Boas, G.
  1935   *Primitivism and Related Ideas in Antiquity*, Baltimore.
Luck, G.
  1997   *Die Weisheit der Hunde: Texte der antiken Kyniker in deutscher Übersetzung mit Erläuterungen*, Stuttgart.
Maccoby, H.
  2003   *Jesus the Pharisee*, London.
MacDonald, D.R.
  2000   *The Homeric Epics and the Gospel of Mark*, New Haven.
  2003   *Does the New Testament Imitate Homer? Four cases from the Acts of the Apostles*, New Haven.
Mack, B.L.
  1988   *A Myth of Innocence: Mark and Christian origins*, Philadelphia.
  1993   *The Lost Gospel: The Book of Q and Christian origins*, San Francisco.
  1997   'Q and a Cynic-like Jesus', in W.E. Arnal and M. Desjardins (eds.) *Whose Historical Jesus?*, Waterloo.
  2001   *The Christian Myth: Origins, logic and legacy*, New York.
Malherbe, A.J.
  1970   'Gentle as a nurse: the Cynic background to I Thessalonians 2', *NT* 12, 203–17.
  1977   *The Cynic Epistles*, Missoula.
  1980   'Medical imagery in the Pastoral Epistles', in W.E. March (ed.) *Texts and Testaments: Critical essays in honour of Stuart D. Currie*, San Antonio 19–35.
  1983a   'Exhortation in First Thessalonians', *NT* 25, 238–55.
  1983b   'Antisthenes, Odysseus, and Paul at war', *HTR* 76.2, 143–73.
  1984   '"In season and out of season"', *JBL* 103.2, 235–43.
  1987   *Paul and the Thessalonians*, Philadelphia.
  1989   *Paul and the Popular Philosophers*, Minneapolis.
  1992   'Hellenistic moralists and the New Testament', *ANRW* II.26.1, 267–333.
  2000   *The Letters to the Thessalonians*, New York.
Marshall, J.W.
  1997   'The Gospel of Thomas and the Cynic Jesus', in Arnal and Desjardins (eds.) *Whose Historical Jesus?*, 37–60.
Martin, R.P.
  1996   'The Scythian accent: Anacharsis and the Cynics', in Branham and Goulet-Cazé (eds.) *The Cynics*, 136–55.
Martin, T.W.
  1997   'The Chronos myth in Cynic philosophy', *GRBS* 38, 85–108.
Meier, J.P.
  1994   *A Marginal Jew: Rethinking the Historical Jesus I*, New York.
Moles, J.L.
  1978   'The career and conversion of Dio Chrysostom', *JHS* 98, 79–100.

1983a ' "Honestius quam ambitiosius?": An exploration of the Cynic's attitude to moral corruption in his fellow men', *JHS* 103, 103–23.

1983b 'The Woman and the River: Diogenes' apophthegm from Herculaneum and some popular misconceptions about Cynicism', *Apeiron* 17, 125–30.

1993 'Le cosmopolitisme cynique', in Goulet and Goulet-Cazé (eds.) *Le cynisme et ses prolongements*, 259–80.

1995 'The Cynics and politics', in Laks and Schofield (eds.) *Justice and Generosity*, 129–58.

1996a 'Cynic cosmopolitanism', in Branham and Goulet-Cazé (eds.) *The Cynics*, 105–20.

1996b 'Diatribe', in S. Hornblower and A. Spawforth, *The Oxford Classical Dictionary*, 3rd edn, Oxford, 463–4.

1997 'Demonax', in D.J. Zeyl (ed.) *Encyclopedia of Classical Philosophy*, Westport, 172–3.

2000 'The Cynics', in Rowe and Schofield, *The Cambridge History of Greek and Roman Political Thought*, Cambridge, 415–34.

Forthcoming a 'Cynicism in Dio Chrysostom'.

Forthcoming b 'Dionysiac *Acts?*'.

Montiglio, S.

2000 'Wandering philosophers in classical Greece', *JHS* 120, 86–105.

Navia, L.E.

1996 *Classical Cynicism: A critical study*, Westport.

1998 *Diogenes of Sinope: The man in the tub*, Westport.

Neusner, J.

1986 'How much Hellenism in Jewish Palestine?', *HUCA* 57, 83–111.

Paquet, L.

1975 *Les Cyniques grecs. Fragments et témoignages*, Ottawa.

Porter, S.E.

1994 'Jesus and the use of Greek in Galilee', in Chilton and Evans (eds.) *Studying the Historical Jesus*, 125–54.

Powell, M.A.

1999 *The Jesus Debate: Modern historians investigate the life of Christ*, Oxford.

Rist, J.M.

1969 *Stoic Philosophy*, Cambridge.

Robinson, J.M.

1994 'The History-of-Religions taxonomy of Q: The Cynic hypothesis', in H. Preissler and H. Seiwert (eds.) *Gnosisforschung und Religionsgeschichte*, Marburg.

1997 'Galilean upstarts: A sot's Cynical disciples?', in W.L. Petersen (ed.) *Sayings of Jesus: Canonical and non-canonical*, Leiden.

Romm, J.

1996 'Dog heads and noble savages: Cynicism before the Cynic?', in Branham and Goulet-Cazé (eds.) *The Cynics*, 121–35.

Rowe, C. and Schofield, M.

2000 *The Cambridge History of Greek and Roman Political Thought*, Cambridge.

Russell, D.A.

1992 *Dio Chrysostom: Orations VII, XII, XXXVI*, Cambridge.

Ste Croix, G.E.M. de
 1981   *The Class Struggle in the Ancient Greek World*, London.
Schmeller, T.
 1987   *Paulus und die 'Diatribe': Eine vergleichende Stilinterpretation*, Münster.
Schofield, M.
 2004   'Epictetus: Socratic, Cynic, Stoic', *Philosophical Quarterly* 54, 448–56.
Seeley, D.
 1992   'Jesus' death in Q', *NTS* 38, 222–34.
 1993   'Rulership and service in Mark 10.41–5', *NT* 35, 234–50.
 1996   'Jesus and the Cynics: A response to Hans Dieter Betz', *JHC* 3, 284–90.
 1997   'Jesus and the Cynics revisited', *JBL* 116, 704–12.
Sevenster, J.N.
 1968   *Do You Know Greek?*, Leiden.
Stowers, S.K.
 1981   *The Diatribe and Paul's Letter to the Romans*, Chico.
Swain, S. (ed.)
 2000   *Dio Chrysostom: Politics, letters, and philosophy*, Oxford.
Theissen, G.
 1978   *The First Followers of Jesus: A sociological analysis of earliest Christianity*,
            London.
 1992   *Social Reality and the Early Christians*, Minneapolis.
Theissen, G. and Merz, A.
 1998   *The Historical Jesus: A comprehensive guide*, transl. J. Bowden, London.
Thiede, C.P.
 2004   *The Cosmopolitan World of Jesus*, London.
Trapp, M.
 2000   'Plato in Dio', in Swain (ed.) *Dio Chrysostom*, 213–39.
Tuckett, C.M.
 1989   'A Cynic Q?', *Bib.* 70, 349–74.
 1996   *Q and the History of Early Christianity: Studies in Q*, Edinburgh.
Vaage, L.E.
 1987   *Q: The ethos and ethics of an itinerant intelligence*, Diss. Claremont College.
 1994   *Galilean Upstarts: Jesus' first followers according to Q*, Valley Forge.
Wendland, P.
 1895   'Philo und die kynisch-stoische Diatribe', in Wendland and Kern (eds.)
            Beitrage zur Geschichte der griechischen Philosophie..., Berlin, 1–75.
 1912   'Die hellenistisch-romische Kultur in ihren Beziehungen zu Judentum und
            Christentum: Die urchristlichen Literaturformen', *Handbuch zum Neuen
            Testament* I 2/3, 75–96.
Wendland, P. and Kern, O. (eds.)
 1895   *Beitrage zur Geschichte der griechischen Philosophie und Religion*, Berlin.
Wright, N.T.
 1991   *The Climax of the Covenant: Christ and the law in Pauline theology*,
            Edinburgh.
 1996   *Jesus and the Victory of God*, London.
Zeller, E.
 1893   'Über eine Beruhrung des jungeren Cynismus mit dem Christenthum',
            SKPAWB 1, 129–32.

8

PHILO'S ADAPTATION OF THE BIBLE
IN HIS *LIFE OF MOSES*

Brian McGing

It would be difficult to imagine better representatives of Mediterranean and Near Eastern cultural encounter than Philo and his home town, Alexandria. The city was exciting, vibrant, dangerous, a sort of New York of the ancient Mediterranean.[1] People flocked to it from all over the known world. If Egyptians, Greeks, Jews and Romans might be identified as the most prominent population strands, Dio of Prusa (*Or.* 32.40) tells us that there were many others there too: settlers from Libya, Cilicia, Ethiopia, Arabia, Bactria, Scythia, India. Philo himself, of course, was a member of a rich, powerful and mostly devout Jewish family.[2] He wrote in Greek – he was obviously highly educated in Greek literature and thought – but was also steeped in the sacred books of Judaism. His interpretation of these books in terms of Greek philosophy is certainly one of the most extraordinary intellectual achievements of antiquity, bridging the worlds of Judaism, Hellenism and, in due course, Christianity. The question of whether he was fundamentally Jewish with a veneer of Greekness, or fundamentally Greek with a veneer of Jewishness[3] represents the sort of unnecessary search for a 'winner' that has sometimes characterized scholarship on the encounter between Judaism and the Greek world. It is a question that fails to accept the possibility of genuine cultural integration: however unusual the result, perhaps Philo's own background and upbringing joined forces with the cultural and intellectual milieu of first-century AD Alexandria to form a person who represents a fusion of Alexandrian Greekness and Alexandrian Jewishness.

My purpose in this paper is to examine briefly some aspects of the composition of Philo's work *On the life of Moses*. We are in the unusual situation of having not just an ancient text, but also its main source, in this case the Septuagint; and I want to concentrate particularly on what Philo does with that source, especially in Book 1. But first, since among his large literary output the *Life of Moses* has attracted little attention from commentators, it may be well to make some brief general points about its character.[4] Although Mark Edwards claims that the work 'does not purport to be a life of Moses,

117

but a commentary on the Biblical account', the opposite would be a more accurate description.[5] In what seems to be a clear programmatic introduction (1–4), it purports precisely to be a life of Moses (Μωυσέως...τὸν βίον ἀναγράψαι διενοήθην), necessary because his laws were famous but the man himself was not well known and even consciously ignored by the Greeks. Stanton notes that in various Jewish writings of this period, while there seems to be a strong biographical interest in the patriarchs, 'the intention is to explain the Biblical text to a new age rather than to furnish biographies of the great men of the past'.[6] This is a statement that could convincingly be applied to Philo's *Moses*: however conscious his choice of the Greek biographical form, it would be difficult to deny that Philo's interest lies at least as much, if not more, in explaining the Bible as in recounting Moses' life.[7] His explanation is offered not in the form of a textual commentary, but in a re-writing of the story. Part of the reason for the biographical form may be the source material. Gregory of Nyssa, it has been argued, in his *Life of Moses*, 'uses the biographical form for the incidental reason that the Genesis text to which he applies his philosophical exegesis happens to be biographically structured'.[8] The choice of form is, I believe, more than incidental to Philo, but the whole Biblical treatment of Moses, the story of his life from birth to death, did perhaps push Philo in a biographical direction.

But does Philo's interest in explaining the Bible disqualify this as a work of biography? Or do its Jewish author and Jewish hero disqualify it as a work of Greek biography? Consultation of classical scholarship on biography would easily lead one to believe that the answer to both questions should be 'yes'. There is not a single mention of Philo in Leo; nothing in Stuart, nothing in Momigliano, nothing in Dihle.[9] He just does not feature in the classic analyses of the development of Graeco-Roman biography.[10] And yet as long ago as 1929, Priessnig identified the literary form of Philo's biographies as Greek.[11] Priessnig was still under the influence of Leo's very rigid categorization of Greek biography, but his argument was persuasive. The chronological account of Moses as king, followed by the topical treatment of him as legislator, High Priest and prophet, finally returning to chronology for the death narrative, is not at all far from Suetonian method; there is no division into public and private life, so characteristic of Suetonius, but Priessnig's analysis and, more recently, Richard Burridge's detailed treatment of the work, leave little serious doubt that the *Life of Moses* belongs, at least formally, in the tradition of Graeco-Roman biography.[12] Of course, exact definition of the genre of biography is not a straightforward matter: one only has to look at the difficulties caused by Isokrates' *Evagoras* and Xenophon's *Agesilaus* to see that: is encomium biography? And the definition becomes harder as you move to later lives – Philostratus, Iamblichus, Porphyry – because these authors very obviously have ulterior motives that take their works some distance away from the biographical details of a life story.[13] Mention of these later lives of holy men may seem to be taking us far away from my purported subject, but I make the detour just to note that Philo's *Moses* generally bears a closer similarity to them than it does to the political, or literary, biographies of the 'canonical' writers like Nepos, Suetonius or Plutarch.[14] This is perhaps hardly surprising given Moses' status as a religious figure, although Philo does also present him as king and political leader. It is tempting to see Philo as representing a strand of biographical writing that points back to Aristoxenus of Tarentum, for example, or others who wrote the lives of 'wise' men like Pythagoras or Socrates;[15] and forward to Philostratus and the late antique biographers of holy men. At any rate, wherever we place him in the history of biographical writing in the Graeco-Roman world, he does not deserve the neglect he has received as a biographer.

The contents of the two books (συντάξεις – 2.1) that make up the work are fundamentally different in character. Book 1 traces the story of Moses' life and career up to the settling of the two cattle-breeding tribes after the defeat of the Midianites (Numbers 31–2). It very largely follows the Biblical narrative chronologically through Exodus and Numbers, with Philo constantly adapting, clarifying, or commenting on the story. This is coupled with occasional sections where Philo adopts an entirely different explanatory mode: he abandons the Bible altogether to offer his own, discursive analysis of a particular subject; the most important example is his discussion of Moses as king (148–62).[16] Book 2 is almost exactly the reverse: apart from the story of Moses' death at the end, which follows Deuteronomy 33–4, the organization and content are now entirely Philo's: Moses is treated under the categories of legislator, High Priest and prophet, and relevant parts of the Biblical story are cited as evidence to illustrate the analysis. As in Book 1, it is not just the Bible that is used as evidence: as proof of the respect in which Moses was held by foreign nations, for instance, Philo recounts the story of the translation of the Hebrew Bible into Greek in Egypt (2.25–44). It is also important to emphasize what Philo himself says about his sources (1.4), that he is basing his biography not only on the sacred books, but also on what he has learnt from the elders of the nation – on what he has read and what he has been told. Theoretically this raises the question of how much of the explanatory material is due to Philo's own interpretation, how much to the oral traditions embroidering the text of the Bible. While the occasional non-biblical coincidences between himself and Josephus (e.g. see below p. 128) point to the common use of such traditions, these coincidences are very rare: Josephus' account of Moses has, on the whole, extremely little in common with Philo's. This can only mean either that Philo has constructed his own interpretation of Moses, or that he has drawn on oral traditions quite different from the ones Josephus used. Whether he has composed it entirely himself, however, or drawn on other traditions, it is quite clear that he is offering what he regards as the best explanations he can devise or find.

How, then, does Philo use his main written source, the Septuagint? There are various compositional techniques we may identify.[17] They are all, ultimately, interpretative strategies: the whole point of re-presenting the story of Moses in the form of a Greek biography was, as Philo says in the introduction, to inform people who did not know about the man himself. The clear implication of this statement, of the choice of the biographical form and of the complaint that Greek writers had ignored Moses, is that Philo was targeting a primarily non-Jewish audience. Why would Jewish people need a new version of Moses' life when they already had the Septuagint? As we will see, Philo's whole treatment of scripture points in the same direction. And yet it scarcely seems necessary to exclude a Jewish readership altogether. Judaism in Egypt had at least to some extent acclimatized to its hellenistic setting, and in the intellectual circles in which Philo moved, fellow Jews may well have been pleased and proud to read a re-telling of the story that they knew would now reach a much wider audience than their sacred texts ever would. In addition it is possible that even law-abiding Jews may have known Moses' laws better than they knew his life story; and even if they did know the story, that is not to say they necessarily understood it: as Philo asserts, 'few people know him as he really was' (αὐτὸν δὲ ὅστις ἦν ἐπ' ἀληθείας ἴσασιν οὐ πολλοί).[18]

1. Omission of Biblical episodes
Philo does not try to reproduce the whole Biblical story. Nor, unfortunately, is there any obvious significance in the scenes he chooses to omit. During the narrative of the plagues he leaves out the Passover instructions of Exodus 12. It is difficult to see anything that could be construed as offensive in it; perhaps he felt that such detailed description of Jewish religious practice simply interrupted the story.[19] Similarly with the death of Aaron in Numbers (20.22–9): it is only a brief notice there, and there is scarcely any significance in its absence in the *Moses*. The meeting of Jethro and Moses in the desert (Exodus 18) is also omitted. It is a moving scene where Moses greets his family and tells Jethro all about his adventures since he last saw him, and God's goodness to Israel. Again, it would be difficult to think of anything particular that Philo was trying to conceal by leaving out the episode. Perhaps he felt that the very human family life and concerns evident in the scene sat uneasily with the frugality and asceticism of Moses' lifestyle that he emphasizes in the biography (1.25–9). The Jethro episode is in fact part

of a much greater omission: in his chronological account of Moses' life in book 1, Philo moves straight from the defeat of the Amelekites (Exodus 17.8–16) to the reconnaissance of Canaan (Numbers 13–14), and in the process leaves out the whole story of Mount Sinai. It is a very strange thing to leave out completely. To be sure, it is a long episode and we might well expect Philo not to reproduce all of it, but along with the plagues and escape from Egypt across the Red Sea, it is a central part of Moses' life. He does deal with elements of the story in book 2 (66–186) when discussing Moses as High Priest, so it is not entirely missing from the biography as a whole and he clearly has no difficulty with the subject. It might be argued that he is saving it up for the second book, where he knows he is going to be dealing with it, but this seems unlikely in view of the fact that he is quite prepared to repeat in book 2, in the section on Moses as prophet, the story of the crossing of the Red Sea and of the Manna, both amply covered in book 1. Perhaps it is a mistake to assume that everything is perfectly planned and executed: almost as strange as the omission of Mount Sinai from book 1 is the inclusion of the Balak and Balaam episode, which has very little at all to do with Moses.

2. Close adaptation of the Biblical text

Numbers 23.7–10

ἐκ Μεσοποταμίας μετεπέμψατό με Βαλακ,
βασιλεὺς Μωαβ ἐξ ὀρέων ἀπ' ἀνατολῶν λέγων
Δεῦρο ἄρασαί μοι τὸν Ιακωβ
καὶ δεῦρο ἐπικατάρασαί μοι τὸν Ισραηλ.
τί ἀράσωμαι ὃν μὴ καταρᾶται κύριος,
ἢ τί καταράσωμαι ὃν μὴ καταρᾶται ὁ θεός;
ὅτι ἀπὸ κορυφῆς ὀρέων ὄψομαι αὐτὸν
καὶ ἀπὸ βουνῶν προσνοήσω αὐτόν.
ἰδοὺ λαὸς μόνος κατοικήσει
καὶ ἐν ἔθνεσιν οὐ συλλογισθήσεται.
τίς ἐξηκριβάσατο τὸ σπέρμα Ιακωβ,
καὶ τίς ἐξαριθμήσεται δήμους Ισραηλ;
ἀποθάνοι ἡ ψυχή μου ἐν ψυχαῖς δικαίων,
καὶ γένοιτο τὸ σπέρμα μου ὡς τὸ σπέρμα τούτων.

From Mesopotamia Balak sent for me,
the king of Moab from the mountains of the east, saying,
'Come here and curse Jacob for me,
come here and denounce Israel for me.'
Why would I curse someone whom the Lord does not curse,
why denounce someone whom God does not denounce?
But I will see him from the top of the mountains,
and from the hills I will descry him.

Behold a people will dwell alone,
and will not be numbered among the nations.
Who has reckoned the seed of Jacob,
and who will number the people of Israel?
May my soul die among the souls of the just,
and may my seed be as the seed of these.

Moses 1, 278–9

ἐκ Μεσοποταμίας μετεπέμψατό με Βαλάκης μακρὰν τὴν ἀπ' ἀνατολῶν
στειλάμενον ἀποδημίαν, ἵνα τίσηται τοὺς Ἑβραίους ἀραῖς. ἐγὼ δὲ τίνα τρόπον
ἀράσομαι τοῖς μὴ καταράτοις ὑπὸ θεοῦ; θεάσομαι μὲν αὐτοὺς ὀφθαλμοῖς ἀφ'
ὑψηλοτάτων ὀρῶν καὶ τῇ διανοίᾳ καταλήψομαι, βλάψαι δ' οὐκ ἂν δυναίμην
λαόν, ὃς μόνος κατοικήσει, μὴ συναριθμούμενος ἑτέροις ἔθνεσιν, οὐ κατὰ
τόπων ἀποκλήρωσιν καὶ χώρας ἀποτομήν, ἀλλὰ κατὰ τὴν τῶν ἐξαιρέτων ἐθῶν
ἰδιότητα, μὴ συναναμιγνύμενος ἄλλοις εἰς τὴν τῶν πατρίων ἐκδιάτησιν. τίς ἐπ'
ἀκριβείας εὗρε τὴν πρώτην καταβολὴν τῆς τούτων γενέσεως; τὰ μὲν σώματ'
αὐτοῖς ἐξ ἀνθρωπίνων διεπλάσθη σπερμάτων, ἐκ δὲ θείων ἔφυσαν αἱ ψυχαί· διὸ
καὶ γεγόνασιν ἀγχίσποροι θεοῦ. ἀποθάνοι μου ἡ ψυχὴ τὸν σωματικὸν βίον, ἵν'
ἐν ψυχαῖς δικαίων καταριθμηθῇ, οἵας εἶναι συμβέβηκε τὰς τούτων.

From Mesopotamia hath Balak called me, a far journey from the east, that he
may avenge him on the Hebrews through my cursing. But I, how shall I curse
them whom God hath not cursed? I shall behold them with my eyes from the
highest mountains, and perceive them with my mind. But I shall not be able to
harm the people, which shall dwell alone, not reckoned among other nations;
and that, not because their dwelling-place is set apart and their land severed
from others, but because in virtue of the distinction of their peculiar customs
they do not mix with others to depart from the ways of their fathers. Who has
made accurate discovery of how the sowing of their generation was first made?
Their bodies have been moulded from human seeds, but their souls are sprung
from divine seeds, and therefore their stock is akin to God. May my soul die to
the life of the body that it may be reckoned among the souls of the just, even
such as are the souls of these men. (Loeb trans.)

This is taken from the story of Balak and Balaam (Numbers 22–4). Philo
reproduces, if not exactly then fairly closely, the actual wording of Balaam's
refusal to curse the Jews. And in the rest of the episode, where Balaam makes
his pronouncements, Philo sticks close to the Greek of the Septuagint.[20] In
spite of this fairly close adherence to the Biblical text, the overall picture
Philo paints of Balaam is much more overtly hostile than Numbers. He has
in fact borrowed a certain amount of direct speech from the story, but he has
not lifted the wording, or indeed the story, wholesale. This is characteristic
of his practice.[21] He does not import whole sections of the Bible. Words and
phrases give clear verbal echoes throughout, and sometimes brief passages,
particularly direct speech, are copied, or remembered, more or less exactly, but

it is important to recognize that Philo's *Moses* is a re-writing, a re-composition of the Bible narrative. The passage cited above is a good example of Philo at work. He has a section where he is sticking close to the actual wording in Numbers; but he cannot quite leave it alone. He avoids Balak's direct speech instructions, adds that Balaam will perceive the Hebrew people with his mind, and restates more clearly his refusal to harm them. He refrains from substantial explanatory comment until he comes to 'a people who will dwell alone, and not be numbered among the nations': this he feels he has to explain. The Jews dwell alone not because they are physically cut off from the rest of the world, but because they do not want to risk losing their own customs by mixing with others. And the notion of Balaam saying 'may my soul die among the souls of the just' worries him too: a soul cannot die, so he qualifies its death as applying just to its 'bodily life' (whatever that may mean).

3. Abridgement

As an opening example I cite the episode in Numbers 13–14 where the Israelites undertake a reconnaissance of the land of Canaan. Philo (1.220–38) follows the story fairly closely to start with. He leaves out the names of the twelve men chosen to inspect Canaan – as we will see (below p. 131), throughout the whole work, he goes to great lengths to avoid names – and Moses' speech to the twelve is a much elaborated version of that in Numbers, but it covers the same ground. Philo then comes to the difficult part of the Biblical story. The scouts agree on their assessment of the land of Canaan, but ten of them argue that it is too strong to attack, while Caleb and Joshua urge an immediate assault. At this the Israelites become openly insubordinate: they tell Moses and Aaron that they would rather have died in Egypt or in the desert, and they talk about appointing a leader to take them back to Egypt. Joshua and Caleb persist with their advice and are nearly stoned. God is furious and threatens to destroy the whole community with pestilence, but is persuaded by Moses' elaborate argument to forgive them. He does, however, sentence them to forty years in the wilderness and refuses to allow any to make it to the promised land, except Joshua and Caleb. And the ten cowardly scouts are destroyed. This part of the story, told at some length in Numbers, is considerably abridged by Philo. He reports the findings of the scouting expedition and the disagreement over the right action to take, but apart from the talk of stoning Joshua and Caleb (who are not named), he says nothing more about the disaffection of the Israelites and compresses drastically the remaining details. God's angry threat is left out and so too Moses' intercession on behalf of the community. It is Moses who becomes indignant and fearful that God will punish the community for not believing his utterances. And indeed the cowardly scouts are struck down. The whole affair is presented as the cause of the Israelites' forty years in the desert, but there is nothing of God's tetchy speeches in which he consigns them to their fate. The uncomfortable elements of the story, showing the Israelites, or God, in a bad light, are either left out or abridged.

The same consideration is probably at work in the abridgement of Exodus 17.1–7 where the Israelites have no water at Rephidim. They complain to Moses, but are not assuaged: 'why did you bring us out of Egypt, only to make us, our children and our livestock, die of thirst?' Moses appeals to Yahweh, afraid the people will stone him. Yahweh tells him to go ahead with some of the elders to the rock at Horeb and strike it with the rod with which he struck the river, and it will produce water for the people to drink. Philo (1.210–11) eliminates the direct speech and reports the episode in much abbreviated form, which leaves out the complaints of the people, any talk of stoning, Moses' appeal to God, and God's advice. He is, no doubt, anxious to avoid an unflattering image of the Israelites, but he is also more interested in offering a rational explanation of why the rock poured out water.

The elimination of direct speech in the Rephidim incident points to what we may identify as a sub-category of abridgement: the reduction of conversational or repetitive direct speech. Philo is quite prepared to make up speeches for Moses (and others) that are not in the Old Testament, and to elaborate considerably on speeches that are there.[22] So, although there are no long, formal orations in Philo, he has no particular problem with speeches. He does, however, cut down considerably on the amount of direct speech in the Bible, particularly conversation. For example, in Exodus 3.7–4.17, where God tells Moses to return and deliver the people out of Egypt, we have a long, drawn-out passage with extended conversation between God and Moses, in which the latter is very reluctant to answer God's call. 'Who am I to go to Pharaoh, king of Egypt, and bring the sons of Israel out of the land of Egypt?', he asks; 'when I tell the sons of Israel the god of your fathers has sent me to you and they ask his name, what will I tell them?'; 'suppose that they won't believe me or listen to my voice?'; 'Please, lord,...I am weak of voice and slow of tongue... send someone else who is up to the job'. God answers all his questions and tries to bolster his confidence by giving him the power to perform various miracles, but finally loses patience: 'And the Lord was roused to anger against Moses'; he gives him the eloquent Aaron as assistant, and tells him to get on with it. In the parallel passage in Philo (1.71–84) God delivers an initial speech as in Exodus; Moses knows the Israelites will not believe him and asks God what to say; God replies and then shows Moses the miracles. Moses believes, but tries to get out of it – 'he was not eloquent, but weak-voiced and slow-tongued', especially since hearing God speak (human eloquence compared to God's was dumbness) and anyway he was a careful person; so he begged God to choose another. 'But God, though approving his modesty' (ἀποδεξάμενος αὐτὸν τῆς αἰδοῦς), Philo says, gave him his brother as helper, and Moses knew he could resist no longer. Philo reduces the amount of conversation and presents a slightly different Moses. The conflation of speeches, of both God and Moses, de-emphasizes the repeated reluctance of the Biblical Moses, who cuts a distinctly weak figure at this point. And the change from divine anger to admiration also helps to show Moses in a better light.

Part of the drama of the Biblical account of the plagues of Egypt (Exodus 7.14–12.36) rests with an almost relentless repetition of action and speech. 'The Lord said to Moses, "Get up early and confront Pharaoh. Behold he will go to the water, and say to him, 'The Lord says this: "Let my people go and worship me in the desert"'(8.16). This and so much else in the episode is repeated time and again with slight variation, but there is none of it in Philo (1.85–147). He tells the story, and indeed expands on the Old Testament in various ways (see below p. 128), but he entirely avoids this particular feature of it. Does he regard it perhaps as unsophisticated, or too characteristically Biblical for his Greek presentation of Moses' life?[23]

In general, abridgement of the Biblical narrative is far less frequent than expansion: Philo leaves out whole sections of the Biblical story, but when he does follow the story he is more likely to elaborate than to abridge.

4. Chronological displacement

In Philo, when Moses had reached the pinnacle of good fortune, regarded as the king's grandson and heir to the throne, Pharaoh adopted a new and impious policy (μέγα καινουργηθὲν ἀσέβημα – 1.33) towards the Israelites. He reduced them to slavery and imposed terrible burdens on them. To supervise their labour he appointed the most pitiless and cruel overseers. Some of the Jews had to make bricks, others fetch the straw for the bricks. They had to build houses, walls, cities, canals, and there was no respite for them. They died in large numbers, their bodies thrown away without burial or mourning (1.34–9). This all leads up to Moses killing the Egyptian overseer and fleeing to Arabia (1.40–7). Philo's source at this point is Exodus 2.11–25 – that is where we are in the Biblical story – but he has also imported material from different parts of Exodus. For instance, it is in Exodus 1.8–22, before the birth of Moses, that we learn of the change of policy towards the Jews. Pharaoh is worried that the people of Israel are too many and too strong. 'And he put overseers over them to do them evil in their labours. And they built strong cities for Pharaoh, Pithom and Rameses and On, which is Heliopolis.' But the Israelites continued to flourish, and the Egyptians were afraid of them. 'And the Egyptians ruled the sons of Israel by force, and burdened their life in wicked labours, digging and brick-making and all the works of the fields, in all their labours with which they enslaved them by force.' Pharaoh goes on to order that the sons of the Israelites be thrown into the Nile; and we have the story of Moses' birth. There is also in Philo at this point material from Exodus 5, where Moses and Aaron have first demanded of Pharaoh to let the Israelites go. The only effect the demand has is to make Pharaoh even more cruel: for instance, he issues specific orders to his taskmasters that the Israelites are to collect their own straw, but not reduce their brick production. What Philo has done is to bring into one place various examples of Pharaoh's cruelty that occur at different chronological points in the Old Testament. The purpose of this displacement is to build up what he feels is a more convincing explanation for the rift between Pharaoh and Moses that ultimately leads to Moses killing the Egyptian overseer. It is in fact part of an elaborate explanation and justification for that killing. I will return to this (see below p. 129).

5. Transfer of an item from one character to another
Philo does not do this very often, but occasionally has cause to. For instance, at 1.112, in response to the plague of gnats/mosquitoes, it is the Egyptians in general who declare 'this is the finger of God'. In Exodus (8.12–15), when the magicians (οἱ ἐπαοιδοί) cannot replicate the plague of gnats, they declare 'this is the finger of God'. Philo's reason for the transfer is fairly clear: he does not like the magicians. In Exodus they appear in the story five times: they could turn a rod into a snake (7.11), they could also turn the Nile to blood (7.22) and produce a plague of frogs (8.3). But they were not able to do the gnats, and could not compete in the matter of boils: indeed they suffered the ignominy of being covered with boils like all the other Egyptians (9.11). Philo mentions them just once (σοφισταὶ καὶ μάγοι – 1.92) right at the beginning of the story, when they turn their staffs into snakes; thereafter he abandons them. As they are the enemies of the Israelites, it is hardly the case that he cuts them out for being generally suspect characters; he could have left them out entirely. His concern is more likely to do with their ability to reproduce any of the miracles God works through Moses and Aaron. The impact of their turning rods into snakes is considerably lessened by the fact that all the snakes they produce are swallowed up by Moses' much superior snake. Philo will accept their presence as long as their inferiority is evident: in Exodus their powers are too impressive for his liking.

There is another minor transfer in the story of the plagues. In connection with the frogs, in Exodus it is Pharaoh who asks Moses and Aaron to beseech God to get rid of them (8.4); in Philo the Egyptian people ask God directly (1.105). This may simply be a matter of not having the Septuagint in front of him; or perhaps Philo consciously attributes a greater role to the people for dramatic purposes. After the death of the first-born the people blame Pharaoh for their woes (it is not in Exodus).

6. Expansion of material by explanatory or dramatic detail

In most circumstances Philo's *Moses* elaborates on what is to be found in the Bible. It is his usual procedure. I examine three examples.

In Exodus 2.15–22 we have the simple and brief story of Moses and the daughters of Jethro at the well. Moses flees from Pharaoh and is sitting at a well when the daughters of Jethro try to water their father's flock. Shepherds drive the girls away, 'but Moses stood up and protected them and drew water for them and watered their flock'. When the girls return, their father asks why they were home so early. They explain what happened. '"And where is he?" he said to his daughters. "Why did you leave the man in that way? Ask him to eat bread." And Moses resided with the man, and he gave Moses his daughter Zipporah as his wife.' And they had a son Gershom. These few lines in Exodus are expanded greatly by Philo (*Moses* 1.51–9).

It is only a small matter, Philo begins in a manner that calls to mind Plutarch (*Alexander* 1), but very revealing. The Arabs breed cattle, he explains, and it is not just men who tend them, but women as well; not just people of humble family, but aristocrats too. He seems to feel it necessary to explain immediately why the priest's daughters were engaged in this menial task. The daughters draw water, taking care to share the work equally, and fill the troughs, but shepherds arrive, and disdaining the weakness of the girls drive them off, so they can use for their own animals the water the girls have drawn. Moses rushes to their assistance and intervenes with a speech. 'Stop this injustice', he berates the shepherds. He accuses them of taking advantage of a lonely spot. 'Are you not ashamed of leaving idle your arms and elbows, you long-haired lumps' (χαῖται βαθεῖαι καὶ σάρκες ὑμεῖς ἐστε); the girls are behaving like young men, and you are behaving like girls; go away; you should have been helping them. For the last part of his speech he is transformed into a prophet, Philo says, frightening the shepherds: the heavenly eye of justice sees everything even in deserted places and has appointed Moses its champion to protect the girls with a great hand, which the greedy cannot see, but the invisible power of which the shepherds will feel if they do not mend their ways. The shepherds immediately submit and water the girls' animals. The girls go home and tell their father, who is annoyed at them for not inviting Moses back. He gives them a brief lecture on gratitude and they go and collect Moses. The father is struck by his face and then by his disposition – 'for great natures are transparent and need no length of time to be recognized' – and gives him his fairest daughter in marriage. 'By that one action he attested all his noble qualities, and showed that excellence standing alone deserves our love, and needs no commendation from anything else, but carries within itself the tokens by which it is known.'

Much of Philo's version is just an expanded dramatization of the Biblical story, although the greater (and manufactured) detail has the important effect of making the incident more easily intelligible than Exodus: it is not simply a matter of telling a better story. Moses as prophet is an addition, but functions as a theological explanation of what is going on. And talk of the transparency of great natures is probably necessary to explain what might appear to be the unseemly haste of Jethro in accepting Moses and giving him one of his daughters as wife. In the corresponding passage in Josephus (*AJ* 2.258–63) there is some of the same detail – Josephus also explains, for instance, why women are tending cattle – so there must be an extra-Biblical tradition here that we do not have and that both Philo and Josephus use. It is, then, difficult to say exactly how much is Philo's expansion. But there is no speech of Moses in Josephus and that looks distinctively Philonic. The whole point of the expansion, however, is clear: it extends the drama of the incident and builds up the character of Moses, making explicit the implications of the Biblical text.

The account of the plagues is one of the central episodes in Moses' life, and without changing the essence of the Bible (Exodus 7.14–12.36), Philo elaborates on it considerably (1.96–139). He reorganizes, rationalizes, categorizes in highly characteristic fashion. The order of the plagues is different from Exodus in order to fit Philo's tidy scheme, which is explained in chapters 96–7. There were ten punishments – the perfect number for the perfect sinners – and they were inflicted by earth, fire, air and water, God's reason being that what he used to produce the world should also be used to destroy the wicked. He distributed the punishments as follows. The first three, made up of the denser elements, earth and water, he gave to Aaron; the second three, consisting of air and fire, the two most productive elements of life, he gave to Moses; the seventh punishment was given to Moses and Aaron together, and the final three were the work of God himself. This is, as far as we can see, entirely Philo's own interpretation of Exodus. It makes rational sense of the story and is very easy for the reader to follow. 'Streamlining' is a good word for the procedure.[24]

Having imposed order on the story he still has to explain details. The turning of the Nile to blood (1.98–101) is very similar to Exodus, but Philo adds that, as water was so important to the Egyptians, water was the first punishment. He also seems to be worried by the statement in Exodus 7.24: 'And the Egyptians all dug around the river to drink water, since they could not drink the water from the river.' His concern is probably that the Old Testament might imply that the Egyptians could drink this water: so he explicitly denies it. He talks of the stench of dead fish and a great multitude of men dying of thirst and lying in heaps, as their relatives did not have the strength to bury them: this is not in Exodus and is clearly the invention of circumstantial detail for dramatic purposes. And, as we have seen above, he is silent about the magicians of Exodus.

The gnats/mosquitoes (1.106–12) need some explanation. Why would God choose to punish the Egyptians with something as petty and insignificant as the gnat – why not bears, lions, panthers, snakes? The answer is twofold: first, God wanted to punish the Egyptians, not destroy them; second, men need the most powerful allies they can get, but God, the highest and greatest power, needs no one. If he does want instruments of vengeance then he provides the slightest and smallest with irresistible and invincible powers.

With the plague of storms (1.113–19), air and heaven, the purest portions of the universe, now take over from earth and water. To emphasize how dreadful the storms are, Philo says you have to remember that Egypt is the only country, apart from southern lands, not to have winter. And we get, not for the first time,[25] a short disquisition on Egyptian weather and why the Nile floods. Winter is not needed in Egypt as the Nile flood serves the purpose of rain; and nature does not waste its effort in sending rain to places that do not need it. This is all by way of explaining how the idyllic weather of Egypt was shattered by the plague of storms.

The plague of darkness (1.123–5) is embellished typically. 'For three days there was darkness over the whole of Egypt. No one could see his brother for three days, and nobody got up from their bed for three days. But for all the sons of Israel there was light everywhere they were.' That is all Exodus (10.22–3) says. Philo speculates on the darkness rather ploddingly – an eclipse or some compaction of the clouds. People threw themselves on their beds for three days, and could not even bring themselves to talk or eat, so depressed by the disaster were they. This raises a practical problem in Philo's mind. What about matters lavatorial? When the needs of nature pressed they had to feel their way along the walls like blind people. Another problem occurs to Philo: why did they not just light fires and torches? The answer: 'the light of artificial fire was partly quenched by the prevailing storm wind, partly dimmed to the point of disappearance by the depth of the darkness'.

The problems posed by the plagues are on the whole practical matters. There is nothing embarrassing that needs justifying. The killing by Moses of the Egyptian overseer, on the other hand, is a good example of an incident that needs special pleading. Philo clearly feels embarrassed by the story in Exodus 2.11–15, in which Moses looks on the burdens of the Israelites and sees one of them being beaten by an Egyptian; he checks that the coast is clear, that there is no one in sight, kills the Egyptian and buries him in the sand.

Next day two Israelites are fighting and when he tries to break it up, one of them questions his authority and asks, 'do you mean to kill me in the manner you killed the Egyptian yesterday?' At this Moses is afraid, realizing he has been found out, and flees. In Philo (1.40–6) this is constructed at greater length and with more care to emphasize the wickedness of the Egyptians and thus Moses' right to take the action he did. We have seen already how the burdens of the Israelites are built up by importing examples of Pharaoh's cruelty from different parts of the Exodus story. We are then told that Moses did all he could to help his people, even though he had no actual powers. He urged the overseers to be less cruel and the workers to be brave. All things in the world, he tells them reassuringly, change to their opposites: clouds to open sky, violent winds to stillness, stormy seas to calm. But his words have no effect. The overseers are ferocious, like wild animals, more unyielding than iron. The cruellest of these Moses kills, and Philo tells us that Moses regarded this killing as a righteous action. 'Righteous it was', he adds, 'that one who lived only to destroy men should himself be destroyed'. The king is annoyed, and his courtiers start a whispering campaign against Moses: he is ambitious, he wants the throne, he will attack you. So Moses retires to Arabia where it was safe for him. Philo does not say Moses was afraid, but it does occur to him that by fleeing, Moses was leaving the Israelites in the lurch; so he has him beseech God to save his people and punish their oppressors, and tells us that God listened to his prayers and very soon judged the land. This is an expanded version of the episode, and there are also some changes in the detail, all resulting in heightened drama and increased justification for Moses' action. His killing of the overseer in Exodus happens very suddenly and might appear a little random and underhand. Philo prepares the ground more carefully, eliminates the unseemly fighting of the two Hebrews and emphasizes Moses' powerful enemies at court who force him to flee. Josephus' narrative in the *Antiquities* (2.254–7) is different again: Moses does not kill anyone but is the victim of an assassination plot hatched by the Egyptian leaders and the Pharaoh who have become jealous of him. This is the same sort of 'cleaning up' process we see in Philo, but carried a stage further.

7. Expansion by allegorical explanation

In most of his writing, allegory is central to Philo's whole working method: it is in particular the device that enables him to interpret Jewish scripture in terms of Greek philosophy. It is ideally suited to textual exegesis.[26] Although the *Life of Moses* involves an implicit interpretation of the Old Testament, it achieves that interpretation largely in the retelling of the story, not by an explicit commentary on the text: there is no contrast set up 'between the biblical text and the interpretation.'[27] Philo could, however, have interpreted his own version of the Bible story allegorically, if he thought it would assist his purpose; and there are occasional outbreaks of the method. The burning bush of Exodus 3 is interpreted as an image of the nation's condition as it then stood, and as a pointer to future events (1.67–70). The twelve springs and seventy palm-trees at Elim (Exodus 15.27) symbolize the twelve tribes and seventy elders of the nation, who are themselves like 'the best of trees' (1.188–90). In the battle against the Amelekites Moses' arms become heavy and light by turn (Exodus 17.8–16), and there is a very laboured allegorical explanation of what this means (1.217–19). Various aspects of the tabernacle (2.81–108), the High Priest's vestments (2.117–35), the nuts that grow on Aaron's branch (2.180–6) are all subjected to detailed allegorical analysis.

In some ways the fact that allegory occurs at all in the *Moses* is more in need of explanation than its absence. Although an effective means of theological exegesis, it does not suit well the form of a Greek biography: it is not, of course, inherently un-Greek, but it may well have appeared to Philo as inherently un-biographical, and too much theologizing could well be unattractive for gentile readers. It really does not assist our understanding of Moses, for instance, to know what the springs and palm-trees of Elim symbolize. I suggest that when Philo does occasionally allegorize in the work, he is forgetting himself. His chosen mode of presentation in the *Moses* is to retell the Biblical story, not to offer a commentary on the scriptural text: allegory suits the latter better than the former, but there are times when Philo just cannot help himself.

8. Avoidance of proper names

One of the strangest features of the *Life of Moses* is the way in which Philo studiously avoids the names of people and places given in the Old Testament, with the regular exception of Moses himself. He offers no explanation for this practice. It starts right at the beginning of the work. Moses was seventh in descent from the first settler who became founder of the whole Jewish nation: why not just say seventh in descent from Abraham? Moses' wife Zipporah, father-in-law Jethro, son Gershom, sister Miriam are not named in Philo. The whole story of the plagues and flight from Egypt is told without naming Aaron, who is a central figure; it calls for considerable ingenuity to avoid his name. During the time in the desert, most of the places the Israelites pass through are not named. In the battle against Amalek (1.214–19), neither Amalek himself nor Aaron nor Hur is mentioned, although curiously Joshua is named once (1.216). The twelve scouts chosen to reconnoitre the land of Canaan (itself not named) are all listed in Numbers, but not in Philo; and when it comes to describing the difference of opinion among the scouts, extraordinary circumlocution is needed not to name Caleb and

Joshua (1.234), even though we have heard Joshua's name just a little before, in connection with the defeat of Amalek. In the description of Edom and the Edomites (1.239–49), which is not in Numbers, but is a summary of the account in Genesis 25.21–34, there is no mention of Edom, Edomites or any of the main characters in the story – Isaac, Rebecca, Esau, Jacob. In the extended story of Balaam (1.263–93), we never hear his name, although curiously Balak is named throughout. The story of the allocation of Transjordan to the Gadites and Reubenites in Numbers 32 has the names of some fifty people and places: in Philo (1.319–33) we get only Moses and the river Jordan. The same tendency is also to be seen in Book 2, although with more theorizing it has less need for proper names. Famous stories like that of Lot and the destruction of Sodom and Gomorrah (2.57–8) are referred to only indirectly – Noah too (2.59–65).

How are we to explain this? It is not an absolute rule, but it is the exception to be given the name of a place or person, and it is clear that Philo often goes to some lengths to avoid doing this. When we do get a name, sometimes it belongs to minor figures or places, and the suspicion must be that they have somehow slipped Philo's guard. This may account for the naming of, for instance, Elim, the watering place (1.188), Sihon, king of the Amorites (1.258), Zelophehad (2.234; 240). It is perhaps less likely that Philo simply forgot his policy when naming Balak seven times, or Phineas four (1.300–14), but although it is difficult to explain the irregularity of Philo's practice, there is no doubt that these are exceptions to a general tendency. Aaron is such an important figure in the Biblical story that by not naming him a single time, it is possible that Philo is protecting the prominence of his hero, the subject of the biography. But there must be more to it than that: otherwise the secondary characters could all have been named. Perhaps the most obvious explanation that comes to mind is that it is all part of the process of hellenizing the Moses story, at least to the extent of not cluttering it up with what might be, to a Greek audience, strange-sounding and difficult-to-pronounce Hebrew names.[28] Josephus provides good support for the notion. Early in the *Antiquities* he alludes to the matter directly (*AJ* 1.129). He has been talking about the nations descended from Japheth, the son of Noah, and points out to his Greek readers, who are perhaps unaware of the fact, that for their pleasure, and for fitting orthography, he has hellenized the names (τὰ γὰρ ὀνόματα διὰ τὸ τῆς γραφῆς εὐπρεπὲς ἡλλήνισται πρὸς ἡδονὴν τῶν ἐντευξομένων), rather than reproducing the usual transliteration of the Septuagint. His inclination at *AJ* 2.176 was not to include the names of Jacob's descendants, on account of their difficulty (δυσκολία), although in that case he decided to go ahead to show that the Jewish people was of Mesopotamian, rather than Egyptian, origin. It was not just that Hebrew names lacked euphony for Greek ears; the Old Testament also presented them, at times, in distractingly long lists. Thus he decided not to name the exiles returning from captivity in Babylon, listed at great length in *Esra* 2, lest he distract his readers from the succession of events and make the narrative difficult to follow (ἵνα μὴ τὴν τῶν ἀναγινωσκόντων διάνοιαν τῆς συναφῆς τῶν πραγμάτων ἀποσπάσας δυσπαρακολούθητον αὐτοῖς ποιήσω τὴν διήγησιν – *AJ* 11.68).[29] If Josephus' solution to the problem of the unfamiliarity of Hebrew names was pragmatic and sensible, Philo's was extremist – eliminate them altogether. When talking about the respect paid to Moses' laws by other nations and the translation of the Hebrew Bible into Greek (2.17–45), Philo is not slow to name the Athenians and the Spartans, the Egyptians and the Scythians, Ptolemy Philadelphus, Alexander, Alexandria and the island of Pharos. These are, presumably, all 'safe' because they are Greek, or at least not Hebrew.

Philo's primary purpose in this work was to present a portrait of Moses to an audience that did not know him. He could have written a commentary on the relevant parts of the Bible, but instead chose to retell the story. This involved an interpretation that he hoped would appeal to his target audience. Philo did not want to clutter his story with Hebrew names, or give it the epic or antiquarian feel of the Bible with its conversation and repetition. Events are dramatized, as we saw with Moses at the well with Jethro's daughters. At virtually every turn dramatic details are added. Pharaoh's daughter who adopted Moses was an only child and herself childless; she wanted a son to inherit her father's kingdom; she was unhappy and always moping at home; she had pretended to be pregnant to pass Moses off as her natural son (1.12–19). None of this is in Exodus; and although it is different from Josephus' elaboration of the story (*AJ* 2.217–37), it may also come from extra-biblical oral tradition. At every turn too, elements that might be thought embarrassing or difficult are played down, eliminated or explained. God is angry with Moses in Exodus; he admires Moses' modesty in Philo. Unsuitable characters like the magicians of Exodus are sidelined in Philo. In the famous story of Balaam's donkey in Numbers, the donkey in exasperation finally addresses Balaam directly. In Philo the donkey does not speak. During the battle in which Amalek was defeated, when Moses held up his hands the Israelites prevailed, when he put them down Amalek prevailed. His hands get heavy and Aaron and Hur have to hold them up. It is a slightly ludicrous scene. In Philo Moses' hands simply get heavy and light by turns and while we get an allegorical interpretation of this, we hear nothing about Aaron and Hur holding the hands up. The killing of the overseer needs very careful explanation in Philo: he would not want his audience to think that Moses might engage in unnecessary violence. So too with the despoiling of the Egyptians when the Israelites leave Egypt (140–2): they did not do this out of avarice; it was just a fair wage for all the work they had done, and reasonable retaliation for their enslavement. Either way their action was right: the Egyptians started it.

Much of this is perhaps not so much 'hellenizing' the story as de-emphasizing the Hebraic. There is also, however, a concerted attempt to present a hellenized Moses. In order to explain him at all, Philo feels he has to make one of the biggest adjustments of all to the Old Testament: Moses becomes king and High Priest, neither of which he was in the Bible. These are presumably categories that make him more understandable in the Judaeo-Graeco-Roman world of contemporary Alexandria. The most sustained hellenizing of Moses undoubtedly comes in the sections of book 1 where Philo takes leave of the Biblical narrative to discuss Moses' education and adolescence (1.20–33) and to analyse him as king (1.148–62). This latter section forms almost exactly the centre of book 1. We find strands of Greek philosophizing, and Hellenistic ideals of kingship mixed with the holy man in partnership with God.[30] It is an extraordinary fusion of Greek and Jewish elements, but deserving of closer attention than the scope of this paper will allow.[31]

Appendix

Philo's *Life of Moses*: structure

Book I. Moses as Philosopher-King (chronological arrangement).
Book II. Moses as Legislator, High-Priest, Prophet (topical arrangement).

BOOK I
INTRODUCTION
1–4   Philo going to write the life of Moses, greatest and most perfect of men. His laws famous, but not the man himself. Greeks ignore him, but waste their skills on comedy and erotic writing. Philo will overlook their malice and tell Moses' life, using the sacred books and what the elders have told him.

I. MOSES' EARLY LIFE IN EGYPT 5–47
(5–19 = Exodus 2.1–10)
5–7   Family background
8–19   Pharaoh's order; exposure by the Nile; adoption by Pharaoh's daughter; early childhood.
20–4   *Education by Greeks and Egyptians.*
25–33 *Adolescence: temperance, control of appetites, asceticism, speech and life in harmony, success, balanced attitude to real and adoptive parents.*
(34–59 = Exodus 2.11–25 + 1.11–14 + 5.6–21)

34–9   Cruelty of Pharaoh to Jewish suppliants.

40–7   Moses' efforts on behalf of the Jews; kills overseer; flees to Arabia.

II. MOSES IN EXILE 48–84

48–50   *Moses trains himself for the best type of life – the theoretical and the practical.*

51–9   Maidens at the well and marriage of Moses to Jethro's daughter.

60–4   *Comparison of shepherd and king; Moses the best shepherd of his time.*

(65–95 = Exodus 3–7.13)

65–70   The burning bush (including allegorical interpretation).

71–84   God and Moses converse, like master and pupil. God urges Moses to take charge of the nation; gives him miracles; grants Aaron as assistant.

III. THE PLAGUES OF EGYPT AND EXPULSION OF THE JEWS 85–147

85–95   Return of Moses to Egypt; Moses and Aaron confront the king; Aaron turns rod into snake, but Egyptians become even harsher.

(96–147 = Exodus 7.14–12.37)

96–7   *Explanation of the 10 plagues, inflicted by earth, fire and water. Plagues 1–3 = denser elements, earth and water > Aaron; plagues 4–6 = two most life-producing elements, air and fire > Moses; plague 7 > Moses and Aaron together; plagues 8–10 > God.*

98–139 The plagues (98–101 Nile to blood; 102–5 frogs; 106–12 gnats; 113–19 storms; 120–2 locusts; 123–5 darkness; 126–9 ulcers; 130–2 dog-flies; 133 foot-and-mouth; 134–9 first-born die).

142–7   Despoiling of the Egyptians; none of the plagues affected the Jews; number and state of departing Jews.

IV. PHILO'S COMMENTARY ON MOSES THE KING 148–62

148–9   *Moses made king not for military exploits, but because of his goodness, nobility of conduct and benevolence; and because God rewarded him with another kingship for giving up the throne of Egypt.*

150–4   *Comparison of Moses with other kings, who promote their own sons and are greedy for material wealth.*

155–9   *God's partnership with Moses: he gives him the wealth of the whole earth, as Moses is a world-citizen (κοσμοπολίτης), and the same title ('for he was named god and king of the whole nation').*

160–2   *Moses living impersonation of the law.*

V. THE CROSSING OF THE RED SEA 163–80 (= EXODUS 13.17–15.21)

163–9   Jews depart Egypt guided by a pillar of cloud; Pharaoh pursues.

170–2   Jews complain to Moses.

173–5   Moses' reply; becomes possessed to prophesy.

176–80 Crossing of the Red Sea.

VI. THIRST AND HUNGER IN THE DESERT 181–213 (= Exodus 15.22–17.7)

181–7   Thirst. Drinking of the water at Marah.

188–90   Elim. 12 springs and 70 palms = 12 tribes and 70 nation heads.
191–209 Hunger. Complaints of the Jews; manna and quails.
210–11   Thirst at Rephidim.
212–13   *Excursus on the wonders of the universe. The familiar despised; the unfamiliar admired.*

VII. The wandering of the Jews 214–62

214–9   Defeat of Amalek and the Phoenicians (= Exodus 17.8–16); allegorical interpretation of Moses' hands.
220–38   Inspection of the land of Canaan (= Numbers 13–14).
239–49   The Edomites (Genesis 25.21–34; Numbers 20.14–21).
250–4   Defeat of the Canaanites (Numbers 21.1–3).
255–7   Jews at the well of Beer (Numbers 21.16–18).
258–62   Defeat of Sihon, king of the Amorites (Numbers 21.20–5).

VIII. The story of Balak 263–318 (= Numbers 22–5; 31)

263–8   Summoning of Balaam.
269–75   Balaam's donkey.
275–93   Balaam's praise of the Jews.
294–9   *Balaam's private advice to use the women to ensnare the Jews.*
300–4   Phineas kills Zimri and Cozbi.
305–18   Phineas leads Jews in victory over Balak; division of the spoils by Moses.

IX. Settling of the two cattle-breeding tribes

319–33 (= Numbers 32)
334   Summary: so much for Moses the king. Next: Moses the High Priest and legislator.

BOOK II

Introduction

1–7   First σύνταξις dealt with Moses the philosopher-king. Philo now presenting three other qualities: Moses as law-giver, High Priest and prophet.

I. Moses as legislator 8–65

8–11   Definition of legislator.
12–45   Moses the best of all legislators, shown by:
 (1)   permanence of his legislation, 12–16;
 (2)   respect paid to his laws by other nations, 17–44 (25–44 story of the Septuagint);
 (3)   greatness of the law itself, 45.
46–52   Analysis of the law into two parts, the historical + commands /prohibitions; explanation of why Moses began with the historical.
53–65   Punishment of the wicked, honouring of the just: Sodom and Gomorrah and Lot, 56–8 (= Genesis 19); flood and Noah, 59–65 (= Genesis 6–9).

II. MOSES AS HIGH PRIEST 66–186

66–140   Instructions given to Moses on Sinai: tabernacle, 71–108; High Priest's vestments, 109–35; basin of bronze, 136–40 (= Exodus 25–28; 38).

141–58   Choice of priests; their purification, dress, anointing (= Exodus 29; Leviticus 8–9).

159–73   Choice of Levites; leads to story of the golden calf; Levites rewarded for their piety (= Exodus 32).

174–86   Challenge of Korah; vindication of Moses' choice of priests and Levites; rod of Aaron (allegorical interpretation of its nuts) (= Numbers 16.1–3; 17).

III. MOSES AS PROPHET 187–287

187–91   Three divisions of prophecy:
(1)   spoken by God in person, interpreted by prophet;
(2)   question and answer;
(3)   spoken by Moses himself, possessed by God.
          Philo says impossible to talk about (1), so he'll concentrate on (2) and (3). Four examples of each:

A. Question and answer 192–245:

192–208 1: the blasphemer (= Leviticus 24. 10–23).

209–20   2: the sabbath-breaker (= Numbers 15.32–6).

221   Both incidents concern punishment of the impious ratified by means of question and answer. Two examples of different kind:

222–32   3: delay of Passover through ritual impurity (= Numbers 9.1–14).

233–45   4: law of inheritance. Daughters of Zelophehad (= Numbers 27.1–11).

B. Prophecies of Moses himself 246–87:

246–57   1: destruction of the Egyptians in the Red Sea (= Exodus 14).

258–69   2: the Manna (= Exodus 16.4–30).

270–4   3: slaughter of the idolaters (= Exodus 32)

275–87   4: destruction of Korah and his people (= Numbers 16).

IV. DEATH OF MOSES 288–92 (= Deuteronomy 33–4)

Notes

[1]   See, for instance, Fraser 1972, 38–92; Haas 1997, chaps. 3–6; Bowman 1986, 209.

[2]   Portraits in Sandmel 1979, 3–16; Williamson 1989, 1–27; Dillon 1996, 139–44. The black sheep of the family was Philo's nephew, Tiberius Julius Alexander – Procurator of Judaea in Claudius' principate and Prefect of Egypt in Nero's – who, according to Josephus (*AJ* 20.100), abandoned his Judaism.

[3]   Discussion in Sandmel 1984, 31–6; Borgen 1992, 122–38.

[4]   There is little that could be called standard bibliography on the *Moses*. Probably the main concern has been to explain how it fits into the overall scheme of Philo's works: see particularly Goodenough 1933, 109–25. Other coverage in Botte 1954, 55–62; Goodenough 1962, 145–52; Arnaldez 1967, 11–21; Holladay 1977, 108–29;

Nikiprowetsky 1977, 194–5; Sandmel 1979, 47–52; Schürer 1987, 854–5.

[5] Edwards and Swain 1997, 229.

[6] Stanton 1974, 127.

[7] Pelling 1980, 139 observes in another context 'a writer's programmatic statements can sometimes be a poor guide to his work'.

[8] Hägg and Rousseau 2000, 9.

[9] Leo 1901; Stuart 1928; Momigliano 1993; Dihle 1970.

[10] More recently, Philo is at least considered in Edwards and Swain 1997, although he manages to make it into two lists: one of works that are biography (229–30), the other of works that are not biography (22–3).

[11] Priessnig 1929, 150–5.

[12] Burridge 1992, 132–53. Burridge's analysis points up an interesting contrast: while classical scholarship has remained largely silent on Philo as a biographer, among scholars engaged in the debate on the genre of the Gospels there is a ready acceptance of the *Moses* as Greek biography: see, for example, Talbert 1978, 97; Guelich 1983, 185–204; Berger 1984, 1234; Aune 1988, 27.

[13] Recognition of this informs Patricia Cox's definition of the Graeco-Roman biography of the holy man: it is 'a narrative that relates incidents in the life of the subject from birth or youth to death. The hero's activities provide points of reference for the insertion of material not always related in an obvious way to the narrative's presumed biographical purpose': Cox 1983, 55.

[14] For discussion of Philo's place, often thought to be central, in the theory of the 'divine man', see Holladay 1977, 24–43; 103–7.

[15] On Aristoxenus see particularly Momigliano 1993, 74–6. On heroes and holy men, and the dubious genre of 'aretology', see Hadas and Smith 1965; Smith 1971, 174–99.

[16] In my schematic analysis of the structure of the work (Appendix, above, p. 134), I have highlighted in italics the most obvious passages in Book 1 where Philo takes leave of the Biblical narrative.

[17] I borrow some terminology from Pelling's analysis of Plutarch's use of his sources: Pelling 1980, 127–40.

[18] Philo's intended audience has been a matter of dispute. Representative of the debate are Goodenough 1933, 109–25, who argued that the *Moses* was a sort of introductory primer to Judaism for interested gentiles; and Sandmel 1979, 47, who thought more of a Jewish audience, particularly Jews who were wavering or not very devout.

[19] He could scarcely have thought that it was unsuitable for his target audience, seeing that in book 2 he goes into great detail on the tabernacle (2.71–108), for instance, and the High Priest's vestments (2.109–35).

[20] See, for instance, Numbers 23.18–24 = *Moses* 1.283–4; Numbers 24.3–9 = *Moses* 1.289–91.

[21] Further examples: Exodus 2.4 = *Moses* 1.12; Exodus 3.13–14 = *Moses* 1.75; Exodus 4.6 = *Moses* 1.79; Exodus 5.2 = *Moses* 1.88; Exodus 14.11 = *Moses* 1.171.

[22] Manufactured speeches at, for instance, 1.54–6 (Moses to shepherds bullying Jethro's daughters); 1.201–2 (Moses to Israelites); 1.296–9 (Balaam to Balak); 1.307–8 (Moses to his troops). Elaboration of Biblical speeches, 1.171–2; 193–5; 223–6.

[23] In Numbers 32, the story of the allocation of Transjordan to the Reubenites and Gadites, the two tribes speak four times, Moses three; in Philo's version there are only three sections of direct speech, two from Moses one from the tribes.

[24] Pelling 1980, 129.

[25] See also 1.5–6.

[26] For a basic description of Philo's allegorizing, and whether it represents Greek or Jewish exegetical method, see Sandmel 1984, 13–22; and bibliography in Borgen 1984, 128–32.

[27] See Mack 1984, 258.

[28] Colson in vol. VI (p. xv note a) of the Loeb briefly refers to what he calls Philo's 'strict economy of names' in the *Abraham, Joseph* and *Moses*. He suggests that, if it is not just a mannerism, it might be to do with his intended gentile audience.

[29] Elsewhere he just says he considers it unnecessary (οὐκ ἀναγκαῖον) to give names: see, for instance, *AJ* 7.369; 11.152; 12.57.

[30] Analysis and bibliography in, for instance, Holladay 1977, 108–29.

[31] My thanks to Christopher Jones who very kindly read a version of this article, and made helpful suggestions.

Bibliography

Arnaldez, R. et al.

1967   *De vita Mosis. Les oeuvres de Philon d'Alexandrie publiées sous le patronage de Lyon*, vol. 22, Paris.

Aune, D.

1988   *The New Testament in its Literary Environment*, Cambridge.

Berger, K.

1984   'Hellenistische Gattungen im Neuen Testament', *ANRW* II, 25.2, Berlin and New York, 1031–1432.

Borgen, P.

1992   'Philo and the Jews in Alexandria', in P. Bilde et al. (eds.) *Ethnicity in Hellenistic Egypt*, Aarhus, 122–38.

Botte, B.

1954   'La vie de Moise par Philon', *Cahiers Sioniens* 8, 55–62.

Bowman, A.K.

1986   *Egypt after the Pharaohs, 332 BC–AD 642*, London.

Burridge, R.

1992   *What are the Gospels? A comparison with Graeco-Roman biography*, Cambridge.

Cox, P.

1983   *Biography in late Antiquity. A quest for the holy man*, Berkeley.

Dihle, A.

1970   *Studien zur griechischen Biographie*, 2nd edn, Göttingen.

Dillon, J.

1996   *The Middle Platonists 80 BC to AD 220*, revised edn, London.

Edwards, M.J. and Swain, S.

1997   *Portraits: Biographical representation in the Greek and Latin literature of the Roman Empire*, Oxford.

Fraser, P.M.

1972   *Ptolemaic Alexandria*, 2 vols., Oxford.

Goodenough, E.R.
  1933   'Philo's exposition of the law and his *de vita Moesis*', *HTR* 27, 109–25.
  1962   *An introduction to Philo Judaeus*, 2nd edn, Oxford.
Guelich, R.
  1983   'The Gospel genre', in P. Stuhlmacher (ed.) *Das Evangelium und die Evangelien*, Tübingen, 183–219.
Haas, C.
  1997   *Alexandria in Late Antiquity. Topography and social conflict*, Baltimore.
Hadas, M. and Smith, M.
  1965   *Heroes and gods: Spiritual biographies in antiquity*, London.
Hägg, T. and Rousseau, P. (eds.)
  2000   *Greek biography and panegyric in Late Antiquity*, Berkeley.
Holladay, C.H.
  1977   *Theios aner in Hellenistic Judaism: A critique of the use of this category in New Testament christology*, Scholars Press.
Leo, F.
  1901   *Die griechisch-römische Biographie nach ihrer literarischer Form*, Leipzig.
Mack, B.L.
  1984   'Philo Judaeus and exegetical traditions in Alexandria', *ANRW* II, 21.1, Berlin and New York, 227–71.
Momigliano, A.
  1993   *The development of Greek biography*, expanded edn, Cambridge, Mass.
Nikiprowetsky, N.
  1977   *Le commentaire de l'Ecriture chez Philon d'Alexandrie*, Leiden.
Pelling, C.B.R.
  1980   'Plutarch's adaptation of his source material', *JHS* 20, 127–40.
Priessnig, A.
  1929   'Die literarische Form der Patriarchbiographien des Philo von Alexandrien', *Monatsschrift für Geschichte und Wissenschaft des Judentums* 73, 143–55.
Sandmel, S.
  1979   *Philo of Alexandria. An introduction*, Oxford and New York.
  1984   'Philo Judaeus: an introduction to the man, his writings and his significance', *ANRW* II, 21.1, Berlin and New York, 3–46.
Schürer, E.
  1987   *The history of the Jewish people in the age of Jesus Christ*. Rev. and ed. by G. Vermes, F. Millar et al., vol. III.2, Edinburgh.
Smith, M.
  1971   'Prolegomena to a discussion of aretologies, divine men, the Gospels and Jesus', *JBL* 90, 174–99.
Stanton, G.N.
  1974   *Jesus of Nazareth in New Testament preaching*, Cambridge.
Stuart, D.R.
  1928   *Epochs of Greek and Roman biography*, Berkeley.
Talbert, C.H.
  1978   *What is Gospel? The genre of the canonical Gospels*, London.
Williamson, R.
  1989   *Jews in the Hellenistic world: Philo*, Cambridge.

9

PORTRAIT OF THE SOPHIST AS A YOUNG MAN

Ewen Bowie

You might easily think that my title had been chosen merely to offer homage to the literary eminence of the city where the most congenial conference that gave rise to this paper took place. Location indeed has something to do with it, but I hope to show that the phrase has some point as a description of Philostratus' *Lives of the Sophists*. Of course the *Lives* are neither restricted to, nor even preponderantly focused upon, the youth of their subjects, unlike one or two ancient works that were so focused because they aimed at filling in a period in an individual's biography that had not already been adequately treated.[1] Rather they are 'true' biographies, taking the subject's life from cradle to grave. But when we compare them with other examples of the genre – those of Nepos, Plutarch, Suetonius, Diogenes Laertius or the *Augustan History* – we find, I think, that Philostratus' subjects are rendered in an agonistic stance constructed in part from their presentation as very emotional figures, acting and reacting in a way more characteristic of youthful immaturity than of adults who might be justifiably content to have achieved a high rank in their society.

That of course may be a contentment hard to acquire in the very competitive society constituted by Greek city elites.[2] For some players, as Plutarch observed in his essay *On Contentment*,[3] one distinction simply whets the appetite for something higher: or, as Philostratus says, trying to excuse the rivalry of Polemo and Favorinus, 'human nature regards ambition as immune to age'.[4] But while some of the strong emotions manifested by sophists can plausibly be related to their highly competitive careers and environment, not all can: anger and envy are predictable responses from a φιλότιμος, grief and lust are surely not, or at least not straightforwardly.[5] I shall shortly consider Philostratus' presentation of each. First, however, whether as a reminder or as more, I offer a very brief sketch of the author Philostratus and his work *Lives of the Sophists*.[6]

Philostratus, usually called the Second, according to the Suda the son of a Verus, was born in an Athenian family with property on Lemnos, an island known to him in his childhood:[7] the date was probably *c.* AD 170.[8] A pupil of

Proclus of Naucratis[9] and perhaps of Damianus of Ephesus, Hippodromus of Thessaly and Antipater of Hierapolis, he had a career like that of many of his subjects in *Lives of the Sophists*. The Suda entry credits him with declamations (μελέται) and a sophistic career in Athens and Rome. In Athens he probably also held high office: if he is the L. Flavius Philostratus of Steiria attested in three inscriptions[10] he was 'hoplite general' (στρατηγὸς ἐπὶ τῶν ὅπλων, a magistrate especially involved with food supplies) between AD 200/201 and AD 210/211,[11] and was also one of the *prytaneis* of the *phyle* Pandionis.[12] He is also probably the sophist Flavius Philostratus honoured by Athens with a statue at Olympia.[13] After moving his sophistic activities to Rome (*c*. AD 203–5) Philostratus was introduced (perhaps before the end of AD 207)[14] to the court of Septimius Severus and Julia Domna and to Julia Domna's coterie of mathematicians and philosophers.[15] He was present when (late in AD 212 or early in AD 213) the sophist Heliodorus 'the Arab' pleaded before Caracalla in Gaul,[16] and perhaps at the imperial visit to Tyana and Antioch in AD 215.[17] An inscription for a statue at Erythrae honouring L. Flavius Capitolinus, son of the sophist Flavius Philostratus,[18] shows that the wife of Philostratus was Aurelia Melitine, that another son and further relatives were senators, and probably that the family owned land at Erythrae.[19]

The *Lives of the Sophists* is one of two biographical works on which at times Philostratus may well have been working simultaneously. The other is 'The story of Apollonius of Tyana' (τὰ ἐς τὸν Ἀπολλώνιον Τυανέα) in eight books, finished after Julia Domna's death in AD 217 (since despite the fact that she commissioned it Philostratus does not dedicate it to her, and since she is referred to by verbs in imperfect tenses);[20] it seems also to have been finished before his completion of *Lives of the Sophists* in AD 237/8, since this work cross-refers to the *Apollonius*.

For the *Apollonius* Philostratus used local oral traditions in cities visited by Apollonius, a four-book work by Moeragenes written early in the second century, a work on Apollonius' youth in Cilicia by Maximus of Aegeae, and a collection of letters, some of which were already attributed to Apollonius in Hadrian's reign.[21] He may also have drawn on two other works attributed to Apollonius: 'On sacrifices' (περὶ θυσιῶν) and 'On astrology' (περὶ μαντείας ἀστέρων).[22] Philostratus played down the role of Apollonius as a magician (μάγος) and stressed his links with the divine in his capacity as a Pythagorean sage who traversed the Roman empire (and even reached Parthia, India and Ethiopia), admonishing individuals and cities, reviving traditional Greek cults and resisting oppression by the 'tyrants' Nero and Domitian. Philostratus presents him as being accompanied by a Platonic interlocutor-figure, Damis of Nineveh, probably invented to be a foil to Apollonius and to allow citation of his 'diaries' to give Philostratus' account more authority than its predecessors. The eight-book structure of the work on Apollonius is among several features that bring it closer to romance than biography.

The *Lives of the Sophists* (βίοι σοφιστῶν) has a very different flavour. Dedicated to Gordian I when proconsul of Africa in AD 237/8,[23] its subject is more central to contemporary Greek society and it is more typical of Greek writing of the period in its version of hellenic cultural identity. Its two books comprise 59 biographies: the majority of these (41, to be precise) are of prominent Greek sophists of the imperial period, starting with Nicetes of Smyrna under Nero and continuing down to Philostratus' own coevals, a sequence for which he coined the enduring term 'New' or 'Second sophistic': the former term was to be ephemeral, the latter to endure, to be revived in the nineteenth century and to be widely and often very loosely applied (sometimes to phenomena quite unrelated to Philostratus' sophists) in the twentieth.[24] The lives of these 'new' sophists, dominated by the much longer accounts of Polemo and Herodes at the end of book 1 and the beginning of book 2 respectively (1.25, 2.1), are preceded by eight lives of philosophers whose presentation also earned them the title sophist (1.1–8), ending with Dio of Prusa and Favorinus, then ten lives of the classical sophists (from Gorgias to Aeschines, 1.9–18) whose authority Philostratus harnesses for his 'Second sophistic'. Philostratus used both his subjects' published works (chiefly declamations) and oral tradition gathered from sophists he himself had heard. His reliability has been questioned,[25] but controls often support his version,[26] and *Lives of the Sophists* is an invaluable, albeit tendentious, Greek cultural history of the period.

Such was Philostratus, such are his *Lives*. Let me now return to the exploration of lust, anger and grief.

Lust

The sophists as portrayed by Philostratus fall unambiguously into the category of sexually active males. Philostratus seems to treat Dionysius of Miletus as exceptional when he notes with praise that, despite his extensive travels, he was never accused of sexual misdemeanours or empty pretentions.[27] Isaeus the Syrian is also commended for abandoning the life of pleasure when he became an adult. He had given his teens over to pleasure, for he easily succumbed to food and drink, wore see-through garments, had frequent affairs and took no steps to disguise himself when painting the town red. But when he reached adulthood he became a new man in many respects: these included giving up sex (τὸ ἐρᾶν μέθηκεν) and when a colleague asked him if he fancied a certain woman (εἰ ἡ δεῖνα αὐτῷ καλὴ φαίνοιτο) he replied (of course in a learnedly allusive way) 'I've stopped having eye trouble' (πέπαυμαι ὀφθαλμιῶν).[28]

By contrast Scopelianus of Clazomenae acquired a common-law wife after his wife's death, and his son tried to dissuade him from this course of action, resulting in her bringing a Potiphar's wife charge against this son. Her plot against the son involved the household meat-chef, who persuaded Scopelianus that his son was trying to poison him and managed to have himself appointed heir. Philostratus comments that this deception should not surprise us, since he ingratiated himself with an old man who was in love and was perhaps going off the rails both because of his age and because of τὸ ἐρᾶν itself.[29] Even Favorinus of Arelate was so over-sexed (θερμὸς οὕτω τὰ ἐρωτικὰ) that, notoriously, he was accused of adultery with the wife of a consul despite his claimed physical condition as a eunuch,[30] and the sexual misconduct of Apollonius of Naucratis (ὄντι δὲ αὐτῷ κακῷ τὰ ἐρωτικὰ) led to the birth of a son out of wedlock.[31]

Anger

Timocrates of Heracleia, the Stoic from whom Philostratus says Polemo drew his qualities of τὸ μεγαλόγνωμον τοῦτο καὶ φρονηματῶδες, was himself immoderately irascible (ἐπιχολώτερος τοῦ ξυμμέτρου) so that when he was lecturing his beard and the hair on his head would stand up as does that of lions when they charge.[32] The comparison to a charging lion is one that begins with the *Iliad*, and its use in a third-century text retains the colour that its ancestry gave it.[33]

There is nothing negative in this presentation by Philostratus of Timocrates' irascibility. His picture of Philagrus of Cilicia is perhaps more ambivalent. At the opening of the *Life* Philostratus characterizes him as the 'hottest and most irascible of sophists' (σοφιστῶν...θερμότατος καὶ ἐπιχολώτατος) to the point where he once cuffed a member of his audience who was snoozing.[34] This is more extreme than the anger (χολή)[35] that Philostratus says was openly shown by Aristides when his performances were not applauded,[36] and sets the scene for a sequence of anecdotes illustrating Philagrus' eristic behaviour: he was excellent at managing arguments, but not at managing his anger in Athens,[37] picking a quarrel with Herodes. Because there is no saloon bar for him to walk into aggressively it is in the Ceramicus that he has to pick his quarrel with Amphicles, a pupil of Herodes. On one occasion he thought himself so effectively into his declamatory part – the perhaps anachronistic situation of Aristogeiton accusing Demosthenes of Medism and Aeschines of Φιλιππισμός – that his capacity to speak was extinguished by his anger.[38] Clearly this is going too far even for Philostratus, and in his conclusion he notes that Philagrus was not unaware of his foul temper[39] and made it a ground for not bringing up a family.

Antiochus of Aegeae also had a capacity for anger which he recognized and offered as a reason for abstaining from local politics, telling his fellow citizens 'It is not you but myself that I fear'.[40] This may have been disingenuous (as the career of Aristides shows, a local magnate might sometimes work hard to evade expensive public offices) but at least the claim must have been plausible.

Such anger can lead to vituperation, λοιδορία, of which Philostratus clearly does not approve: 'for vituperation is self-indulgent, and even if it is true, it does not release from blame the man who speaks on such matters.'[41] We may note too that Philostratus classes criticism by the δῆμος of its political leaders as λοιδορία.[42] Thus he commends Scopelianus of Clazomenae for his dismissal of 'those who were vituperative in their speeches and thought they were making a display of their anger';[43] and his report of verbal attacks, λοιδορίαι, on Herodes by the Cynic Peregrinus comes out very much in favour of the witty and self-controlled retort of Herodes.[44] Likewise Hadrianus of Tyre is praised for dismissing as flea-bites the λοιδορίαι of Chrestus and of one of his fans who 'was fond of vituperation and would bark.'[45] Then again Hippodromus of Larissa is commended for his oblique and irenic response to a coarse attack by Proclus of Naucratis that included him in its λοιδορησμοῖς. Philostratus gets the unusual word from Aristophanes' *Frogs*.[46]

Grief

For Philostratus different reactions to pain or to distress can be equally commendable. Polemo jokes about the pain caused by his serious arthritis: 'I need to eat, but I have no hands; I need to walk, but I have no feet; but when I need to feel pain, then I have both feet and hands.'[47] By contrast Euodianus, also of Smyrna, shows extreme restraint at his son's death, uttering nothing feminine or ignoble, but simply repeating ὦ τέκνον three times at his funeral.[48]

Philostratus has several pages on Herodes' manifestation of grief. When his wife Regilla died, around AD 160 or 161, in the eighth month of a pregnancy, an accusation was brought by her brother that his freedman Alcimedon had struck her on Herodes' orders and that this had caused her death. Herodes' defence was assisted, Philostratus claims, by his extreme manifestations of grief:[49] building a theatre in her memory,[50] postponing his consideration for a second consulate,[51] and redecorating his house in black, using amongst others the black marble from Lesbos.[52] Although Herodes' grief for the death of his daughter Athenais was assuaged by the honours decreed to her by Athens, when his other daughter Elpinice died he 'lay on the floor, beating the ground and yelling "Daughter, what shall I consecrate to you? What shall I bury with you?"'[53] In having Herodes throw himself on the ground Philostratus recalls the behaviour of Achilles and Priam in the *Iliad* when they hear of the deaths of Patroclus and Hector.[54]

On one spectacular and well-known occasion, again in the *Life* of Herodes, anger and grief worked together. Herodes Atticus had been called to the emperor's court at Sirmium to defend himself against charges brought by his political enemies in Athens. His retinue included the twin daughters of one of his freedmen, nubile and remarkable for their beauty, whom Herodes had brought up and had employed to serve drinks and short-eats at his parties.[55] These twins were killed by a lightning-strike on the tower where they were sleeping, and when Herodes entered the court the disaster had made him suicidal.[56] In consequence, says Philostratus, he openly attacked the emperor Marcus, not resorting to allusive rhetoric to manage his anger.[57] Although the biographer goes on to commend Marcus for his control of his own anger,[58] and although he seems to judge Herodes' anger as potentially self-destructive, the whole incident is told in a way that makes it add to, rather than detract from, our image of Herodes' greatness.

Taken together, these strongly felt and ostentatiously displayed emotions contribute to an impression of individuals who are larger than life and who are conscious of the gap that divides them from ordinary mortals, though they must also be aware of limits. If they overestimate themselves they can be criticized as 'swollen with pride' or susceptible to uppityness.[59] Philostratus offers the anecdote of Polemo in AD 134/5 throwing the governor of Asia out of his house – this was the future emperor Pius – as an illustration of his being arrogant, ὑπέρφρων. He wraps up Polemo's conduct in a γνώμη: 'For in fact Polemo was so arrogant that he had exchanges with cities from a stance of superiority, with rulers from the stance of one not inferior, and with the gods from the stance of an equal.'[60] A few lines later this quality is termed τὸ μεγαλόγνωμον τοῦτο καὶ φρονηματῶδες, 'this grandeur of spirit and proud self-esteem.' The word φρονηματώδης seems to be a recent coinage, perhaps even by Philostratus himself, who had earlier used it in the *Heroicus* (19.3 = p. 20.9 De Lannoy) of Hector as represented in his statue at Ilion.[61] The term τὸ μεγαλόγνωμον is again one used elsewhere by Philostratus, in *Letter* 73 (addressed to Julia Domna), where he links it with 'haughtiness' (τὴν ὄφρυν) as a literary quality of Critias and Thucydides, but it has Xenophontic ancestry. The literary lineage of ὑπέρφρων is telling; it is used twice in Aeschylus' *Seven against Thebes*, first of the symbol on Tydeus' shield (ὑπέρφρον σῆμα, 387), then in Eteocles' praise of his own champion as στυγοῦνθ' ὑπέρφρονας λόγους (410). Next we (and perhaps too Philostratus) can find it in Sophocles' *Ajax*, where Agamemnon uses it to characterize Teucer's praise of his brother Ajax: ποίου κέκραγας ἀνδρὸς ὧδ' ὑπέρφρονα (1236).[62] The contexts and the word with which it linked (τὴν ὄφρυν) show that τὸ μεγαλόγνωμον is a more self-regarding quality than μεγαλοψυχία and μεγαλοφροσύνη, attributes that Philostratus predicates exclusively of Atticus, the father of Herodes, in respect of his generosity with his huge fortune:[63] we are left to imagine what this quality would have been if father Atticus had himself been a distinguished sophist.[64]

One physiological manifestation of a speaker's sense of importance is his manner of delivery. Philostratus describes vigorous speaking with the verb πνεῖν. Thus when Dio restored order among the Danube legions he 'threw himself vigorously into a denunciation of the tyrant (i.e. Domitian)';[65] although Scopelianus declaimed with distinction (ἐπιφανῶς), in the courts he had a more vigorous delivery;[66] when Lollianus purported to oppose Athenian plans to sell the islands he 'breathed' the phrases 'Abolish, Poseidon, your favour to Delos; allow her, now that she is being sold, to escape';[67] Philostratus' epitaphic notice for Apollonius of Athens includes the phrase 'after also speaking with great vigour before the Athenian people'.[68] The noun 'breath' (πνεῦμα) can sometimes mean little more than 'eloquence',[69] and can even be qualified;[70] but otherwise, like the verb, it relates to vigorous delivery: just as Homer, in Hippodromus' phrase, was the voice (φωνή) of the sophists, so too was the famously vehement Archilochus their πνεῦμα.[71] Gorgias is credited with introducing it into rhetoric.[72] In the case of Ptolemaeus of Naucratis it is coupled with τὸν ῥοῖζον,[73] a term also used of Hadrianus of Tyre and (by implication) Polemo.[74] The lack of τὸ πνεῦμα or of attention to it is a weakness in Apollonius of Naucratis and Aspasius of Ravenna.[75] It is a corollary of such vigour that delivery is often excited: especially striking is Philostratus' claim that Polemo would stamp his feet at key points in his argument 'no less than the horse in Homer'.[76]

Youthfulness

These sophists of course display their vigour and πνεῦμα at all stages of their career. But their profession keeps them in continued contact with the young, and in some cases Philostratus suggests that to some extent they protract their youth. When Hadrianus of Tyre was appointed to the imperial chair of rhetoric in Athens, shortly before AD 176, he made himself vastly popular by joining his pupils in entertainments, drinking, hunting and attending festivals, sharing their various youthful pursuits.[77] The first and distinguished period of Aspasius' tenure of the chair at Rome was when he was young.[78] Even when a sophist's body ages, his mind can remain young, as in the case of Philostratus' own teacher Damianus: 'I saw a man who resembled Sophocles' horse,[79] for although he seemed sluggish on account of his age he would recover a youthful energy in our tutorials.'[80] In this respect Damianus resembles the sophistic culture-hero Gorgias, of whom Philostratus claims that at his death at the age of 108 it was said that his body had not been subverted by age, but he lived out his life in good shape and with the senses of a young man.[81] Occasionally a sophist dies in his literal prime, deprived of the chance to acquire further fame, like Athenodorus of Aenus.[82] One sophist, the handsome Alexander of Seleuceia, was rumoured to be resorting to artificial means to maintain his youthful appearance,[83] a habit which laid him open to being got at: when he was on an embassy to the emperor, probably Pius, and thought the emperor was not paying proper attention, he said loudly 'Pay attention, Caesar'. Pius' reply was swift; 'I am paying attention and know who you are: you are the man who shapes his hair and polishes his teeth and files his nails and is always fragrant with perfume.'[84] Others kept themselves trim by going to the gym: Rufus of Perinthus was said to toughen his body by gymnastic training, following a strict diet and putting his body through exercises like athletes.[85]

What should we conclude from this apparent emphasis in Philostratus' presentation? It might be argued that it is not sufficiently different from what we find, for example, in Plutarch for it to deserve to be considered anything more than an insignificant variation. To meet that argument would require a confrontation of Philostratean with Plutarchan passages for which there is no space here. I must move on with the provisional hypothesis that there is indeed something different in Philostratus. I shall give my interpretation briefly, and hope it may provoke debate.

Two sets of data are relevant. To one I have alluded from time to time – the use of language that recalls Homer and (less often) tragedy. I suggest that one component of Philostratus' presentation of these 41 members of the Greek elite who over almost two centuries demonstrated their natural and acquired skills in competition and sometimes conflict with each other is a degree of assimilation to the heroes of Homeric epic, particularly to those of the *Iliad*. These heroes provided Greeks with their earliest and in most eyes most formative models of grand displays of lust, grief and anger, as well, of course, as their earliest examples of persuasive rhetoric. And with the exception of Nestor, Phoenix and Priam the *Iliad*'s heroes are all young men.

That observation leads to the second set of data: the constituents of the *Heroicus*. The *Heroicus*, by the same Philostratus, is a dialogue in which an unnamed Phoenician sailor learns from a vintner in the Thracian Chersonese of the latter's encounter with the ghosts of heroes of the Trojan war. It is a variant on the popular game of 'correcting' Homer and other archaic poets.[86] Reference to the second Olympic victory of (T. Aurelius) Helix puts the *Heroicus* no earlier than AD 213[87] and perhaps after AD 217,[88] but not, I should guess, long after either date. The major part of the dialogue is a long sequence of portraits of heroes both Greek and Trojan – Hector, Palamedes, Achilles, Antilochus, Patroclus, Telephus, Nestor, Diomedes, Sthenelus, Philoctetes, the Atreidae, Idomeneus, Locrian Ajax, again Palamedes,

Odysseus, Ajax, again Hector, Aeneas, Sarpedon, Paris, Euphorbus – then back to Achilles. The *Heroicus* shows Philostratus using what I am tempted to call the 'portrait gallery format' in a work probably composed some 20 years before the completion of the *Lives*. He uses it again, in literal gallery format, in the *Imagines*, in my view a work certainly by our Philostratus, but impossible to date.

The Homerizing of the *Heroicus* is very much 'in your face'. The Homerizing of the *Lives* is subtler, and to see the extent to which it operates some knowledge of the *Heroicus* helps. Once seen, it can explain one or two other puzzles. Why two books? – unusually so advertised by Philostratus in his preface. Because *Iliad* and *Odyssey* together make two books (a fact fundamental to ancient perceptions of Homer, cf. the Archelaus relief in the British Museum). Why have two outstanding sophists each given a disproportionately long *Life*, one at the end of Book 1, one at the start of Book 2, the pair flanked by a cohort of 38 others? I would suggest the model of Achilles and Hector in the *Iliad*.

Notes

[1] As perhaps the work of Maximus of Aegeae on Apollonius of Tyana, cf. Philostr. *VA* 1.3 claiming that it comprised πάντα concerning Apollonius' time in Aegeae, with Bowie 1978, 1684–5.

[2] For an excellent recent discussion cf. Schmitz 1997, esp. 97–135.

[3] Plut. *De Tranquillitate Animi* 10 = *Mor.* 470b–c.

[4] τῆς ἀνθρωπείας φύσεως τὸ φιλότιμον ἀγήρων ἡγουμένης, *VS* 1.8.491, with ἀγήρων perhaps echoing Sarpedon's expression of *philotimia* at *Il.* 12.323...εἰ μὲν γὰρ πόλεμον περὶ τόνδε φυγόντε αἰεὶ δὴ μέλλοιμεν ἀγήρω τ' ἀθανάτω τε ἔσσεσθ', οὔτε κεν αὐτὸς ἐνὶ πρώτοισι μαχοίμην οὔτε κε σὲ στέλλοιμι μάχην ἐς κυδιάνειραν. For the self-constructions of Polemo and Favorinus see esp. Gleason 1995, and for an exploration of that of Polemo, Campanile 1994.

[5] There is of course a clear link between the real or seeming exercise of power and the pursuit and availability of objects of lust, but I cannot pursue that topic here.

[6] For the biographies of the Philostrati and the problems of attributing transmitted and attested works to each see especially Münscher 1907, Anderson 1986, Flinterman 1995, Billault 2000.

[7] *VA* 6.27, cf. *VS*. 1.21.515–16.

[8] Cf. Avotins 1978a.

[9] *VS* 2.21.602.

[10] Traill 1971, nos 13 and 14, *IG* 2–3² 1803, cf. Traill 1971, 323–5.

[11] Follet 1976, 101–2.

[12] Traill 1982, 231–3, no. 34.

[13] *Syll.*³ 878.

[14] For the chronology cf. Flinterman 1995, 19–22.

[15] Philostr. *VA* 1.3.

16 Philostr. *VS* 2.32.625–6.

17 Cassius Dio 77.18.4.

18 *I Erythrae* 63 = *Syll.*³ 879.

19 Cf. Philostr. *Epist* 45.

20 Philostr. *VA* 1.3.

21 Philostr. *VA* 1.2, 7.35, 8.20.

22 Philostr. *VA* 3.41, cf. 4.19.

23 Philostr. *VS* pref. 480 with Avotins 1978b, 242–7.

24 For pertinent observations see Whitmarsh 2001, 41–5.

25 Jones 1974.

26 Swain 1991.

27 οὔτε ἐρωτικήν ποτε αἰτίαν ἔλαβεν οὔτε ἀλαζόνα, *VS* 1.22.524.

28 *VS* 1.20.513: the allusion is to the remark of Sophocles as reported in Plato, *Republic* 329c.

29 ἐπεὶ πρεσβύτην ἐρῶντα ἔθελξεν ἴσως που καὶ παραπαίοντα ὑπὸ ἡλικίας καὶ αὐτοῦ τοῦ ἐρᾶν, *VS* 1.21.517.

30 *VS* 1.8.489.

31 ἐξ ἀδίκων γάμων, *VS* 2.19.599.

32 ὡς ὑπανίστασθαι αὐτῷ διαλεγομένῳ τήν τε γενειάδα καὶ τὰς ἐν τῇ κεφαλῇ χαίτας, ὥσπερ τῶν λεόντων ἐν ταῖς ὁρμαῖς, *VS* 2.25.536.

33 Pollux of Naucratis also associated anger with lions in the extract from one of his διαλέξεις cited at *VS* 2.12.593 (talking of Proteus): καὶ ἐς λέοντα θυμοῦται καὶ ἐς σῦν ὅρμαι.

34 λέγεται γὰρ δὴ νυστάζοντά ποτε ἀκροατὴν καὶ ἐπὶ κόρρης πλῆξαι, *VS* 2.8.578.

35 χολή can be a quality of delivery rather than of the deliverer, cf. (of Aristocles of Pergamum) χολή τε γὰρ ἄπεστι τοῦ λόγου καὶ ὁρμαὶ πρὸς βραχύ, *VS* 2.3.568. It is related to θυμός *VS* 1.17.504, 1.21.519.

36 οὔτε ἐκράτει χολῆς ἐπὶ τοὺς μὴ ξὺν ἐπαίνῳ ἀκρωμένους, *VS* 2.9.582.

37 οὐ μετεχειρίσατο Ἀθήνησιν εὖ τὴν ἑαυτοῦ χολήν, *VS* 2.8.578.

38 ἐσβέσθη τὸ φθέγμα ὑπὸ τῆς χολῆς *VS* 2.8.580.

39 τὸ ἐν αὐτῷ δύστροπον, *VS* 2.8.581.

40 οὐχ ὑμᾶς, εἶπεν, ἀλλ' ἐμαυτὸν δέδοικα, εἰδώς που τὴν ἑαυτοῦ χολὴν ἄκρατον καὶ οὐ καθεκτὴν οὖσαν, *VS* 2.4.568.

41 ἀσελγὴς γὰρ ἡ λοιδορία, κἂν ἀληθὴς τύχῃ, οὐκ ἀφίησιν αἰσχύνης οὐδὲ τὸν ὑπὲρ τούτων εἰπόντα, *VS* 1.8.491.

42 *VS* 1.19.511.

43 τοὺς δὲ λοιδορουμένους ἐν τοῖς λόγοις καὶ θυμοῦ τινα ἐπίδειξιν ἡγουμένους ποιεῖσθαι γραίδια ἐκάλει μεθύοντα καὶ λυττῶντα, *VS* 1.21.519.

44 ἔστω, ἔφη, κακῶς με ἀγορεύεις, πρὸς τί καὶ οὕτως, *VS* 2.1.563.

45 The unnamed Athenian...φιλολοιδόρως εἶχε καὶ ὑλακτεῖ, and Hadrianus put up with it, δήγματα κόρεων τὰς τοιούτων λοιδορίας καλῶν, *VS* 2.10.587–8.

46 *VS* 2.27.617, Aristophanes *Frogs* 758.

47 δεῖ ἐσθίειν, χεῖρας οὐκ ἔχω· δεῖ βαδίζειν, πόδες οὐκ εἰσί μοι· δεῖ ἀλγεῖν, τότε καὶ πόδες εἰσί μοι καὶ χεῖρες, *VS* 1.25.543.

48 *VS* 2.16.596.

49 τὸ ὑπερπενθεῖν ἀποθανοῦσαν, 2.1.556.

50 The Odeion at Athens, cf. Paus. 7.20.6.

[51] *PIR* thinks that what is referred to was more probably the *sortitio* for the proconsulate of Asia or Africa, cf. Ameling 1983, ii.7–9.

[52] *VS* 2.1.556.

[53] τί σοι, θύγατερ, καθαγίσω; τί σοι ξυνθάψω; *VS* 2.1.558.

[54] *Iliad* 18.22–7, 22.414–15.

[55] δίδυμοι κόραι πρὸς ἀκμῇ γάμων θαυμαζόμεναι ἐπὶ τῷ εἴδει, ἃς ἐκνηπιώσας Ἡρώδης οἰνοχόους ἑαυτῷ καὶ ὀψοποιοὺς ἐπεποίητο θυγάτρια ἐπονομάζων καὶ ὧδε ἀσπαζόμενος, *VS* 2.1.560.

[56] ὑπὸ τούτου δὴ τοῦ πάθους ἔκφρων ὁ Ἡρώδης ἐγένετο καὶ παρῆλθεν ἐς τὸ βασίλειον δικαστήριον οὔτε ἔννους καὶ θανάτου ἐρῶν, *VS* 2.1.560.

[57] οὐδὲ σχηματίσας τὸν λόγον, ὡς εἰκὸς ἦν ἄνδρα γεγυμνασμένον τῆς τοιᾶσδε ἰδέας, μεταχειρίσασθαι τὴν ἑαυτοῦ χολήν, *VS* 2.1.561. For λόγοι ἐσχηματισμένοι cf. Russell 1983, 36 with n. 94, Rutherford 1998, 116–17.

[58] Philostratus also commends monarchs for control of anger in the context of Hadrian's relations with Favorinus, βασιλεὺς δὲ κρείττων, ὅτε χώσεται ἀνδρὶ χέρηι (*Iliad* 1.80) ἢν ὀργῆς κρατῇ, καὶ θυμὸς δὲ μέγας ἐστὶ διοτρεφέων βασιλήων ἢν λογισμῷ κλάζηται, *VS* 1.7.489. Note too that Marcus' own grief for Faustina is referred to by the lower-key term ὀλοφυράμενος, *VS* 2.1.562.

[59] τετυφωμένον *VS* 2.11.592, ἀγερωχία, *VS* 1.16.501 (of Thessalians), 1.25.531 (of Smyrniotes), 2.11.591 (of the sophist Chrestus of Byzantium, who successfully controls his), 2.16.596 (of the Dionysiac *technitae*).

[60] ὑπέρφρων γὰρ δὴ οὕτω τι ὁ Πολέμων, ὡς πόλεσι μὲν ἀπὸ τοῦ προὔχοντος, δυνάσταις δὲ ἀπὸ τοῦ μὴ ὑφειμένου, θεοῖς δὲ ἀπὸ τοῦ ἴσου διαλέγεσθαι, *VS* 1.25.535.

[61] καὶ γὰρ φρονηματώδης δοκεῖ καὶ γοργὸν καὶ φαιδρόν, Philostr. *Heroicus* 19.3 = p. 20.9 De Lannoy.

[62] That it is used eight times by Plutarch, once by Josephus, once by Longinus, and twice by Arrian shows that it had found a firm place in imperial Greek prose before Philostratus. But Philostratus is likely to have remained sensitive to its tragic roots.

[63] *VS* 2.1 548, 549.

[64] For the possibility that he was at least a *rhetor* and is introduced by Plutarch into his *Quaestiones Convivales* 8.4 and 9.14 cf. Bowie 2002, 42–3.

[65] ἐπὶ μὲν τὴν κατηγορίαν τοῦ τυράννου πολὺς ἔπνευσεν, *VS* 1.7.488.

[66] πολλῷ δὲ μεῖζον ἐν τοῖς δικαστηρίοις πνεύσαντα, *VS* 1.21.516.

[67] ὧδε ἔπνευσεν· λῦσον, ὦ Πόσειδον, τὴν ἐπὶ Δήλῳ χάριν, συγχώρησον αὐτῷ πωλουμένῳ φυγεῖν, *VS* 1.23.527.

[68] πολὺς καὶ ἐν τῷ Ἀθηναίων δήμῳ πνεύσας, *VS* 2.20.602.

[69] e.g. of Critias, *VS* 1.16.503, and note τοῦ φωνητικοῦ πνεύματος of the breath needed to make sounds, 2.8.580.

[70] Thus Herodes had τὸ πνεῦμα οὐ σφοδρόν, *VS* 2.1.564.

[71] τὸν δὲ Ἀρχίλοχον πνεῦμα, *VS* 2.27.620.

[72] ὁρμῆς τε γὰρ τοῖς σοφισταῖς ἦρξε καὶ παραδοξολογίας καὶ πνεύματος καὶ τοῦ μεγάλα μεγάλως ἑρμηνεύειν, *VS* 1.9.492.

[73] τὸν γὰρ ῥοῖζον καὶ τὸ πνεῦμα, *VS* 2.15.595.

[74] *VS* 2.10.589.

[75] *VS* 2.19.599, 33.627.

[76] καὶ κροαίνειν ἐν τοῖς τῶν ὑποθέσεων χωρίοις οὐδὲν ἧττον τοῦ Ὁμηρικοῦ ἵππου (i.e. *Iliad* 6.507) *VS* 1.25.537.

Ewen Bowie

[77] ὑπεποιεῖτο δὲ αὐτοὺς παιδιαῖς καὶ πότοις καὶ θήραις καὶ κοινωνίᾳ πανηγύρεων Ἑλληνικῶν, ἄλλα ἄλλῳ ξυννεάζων, *VS* 2.10.58).

[78] νεάζων ἔτι εὐδοκιμώτατος, *VS* 2.33.627.

[79] Sophocles, *Electra* 25 (Orestes addressing his old *paidagogos*).

[80] εἶδον ἄνδρα παραπλήσιον Σοφοκλείῳ ἵππῳ, νωθρὸς γὰρ ὑφ᾽ ἡλικίας δοκῶν νεάζουσαν ὁρμὴν ἐν ταῖς σπουδαῖς ἀνεκτᾶτο, *VS* 2.24.606.

[81] λέγεται...μὴ καταλυθῆναι τὸ σῶμα ὑπὸ τοῦ γήρως, ἀλλ᾽ ἄρτιος καταβιῶναι καὶ τὰς αἰσθήσεις ἥβων, *VS* 1.9.494.

[82] ἐτελεύτα ἥβων ἔτι ἀφαιρεθεὶς ὑπὸ τῆς τύχης τὸ καὶ πρόσω ἐλάσαι δόξης, *VS* 1.9.494.

[83] διαβολαὶ δὲ ἐπ᾽ αὐτὸν ἐφοίτησαν, ὡς νεότητα ἐπιποιοῦντα τῷ εἴδει, *VS* 2.5.570.

[84] πρόσεχέ μοι, Καῖσαρ...προσέχω, ἔφη, καὶ ξυνίημί σου· σὺ γάρ, ἔφη, ὁ τὴν κόμην ἀσκῶν καὶ τοὺς ὀδόντας λαμπρύνων καὶ τοὺς ὄνυχας ξέων καὶ τοῦ μύρου ἀεὶ πνέων, *VS* 2.5.571.

[85] ἐλέγετο δὲ καὶ γυμναστικὴ κρατύνειν τὸ σῶμα ἀναγκοφαγῶν ἀεὶ καὶ διαπονῶν αὐτὸ παραπλησίως τοῖς ἀγωνιζομένοις, *VS* 2.17.598.

[86] Cf. Dio of Prusa, *Oration* 11, and Dictys of Crete.

[87] Münscher 1907, 497–8, 553–4.

[88] Jüthner 1909, 87–9.

Bibliography

Ameling, W.
1983   *Herodes Atticus.* Subsidia Epigraphica 11, 2 vols., Hildesheim, Zürich and New York.

Anderson, G.
1986   *Philostratus*, London, Sydney and Dover, N.H.
1993   *The Second Sophistic*, London and New York.

Avotins, I.
1978a   'The year of the birth of the Lemnian Philostratus', *Antiquité Classique* 47, 538–9.
1978b   'The date and recipient of the *Vitae Sophistarum* of Philostratus', *Hermes* 106, 242–7.

Billault, A.
2000   *L'Univers de Philostrate.* Collection Latomus, vol. 252, Brussels.

Bowersock, G.W.
1969   *Greek Sophists in the Roman Empire*, Oxford.

Bowie, E.L.
1978   'Apollonius of Tyana: tradition and reality', in *Aufstieg und Niedergang der römischen Welt* II.16.2, Berlin and New York, 1652–99.
1994   'Philostratus, writer of fiction', in J.R. Morgan and R. Stoneman (eds.) *Greek Fiction*, 181–99.

Campanile, M.D.
1999   'La costruzione del sofista. Note sul βίος di Polemone', *Studi Ellenistici*, (ed. B. Virgilio) 12, 269–315.

Civiletti , M. (ed., transl. and comm.)
2002   *Filostrato. Vite dei sofisti. Testo greco a fronte*, Milano.

152

Flinterman, J.J.
  1995 *Power, Paideia and Pythagoreanism*, Amsterdam.
Follet, S.
  1964 'Deux épigrammes peu connues attribuées à Philostrate', *Revue de Philologie* 38, 242–52.
  1976 *Athènes au IIe et au IIIe siècle. Études chronologiques et prosopographiques*, Paris.
Gleason, M.W.
  1995 *Making Men. Sophists and self-presentation in ancient Rome*, Princeton.
Jones, C.P.
  1974 'The reliability of Philostratus', in G.W. Bowersock (ed.) *Approaches to the Second Sophistic*, 11–16.
Jüthner, J.
  1909 *Philostratos über Gymnastik*, Leipzig and Berlin.
Mestre, F. and Gómez, P.
  1998 'Les sophistes de Philostrate', in N. Loraux and C. Miralles (eds.) *Figures de l'intellectuel en Grèce ancienne*, Paris.
Münscher, K.
  1907 'Die Philostrate', *Philologus Supplementband* 10, 467–558.
Russell, D.A.
  1983 *Greek Declamation*, Cambridge.
Rutherford, I.
  1998 *Canons of Style in the Antonine Age*, Oxford.
Schmitz, T.
  1997 *Bildung und Macht*, Zetemata 97, Munich.
Solmsen, F.
  1941 'Philostratos, (9)–(12)' in *RE* 20.1, 124–77.
Swain, S.C.R.
  1991 'The reliability of Philostratus' Lives of the Sophists', *Classical Antiquity* 10, 148–63.
  1996 *Hellenism and Empire*, Oxford.
Tobin, J.
  1997 *Herodes Attikos and the City of Athens. Patronage and conflict under the Antonines*, Amsterdam.
Traill, J.S.
  1971 'Greek inscriptions honoring Prytaneis', *Hesperia* 40, 309–29.
  1982 'Prytany and ephebic inscriptions from the Athenian Agora', *Hesperia* 51, 197–235.
Whitmarsh, T.
  2001 *Greek Literature and the Roman Empire. The politics of imitation*, Oxford.

10

HOLY AND NOT SO HOLY: ON THE INTERPRETATION OF LATE ANTIQUE BIOGRAPHY

John Dillon

The stimulus for this paper arises from a re-reading of a thought-provoking, but ultimately rather annoying work, Patricia Cox's *Biography in Late Antiquity: A quest for the Holy Man*,[1] composed some decades back now. This work, as I say, has much to commend it, but there are some aspects of her treatment of the subject that disturb me, particularly as they seem to represent a tendency in modern literary criticism, and it is on those that I would like to base my remarks here.

As her subtitle suggests, Cox sees the two biographers that she selects for treatment, Eusebius (in his portrait of the Christian Father Origen), and Porphyry (in his *Life of Plotinus*), as being primarily concerned with the presentation of models of the Holy Man. 'In Eusebius' case,' she says (p. 70), 'the ideal of the sage is imposed on Origen, and to some extent the facts of the churchman's life form a kind of historical clothing for the model Eusebius develops.' In the case of Porphyry (precisely, I think, because Porphyry adopts a more straightforwardly factual approach to his subject) she goes rather further, discerning various arcane motifs in Porphyry's narrative.

First of all, since Plotinus himself, speaking about the recognition of God in the self (in *Enn.* 6.9.10–11), speaks of the impossibility of conveying the mystical experience literally, and also warns against spreading abroad (ἐκφέρειν) the divine mysteries, she assumes that Porphyry is bearing these precepts in mind when composing his biography, and is consciously presenting us just with an outer shell, within which we are encouraged to seek the truth (p. 102).[2] Then, because Plotinus says, at *Enn.* 6.8.13, 49–50, that 'everywhere one must use "so to speak" (οἷον),' she takes this as an excuse for applying this precept to his biography (p. 103). But Plotinus made this remark only with reference to speaking about the activities of the One, and there is no indication at all that Porphyry is using it as a guiding principle for presenting Plotinus himself.

On the basis of such passages as these, she launches forth as follows (p. 107):

> In the following pages, biography will be considered as a quest for meaning, an interpretative effort that resists making a 'common story' out of the 'vision that baffles telling'.[3] The text, in this case, is a life, the life of Plotinus, and the vision is the dark and obscure cry of man's being that sounded through Porphyry and made his interpretation a song full of echoes. The biographical telling is indeed baffling, for the echoes come forth as 'real beings' like Odysseus and Socrates, who give shadowed form to the mystery we call Plotinus. Nature, we have said, is riddling; so too is the meaning of a man's life. In Porphyry's biography the soulfulness of Plotinus shines like a face reflected in many mirrors. What we can know about a life is its veil of images; biographical interpretation is a labyrinthine tracing and a weaving together of the tracks of soul in life.

I am sorry to say that when I read this sort of thing, I tend – entirely metaphorically, of course – to reach for my revolver. If this is where the Quest for the Holy Man in late antique biography is getting us, I feel that it is time to call a halt, and reconsider our premises.

However, if I do not feel that this sort of thing is going on in the biographical efforts of either Eusebius or Porphyry, then it is incumbent on me to suggest what I do think is going on. Are these people writing straightforward biographies in the modern sense (and what *is* the modern sense, after all?), or are they indulging in some sort of hagiographical activity, seeking primarily to present to their contemporaries (and to posterity) a model of the holy man to be admired and imitated? Obviously the same standards of objectivity do not hold for ancient biography as for modern, nor indeed are the records often there which would permit such objectivity, but I think it is important that we try to preserve a distinction, even so, between 'straight' biography and hagiography, and it is this that I fear that Patricia Cox is tending to blur. The methods and purposes of, say, Philostratus in writing his *Life of Apollonius of Tyana*, Porphyry and Iamblichus in their lives of Pythagoras, or Athanasius in his *Life of Antony*, may, I think, be distinguished from those of Eusebius in his life of Origen (in the *Ecclesiastical History*), Porphyry in his *Life of Plotinus*, or even Marinus in his *Life of Proclus*, and Damascius in his *Life of Isidore*.[4]

Admittedly these are borderline cases. If Eusebius is wearing one hat in his *Ecclesiastical History* (*HE*), he was very likely wearing another in his (now lost) joint venture with Pamphilus, the *Apology for Origen*, on which he draws extensively for his account in the *HE*. And whatever about Porphyry and Damascius, Marinus in his *Life of Proclus* explicitly uses as a structuring principle of his biography the Neoplatonic sequence of levels of virtue, all of which Proclus can be shown to exemplify, a procedure which brings him close to hagiography. Again, the worthy Eunapius, in his *Life of Iamblichus*,[5] tells us on the one hand what we would regard as a number of pious fictions, such as the raising up by Iamblichus of two spirits out of adjacent hot springs at Gadara, during a visit there of the members of the School, but at the same time (*VP* 459–60) he goes out of his way to abjure what might normally be termed hagiography:

> Even more astonishing and marvellous things were related of him, but I wrote down none of them, since I thought it a hazardous and sacrilegious (*theomises*) thing to introduce a spurious and fluid tradition into a stable and well-founded narrative.
> (transl. W.C. Wright)

In view of Eunapius' actual practice this remark may seem amusing, but as a statement of policy I think it is important. Eunapius is well aware that a hagiography of Iamblichus could have been written (and that Christian writers were already hard at work composing such documents for their chosen holy men), but he himself would regard such an enterprise as irresponsible, if not worse, and he sees himself as doing something different. The contrast between a συγγραφὴ στάσιμος καὶ πεπηγυῖα and ἀκοὴ διεφθαρμένη καὶ ῥέουσα at least betokens a consciousness of a difference between securely-attested fact and piety-driven rumour – even if the incident at Gadara is presented as belonging to the former category!

It is certainly a distinction acknowledged at various points by both Eusebius and Porphyry. Eusebius, after all, distinguishes at the beginning of his biography (*HE* 6.2.1) between documentary evidence (τινὲς ἐπιστολαί, sc. of Origen himself and others, preserved in the archives at Caesarea), and tradition (ἱστορίαι, preserved by those who knew him in later life).[6] Eusebius is quite good about using 'they say' or 'it is said' in this latter case;[7] otherwise he bases himself explicitly on one letter or another – not, admittedly, the most reliable of sources, even in the case of very saintly men, since they are always to some degree apologetic, but at least primary documents of a sort.

The famous incident of Origen's self-castration (*HE* 6.8.1–3) presumably did not figure in any of Origen's letters, but it is not mere hearsay either. Eusebius tells us that it was brought up by Bishop Demetrius of Alexandria in the indignant broadside that he launched in 232 against Theoctistus of Caesarea for ordaining Origen to the priesthood (6.8.4–5). Eusebius condemns this as *diabolē*, but he does not seek for a moment to deny it. Modern authorities who wish to do so, on the basis of Origen's later determinedly non-literal exegesis of the passage in Matthew (19.12),[8] which had allegedly earlier prompted him to this act, seem to me misguided. Certainly Origen goes out of his way in his commentary to deprecate those who, through excess of zeal, have ventured to take this exhortation literally, but one can perfectly take this as rather poignant self-criticism, the significance of which those who knew the facts would appreciate. At any rate, Eusebius is here behaving like a responsible historian.

That he is perfectly capable of lapsing into hagiography, however, is shown by a rather Herodotean digression that he makes not long after this in his narrative, when he pauses to celebrate the saintly predecessor of Alexander in the see of Jerusalem, Narcissus (6.9–11). Narcissus is presented purely as a figure of pious legend, in a sequence of hagiographical tales. First, he changes water into oil for the lamps at the Easter ceremony, when oil had run out. Then certain low fellows wreak destruction upon themselves by bringing false accusations against him. Then he retires into the desert for many years, during which three other bishops occupy the see in turn, before returning suddenly 'as if coming to life again' (ὥσπερ ἐξ ἀναβιώσεως). Finally, when he is already 115 years of age, Alexander is brought in to share the burdens of episcopacy with him. This is plainly the very stuff of hagiography, and it is what Eusebius is *not* doing in his *Life of Origen*, apologetic as that document is.

To turn to Porphyry, we have once again, it seems to me, a man who, though he greatly reveres his subject, is yet simply concerned to give as much accurate information about him as he can, in an effort to throw light on his character. About his subject's later life he is of course in a much better position to write than was Eusebius, since he knew his subject personally, but as regards Plotinus' early life his situation is actually much worse, since Plotinus could not be induced to talk about it (*V. Plot.* 1), and no other source of information was available. Porphyry does allow (chap. 3) that Plotinus from time to time mentioned incidents from his early life, but all he in fact records are three very widely spaced ones, the first (a detail much cherished by the psychoanalytically-minded) his being reproved by his nurse for still wanting to suck her breasts at over seven years of age; the second his turning to philosophy and discovery of Ammonius Saccas, in his twenty-eighth year; and the third, in his thirty-ninth year (243 AD), his joining the personal staff of the Emperor Gordian in his expedition against the Persians, in the hope of getting to consort with the Magi, and ultimately the Brahmans.[9] Porphyry does not offer comments on these data – no Freudian reflections on late breast-feeding, no explanation of where Plotinus had been, or what he had been doing, up to the age of twenty-seven, no background to his leaving Ammonius to join Gordian's ill-fated expedition,[10] which even at the best of times would hardly have put him in the most promising position to have meaningful contact with any Magi.[11] Such matters, it seems, are not germane to Porphyry's purpose, which is to present a profile of the mature Plotinus, author of the *Enneads*.

Even the study of the mature Plotinus, however, presents difficulties. It must be divided into two periods, the first from Plotinus' arrival in Rome in

244 to Porphyry's own arrival, nineteen years later, in 263, and the second from 263 to Plotinus' death in 270 – with the proviso that for the last year or so of his life Porphyry was no longer with him, but was roosting in Lilybaeum in Western Sicily, recovering from a mental breakdown, so that he has to rely for his account of Plotinus' last days once again on oral reports, chiefly from the physician Eustochius. It is this latter who provides the edifying account of Plotinus' last words, and of the snake crawling under the bed and out through a hole in the wall (*V. Plot.* 2).

Most of the incidents which modern critics tend to pick on as hagiographical, or at least improbable, seem, from Porphyry's way of presenting them, to date from the period before he was present:[12] for instance, the magical attack on Plotinus by Olympius that backfired, and the evocation of his guardian daemon (which turned out to be a god) by a visiting Egyptian priest (both told in chap. 10). In connection with the latter incident, Porphyry makes the rather 'hagiographical' remark, 'Plotinus certainly possessed by birth something more than other men,' but otherwise, as has been well pointed out long since by A.H. Armstrong,[13] there is nothing in these stories that would be regarded as in the least 'supernatural' or improbable by a late antique audience. Magical practices and the summoning up of spirits were a part of 'normal' life, and provided for in their philosophy, including that of Platonism. Other stories, such as that involving his unusual degree of discernment of character (περιουσία ἠθῶν κατανοήσεως, chap. 11), which enabled him to discern from among the household slaves the thief of a necklace, and to sense that Porphyry was suffering from a fit of depression and contemplating suicide, are designed, perhaps, to present Plotinus as a sage on the model of Pythagoras, but are otherwise presented quite factually, and are not in themselves totally improbable.

Indeed, the whole tone and structure of the *Life of Plotinus* is such as to give the lie to Patricia Cox's imaginative interpretation. Plotinus undoubtedly *was* a remarkable man, and he is presented as such, but such 'warts' as he had are also presented factually. He was rather disorganized in his writing habits (though his concentration was remarkable), his spelling, writing and punctuation were awful, he would not read over what he had written (bad eyesight the excuse, chap. 8), and he committed solecisms in speech (one even wonders if he suffered from mild dyslexia? – chap. 13). None of these, of course, are moral failings – more the complaints of an exasperated editor – but one would not expect to hear of the existence of these, nor is it necessary to suppose that Plotinus had any serious ones.

In general, the main fault that I would find with Porphyry as a biographer is one which is almost universal, I regret to say, in late antique biography, the presentation of a sequence of facts or events without any adequate background or connection with one another. Situations are simply presented to us – Plotinus living in the house of the lady Gemina (chap. 9), for example,[14] or being highly regarded by the Emperor Gallienus and his wife Salonina (chap. 12); characters pop up and disappear again – the wicked Olympius, who had been briefly a student of Ammonius (chap. 10), Polemon, who was amorous and short-lived, as Plotinus had predicted (chap. 11), Eubulus, the Platonic Successor, sending queries from Athens (chap. 15); and we shift from topic to topic on the basis of a fairly loose association of ideas. But to a certain degree such complaints are unreasonable. This biographical essay is not being composed for *us*, but for a relatively small circle of those who know the basic situation already, for whom elaborate background explanations would be superfluous and tedious. We should be grateful for what we have, without trying to read into Porphyry's narrative concepts that can never have entered his head.

Eusebius and Porphyry, then, are misjudged if they are seen as fixing their gaze on some ideal of the Holy Man, and then composing lives to exemplify this. If we turn to such a figure as the pious Marinus of Neapolis, on the other hand, in his *Life of Proclus*, we are in a rather different thought-world. Marinus, as I have mentioned earlier, explicitly sets out to show how his hero, Proclus, exemplified all the virtues in the Neoplatonic canon from the lowest to the highest (*V. Procl.* 2–3), and this colours his whole approach to his subject.[15] All the major events in Proclus' life, and all his significant decisions, are directed by some god or other, primarily Athena, but also Apollo (patron god of his home town of Xanthus in Lycia), and Asclepius. Athena arranged that he be born in Constantinople (chap. 6), and then later directed him in a dream to go and study philosophy in Athens (chap. 9). Once in his youth, when he was very ill, a beautiful boy appeared to him and announced that he was Telesphorus, the messenger of Asclepius (chap. 7). He instantly recovered, and was ill only two or three times in his life after that (chap. 3). His arrival in Athens was marked by two omens: first, he sank down exhausted during his walk up from the Piraeus with his friend Nicolaus, and found that he had chosen a shrine of Socrates, and had taken his first drink of Attic water from the spring there; and secondly, when he had arrived in the city, and went to visit the Acropolis,[16] the gatekeeper, who was just about to close the gate, said to him, 'Truly, if you had not come, I would have closed up!', and this Marinus takes to indicate that Athens itself was welcoming him as the last hope of Hellenism (chap. 10). Then later, when the Christians desecrated the Parthenon by removing the great chryselephantine statue of Athena and taking it to Constantinople, the goddess appeared to him in a dream, and announced that she was moving in to live with him.[17] And so on. It is certainly possible to extract factual information from Marinus' work, but essentially we are in the realm of hagiography, and hagiography composed by a rather dull dog.

When we come to Damascius' *Life of Isidore*,[18] on the other hand, which is my ultimate goal in this discourse, the situation becomes much more interesting. First of all it must be said that we do not have the full text of Damascius' work, but only an extended précis, or rather two of them, by Photius in his *Bibliotheca* (codd. 181 and 242), supplemented by a series of more or less verbatim extracts from the *Suda*, and this makes a proper literary appreciation difficult; but what we appear to have is a work which makes use of all the flowers of late antique rhetoric in the cause of celebrating the virtues of Isidore, Damascius' philosophical mentor, enlivened by a wide-ranging and lively survey of the philosophical scene in both Alexandria and Athens for the previous hundred years or so (taking the *Life* to have been composed in approximately 520 AD). As one wades through the turgidity of the introductory part, one could be excused for anticipating another hagiography in the style of Marinus. But one would be wrong. Damascius is *not* a dull dog. He has a waspish gift of characterization and a love of gossip and well-turned anecdotes that make his tale, if not entirely reliable, at least good reading.

His own contempt for ill-informed pieties comes out in an anecdote that he tells of the philosopher Hypatia, back at the beginning of the previous century.[19] She was devoted to chastity, but very beautiful, and in consequence had many admirers. One young man in particular was quite unable to conquer his passion, haunted her philosophy lectures, and plagued her with his attentions. 'Ignorant accounts (οἱ ἀπαίδευτοι λόγοι) say that Hypatia cured him of his disease through the power of music.' Rubbish, says Damascius; the truth is that she cured him by taking a used sanitary napkin and shoving it under his nose, saying, '*That's* what you're in love with, young man – nothing beautiful!'

For many of the stories he tells we unfortunately lack a context, since we have them only in the form of disconnected entries in the *Suda*, but at least some of them sound as if they were told for their own sake, in an amiably Herodotean way.[20] But Damascius is not just rambling; rather he is building up an elaborate tapestry of fifth-century intellectual life, against which to set the character of his chosen hero. The tone of his narrative is generally celebratory, but he does not pull his punches either. His judgements on his predecessors, including even his chief subject, Isidore, are often less than flattering. Of Proclus' pupils and associates, Marinus is portrayed as distinctly second-rate;[21] Domninus was a competent mathematician, but not much of a philosopher (§89A Athan.); furthermore, his conduct was not always edifying – he was quite prepared to eat pork, though it was against Syrian custom, when it was prescribed for medical reasons (admittedly, by Asclepius himself, in a dream). Proclus' fellow-pupil Hermeias was a decent fellow (*epieikēs*), but not very bright, nor inventive in argument, nor even a very determined seeker after truth (§54 Athan.)

And so on. Even his avowed hero Isidore does not escape unscathed, despite the celebratory tone with which Damascius starts out. It is revealed that his sense-perceptions and memory were not as sharp as they might have been (§14);[22] he was somewhat more choleric than ideally became a philosopher, and this led to his getting on the wrong side of many people (§15); he was somewhat naïve in practical matters, being often taken in by frauds who made pretensions to high-mindedness (§17); and, while not being exactly miserly, he was a very careful housekeeper (§24). Damascius in this connection provides a nice little illustration:

> When there were many of us gathered together to dine with him, he would sometimes just set before us as dessert three or four walnuts each, or perhaps five or six dried figs. And if any of us plucked up the courage to ask for more, he would add perhaps two or three more, with a very solemn countenance, quite oblivious to the laughter of the younger generation.

However, we must not exaggerate the critical tendencies of Damascius. The *Life of Isidore* is not really the fifth-century AD equivalent of *Eminent Victorians*. The overall tone is, as I have said, celebratory and edifying. Indeed, what is interesting about Damascius' work in the present context is how near it comes to what we think of as hagiography without, in my view, coming into that category. Right from the outset, in his introduction (§§5–6), he makes clear that he is telling us about a *theios anēr*, a divine man, to the recital of whose life and deeds a certain style of writing is appropriate – that is to say, one dignified and not too flowery (at least by the standards of the time). Damascius is obviously well aware of the conventions of encomiastic biography, which he does not feel precluded from making use of, at least to a certain extent. Indeed, there are indications at various points throughout his narrative that he has in mind such a work as Iamblichus' *Bios Pythagorikos*, analogies to which are duly noted by Clemens Zintzen in his edition.[23]

As in the case of Pythagoras, we are concerned first with the divine origin of Isidore's soul, which involves Damascius in a long excursus on the ancient Egyptian theory of the immortality of the soul, and the theology of Isis and Osiris (§§1–4 Athan.). Unfortunately, the fragmentary state of the work denies us the opportunity of seeing what exactly Damascius is building up to, but the implication seems to be that Isidore is a sort of *boddhisattva*, come down for the salvation of the human race (cf. §§5–6, 13). Damascius in this connection stresses the importance of Isidore's reception of prophetic dreams (§§9–11).

He turns next to a description of Isidore's outward appearance, and here he rather goes to town (§13, *Epit. Phot.* 16):

Isidore's appearance was intellectual and authoritative (ἔμφρων καὶ πρεσβυτικός), and indeed solemn and resolute in manner. His face was almost square, a sacred image of Hermes Logios himself.[24] As for his eyes, how can I describe the truly charming attractiveness (Ἀφροδίτη) that sat upon them, how can I indicate the supreme degree of wisdom (Ἀθήνη) that infused them?

He goes on about the eyes for some time in this vein, emphasizing the wondrous union of opposites (Aphrodite and Athena) that they manifested, and ends: 'In a word, his eyes were accurate images of his soul, and not only of that, but of the divine influence that infused it (τῆς ἐνοικούσης αὐτῇ θείας ἀπορροῆς).' The eyes, of course, are the most significant physical aspect of a divine man, or indeed of any intellectually distinguished individual, so one should not be surprised that they receive special attention.

All this, however, leads up, in §14 (*Epit. Phot.* 17), to the revelation to which I have alluded earlier, that Isidore's sense-perceptions and memory were not of the best. Damascius here, as I have mentioned (n. 22 above), does provide a graceful explanation of this weakness, but at the same time honesty forbids him to gloss over such facts. He also adds, however, rather waspishly, that he has come upon many people who have all the external characteristics of a philosopher – sharp observation, good memory, and so on – but who inside are totally lacking in true wisdom.

The *Life* is arranged, then, so far as we can see, in such a way as to provide at the outset a sketch of Isidore's appearance, character, and way of life, broadly arranged according to levels of virtue, followed by some discussion of his philosophical influences – principally, after Pythagoras and Plato himself, Iamblichus and Syrianus (§34), though he also took a lively interest in the ancient wisdom of Egypt – and of his teaching style. Here again, we can read between the lines of Damascius' encomium to gather that Isidore was not very widely read ('he shunned the noisy babble of books', §35A – with a reference to *Rep.* II 364E) – though this was balanced by his great insight into the truth. Nor was he a very *perspicuous* lecturer (§37D): 'In his expositions he was somewhat deficient in ability to explain his ideas clearly; but even here he was not left without help from natural ability or application, but he made every effort to improve his clarity.' He disdained rhetorical embellishment, but clung fast to the metaphysical truth (*ta pragmata*), so that the most complimentary thing that one of his students could find to say about him was that 'the man uttered not so much words (*logoi*) as the essences of the things themselves (*pragmatōn ousiai*).' Such lecturers are not unknown today, I think, not least in the field of philosophy.

John Dillon

It is not possible, or necessary, on the present occasion to journey through the vast panorama which makes up the body of the *Life of Isidore*. Certain characteristic aspects of it have been mentioned earlier. They do not escape the notice of Bishop Photius, in his summing up of the work in the *Bibliotheca* (Test. III Athanassiadi; p. 317, 24 ff. Zintzen). All those, he notes, whom Damascius sets out to praise, including even his chosen hero and mentor, he ends up by undermining and shooting down (κατασύρων καὶ ῥίπτων χαμαί), while subtly and gradually arrogating all honour to himself. So and so was distinguished for intelligence – but then we learn that he was not all *that* intelligent; another man was widely learned – but we discover presently that he was not universally learned; and even people celebrated for virtue turn out after all to be lacking in one or more of the virtues.

Photius is by no means a friendly critic of Damascius – he strongly objects to his 'impiety' (that is, his uncompromising Hellenism), and his repeated digs at Christianity – but in noting this characteristic of his work we must admit that he has hit the nail on the head. We, of course, are not complaining. Damascius has written something much more interesting than a hagiography. It is the portrait, not only of a man, but of an age, observing the contemporary conventions of encomiastic biography, but undercutting them at the same time, in the interests, perhaps, of truth, perhaps (as Photius would suggest) of self-aggrandizement – or perhaps, to judge somewhat more charitably, of both. The effect is certainly remarkable and unexpected. It is rather as if an ancient, gold-encrusted icon of some whiskery old saint looked out at one from the iconostasis of late antiquity – and *winked*.

In conclusion, I would like to suggest that, in considering the various examples that we have of biography from late antiquity, we should not be too quick to assume that we are dealing with the presentation of idealized archetypes, or the manipulation of empty rhetorical conventions. Certainly there were conventions of encomiastic biography that had grown up over the centuries, and the distinction between the credible and the incredible is not generally drawn where we would draw it today, but I would suggest that the purposes of biography were then more or less what they are now,[25] that is, to present a portrait of a life for our edification and instruction. Rather than try to make a rigid distinction between biography and hagiography in late antiquity, I think we would do better to think in terms of a sliding scale between theoretical extremes of factuality and fantasy, on which all the works that we have been here discussing can find their place in sequence. We might place Porphyry's *Life of Plotinus* nearest to the factual end, followed, perhaps, by Eusebius' study of Origen, and then Damascius' *Life of Isidore*, with the worthy Marinus, in his *Life of Proclus*, coming nearer to the fantastical end of the scale, in close proximity to such works as Eunapius' *Life of Iamblichus*, and most of the lives of the Christian saints, such as that of Antony. But all, I think, may be accommodated on one scale.

As for the 'quest for meaning' of which Patricia Cox speaks in the passage I quoted at the outset, that is surely there, but it is present, I would suggest, also in the decision of any modern biographer to select one life or another for study and presentation. In asking what these men of late antiquity were about, we are involved in asking what the real purpose and justification of biography is even now.

Notes

[1] Cox 1983.

[2] More appropriate, I think, if one is to go in search of motifs, is the recent suggestion of Edwards 1993, 480–90, that Porphyry's purpose in beginning his biographical sketch with the account of Amelius' efforts to get a portrait made of Plotinus (very much against his will), is to suggest that Porphyry's own pen-picture, emphasizing as it does Plotinus' *ethos*, gives a far truer picture of the man.

[3] A reference back to *Enn.* 6.9.11.

[4] This last renamed by Polymnia Athanassiadi, following the *Suda*, in her recent excellent edition, as *The Philosophical History* (which is indeed a more accurate title), but it must be recognized that Bishop Photius, in recording his reading of it in the *Bibliotheca*, does precisely complain of the title 'Life of Isidore', on the grounds that it is about far more than Isidore – so that was plainly the title that he had for it.

[5] In his *Lives of the Philosophers*, 457–61 Boissonade.

[6] Cf. 36.4. Since some of those survived even to Eusebius' own day, they cannot have had first-hand knowledge of Origen's early years.

[7] e.g. Leonides is only ὁ λεγόμενος πατήρ of Origen (6.1.1), and the account of Origen's early education is a βεβοημένος λόγος (cf. μνημονεύουσιν, 6.2.11); and λέγεται that he went without shoes for many years, and without drinking wine (6.3.12).

[8] *Comm. in Matth.* 15.3.

[9] The date of his birth (204/5) seems to have been winkled out of him by his doctor, Eustochius, who learned that he was 66 at the time of his death (*V. Plot.* 2).

[10] Gordian was assassinated by members of his own staff, led by the man who succeeded him on the throne, Philip the Arab, before he could come to grips with the Persians. The fact that Plotinus felt it necessary to flee (*V. Plot.* 3) indicates that he was attached to Gordian's personal retinue, no doubt the result of an introduction by a well-placed friend of the family.

[11] A modern analogy would be, perhaps, an idealistic young German admirer of French philosophy in the 1940s who joined in the occupation of Paris in the hope of meeting Jean-Paul Sartre.

[12] The latter incident, Porphyry suggests, led Plotinus to compose his essay 'On our Allotted Guardian Spirit' (*Enn.* 3. 4), which is one of those composed before Porphyry's arrival (no. 16 in the chronological list).

[13] In his sensible discussion of the question 'Was Plotinus a magician?', Armstrong 1955, 73–9, answering a rather tendentious article of Merlan 1953, 341–8.

[14] As regards Gemina, I like the suggestion of Saffrey (1992, 32) that this lady is none other than Afinia Gemina Baebiana, widow of the Emperor Trebonian (251–3). If we could know this, it would explain a lot about Plotinus' status (though we would still like to know how he came into contact with her in the first place!), but we are not going to learn this sort of thing from Porphyry.

[15] Indeed, the full title of the work is *Proklos, ē peri eudaimonias*, which rather sets the tone.

[16] I take this to be the meaning of Marinus' slightly cryptic expression ἀναβάντι δὲ αὐτῷ καὶ εἰς τὴν ἄκραν, but it could, I suppose, simply refer to his arriving at the gate of the city.

[17] He was established by this time in a large house at the southern foot of the Acropolis, which has now been identified with reasonable probability by archaeologists. The exact date of the removal of the statue is unfortunately unknown.

[18] I have given reasons above (n. 4) for preserving this title, rather than adopting Athanassiadi's choice, *The Philosophical History*.

[19] Fr. 102 Zintzen; §43A Athanassiadi. There is an excellent study of Hypatia by Maria Dzielska, *Hypatia of Alexandria*, Cambridge: Harvard University Press, 1995.

[20] Why, for instance, are we informed that the grammarian Ammonianus, a kinsman of the philosopher Syrianus, had a donkey who was so fond of listening to lectures on poetry that it would stop eating in order to do so, even if it had been deliberately starved beforehand (§47 Athan.)? Why are we told that Hierax of Alexandria once saw a *panikon zōion* (a faun?) on its way from Ethiopia to Constantinople, as it was being conveyed through Alexandria (it uttered a squeaking or chirping noise) (§58B Athan.)? Why is it important that the horse of the philosopher-statesman Severus (cos. 470) emitted sparks when it was rubbed down (§51 Athan.)? Doubtless the answers lie in the reams of text that are lost to us.

[21] §97F Athanassiadi (*Epit. Phot.* 144): 'Judging from both his discourses and his writings (which are few enough in any case), Marinus did not "reap the deep furrow" (cf. Aesch. *Septem* 593) of ideas from which shoots forth the wise contemplation of the true nature of beings.' The Aeschylus reference, doubtless borrowed from Plato's use of it at *Rep.* II 362A, serves to intensify the put-down.

[22] Though Damascius here does provide a graceful explanation of this peculiarity: God wished to make clear that Isidore was most truly his soul, and not his more external manifestations.

[23] e.g. *Epit. Phot.* 5 (θεοκρασία); 18 (ἀληθινὴ φιλία); 32; *Suda* Frs. 50 (σοφὸς οἰκίας διαθέτης) ; 60 (ἐχέμυθος). There are also various reminiscences of, or at least analogies to, the *De Mysteriis* and the *Protrepticus*.

[24] Damascius elsewhere, in his *Commentary on the Parmenides*, §261, mentions the connection between Hermes and squareness, attributing the doctrine to the Pythagorean Philolaus.

[25] Or were at least until quite recent times; it sometimes seems now as if the purpose of most biography is to *demolish* reputations, rather than to establish them.

Bibliography

Armstrong, A.H.
1955 'Was Plotinus a magician?', *Phronesis* I, 73–9, reprinted in *Plotinian and*

Christian Studies, London 1979.

Athanassiadi, P.
1999   *Damascius* Life of Isidore, Athens.

Cox, P.
1983   *Biography in Late Antiquity: A quest for the holy man*, Berkeley and Los Angeles.

Dzielska, M.
1995   *Hypatia of Alexandria*, Cambridge.

Edwards, M.
1993   'A portrait of Plotinus', *CQ* 43, 480–90.

Merlan, P.
1953   'Plotinus and magic', *Isis* 44, 341–8.

Saffrey, Fr H.-D.
1992   *Porphyre, La vie de Plotin*, II, ed. L. Brisson et al., Paris, 32.

11

JUSTICE FOR JUSTUS:
A RE-EXAMINATION OF JUSTUS OF TIBERIAS' ROLE IN JOSEPHUS' *AUTOBIOGRAPHY*

Zuleika Rodgers

The writings of Josephus provide us with an incomparable source for the study of Judaism in the Hellenistic and Roman periods, giving rise to a large body of secondary literature – concordances, articles and monographs – dealing with various aspects of his work. Yet in many ways, this author remains an enigma, despite the fact that his own story is inextricably bound up with those very writings. While Josephus certainly provides information about the important events of his life, his education and literary career, much remains debated, especially his motivation for writing.[1]

Scholarship is divided on the subject of what Josephus wished to achieve personally and nationally through his literary endeavours. Per Bilde has constructed two broad categories into which modern Josephus scholarship can be placed: classical and modern conceptions.[2] The first group takes a harsher view of Josephus: when he was not self-serving, he was grovelling in servitude to the Roman leadership, but in the reign of Domitian he underwent a radical transformation (perhaps as a result of losing imperial favour), which produced a new religious and nationalistic outlook in *Antiquitates Judaicae* (*AJ*). Essentially, then, two distinct phases are isolated in Josephus' career, which stand in stark contrast with each other.[3]

The second trend in scholarship maintains that Josephus consistently concerned himself with the issues surrounding Jewish existence in the Roman Empire and the preservation of Jewish rights.[4]

Josephus' shortest work, known as the *Vita* (*V*), is the first complete extant example of an autobiography, and as an account of his life it should offer us an insight into his intellectual and personal development. The work is replete with personal statements and explanations but difficulties arising in the narrative mean that *V* often obscures as much as it reveals. First, the scope of *V* is limited: the main body of the text is concerned with Josephus' activities during the war against Rome, and more specifically, the five to six months he spent as a commander in Galilee (*V* 28–413), omitting even his capture by the Romans at Jotapata. This account is set within a short auto-biographical sketch of his early and later life with some comments about his ancestry. Secondly, this account is at variance with that provided in *Bellum Judaicum* (*BJ*) 2.556 f. For example: the description of Josephus' mission to Galilee in *V* has been seen as conflicting with the account in *BJ* (the mission in *V* is pacific while in *BJ* it is bellicose); the chronology of events is altered; and the relationship between Josephus and his local rival, John of Gischala, undergoes some modification. Furthermore Josephus includes in *V*'s version of events a thus far unmentioned rival, Justus of Tiberias. Justus is accused of bringing ruination to his people (*V* 41), a puzzling charge since in *BJ* Josephus lays blame on many others but never took the opportunity to mention Justus. As the story unfolds in *V*, Justus' role in events is negligible and the outcome would not be substantially different without him among the *dramatis personae*. However, Josephus also tells us that Justus wrote an account of the same events (*V* 40) and he dedicates an excursus to an attack on this man and his work (*V* 336–67). Justus' work has not survived, however, and so we can only access the debate from Josephus' account.

The introduction of the figure of Justus of Tiberias is the most significant alteration that Josephus makes in his retelling of the story of the war in Galilee, and if *V* is to reveal something of Josephus' personal and literary programme in the 90s, we must explain Justus' role. Did he motivate Josephus to write *V* or at least part of it? What was the nature of the debate between Justus and Josephus and why would Josephus have felt the need to reply?

These questions lie at the heart of scholarship on *V*. Various degrees of influence have been assigned to Justus and numerous theories regarding the nature of the debate have been put forward. The traditional approaches focus on the historiographical (Josephus was defending *BJ*), the moral (Josephus was reacting to charges of tyranny and abusive behaviour in Galilee and, in particular, in Tiberias), and the personal (he was providing an apologia for his character).[5] *V* then is understood either as a unified narrative or as a reworked source, which provided a response to Justus – either partially or completely – although some topics do not seem related to their debate; hence the existence of other critics is suggested.[6] The context for Josephus' response is reconstructed in a number of ways: his livelihood as the representative of Jewish tradition was jeopardized, he was motivated out of pride and wished to court the favour of the Yavnean rabbis, and he was covering up his revolutionary activity in a period when this might come back to haunt him.[7]

Underlying all these views is the understanding that *V* is essentially apologetic and defensive and that Josephus offers excuses and explanations to exculpate himself from various charges. In contrast to these traditional readings, a very different approach to *V* has been offered by Bilde, who stresses the importance of seeing *V* within its literary context.[8] He suggests that the purpose of *V* is two-fold: to establish Josephus' credentials for writing *AJ* and to explain his involvement in the war as part of his qualifications for writing its history in *BJ*. In this way, *V* holds an important position in the corpus of Josephus' writing: it is not simply an apologetical appendix to *AJ* but an autobiography that presents the author's qualifications for his literary endeavours.

Drawing on this approach, Steve Mason has recently offered an alternative interpretation grounded in the literary and historical context of first-century CE Rome.[9] He now rejects the view (which he had formerly supported) that Justus is a motivating factor for *V* and notes the failure of those scholars who posit such a role for Justus to propose a realistic context in Rome for the debate, or to explain all the various features of *V*.[10] His work has revealed Josephus' familiarity with and reliance upon the rhetorical traditions and social expectations of the elite in Rome at this time. This invaluable research demands that any future discussion of the role of Justus in *V* take into account the socio-rhetorical features highlighted by Mason.

In this essay, I shall outline Mason's conclusions regarding the nature of *V* and, in light of his findings, re-examine the question of Justus' role in *V*. Is it possible to find a place for Justus once we take account of the literary and historical context revealed by Mason's work?

I. Mason on *Vita*
(i) *Critique of scholarship on Justus*
Mason has highlighted some serious questions that traditional proposals regarding Justus' role in *V* cannot adequately answer. Would a revolutionary past really be of harm to Josephus, especially in light of the fact that he had written *BJ* from the perspective of a military general? If he had been charged with warmongering, how could he have been simultaneously condemned as a traitor and what concern would it have been to the Romans if he had been charged with tyrannical behaviour decades earlier? Furthermore, as *V* often contradicts the version in *BJ* rather than attempting to defend it, Mason cannot accept that *V* could have been any sort of response to a critique of the earlier work. *V* itself is full of internal inconsistencies and such a work could not presuppose an audience critical of *BJ* who were looking to *V* for explanations.

Furthermore, structurally, *V* does not live up to a Justus-oriented apologetic, since Justus is only directly addressed near the end of the work (*V* 336–67). Even this excursus is an attack on Justus and could not work as a defence. Mason does allow for the possibility that Josephus may have envied Justus on a literary level and might have employed him as a source.

Mason also criticizes scholars for viewing the opening remarks of *V* as mere artifice to give the impression of a life story. *AJ* 20.262–7 supplies an introduction for *V* and while this does not mention Justus it does focus Josephus' interest on his ancestry. It is the thematic relationship between *AJ* and *V*, which has often been viewed as incidental, that Mason sees as providing the key for understanding the nature and purpose of *V*. In an earlier examination of *AJ*, Mason proposes that Josephus' aim there was 'to provide a handbook of Judaean law, history and culture for a Gentile audience in Rome that is keenly interested in Jewish matters'. As *AJ* depicts the history of the Jewish constitution (πολιτεία), which is aristocratic and priestly in focus, so *V* mirrors Josephus' public life and behaviour as a priestly aristocrat. It is the character (ἦθος) of the members of a society that determines its worth, and so while *AJ* describes the heroes of Jewish history, *V* emphasizes the character of the author Josephus. Both *AJ* 20.267 and *V* 430 point to the fact that Josephus, having finished this great literary project, undertook to write about the events of his life (public and military) and his ancestry. Josephus' time in Galilee was the only example from his life of such civic and military activity and so this short period became the focus of his story, and this explains the disproportionate nature of the account. *V*, he concludes, is grounded in this context and is concerned not with matters of history, primarily, but with the virtues of Josephus' character. Furthermore, since *AJ* and *V* are inextricably linked in both structure and concern, Mason concludes that they share the same sympathetic Graeco-Roman audience.

(ii) *Literary and historical contexts for* Vita

For an historical context in which to understand the themes and values in *V*, Mason looks to the world of the hereditary aristocracies of Rome and the eastern Mediterranean. There was an expectation for individual members of the ruling class to enter into public service and they usually followed a predictable career path. After a period of military service, these men took up civic duties, for example, in the judiciary, government, or priesthood. Authority and efficacy in their careers originated with the superiority of their characters. Products of an educational system and culture that featured the art of rhetoric, in retirement they often cultivated a literary career. *V* outlines Josephus' life accordingly, emphasizing the excellence of his character through the stages of his career (public service as a diplomat followed by his military experience), all the while displaying his rhetorical skills. Thus Josephus fulfils the expectation of a man of his class and background.

Mason also notes other traditional Roman values that appear in *V*: Josephus' leadership and power are based on trust (*fides*) and authority (*auctoritas*) while the themes of friendship and enmity in public life dominate the descriptions of his relationships in both Galilee and Jerusalem.

To appraise Josephus' *V* within its contemporary literary context, Mason chooses four categories: rhetoric, autobiography, advice to a public figure, and models for the military leader.

First, Mason examines Josephus' relationship to rhetoric and finds that *V* displays characteristics of contemporary Roman rhetoric. The lack of concern with the accuracy of historical reconstruction, the emphasis on Josephus' character, and the vilification of his enemies can be explained by recourse to Roman rhetoric. Josephus is happy to rearrange events or introduce new details over against *War* (often contradicting the earlier work) in order to demonstrate the virtues that make up his character. The narrative acts as a background, providing a moral lesson in which the excellence of Josephus' character is described and he is portrayed in stark contrast to his various adversaries. The virtues ascribed to Josephus were ones not only familiar to a Roman audience but those expected of a member of the aristocratic elite. Thus Mason proposes that, 'Although Josephus' *Life* leaves all sorts of loose ends on the historical and literary levels, the entire book – virtually without remainder – works as a statement of these widely understood virtues, explicated through a more or less chronological review of his origins and public life'.

Turning his attention to the category of ancient autobiography, Mason notes the rise in popularity of celebratory self-description among political and literary figures. Since Josephus' source, Nicolaus of Damascus, appended an autobiography to his universal history, it is not unusual that we should find Josephus adding an account of his life to *AJ*.

The ambition of many aristocrats was a successful political career and Mason next focuses on the 'advice for public figures' found in ancient sources. In particular, he concentrates on the advice for politicians offered in Plutarch's *Precepts of Statecraft* and reveals the many parallels found in *V*. To enter public life, one must do so with clear convictions (*V* 12), usually after an apprenticeship or an unusual achievement (Josephus' diplomatic mission and subsequent military leadership, *V* 17–29). Success in providing leadership for the people is tied to the character of the leader (*V* 80–4 provides a brief synopsis of Josephus' character), who should be an accomplished orator with the ability to sway the masses (Josephus makes a number of speeches in *V* which display this ability). Leaders need to listen to the people in order to rule (*V* 30–61 describes how Josephus ascertains the situation in Galilee from the locals), should not directly challenge them but use tactics or double-speak to trick and bring them over to his point of view (Josephus regularly employs diversionary tactics to direct the Galilean mob away from their violent ambitions). The politician should choose his friends with care and reward them where appropriate (*V* 79 tells how Josephus befriends local Galileans as a means of eliciting their support and *V* 81, 419–21, describes the favour he extends to friends and family) while treating his enemies fairly and putting aside personal animosity for the sake of the state (John of Gischala is presented as threatening the stability of the state and Josephus emphasizes how moderately he treated him). The ability to delegate is necessary for the smooth running of the state (Josephus describes how he divided the labour with his associates, *V* 79, 86), while forethought (πρόνοια) for the common good is essential for successful leadership (Josephus continually writes of his efforts to 'make provision' for the area). Roman domination provides the context for two pieces of advice: the politician should understand the limitation of his own power and function under Roman rule while simultaneously avoiding needless reliance upon Rome by dealing with internal problems (Josephus' task in *V* seems to be directed at avoiding contact with Rome). The ultimate goal of these skills and tactics is to achieve tranquillity and avoid civil discord (στάσις) (this theme not only appears as the aim of Josephus' mission throughout *V* but also features in *BJ* and *AJ*).

Mason notes that Plutarch's essay highlights the problems faced by the ruling elite under Roman domination; Josephus' stories of double games and clever stratagems to trick the masses into believing they had his support reflect the predicament of his class. Thus we cannot read *V* as trying to hide or explain away Josephus' revolutionary past but rather as an explanation of his tactics whereby he pretended to support a war he did not believe in so as to pacify the rebels (*V* 17–22).

Finally Mason looks to military literature for parallels since Josephus presents himself as a general (στρατηγός). The commentaries of Iulius Caesar and Sextus Iulius Frontinus' military handbook provide a context for understanding certain aspects of *V*. Similarities in the description of opponents and Caesar's clemency towards them can be found in the former, while in the latter Frontinus advises employing stratagems in warfare and he uses the same Greek term, στρατηγήματα, found in *V* to describe the tricks Josephus used to avoid violence.

Mason, then, suggests that Josephus did not write out of self-defence but from a position of strength as an author with powerful friends and a sympathetic audience. As an aristocrat, he presented an account of the period of his life dedicated to public service and was concerned not with the accuracy of historical detail, but with the presentation of the virtues of his character and the failings of his opponents. *AJ* provided a survey of the Judaean constitution based on the characters of its heroes and in *V* Josephus exemplified those very qualities. The priestly aristocratic constitution praised in *AJ* is reflected in the actions of the priestly aristocrat, Josephus, in *V*. Perhaps Justus or others did attack Josephus but he was not forced into defending himself in *V*, where his adversaries appear not as serious threats but as literary figures who provide Josephus with unvirtuous opposition for him to overcome successfully. His avaricious priestly colleagues, the power-hungry John of Gischala, the misguided Jonathan with his delegation colleagues, and Justus, the self-serving rabble-rouser, are included in a motley crew of antagonists encountered by Josephus in Galilee. Josephus, in contrast, attained his position as an aristocratic man of character who is neither rapacious nor tyrannical and cares only for the maintenance of order in Galilee

Do Mason's invaluable insights into many features and themes in *V* render it impossible to recover a more active role for Justus? Do his conclusions preclude assigning some significant responsibility to Justus for Josephus' writing of *V*? In the next section, I will focus on the presentation of Justus in *V*.

II. Justus in *Vita*

(i) *Justus' role in the rebellion*

As noted above, the most striking difference between *BJ* and *V* is the inclusion of the figure and actions of Justus of Tiberias in *V*, absent in *BJ*. Although the situation in Tiberias is discussed in the earlier work, neither Justus nor his father Pistus (nor his brother or brother-in-law) is included in the narrative. While others hostile to Josephus in Tiberias – Jesus son of Sapphias and Cleitus – figure in both accounts (*BJ* 2.599, 642), Justus does not. No names are supplied in *BJ* 2.639–41 where Josephus describes his taking captive the Tiberian council and principal men, whereas in the version of *V* 175 Justus and his father Pistus are among those incarcerated.[11] John of Gischala receives support from Justus while he is at Tiberias according to *V* 88, but in the parallel account of *BJ* 2.615–6, though John bribes or blackmails the citizens to revolt, the recipients of the bribes are not identified.

The first mention of Justus in *V* occurs in Josephus' description of the situation at Tiberias. We are told that there were three factions: Justus was the leader of the third party, which although not openly hostile to Rome, in reality wanted war in order to obtain power in Galilee (*V* 34–7).[12] Justus attempted to persuade his fellow citizens to take up arms against King Agrippa II in order to regain their city's former status, which was lost during his reign (*V* 37–8). Sepphoris was now the capital of Galilee and Justus proposed that they could procure the aid of the Galileans, who hated that city for remaining loyal to Rome (*V* 38–9). Josephus comments that Justus was an able orator with a Greek education who used rhetorical tricks to convince his audience, and that he later employed his skills to write a distorted history of these events. Furthermore, he lived a sordid life and was the cause of Galilean ruination (*V* 40–2). Josephus follows with a note about how Justus then forced the populace to attack the villages of Gadara and Hippos, which were situated on the borders of Tiberian territory with Scythopolis (*V* 42).

Justus' next appearance in the narrative is linked with John of Gischala's visit to Tiberias, where Justus is hoping to gain the people's support against Josephus. We are told that Justus and his father, Pistus, were eager to offer their support to John (*V* 88).[13]

Our next encounter with Justus is in *V* 155: here Josephus describes how the citizens of Tiberias wished to ally themselves with Agrippa and defect from Josephus. Josephus prevents this by creating the illusion of a supporting fleet, and in the process he takes Justus prisoner. It seems from the following narrative that Justus was a member of the governing body of Tiberias who was inviting the king to protect them. That evening Josephus hosts a dinner for Justus and his father where the conversation hints at this.

> I sent for those of the mob of the Tiberians who were in prison – Iustus and his father Pistus were among them – and made them my dinner guests. After the banquet I said: 'I myself know very well that the power of the Romans is utterly overwhelming; but I have kept quiet about it because of the bandits.' I counselled them to do the same, to wait patiently for the necessary amount of time and not become upset with me as general, for they would not easily find the opportunity to meet someone else who was similarly mild. I also reminded Iustus that before I came along from Jerusalem, the Galileans had cut off his brother's hands, adducing wrongdoing prior to the war in the form of forged letters by him, and that after Philip's withdrawal the Gamalites had risen against the Babylonians and disposed of Chares – he was Philip's relative – and how they had with no greater consideration disciplined Iesous, that man's brother and the husband of Iustus' sister. These things I discussed with Iustus' group after the banquet.　　　　　　　　　　　　　　　　　　　(*V* 175–8)

Here Josephus asserts his leadership after quelling the Tiberians' attempt to go over to Agrippa and the Romans. He reminds Justus of the suspicion and enmity with which the Galileans regarded him (as opposed to Josephus' constant refrain about his own popularity with them). Other issues mentioned here are: the Galileans' hatred of Sepphoris because of that city's pro-Roman stance (and how they wished to punish them for it) and how Philip ben Jacimus remained faithful to Agrippa and the Romans. By these references Josephus also reveals that Justus was part of a pro-Roman or at least moderate faction sometime during this period in Tiberias and so consequently should fear the Galileans. His family moreover shared similar sentiments.[14]

As a member of the council in Tiberias, Justus must have been an important person locally. If this had not been the case, Josephus would not have missed an opportunity to inform us of the matter. Some scholars have rejected the historicity of Josephus' claim that there was a third faction in Tiberias and Mason draws attention to the way in which Justus' position is a mirror image of his own.[15]

It would be useful at this stage to digress in order to offer some comments regarding the difficulty of reconstructing the historical situation during these early days of the Jewish rebellion against Rome. Cohen outlines some of the restrictions that obstruct our view of the events: it must have been a confusing period, in which it was difficult to know to whom or to which group to declare one's loyalty, and allegiances surely were modified or intensified as the situation developed.[16] A clear identification of the different positions is impossible because factionalism was rife among the ruling class and this phenomenon does not seem to have emerged only in 66 CE.[17] The debate regarding the Judaean aristocracy's involvement in the rebellion is tied to a reading of Josephus' *BJ* and *V* in which scholars discern an attempt by Josephus to exculpate this group from either the responsibility for starting the war or from willing participation.[18] The 'pro-war' camp represented a whole spectrum of social groups and opinions as to the aims and methods of the revolt. Some scholars, however, reject any position other than either pro- or anti-Roman, precluding a moderate stance.[19]

Others see the provisional government of the High Priest Ananus in Jerusalem as representing a moderate position producing hesitant actions.[20] This position was one that did not preclude the elite from involvement at the outset as a form of protest, but in spite of their necessary preparations for war this group planned to hold out for an agreement with the Romans.[21]

There is some agreement that individuals or groups shifted allegiances. Cohen allows that certain members of the ruling class only involved themselves in war insofar as it was advantageous; when it ceased to be so, they could just as easily detach themselves again (e.g. Philip ben Jacimus, Saul, and Costobar).[22] It is important to keep in mind that opposition to certain aspects of Roman rule does not directly correspond with a desire to fight a full and uncompromising war with a powerful empire. Hence, different individuals may have joined in with the initial euphoria but kept their options open in terms of controlling the situation, so as to negotiate in the future. In this way, some may even have been involved in the initial battle with Cestius but still lacked any hope for the long-term outcome of such a war. It seems inconceivable that the members of the upper class who stayed on in Jerusalem were anything other than wholly committed to a war in which they had most to lose. Consequently they could not hand over responsibility to a group whom they may have perceived as socially disaffected and unsuitable to lead the people because they were not part of the traditional elite.[23]

Josephus' assertion that Justus was a supporter of the rebellion is unsubstantiated by the narrative. Justus was a responsible member of the Tiberian government who, along with other members of the ruling class in Tiberias, opposed the demolition of Antipas' palace. We also hear how his brother suffered at the hands of the pro-rebellion Galileans in Gamala (*V* 177). We do learn, admittedly, that Justus led or incited attacks on the Decapolis, did not abandon his city when the rebellion broke out, and only fled to Agrippa after the second revolt of Tiberias (*V* 390–3).[24] Justus' position may represent a moderate approach to the rebellion: he certainly was not eager for rebellion but remained in Tiberias when the revolt broke out, perhaps in the hope of using his position to influence the citizens against rebelling.[25] In many ways, this position is similar to the one Josephus claims for himself in *V* – the aristocratic politician playing double games with the mob. Certainly Josephus' invective does not prove Justus' pro-rebellion sentiments.[26]

Josephus' description of Justus as a power-hungry demagogue is part of the literary degradation of his opponents and it places him in stark relief to the aristocratic Josephus. Mason notes that this portrait of Justus was designed to elicit a censorious response from his audience and Josephus' condemnation of Justus' Greek education would also have resonated with the readers.[27]

Justus is also described as supporting John of Gischala. Perhaps Justus did support John rather than Josephus, but as Mason observes Josephus reveals this connection in order to tarnish Justus' reputation.[28]

To summarize, we have seen that Justus figured little in the actual events and does not seem to be playing an active or vital role in the story. It is clear, however, that he did hold an important position in Tiberias and consequently would have had some part to play in the affairs of the city. Moreover, Josephus devotes a section of the work to Justus and it is to this we must look in order to discover more about the person of Justus and his relationship with Josephus.

(ii) *Excursus on Justus: V 336–67*

The excursus in *V* 336–67 opens and closes with a literary attack in which Josephus charges that Justus lied about both Josephus and the events in Tiberias (*V* 336–8 and *V* 357–67). Josephus accuses Justus of parading mendacity as historical writing and compares him to a forger of contracts.[29] Josephus explains his own omission of certain details concerning Justus from his earlier work as a sign of his moderation (*V* 338–9). In summing up, again Josephus returns to matters historiographical: Justus cannot claim to write an eye-witness account as he was neither present in Galilee during those times, especially at the siege of Jotapata (which he has dared to describe nonetheless), nor in Jerusalem (*V* 357–8). Furthermore, since he had not fought at the capital he might have made up for the deficiency by consulting the 'Commentaries of Caesar', but he did not do so (*V* 358). Josephus demands that Justus explain the delay in his publication, for he had composed the work twenty years earlier. Was he not confident about its content? Josephus offers an explanation himself, charging that Justus delayed publication until Vespasian, Titus, Agrippa, and family were no longer alive and thus could not testify to the factual veracity or literary quality of the work (*V* 359–60). Josephus compares his own work, which he claims he showed, not long after the events described therein, to Vespasian and Titus, and he was rewarded by their response (*V* 361). Again unlike his opponent, his work also received affirmation from Agrippa, who he claims wrote sixty-two letters attesting to the veracity of Josephus' work: this Agrippa did with sincere intentions, not from irony, as Justus would surely like to suggest (*V* 364–7).

The next part of the excursus takes up the issue of the war, with a specific focus on Tiberias. Josephus claims the following:

V 340–1: Justus blames Josephus and the Galileans for the revolt of Tiberias against the Romans and Agrippa.

V 341–4: Josephus retorts that Justus and the Tiberians were at war with the Syrian Decapolis even before Josephus received his commission in Jerusalem. This is attested in the *commentarii* of Vespasian and by the fact that Justus' punishment was called for by the victims. Justus escapes the death penalty only by Berenice's intercession. Josephus will prove this by referring to Justus' later career.

V 345–8: Again Josephus restates that Justus and the other Tiberians were anti-Roman. He contrasts Tiberias with Sepphoris and the latter's ability both to remain faithful to Rome and to stand up to Josephus. The citizens of that city even desisted from aiding Jerusalem and the Temple because of their anti-war stance.

V 349–53: In contrast, Tiberias was situated near Roman allies and far from revolutionary centres. The city was well armed and could easily have followed Sepphoris, but it did not do so. Justus had charged Josephus with the responsibility for its insurrection, but Josephus asks who was to blame later, after he had been captured, when the city could have easily surrendered, rather than waiting until Vespasian's forces arrived. The only reason Tiberias survived was Agrippa's request. Hence the fault lies with the Tiberians.

V 353–4: Josephus treated the Tiberians mildly but they slaughtered their own, not out of loyalty to Rome but because of internecine tensions. He reminds Justus that two thousand Tiberians were present during the siege in Jerusalem.

V 354–6: Justus may claim exemption as he fled to the king, but that was simply out of fear of Josephus. Even Agrippa, his great patron, punished Justus a number of times for his actions.

(iii) *Charges and counter-claims*

Josephus' attention to contrasting his own work with that of his Tiberian rival suggests that part of the debate between these two men was historiographical. The literary charges Josephus employs have been shown to be standard techniques of refutation, but this does not in any way preclude the possibility that there was an underlying need to protect his interests as an historian.[30] Agrippa's letters are not entirely complimentary and the second of these presumes that Josephus omitted details of which the king wished to inform him.[31] Josephus even proffers excuses for now including matters he had formerly omitted. Josephus is eager to claim that *BJ* received Agrippa's approval for his work, and this indicates that Justus did comment critically on the literary nature of Josephus' earlier work, *BJ*.[32] However, as we noted earlier, Mason criticizes the traditional views about this element of the debate since Josephus does not attempt to defend in any detail his version of events as presented in the earlier work.[33]

Josephus did write a history of events in which he played a role and, as such, the truthfulness of his account is bound up with the presentation of his actions: any historiographical criticism that went beyond the merely stylistic would surely touch upon his actions as he related them.

The issue of who was to blame for the revolt of Tiberias is presented as a crucial subject for Justus and Josephus.[34] Josephus attempts to deflect blame by claiming that it was actually Justus and the Tiberians who were eager for war.[35] It seems odd that Josephus would attempt to cover up his own revolutionary activity: he had proudly described his campaign in *BJ*; he admits earlier in *V* 82 that he took Tiberias four times; and in *V* 155–73 he describes how he prevented the city from going over to Agrippa.[36] After this excursus against Justus, he refers again to an episode in which the Tiberians attempted to ally themselves with Agrippa but he intervened and so prevented them both from being attacked by the Galileans and from achieving their aim (*V* 381–9).

His counter-attack on Justus and the Tiberians also does not make much sense within this context. The accusation regarding the hostilities with the Decapolis fails to prove much; he had already presented an explanation for the revolution, partially based on the fact that the Jews had been treated badly by their Gentile Syrian neighbours (*V* 24–7).[37] Commenting on Justus' later career, he attests to the fact that he was punished by the king, but also reveals that he was pardoned.

Josephus' comment in *V* 353 reveals a shift in focus for the debate to the subject of internal divisions within Tiberias. Josephus claims that he himself never killed any of the citizens, but they turned on each other, not in a struggle to remain with Rome but because of political wrangling (*V* 353). Here, as in the rest of the book, the rebellion against Rome does not play a role and Josephus concerns himself only with intra-Jewish struggles and his fair treatment of his people.

This leads us to suggest that Justus' accusations were concerned with Josephus' and the Galileans' cruel behaviour towards the Tiberians and the way in which Josephus, in his attempt to control Tiberias, actually strengthened the divisions and led them towards civil disaster. This would explain why Josephus makes no effort in the narrative of *V* to hide his revolutionary dealings with Tiberias. However, the theme of civil strife (στάσις) is one he addresses throughout all his works and it arises here also.[38] Being sensitive to this issue, Josephus does not explicitly state it as a charge but rather expands the accusation from internecine conflict to revolt against Rome, which was the ultimate outcome.

If this is the real focus of the debate, it would explain other features in *V*. Jotapata, for example, was an important subject for Josephus in *BJ*, and even though it would seem that Justus had mentioned this episode in his life, Josephus shrugs it off with a brief comment about his lack of information (*V* 357). A recurrent theme in *V* is the moderation that Josephus displayed towards his enemies, especially John and Tiberias.[39] This was implemented usually through his control of the Galileans who desired to punish them, either for their lack of loyalty to Josephus or for their pro-Roman tendencies.[40] Justus would have included the Galileans as Josephus' partners in crime, especially since his own family had fallen victim to them (*V* 177).[41] Perhaps Justus had described Josephus' lack of control over this group, since Josephus now stresses how Tiberias had been saved from the wrath of the Galileans as a direct result of his influence (*V* 99, 381, 384).

The moderation that Josephus claimed he displayed towards all in Galilee he especially emphasizes with regard to Tiberias.[42] His depiction of the events confirms that the topic of civil discord was important to him, for he shows that the divisions in Tiberian society existed before his arrival: even before the outbreak of war Justus and the Tiberians had persecuted the Galilean population (*V* 392). Later, Josephus' adversaries, John and the delegation, were the fomenters of strife, in Galilee and particularly in Tiberias. This theme of civil discord is also important with regard to his treatment of Justus, who is presented as specializing not only in anti-Roman feeling but also in dissension among Jews themselves (e.g., against Sepphoris).

The final topic covered by Josephus in the excursus is Justus' relationship with Agrippa: the attack is informed by a polemical desire to denigrate Justus' character and relationship with the monarch. Agrippa's punishment of Justus is not clearly outlined and Josephus does not provide the actual allegations brought against his rival.[43] That Josephus bothers to provide evidence that the king gave his work approval, denying the charge that he did so out of irony, could lead us to surmise that Justus mentioned something of Agrippa's attitude towards Josephus.[44] In reaction, Josephus turns the charge back on his rival, and tarnishes Justus' association with Agrippa. Josephus could not have issued such a vehement denunciation without some evidence for a chequered relationship between Justus and Agrippa, but his account is no doubt distorted.[45]

Josephus' polemic against Justus cannot prove him to have been an instigator of rebellion against the king and the Romans, but it does suggest that he was a player in Jewish politics and responsible for inner tensions among different Jewish groups. Perhaps, then, the subject of civil discord is where the real debate lay. If so, there would be no need for Josephus to defend *BJ* and in *V* he focuses on showing how he, as an aristocrat skilled in the art of leadership, aimed to keep Galilee from civil discord. It is noticeable that throughout *V* Josephus reminds the reader of his own horror of civil war and stresses the correct behaviour that ought to be displayed towards members of one's own race.[46] Not only is Justus the inferior historian in comparison with Josephus, but also Justus, and not the popular, moderate Josephus, is responsible for civil strife.

In *V* Josephus attacks Justus' character by claiming that his actions promoted civil discord, which led to disaster for Tiberias, while in contrast Josephus' own virtuous character was aiming to bring stability to Galilee and avoid *stasis*, a duty incumbent on any responsible member of the aristocratic elite. Mason proposes that Josephus' opponents are presented as polar opposites to provide foils for his self-presentation and we have noted the parallels between Justus and Josephus. Bringing together the foregoing analysis with Mason's work on *V* in its historical and literary contexts, I should like to propose a different way of viewing both the content and context of the debate between Justus and Josephus.

III. Justus and Josephus' *Vita*

Unfortunately, since the literary output of the Tiberian historian has been lost to us, it is only possible to reconstruct something of it from the testimony of other writers. Josephus' description mentions that Justus wrote a 'history of these events', referring primarily to the situation in Tiberias during the war (*V* 40), and in the excursus he repeats this (*V* 338). Josephus also criticizes him for his account of Jotapata and Jerusalem, so we can surmise that these were included in Justus' work. This is the sole evidence that we can directly take from his rival, and it simply suggests that he wrote an account of the war in which he mentioned Josephus, Galilee, and the siege of Jerusalem.

The evidence for Justus' work from non-Josephan sources poses many problems, since notices in other authors often depend on Josephus rather than being independent witnesses. In the ninth century, Photius, the Patriarch of Constantinople, includes a reference to Justus in which he mainly relies on Josephus but adds an independent note that Justus wrote a 'Chronicle' on the Jewish kings, which begins with Moses and ends with the death of Agrippa II.[47] Mason reminds us how important was the subject of the war in Agrippa's career, and so argues that Justus must have mentioned it within this context.[48] Justus was Agrippa's secretary and owed him his life. He had abandoned the revolution and taken refuge with the king. His account of the war surely glorified his now dead benefactor's role in those days.

Justus' focus on the monarchy in Judaean history must have emphasized the importance of this aspect of the political culture, and this would differ significantly from Josephus' presentation of the priestly aristocracy as the traditional and legitimate form of government. This basic difference in ideology may well have been important for their debate.

Justus' own position during the war does not seem to have been so very different from that of Josephus. He may well have been playing a double game, not unlike that described by Josephus in their dinner-table conversation (*V* 175–6).[49] Neither foresaw the war's ultimate direction and both perhaps hoped for an early end to the hostilities. As Josephus became more involved on account of his official position and so could not abandon the province, he ultimately went the way of the revolutionaries. Justus, unable to accept the Galilean attitude toward his city, and suffering personal loss, but lacking any official role such as might have forced him to remain, abandoned the war he had never really wanted.

Thus Josephus and Justus parted company even though there had been no major differences politically *vis à vis* the Romans during the early stages of the war. Both ended up in Rome and both attempted to present Jewish history in Greek terms.[50] Justus was in the service of Agrippa and reportedly penned his work during the decade following the war, but for some reason it was only published after the monarch's death.[51] The similarities between Justus and Josephus can explain much of the animosity: it is the sort which occurs not between those from radically different positions but between those of the same political cast who subsequently choose different expressions of those views and go their separate ways.

Well educated and as Agrippa's secretary, Justus surely mixed in elite circles and, not unlike Josephus, he must have been familiar with their values and social expectations. Clearly then any effective attack on Josephus who was courting this sort of audience must have been presented in terms they would understand. Furthermore, to discredit Josephus, the rhetorically-trained Justus would have focused on Josephus' character. To do this, he presented Josephus' actions during the war as those of a power-hungry autocrat who recklessly led Galilee, and in particular his home-town Tiberias, towards civil strife. Perhaps Justus also mentioned Josephus' close ties with John of Gischala whose reputation as a hardened rebel would have been well known in Rome. Mason has shown how Josephus' presentation of the virtues of his character is central to *V* and is sharply contrasted with his opponents but denies that Justus, who is only addressed later in the work, was a motivating factor for Josephus' writing of *V*. If Justus, however, attacked Josephus' character, he must be assigned a more influential role in *V*.

Josephus may well have been planning to append an autobiographical section to *AJ* (Mason highlights the structural links) but this attack by Justus focused Josephus' attention on the intra-Jewish conflicts in Tiberias. As Mason reminds us, his time in Galilee was his only example of civic or military duty, but within this period *V*'s narrow focus on the interaction between competing groups in Tiberias and Galilee, without any reference to his later encounters with Roman forces, demands further explanation. Justus provides us with the reason for this concentration on issues surrounding the behaviour of competing groups who all seem to share a similar attitude to the rebellion. In response, Josephus offers a summary of the power games played by John, Jonathan and the delegation, and Justus, whom he views as the real culprits who led Galilee to disaster. In contrast, he celebrates his own actions and relationships, describing them as guided by his desire to prevent civil discord and in line with those expected of an aristocratic politician.

What could have been the context for such a debate? Mason has clearly shown that Josephus expected a sympathetic audience for *AJ* and *V*. He presents himself as a Judaean aristocrat who embodies the values of his audience and who reflects the priestly aristocratic virtues so highly praised in *AJ*. He is thus qualified to write about Judaean history and culture. Justus, similarly, must have thought that he was qualified to write about Judaean history, because of his links with Agrippa and in light of his own literary abilities, which Josephus acknowledges.[52] These authors were competing as historians but from very different perspectives, one focused on the priesthood and the other on the monarchy.

Mason has challenged scholarship to provide a context for the debate and to explain what could have threatened Josephus in this period. He also notes that Josephus presents his life story as an appendix to *AJ* and this account 'is not that of an intellectual but of a public figure – in Judea and Galilee.'[53] Perhaps, then, it is a political matter that separates these two historians.

We have seen that Justus and Josephus were not very different in their approach to the Romans at the start of the war, and there seems no reason to assume that this agreement changed. Politically, Josephus saw the future of the Jews in cooperation with the ruling power; surely, from what we know of the Tiberian's career, Justus did not fundamentally disagree. Thus it must have been an intra-Jewish political matter that divided these two men. For Justus to bother attacking Josephus, the latter must have gained an elevated position in Rome, which at least gave him credibility in the eyes of some Romans. He had just completed his major work, *AJ*, and may have been planning his *CA*. These works attempted to present Judaism to the Graeco-Roman world, and by undertaking such an ambitious cultural project, Josephus was posing as a credible representative for Judaism and the Jews. Significantly, he often implies parallels between himself and the great figures of Jewish history.

It is against this backdrop that the debate between Justus and Josephus ought to be interpreted. Josephus, in taking on the role of Judaism's representative, clashed with Justus. They parted company on the subject of Jewish politics. This may have been the case also in 66/67 CE . Justus as a faithful aide to Agrippa may well have assumed that monarchical politics culminating in the Herodian dynasty, whose major representatives were all well placed in Rome, represented the best of Judaean culture. There were inevitable tensions in Josephus' position, by contrast, as the differences between *War* and *Antiquities* make clear: he wanted to claim Herod as a model of good Judaean-Roman cooperation (*BJ* 1 and the decrees of *AJ* 14), but could not resist using his reign to illustrate the evils of monarchy (*AJ* 14–17); he needed to trade on Agrippa's standing during the war and alleged favourable reception of his work (*BJ* 2), but again could not resist digs at the shortcomings of Agrippa's reign and even character (*AJ* 20.189–91, 145–6, 211–12, 214, 216–18). A faithful and cultured assistant of the king's, such as Justus, was extremely well positioned to expose these inconsistencies and challenge Josephus' assumption of Agrippa's mantle after the king's death. He scorned Josephus by presenting him as one who tore apart the body politic in Tiberias, creating civil tension and undoing the work of the city's elite.

Josephus' sympathetic audience might have felt betrayed when they discovered that this champion of Judaean culture had actually been responsible for civil strife in Galilee and acted against the interests of Agrippa, his ostensible patron in Rome. Such accusations could damage the reputation of this author who set himself up as the literary spokesman of his people. In *V*, Josephus takes the opportunity to quell any doubts about his credentials as a Jewish politician and, incidentally, as a friend of the respected king.

He provides a link between his character and the Judaean constitution as described in *AJ*.

IV. Conclusion

If we adopt the growing scholarly opinion that from the beginning of his Roman career Josephus was concerned to defend and explain Judaean customs (see introduction above), then with the death of King Agrippa II in the later phase of Domitian's reign (*c*. 92–93), he may have felt even more keenly the need to maintain this role. Although not perhaps of the same standing as his father, the loyal client king Agrippa II had been regarded in Rome as chief representative of the Judaean people, and on terms the Romans could accept – in sharp contrast to the priestly aristocracy, who had evidently failed so catastrophically to maintain order in Jerusalem. Josephus' attempt to co-opt Agrippa (and at times the whole Herodian line) for his nationalistic purposes provided an easy target for someone who was close to the king and supported the client kingship as the best model of Roman-Judaean relations. Such a figure was Justus of Tiberias. He was in a position to undo some of Josephus' most important constructions in *BJ*, and on the other side, to present the Jerusalemite priest as the one who interfered in the prominent city of Tiberias to sow unrest (whether this could have been avoided or not, given Josephus' role) and turn the city against the king. It is possible to accept Mason's basic explanation of *V*'s context and main motives, while also allowing that Justus, by bringing together challenges of character, patronage, and political philosophy in his portrait of Josephus, managed to 'get under the skin' of the author whose work would end up triumphing in western history.

Josephus had previously enjoyed favour at the imperial court and, with the death of Agrippa, he may have felt that in the tense time of Domitian's reign, he could fill the role of advocate of the Jewish people. Agrippa I had managed to negotiate successfully on behalf of the people and Agrippa II, in spite of his inadequacies, at least represented the nation somewhat, if only in the eyes of the Romans. With his death, Josephus could have seen himself as a successor, not in terms of monarchy but as a member of the aristocratic priesthood, those other traditional leaders of the people. Justus' attack threatened such ambitions and Josephus, in response, celebrates the very aspects of his character and career that make him a model representative for his people[54]

Notes

[1] The field of Josephan studies is enjoying a period of unprecedented activity with new approaches and questions which seriously engage his work in its historical and

literary contexts. This trend parallels other literary studies of ancient authors rather than focusing on Josephus as a 'faulty' source for reconstructing the world of ancient Judaism and early Christianity. Two volumes of the new translation and commentary published by Brill and edited by Steve Mason have already been published and a website dedicated to expanding this project to include a history of reception, bibliography and archaeological index is already online (www.paceweb.yorku.ca). This growing interest is reflected in the work of individual scholars, while the International Josephus Colloquium and the Josephus Seminar at the annual meeting of the Society of Biblical Literature provide a useful arena for sharing new ideas and approaches.

When directly quoting from *V* in this paper, I use the new translation by Mason 2001.

[2] Bilde 1988, 123–71. For the purpose of this paper, these categories have been described in very general terms and, it must be added, the scholars cited often diverge from one position on particular points. Bilde's own work has done much to advance the second line of interpretation.

[3] Of the scholars mentioned in this paper, Laqueur 1920; Schalit 1933, 67–95; Cohen 1979; and Schwartz 1990 could generally be seen to represent this group.

[4] Works cited in this paper which follow this trend include Rajak 1983; Rajak 1987, 81–94; Mason 1991; Mason 1998, 64–103; Mason 2001.

[5] Laqueur 1920, 6–32, views the debate as mainly historiographical with Josephus defending the veracity of *BJ* which Justus charged was inaccurate as it covered up the real situation in Galilee. Schalit 1993, 71–95, and Rajak 1987, 85–6, propose that Josephus' actions in Galilee were under attack by Justus, while Cohen 1979, 120, agrees that his behaviour was part of the debate but adds that Justus must also have attacked his character.

[6] Laqueur 1920, 56–79, and Cohen 1979, 67–83, are proponents of the theory that Josephus relied upon a source for *V*. Laqueur 1920, 21, the early Rajak 1973, 345–68, and the early Mason 1991, 322–4, conclude that Justus is the main target for *V* while Cohen 1979, 151–60 and Rajak 1983, 152–3, and 1987, 85–7, suggest that since some issues which appear in *V* could not have been part of the debate with Justus, other critics are also targeted.

[7] These views are respectively presented by Laqueur 1920, 21; Cohen 1979, 140 and 145; and Rajak 1983, 152–3 and 1987, 85–7.

[8] Bilde 1988, 107–13. Neyrey 1994, 177–206, also focuses on the ancient literary context of *V* and proposes that this work should be understood as an encomium as described in *progymnasmata* or ancient writing guides.

[9] Mason 2001, XIII–L.

[10] What follows is based closely on Mason 2001, XIII–L. Rather than footnote every point I refer the reader to those pages.

[11] Mason 2001, 41, n.210, comments on the comic possibilities of the names 'Justus' and 'Pistus'.

[12] Mason, 2001, 39, n. 196, addresses some of the difficulties in accepting the existence of a third party as described by Josephus.

[13] In Josephus' description of John's later attempt to induce Tiberias (as well as Sepphoris and Gabara) to support him, John is successful only in so far as the Tiberians befriend him; they do not revolt outright (*V* 124) and the personal names of those involved are not provided.

[14] *V* 186 has slightly different information: it is not his brother-in law but his brother who has his hands cut off by the Galileans.

[15] Cohen 1979, 133–4; Mason 2001, 39.

[16] Cohen 1979, 181–99.

[17] Goodman 1987, 156, 167–8, believes that Josephus' attempt to portray his colleagues in Jerusalem as moderate is unfounded, for the ruling class did indeed commit themselves to the rebellion. Goodman admits that partisan loyalties were not immune to modification during this tense period but asserts that, in general, the various factions during the revolt mirror earlier alliances. He contends (172–4) that the ruling class provided the impetus for the rebellion and that without their leadership and involvement, it would never have taken place. Price 1992, 11–50 and 27–32, similarly believes that although disunity reigned among the aristocracy they were, for the most part, pro-rebellion.

[18] The issue for scholars here is whether those aristocrats who remained in Jerusalem after Cestius' defeat could have been pro-Roman. Goodman 1987, 157–9, notes that the elite must have taken at least precautionary measures even before Cestius' arrival, for weapons were manufactured and revolutionary coins were minted. Those who took part in such activity before Cestius' defeat and remained thereafter could not have been in any way pro-Roman. Aristocrats who opposed continuing, such as Saul, Costobar and Philip ben Jacimus, made the decision to quit the capital. Price 1992, 32–6, surmises that the aristocracy would not have been accepted as leaders by the rebel factions if they had not taken part in Cestius' defeat. Those who stayed in the city, he concludes, colluded with other rebels.

[19] Cohen 1979, 185–6, notes that Ananus is never called a moderate (μέτριος) and since Josephus actually led the war in Galilee he could not have been allied to such a group. Goodman 1987, 155 and 167, accepts that some members of the ruling class may have been moderate insofar as they hankered for Roman domination since it provided them with a route to power, but he ultimately rejects this as a realistic position because of the evidence that so many fought. This elite, Goodman believes, had most to lose and so supported the rebellion often for practical rather than ideological reasons. Price 1992, 137–8, insists that the term (μέτριοι) should be totally abandoned as Josephus only employs it four times in *BJ* and, in spite of his aim, Josephus cannot attach it to any named individuals. He concludes that the moderate position is simply the product of scholarship.

[20] Rajak 1983, 128–9, supports the existence of a group whose political preference was moderate but who could not maintain such a position during a time of *stasis* and had to commit to one side or the other, even though they may not have been ideologically inclined to do so. She dismisses any evidence for the contrary based on the fact that the word μέτριος is not employed. Mendels 1997, 361–70, discerns the existence of a moderate group with whom the extremists formed a short-lived alliance.

[21] Rajak 1983, 128–9, suggests that involvement by this group could have been for a number of reasons, such as concern for the Temple, religious and national patriotism, as well as vain hope and indecision. Mendels 1997, 363–4, sees this group simply preparing for defensive action, presumably in the hope of coming to an agreement with the Romans. Although coins were minted, there was no traditional declaration of independence or centralization of the army in the Hasmonaean way. Furthermore, when Vespasian arrived, there was no united front.

²² Cohen 1979, 184–5.

²³ *Contra* Goodman 1987, 167–9. He explains the elite's involvement in the rebellion as part of their attempt to maintain their power, which had been undermined through their further alienation from Rome. They needed to establish an independent Jewish state to achieve their former eminence.

²⁴ Although others in Tiberias such as Herod, son of Miarus, and Herod, son of Gamalus, did not launch an attack upon territory belonging to Agrippa II, Justus' involvement with attacks on some cities of the villages of the Syrian Decapolis is likely not to be a complete fabrication. The atmosphere at the outbreak of war was one in which underlying tensions among different sections of the population surfaced and resulted in hostilities, hence Justus' action against the Decapolis was not a sign of his revolutionary credentials. Mason 2001, 47 n.254, suggests that Justus may have been responding to the cruel treatment of Jews by the Scythopolitans mentioned in *V* 26.

²⁵ Mason 2001, 42, n.216, calls into question the possibility of Justus' holding the position ascribed to him by Josephus. He also notes the difficulty Josephus encounters in trying to present Justus as a hawk.

²⁶ Justus appears again when Jonathan and the delegation from Jerusalem go to Tiberias in search of support, having been invited by Jesus the chief magistrate (*V* 271–303). While there, Josephus tells how they persuaded some who were in disagreement with him to defect but no names are given. The following day they met in the prayer-house, where Jonathan and Jesus made speeches against Josephus' leadership. Justus, we are informed, '...came forward and praised Iesous who had said these things; accordingly, he persuaded some of the populace' although his words are not reported (*V* 279). Justus, however, is not named in any of the incidents following this story (*V* 284, 299–300).

²⁷ Mason 2001, 45, n.242 and 45–6, n.245, notes that in spite of the ubiquity of Greek rhetorical training in Roman education, Josephus plays to the Roman prejudices by contrasting his (and Roman) preference for truth over rhetoric.

²⁸ Mason 2001, 47–8, n.257 and 69, n.466. John, a key figure in the triumph who is also mentioned by Tacitus, would have been well known in Rome as a rebel leader.

²⁹ Mason 2001, 137, n.1375, draws attention to the fact that Josephus uses the adjective for 'forged' (πλαστός) only twice, both times in *V*, here and in reference to Justus' brother (*V* 177).

³⁰ Cohen 1979, 114–17 and 128–9, provides other examples of charges of forgery against historians and official secretaries, as well as that of lack of autopsy. He also notes that both *V* and *CA* are replete with common methods of historiographical slights. Moessner 1996, 105–22, esp. 108–20, takes up this topic in the context of defining Josephus' criteria for historiographical accuracy and shows that even as Josephus concerned himself with defence and attack about his and Justus' actions and character, our author maintains a 'theoretical consistency' in that he reveals that Justus fell short of the standard for history writing as presented in *CA* 1.53–4. Mason 2001, 137, n.1373 and 146, n.1474, also draws attention to Josephus' use of stock charges found elsewhere in Josephus' works and among other ancient historians.

³¹ Cohen 1979, 115–16, n.59, suspects that the sixty remaining correspondences which may have been in circulation were not as positive or that Justus had access to others, also of a less affirmative nature. Mason 2001, 149, n.1499, notes that Josephus elsewhere mentions that he sold his work to Agrippa and family (*CA* 1.51).

³² Laqueur 1920, 15–17, draws our attention to the similarities between the

historiographical critique in *V* 336–9 and 357–67, which specifically concerns Justus, and the general polemic offered in *CA* 1.46–56, in terms of both language and concerns. Rajak 1983, 153, reminds us that the tension between Josephus and Justus goes beyond the Tiberias issue as they are competing authors and might attempt to deride the other's work.

[33] Laqueur 1920, 6–23, proposes that Justus attacked Josephus' style to which Josephus, the less talented writer of Greek, had to find a different response. Thus Josephus directed his polemic against Justus' accuracy as a historian as well as against Justus the man. Cohen 1979, 118, n. 70 and 126, notes that in some cases Josephus even offers an entirely different picture and concludes that Justus' attack mainly addressed Josephus' character and actions.

[34] Cohen 1979, 126–8, posits responsibility for the revolt of Tiberias among Justus' charges while Mason 2001, 139, n. 1397 and 143, n. 1431, identifies this as the only charge Josephus confronts but notes that he does not attempt to defend himself.

[35] Mason 2001, 141, n. 1408.

[36] Mason 2001, 136, n. 1368, argues that Josephus could not and does not defend himself against this charge since *BJ* and *V* unequivocally present him as a general fighting a war against the Romans.

[37] Mason 2001, 140, n. 1400, suggests that Justus might not have considered an attack on the villages of the Decapolis as anti-Roman or anti-Agrippa.

[38] Mason 2001, 28, n. 124, cites other scholars who have commented upon this theme in Josephus' works and identifies this as a central concern in *BJ* and a minor one in *AJ*. In his literary assessment of *V* as summarized above, he notes that the aim of the successful aristocratic politician is the maintenance of concord and tranquillity among the populace.

[39] Mason 2001, 138–9, n. 1390 and 67, n. 443, notes that this is a major theme in *V*, which separates the aristocrats from the rebels. He also that comments in *V*, Josephus wishes to show his *clementia* in his dealings with Tiberias (and other Galilean cities). Cohen 1979, 123–5, identifies examples of Josephus' displays of *clementia* towards John of Gischala and others in *V*.

[40] In *V* 82 Josephus claims that he did not punish the people of Sepphoris, Tiberias, and Gabara when he took their cities nor did he take measures against John when he was at his mercy. Mason 2001, 67, nn. 441, 443, 445, highlights the difficulty of substantiating Josephus' claims about the storming of these cities from the narrative in *V*. In *V* 103, 306–8, and 368–9 Josephus mentions how he restrains the Galileans from punishing John but it is difficult to find occasions in the text when John was seriously threatened by Josephus.

[41] Mason 2001, 139, n. 1395, finds the relationship between Josephus and the Galileans revealing since much of *V* is concerned with his gaining control of this group, who then become a weapon against all his opponents. Josephus' popularity with the Galileans and his ability to control them is a refrain throughout *V* and he emphasizes his ability to control this group (*V* 30, 97, 100, 103, 244, 262–6, 307, 329, 369, 377–9, 385, 389).

[42] *V* 82, 98, 385.

[43] Cohen 1979, 117–18, highlights the difficulties in making sense of all the incidents in the polemic. Mason, ibid. 144, nn. 1453, 1456, 1463, surveys the slights Josephus makes about the relationship between Justus and Agrippa and notes that his claims are probably exaggerated or based on hearsay.

[44] Mason 2001, 149, n. 1499, 150, n. 1504, suspects that Justus claimed the king as his source for the war and now Josephus undermines this by showing that the king favoured his work and had a difficult relationship with Justus.

[45] Mason 2001, 144, n. 1453, suggests that although Agrippa imprisoned Justus, he seems to have been compelled to do so to prevent harsher punitive measures being taken by Vespasian. He also notes that Josephus takes what was probably one event and misrepresents it as two.

[46] *V* 26, 128, 141, 171, 286–7, 376, 378 uses the terms ὁμόφυλος and ὁμόεθνος.

[47] For this text, Henry 1959, cod. 33 and FGrH 734 T1–6 and F1–6, 695–9. Scholars debate the question of whether or not this 'Chronicle' is a distinct work from the war account. For a detailed discussion of Justus' work, see Rajak 1973, 358–70; Cohen 1979, 141–3; Mason 2001, 136–7, n. 1371.

[48] Mason 2001, 136–7, n. 1371.

[49] Rajak 1987, 90–1, sees Justus' position as ambiguous at this stage of the war. Mason 2001, 42, n. 219, notes that Justus and Josephus must not have been that different politically. Cohen 1979, 137, n. 126, in discounting almost all the evidence in Josephus as his biased 'glosses', rejects suggestions that Justus was anything but a constant pacifist.

[50] Rajak 1987, 92–3, outlines these similarities. Schwartz 1990, 144–5, attempts to reconstruct the events of Justus' life after his defection to Agrippa. He asks about the importance of Justus' position and proffers the suggestion that maybe Josephus named his son after Justus (circa 75 CE) because of Agrippa's trip to Rome and Justus' position.

[51] Many reasons have been offered for this delay in publication. It is an issue because Josephus made it so and, as Rajak points out, this is a commonplace criticism; Rajak 1987, 82–3. Cohen 1979, 137–8, summarizes some explanations for this delay while Mason 2001, 148, n. 1489, notes that this delay may have been claimed as a virtue by Justus because he could not be charged with indulging in flattery while Agrippa II was still alive.

[52] Mason 2001, 136–7, n. 1371, observes that Justus must have relied upon his link with Agrippa to give him legitimacy as a historian and so Josephus challenges his relationship with the monarch.

[53] Mason 2001, xliii.

[54] Rajak 1983, 225–6, discounts a diplomatic career for the later Josephus (unlike Nicolaus of Damascus) and suggests that he restricted himself to presenting Judaism to a partially hostile and partially sympathetic Gentile world. Cohen 1979, 236–7, declines to outline a real role for Josephus in this period of his life but interprets what he sees as Josephus' new nationalistic outlook as part of his religious bias which was very much in favour of the Pharisees. He proposes the possibility that, as Josephus aligned himself with the emerging Rabbinical power, he may have hoped to represent them in Rome. Schwartz 1990, 214–16, thinks it most likely that Josephus remained publicly active in Jewish affairs, and the propagandistic interests which he displays in *AJ* and *CA* confirm this: his promotion of the observance of Jewish laws and his interest in Jewish leadership in the Gentile Diaspora lead him to conclude that Josephus is involved in a type of advertising campaign on behalf of the law-conscious early Rabbinic movement as the legitimate leaders of the Jewish people. Schwartz does recognize that the one group whom Josephus consistently portrays in a positive light is his own clan, the upper priesthood, who probably did not suffer such losses as the high priesthood.

Bibliography

Bilde, P.

1988   *Flavius Josephus between Jerusalem and Rome. His life, his works, and their importance*, Sheffield.

Cohen, S.J.D.

1979   *Josephus in Galilee and Rome: His* Vita *and development as a historian*, Leiden.

Goodman, M.

1987   *The Ruling Class of Judaea. The origins of the Jewish revolt against Rome* AD *66–70*, Cambridge.

Henry, R.

1959   *Photius,* Bibliothèque. Tome 1, Codices 1–83, Paris.

Laqueur, R.

1920   *Der jüdische Historiker Flavius Josephus*, Giessen.

Mason, S.

1991   *Flavius Josephus on the Pharisees: A compositional-critical study*, Leiden.

1998   ' "Should any wish to enquire further", (*Ant.* 1.25): The aims and audience of Josephus', *Judaean Antiquities/Life*', in S. Mason (ed.) *Understanding Josephus. Seven perspectives*, Sheffield, 64–103.

2001   *Life of Josephus. Translation and commentary*, Leiden.

Mendels, D.

1997   *The Rise and Fall of Jewish Nationalism. Jewish and Christian ethnicity in ancient Palestine*, Grand Rapids.

Moessner, D.P.

1996   ' "Eyewitnesses", "Informed Contemporaries", and "Unknowing Inquirers": Josephus' criteria for authentic historiography and the meaning of παρακολουθέω', *NovT* 38, 105–22.

Neyrey, J.H.

1994   'Josephus' *Vita* and the encomium: a native model of personality', *JSJ* 25, 177–206.

Price, J.J.

1992   *Jerusalem Under Siege. The collapse of the Jewish state 66–70* CE, Leiden.

Rajak, T.

1973   'Justus of Tiberias', *CQ* 23, 345–68.

1983   *Josephus. The historian and his society*, London.

1987   'Josephus and Justus of Tiberias', in L.H. Feldman and G. Hata (eds.) *Josephus, Judaism and Christianity*, Leiden, 81–94.

Schalit, A.

1933   'Josephus und Justus. Studien zur Vita des Josephus', *Klio* 26, 67–95.

Schwartz, S.

1990   *Josephus and Judaean Politics*, Leiden.

12

SACRED WRITING, SACRED READING: THE FUNCTION OF AELIUS ARISTIDES' SELF-PRESENTATION AS AUTHOR IN THE *SACRED TALES*

Alexia Petsalis-Diomidis

Introduction: autobiography within an Asklepian votive offering

Almost two hundred years after his death in the late second century AD, Aelius Aristides was admired and imitated by the orator Libanios. Libanios' admiration for Aristides was of a personal as well as a literary nature: he wanted to acquire a portrait of him, and he asked at least two acquaintances to help him find one. On receiving a painted portrait from his friend Theodoros, then governor of Bithynia, he sent him this letter:

ἔχω τὸν Ἀριστείδην, πρᾶγμα πάλαι ποθούμενον, καὶ σοὶ χάριν ἔχω μικροῦ τοσαύτην, ὅσηνπερ ἄν, εἰ αὐτὸν ἡμῖν ἀναστήσας τὸν ἄνδρα ἐπεπόμφεις. καὶ παρακάθημαί γε τῇ γραφῇ τῶν ἐκείνου τι βιβλίων ἀναγιγνώσκων ἐρωτῶν αὐτόν, εἰ αὐτὸς ταῦτα. εἶτ' αὐτὸς ἀποκρίνομαι ἐμαυτῷ· 'ναί, ταῦτά γε ἐκεῖνος·' καὶ γὰρ ἔπρεπε τοιούτων λόγων τοιαύτην μορφὴν εἶναι μητέρα· οὕτω πάντα θεοειδῆ καὶ καλὰ καὶ κρείττω τῶν πολλῶν.[1]

I have the portrait of Aristides, something I have long desired, and I am almost as grateful to you as if you had resurrected the man himself and sent him to me. And I sit by his portrait, read some book of his and ask him whether he was the one who wrote that. Then I answer my question myself. 'Yes, he did that.' Indeed, it was only proper that such a handsome figure should produce such eloquence.

This passage suggests how strongly the character of Aristides emerges from his writings. Firstly Libanios' desire to see the person Aristides arises solely from his study of the latter's public orations. Secondly this powerful mental image of Aristides has to be re-adjusted in the light of the new visual image of Aristides, through the process of concurrent viewing and reading. The strength of Libanios' mental image of Aristides is further suggested later in the letter when it is revealed that he had already rejected the first portrait of the orator he had been sent because it did not look like the man who emerges from Aristides' writings:

ἐγὼ δὲ ἠπίστουν τοῦτον ἐκεῖνον εἶναι· τῆς τε γὰρ νόσου τῆς πολλῆς ἀπᾴδειν τὸ πρόσωπον τήν τε κόμην ἄλλον τινὰ μηνύειν. οὐ γὰρ εἶχον εὑρεῖν, ἐξ ὅτου τοσαύτην ἔθρεψεν ἄν.[2]

But I could not believe that this was Aristides, for the face seemed to be out of keeping with his serious illness and the hair indicated that it was someone else, for I could not see how he should have such a growth of it.

Libanios had concluded that this image was in fact a depiction of Asklepios, the god whom Aristides worshipped above all others, and in a neat reversal he decided to place what he took to be the image of the god in the temple of Olympian Zeus at Antioch. In fact, the arrival of the second identical portrait from Theodoros convinced Libanios that his attribution had been wrong. But the healthy aspect of the man depicted still troubled him, and at the end of the letter he requests that Theodoros ask around for an explanation of Aristides' abundant hair growth. Libanios' fascination with Aristides' physical appearance is confirmed at the end of the letter where he urges his friend to acquire on his behalf a full-length image of Aristides because he was 'awfully eager to see the hands and feet' (ἐπιθυμῶ γὰρ δεινῶς χεῖράς τε καὶ πόδας ἰδεῖν).[3]

Libanios' distinct sense of Aristides' personality and body was rooted in Aristides' self-presentation in his orations, above all in the Ἱεροὶ Λόγοι, *Sacred Tales*. This work, written *c.* 170 AD, is said to be a thank offering to Asklepios and consists of an account of the god's exertions (ἀγωνίσματα) in favour of Aristides.[4] It is written in the first person and its pronounced focus on Aristides' person – in particular on his relationship with the god, on his body and his practice of oratory – has led some modern scholars to interpret the *Sacred Tales* as an 'autobiography'.[5] Indeed Libanios used the *Sacred Tales* as a literary model for what is perhaps the first clearly autobiographical work produced in Europe Βίος ἢ περὶ τῆς ἑαυτοῦ τύχης, *Autobiography*. But while there are significant autobiographical dimensions in the *Sacred Tales* I would argue that locating it within a distinctly autobiographical rather than aretalogical genre has resulted in the distortion of the text and in very bad press for the author.[6] In effect this self-proclaimed thank offering to Asklepios has often been seen as a thinly veiled autobiography which uses the god as an excuse to trumpet the author's own talents and successes. Seen primarily as an autobiographical account Aristides' exclusive focus on himself, his body, his oratory, his dreams and 'his' god, to the exclusion of any other significant characters or relationships, makes the work appear to be the bizarre product of a highly self-absorbed author. The repeated assertions of the god's involvement in all aspects of Aristides' life (from public oratorical performances through to intimate bodily functions) are also unusual and problematic. These judgements are often accompanied by dislike and even contempt for Aristides if the text is seen through a Christian (or implicitly Christian) prism. Such a perspective transforms Aristides' focus on himself and his body into self-absorbed hypochondria, and his assertion of the constant involvement of the god into arrogance and superficial religiosity.[7]

If, however, the *Sacred Tales* is seen primarily as praise of the god through the personal testimony of the author, what appears bizarre in a purely autobiographical account falls into place. An exclusive personal focus in an aretalogy is innovative and can be seen on the one hand against the general background of an increasing focus on the individual in this period and on the other in the context of the traditional practices of the cult of Asklepios.[8] Aristides' exclusive focus on himself – on the favours he had received from the god – and the importance he accords to his personal testimony of salvation are features of both inscriptional and sculptural thank offerings found at healing sanctuaries dedicated to Asklepios. Moreover, such dedications focus on the bodies of pilgrims, just as the *Sacred Tales* focus on Aristides' body. This text is also established within the discourse of Asklepian dedications of praise and thanks by explicit statements that it is a thank offering to the god and that it was ordered by him (the latter being a common feature of Asklepian dedications).[9] The title of the work, revealed to Aristides' foster father in a dream, supports this interpretation: a ἱερός λόγος, essentially an aetiological account of a religious ceremony, usually involved the narration of the deeds of the god.[10] Most fundamentally the title defines the work as 'of' the god – not just about the god but also belonging to the god. In the opening chapter Aristides describes his task as telling 'the exertions of the god as many as I have enjoyed to the present day' (τὰ τοῦ Σωτῆρος ἀγωνίσματα, ὅσων ἀπέλαυσα εἰς τήνδε τὴν ἡμέραν):[11] the involvement of the god in every episode, however minor, is axiomatic in such a work.

The autobiographical element of Aristides' literary thank offering to Asklepios is, in common with other Asklepian dedications, very prominent. This operates on a number of levels, most obviously through the first-person narration of episodes of Aristides' life which are linked to the intervention of Asklepios. Aristides' self-presentation as a great orator is another autobio-graphical aspect of the text. Through a series of references he actively fashions himself on the models both of the great classical orator Demosthenes, and the skilful speaker and long-suffering traveller Odysseus.[12] His oratorical successes and difficulties in the face of his illnesses are recurring themes.[13] The composition and performance of speeches and hymns as therapy is another aspect of this presentation.[14] The published (and still extant) speeches he wrote during the 'kathedra' (his two-year stay at the Asklepieion of Pergamon) are specifically named in the *Sacred Tales*.[15] The prominence of oratory in Aristides' literary self-presentation should be seen in the context of the high level of public interest in the great orators of the time.[16]

On a more subtle level, though, an important element of Aristides' self-presentation in the *Sacred Tales* is as author of that very text. It is this auto-biographical aspect of the *Sacred Tales* which is the focus of this paper. In my analysis I first examine ways in which Aristides brings attention to himself as author of the *Sacred Tales*, secondly I explore the details of this authorial self-portrait, and thirdly I raise the question of the purpose of this self-presentation. I argue that Aristides' self-presentation as author of the *Sacred Tales* is intimately bound to the religious purpose of the work. In particular I demonstrate that this theme is used to present the process of writing the *Sacred Tales* as a religious act, and at the same time to elicit a religious reading from the audience.

One narrative among many: the *Sacred Tales* as *text*

Throughout the *Sacred Tales* Aristides refuses to allow the implicit conflation of the events he describes with the text through which he describes them. He sets up and continually emphasizes the distinction between the deeds of the god in his favour (life) and their inadequate description (text). One of the principal ways in which he achieves this is through self-conscious references to other texts which have been written or potentially could be written about these same experiences. He uses these imaginary or unpublished texts as an indication to the reader of what the *Sacred Tales* is *not*. He writes, for example, that he had kept a record of his dreams at the command of Asklepios, and he refers to this as an ἀπογραφή, 'written list', and also as διφθέραι 'parchment books'.[17] Many scholars have interpreted these references literally and argued over whether Aristides used these records in the composition of the *Sacred Tales*, with implications for the 'accuracy' of the work.[18] Pearcy has convincingly argued that the literary function of these dream books is as a foil against which to read the *Sacred Tales* itself:[19] whereas the dream books are said to give an exact account of the revelations of the god, the *Sacred Tales* is a summary of the events and conveys the telescoped essence of the experience, its meaning, as far as that can be expressed in words. It is explicitly presented as a selective and not a comprehensive account. The disordered chronology of the events and dreams described in the *Sacred Tales* – a feature for which Aristides has been severely criticized by modern scholars – can be read as part of this 'essential' rather than exhaustive discourse.[20] Aristides at one point suggests that he has made a considered choice *not* to relate all his dreams (in the manner, presumably of the dream books) but instead to summarize them according to a scheme:

ὅτι μὲν δὴ τῷ παντὶ φρικωδέστερον καὶ ἐναργέστερον αὐτὰς τὰς ὄψεις καθαρὰς διηγεῖσθαι δῆλον, ἀνάγκη δὲ ἐπὶ τῶν πλείστων χρῆσθαι τῇ ὑποθέσει ἥπερ ἐνεστησάμην καὶ κεφάλαια ἐπιτρέχειν, ὅπως ἂν ἀπαντᾷ τῷ λόγῳ.[21]

It is evident that it would be in every way more awesome and clearer to narrate the simple visions themselves, but in most things it is necessary to use the plan that I have instituted and to discuss summarily the main points, as they occur in the tale.

Repeated assertions that the *Sacred Tales* is a summary of the events, and references to another text about the same events (the dream books), on the one hand signal to the reader the author's understanding of the nature of this text, and on the other, implicitly reinforce his or her awareness of the *Sacred Tales* as a *text* distinct from the events themselves.

Aristides explains to the reader that his decision to summarize the events is due partly to his lapse of memory about events stretching back over thirty years, but fundamentally to the inadequacy of words in describing the deeds of the god.[22] In the narrative account of the beginning of Asklepios' revelations at Pergamon Aristides combines this theme of his inadequacy as an author with the theme of the dream books:

τὰ δ' ἐντεῦθεν ἔστι μὲν οὐ κατ' ἄνθρωπον διηγήσασθαι, ἐγχειρητέον δέ, ὥσπερ ὑπεθέμην, ἐξ ἐπιδρομῆς ἔνια αὐτῶν διελθεῖν εἰ δέ τις τὰ ἀκριβέστατα γνῶναι βουλήσεται τῶν γεγενημένων ἡμῖν παρὰ τοῦ θεοῦ, ὥρα τὰς διφθέρας αὐτῷ ζητεῖν καὶ τὰ ὀνείρατα αὐτά. καὶ γὰρ ἰάματα παντὸς εἴδους καὶ διαλόγους τινὰς εὑρήσει καὶ λόγους ἐν μήκει καὶ φάσματα παντοῖα καὶ προρρήσεις ἁπάσας καὶ χρησμῳδίας περὶ παντοδαπῶν πραγμάτων, τὰς μὲν καταλογάδην, τὰς δὲ ἐν μέτροις γεγονυίας, καὶ χαρίτων πάντ' ἄξια τῷ θεῷ μειζόνων ἤ τις ἂν εἰκάσαι.[23]

To narrate what came next is not within the power of man. Still I must try, as I have proposed to do, to recount some of these things in a cursory way. But if someone will wish to know precisely what has befallen us from the god, it is time for him to seek out the parchment books and the dreams themselves. For he will find cures of all kinds and some discourses and full scale orations and various visions, and all the prophecies and oracles about every kind of matter, some in prose, some in verse, and all deserving of a gratitude to the god greater than one might expect.

Here Aristides refers the reader 'out' of the *Sacred Tales* to the dream books for an account that would do justice to the events. The rhetorical nature of this statement is suggested not only by the fact that the dream books were not published, but also by Aristides' own admission five chapters previously that the dream books were in fact incomplete (he was not assiduous in keeping the records from the start), did not give the context of the dreams, were chronologically confused, and, above all, were partially lost.[24]

197

So this invitation to the reader to consult the dream books has a similar function to the evocation, at the beginning of the *Sacred Tales*, of an imaginary record of the totality of events:

ἑκάστη γὰρ τῶν ἡμετέρων ἡμερῶν, ὡσαύτως δὲ καὶ νυκτῶν, ἔχει συγγραφήν, εἴ τις παρ᾽ ἓν ἢ τὰ συμπίπτοντα ἀπογράφειν ἠβούλετο ἢ τὴν τοῦ θεοῦ πρόνοιαν διηγεῖσθαι, ὧν τὰ μὲν ἐκ τοῦ φανεροῦ παρών, τὰ δὲ τῇ πομπῇ τῶν ἐνυπνίων ἐνεδείκνυτο, ὅσα γε δὴ καὶ ὕπνου λαχεῖν ἐξῆν·[25]

For each of our days, as well as our nights, has a story, if someone, who was present at them, wished either to record the events or to narrate the providence of the god, wherein he revealed some things openly in his own presence and others by the sending of dreams, as far as it was possible to obtain sleep.

Elsewhere he implies that a complete narrative such as this is by its very nature an impossibility:

τίς κεν ἐκεῖνα πάντα γε μυθήσαιτο καταθνητῶν ἀνθρώπων; οὐ γὰρ πεντάετες οὐδ᾽ ἑξάετες οὐκ ἀρκεῖ, ἀλλ᾽ οὐκ ἐλαττόνων ἴσως ἐστὶ χρόνων ἡ διήγησις ἢ ἐν ὅσοις τὰ πράγματα ἐγίγνετο.[26]

'What mortal man might tell all these things?' 'For neither five nor six years' are sufficient, but the narration perhaps needs no less time than that, in which the events took place.

This suggestion that a full narration of the events would take as much time as it took to live through the events, implicitly raises the issue of the relationship of the text to the events it describes. In effect Aristides again refers the reader 'beyond' the *Sacred Tales*, but this time to the events themselves.

Frequent references to other real or potential texts about the deeds of the god help to define through contrast the nature of this innovative Asklepian literary thank offering. On another level these references continually remind the reader that this is one particular view of the deeds themselves, to which he or she is constantly referred. Overall the effect is to emphasize the *Sacred Tales* as a *text*, as a literary mediation between the events and the audience, and thus implicitly to emphasize its author Aristides.

Aristides the reluctant, divinely-inspired author

Aristides also makes explicit references to his authorship of the *Sacred Tales*. Throughout he presents himself as an unwilling author because the task of describing the divine in words is impossible. In the two passages which deal directly with the issue of his motivation for writing the *Sacred Tales*, Aristides states that he long resisted his friends' requests that he write about the favours he received from the god because of the impossibility of remembering and describing all of them.[27] The stated purpose of the work is to praise and thank the god for his deeds, and it is suggested that an incomplete account would in some way pollute them:

χρόνου δὲ αὖ προελθόντος ἕν τι τῶν ἀδυνάτων εἶναι ἐδόκει καὶ μνημονεῦσαι ἕκαστα καὶ δι᾽ ἀκριβείας εἰπεῖν· κρεῖττον οὖν εἶναι σιωπᾶν ὅλως ἢ λυμήνασθαι τοσούτοις ἔργοις.

Again as time passed it seemed to be an impossibility to remember each thing and to tell it precisely. So I thought that it was better to keep completely silent than to spoil such great deeds.[28]

Aristides' preference was to maintain a religious silence on the subject, not to use words (λόγοι) to describe his contact with the divine. His reluctance is said to be overcome only through divine revelations which compelled him to make this thank offering.[29] The initial decision to write the *Sacred Tales* is thus presented as a religious, votive act. The *text* as an object is thus implicitly presented as a comparable thank offering to others made by Aristides *within* the text, such as a silver tripod, a ring or a blood sacrifice.[30] And the *act* of writing the text is presented as the obedient response to the god's revelation, and thus qualitatively comparable to other commands which Aristides obeys *within* the text, ranging from making extempore speeches to bathing in freezing rivers, vomiting and receiving enemas.[31]

The intensity of this relationship of submission is in fact dramatized throughout the *Sacred Tales* by Aristides' invitation to the god to lead him as he composes:

ὑπόλοιπον οὖν ἐστι κεφάλαια λέγειν, ἄλλα ἄλλοθεν ἀναμιμνησκόμενον, ὅπως ἂν ὁ θεὸς ἄγῃ τε καὶ κινῇ. καλοῦμεν δ᾽ αὐτὸν καὶ πρὸς αὐτὰ ταῦτα ὥσπερ πρὸς ἅπαντα·[32]

The only thing left is to speak in summary fashion, as I remember different things from the different sources, however the god will lead and stimulate me. We call on him even in this, as in all things.

The function of this passage as more than a conventional invocation to a divine power is suggested by a series of passages in which Aristides directly addresses the god and publicly consults him on the direction of the narrative.[33] In one instance the god is presented as altering the course of the text by manifesting himself to Aristides in a dream in the days when he was writing.[34] Intense and personal communication between Aristides and the god – a theme which surfaces in most episodes and in fact underpins the whole of the *Sacred Tales* – is thus dramatized in a present and immediate way on the level of literary composition. These passages not only express the intimacy of the relationship between Asklepios and Aristides, they also have implications for the status of the text as divinely authored (or perhaps co-authored).

But as we have seen, Aristides insists on the inadequacy of his words in conveying the reality of the experience, even in the summarized, planned and divinely-directed *Sacred Tales*. Repeated referrals of the reader beyond the text to other real or imaginary texts and to the events themselves is one aspect of this theme. Another is implicit or explicit invitations to the reader to imagine more than Aristides can describe in words. The reader is asked to actively participate in the reading of the text by drawing on her or his own religious sensibilities and experiences. In a dream narrative in the second sacred tale Aristides gives a vivid and moving description of his encounter with Asklepios:

καὶ γὰρ οἷον ἅπτεσθαι δοκεῖν ἦν καὶ διαισθάνεσθαι ὅτι αὐτὸς ἥκοι, καὶ μέσως ἔχειν ὕπνου καὶ ἐγρηγόρσεως καὶ βούλεσθαι ἐκβλέπειν καὶ ἀγωνιᾶν μὴ προαπαλλαγείη, καὶ ὦτα παραβεβληκέναι καὶ ἀκούειν, τὰ μὲν ὡς ὄναρ, τὰ δὲ ὡς ὕπαρ, καὶ τρίχες ὀρθαὶ καὶ δάκρυα σὺν χαρᾷ καὶ γνώμης ὄγκος ἀνεπαχθής, καὶ τίς ἀνθρώπων ταῦτα γ᾽ ἐνδείξασθαι λόγῳ δυνατός; εἰ δέ τις τῶν τετελεσμένων ἐστίν, σύνοιδεν τε καὶ γνωρίζει.[35]

For there was a seeming as it were to touch him and to perceive that he himself had come, and to be between sleep and waking, and to wish to look up and to be in anguish that he might depart too soon, and to strain the ears and to hear some things as in a dream, some as in a waking state. Hair stood straight, and there were tears with joy, and the pride of one's heart was inoffensive. And what man could describe these things in words? If any man has been initiated, he knows and understands.

Aristides' description is in fact very effective in conveying the sense of divine presence *as far as words go* – not least through his elliptical style – but in addition the conclusion of the passage clearly aims to elicit a personal response or memory in the reader. Later in the fourth sacred tale, Aristides invites a similar elaboration in the mind of the reader retrospectively on all the narrative of the *Sacred Tales*:

τὰ μὲν περὶ τοὺς λόγους καὶ ὡς κατέστησεν ἡμᾶς ἐξ ἀρχῆς εἰς αὐτοὺς καὶ ψῆφον ὁποίαν τινὰ ἤνεγκε περὶ αὐτῶν καὶ ὅσα εἰς τοῦτο φέροντα ἐχρημάτιζεν καὶ τοὔνομα ὡς πρὸς τῷ ἀρχαίῳ τὸν Θεόδωρον προσέθετο καὶ περὶ τῆς αὐτοῦ φύσεως ὁποῖ᾽ ἄττα ἔδειξεν καὶ ὅσα τοῦ τύπου τούτου, πάντα μὲν οὐδ᾽ ἐγγὺς εἴρηται, ὅσα δὲ ἦν ἔναυλα καὶ ἀφ᾽ ὧν ἔξεστι περὶ τῶν ἄλλων τεκμαίρεσθαι.[36]

As to the practice of oratory, how he brought us to it in the beginning, and what was his verdict about our career, and all the oracles which he gave pertaining to this, and how he added 'Theodoros' to my old name, and what sort of things he revealed concerning his nature, and as much as there is of this character, not nearly all has been said, but as much as was ringing in my ears, and from which it is possible to conjecture about the rest.

This passage paradoxically both emphasizes the divinely-inspired act of composition, but simultaneously draws back from the conclusion that the resulting text adequately conveys the deeds of the god. Aristides' earlier expression of his concern not to pollute the deeds of the god through his inadequate words (his self-presentation as a reluctant author), in combination with the god's insistence on publicizing these deeds and his participation in the process of composition (his self-presentation as a divinely-driven and divinely-inspired author), together invite a religious reading of the text. The reader is made aware that this partial and fragmented account of the deeds demands the active involvement of the imagination for an understanding of the reality of Aristides' experience. The invitation to 'imagine the rest' is thus an important mechanism by which the reader is drawn in and implicated in the religious discourse of the *Sacred Tales*.

Describing writing and not writing

In addition to Aristides' depiction of the god's participation in the process of composition of the *Sacred Tales* he makes numerous references to his own authorial choices at various points in the narrative. As we have seen, the use of references to other potential texts is one such element, as is the repeated statement that the *Sacred Tales* is a summary. Other aspects include telling the reader that he has finished a particular episode, or that he will now start a new story, telling the reader that he is changing the plan of composition, and justifying his inclusion of certain elements not usual in a narrative of Asklepian deeds.[37] This technique reinforces the sense of the *Sacred Tales* as a text, as one particular version of the events, and it keeps the image of the author Aristides firmly in the reader's mind.

The process of composition is also dramatized by statements about what Aristides is *not* going to tell the reader: he self-censors himself in order to avoid revealing religious experiences and truths that are not meant for the uninitiated.[38] While most of the instances in which Aristides withholds stories are to do with divine revelations, there are also some examples where self-censorship is applied to his own achievements on account of modesty and because they are tangential to the subject of the achievements of the god, and others where it apparently operates because of the need to press ahead with the story and not linger unnecessarily.[39] Two further aspects of the break-down of words which I have already touched on are statements about the fundamental inadequacy of words in describing the divine, and statements about the lapse of memory which prevents describing and naming.[40] On another level, words cannot be used to describe the god's future exertions in favour of Aristides, as the relationship is envisaged as ongoing.[41] Invitations to the reader to imagine what Aristides cannot describe are closely linked to such break-downs. Aristides' reputation as a great orator, and indeed his self-presentation as such in the *Sacred Tales*, render this failure of words particularly striking. These 'negative' references are tantalizing, and are comparable to references to texts which Aristides is *not* going to offer to the reader (the dream books and the potential narrative of the totality of events).

This theme of the break-down of words self-consciously underlines the process of writing, and in particular the process of writing about the divine. Such references to the process of composition and changes of plan, in combination with the disordered chronology and elliptical style mentioned above, have in fact been so persuasive that some scholars regard the *Sacred Tales* as an unpolished text, written in haste and not revised.[42] Without necessarily implying that Aristides' experience of composition was not that described in the text, and certainly without implying a calculated manipulation of the reader, it seems to me highly unlikely that a writer and orator of Aristides' stature would have been unaware of the impact of these instances of the break-down of his words. Fundamentally the break-down of normal discourse in the description of the divine, and in particular the withholding of religious knowledge from the uninitiated, dramatize the very experience they ostensibly fail to describe by emphasizing its 'otherness'. In another second-century narrative of sacred travel, Pausanias' *Description of Greece*, discourse similarly breaks down at crucial moments in relation to religious images and mysteries, thereby conveying its importance and its operation on a sphere not susceptible to normal description.[43] This feature speaks volumes about the author's relationship with the divine, but crucially it also sets the reader within a religious framework by not allowing him or her to read about certain aspects of the divine. It can be interpreted as an invitation not only to imagine what is not expressed in words but also to search out the experience by making the sacred journeys which the authors are describing.

Most instances of self-censorship are articulated by means of simple statements that Aristides may not reveal a particular dream. In the fourth sacred tale he brings up the issue in a novel way and in fact relates the revelatory dream:

τὰ δ' ἐντεῦθεν ἤδη, εἰ μὲν θέμις, εἰρήσθω καὶ γεγράφθω, εἰ δὲ μή, τοσοῦτον σοί μελήσειεν, δέσποτα Ἀσκληπιέ, ἐπὶ νοῦν ἀγαγεῖν μοι διαγράψαι παντὸς δυσκόλου χωρίς. ... καὶ ταῦτα μὲν ἡμῖν εἰρηκόσι μηδὲν ἔλαττον εἴη τῆς πρόσθεν τιμῆς παρὰ τοῦ θεοῦ.[44]

As to what comes next, if it is fitting, let it be said and written, and if not, may you be fully concerned, Lord Asklepios, to prompt me to describe it without causing any disagreeableness. ... And now that we have said these things, may we have not less honour than before from the god.

This passage combines the theme of revelation of religious knowledge with that of divine participation in the process of composition. The relationship of Aristides and Asklepios is thus powerfully enacted and becomes present to the reader.

Conclusions: writing, pilgrimage and religious transformation

Aristides' references to writing the *Sacred Tales* dramatize the immediacy of the author and imply an experiential process of composition. The text as a whole reflects the unfolding experiential nature of contact with the god through instances of the break-down of words, unexpected and self-conscious changes in the direction of the narrative, all in the context of the participation of the god in the act of composition. I suggest that this is related to Aristides' treatment of the subject of the *Sacred Tales*: the favours bestowed by the god on Aristides are translated into the unfolding relationship of Aristides with the god, Aristides' changing understanding of his pilgrimages, and his religious transformation. In the fourth sacred tale Aristides explicitly describes how his understanding of his pilgrimage to Asklepios at Pergamon changed through the process of the pilgrimage:

ἐκέλευε δὲ καὶ συντιθέναι λόγους, οὐ μόνον ἐκ τοῦ παραχρῆμα ἀγωνίζεσθαι, καὶ προσέτι γε ἐκμανθάνειν ἔστιν ὅτε κατὰ ῥῆμα. καὶ μοι τὸ πρᾶγμα πολλὴν παρεῖχε τὴν ἀπορίαν οὐδὲν τῶν ὕστερον οὔτ' ἐνθυμηθῆναι δήπου δυναμένῳ οὔτε πιστεῦσαι τί ποτ' αὐτῷ βούλεται ταῦτα. πάνυ γοῦν ἐν τούτοις ἐμοὶ...ποῦ δὲ ἔξεστι σχολάσαι τοσοῦτον, σωθῆναι πρότερον ἦν· τῷ δέ, ὡς ἔοικεν, ἅμα μὲν σοφίσματα ταῦτ' ἦν εἰς τὰ παρόντα, ἅμα δ' ἐδόκει τι κρεῖττον αὐτῷ ἢ σῶσαι μόνον. ἔσῳζεν οὖν διὰ πλείονος ἀξίων ἢ ὅσουπερ ἦν τὸ σωθῆναι.[45]

But the god also ordered me to compose speeches, not only to contend extemporaneously, and besides sometimes to learn them word for word. And the matter afforded me much difficulty, for neither was I at all able to conceive of any of the things which were to follow, nor could I trust his purpose. Indeed in these circumstances – how could I have so much ease – first I had to be saved. Yet, as it seems, these were his contrivances for the present, but at the same time it occurred to him to do something greater than just to save me. Therefore he saved me by means worth more than the act of being saved.

Whereas when Aristides first went to Pergamon he hoped that Asklepios would cure him once and for all in order that he might resume the practice of his oratory, he slowly realized that the contact he established with the god was more valuable to him (and to his oratory) than a simple return to health. Pausanias' statement towards the end of the *Description of Greece*, that his appreciation of the significance of myth had changed in the course of his journey, can be seen as a parallel to Aristides' new understanding of the divine through his pilgrimages.[46] Aristides' personal transformation through contact with the divine is also signalled by his adoption of a new name given to him by Asklepios: Theodoros, to signify that his whole existence is a gift of the god.[47]

I have argued that Aristides' emphasis on himself and his body in the *Sacred Tales* – the autobiographical dimension – makes sense within the context of Asklepian votive offerings. The stories of Aristides' treatments share many features with those inscribed on marble plaques in Asklepieia, not least in the Pergamene Asklepieion.[48] Aristides' emphasis on his authorship of the *Sacred Tales* throughout that text is a remarkable aspect of his self-presentation. He achieves this heightened awareness of his authorship by reminding the reader that the *Sacred Tales* is a *text*, in other words, by constantly rupturing the reader's illusion of the immediacy of the events described through a series of references to other real or potential texts about the same subject, and by references to the process of composition, including divine participation. A particularly striking technique is an 'articulated' break-down of words, both generically in relation to the divine (expressions of the inadequacy of words) and specifically in the context of revelatory dreams (advertised self-censorship). All this has the effect of presenting the act of composition as a religious process. The corollary of the break-down of words and of invitations to the reader to imagine what Aristides cannot (or will not) describe is that the act of reading is also fashioned as a religious process. The text is thus profoundly religious in intent and effect. I have further suggested that the presentation of Aristides' authorship of the *Sacred Tales* as an experiential process is linked to the transformational nature of contact with the divine, and that the text reflects this in a highly sophisticated way. The interpretation of the *Sacred Tales* within the discourses of travel and pilgrimage further illuminates this text. The experiential tone of writing can be seen as reflecting the author's/pilgrim's developing understanding of the meaning of his pilgrimage. More broadly the process of writing about pilgrimage, and fashioning the self within such writing, is an important feature of pilgrimage cross-culturally. It is within the context of the discourses of Asklepian pilgrimage that the autobiographical features of the *Sacred Tales*, and in particular the presentation of Aristides as author, are to be interpreted.

Notes

[1] Libanios *Letters* no. 143.1–2 (A.F. Norman 1992, 294–5).

[2] Libanios *Letters* 143.3.

[3] Libanios *Letters* 143.5.

[4] Aelius Aristides *Sacred Tales* (henceforth *ST*) I.1, also II.1–4. For the text see Keil 1958; translations are from Behr 1981.

⁵ The *ST* is written in the first person singular and occasionally the first person plural. See Boulanger 1923, 163 ('Ces extraordinaires mémoires, qui nous ont fourni déjà tout l'essentiel de la biographie d'Aristide, renseignent abondamment sur son caractère et ses idées religieuses.') and Behr 1968, 23 'At this point begins the period covered by the *Sacred Tales*, which, except for the gap of ten years (155–65 AD), contain the account of the next twenty-six years of Aristides' life'.

⁶ On the difficulty of categorizing the *ST* see Quet 1993, 249–50.

⁷ See for example Boulanger 1923, 172; Phillips 1952; Festugière 1954, 97–8, 103; Gourevitch and Gourevitch 1968; Behr 1968, 44–6; Bowersock 1969, 72; Reardon 1971, 258, 261, 262; Misch 1973, 495–510 (especially 502, 506–8); Brown 1978, 27–53 (especially 41); MacMullen 1981, 9, 15; Lane Fox 1986, 160; Hoffmann 1998, 54. In contrast see Pearcy 1988; Dodds 1990, 41–3, 52; Quet 1993; Cox Miller 1994, 184–204; Perkins 1992 and 1995, 173–90; King 1999; Rutherford 1999.

⁸ See Brown 1978 and Foucault 1990. On holy men in particular and their representation in literature see Bieler 1935–6, Smith 1971, Brown 1981, Fowden 1982 and Cox 1983, Van Dam 1993, Anderson 1994, Potter 1994, Francis 1995, Frank 1998. On authorial self-narrative in the context of 2nd-century literature see Said 1993 and Reardon 1999. On the originality of the project of the *ST* see Quet 1993, 239.

⁹ *ST* I.1 and II.1–3. Stories of Asklepios discussing the kind of thank offering with the incubant or ordering a particular one during his manifestations to pilgrims occur in the Epidaurian miracle inscriptions: LiDonnici 1995, 88–9 (A4), 92–3 (A8), 96–7 (A15), 104–5 (B5). The practice is also referred to in the 2nd-century *Lex Sacra* from the Asklepieion of Pergamon where the pilgrim is required to offer 'anything else the god should require' (Wörrle 1969, lines 33–4). The sense of communication between the pilgrim and the god in the course of incubation is conveyed by phrases in 2nd century Pergamene votive inscriptions such as κατὰ ἐπιταγήν 'in accordance with command' (Habicht 1969, nos. 72, 139), κατὰ συνταγήν 'in accordance with a command' (Habicht 1969, nos. 69, 120, 123), κατὰ κέλευσιν τοῦ θεοῦ 'in accordance with the order of the god' (Müller 1987, 194, line 6), κατ' ὄνειρον and κατ' ὄναρ 'in accordance with a dream' (Habicht 1969, nos. 75, 76, 77, 91, 116, 117, 127) and κατὰ ἐνυπνίου ὄψιν 'in accordance with the vision of a dream' (Habicht 1969, no.132).

¹⁰ *ST* II.9. Boulanger 1923, 163 and Festugière 1954, 88. See Weiss 1998, 30–7 for an interpretation of the title as a reference to Aristides becoming 'a god in the cult of rhetoric'.

¹¹ *ST* I.1.

¹² References to Demosthenes *ST* I.16, IV.15, IV.18, IV.19, IV.97, V.63. References to the *Odyssey* include *ST* I.1, II.60, II.65, V.12, V.44. On Aristides' use of Homer see Kindstrand 1975, 73–97.

¹³ References to his successes include *ST* I.49, IV.49, IV.78, IV.87, IV.102, V.16.

¹⁴ Examples of therapeutic composition or performance include *ST* I.73, IV.4, IV.17–18, IV.22, IV.30, IV.38.

¹⁵ *ST* IV.25 (*In Defence of Running*, prose hymns *Athena* and *Dionysos*), V.39 (*Against the Sophists* Oration 34).

¹⁶ See Bowersock 1969 and Gleason 1995. Philostratos' *Lives of the Sophists* is an example of the interest in orators and their lives.

¹⁷ *ST* II.2, II.3, II. 8, III.26, III.30, IV.25, V.45.

¹⁸ For example Boulanger 1923, 165, 169, Dodds 1990, 40, Behr 1968, 116, Schröder

1988. Aristides does, however, state that he does not use the dream books *ST* II.3.

[19] Pearcy 1988. For Aristides' statements that the *Sacred Tales* is a summary see *ST* I.1, II.4, II.18, II.29, II.60, III.5, III.13.

[20] On the 'disorganization' of the text see Boulanger 1923, 165 ('la confusion dépasse encore tout ce qu'on pouvait craindre'), Behr 1968, 110, 116–21 ('the result is unbeliev-able confusion'), Reardon 1971, 256 ('ce journal manque entièrement de forme ... c'est un assemblage très confus d' événements de toutes sortes') and Bompaire 1989, 30 ('tissu d'observations directes et décousues'). For interpretations of the literary effect of the 'disorder' of the text see Pearcy 1988, 383–4, Quet 1993, 221–3, 230–6; on the elliptical style of the *ST* suggesting urgent divine inspiration see Weiss 1998, 53–4 and 58.

[21] *ST* II.29.

[22] *ST* II.1–4. Statements about Aristides' inability fully to describe what happened in words include: I.1–2 (not even if he could surpass all human strength, speech and wisdom could he do justice to the events; the task is impossible), I.3 (each day merits a narrative), II.1–4 (it is impossible to remember each deed and tell it precisely), II.6 (other symptoms which are impossible to describe), II.8 (it is not within the power of man to narrate what came next), II.22 (who could indicate what came next?), II.49 (the experience is easy for a god to understand, not easy for a man to conceive or write about), II.56 (who can understand what his physical state was? only those who were present), II.58 (the full narrative would take as long as the actual events), II.67 (you could not put into words what happened), II.80 (impossible to tell how often he was commanded to bathe), III.30 (it would be possible to tell countless other things relating to the god's drug recommendations), V.39 (whatever the reader might conceive or declare, he will say less than what happened then). References to Aristides not remembering particulars include: I.65 (he relates the cures which he remembers), I.66 (he cannot remember the particulars of a drug), II.1 (the impossibility of remembering each thing), II.11 (he cannot remember all the events but only his gratitude because of them), II.18 (he gives a summary of the dream and would like to be able to recount it in detail), III.21 (he recalls a dream unclearly), III.26 (he cannot remember two of the four ingredients of a remedy recommended by the god, and will add them if the book of dreams turns up), III.44 (because many years have passed he cannot remember how he used an egg in a remedy), IV.15 (it is impossible to say which of the dreams came first), IV.40 (he cannot remember the order of the dreams).

[23] *ST* II.8.

[24] *ST* II.2–3.

[25] *ST* I.3.

[26] *ST* II.58

[27] *ST* I.1 and II.1.

[28] *ST* II.1.

[29] *ST* II.2.

[30] *ST* IV.45 (tripod), II.27 (ring and blood sacrifice), III.13 (continuous sacrifices).

[31] For example *ST* I.59.

[32] *ST* II.4.

[33] The tradition of invoking a divinity to help with the process of composition is established at the opening of Homer's *Iliad* and *Odyssey*. An example of Aristides' direct appeal to the god for guidance in the full flow of the text occurs in *ST* II.24: 'But as to what follows it is your task, O Lord, to make clear and to reveal, by saying what and by

turning where, we would do what is gratifying to you and would best continue our tale. Since I have mentioned the river and the terrible winter and the bath, am I next to speak of other things of the same category and am I to compile, as it were, a catalogue of wintry, divine, and very strange baths? Or dividing up my tale, shall I narrate some intermediate events? Or is it best to pass over all the intermediate things and give conclusion of my first tale, how the oracle about the years held and how everything turned out?' See also *ST* IV.50–1.

³⁴ *ST* IV.68–9. See also IV.13.

³⁵ *ST* II.32.

³⁶ *ST* IV.70.

³⁷ References to the process of composition in the *ST* include: I.1 (he will talk in summary fashion like Helen), I.4 (now he wishes to indicate the condition of his stomach), I.59 (what should he say about the matter of not bathing?), I.61 (so much for the story of his stomach), II.4 (he will speak in summary and calls on the god), II.10 (he wishes to recall strange happenings), II.11 (where should he begin?), II.12 (why should he mention people's pleasure at seeing him in Smyrna?), II.18 (this is a summary of the vision), II.24 (should he talk of this or that?), II.29 (he must go on in summary), II.36–7 (he returns to the theme), II.45 (should he talk about baths?), II.60 (he will try to speak cursorily), II.71 (returning to the theme of the baths), II.73 (he urges himself to recall the commandments of the god), III.5 (this is a summary of the dreams), III.6 (he will omit the return journey because of the abundance of stories and troubles), III.13 (he recollects in summary), III.41 (he has finished the story of the earthquake), III.49 (it is necessary to recount something even more frightening), IV.12 (it would probably be best to speak next of his visions concerning oratory), IV.13 (the original plan of composition has changed), IV.27 (it lies outside his plan to tell of the many other things), IV.28 (he wishes to speak of a dream), IV.38 (story follows story), IV.63 (he had determined to bring his speech on this subject to an end at this point, but another wonderful thing occurs to him), IV.68–9 (Asklepios intervenes with a particular dream), IV.70 (not all has been said about the benefactions, only that which was ringing in his ears), IV.71 (he will return to the story), IV.100 (he urges himself to recall an earlier event), V.34 (he will not say more on this subject), V.35 (it is not seemly to recount what happened), V.36 (he *will* recount stories about the god's help to his oratory), V.49 (it is better to narrate the dream itself, for it is still ringing in his ears and there is no need to omit it).

³⁸ Self-censorship due to religious reasons: *ST* I.71, III.46, III.48, IV.50–1, IV.80 (unclear whether in this instance reticence is due to self-censoring or forgetting), V.49 (here he says there is no reason to omit it).

³⁹ Self-censorship on the subject of his oratorical achievements on account of modesty: e.g. II.12, IV.27, V.34–7.

⁴⁰ See above n. 22.

⁴¹ For example *ST* II.2 and IV.68 (dream visions occur in 'the present' i.e. the time of composition).

⁴² See for example Boulanger 1923, 169 ('[Les *Discours Sacrés*], composés au hasard, de l'inspiration et de souvenirs, écrits à la diable, en style d'improvisateur'), and Festugière 1954, ('the *Sacred Discourses* are written slapdash, in a style which is simple, rapid, at times even incorrect'), and Gourevitch 1984, 17 ('il nous livre par eux [les *Discours sacrés*] un matériel presqu'entièrement à l'état brut').

⁴³ For example Pausanias *Description of Greece* 1.38.6–7 (the Eleusinian Mysteries),

4.33.4–5 (the rites of Demeter and Kore at the Karnasian Grove), 2.10.2–3 (the statue of Karnean Apollo at the sanctuary of Asklepios at Sikyon), 2.35.8 and 11 (the image of Demeter on Mt Pron). For a full list see Elsner 1995, 150 n. 69. For a discussion see Habicht 1998, 156 and Elsner 1992, especially 20–5.

[44] *ST* IV.50–1.

[45] *ST* IV.29.

[46] Pausanias *Description of Greece* 8.8.3: 'When I began to write my history I was inclined to count these legends as foolishness, but on getting as far as Arkadia I grew to hold a more thoughtful view of them, which is this. In the days of old those Greeks who were considered wise spoke their sayings not straight out but in riddles, and so the legends about Kronos I conjectured to be a sort of Greek wisdom. In matters of divinity, therefore, I shall adopt the received tradition.'

[47] References to Aristides' new name Theodoros occur in *ST* IV.53 and IV.70. See also Cagnat 1911, 369–70 no. 1070 for an inscription from Alexandria where Aristides is honoured as Publius Aelius Aristides Theodoros. The adoption of a religiously significant name also occurs in the story of the 1st-century Christian martyr St Ignatius, who added Theophoros ('bearer of God') to his name (*Letter to the Ephesians*, salutation). See Camelot 1969, 56, note 1. Passages in the *ST* which convey Aristides' sense of profound religious and physical transformation include: I.48 (he is no longer easily recognized following a revelatory dream), II.27 (the god requires him to cut off some part of his body, but a ring is substituted), III.15 (the god requires him to knock out his bones and cut out his tendons, but an application of olive oil is substituted), II.13–14 (shipwreck symbolically enacted), IV.11 (symbolic burial).

[48] For example the inscriptions of Julius Meidias in Habicht 1969, no.139, and of Aelius Theon in Müller 1987, 194.

Bibliography

Anderson, G.
1994   *Sage, Saint and Sophist: Holy men and their associates in the early Roman empire*, London.

Baslez M.-F., Hoffmann, Ph. and Pernot, L. (eds.)
1993   *L'invention de l'autobiographie d'Hésiode à Saint Augustin*, Paris.

Behr, C.A.
1968   *Aelius Aristides and the Sacred Tales*, Amsterdam.
1981   *The Complete Works of P. Aelius Aristides*, vol. II: Orations XVII–LIII, transl. and comm., Amsterdam.

Bieler, L.
1935–6   ΘΕΙΟΣ ΑΝΗΡ: *das Bild des 'göttlichen Menschen' in Spätantike und Frühchristentum*, Vienna.

Bompaire, J.
1989   'Le Sacré dans les discours d'Aelius Aristides, (XLVII–LII Keil)', *Revue des Etudes Grecques* 102, 28–39.

Boulanger, A.
1923   *Aelius Aristide et la sophistique dans la province d' Asie au IIe siècle de notre ère*, Paris.

Bowersock, G.W.
1969 *Greek Sophists in the Roman Empire*, Oxford.

Brown, P.
1978 *The Making of Late Antiquity*, Cambridge, Mass.
1981 *The Cult of the Saints: Its rise and function in Latin Christianity*, London.

Cagnat, R. et al. (eds.)
1911 *Inscriptiones Graecae ad Res Romanas Pertinentes*, vol. I, Paris.

Camelot, P.Th.
1969 *Ignace d'Antioche Polycarpe de Smyrne. Lettres. Martyre de Polycarpe*, Paris.

Cox, P.
1983 *Biography in Late Antiquity: A quest for the holy man*, Berkeley.

Cox Miller, P.
1994 *Dreams in Late Antiquity. Studies in the imagination of a culture*, Princeton.

Dodds, E.R.
1990 *Pagan and Christian in an Age of Anxiety*, Cambridge, 41–5.

Elsner, J.
1992 'Pausanias: A Greek pilgrim in the Roman world', *Past and Present* 135, 3–29.
1995 *Art and the Roman Viewer. The transformation of art from the pagan world to Christianity*, Cambridge.

Festugière, A.-J.
1954 *Personal Religion among the Greeks*, Berkeley, 85–104.

Foucault, M.
1990 *The History of Sexuality*, volume III, London.

Fowden, G.
1982 'The pagan holy man in late antique society', *Journal of Hellenic Studies* 102, 33–59.

Francis, J.A.
1995 *Subversive Virtue. Asceticism and authority in the second century pagan world*, Pennsylvania.

Frank, G.
1998 'Miracles, monks and monuments: the *Historia Monachorum in Aegypto* as Pilgrims' tales', *Frankfurter*, 483–505.

Gleason, M.
1995 *Making Men. Sophists and self-presentation in ancient Rome*, Princeton.

Gourevitch, D.
1984 *Le Triangle Hippocratique dans le monde Gréco-Romain*, Rome.

Gourevitch, M. and Gourevitch, D.
1968 'Aelius Aristide ou mémoires d'un hystérique au IIe siècle', *Information psychiatrique* 44, no. 10, 897–902.

Habicht, C.
1969 *Altertümer von Pergamon* VIII.3 *Die Inschriften des Asklepieions*, Berlin.
1998 *Pausanias' Guide to Ancient Greece*, Berkeley.

Hoffmann, A.
1998 'The Roman remodeling of the Asklepieion', in H. Koester (ed.) *Pergamon Citadel of the Gods*, Harvard Theological Studies 46, 41–61.

Jones, W.H.S. et al. (eds.)

1988–95   *Pausanias* Description of Greece, vols. I–V, Loeb Classical Library.

Keil, B.

1958   *Aelii Aristidis Smyrnaei quae supersunt omnia*, vol. II: *Orationes* XVII–LIII *Continens*, Berlin.

Kindstrand, J.F.

1975   *Homer in der zweiten Sophistik: studien zu der Homerlekture und dem Homerbild bei Dion von Prusa, Maximos von Tyros und Ailios Aristides*, Uppsala.

King, H.

1999   'Chronic pain and the creation of narrative', in J.I. Porter, *Constructions of the Classical Body*, Ann Arbor, 269–86.

Koester, H. (ed.)

1998   *Pergamon Citadel of the Gods*, Harvard Theological Studies 46.

Lane Fox, R.

1986   *Pagans and Christians in the Mediterranean World from the Second Century* AD *to the Conversion of Constantine*, London.

LiDonnici, L.R.

1995   *The Epidaurian Miracle Inscriptions*, Atlanta.

MacMullen, R,

1981   *Paganism in the Roman Empire*, New Haven.

Misch, G.

1973   *A History of Autobiography in Antiquity*, vol. II, Westport, Connecticut.

Müller, H.

1987   'Ein Heilungsbericht aus dem Asklepieion', *Chiron* 17, 192–233.

Norman, A.F. (ed. and transl.)

1992   *Libanios Autobiography and Selected Letters*, vol. II, Cambridge, Mass. and London.

Pearcy, L.T.

1988   'Theme, dream and narrative: reading the *Sacred Tales* of Aelius Aristides', *Transactions of the American Philological Association* 118, 377–91.

Perkins, J.

1992   'The "self" as sufferer', *Harvard Theological Revue* 85, 245–72.

1995   *The Suffering Self: Pain and narrative representation in the early Christian era*, London.

Phillips, E.D.

1952   'A hypochondriac and his god', *Greece and Rome* 21, 23–36.

Potter, D.

1994   *Prophets and Emperors. Human and divine authority from Augustus to Theodosius*, Cambridge, Mass.

Quet, M.-H.

1993   'Parler de soi pour louer son dieu: le cas d'Aelius Aristide (du journal intime de ses nuits aux *Discours Sacrés* en l' honneur du dieu Asklépios)', in Baslez, Hoffman, Pernot (eds.) *L'invention de l'autobiographie d'Hésiode à saint Augustin*, 211–51.

Reardon, B.P.

1999   'Achilles Tatius and ego-narrative', in S. Swain (ed.) *Oxford Readings in The Greek Novel*, Oxford, 243–58.

Rutherford, I.C.

    1999   '*To the land of Zeus...*: patterns of pilgrimage in Aelius Aristides', *Aevum Antiquum* 12, 133–48.

Saïd, S.

    1993   'Le "je" de Lucien', in Baslez, Hoffman and Pernot (eds.) *L'invention de l'autobiographie d'Hésiode à saint Augustin*, 253–70.

Schröder, H.O.

    1988   'Publius Aelius Aristides. Ein kranker Rhetor im Ringen um den Sinn seines Lebens', *Gymnasium* 95, 375–80.

Smith, M.

    1971   'Prolegomena to a discussion of aretalogies, divine men, the Gospels and Jesus', *Journal of Biblical Literature* 90, 174–199.

Van Dam, R.

    1993   *Saints and their Miracles in Late Antique Gaul*, Princeton.

Weiss, C.

    1998   'Literary turns: the representation of conversion in Aelius Aristides' *Hieroi Logoi* and in Apuleius' *Metamorphoses*', PhD dissertation, Yale University.

Wörrle, M.

    1969   'Die Lex Sacra von der Hallenstrasse (Inv. 1965, 20)', in Habicht, *Altertümer von Pergamon* VIII.3 *Die Inschriften des Asklepieions*, Berlin, 167–90.

13

DREAMS OF GLORY:
LUCIAN AS AUTOBIOGRAPHER

Noreen Humble and *Keith Sidwell*

Lucian's claim to be considered in a volume on ancient biography perhaps ought to rest on the three works that fall in some measure into that category. These are *Demonax*,[1] the life and jokes of the philosopher of that name,[2] *Alexander the False Prophet*, which is an indictment of the originator of the cult of Glykon, son of Asclepius, at Abonuteichos on the Black Sea, and *The Passing of Peregrinus*, an account of the self-immolation of the Cynic philosopher from Parion at the Olympic Games of AD 165. But one of the remarkable facts about these biographies – if that term is applicable – is that Lucian the narrator is so firmly implicated in them in autobiographical mode.[3]

In *Demonax* Lucian claims to have spent a great deal of time with the philosopher (1), which is presumably supposed to guarantee the accuracy of his account. In the other two works, the involvement is of a similar nature, but greater still. Between chapters 53 and 57 of *Alexander the False Prophet*, Lucian relates his own attempts to trick the oracle, a personal encounter with the prophet, his claim that Alexander had tried to have him drowned and his frustrated attempt to prosecute, giving his own name at 55 as it were as a *sphragis* to guarantee authenticity. In *The Passing of Peregrinus* he is involved in the narrative at a much earlier stage, intimating at chapter 2 that he had put himself in danger of physical attack by mocking Peregrinus' suicide at the very scene. The rest of the story is narrated as Lucian's eye-witness account of the build-up and the aftermath, including his own contribution to the apotheosis (a vulture rises from the pyre) and a final claim to have travelled on the same ship as Peregrinus and seen for himself the inconsistency between his philosophy and his behaviour (43–5).

In other respects, too, Lucian seems an especially self-revealing author. His literary defences are sometimes in his own voice as narrator (e.g. *To the one who said 'You're a Prometheus in words'*), but sometimes involve him, slightly disguised as a character in a comic dialogue (as the 'Syrian' in *Double Indictment* and 'Parrhesiades' in *The Fisherman*). He involves himself as

narrator in his literary satire the *True History* and possibly in an account of
another satirical philosopher, *Nigrinus*. In other dialogues, he seems to be
barely disguised under the similar name of Lykinos (e.g. *Hermotimus, The
Ship, Lexiphanes, Essays in Portraiture* and *Essays in Portraiture Defended*).
In all of this, one may see him following and mixing (as he claimed he did
in *Double Indictment* and elsewhere) two distinct literary traditions. One
is that of the Platonic dialogue, which makes constant use of the figure of
Socrates, but never allows the author himself to feature. The other is Old
Comedy, which was perceived in the scholarship of the Alexandrian tradition
as a highly autobiographical genre, with poets often appearing on stage in
their own plays, voicing their views of themselves and their rivals in *parabases*
and not afraid to put details of their personal lives and tribulations into
them as well (as for instance the battle between Kleon and Aristophanes),
but sometimes apparently disguising themselves a bit (as with Dicaeopolis
in *Acharnians*). Scholars have not resisted the temptation to try to make
sense of this data as material for Lucian's biography, and there is a venerable
tradition from Croiset's *Essai sur la vie et les oeuvres*, through Schwartz'
Biographie de Lucien to Jones' *Culture and Society in Lucian* which in less
and more sophisticated ways attempts this task. In stark opposition to this
trend of thinking is the recent article by Suzanne Saïd, 'Le "je" de Lucien'; her
conclusion is that 'malgré l'omniprésence de "je", l'oeuvre de Lucien est…aux
antipodes de l'autobiographie'.[4]

Certainly the avowedly literary nature of this autobiographizing should
give us pause. The audience to whom it is addressed shares a mode of
perception schooled by wide knowledge of the classics and the models of
interpretation handed down with them.[5] Our ways of reading this mode are
affected not least by the existence in our culture of the notion of autobiography as a mirror of the human soul. Augustine's *Confessions* are traditionally regarded as the first real autobiography in this sense.[6] However, we may
with care be able to approximate the cognitive process of Lucian's putative
audience and we should certainly attempt to do so, before we try to judge
(however provisionally) the truth status of material presented in the autobiographical form. This paper will attempt to do this with Lucian's *Dream*,
a work which attracted the sub-title *Bios Loukianou* at some time during its
transmission and which has been the natural starting-point for all attempts
to tell Lucian's own story.[7]

In this short work, addressed to a group of people to whom the author has
returned (18: οἷος…πρὸς ὑμᾶς ἐπανελήλυθα – Syrians, perhaps the people of
his native Samosata), Lucian relates how he chose his career-path. The first
four chapters sketch the family conference at which he is entrusted to his
uncle to begin an apprenticeship as a sculptor, and go on to relate his uncle's

decision to throw him in at the deep end with a chisel, a piece of stone and a tag from Hesiod, his botched first bash, his beating by the furious uncle, and his (successful) complaints to his mother about her brother's treatment of him. The next twelve chapters describe a dream, which is introduced by a quotation from the *Iliad*. In this dream, two women personifying Sculpture and Culture (Παιδεία) appear to Lucian, and, after playing tug-of-war with him, ask him to choose between them. Each gives a speech, Sculpture first and Culture second. Lucian has no problem in running to the side of Culture before she has even finished her piece (14). She then promises him unparalleled success in the world in return for the justice of his judgement, taking him above the earth in a chariot drawn by winged horses, from which he hears the applause of the peoples from east to west over whom, like Triptolemus, he scatters he does not remember what, and from which he finally steps down dressed in clothing of a superior cut to that which he wore on mounting. In the coda (17–18), the author envisages the critical response of his audience to this childish vision ('Does he think we are dream interpreters?'), but defends himself by claiming he has a purpose in having related it, as did Xenophon, he adds, when he recounted a particular dream in the *Anabasis*. Lucian's purpose is to induce the young to turn to the better path and take a firm hold on culture, and not ruin a noble nature because of poverty. He himself will be their role-model, given the difference between his status then and now on his return.

The piece has seemed straightforward enough to most Lucian scholars. Lucian is asked to choose between a manifestly better and a manifestly worse course. He chooses the better and this choice is then used as an *exemplum* for young men to follow. Consequently, an historian as acute as C.P. Jones can conclude:[8]

> Although Lucian has evidently passed his experiences through a prism of literature, it does not follow that they are fiction: at least when mentioning external, verifiable facts he must be supposed to have respected the knowledge already possessed by his hearers and readers. It can be accepted that he was originally of modest means, though not so modest as to put a life of culture out of the question…What Lucian says of his chosen profession is studiously vague, but again not implausible… Even his claim to have been guided by a 'clear' dream may have a basis in reality… Lucian could have embroidered his memories of an actual dream to make them more literary, though since dreams and the recollection of them tend to be influenced by cultural patterns the embellishment may be in part unconscious. The *Dream*, therefore implies that…Lucian had turned away from an intended career early in youth and taken up another which, it is strongly hinted, involved travel and public speaking.

While the literary substructure of this piece has generally not been missed

– editors duly note but rarely discuss the references to Hesiod, Homer, Xenophon and others – there is little agreement concerning the degree to which the complex web of allusions contributes to the meaning or message of the work. Jones, just cited, represents one extreme with his suggestion of unconscious embellishment. Somewhere in the middle ground is Branham who attempts at least to include in his interpretation of the work an explanation of why Lucian engages in literary games:[9]

> His consequent decision to pursue the liberal arts of eloquence is offered ostensibly as an edifying example of the powers of *paideia* (18), but his praise of 'culture' coincides rhetorically with an artful celebration of the speaker's own powers as self-praise becomes the vehicle for demonstrating the special mastery the speaker's reputation implies. Thus the dream Lucian 'remembers' is a comic transfiguration of the famous Choice of Heracles as reported by Xenophon...

A recent article by Deborah Gera looks far more closely at this 'comic transfiguration' and analyses acutely its complexity, focusing upon the ambivalence given to Culture through a full comparison with the short-cuts-to-culture rhetoric teacher of *A Professor of Public Speaking*.[10] Her conclusion, that 'one can perhaps sense underneath the surface the disillusionment or disappointment Lucian feels with the path he has chosen',[11] accounts for the work's texture, but in a way which accepts in too modern a sense the autobiographical framework. At the other end of the spectrum, Saïd, also using similarities between the *Dream* and *A Professor of Public Speaking*, which she takes as a personal satire on Pollux of Naucratis, concludes: 'If the same clichés can be used to represent in this way the same and the other in turn, this is the best proof we have of the ironic distance Lucian knows how to keep between himself and others'.[12]

Recent scholarship on the *Dream*, then, agrees in focusing upon the artfulness of its literary structure and its irony, but disagrees about the conclusions to be drawn from these facts about its status as autobiography. What follows is an attempt to show, through closer interpretation of the literary reminiscences and models of this piece, that Lucian is not engaging in extravagant self-praise (Jones, Branham), that when other aspects are taken into account, the 'external, reliable facts' Lucian knows his audience to possess will turn out to be different from those inferred by Jones, that the literary reminiscences do not necessarily completely divorce the work from Lucian's own reality (Saïd), but that Gera's sense of an underlying pessimism about Culture is a misreading.

The first literary citation of the piece, Lucian's uncle's brusque use of the tag 'the beginning is half of the whole' (3: ἀρχὴ δέ τοι ἥμισυ παντός) is marked as a non-literary reference (τὸ κοινὸν, 'the commonplace', is Lucian's word) and no source is named. At the same time, of course, the learned audience to whom this piece is addressed is fully expected to know that its source is Hesiod and to see how appropriate it is for a workman since it is from *Works and Days*.[13] Thus the positive fruit of the learning obtained by Lucian is already on display in contrast to the banausic occupation of his uncle as he moves towards the dream itself.

But this is not the first literary reminiscence. Already in chapter 2, Lucian has represented his father as making inferences about his aptitude for sculpture from his wax-modelling which apparently occurred during classes at school.[14] The similarity of substance and context to Aristophanes *Clouds* 877–81[15] has not gone unnoticed.[16] In this passage Strepsiades, who has himself failed to learn the Socratic arguments which will secure the family's financial future, introduces his son Pheidippides to Socrates as a more plausible substitute. The arguments he employs rest on Pheidippides' sculptural abilities as a child. He will surely be able to learn the arguments because he was so handy with clay, figwood and pomegranate peel, carving houses, boats, carts and frogs. Lucian's father recalls his son's sculptural abilities with wax and his more Promethean products, cattle, horses or human beings,[17] but presumes that these predict a future as a sculptor. A cultivated reader must stop and consider whether the parallel, which suggests that Lucian could learn rhetoric quickly and easily, bodes well for Lucian given his knowledge of the outcome in the comedy. Perhaps the central point, however, is that both Pheidippides and Lucian will grasp rhetoric firmly enough to be able to subvert traditional categories.[18]

That the childish Lucian of the proposed time of the narrative may be incapable of sorting out niceties is suggested by a couple of small details. First of all, he insists that it was the beating which induced the dream (4, 16) and pushed him towards the choice of Culture in it (14). But earlier he mentions that he had been beaten at school for making wax models. He does not see the similarity in the necessity for physical violence which his own evidence suggests is there for both Sculpture and Culture. Secondly, these wax models were what induced him to hope that he could learn the trade of sculpture 'in a short time' (βραχεῖ, 2). The theme of *A Professor of Public Speaking* is here also, then, and we are warned from the beginning that the boy Lucian imagined that the acquisition of a skill (τέχνη, 3) could be done in short order. It should also be noted that Hesiod, cited in the next chapter (3), is also in Lucian the model of the person who learned his craft without any effort (cf. *A Professor of Public Speaking* 4 and *Ignorant Book-Collector* 3).

That the dream itself will be a complex mixture of positive and negative is also implied by the quotation, in chapter 5, from Homer *Iliad* 2.56–7:

θεῖός μοι ἐνύπνιον ἦλθεν ὄνειρος ἀμβροσίην διὰ νύκτα·

a divine dream came to me in my sleep in the ambrosial night.

In the *Iliad* the words are put into the mouth of Agamemnon when he addresses the assembly after he has been sent a dream by Zeus. However, the reader of the *Iliad* knows, as Agamemnon does not, that this is a false dream (2.5–15) whose purpose is to fulfil Thetis' promise to Achilles to inflict a defeat upon the Greeks. Lucian's astute reader is thus forewarned that the dream about to be reported is not all that it seems. However, we must wait a while to discover in what respect the dream is false.

The centrepiece of the work is the actual dream, which is based on Prodicus' Choice of Heracles (Xen. *Mem.* 2.1.21–34). The choice seems straightforward: Sculpture is ugly and harsh, Culture beautiful with promises of fame. Gera, however, carefully points out the complexities.[19] Sculpture and Culture appear in a comic or negative light at the opening as they tug at the young Lucian. The unattractiveness of Sculpture is so exaggerated[20] as to make the choice no choice at all; yet at the same time Lucian also gives Sculpture characteristics (squalid, austere and masculine) associated with Virtue in Prodicus' tale and with another of Lucian's characters, the old-fashioned teacher in *A Professor of Public Speaking*. Indeed the new-fangled teacher in the same work bears more than a passing resemblance to Culture in the *Dream*, concerned as both are with appearances and promising fast and easy fame. In general in stories of this sort it is the hard road which leads to Virtue, the easy road to Vice. But lest we begin to think these are the only complexities – that while in physical terms there is no choice, Culture is actually equivalent to Prodicus' Vice – Gera also draws attention to the fact that Sculpture also promises eternal fame while Culture does promise to nourish Lucian's soul with qualities associated with Virtue in Prodicus' tale. Nothing in this dream is completely straightforward. However, in the last chapter of the whole piece Lucian does make it clear, that Culture was nonetheless the correct path to choose (18).

But there are further literary allusions which add to Lucian's eventual point. First, within the dream, near the end of her speech Culture uses as an argument the example of Socrates (12), to support her case that education is a better goal than sculpture, since, so she claims, Socrates left a life of sculpture for one of culture. While the connection of Socrates and his family with the plastic arts was well established in the biographical tradition,[21] Socrates is not the best example of easy learning leading to wealth (the promise just given to Lucian). The reader would instead associate with Socrates a life of relative poverty, stating of unpopular opinions, taking people down a peg, and dissociation from political life and power. And this would resonate with what the original audience, familiar with Lucian's works and life, might well have seen as Lucian's mission. For example, in the *Demonax*, Lucian lionizes Demonax (*Dem.* 2) and images him as a new Socrates (*Dem.* 11). And an anecdote in Galen[22] about Lucian's literary fraud (a new work of Heraclitus) perpetrated on a philosopher to expose his pretensions suggests Lucian might have seen himself as a philosopher in the Socratic mode. It is perhaps also significant that Lucian makes poverty and the pursuit of Culture a central theme in his conclusion (18).

Secondly, the dream is followed by Lucian's accounts of the complaints of his audience about the length and the incomprehensibility of the dream (17): 'Surely', he has his proposed audience say, 'he does not take us for dream interpreters?' Clearly the puzzlement of his audience is evidence that the dream as noted earlier, whatever it did mean, was *not* completely straightforward. In answer to their imagined disgust and puzzlement, Lucian draws a parallel with a dream of Xenophon which, he says, was recounted because it had some usefulness. Lucian is referring to *Anabasis* 3.1.11–13. Xenophon's dream is not as complex as Lucian's: there is a clap of thunder and a lightning bolt appears to strike his father's house. Xenophon, however, could not decide upon waking whether the dream was from Zeus and auspicious ('because in the midst of hardships and perils he had seemed to behold a great light from Zeus') or from Zeus the King and inauspicious ('since the fire appeared to blaze all about, he might not be able to escape from the Great King's country and be shut in on all sides by various difficulties').[23] Crucially, then, Xenophon states that 'what it really means to have such a dream one may learn from the events which followed the dream'. The events that follow show Xenophon exhorting himself to take action so that he and the rest of the army do not end up unable to escape from the King's country. He convinces the others to rouse themselves, takes partial command of the army, and the army eventually makes its way back to safety. So in light of the events which followed, the negative interpretation of the dream was incorrect – just as for Lucian it was right not to follow Sculpture. It is notable, however, that on the positive interpretation Xenophon's dream was merely auspicious, and it did not predict exactly what was going to happen. Its usefulness was that it warned him that a decision was necessary. In exactly the same way, then, Lucian is warning his audience that while he made the right decision in avoiding a sculptural career, the full consequences of his decision to follow Culture, while certainly auspicious, could not be predicted precisely from the dream he recounts. The framework for Lucian's dream is constructed through the Iliadic dream *and* the Xenophontic dream. The former warns the audience, who would have known Lucian's actual status, that what he dreamt was not what would happen, and thus helps to establish an ironic distance between the childish vision and the mature narrator. The dream, however, cannot be totally false because the Xenophontic dream confirms the correctness of the decision taken. The question that still remains for us, then, is how to reconcile these two literary allusions with each other: how can the dream be both false and the decision correct at the same time?

What actually happened to Lucian is, as Jones rightly remarked, known to his present audience, and not to us.[24] Scholars, Gera included,[25] have interpreted the last part of the dream (15–16), where Culture raises Lucian aloft in a winged chariot, as a statement of his own perception of the success he has achieved as an orator. The literary structure and substructure suggest that this interpretation is wrong.

Harmon's introduction in the Loeb is even now not unrepresentative of views of this aspect of the piece: 'it would seem to have been composed on his first return to Syria, after the visit to Gaul that made him rich and famous'.[26] For Jones, what he scatters Triptolemus-like is speeches,[27] and for Branham, the chariot-journey, though 'comically heroic', nonetheless is 'rhetorically effective', even while 'wryly distanced',[28] and finally, Gera remarks 'surely it is significant that what Lucian remembers from this ride is the praise of those who saw him from below, while he forgets the kind of seeds he has sown to them.'[29]

But such self-praise in this section would be wildly overblown in comparison with Lucian's presentation of himself elsewhere where he always manages to keep the 'wry distance' which Branham mentions. Here that distancing occurs in the mouth of the present speaker as opposed to the child (emphasized again right at the end of 16, just before the imagined response of the audience). We might justifiably ask, 'what does the child Lucian imagine he is being promised by Culture as his reward?' The winged chariot is used in an ironical context in *A Professor of Public Speaking* 26, by the false guide to the youth wishing to pursue rhetoric. Moreover, although Triptolemus appears to be a positive model, the mention of Pegasus (15) would surely, in the context of a human entering the realm of the gods, induce the educated listener to recall Bellerophon and his fate. Nor is it clear that Jones' interpretation of what is scattered as 'speeches' is correct. Lucian leaves it deliberately vague. But when he returns, what he thinks he has been promised is more than hinted at in the description of his clothing. Now he is 'a grandee' (16: εὐπάρυφος). Elsewhere in Lucian, this word implies high social status. At *On Salaried Posts in Great Houses* 9 it is linked to the word 'aristocracy' (εὐπατρίδαις) and at *Demonax* 15 it refers to the Macedonian nobility. In the same work at 41, one of the 'grandees' is said to be preening himself on the width of his purple stripe. The image shown to Lucian by Culture is of a grandee, and this chimes in with the phrase she uses at 13, where fine dress (σχῆμα εὐπρεπές) is linked directly not only with praise following from successful rhetoric (τὸ ἐπὶ λόγοις εὐδοκιμεῖν) but also with real power (δύναμιν καὶ ἀρχὰς) and the material benefits it implies (προεδρίας).

What kind of grandee might his audience be expected to bring to mind, though? Whitmarsh suggests that there is a 'hint at a senatorial position' but that we have no evidence of Lucian holding such a position.[30] The literary substructure outlined above, however, certainly suggests it must be something never attained by Lucian and probably so absurd as to be unattainable except in the mind of a foolish child (as Lucian represents himself as having been). There were examples of orators among the Roman nobility of Greece who attained high office in the empire. Herodes Atticus, consul in AD 143, is perhaps the most notable one mentioned by Lucian (*Dem.* 24, 33). What he scattered might represent the euergetism of such a nobleman, his buildings and other gifts to the people of the empire, which certainly would have been greeted with praise. But possibly an even greater absurdity was intended. The chariot allows a view not just of one region, but of the whole panorama from east to west, and it is not just the odd city which seems to be involved, but the whole world (πόλεις καὶ ἔθνη καὶ δήμους, and the implications of Triptolemus' gift of agriculture to everyone, 15). The greatest euergetist of all, of course, would be an emperor, who gives largesse in the form of corn-doles (and sometimes cash) to the people and is always greeted with praise as he passes through the empire (cf. Suetonius *Augustus* 98.2). The absurdity of this childhood vision might be underlined, and its potential danger lessened, by a final literary undercurrent. Athenaeus (4.152d) tells us that the historian Posidonius reported that the Gaul Lovernius, to win the favour of the mob, rode in a chariot through the fields scattering gold and silver among the myriads of Celts who followed him. Later he was deposed by the Romans. Lucian too is a barbarian, inclined like Lovernius to envisage a quite impractical future for himself.

The import of the dream is now clear enough, as is the answer to the question how the dream can be both false and the decision correct at the same time. Lucian was enticed into the right course, but he chose it for the wrong reasons. His imagination told him that Culture could make him into a senator or even an emperor. This was absurd and what completes the ironic impact of the piece is surely the knowledge which the present audience has about his position.

And what is that? Lucian had obtained a relatively well-paid position in Gaul, but that was not one of the plum jobs or in one of the most highly regarded areas. He had always had to rely on patronage (see *The Scythian*) rather than to extend it to others, and the idea that he attempted to enter the imperial court under Lucius Verus relies upon straightforward readings of *Essays in Portraiture* and *Essays in Portraiture Defended* which have recently been challenged.[31] He must have had some pull, to have obtained the post of 'introducer' (εἰσαγωγεύς) in Egypt in the entourage of the governor,[32] but this was probably later. His audience can of course tell from his speech itself that he has attained the highest level of literary competence, and perhaps the main point of the discourse is to show that delusions about the social status conferred by literary learning do not affect the actuality – that such learning of itself provides a worthwhile self-definition as well as entry to an exclusive club. His final remark in any case seems in the context to imply that he is content with his lot,[33] though it would be crass to read any more into the irony of his ability only to claim no lower fame than the 'workmen' in whose number he might have been counted had he stuck with Sculpture. The Lucian of the *Dream*, like the Lykinus at the end of *The Ship* (46), seems to have learned that wishful thinking is much less worthwhile than trying to face facts.

In the end, autobiography is only an ideology of the self. The cleverer the writer, the less easy it is to pull the threads that will deconstruct the construct. All we can do in the case of Lucian is to trace the fault-lines (if any) in his use of the 'I' mode. But this can tell us little except perhaps where to place works in whatever ideological spectrum we can conjure from his oeuvre. Maybe the *Dream* has more in common with Lucian's 'comic dialogue' phase than Gera thinks, and the literary self-mockery marks it as contemporary with that self-reinvention proclaimed so memorably in the *Double Indictment*. It may even be the case that the motif of a dream which predicts a fabulous career contains a sardonic reflection on a contemporary fashion.[34]

But as to Jones' inferences about Lucian's early life, who knows? On that front perhaps little has changed even now; the modern genre is subject to the same problems of interpretation. Consider this snippet from a review of the 'autobiography' of Sumner Redstone, head of the Viacom media empire:[35]

> In 1984, Lee Iacocca, chairman of the resurgent Chrysler corporation, published his autobiography. It was a charming book in which Iacocca came across as a homespun, no-nonsense man of the people...Iacocca followed the dramatic prologue with a chapter on his humble origins. Now every chief executive has humble origins. Iacocca spoke of an early mentor...who instilled lessons that guide him still. Sure enough, now there are gruff no-nonsense men instilling lessons that guide chief executives to this day...Iacocca's legacy wouldn't matter so much if chief executives were, in fact, homespun men of the people... But they aren't. Redstone's attempt to play the humble-beginnings card, for instance, is compromised by the fact that he didn't have humble beginnings.

Acknowledgements
We would like to thank the participants in the discussion at the Biographical Limits Conference for their stimulating insights and also David Braund for particular help on the Roman purple.

Notes

1 Throughout English titles for Lucian's works follow those in the Loeb translations.

2 Whether or not Demonax actually existed does not alter the generic style of the work.

3 See further Bompaire 1993 and even more so Saïd 1993.

4 Saïd 1993, 270.

5 See, for example, Branham 1989 and Swain 1996, 1–131.

6 See, for example, Misch 1950, 17 and Pascal 1985, 21.

7 For example, Jones 1986, 8, though for a sceptical view see now Goldhill 2002, 63–4 and 67–9.

8 Jones 1986, 9–10.

9 Branham 1989, 28.

10 Gera 1995.

11 Gera 1995, 250.

12 Saïd 1993, 270.

13 Hesiod *Op.* 40: οὐδὲ ἴσασιν ὅσῳ πλέον ἥμισυ παντός, 'nor do they know by how much the half is greater than the whole'. Cf. also Lucian *Hermotimus* 3: ἀλλὰ τήν γε ἀρχὴν ὁ αὐτὸς οὗτος Ἡσίοδος ἥμισυ τοῦ παντὸς ἔφη εἶναι 'but this same Hesiod said that the beginning is half of the whole'.

14 Romm 1990, 95–8 has an interesting discussion on the metaphoric relationship between the softness of wax and the hardness of stone on the one side and the flexibility of Lucian's literary techniques on the other.

15 Aristophanes *Clouds* 877–81:

θυμόσοφός ἐστιν φύσει.
εὐθύς γέ τοι παιδάριον ὂν τυννουτονὶ
ἔπλαττεν ἔνδον οἰκίας ναῦς τ' ἔγλυφεν
ἁμαξίδας τε συκίνας ἠργάζετο
κἀκ τῶν σιδίων βατράχους ἐποίει, πῶς δοκεῖς;

He is naturally clever. Why when he was just a tiny little lad he used to mould houses inside and carved ships and made wagons out of fig-wood and frogs from pomegranate peel, ever so well.

16 Bompaire 2000, 531 and Saïd 1993, 267.

17 Though the word 'Promethean' here is our own addition, it is possible that Lucian was nicknamed Prometheus (see his *To one who said, 'You're a Prometheus in words'*) and consequently that he expects that sobriquet to resonate with this passage. See further Romm 1990.

18 Romm 1990, 95–8 discusses the wax as a metaphor for the plasticity of Lucian's literary art but does not draw this particular parallel.

19 Gera 1995.

20 Perhaps, as Saïd 1993, 268 points out, resembling, in the young child's dream, his uncle who so recently beat him.

21 Aristoxenus fr. 5 is the earliest reference. It certainly at some point becomes part of the biographical tradition, e.g. D.L. 2.18. In Plato all that is found is mention of Daedalus as Socrates' ancestor (see *Euthyphro* 11b, *Alcibiades* 1.121a).

22 Strohmaier 1976.

23 Xen. *An.* 3.1.11–12:

ἔδοξεν αὐτῷ βροντῆς γενομένης σκηπτὸς πεσεῖν εἰς τὴν πατρῴαν οἰκίαν, καὶ ἐκ τούτου λάμπεσθαι πᾶσα. περίφοβος δ᾿ εὐθὺς ἀνηγέρθη, καὶ τὸ ὄναρ τῇ μὲν ἔκρινεν ἀγαθόν, ὅτι ἐν πόνοις ὢν καὶ κινδύνοις φῶς μέγα ἐκ Διὸς ἰδεῖν ἔδοξε· τῇ δὲ καὶ ἐφοβεῖτο, ὅτι ἀπὸ Διὸς μὲν βασιλέως τὸ ὄναρ ἐδόκει αὐτῷ εἶναι, κύκλῳ δὲ ἐδόκει λάμπεσθαι τὸ πῦρ, μὴ οὐ δύναιτο ἐκ τῆς χώρας ἐξελθεῖν τῆς βασιλέως, ἀλλ᾿ εἴργοιτο πάντοθεν ὑπό τινων ἀποριῶν. ὁποῖόν τι μὲν δὴ ἐστὶ τὸ τοιοῦτον ὄναρ ἰδεῖν ἔξεστι σκοπεῖν ἐκ τῶν συμβάντων μετὰ τὸ ὄναρ.

[24] Jones 1986, 9.

[25] Gera 1995, 248.

[26] Harmon 1921, 3.213. It should be noted that this claim derives from Lucian's *Double Indictment* 27, where it is Rhetoric who mentions the fact, not the Syrian who is a surrogate for Lucian (see Swain 1996, 310).

[27] Jones 1986, 10.

[28] Branham 1989, 29.

[29] Gera 1995, 248.

[30] Whitmarsh 2001, 124 n. 121.

[31] See Jones 1986, chap. 7 and Swain 1996, 315 for straightforward readings and for the challenge, Sidwell 2002.

[32] Jones 1986, 20–1, with n. 80.

[33] *Contra* Gera 1995.

[34] e.g. the dream of Galen's father, Galen 10.609, 14.608, 19.43 (Kühn) and more generally Bowersock 1969, 60, 73–4 and 1994, 77–97 on the importance of predictive dreams to the upper classes in particular.

[35] *Guardian* 4th September 2001 Part G2, p. 16, by Malcolm Gladwell.

Bibliography

Bompaire, J.

1993   'Quatre styles de l'autobiographie au IIe siècle après J.-C.: Aelius Aristide, Lucien, Marc-Aurèle, Galien', in M.-F. Baslez, P. Hoffmann and L. Pernot (eds.) *L'invention de l'autobiographie: d'Hésiode à Saint Augustin*, Paris, 199–209.

2000   *Lucien écrivain: imitation et création*, Paris. Reprint of 1958 edn.

Bowersock, G.W.

1969   *Greek Sophists in the Roman Empire*, Oxford.

1994   *Fiction as History: Nero to Julian*, Berkeley.

Branham, R.B.

1989   *Lucian and the Comedy of Traditions*, Cambridge, Mass.

Croiset, M.

1882   *Essai sur la vie et les oeuvres de Lucien*, Paris.

Gera, D.L.

1995   'Lucian's choice: *Somnium* 6–16', in D. Innes, H. Hine and C. Pelling (eds.) *Ethics and Rhetoric: Classical essays for D. Russell on his 75th birthday*, Oxford, 237–50.

Goldhill, S.

2002   *Who Needs Greek? Contests in the cultural history of Hellenism*, Cambridge.

Harmon, A.M.
1921   *Lucian*, vol. 3, Loeb, Harvard.
Jones, C.P.
1986   *Culture and Society in Lucian*, Cambridge, Mass.
Misch, G.
1950   *A History of Autobiography in Antiquity*, 2 vols., London.
Pascal, R.
1985   *Design and Truth in Autobiography*, Cambridge, Mass.
Romm, J.
1990   'Wax, stone, and Promethean clay: Lucian as plastic artist', *Classical Antiquity* 9, 74–98.
Saïd, S.
1993   'Le "je" de Lucien', in M.-F. Baslez, P. Hoffmann and L. Pernot (eds.) *L'invention de l'autobiographie: d'Hésiode à Saint Augustin*, Paris, 253–70.
Schwartz, J.
1965   *Biographie de Lucien de Samosate*, Brussels.
Sidwell, K.
2002   'Damning with great praise: paradox in Lucian's *Imagines* and *Pro Imaginibus*', in K. Sidwell (ed.) *Pleiades Setting*, Cork, 107–26. Available online at http://www.ucc.ie/academic/classics (click on Departmental Publications).
Strohmaier, G.
1976   'Übersehenes zur Biographie Lukians', *Philologus* 120, 117–22.
Swain, S.
1996   *Hellenism and Empire: Language, classicism, and power in the Greek world, AD 50–250*, Oxford.
Whitmarsh, T.
2001   *Greek Literature and the Roman Empire*, Oxford.

14

THE CYNIC AND CHRISTIAN LIVES
OF LUCIAN'S *PEREGRINUS*

Jason König

I

Lucian's work *On the Death of Peregrinus* both parodies and brilliantly manipulates biographical and autobiographical convention. The text is a satirical account of the suicide of the Cynic philosopher Peregrinus, who burned himself to death at the Olympic games of AD 165.[1] The first half is taken up with description of a speech in Elis several days before the beginning of the festival, by Peregrinus' sidekick Theagenes, who eulogizes Peregrinus extravagantly and advertises the forthcoming attraction of his self-immolation. An unnamed second speaker then denounces Peregrinus with a long account of his fraudulent career, during which Peregrinus has (allegedly)[2] taken on a number of different philosophical and religious identities, Cynicism and Christianity at most length. In the second half of the work we hear about the suicide itself – which turns out, on Lucian's account, to be a great anti-climax – and about the rumours which began to proliferate even within hours of Peregrinus' death, some of them started mischievously by the narrator himself.

Death is often a defining moment in ancient biographical literature, a moment which is emblematic of the subject's character, and a moment which brings in its wake the first glimpses of posthumous glory and immortality, in the funeral celebrations which follow. But in Peregrinus' case it brings only anti-climax. Even the title of the work signals Lucian's undermining of Peregrinus' autobiographical pretensions. Lucian makes this a 'Death' of Peregrinus, rather than a 'Life', as we would more naturally expect a biographical work to be entitled.[3] The text 'puts an end' to Peregrinus in unmasking the autobiographical deceptions on which his reputation is based, offering him only a mocking travesty of textual immortality, and dramatizing the narrator's own skills of manipulative self-presentation by contrast.

The title of the work thus immediately hints at Lucian's engagement with biographical convention. In what follows I wish to look a little more closely at the contours of that engagement in the rest of the work. In doing so, I have

227

two main aims, both of which, I hope, will have some relevance to the wider themes of this volume. First, I will argue that Lucian flaunts his ability to beat Peregrinus at his own game, in order to convey a characteristically Lucianic impression of the theatrical nature of all biographical and autobiographical representation, and of the difficulties of controlling such theatricality. Secondly, I wish to suggest that Christian and non-Christian biographical material are intertwined with each other throughout the work, especially in the description of the hours leading up to Peregrinus' death, in ways which contribute to the same effect.

The foregrounding of autobiographical theatricality is prominent from the beginning of the work. Peregrinus, Lucian suggests, has lurched from one piece of frantic self-promotion to the next throughout his career, trying out an opportunistic and often indiscriminate mixture of different personas and philosophical allegiances in an attempt to gain glory, and perverting all of the traditions he touches in the process. His glory-seeking suicide has similar characteristics. Peregrinus (allegedly) stages his own death for maximum publicity, and in doing so claims to be following a number of prestigious role models. And yet, despite the calculating nature of his self-advertisement, he is ultimately unable to claim full control over his own self-representation. Lucian's Peregrinus constructs his own life, autobiographizes himself, by imitating iconic philosophical and religious figures. But in Lucian's hands those imitations constantly threaten to spiral into absurdity. Similarly, Lucian satirizes the Cynic and Christian followers of Peregrinus, who perpetuate his self-dramatizations in their biographical accounts of him.[4]

By contrast, Lucian – or at least the first-person narrator whose voice Lucian inhabits (more on that distinction in a moment) – manages the process of manipulative autobiography more successfully. We are often told that biography and autobiography are almost inevitably connected with each other.[5] That may have been the case particularly within the ancient world, when the writing of biography was related in many ways to the practices of eulogistic speech-making, where the speaker's own character was always on display together with that of his subject.[6] Lucian pushes that association to its limits throughout the *Peregrinus*. The author, like the narrator whose mask he hides behind, matches his subject's creative self-fashioning by his own more sophisticated manipulations of other people's perceptions, and his own more sophisticated ability to switch between a range of different personas. He repeatedly compares himself with the man he is satirizing, revelling in his ability to outdo Peregrinus. And he hints at the possibility that we, his readers, may be just as much at the mercy of his own narrative control as the gullible onlookers who fall for his invented rumours, so he claims, after Peregrinus' death.

In what follows I will use the name 'Lucian' to describe both Lucian the author and Lucian the first-person narrator, while trying as far as possible to flag the moments within the narrative where the possibility of divergence between the two is made most conspicuous. The text suggests that the narrator is a mouthpiece for the authentic and trustworthy voice of the author, and yet it never allows us to be fully confident of that voice's authenticity. How far are we to take the narrator's debunking of Peregrinus as a reflection of the author's own opinion? To what extent is the narrator himself to be suspected of untrustworthiness or ludicrousness? Are we really meant to believe what he tells us about Peregrinus?

The difficulty of answering those questions contributes to the text's broader thematic preoccupation with the difficulties of finding any firm ground beneath the shifting surfaces of self-presentation. Peregrinus is an extreme example of fakery, but he may not be the only one. Lucian throughout his writing relies on techniques of mask-swapping and ironic role-playing, which make him an always-elusive figure, hard to pin down to any one set of opinions.[7] One effect of that strategy is to confront us repeatedly with the untrustworthy characteristics of any kind of self-description. In the *Peregrinus* that technique is pushed to its extreme. The text not only suggests that the real Lucian is to be linked with the narrator, and perhaps with the anonymous second-speaker who attacks the encomium of Peregrinus given by Theagenes, but also hints, more audaciously, that Lucian's true face may be not be so easily distinguishable from Peregrinus' own. 'Lucian', as he appears to us in this work, is always the product of rhetorical sleight of hand. The author is never reliably identifiable with the face he presents to us. The text draws attention to the constructedness of Lucian's masks as much as it does to those of Peregrinus.

My first aim, then, is to explore Lucian's representations of the processes of biographical theatricality, paying particular attention (especially in the final section of the article), to the ways in which both author and narrator, as far as they can be separated, are implicated in the techniques they expose. My second aim, in many ways connected with that, is to explore the ways in which Christian and non-Christian biographical traditions are intertwined with each other in this text. Christian and non-Christian biographical traditions are interwoven not only within the account of Peregrinus' Christian phase in the first half of the work, but also in the report of Peregrinus' death in the second half, which has a number of striking intertexts with the crucifixion narratives of the Gospels. Lucian compares Peregrinus with Jesus on the cross, while simultaneously ascribing to him a bewildering range of other biographical models, in order to foreground the opportunistic and indiscriminate nature of Peregrinus' self-dramatization. He represents Jesus as a self-promoting sophist,[8] a judgement which may have contributed to the widespread criticism of Lucian by later Christian readers.[9] According to Lucian at least, Peregrinus' imitation of Jesus' self-dramatization (amongst other models) takes the strategy of opportunistic self-staging to an even more extreme level.

That argument may have some relevance for our wider understanding of the influence of Christian biography on non-Christian 'Lives', although it is extremely difficult to pin down the significance of this one example of self-conscious gospel imitation within any broader context. Glen Bowersock has recently drawn attention to the presence of 'Christian' motifs within non-Christian narrative of the first to third centuries AD, arguing from this evidence that the Gospels had a widespread influence on contemporary culture even very soon after they were written.[10] His overall argument is not implausible. It has, however, attracted some sceptical responses, especially in relation to many of his individual examples (of which the *Peregrinus* is one).[11]

I want to suggest here that there are several methodological problems which hold back this debate from any fruitful progress. For one thing, there is a tendency to assume a self-evident significance for 'allusions' to Christian texts, as if their very presence is significant enough not to require any further interrogation. Bowersock, for example, tends not to examine the question of how or why these Christian motifs may have been exploited within any particular text.[12] Close examination of that sort, I will suggest, is crucial for any attempt to approach a broad picture of how early Christian narrative was used and valued by contemporary non-Christian authors. Some authors have disputed the claim that there are Christian motifs in the second half of the *Peregrinus*,[13] but in this case Bowersock seems to me to be right to suggest that there are details which point to a degree of familiarity and engagement with Christian narrative. The fact that Lucian has discussed Christian practice explicitly and at length in the first half of the work, mentioning Christ's crucifixion twice, strengthens the likelihood that the Christian motifs of the second half would have played a thematically significant role for some readers. Bowersock, however, discusses these details without giving much attention to the rest of the work, and so leaves open the challenge of exploring the effects they achieve in their narrative context. Analysing those effects is one of the main aims of this article.

Even then, however, it is hard to extrapolate from this one example to a broad vision of contemporary opinion. Lucian's insistent linking of Christian narrative with Peregrinean trickery – albeit in a way which also signals some differences between them, as we shall see – may be a sign that some features of Christian narrative were more widely known than has usually been thought, not least through an association between the

Christian Gospels and theatrical techniques of biographical trickery of the kind discussed in the late second-century anti-Christian work of Celsus.[14] However, it would surely require a more detailed thematic analysis of the use of this material in all of the places it appears for us to begin to outline a broad view of the effects Christian narrative details commonly achieved in non-Christian narrative contexts.

The *Peregrinus*, then, offers a thematically consistent and sustained view of the significance of Christian narrative, in fact it is unusually explicit in marking out its relations with Christian narrative traditions. In that sense it offers, I will suggest, an important – though in some ways untypical – example of close relations between Christian and non-Christian narrative.

Moreover, despite my own argument in what follows that Lucian is at least to some degree in control of the Christian material he draws on, it also seems important to be suspicious of any rigid insistence on 'demonstrable' intentionality on Lucian's part as a necessary ingredient of 'authentic' intertextual reference[15] (an insistence which has been evident especially in the work of those who have disputed the possibility that the appearance of 'Christian' motifs in non-Christian works could be a sign of Christian 'influence' at this early stage in Christian history). A precise model of deliberate allusion seems particularly inappropriate for most of the appearances of Christian material that we find in the non-Christian literature of this period. In other words, the assumption that authors and (especially) readers of non-Christian writing must be engaging with Christian texts carefully and deliberately if they are to be taken as doing so at all seems to me to be unnecessarily restrictive. Christian story-telling – which was itself very far from uniform – participated in a wide network of narrative traditions, both drawing on and contributing to those traditions through oral as much as written communication. Half-remembered stories, imperfectly distinguished from each other, must have influenced non-Christian writers at least as often as closely recalled and easily identifiable Christian narrative traditions. The Christian nature of certain types of narrative material must often have been only half acknowledged by their readers (or even their authors), or else acknowledged only by a small proportion of their readers. Even within the *Peregrinus*, where Christian influence on the text seems more carefully controlled than it often is elsewhere, intertexts with Christian crucifixion narratives do not necessarily imply any exact or detailed knowledge of these texts on Lucian's part, or any required knowledge of the same on the part of his readers.

Moreover, the *Peregrinus* advertises its own conformity with precisely this kind of flexible intertextual model, in repeatedly and self-consciously hinting at the impossibility of controlling 'allusion'. Lucian's *paideia* refuses to proceed by any orderly, easily trackable method. Instead, he courts an impression of deliberate indiscriminateness in his own ascription of biographical models to Peregrinus.[16] This ability to mix together a wide range of different sources is represented as a more successful version of Peregrinus' own indiscriminate appropriation of role models. The *Peregrinus*, in other words, is a text which knowingly undermines rigid models of intertextual exchange. The effects I outlined earlier in this section, whereby Lucian satirizes Peregrinus' attempts to control his own autobiographical 'imitations', themselves thematize precisely the point I have been making here in discussing the text's engagement with biographical tradition. We should surely be cautious about insisting on intentionality and close control over literary allusion in a text where Peregrinus' attempts at that kind of control within his own life are so ruthlessly subverted. The dizzying and deliberately chaotic proliferation of intertextual links that the text revels in is itself a metaphor for the techniques of multiple imitation which both Peregrinus and Lucian (author and narrator alike) use in their self-presentations.

II

Peregrinus is remarkable above all for the great range of models he appropriates. His further name 'Proteus', which Lucian mentions in the work's opening lines, linking him with the shape-changing sea-god of the *Odyssey* (discussed further below), foregrounds that characteristic immediately. I wish to focus in everything that follows on the way in which Peregrinus, by Lucian's account, combines many different models for his own life in such a way as to elide the differences between them. Lucian pursues that impression partly in order to show how Peregrinus' glory-seeking has imposed itself on gullible victims (as Lucian represents them) in a uniform and indiscriminate way. Mark Edwards has demonstrated this effect convincingly for the first half of the text.[17]

In this section I want to discuss especially the way in which Lucian's Peregrinus superficially and distortingly accommodates himself with a range of different philosophical attitudes towards death and suicide. I will then argue, in section three, that Lucian's use of a gospel-narrative framework for Peregrinus' death in the second half – in combination with many other models – contributes to the same impression of blurring between different biographical models. In the final section I will turn to the author/narrator's own self-representation to reveal something of his own surprisingly close connections with Peregrinus.

One of the things which reinforces the impression of Peregrinus' opportunistic eclecticism is Lucian's engagement with contemporary debate about the value of Peregrinus' death. Peregrinus was a controversial figure. We have extensive evidence for both praise and criticism of him from many different perspectives.[18] Some of these accounts contradict the impression we receive from Lucian's account. Many writers were apparently convinced of his philosophical credentials. Aulus Gellius, for example, describes him as 'serious and resolute' ('gravem et constantem'; *Noctes Atticae* 12.11), and records him saying that the wise man would not commit a sin even if he knew he would remain undetected. That portrait, of a man conspicuously not interested in surface appearances, is about as far removed from Lucian's version as one could imagine. Others give valuations of the suicide which are very different from Lucian's own. Lucian's text, I will argue, responds to those views by acknowledging that Peregrinus' suicide could in theory have been admired from a great range of philosophical perspectives, if it had been done with the right motives, but he also stresses the fact that Peregrinus (as this text describes him) was acting for the wrong reasons, that he perverted all of the potentially admirable philosophical viewpoints he got his hands on.

The ease with which Peregrinus is able to swap between different life stories within Lucian's version of his life is of course partly explained by the fact that there was a great deal of shared ground between the different philosophical groups of this period. That was true not least for Cynicism and Christianity, which seem to have had influence on each other, and which certainly shared a sufficient number of characteristics to be confused with each other by outsiders, although that shared ground often seems to have intensified rivalry between the two groups rather than the opposite.[19] We often see signs of a self-conscious eclecticism within the philosophical culture of the Roman Empire, in Cynicism perhaps more than anywhere. However, there may also have been commonly envisaged limits on the degree to which eclecticism was acceptable.[20] Lucian's representation of Peregrinus is certainly in line with that conclusion. He is firm about demonstrating that Peregrinus' eclecticism is of the wrong sort, opportunistic and absurd (as we shall see further in a moment in looking at the distinction between Peregrinus and Demonax, who is represented by Lucian as a more admirable model of philosophical eclecticism).

Theorization of death – especially suicide and resurrection – was one of the areas where the shared ground between different philosophical and religious groups was most apparent, but also, paradoxically, one of the most important and hotly contested focuses for religious boundary-definition.[21] Lucian's concentration on the moment of Peregrinus' death and on the many false starts leading up to it (for example, his failed Christian martyrdom and his many advertisements for the suicide), can be partly explained by his desire to exploit this background of doctrinal overlap in order to reflect on Peregrinus' boundary-blurring self-promotion.

How would Peregrinus' suicide (as Lucian describes it) have been viewed from the many different perspectives which the text hints at?

Lucian's Peregrinus had (allegedly) been living as a Cynic for some time when he died, and his decision to die need not have been incompatible with that purported allegiance, since Cynicism[22] – like Stoicism[23] – sanctioned suicide in cases where it was no longer possible to continue living a virtuous life. We hear of Cynics – including (according to some accounts) Diogenes himself, the founding father of Cynicism[24] – committing suicide under those circumstances. It was important not to kill oneself for the wrong reasons, however. The glory-seeking motives Lucian ascribes to Peregrinus are at odds with the requirement that one should only commit suicide when one is no longer capable of virtuous self-sufficiency.[25]

Suicide was also compatible with Epicurean belief but, again, only when carried out for the right reasons, when 'the prospects for an acceptably pleasant subsequent life are irretrievably slight'.[26] There are hints of an Epicurean perspective within Lucian's text. In 23, for example, we hear that Peregrinus *claimed* that he was attempting to banish the fear of death. Once again, however, the match is a very superficial one, not least because Peregrinus' deeply ingrained desire for worldly glory and for the 'immortality' of fame was one of the things Epicurean teaching most consistently condemned. Epicurean writing also warns of the way in which fear of death can paradoxically be a motive for suicide, and treats this as one of the least acceptable motives possible. Lucian's Peregrinus is afraid of death himself. In 43, for example, Lucian describes Peregrinus' fear during a storm at sea:

> ...he started to wail with the women, this admirable man who was thought to be superior to death. (*Peregrinus* 43)[27]

Freedom from fear is one of the prime goals of Epicurean *ataraxia*. That state is often described through the imagery of quiet seas after a storm.[28] By exposing Peregrinus' cowardliness, and his failure to conform to Epicurean demands for 'calm' in the face of the insignificant storms of life which threaten bodily harm, Lucian sabotages any claim on his part to be an Epicurean role model.

Platonic doctrine did allow for the possibility of suicide in certain limited circumstances, although it inclined towards prohibition of self-killing even more strongly than the schools I have already discussed.[29] The tendency to reject suicide intensified within later Platonic thinking, responding in part to Pythagorean doctrine (although that tendency is most striking in the centuries after Lucian was writing).[30] The classic Platonic discussion of suicide is in the *Phaedo*, where Socrates elucidates Pythagorean prohibitions of suicide, while nevertheless leaving open the possibility that suicide may sometimes be acceptable, if one is under divine compulsion.[31] Socrates is presumably under that kind of compulsion himself, since he seems to have at least a hand in his own death (for example because of his famous refusal to escape from punishment by adopting a more compromising attitude during his trial), although the text stops short of describing the submission to execution (which requires him to drink hemlock by his own hand) as an act of self-killing. In Lucian's account, Peregrinus' followers, both Cynic and Christian, use Socrates as a model for his death; in fact the *Phaedo* – which was one of the most famous and influential models for later biographical writing, as well as later discussions of suicide – is twice evoked explicitly, in Lucian's description of the Christians gathering around Peregrinus in his prison cell (*Peregrinus* 12), and in his mockery of the Cynics who loiter around the pyre after Peregrinus has died, as if they are the companions of Socrates waiting for a painter to paint their portraits (37). Lucian's Peregrinus follows a Socratic model, then, but his unnecessary self-immolation is absurdly inconsistent with the possibilities for divinely sanctioned suicide which the *Phaedo* leaves open.[32]

There are also repeated suggestions in Lucian's account – as in the work of other contemporary commentators on Peregrinus – that he was imitating Brahmans who had famously burned themselves to death in public.[33] The beliefs which were ascribed to them as motives for self-immolation are much harder to reconstruct than they are for the philosophical positions I have outlined. Lucian himself gives the impression that he has no clear idea of the motives for Brahmanical suicide. Despite that imprecise knowledge, however, he is still keen to represent Peregrinus' imitation of their example as inadequate and superficial. In 25, for example, Lucian reminds us that even the Indians may have glory-seekers amongst them; but then contrasts the Brahmans' admirably impassive acceptance of pain and gradual death with Peregrinus' sensational and cowardly plan to leap into the pit in which his pyre was located, so that he would die within seconds.[34]

Finally, there was also debate about the value of suicide amongst Christians in this period.[35] The Christian prohibition of suicide, influenced by traditions of Platonizing Christianity, and partly in reaction to excessive enthusiasm for martyrdom, was crystallized only in the writing of Augustine.[36] Before Augustine we often find Christians speaking in praise of suicide in some contexts. Peregrinus' own death seems to have been compatible with Christian admiration from the perspective of some authors. Tertullian, for example, probably influenced by Stoic and Cynic traditions,[37] uses Peregrinus as an example of noble suicide in *Ad Martyras* 4. He includes Peregrinus in a long list of pagans who have had admirable deaths by suicide, and then says that it is *even more* noble to die like this for Christian principles.

Lucian exploits the Christian reputation for eye-catching martyrdom in his satire of Peregrinus,[38] associating him with stereotypical Christian sensationalism. Strikingly, however, he chooses not to extend that criticism to Peregrinus' Christian followers, blaming instead their gullibility (as he represents it):

> For the wretches have convinced themselves entirely that they will be immortal and live for ever, and for that reason they despise death and willingly give themselves into custody. (*Peregrinus* 13)[39]

He seems keen to exonerate the Christians themselves from the charge of glory-seeking, in order to enhance the impression of Peregrinus' manipulative nature by contrast. By comparison with him the Christians, those most spectacular of suicides, are innocents who have beguiled themselves into false belief. Peregrinus' appropriation of Christian identity, as Lucian describes it, thus follows the pattern I have argued for in relation to a number of other philosophical and religious influences on him, in the sense that his own motives are almost unconnected with the beliefs of those he purports to represent.

There are many different perspectives, then, from which Peregrinus' suicide might have been envisaged as admirable.[40] Peregrinus, however, on Lucian's account, is not a reliable representative of any of them. The debate between modern scholars about which of the philosophical and religious influences on Peregrinus were most significant at different times in his career has often ignored the fact that Lucian deliberately makes that difficult for us to judge. Peregrinus' Cynic and Christian followers, meanwhile, are mocked by Lucian for their naïveté, which allows their beliefs to be manipulated, so much so that they become in many ways indistinguishable from each other. They, too, in Lucian's account of them, fail to respect the boundaries between their own beliefs and those of rival groups, only in their case it is more from stupidity than calculation.[41]

Peregrinus' perversion of philosophical norms is implicitly connected in Lucian's text with the manipulation of biographical convention, both by Peregrinus himself and by his followers. Most significantly, Lucian exposes Peregrinus' perversion of the conventions of philosophical death within biographical writing. Philosophers, as they are described in their biographies, tend to die bravely but unobtrusively. Diogenes Laertius, in his *Lives and Opinions of Eminent Philosophers*, repeatedly introduces brief descriptions of his subjects' deaths, deaths which often showcase the philosophers' bravery in the face of pain and misfortune, and in a number of cases are self-administered, but which are nearly always unobtrusive. In a few cases also he describes posthumous honours, especially widely-attended funeral processions which testify to the popularity of the deceased. And he often records epigrams composed to celebrate the life of the philosopher in question, regularly including epigrams he has composed himself, with the implication that his own writing participates in the processes of commemoration and immortalization. Lucian's Peregrinus attempts to combine the defining moments of death and funeral commemoration into one, mixing the defining moment of his death with the moment of cremation, dying on his own funeral pyre. But he seems to have forgotten that his proclaimed philosophical allegiances should lead him to a less theatrical method of leaving the physical world.

In many ways Lucian's Peregrinus is closer to the biographical traditions applied to wonder-workers and holy-men like Apollonius of Tyana, whose lives end in a blaze of glory.[42] Even here, however, he falls short of his role models by the incompetence of his attempted sensationalism. His attempt to conjure up a glorious afterlife by orchestrating the moment of his own destruction falls flat. That anti-climactic combination does make a formative contribution to Peregrinus' self-definition, but it does so in ways he has failed to anticipate, contributing above all to the absurdity of his reputation, at least as Lucian paints it. One of the functions of biographical writing is to bring a kind of immortality to its subjects, by keeping alive the deeds of great men. Lucian's biography of Peregrinus offers him only an absurd travesty of literary commemoration.

For any reader who knows Lucian's other writing there is as an implicit contrast between Peregrinus and Demonax, another Cynic philosopher, who was the subject of one of Lucian's other biographical texts.[43] The difference between them (which is signalled briefly in the *Demonax*, though not in the *Peregrinus*)[44] illustrates some of the distinctive problems involved in Peregrinus' overstepping of philosophical and autobiographical limits. Demonax, like Peregrinus, displays an eclectic kind of Cynicism, but his motives for doing so are represented as being very different. He makes no attempt to control his own self-representation, preferring to let his life emerge from disparate details, just as Lucian lets Demonax's life emerge from disparate details through the disjointed form of his biographical writing within the text, which consists of a loosely combined collection of anecdotes. Peregrinus, by contrast, tries to control too much, swinging very self-consciously between different labels and different ideals. His eclecticism, it seems, is flawed.[45] Demonax also provides an example of how a Cynic philosopher can commit suicide in a way which is compatible with philosophical principles, without the aim of self-glorification. He starves himself to death when he realizes he is no longer able to maintain his self-sufficiency, leaving instructions that no one should waste energy over his burial, in a scene which takes up only a few sentences at the end of Lucian's narrative. The Athenians insist on giving him a public funeral, however, which attracts many more people than are present at the pyre of Peregrinus.[46]

III

I have argued, then, that Lucian shows Peregrinus making the boundaries between different groups (Cynics and Christians especially) irrelevant, as if his actions and his insidious influence (as Lucian represents it) are identical whichever group he claims to belong to (although he does not get away with this all the time, and there are occasions when his opportunistic attitude to these boundaries comes up against obstacles, for example when his otherwise gullible Christian followers object to his violation of their dietary laws and expel him; *Peregrinus* 16). I have also suggested that there are implicit links between the *Peregrinus* and Lucian's *Life of Demonax*. Demonax represents a more positive paradigm of some of the biographical and philosophical traditions Peregrinus perverts.

How does Lucian's *description* of the suicide itself help to articulate these impressions? And do the intertexts between Lucian's text and the Gospel crucifixion narratives play any role in fulfilling these wider aims? Christopher Jones has argued for a clear separation between Peregrinus' Cynic and Christian phases, listing a fascinating range of non-Christian parallels for Peregrinus' activity during the Cynic stage of his career.[47] However, he seems to me to overstate his case in arguing that reminiscences of Christian narrative within the account of Peregrinus' death should not be taken as such simply because they *can* be explained in purely 'pagan' terms.[48]

For one thing, as I have argued, the concept of deliberate and undeniable allusion may not be the only one which is relevant for intertextual study of this sort, especially for culturally 'marginal' narrative traditions like the far-from-uniform set of Christian stories which the Gospels arose from and perpetuated. The influence of Christian material on this account may be a sign of the gradual spread of familiarity with Christian narrative even if it is being used without careful planning by Lucian himself, and even if only a small proportion of his readers would have noticed it.

That said, it also seems likely, given the tendency to eclecticism which Peregrinus displays in relation to non-Christian traditions at this point in the story,[49] and in other parts of the text, and given the frequency with which Lucian refers to Christian narrative material at other points in his account, that Lucian is here exercising at least a degree of control over the Gospel reminiscences I will discuss, even if he does not choose to draw attention to that control in any precise terms. I will argue here that Lucian's comparisons between Peregrinus' suicide and Jesus' death on the cross potentially contribute to the impression that Peregrinus himself was still unable or unwilling to settle on one biographical model, even (or perhaps especially) at the moment of his death. They also suggest that Peregrinus loses control over his own self-portrayal, acting in ways which resemble inept versions of Jesus' manipulation of gullible opinion (as Lucian portrays it) even when they are not intended to, if Lucian chooses to represent them as such.

In *Peregrinus* 32 the slanging match between Theagenes and his unnamed respondent with which the work has opened finally draws to a close, and the scene shifts to Olympia, where we see Peregrinus speaking on his own behalf in a scene which briefly replays the absurdity and turmoil of the previous exchange of speeches in Elis. Lucian tells us that he stayed on the edges of the crowd, preferring not to give Peregrinus too much of his attention. His strongest impulse is to laugh, not only at the indignity of Peregrinus' self-advertisement, but also at the ineptitude of it. Peregrinus, Lucian tells us, was so taken up with the temporary success of his self-publicization that he could not see how insignificant the crowds gathering around him really were:

> ...not knowing, poor fool, that even those who are being led away to the cross, or those who are in the power of the public executioner, have many more people following after them.   (*Peregrinus* 34)[50]

On its own, of course, a reference to crucifixion need not be taken as a deliberate allusion to Christian precedents. In the context of Lucian's text, however, which twice mentions the crucifixion of Jesus outside the account of Peregrinus' suicide, the reference seems pointed. In 11, for example, we have heard that Peregrinus' Christian followers had worshipped him in second place, after 'that man who was crucified in Palestine'.[51] Later, in 13, Lucian notes Jesus' deception of his gullible followers, describing him scathingly as 'that crucified sophist',[52] an image which suggests a parallel between Jesus' manipulation of opinion (as Lucian portrays it) and Peregrinus' own deceitfulness. When read with these other passages in mind, it seems to me hard to avoid the conclusion that the passing reference to crucifixion in 34, immediately before the shift to the scene in front of Peregrinus' pyre, is likely to recall the Christian themes of the early part of the work for some of Lucian's contemporary readers. It sets up the crucifixion of Jesus – unobtrusively but artfully – as one of many models for the suicide description which follows. In the process it implies that Jesus' following was largely due to sensation-hunting crowds rather than anything more. Peregrinus exploits the same hunger for sensation (as Lucian portrays it), only far less successfully.

Similarly, after the death of Peregrinus has been described, in the very closing sentences of the work, Lucian mocks Peregrinus for his vanity in taking medication to improve his eyesight, even though he was planning to burn himself to death only a few days later:

> it is as though a man about to go up on the cross should treat the bruise on his finger.   (45)[53]

This echoes the tradition of mocking Jesus for his weakness before death, as Celsus did with reference to Jesus' prayer to be released from suffering.[54] Peregrinus had worried about death itself in similar terms, as we learn shortly before this passage, in 43–4, discussed above. Here, in this climactic image of vain complaints about a minor ailment, Peregrinus is doing something even more absurd than Jesus (as he is represented by Celsus and others), complaining over something very much more trivial. Once again, it seems, Lucian's Peregrinus not only reproduces the fraudulence and hypocrisy associated with Christian stories by critics like Celsus, but also intensifies it, carrying it to ridiculous extremes. This final return to Jesus as an implicit model for Peregrinus is a conspicuous concluding detail in a series of recurrent references to crucifixion. That recurrence echoes the way in which Peregrinus' own imitations of Christianity have a degree of consistency, reappearing even after he has renounced any explicit Christian allegiance. Such consistency may be partly a result of Peregrinus' calculating eclecticism, but it may not be entirely under Peregrinus' own control. In this case, at least, his imitation of Jesus' alleged weakness is presumably an unwitting one.

After the initial description of Peregrinus' speech-making in Olympia, Lucian moves on to the burning itself. This eventually takes place several days after the end of the festival. Lucian represents the delay as a result of Peregrinus' cowardly procrastination, although the same detail could equally well have been used to argue that Peregrinus was not interested in attracting a large crowd. The aggressive advertisement of Peregrinus' connections with distinguished role models who were mentioned in the speech of Theagenes is not continued here, as if Peregrinus and his companions are silenced by being finally confronted with the reality of the moment they have been imagining for so long. Even here, however, there are signs that Peregrinus is trying to play a great range of roles at the same time. In 36, for example, Lucian describes the way in which he removed his Cynic clothing before jumping, taking off his wallet and cloak, and laying aside the Herakles-club which he used to carry around with him. Herakles was an icon of Cynic virtue, not least because of the way he had burned himself to death when suffering unbearably, and Peregrinus' club-carrying is therefore an ostentatious reminder of his continued claim to Cynic identity. The allusion to Plato's *Phaedo* after the suicide, in 37, which I discussed above, reminds us of Peregrinus' Socratic pretensions. There is also a reference in 39 to the habits of the Brahmans (although it turns out that Peregrinus has failed to conform to these, having burned himself at the wrong time of day).[55]

That medley account of the moment of burning and of Peregrinus' preparation for it also contains one detail which might for some readers have given the impression of being a muddled imitation of the Christian crucifixion stories. In 36, just before Peregrinus leaps on to the fire, we hear that he entrusts himself to the spirits of his mother and father:

'Spirits of my mother and my father, receive me with favour.' Having said that he jumped into the fire...[56]

That seems to echo the final words of Jesus on the cross, as reported by Luke:

and having cried out in a loud voice, Jesus said, 'Father, into your hands I shall commit my spirit.' And having said those words, he expired.
(Luke 23.46)[57]

Jones downplays this possibility, pointing out that there are plenty of models for this sort of address to paternal and maternal *daimones* in non-Christian prayers to the underworld.[58] Once again, however, it seems likely, given the depth of reference to Christian practice and narrative tradition elsewhere in the text, that these Christian and non-Christian influences could have stood together, at least for some readers, in a way which is consistent with the effects of blurring between different religious and philosophical influences that Lucian is trying to achieve throughout the work.

As we read on we find more examples. On his way back from the pyre, the narrator meets people who have got the time of the firework display wrong, and describes everything to them:

If I saw a man of taste, I would recount everything which happened without embellishment (ψιλά), as I have to you. But for the stupid people, those who listened open-mouthed to any story they heard, I made up my own tragedy (ἐτραγῴδουν τι παρ' ἐμαυτοῦ), saying that when the fire was kindled, and Peregrinus went up to it and threw himself in, there was first of all a great earthquake, and a bellowing of the earth, and then a vulture flying out of the middle of the fire went up to the sky, saying in a human voice, 'I have finished with the earth, and I'm going to Olympus.' (39)[59]

The claim to be offering a narrative which is unembellished, bare, accurate (ψιλά) is one we might be suspicious of, given our experience in the preceding chapters of this narrator's manipulative story-telling style (more on that in the next section). Later he meets an old man (40) who looks trustworthy on the surface, but ends up repeating the invented detail of the vulture back to him, claiming to have seen it himself, and combining that claim with an entirely different story of Peregrinus' resurrection:

...how he had seen Peregrinus after the burning in white clothing, only a little while ago, and had only just left him wandering around in the Stoa of the Seven Voices, shining and crowned with an olive crown.[60]

It is tempting to feel that Lucian's choice of the Stoa of Seven Voices as the venue for this imaginary reappearance – a building on the east side of the Olympic sanctuary which was famous for its echoes – is intended to add to a sense of the multiplicity of voices contributing to Peregrinus' 'immortality', partly in the sense that there are many different people making up their own stories, but perhaps also in the sense that these stories have arisen from a very wide range of sources.

Clearly many of these details again have 'pagan' precedents. Jones gives most of his attention to these, suggesting that there is no need to posit Christian influence. In Plutarch's *Life of Romulus* 28.1 and 28.3, for example, Romulus appears after death dressed in armour with an olive crown. The olive crown is also reminiscent of the traditional garland for Olympic victors, drawing on a long tradition of representing philosophical prowess by athletic imagery. In foregrounding these intertexts Jones rejects the possibility that there is any reference to the 24 elders who are described in Revelation 4.4 wearing gold crowns and dressed in white.[61] The non-Christian influences are strong, and Jones is no doubt right to suggest that we cannot be sure that Lucian has this passage from Revelation in mind. Nevertheless, it seems wrong to assume that the existence of adequate non-Christian parallels in itself precludes the possibility that some readers would have sensed Christian overtones at this point. The likelihood that these intertexts with Christian narrative would have been conspicuous for some readers surely gains force from the weight of Christian material elsewhere within the work.[62] And if these references were ever thought of as significantly related to New Testament texts, they would – once again – clearly have been appropriate to the wider aims of the work as a whole.

In some cases the parallels with Christian narrative are more sustained than the links with pagan material which Jones cites. I am not suggesting that they outweigh those references, rather that the two potentially work together, offering a variety of shades of significance which different readers would have responded to in different ways. Matthew 27, for example, contains details – of an earthquake and of the reappearance of bodies from the grave – which are similar to those in *Peregrinus* 39–40, in a combination which is not present within any of the non-Christian parallels usually cited for that passage:

And look, the veil of the Temple was torn into two from the top to the bottom; and the earth shook and the rocks were torn apart; and the tombs were opened, and many bodies of holy men who had died were awoken; and coming out of the tombs, after his resurrection, they went into the holy city, and appeared to many people.   (Matthew 27.51–3)[63]

The credulous bystanders react to Peregrinus, the text suggests, not only by swallowing his self-fabrications, but also by replaying and extending them. The narrator himself does something similar, although more knowingly and ironically, exposing the charlatanism of Peregrinus' self-presentation by mockingly colluding with his strategy of imitating an indiscriminate mixture of philosophical and religious role models, Christian role models included.

IV

I hope to have shown, then, that the frequency of Lucian's (at times superficial) engagement with Christian ideas elsewhere in this text – most importantly his two explicit references to Jesus' crucifixion in *Peregrinus* 11 and 13 – makes it likely that the Gospel reminiscences within the account of Peregrinus' suicide could have been seen as significant by readers with some – even vague – knowledge of Christian narrative. These reminiscences potentially play an important role within Lucian's portrayal of Peregrinus' boundary-traversing theatricality.

How, finally, does Lucian, whether as author or as narrator, situate 'himself' in relation to the imagery of deceptiveness which is applied to Peregrinus?

The actions of Peregrinus, as we have seen, are repeatedly described in theatrical terms,[64] but that imagery is also implicitly associated with the narrator. Immediately after his introductory remarks, for example, Lucian describes Peregrinus' death as the latest act in a long drama:

> The complete staging (διασκευή) of the event was as follows. You know what the playwright (τὸν ποιητήν) [i.e. Peregrinus] was like, of course, and what great performances he put on (ἡλίκα ἐτραγῴδει) throughout his life, surpassing Sophocles and Aeschylus'. (*Peregrinus* 3)[65]

The phrase 'throughout his life' (παρ' ὅλον τὸν βίον) is perhaps meant to remind us that Peregrinus' theatricality has been directed in particular at manipulation of biographical convention, imitating the lives of famous figures as they are described in biographical texts. The sentence as a whole has a sarcastic tone, as if Lucian the narrator is sharing a private joke with his friend from a position of superiority. But does it also deliberately flirt with the impression of grudging admiration, lying behind its sarcastic surface? Certainly it suggests that Lucian and Kronios have a long familiarity with Peregrinus' trickery, and that they have taken a certain pleasure from their observation of it. It also hints at an equation between Lucian and Peregrinus by its references to the processes of scene-setting. Lucian's Peregrinus stage-manages the incident itself, just as Lucian stage-manages his telling of it within the text. The transferability of Peregrinean theatricality to the narrator himself is even more conspicuous later, for example in 39, where Lucian claims to have made up his own tragedy (ἐτραγῴδουν τι παρ' ἐμαυτοῦ).[66]

There are also moments when Lucian the narrator seems more closely associated with the companions of Peregrinus than he pretends to be. That dissonance between implicit association and ostensible dissociation may be a deliberate attempt on Lucian's part to draw attention to the skill with which he has disguised the connections between them. It is as though he cannot resist the opportunity to show his own Peregrinean qualities peeping out from beneath their irreproachable disguise. He declares his own lack of interest in Peregrinus at several points. In 32, for example, he claims that he left halfway through the speech of Peregrinus in Olympia. Similarly, in 35 he claims that he stayed at Olympia beyond the end of the festival only because he could not get any transport. He praises the contests he has just witnessed as the best of the four Olympics he has seen, suggesting that this was the spectacle he was really interested in, whereas he went to watch Peregrinus simply to fill in some spare time. This ostentatious parade of lack of interest is compromised, however, by an increasing impression that he and Peregrinus have been dogging each other's footsteps for some time. For example, the mention of the narrator's three previous visits to the Olympics in 35 might remind us of Peregrinus' notorious exploits at previous occurrences of the festival, mentioned in 19–20, reinforcing the impression that he and Peregrinus have come across each other many times before. That effect is intensified in 43–4, where he describes a ship journey they once shared across the Aegean. Even the imagery used to describe Peregrinus' deranged followers in the opening paragraphs of the work slyly suggests that Lucian himself is related to them. In 2, for example, he explains:

> I was nearly torn apart by the Cynics (Κυνικῶν), like Aktaion by his dogs (κυνῶν), or like his nephew Pentheus by the Maenads.[67]

The imagery of destruction at the hands of one's own people has disturbing implications. Is the narrator like Pentheus, at risk of being torn apart by his own relatives? Is Lucian threatened by the dog-like Cynics in the same way as Aktaion by his dogs, both of them menaced by their own creatures? We cannot discount the possibility – so the similes seem to be warning us – that Lucian is, deep down, one of them.

Peregrinus' capacity to switch between different allegiances is also relevant to Lucian's self-representation, both as narrator, in this text, and also as author, through its similarity with the characteristics Lucian displays throughout his work. Peregrinus named himself Proteus in imitation of Homer's shape-changing and prophetic sea-god, as if claiming divine status for himself, as Lucian reminds us repeatedly within his account.[68] In

Lucian's hands, however, the image comes to have less complimentary effects. Menelaus, in *Odyssey* 4, following the instructions of Proteus' daughter, holds on to the god as he changes himself into many different forms, until finally Proteus' repertoire is exhausted and he reveals what Menelaus has come to demand. Lucian, similarly, holds on to Peregrinus through all of his different incarnations, until finally the underlying truth of his identity is revealed, except that in Peregrinus' case that true image is very much less flattering.

Perhaps we are to imagine that it is only the narrator's own greater mastery of Peregrinean skills of trickery which allows him to unmask the impostor, just as he is able to detect and unmask the fraudulent prophet Alexander, according to his own account, because of his own greater control over the skills on which Alexander relies.[69] That possibility is made more likely by the fact that the imagery of shape-changing and disguise is also applicable to Lucian himself – both in this incarnation as narrator and in the other works of Lucian the author – in a variety of ways.[70] I have suggested already that Lucian in other works matches Peregrinus' refashionings by his own strategy of inhabiting a range of different masks within his own texts, and that the anonymous respondent to Theagenes in Elis fits in with that pattern.[71] He also takes on a great range of different philosophical viewpoints in his work, using a Cynic voice perhaps most often of all.[72] The eclectic Cynic Demonax, discussed above, is one of the figures he links himself with most strongly.[73] Lucian thus risks association with Peregrinus through their shared strategy of switching between different philosophical viewpoints. And yet he distances himself from that model, partly – in the *Demonax* – by implying a contrast between Peregrinus and Demonax, and by his own association with the latter, casting Peregrinus' shape-changing as an absurd perversion of his own more valuable philosophical selectiveness.

There are times, then, when Lucian – both as narrator and author – seems to be suggesting a clear separation between himself and his subject, despite superficial resemblances, because of the crucial contrast between Peregrinus' self-advertising charlatanism and his own integrity and lack of interest in worldly glory. I have also suggested, however, that the text constantly makes such a separation difficult to maintain. It is hard to avoid the impression that the difference between them is one of competence, not of morality; that the important distinction between them lies not in their different motives, but simply in the fact that Lucian himself is *better* at manipulating perceptions than his rival is. Certainly the narrator's retiring self-presentation is (deliberately?) unconvincing. He presents the *Peregrinus* as a private letter to his friend Kronios, as if he is keen to suggest that he has no interest in public opinion, or in debating Peregrinus' reputation openly. However, the text also exposes the disingenuousness of that claim as soon as any reader other than Kronios begins to read it. The very fact that we are reading it implies that it is not as private as it purports to be. In many ways, Lucian is an Odyssean figure, flaunting his own control over the narrative, and maintaining a cunning anonymity in a way which allows him to survive beyond the death of Peregrinus, to the end of the story.[74] Peregrinus seems to have been worshipped as a cult figure after his death, an outcome which Lucian pretends to anticipate, representing his own after-the-event knowledge as prophetic. Lucian subverts the immortality which that cult implies, replacing it with a very different, and less flattering, kind of immortality for Peregrinus, determined by his own narrative priorities. He revels in his own ability to manipulate Peregrinus' reputation, and his own. Unlike Peregrinus, who (as we hear in 42), is not even able to profit from his notoriety, Lucian himself is alive to enjoy his glory. He can recreate himself, and his rivals, repeatedly, as often as he wishes, in his speech and in his writing.

It is tempting to sidestep the disturbing implications of Lucian's cunning self-representation by assuming that we, at least, are not subject to his deception. However, even that consolation is hard to maintain, and there are repeated hints that Lucian's readers risk being just as much under his spell as the ignorant men he mocks. The description of Lucian's fabrications after the suicide is a good example. In 39, he explains that he told the true story to men of taste, and deceived only those who looked stupid. In 40, he then comes across the gossiping old man whose claims I discussed in the previous section.

> When I had returned to the festival I met a grey-haired man who looked trustworthy, to judge by his face, and by his beard and his general air of respectability.[75]

The old man is reliable and dignified on the surface, but turns out to be just as gullible and incompetently deceptive as the other men Lucian has criticized. Is the old man an image for Peregrinus, who hides his disreputable aims beneath a mask of respectability? Or does Lucian include him here to warn us that the honesty he had proclaimed towards men of taste in 39 (and, implicitly, towards his readers) may not be what it seems? Why should he tell the truth to anyone, us included, if men who look reliable turn out to be no better than the worst of the gossiping bystanders? And if that is the case, could the old man even be an image for Lucian himself (as far as we can locate him at all), who, like Peregrinus, hides deep-rooted manipulations of the truth beneath a trustworthy facade?

I have suggested, then, that Lucian's text is largely dedicated to exposure of Peregrinus' theatrical deceptions, and that he achieves that effect in part by the technique of linking Peregrinus' biography with the traditions of Christian life-telling. That effect is compromised, however, by the way in which he flirts – in his narratorial voice – with an association between those deceptive forms and his own narrative techniques, which at times even allows a note of admiration for Peregrinus' self-fashioning to creep through. Ultimately, Lucian's scorn for Peregrinus is not about his fraudulence, but about his incompetent application of that fraudulence, which can never come close, he suggests, to the brilliance of his own biographical and autobiographical control. Lucian decries love of glory and the exploitation of gullibility while indulging in it, all the time daring us to side with Peregrinus and his stupid followers in order to accuse him of such indulgence. He demands our collusion in his almost irresistible mockery of Peregrinus. And yet at the same time the authority of the narrator's voice is questionable. We are continually prompted to suspect that the presiding genius of the work may himself be beyond capture, always receding behind new layers of deceptive and dubious self-dramatization.

V

This chapter has been centred around two main arguments. First, I have suggested that the material Lucian presents in his description of Peregrinus' final hours is closely in dialogue with the Gospel narratives of the crucifixion, in a way which at least some of his contemporary readers might have sensed, prompted perhaps by more explicit references to Christian practice and Christian biography elsewhere in the text, although the degree of Lucian's own knowledge of these things is hard to judge given the deliberate impression of indiscriminate eclecticism with which the work is imbued. I have argued that these fleeting intertexts with Christian narrative traditions enhance the impression of Peregrinus' fleeting association with a wide and inconsistently applied range of biographical paradigms. Through that deliberately jumbled mixture Lucian represents biographical writing and auto-biographical self-presentation, Christian and otherwise, as processes which are always open to opportunistic manipulation, albeit manipulation whose effects may be hard to control.

Whether that conclusion has implications for our understanding of the use of Christian narrative material by other non-Christian authors is less clear. There are many texts from this period which contain what look like 'Christian' motifs. Moreover, some non-Christian writing, like the work of Celsus, shares the preoccupation with Christian theatricality and deception which we find in the *Peregrinus*. However, that evidence on its own is not enough to prove a widespread knowledge of the Gospels or a widespread association of Christian narrative traditions with connotations of biographical trickery, not least because in other cases the thematic significance of these 'gospel motifs' does not obviously match those patterns. The *Peregrinus* may in fact be unusual in the depth of its engagement with Christian story-telling. It seems to me that progress can be made in uncovering the complex contours of non-Christian attitudes to Christian narrative only by paying close attention to the themes and agendas which inform the texts in which these motifs are found, as I have tried to do here for the *Peregrinus*.

My second point is that Lucian weaves his own self-presentation in with the scathing biography of his subject, in a way which makes his criticism of Peregrinus far from straightforward. In doing so, he exposes, once again, the theatricality of all self-presentation, and satirizes, but also exploits, the reliance on role models which is central to so much of the rhetorical self-promotion and biographical writing of the ancient world. He represents himself – through his narratorial voice, whose own authenticity and authority are never quite guaranteed – as someone who has very far outdone Peregrinus' opportunistic and parasitic self-fashioning, and Jesus' (as Lucian represents it) slightly less incompetent version of that. He revels in the possibility that he may have even us, his readers, under his control, hinting at the enormity of his own manipulation of the truth without ever giving us enough evidence to accuse him of it. In that sense, Lucian, for one, represents Christian biographical tradition, like the other traditions on which Peregrinus has drawn in his life and his death, not as an alien narrative form of which he happens to be aware, but rather as something familiar, as another version of the much larger system of fictionalization and self-fictionalization over which he repeatedly and ironically proclaims his mastery.

Acknowledgements

I am grateful especially to Tim Whitmarsh and Alice Weeks for comments on recent drafts of this article; and to James Warren and Lucy Grig for discussion of a much earlier version.

Notes

[1] On the date of Peregrinus' death, see Jones 1986, 124–5, esp. n.34.

[2] I hope it will be clear in everything that follows that my discussion of Peregrinus and his followers is intended primarily as a discussion of Lucian's representation of them, not of the historical reality lying behind that representation, unless otherwise specified.

[3] See Edwards 1997, 230–31 on the title βίος in this period, with a number of examples, although he notes that the word was much less common as a generic marker of biographical writing in this period than it was in late antiquity.

[4] For example, Theagenes (who later seems to have preached Peregrinus' virtues in Rome) eulogizes Peregrinus in *Peregrinus* 4–6, comparing him with an absurdly extravagant range of philosophical and even divine figures; see Jones 1986, 131 on Theagenes, and on the *Apologies of Peregrinus* which were written after Peregrinus' death (whether

by Theagenes or others is not clear).

⁵ e.g. see Marcus 1994, 273–4.

⁶ Hägg and Rousseau (eds.) 2000, 2–5 discuss the way in which a spoken panegyric involves enhancement of the speaker's reputation as well as eulogy of its subject. They take written biography and panegyric as separate (though related) genres. They also suggest that biography is paradoxically even more likely than panegyric to involve authorial self-projection, and distortion of the truth, because the author's own presence is more easily disguised: '…without our noticing it, the biographical subject often merges with the biographer's own persona and agenda into one ideal whole…' (3).

⁷ e.g. see Branham 1989, e.g. 209–10 on the common Lucianic strategy of 'ironic impersonation of a didactic voice' (210). That quotation comes from his concluding remarks on the *Alexander*, a text which has a great deal in common with the *Peregrinus*, in the sense that both works are dedicated to the exposure of a fraudulent philosopher, and both of them draw similar links between manipulative author and manipulative subject; for that point see Clay 1992, 3430–8 and (especially) 3445–8, who provides the best analysis of the complexities of Lucian's self-representation in the *Peregrinus*; by contrast, Branham 1989, 193–5 underestimates the extent to which the *Peregrinus*, like the *Alexander*, problematizes the character of its narrator, and parodies traditional biographical forms in the process. On Lucian's role-playing, see also Whitmarsh 2001, 247–94; Saïd 1993.

⁸ e.g. at *Peregrinus* 13, discussed further below.

⁹ e.g., see Clay 1992, 3437, n. 74; Baldwin 1973, 97–103.

¹⁰ See Bowersock 1994, esp. 115–16 on the *Peregrinus*.

¹¹ e.g., see Demandt 1997, esp. 742–3.

¹² e.g. in his concluding remarks (ibid. p. 143) he suggests that '[t]he stories of Jesus inspired the polytheists to create a wholly new genre that we might call romantic scripture'; this may well be right (although it may be only a part of the story), but it still leaves open the challenge of explaining what was at stake within such manipulations of Christian material, taken both individually and collectively.

¹³ Most forcefully Jones 1993.

¹⁴ e.g., see Bowersock 1994, esp. 2–3 on Celsus' criticism of Christian mendacity; Bowersock compares Celsus' preoccupations with Lucian's obsessive interest in the fictionality of all ostensibly reliable narrative; that comparison seems especially important in the context of Lucian's explicit engagement with Christian ideas in the *Peregrinus*. It has sometimes been argued (e.g. by Baldwin 1973, 29–30, following the claims of the scholiast to Lucian's *Alexander*) that the Celsus against whom Origen defended Christian belief is the Celsus to whom Lucian addressed his *Alexander* (another work which juxtaposes a fraudulent philosopher with Christians, who are portrayed as surprisingly right-minded by comparison); for an opposing argument see Chadwick (ed.) 1953, xxiv–xxvi.

¹⁵ As Hinds 1998, and many others, have recently pointed out for a great range of other texts and genres.

¹⁶ However, see Jones 1986, 122 and Betz 1959 on signs of surprisingly detailed knowledge of early Christian practice within the first half of the work; they contradict Bagnani 1955, who over-emphasizes Lucian's ignorance of Christianity.

¹⁷ Edwards 1989. Jones 1986, 123 (following Schwartz 1963, 98 and others) notes the fact that Peregrinus is described wearing Cynic clothes while he was still a Christian (in

Peregrinus 15), and explains this anomaly by the suggestion that Lucian has twisted the order of events, delaying his account of Peregrinus' apostasy 'in order to give an unflattering motive for...Peregrinus' quarrel with his home city'. The 'anomaly' might equally be explained as a deliberately planted sign of Peregrinus' disrespect for philosophical boundaries; those two explanations seem entirely compatible with each other.

[18] See Jones 1986, 130–2 for a good overview, with the observation that 'contemporary references to Peregrinus almost always have a combative tone, as if their authors were touching on a sensitive topic' (131).

[19] e.g. see Branham 1996, 19 for an overview of that ambivalent relationship; Downing 1993 and 1992, who argues for Cynicism as a crucial influence on early Christianity; Dorival 1993, who charts (mainly but not exclusively critical) attitudes towards Cynicism in the writing of the Church Fathers; cf. Goulet-Cazé 1990, 2806–18 on Cynicism's similar relations of mutual borrowing and resistance with other philosophical schools.

[20] See the essay of John Moles in this volume.

[21] e.g., see Davies 1999, esp. 1 on distinctive Christian attitudes: '...it was on matters to do with death that "Christianity" successfully defined an identity for itself that was both distinctive and, at the same time, sufficiently eclectic as to enable it to relate to aspects of some of the other religious cultures within which it found itself'.

[22] See Droge and Tabor 1992, 23–6; van Hooff 1990, 188–9.

[23] See Cooper 1999, 531–6; Droge and Tabor 1992, 29–39; van Hooff 1990, 189–91.

[24] See Diogenes Laertius, *Lives and Opinions of Eminent Philosophers* 6.76–7.

[25] On Peregrinus' perversion of respectable Cynicism, see Branham 1996, 17, n. 56; Niehues-Pröbsting 1979, 201–12. Hornsby 1933, discusses Peregrinus' misapplication of Cynic doctrine, but also collects evidence which suggests that some elements of his death (for example its mystical overtones, and the attribution of divine status to Peregrinus) may have been more widely paralleled within Cynic tradition than at first sight seems likely.

[26] Cooper 1999, 537; cf. Droge and Tabor 1992, 26–9; van Hooff 1990, 189.

[27] ...ἐκώκυε μετὰ τῶν γυναικῶν ὁ θαυμαστὸς καὶ θανάτου κρείττων εἶναι δοκῶν. Similarly, in 44, Lucian describes Peregrinus' illness several days before the suicide, and his terror at the prospect of dying without achieving the notoriety he had planned.

[28] e.g. see Epicurus *Ep. Men.* 128; Diogenes Laertius 9.45, on Democritus; cf. 9.68 on Pyrrho's calm during a storm at sea; I am grateful to James Warren for this point.

[29] See Cooper 1999, 520–6; Droge and Tabor 1992, 20–2; van Hooff 1990, 191–2.

[30] See Cooper 1999 537–40; Droge and Tabor 1992, 39–42; van Hooff 1990, 192–3.

[31] *Phaedo* 61c–62c, discussed by Cooper 1999, 520–3; Droge and Tabor 1992, 20–2.

[32] Lucian's addressee, Kronios, was probably a Platonist himself (see Jones 1986, 20); any Socratic pretensions Peregrinus and his followers may have had must have seemed particularly absurd to a reader who was aware of that.

[33] On these Brahman suicides, see van Hooff 1990, 37–8, with reference to Strabo 15.1.73 and Cassius Dio 54.9.10.

[34] The same contrast is implied at *Runaways* 6–7.

[35] Jones 1993, 314 underestimates this.

[36] e.g. see Bowersock 1995, 59–74; Droge and Tabor 1992; van Hooff 1990, 193–7.

[37] See Bowersock 1995, 63–4 on Stoic influences on Tertullian's views about suicide;

cf. Downing 1993, 295–7, who discusses Cynic influences on Tertullian's work more broadly.

[38] e.g. see Perkins 1995, 20–2, who argues that 'if Christianity was known at all, it was known for its adherents' attitude toward death and suffering' (20), using the *Peregrinus* as one of her main illustrations of that.

[39] πεπείκασι γὰρ αὑτοὺς οἱ κακοδαίμονες τὸ μὲν ὅλον ἀθάνατοι ἔσεσθαι καὶ βιώσεσθαι τὸν ἀεὶ χρόνον, παρ' ὃ καὶ καταφρονοῦσιν τοῦ θανάτου καὶ ἑκόντες αὑτοὺς ἐπιδιδόασιν οἱ πολλοί.

[40] Empedocles' suicide – committed by jumping into the crater of Mount Etna – is another important model for Peregrinus, according to Lucian's account, and is mentioned in *Peregrinus* 1 and 4; in the first of those passages Lucian reminds us that Empedocles (unlike Peregrinus) killed himself without anyone watching. See also Pack 1946 on the possibility that Peregrinus and his followers were influenced by 'contemporary speculation on the ascent of the soul' from a Neoplatonic and Pythagorean perspective; neither of these schools, however, sanctioned suicide as a direct means of achieving that ascent, as I have already suggested.

[41] Schwartz 1963, 61–7 suggests that the sensationalism of public opinion is Lucian's main target in this work, and that his unfair distortions of Peregrinus' reputation are a side-effect of that project (the latter point seems to me to be an overstatement).

[42] e.g., see Anderson 1994, 108–12.

[43] On the Cynicism of Demonax, see Clay 1992, 3425–9; Branham 1989, 57–63.

[44] Peregrinus makes an appearance in *Demonax* 21, criticizing Demonax for laughing too much and for not being dog-like enough, in other words not being enough of a Cynic. Demonax rejects that criticism and rebukes Peregrinus in turn for being inhuman; that response may imply that Peregrinus is wearing his Cynic mask too uncompromisingly, in line with the inflexible nature of his role-playing in the *Peregrinus*; cf. Branham 1989, 62–3 for the point that Demonax is criticizing Peregrinus here for his lack of humour.

[45] Lucian praises Demonax's eclecticism explicitly in *Demonax* 5.

[46] *Demonax* 65–7.

[47] Jones 1993, expanding on some aspects of his reading in Jones 1986, 117–32.

[48] e.g., see Jones 1993, 315, concluding his analysis of *Peregrinus* 40 (discussed further below), where Lucian invents the story that Peregrinus appeared after death wearing an olive crown: 'La couronne de Pérégrinus héroïsé s'explique donc par une tradition purement grecque'.

[49] Eclecticism which Jones himself draws attention to: see Jones 1993, 316.

[50] οὐκ εἰδὼς ὁ ἄθλιος ὅτι καὶ τοῖς ἐπὶ τὸν σταυρὸν ἀπαγομένοις ἢ ὑπὸ τοῦ δημίου ἐχομένοις πολλῷ πλείους ἕπονται.

[51] τὸν ἄνθρωπον τὸν ἐν τῇ Παλαιστίνῃ ἀνασκοπολισθέντα.

[52] τὸν...ἀνεσκολοπισμένον ἐκεῖνον σοφιστήν.

[53] ὅμοιον ὡς εἴ τις ἐπὶ σταυρὸν ἀναβήσεσθαι μέλλων τὸ ἐν τῷ δακτύλῳ πρόσπταισμα θεραπεύοι.

[54] e.g., see Bowersock 1994, 74–5, on Origen, *Contra Celsum* 2.24.

[55] See Jones 1993, 311–12 on Lucian's references to Brahmanic practice, which may, he suggests, reflect real-life eastern influences on Peregrinus.

[56] Δαίμονες μητρῷοι καὶ πατρῷοι, δέξασθαί με εὐμενεῖς. ταῦτα εἰπὼν ἐπήδησεν ἐς τὸ πῦρ.

[57] καὶ φωνήσας φωνῇ μεγάλῃ ὁ Ἰησοῦς εἶπεν· Πάτερ, εἰς χεῖράς σου παρατίθεμαι τὸ

πνεῦμά μου. τοῦτο δὲ εἰπὼν ἐξέπνευσεν.

58 Jones 1986, 128.

59 εἰ μὲν οὖν ἴδοιμί τινα χαρίεντα, ψιλὰ ἂν ὥσπερ σοὶ τὰ πραχθέντα διηγούμην, πρὸς δὲ τοὺς βλᾶκας καὶ πρὸς τὴν ἀκρόασιν κεχηνότας ἐτραγῴδουν τι παρ’ ἐμαυτοῦ, ὡς ἐπειδὴ ἀνήφθη μὲν ἡ πυρά, ἐνέβαλεν δὲ φέρων ἑαυτὸν ὁ Πρωτεύς, σεισμοῦ πρότερον μεγάλου γενομένου σὺν μυκηθμῷ τῆς γῆς, γὺψ ἀναπτάμενος ἐκ μέσης τῆς φλογὸς οἴχοιτο ἐς τὸν οὐρανὸν ἀνθρωπιστὶ μεγάλῃ τῇ φωνῇ λέγων, Ἔλιπον γᾶν, βαίνω δ’ ἐς Ὄλυμπον.

60 καὶ ὡς μετὰ τὸ καυθῆναι θεάσαιτο αὐτὸν ἐν λευκῇ ἐσθῆτι μικρὸν ἔμπροσθεν, καὶ νῦν ἀπολίποι περιπατοῦντα φαιδρὸν ἐν τῇ ἑπταφώνῳ στοᾷ κοτίνῳ τε ἐστεμμένον.

61 Jones 1993, 314–15.

62 For brief acknowledgement of the significance of the Christian intertexts within this part of the narrative, see Clay 1992, 3437 (with reference to Matthew 28.3 and Luke 24.4, which parallel the detail of Peregrinus' white clothing); cf. Bowersock 1994, 115–16.

63 καὶ ἰδοὺ τὸ καταπέτασμα τοῦ ναοῦ ἐσχίσθη ἀπ’ ἄνωθεν ἕως κάτω εἰς δύο, καὶ ἡ γῆ ἐσείσθη, καὶ αἱ πέτραι ἐσχίσθησαν, καὶ τὰ μνημεῖα ἀνεῴχθησαν καὶ πολλὰ σώματα τῶν κεκοιμημένων ἁγίων ἠγέρθησαν· καὶ ἐξελθόντες ἐκ τῶν μνημείων μετὰ τὴν ἔγερσιν αὐτοῦ εἰσῆλθον εἰς τὴν ἁγίαν πόλιν, καὶ ἐξεφανίσθησαν πολλοῖς.

64 For examples other than those discussed in the main text, see *Peregrinus* 15 and 36; cf. Clay 1992, 3415–17.

65 Ἡ δὲ πᾶσα τοῦ πράγματος διασκευὴ τοιάδε ἦν. τὸν μὲν ποιητὴν οἶσθα οἷός τε ἦν καὶ ἡλίκα ἐτραγῴδει παρ’ ὅλον τὸν βίον, ὑπὲρ τὸν Σοφοκλέα καὶ τὸν Αἰσχύλον.

66 Cf. *Peregrinus* 37, where Lucian imagines his friend laughing at the last act of the play (τὴν καταστροφὴν τοῦ δράματος); he is deliberately unclear about whether the play is Peregrinus' or his own; cf. Whitmarsh 2001, 247–94 (esp. 254–65) on Lucian's preoccupation with the imagery of theatre and spectacle elsewhere in his work.

67 ἀλλ’ ὀλίγου δεῖ ὑπὸ τῶν Κυνικῶν ἐγώ σοι διεσπάσθην ὥσπερ ὁ Ἀκταίων ὑπὸ τῶν κυνῶν ἢ ὁ ἀνεψιὸς αὐτοῦ ὁ Πενθεὺς ὑπὸ τῶν Μαινάδων.

68 Philostratus *VA* 1.4 reports a similar story that Apollonius of Tyana was a reincarnation of Proteus; that may be another sign that Lucian wishes to represent Peregrinus as someone who perverts images which in other contexts could have more positive connotations; and it may even be a sign of the importance of Apollonius as yet another role model for the historical Peregrinus, or at least a sign that Lucian is keen to suggest similarities between them.

69 On the *Alexander*, see Branham 1989, 181–210.

70 Cf. Whitmarsh 2001, 122–8, amongst many others, on Lucian's preoccupation with the theme of cultural hybridity.

71 See Jones 1986, 118–19.

72 See Branham, 1996, 16–19.

73 See Jones 1986, 98 on Demonax as a model for Lucian.

74 The Odyssean parallel is not one which the text marks in many places. However, the phrase μυρίας τροπὰς τραπόμενος ('having turned thousands of turns', 'having made thousands of changes'), applied to Peregrinus in the opening lines of the work (*Peregrinus* 1), echoes the Odyssean epithet πολύτροπος ('versatile', 'much-travelled'), with the implication that Peregrinus has attempted, with absurd extravagance, to imitate and surpass Odyssean multi-facetedness.

75 ἀπελθὼν δὲ ἐς τὴν πανήγυριν ἐπέστην τινὶ πολιῷ ἀνδρὶ καὶ νὴ τὸν Δί’ ἀξιοπίστῳ τὸ πρόσωπον ἐπὶ τῷ πώγωνι καὶ τῇ λοιπῇ σεμνότητι.

Bibliography

Anderson, G.
  1994   *Sage, Saint and Sophist. Holy men and their associates in the early Roman Empire*, London.

Bagnani, G.
  1995   'Peregrinus Proteus and the Christians', *Historia* 4, 107–12.

Baldwin, B.
  1973   *Studies in Lucian*, Toronto.

Betz, H.D.
  1959   'Lukian von Samosata und das Christentum', *Novum Testamentum* 3, 226–37.

Bowersock, G.W.
  1994   *Fiction as History*, Berkeley, Los Angeles and London.
  1995   *Martyrdom and Rome*, Cambridge.

Branham, R.B.
  1989   *Unruly Eloquence. Lucian and the comedy of traditions*, Cambridge, Mass.
  1996   'Introduction', in Branham and Goulet-Cazé (eds.) *The Cynics*, 1–27.

Branham, R.B. and Goulet-Cazé, M.-O. (eds.)
  1996   *The Cynics. The Cynic movement in antiquity and its legacy*, Berkeley, Los Angeles and London.

Chadwick, H. (ed.)
  1953   *Origen, Contra Celsum*, Cambridge.

Clay, D.
  1992   'Lucian of Samosata. Four philosophical lives, (Nigrinus, Demonax, Peregrinus, Alexander Pseudomantis)', *ANRW* 2.36.5, 3406–50.

Cooper, J.M.
  1999   'Greek philosophers on euthanasia and suicide', in *Reason and Emotion. Essays on moral and ethical theory*, Princeton, 515–41.

Davies, J.
  1999   *Death, Burial and Rebirth in the Religions of Antiquity*, London and New York.

Demandt, A.
  1997   Review of Bowersock 1994, *Gnomon* 69, 740–3.

Dorival, G.
  1993   'L'image des cyniques chez les Pères grecs', in Goulet-Cazé and Goulet (eds.) *Le cynisme ancien et ses prolongements*, 419–43.

Downing, F.G.
  1992   *Cynics and Christian Origins*, Edinburgh.
  1993   'Cynics and early Christianity', in Goulet-Cazé and Goulet (eds.) *Le cynisme ancien et ses prolongements*, 281–304.

Droge, A.J. and Tabor, J.D.
  1992   *A Noble Death. Suicide and martyrdom among Christians and Jews in antiquity*, San Francisco.

Edwards, M.J.
  1989   'Satire and verisimilitude. Christianity in Lucian's *Peregrinus*', *Historia* 38, 89–98.
  1997   'Epilogue. Biography and the biographic', in M.J. Edwards and S. Swain (eds.)

Portraits. Biographical representation in the Greek and Latin literature of the Roman Empire, Oxford, 227–34.

Goulet-Cazé, M.-O.
1990   'Le cynisme à l'époque impériale', in *ANRW* 2.36.4, 2720–833.

Goulet-Cazé, M.-O. and Goulet, R. (eds.)
1993   *Le cynisme ancien et ses prolongements*, Paris.

Hägg, T. and Rousseau, P.
2000   'Introduction. Biography and panegyric', in T. Hägg and P. Rousseau (eds.) *Greek biography and panegyric in late antiquity*, Berkeley, Los Angeles and London, 1–28.

Hinds, S.
1998   *Allusion and Intertext. Dynamics of appropriation in Roman poetry*, Cambridge.

Hooff, A.J.L. van
1990   *From Autothanasia to Suicide. Self-killing in classical antiquity*, London and New York.

Hornsby, H.M.
1933   'The cynicism of Peregrinus Proteus', *Hermathena* 48, 65–84.

Jones, C.P.
1986   *Culture and Society in Lucian*, Cambridge, Mass.
1993   'Cynisme et sagesse barbare. Le cas de Pérégrine Proteus', in Goulet-Cazé and Goulet (eds.) *Le cynisme ancien et ses prolongements*, 305–17.

Marcus, L.
1994   *Auto/biographical Discourses. Studies in theory and practice*, Manchester.

Niehues-Pröbsting, H.
1979   *Der Kynismus des Diogenes und der Begriff des Kynismus*, Munich.

Pack, R.
1946   'The volatilization of Peregrinus Proteus', *AJP* 67, 334–45.

Perkins, J.
1995   *The Suffering Self. Pain and narrative representation in the early Christian era*, London and New York.

Saïd, S.
1993   'Le "je" de Lucien', in M.-F. Baslez, P. Hoffmann and L. Pernot (eds.) *L'invention de l'autobiographie d'Hésiode à Saint Augustin*, Paris, 253–70.

Schwartz, J.
1963   *Lucien de Samosate*. Philopseudes *et* De morte Peregrini, Paris.

Whitmarsh, T.
2001   *Greek Literature and the Roman Empire. The politics of imitation*, Oxford.

15

BREAKING THE BOUNDS:
WRITING ABOUT JULIUS CAESAR

Christopher Pelling

I. Introductory: person and genre

Caesar was a bounder: a person who operated on, and broke, the boundaries of his world. He broke through the boundaries of the physical world, bridging the Rhine, crossing the Ocean to get to Britain and 'advancing Rome's empire outside the human world'.[1] He broke through the more figurative bounds as well, changing the rules of Roman public life: if Sulla had not understood the political ABC,[2] Caesar changed it to make a language all his own. And at the end he was pressing on the bounds of mortality itself.

This paper will explore the way in which this 'boundary-breaking' affects not only Caesar the historical figure, but also the people who came to write about him. The relevant boundaries now will be those of genre. Just as the historical Caesar changed the rules of his world, so writing about Caesar forces the writer to change the rules as well: so it is no surprise that generic questions frequently become so difficult when we look at Caesar-literature. If you are writing history, you find yourself having to write biography instead; if you are writing biography, you find yourself writing history. Something like that may already be true of his own *commentarii*. Are they really, in any sense at all, only a draft for later, 'proper' historians to come to and elaborate? Or are they already playing for the verdict that Cicero and Hirtius swiftly give them, that they take away rather than offer an opportunity to later writers (*Brut.* 262, Hirt. *B.G.* 8 proem 5)?[3] Do Caesar's acts themselves have a 'finish' – so complete, so polished, so definitive – such that Caesar's own writing about them is equally a sort of last word, with the rhetorical simplicity to give a simple message, 'job done, nothing more to say'? Then there is Velleius; and for Velleius it is Caesar's consulship which 'grabs the writer and, eager though he may be to hurry on, forces him to delay and to talk about him'('scribenti manum inicit et quamlibet festinantem in se morari cogit', 2.41.1); this is what changes[4] these 'hurrying', summary *Historiae* into a sequence of 'Caesarian', 'Augustan', and 'Tiberian' narratives.[5]

What about Lucan? Is that 'epic' as epic would be expected? Surely not, given that so many of the generic expectations are put into reverse in this fragmented, godless, untriumphant world: this is more anti-epic, not epic. 'To the victors belongs epic, with its linear teleology...':[6] there was something about epic, at least Virgilian nationalistic epic, which at least allowed and probably insisted that the natural reading was 'with the grain', the grain of a triumphant story of the birth of a nation, so that there could at least be some feeling that it all made sense. But the world of Lucan is not like this; we are now in a world of an epic which can only be written as anti-epic – or perhaps 'spaghetti epic', as Michael Comber put it.[7] In part, that is a matter of ideology. If epic takes over the traditions of the past as well as the form, it had a problem: for those traditions were such that, when confronted with the birth of the present, the only reading which could now dominate was a reading *against* history's grain, a reading that the world did not make sense at all. In part it is a point of literary development too. Of course there was an anti-epic nestling within Virgil too, the story of the victim's voice rather than the conqueror's; but it was an anti-epic which could be restrained or balanced, where the generic struggle might finally be resolved in terms of the great Roman juggernaut triumphantly rolling on.[8] But now the squeal of the hedgehog beneath its wheels could not be so stilled; not now that Virgil had done what he had to epic, working out so many of its implications; not now that Caesar had done what he had to Rome.

This paper will explore related themes in Greek and in prose, exploring the generic play with history and biography in Plutarch, Appian, and Cassius Dio. Talk of 'genre' is of course problematic. There have been those, especially Rosenmeyer, who have denied that 'genre' is a useful concept at all for ancient writers: for them, it is more a question of more or less subtle and innovative *imitatio*, of basing oneself on (as he puts it) a 'father-figure'.[9] These are the issues aired in Christina Kraus' collection on *The Limits of Historiography: Genre and narrative in ancient historical texts* (Brill 1999), and I had my own say in that volume.[10] I argue there that genre is indeed a useful concept for history, and that at least by this stage one could talk of *historia* and conjure up a certain set of expectations. If one could not, Plutarch's famous distinction between 'writing *Lives*' and 'writing history' in *Alexander* 1 could not have been drawn so economically and allusively.[11] At the same time genre is not straitjacketing. We should think of 'on-the-whole' generic expectations, an acceptance that certain features of a genre will *probably* appear in a text, but also an acceptance that they may not; genre is a shifting and changing target, in Alastair Fowler's words more a pigeon than a pigeon-hole.[12] But prose genres do not necessarily work in the same way as poetic ones, and expectations in prose can be even looser and more provisional; and Greek imperial historical writing is even more loose and provisional in this regard than Latin. An audience picking up Latin *Annales* or even Latin *Historiae* would have much firmer on-the-whole expectations of what they will find, though even they may find that those expectations are not wholly met or are met in an interestingly different way – as in Tacitus, and indeed as already in Livy. That readiness to renuance one's expectations will be even greater with an Appian, a Plutarch, or a Cassius Dio.

Quite often, indeed, we should talk of these writers *themselves* creating and then recreating their generic expectations as they go, operating doubtless against templates offered by past writers, but creating their own particular rules of the game as they go on.[13] A good deal of what I will say can be put in those terms, with writers intimating that their own work redefines its rules when Caesar arrives. We will still, however, find that generic distinction between biography and history a useful one. It may be that an Appian or a Dio redefines Caesarian history into something suggestively close to biography; and that is *felt*, it is an expressive generic point. This is not far from the sort of generic analysis that Gian Biagio Conte gives of the *Tenth Eclogue* and of the *Aeneid*: it is expressive that pastoral is in danger of toppling over into elegy or that epic is in danger of tipping into tragedy, even though the reader remains utterly clear that the borders are not finally breached, that the poem remains pastoral or epic.[14] The expressive thing is the area of the genre within which the poem is manoeuvring, the border-country in which it finds itself.

As Conte stresses, this generic point has an ideological aspect. Tragedy *cannot* be allowed to take over Virgilian epic, not this epic of Rome. John Marincola applies a similar approach to Tacitus' *Agricola*:[15] will this biography remain biographical, or will it have to transform itself into a straight historical narrative? That question too has ideological implications: is there still room to tell a private individual's story under the principate? And I have applied a similar approach to Cassius Dio, this time with the emperor himself: will imperial historiography blur over into being pure biography, so that even if Dio starts by aspiring to be a Tacitus he ends by having to be a Suetonius?[16] The answer may be yes, there is room for Agricola's biography, and no, imperial historiography can stay as history – but, in each case, only just, and that 'only justness' will be the more interesting interpretative point.

II. Cassius Dio

Let us start with Dio, given that the relation between a 'biographical' and a more annalistic structure is clearly an issue once he moves on to the imperial books. The phenomenon there is well known. Imperial reigns tend to start in a 'biographical', almost Suetonian way, with a characterizing survey of the new princeps and his past life; such an arrangement, often in categories, persists into the early chapters, and it also sometimes reasserts itself towards the end of a reign; but the middle sections are more standardly historiographic and annalistic, going through events year by year.[17]

Those are the principate books: what is interesting here is how Dio leads up in the late Republic to that sort of qualified 'biostructuring'.[18] Do the great individuals of the late Republic come close to imposing their own structure on events? We can only begin when the triumph of the big men is already underway, with the start of our continuous text in Book 36. And we do indeed find a measure of Republican 'biostructuring', but it is more limited than we might expect. *Conceptually* or *interpretatively* Dio is already seeing history as dominated by the great men, in many areas more than Appian does, and particularly by their antagonisms, so that (as we shall see) elaborate implicit *synkrisis* underlies a lot of the presentation. That is true from the outset of the continuous text, with the contrast of Lucullus and Pompey, and much of the early emphasis there is on what a difference a leader can make (especially 36.16). But that interpretative stress on the big players does not mean that the narrative breaks up *formally* into biostructured panels. Naturally enough, we can see narrative shaping towards this imperial pattern as Caesar comes to dominate more, but still the Catilinarian conspiracy account could have been organized more sharply around either Catiline or Cicero; much of the fifties narrative could have centred more on either Cicero or Pompey; even Caesar's own campaigns allow surprising space and focus to the lieutenants as well as to Caesar himself.[19] It is with the introduction of Octavian at the beginning of Book 45, and the elaborate biographical survey of his earlier life and character, that the formal style of the principate books takes firmer shape.[20]

Still, this shift towards biostructuring remains interesting and expressive, and it is a point about historical interpretation as well as about literary form. Interpretatively, it is important that the shift is taking place; it is just as important that it is not complete. Take the closing chapters of book 43, when the end is beginning to approach, Caesar is making mistakes which trigger his end, and various rings are beginning to close. Some of those rings are indeed very Caesar-shaped, 'biographical' points about his life. When he wears his triumphal garb and laurel crown, excusing it by his baldness, this is related to the attention he had always paid to rather foppish clothing. Dio reminds us of Sulla's remark about Caesar as a young man, 'beware the badly-belted boy' (43.43.4). But that comes just before and just after points where the ring is much bigger. Just after, we go on to the statue erected 'to the Invincible God' in the temple of *Quirinus*, so that we are reminded of Rome's first king; and then to another statue put up on the Capitol, so that there were statues of the seven kings there and now of Caesar too (43.45.2–4). Just before we had Caesar wearing the boots of the Alban kings (43.43.2), and also his institution of permanent annual games to celebrate the Parilia – so, again, right back to Rome's beginnings rather than Caesar's own (43.42.2–3).

The point, though, is that these games were 'not at all to celebrate Rome's birthday but because the news of Caesar's victory had arrived on the day before, towards evening' (43.42.3). It is precisely because a point which should have been about Rome has become one about Caesar that the crisis comes. This is inflammatory, just as the triumph Caesar has just been celebrating over other Roman citizens was inflammatory (42.1). There are pointers here towards the principate: we have indeed just had an omen, a palm which stood on the battlefield of Munda sending forward a shoot after the victory – and Dio observes that Caesar took it as a good omen for himself, whereas in fact it related to the young Octavius, there with him on the campaign (41.3).[21] But those pointers towards the principate combine with, indeed are largely the same as, the indications that this is why Caesar is killed, why the omen is not good for him after all. Rome is not yet ready for such displays; we have not got to the principate *yet*. The real irony about the statue was that there were not merely those seven kings' statues on the Capitol, but also an eighth, that of 'the Brutus who overthrew the Tarquins'. It was next to Brutus that the statue of Caesar was placed, 'and this in particular was the reason that spurred Marcus Brutus to plot against him' (43.45.4). Conspiracy, then, is in the air, just as 'conspiracy' was the way in which Dio painted that vital step in Caesar's career, the forming of the first triumvirate (38.2.2 in particular, συνωμοσία).[22] This is another ring that is beginning to close, this time again a more Caesar-shaped one. Conspiracy is coming back to destroy the man whom conspiracy made great.

So we can see Caesar *trying* to turn history into biography, and we can see him failing: both the attempt and the failure are interpretatively most expressive. But it is not just Caesar's person that shapes and reshapes his narrative in this way, not just Caesar who points how far we have moved towards the principate. True, from the moment Caesar is introduced we have a clear idea of where he is going (ambitions, long-term plotting, clear-sightedness and so on):[23] as focalized through him, history is shaping towards one-man rule, and rule of this one man in particular. But Dio uses his implicit synkriseis much more subtly. It is the contrasts of Caesar with others, and indeed of others with one another, which so often underline the way in which things are going.

I shall take three examples.

(a) *Caesar and Cicero*, and in particular the different ways in which they play off Pompey. Caesar's first entry (and almost Cicero's first entry too[24]) in the extant text is at 36.43, when both men are supporting the *lex Manilia*.

> The two men who particularly urged this were Caesar and Marcus Cicero. They supported the proposal not because they thought it in the city's interests, nor to ingratiate themselves with Pompey. It was rather that they could see that it was going to happen in any case; and Caesar was firstly cultivating the people because he saw how much more powerful they were than the senate, secondly laying the grounds for something similar to be voted to himself in the future, and thirdly trying to make Pompey the object of envy and unpopularity through these grants so that people would tire of him all the quicker. Cicero thought it right that he himself should lead the state, and was making a demonstration to the masses and to the men of power that, whichever side he supported, he would certainly build them up (ἐπαυξήσει). He vacillated and sometimes supported one side, sometimes the other, so that both sides would take him seriously...

Here Caesar is already doing what he so often does later, playing subtly with a view to his own future. He is preparing the masses with an eye to getting a similar command for himself at some time, and also trying to create an atmosphere where Pompey will run into more 'envy', φθόνος. ('Envy' is a recurrent theme when Caesar and Pompey are in point, as we shall see,[25] but already Pompey is well aware of the dangers.[26]) Cicero is more concerned with the present, to demonstrate that it will make a difference if he throws his authority into the ring: whichever of the powerful he supports he will be able to 'build them up'- ἐπαύξησει, an interesting word, with its suggestion of rhetorical *auxesis* as well as of power politics. Cicero wants to be a decisive factor in the balance *for others*; Caesar wants to outstrip others, and (by implication) to do without any balance at all. Whether or not Cicero's style belongs to the past, Caesar's certainly belongs to the future; and, unsurprisingly, the contrast of the two continues in similar terms. The next time Cicero and Caesar are treated in close juxtaposition, it is at 37.37–8, where Caesar is assiduously courting the demos and becoming pontifex maximus, and Cicero is in bad popular odour after executing the Catilinarians. Then at the end of his consulship Caesar is deftly restrained, biding his time in handling his enemies, but Cicero, roisteringly tactless as ever, is easy meat for Clodius (38.11–12).

  (b) *Cicero and Pompey*. Other comparisons too with Cicero play up the rhetorical side; indeed the animus is often greater,[27] with Cicero as *windbag*, as the person who just cannot keep his mouth shut. There is a contrast here even with Cato, who finds Cicero irritating too (39.22.1): when he speaks it is more effectively – but only to filibuster, speaking out the day till nightfall (39.34), a more realistic response to political realities. But the contrast is especially with Pompey. When both are hounded by Clodius, Cicero again cannot hold his tongue (39.22 as well as the 38.12 case); Pompey can and does (note in particular the long study, just after the Cicero passage, at 39.24–6). That is part of his distinctive enigmatic quality, even furtiveness. But it is interesting too that this furtiveness is gradually put aside during the fifties: Pompey is forced more and more into the open by the pressure of events. Thus Pompey is more open in the manoeuvrings of 56 than he is in Plutarch, and is readier to come clean about his planned candidature for the consulship (39.30.2: contrast *Pomp.* 51.7, *Crass.* 15.2). That leads to some famous brushes between Cicero the wordsmith and Pompey the powerful; over Gabinius, when Pompey again comes into the open in the man's defence and leaves Cicero helpless (39.63); with Milo, when Cicero's silver tongue is so memorably stilled (40.54: that famous instance should be seen as part of this larger pattern); and again with Plancus (40.55).

(c) So *Pompey and Caesar* both emerge from these synkriseis as the men with the nose for power. Cicero floods the world with words; Pompey and Caesar fend him off with disingenuousness, though it comes in different forms. By the end of the fifties Dio's Pompey is rather less underhand and secretive than his Caesar, and also than Pompey himself is in other authors. But he is shrewd too, again shrewder than he is in other authors: this Pompey is well aware of the dangers of envy, for instance, especially when ruling alone in 52 (40.51.1); and once the war comes he avoids boastfulness about his successes over citizens (41.52.1). By then Caesar is much less concerned about what people thought or disliked about him, especially when he is bestowing honours on himself (41.54.1). So there are dangers here that Pompey senses, and the young Caesar sensed too – this, we saw, was why he supported the big Pompeian commands in the sixties, trying to engineer envy against the great man (above, p. 260). The older Caesar learns some lessons from Pompey (for instance, the lesson that it is not a good thing to make too much of citizen dead, 42.18.1), but not enough. When he tries to play the game of disingenuousness at Rome, he cannot carry it off. When he pretends to be grieved by Pompey's death, his hypocrisy is so transparent that people laugh at him (42.8.2–3); when he returns and makes a reassuring speech, people do not believe him, at least until they can see words backed up by deeds (43.18.6).

There are various ways here in which Caesar's mistakes anticipate his downfall,[28] but there is more to it than that. We can feel the way to the principate shaping in lots of ways. There is not merely the simple point, made recurrently and in several ways, that all these people are going to impose their own rule in the end; they may be different, but all are aiming at power, and whoever wins the consequences will be the same (esp. 41.53–9).[29] There are also the distinctive *features* of Dio's principate which are already shaping, conspiracy, disingenuousness, furtiveness, hypocrisy, and deceit, including the disingenuousness and flattery which *all people* at Rome now have to practise as they mould their reactions to the shifting news of the war, 42.17–18; or the distrust, the feeling that no one can speak freely, and the ubiquitous mutual slanderings as they wait for Caesar's return, 42.27–8. The dominating individuals are being used to plot the move towards principate in subtler ways than simply tracing Caesar's personal takeover.

If we are moving towards one man's rule, it is not just one man's doing. There is a wider historical vision here, and not at all an unrespectable one. Dio is very, very smart.

III. Appian

Appian is smart too, but his smartness comes out in different ways. In his overall *Proem*, Appian has a clear strategy for organizing the entire *History*, and that extends to the way he plans to divide up the *Civil Wars*. 'It is divided up', he says, 'by the generals who lead the factions', ἐς τοὺς στρατηγοὺς τῶν στάσεων διῄρηται (*Proem* 14.59)[30]; book 1, Marius and Sulla, book 2, Pompey and Caesar; book 3, Antony and Octavian against Caesar's murderers; then (i.e. books 4 and 5) Antony and Octavian in civil war (*stasis*) against one another. That is the plan, of course a simplified one. Book 1 is enough to show that, where the *stasis* begins as less a matter of personalities, more of bigger themes and collectives – Italian unrest, *dēmos* against *boulē*, and so on – and the personalities gradually emerge from it, first the Gracchi, then several others before we reach 'Marius and Sulla'. But the pattern in book 2 is a particularly interesting one, as this 'Pompey and Caesar' book is overtaken by events and becomes Caesar's book alone, and history becomes a sort of biography.

'Pompey and Caesar': that is how Book 2 itself begins as well, heralding the war of the two and the deaths of the two: '...until C. Caesar and Pompey the Great fought one another, Caesar killed Pompey, and some men struck Caesar down in the senate house on the grounds that he had aspirations to be king' (1.1). It duly begins by setting out the relative statures of the two. Pompey is introduced for his *achievements*, the victories over Mithradates and the pirates, Caesar for his *qualities*, audacity, rhetorical skill, and ambition (1.2–3).

We are given an immediate narrative clue that this is not going to be an even balance. There was an obvious point to begin 'Caesar and Pompey's' book, especially for an author so steeped in Pollio, and that was the year 60.[31] The book would then begin with their friendship; it would trace how friendship became enmity, and dragged the state into war. But that is not where Appian begins. Instead it is with Catiline, relevant for Caesar in two distinct ways: first, of course, because it is Caesar's first major bow on the stage; secondly, because it heralds so many of the themes which will come back with Caesar himself. Appian makes the relevance clear. Catiline 'too' is full of ambition (2.4), and that 'too' must refer back to the ambition of Caesar introduced a page before (1.3); even 'monarchy' comes in at an early stage, with Catiline aiming for 'tyranny' (2.4) and disdaining constitutional methods as 'not bringing monarchy in any quick or sure way' (2.6). Catiline too, when military action looms, acts decisively, 'putting his trust in speed' (3.10, cf. Caesar at 34.136 etc). Caesar will be a much more menacing equivalent. (These are points which could be made about Sallust's presentation too: Appian may have got the idea from him, if – as is very likely – he drew at least the first part of the Catiline narrative from the *Bellum Catilinae*. We can get too obsessed with always thinking of Pollio when we read Appian.)

Appian did not have to do it this way. Even after he had decided to include Catiline, he did not have to put him here: he could have put him at the end of Book 1, just as – significantly – he had put Pompey's earlier exploits against Sertorius and Spartacus in Book 1.[32] He had there represented Sertorius' war as 'the remaining one of the Sullan events', 1.108.505; he could easily have treated Catiline under a similar rubric, especially again for someone who knew his Sallust.[33] He could then have used the pact of 60 to give a powerful new start to Book 2. Even once he had decided to start with Catiline, he could have brought Pompey even into this story, as the great presence in the East on whom all people had their eye. But he does not. We already have a clear hint whose story this is really going to be.

As the narrative goes on, the contrast with Pompey develops. Appian's Pompey is distinctively a passive figure, someone to whom things happen. Trains of action start from others: Pompey is usually at the end of those chains, reacting to what others do, and often reacting impulsively. He is prey to others, not driving them. There are even echoes of Thucydides' Nicias, always a bad sign.[34] Caesar on the other hand tends to start those chains, but only start them. He is extremely good at setting things up so that others get his own way (at least in politics: it changes a little when the fighting starts). That does not mean he is making every call himself; the tribunes, for instance, Curio and Antony, are more clearly acting on their own initiative in Appian than in Dio or Plutarch.[35] They are their own persons, but Caesar has bought or acquired the right persons, Pompey is prey to the wrong ones.

Pompey reacts to others, often the senatorial grandees – the Marcelli in the run-up to the war, the bellicose up-and-at-them types on the battlefield of Pharsalus. He also has to react to Caesar himself, especially once the fighting starts.[36] Pompey sometimes manages that reaction very well, especially when it is a matter of shrewd professional soldiering – that is why he comes so close to final success at Dyrrhachium[37] – but then he finds himself confronted by the bewildering; Caesar changes the rules; and the narrative tone and register move as well. It may be a move to a more dramatic set-piece: the crossing of the Rubicon itself (35.137–40), Caesar hiding in the small boat to cross the Adriatic back to Italy (56.234–58.241).[38] It may be a sharp focusing in on a sensational vignette on the battlefield: Scaeva at 60.247–50, Crassinius at 82.348. It may just be a more globalized description of the army as a whole, but the army acting in a way in which armies usually do not: there is something 'demonic', superhuman (σπουδῇ δαιμονίῳ, 66.274), about their speed and enthusiasm; there is something divine in their change of heart at 63.262 ('a god was leading them to repentance'), so that even Dyrrhachium reinforces rather than wrecks their morale (62.257–63.264).[39]

One particular image which is interesting here is that of wild beasts, θηρία· a fairly conventional image, one would think, but one which recurs much more frequently in this part of the *Civil War* than anywhere else in Appian.[40] Thus Caesar's men are repeatedly θηρία: 61.252, 71.297, 75.312, and in retrospect at 151.632. Nor is that the end of it, for bestiality is infectious: Cato too dies like a θηρίον, 99.412, 101.420. And another hunt looms: that hunt where Caesar himself is the final prey and victim, and he too dies on the Ides 'like a wild beast', 117.493, 147.612. Cinna the poet is then hunted down 'like a wild beast' too (θηριωδῶς, 147.613).[41] Once again Caesar has changed the rule-book, so much so that his men are no longer acting like men. They are subhuman as well as superhuman. And once the rule-book is changed the author of that change is vulnerable too. We again see how a dominant thematic strand has come to be one man's story, what he has made of his troops, what comes back to destroy himself.

How much of all this is Appian himself, and how much is owed to Pollio?[42] We cannot know, and for our purposes it does not matter all that much: it anyway shows one interesting way in which the story could be treated, and was. But there are some indications. Several similar points could be made about Plutarch, but are much less true of Dio: in particular, that picture of Pompey as prey, as the person to whom things happen;[43] the person who at Pharsalus is overborne by the same people whom he could never manage in politics, and cannot manage now.[44] In Plutarch too Caesar is struck down like a wild beast (*Caes.* 66.10), after Pompey was earlier struck by noticing how bestial was the behaviour of Caesar's troops (*Caes.* 39.3).[45]

One could also think of the paradox of Pollio, as presented in modern reconstructions. On the one hand we have Syme's Pollio, the pre-author of *Roman Revolution*, acid, terse, incisive, and cynical; that Pollio is still visible in Morgan 2000: esp. 62–3. On the other, there is the much more sensational Pollio whom we can trace in most of the passages more plausibly tracked back to him – the Pollio who told the Rubicon story, or Curio's campaign, or Caesar's gloomy utterances on the Pharsalus battlefield: a Pollio with much more taste for the dramatic.[46] Not of course that vividness and incisive analysis cannot co-exist; one need only think, once again, of Thucydides. But Pollio too may well have found his narrative style veering wildly as Caesar makes events veer. It would not be surprising if some of this were Appian reacting to things already in Pollio, reproducing some points, responding in other cases to hints which were already there. But it is hopeless to try to separate out more exactly which of them is responsible for what.

So: Caesar is dead. What happens now? Brutus and Cassius may think that this will mark a return to what they call 'democracy', and if they were right this would be mirrored by a return to the earlier norms of the narrative game. Things once again might start from the senate or the *dēmos*, as they had at the beginning of Book 1, and to an extent had again at the end of Book 1 after Sulla's death.[47] But in fact the narrative is not like that at all. Senate and *dēmos* are felt as forces, but they too are reacting, not initiating.[48] And Brutus, Cassius, and the rest cannot just go back to where they were, cannot carry on playing as they used to play. The force that dominates the narrative is still Caesar. Antony explains how little freedom of action the senate really has to alter any of Caesar's *acta* (133.555–134.562); it emerges soon enough that they do not really want to. The idea of Caesar's curse starts to be important, too: that curse which will be traced through the narrative of Book 3 as well, as the final sentence of the book promises: the next book will trace how the murderers were punished.[49] The first sentences of Book 3 go on to put the theme in the same terms. Caesar cannot be erased from the narrative, his name remains the governing theme, and when we do get the focus shifting to the later generals they are by then struggling for the monarchy that he established.[50]

The clearest marker of how the narrative texture has changed is the final section of Book 2, the extended comparison of Alexander and Caesar (2.149.619–154.649). No mention of Pompey there, the man who had himself so often been compared to Alexander;[51] remarkably, the only time the word Πομπήιος appears in that epilogue is referring not to the great Pompey but to his son Gnaeus twice (150.630, 152.638). There is doubtless some relation to Plutarch in this epilogue,[52] though it is not clear quite what it is. Might Appian be borrowing from a (lost) *synkrisis* to Plutarch's own *Alexander and Caesar*, as some have thought? Or did Plutarch leave that pair without a *synkrisis*, as I will suggest below (p. 268)? In that case, was Appian making a parade of filling the gap?[53]

However precisely we envisage that relation to Plutarch, the important point is that Appian's history has now become Plutarchan, a biographical tale. History has become biography, or come as close to it as it ever gets. Or, if we prefer to put it a different way, Appian's initial programme has had to be revised, and he cannot make it simply a sequence of X against Y, then A against B, then P against Q. Games for two have yielded to games for one.

IV. Plutarch

Alexander 1 is often quoted as the key to Plutarch's biographical technique:[54]

> For it is not histories we are writing, but *Lives*. Nor is it always the most famous actions which reveal a man's good or bad qualities: a clearer insight into a man's character is often given by a small matter, a remark or a jest, than by engagements where thousands die, or by the greatest of pitched battles, or by the sieges of cities.
> (*Alex.* 1.2)

It is important to notice that he says it here, at the beginning of the pair *Alexander–Caesar*. It is fair to ask, too, how far the pair, especially *Caesar*, really delivers what we should have expected from this initial programme. Does *Alexander–Caesar* really dwell on all those 'little things'? Not altogether. *Caesar* in particular has very little time for the 'smaller things' of Caesar's life: even his love-life is given very little space,[55] much less space than the equivalent themes in *Pompey* or *Cato Minor* or *Brutus*. In fact, one important story in Caesar's love-life, his alleged affair with Servilia, is mentioned in *Cato* and in *Brutus* but not in *Caesar* itself (*C. Min.* 24.1–3, *Brut.* 5). And when Caesar is allowed a 'remark or a jest', it is hardly on the private and more intimate themes: 'this is what they wished' on the battlefield of Pharsalus (46.1), or 'today the enemy had victory in their grasp – if only they had had a victor to command them' at Dyrrhachium (39.9), or indeed 'let the die be cast' (32.8). This is pre-eminently a *Life*, and a pair, which dwells on 'engagements where thousands die...'

It is better, I suggest, to see that preface to *Alexander* as introducing a polarity of 'small things' and 'big things' which prepares for a variety of interactions through the pair, and as we go on it may prove more difficult to keep small things and big things so separate. In *Alexander* it is in many ways the little things, the remarks and jests which go astray, which mark his decline, even destroy him – the exchanges with Cleitus or Callisthenes, the bizarre and macabre goings-on at Babylon at the end. In *Caesar* it may be more that Caesar has so little time for anything other than 'big things', no time for instance for love,[56] no time to become the great orator which his nature would have allowed him to be (*Caes.* 3). Instead it is Cicero who becomes the topmost orator, and Caesar can only be second-best. If we look for 'remarks and jests', it tends indeed to be Cicero's remarks that are the most effective – those witticisms which chart and even orchestrate the growth of opposition to Caesar in power.[57] Initially things are good: 'by raising Pompey's statues he has firmly fixed his own' (57.6); but before long 'let us hurry to greet the new consul before he demits office' (58.3), and the calendar is 'obeying orders' (59.6). Little things have a way of biting back, and affecting those big things after all. However precisely we put it, we certainly cannot say that *Caesar* avoids the big public themes; indeed it is in many ways the most 'historical', least intimate and personal of all the *Lives*.[58] Our knowledge of Caesar's more personal side comes not from Plutarch but from Suetonius, whose category-approach is so well suited to providing a 'rounded' portrait. In Plutarch it is precisely the public man whom we see.

So *Alexander* 1 is most interesting in generic terms. It can still be quoted as the key to Plutarch's normal biographical style – but it creates an expect-ation, perhaps rather reinforces an expectation already created by Plutarch's own earlier *Lives*, which this particular pair only partly fulfils. Yet again *Caesar* has defied generic expectation, but this time it is biography which has to become history. The leading themes of the *Life* are historical ones: the factors which build Caesar's power – the support of the *dēmos* for which he plays, the enthusiasm of his friends, the backing of his troops – and yet then go on to destroy him, when they all turn sour, when friends and troops behave badly, when the *dēmos* turns against him (esp. *Caes.* 51).[59] Of course his *ethos* matters, but in terms of the qualities which win that popularity and that friendship, the charismatic quality of the public man.[60] This could so easily have become a *Life* more like *Cicero* or even *Brutus*, building more on the other aspects of this multifaceted character: the man of letters, not merely the influential orator, which he might have become; the intellectual as well as the vanquisher. But that was not the way to write Caesar's life. Power is all.

And was it worthwhile? Has Caesar had to give up too much? That is a question Plutarch leaves us with at the end:

> He had sought dominion and power all his days, and after facing so many dangers he had finally achieved them. And the only benefit he reaped was its empty name, and the perils of fame amid his envious fellow-citizens.
>
> (*Caes.* 69.1)

This may not be quite the *envoi* which the *Life* itself has led us to expect;[61] but, taken in the context of the whole series of *Lives*, it has a point. If eventu-ally this pair has almost toppled over into history, we do not forget that it started by signalling itself as biography; and we may wonder whether Caesar himself, and Alexander himself, would not have been happier persons if it had stayed that way, if Caesar had had time to be an orator and a lover and have a more regular *Life* written about him. And, given the moral purpose of the *Lives*, we may wonder too whether we might do better to mould our own lives on the more rounded figures who can be given more rounded and regular *Lives*.

We dwelt earlier on the presence of a *synkrisis* at the end of Appian's second book; we should also make something of the absence of a *synkrisis* at the end of *Alexander–Caesar*. This is a scholarly puzzle. Some think that Plutarch wrote one and that it has been lost, along with those to three other pairs (*Pyrrhus–Marius*, *Themistocles–Camillus*, and *Phocion–Cato Minor*). In 1956 Erbse suggested that there were reasons why Plutarch might have chosen not to write formal synkritic epilogues for those four pairs, and in 1997 I joined in on Erbse's side, arguing that in those four pairs the closural rhythms of the second *Life* all have something odd and irregular about them: it looks as if they are crafted to be 'the end' of a pair in a way that most second *Lives* are not.[62] *Caesar* in particular has that marvellous closing scene at Philippi where Caesar's 'great spirit' (μέγας δαίμων) appears to Brutus, and one can understand why Plutarch chose not to compromise it by adding anything else. That, prudently, is where I left the argument in 1997, but there may be a further point as well. If Appian's comparison is appropriate because history has almost become biography, Plutarch's lack of one is equally appropriate because, in his terms, biography has almost become history. The story is no longer just Caesar's own. The important perspective is no longer the comparison with another individual, even one as great as Alexander; we have gone beyond that, the gods themselves are involved, Caesar's spirit is hounding down his killers, and his personal strengths and defects are no longer what the story is about.

One last point. I suggested that 69.1 makes better sense when we remember the norms of other *Lives* as well, all the things that a more rounded story might have been able to tell. One great step of the last generation, as we have just seen, was to see the unit of Plutarch's biographies as the pair as much as the *Life*. We should now take the further step, and see individual *Lives* more in the context of the series as a whole.[63] In the case of *Caesar*, especially the end of *Caesar*, this is particularly interesting. Dio, we saw, made play out of the Romulus connection: thanks to Caesar's regal behaviour the age of the kings is coming back, but it has not come yet, and that is why Caesar dies.[64] Plutarch has something of the same. By this stage of the production of the *Lives* he had almost certainly already written *Theseus–Romulus*:[65] and how did Romulus meet his end?

> This was Romulus' last war [cf. *Caes.* 56.7, 'this was Caesar's last war' – just before everything goes sour]. Next came the experience that falls to most, indeed virtually all who are raised to power and majesty by great and paradoxical successes; Romulus did not escape this either. His career had given him (over?-)confidence (ἐκτεθαρρηκώς); he became haughtier in spirit and abandoned his popular manner (ἐξίστατο τοῦ δημοτικοῦ), shifting to a monarchy which gave offence and pain. This came about in the first place because of the way in which he presented himself... (*Rom.* 26.1)

Then we move into a description of Romulus' purple robes, his kingly throne, his bodyguard and so on. The similarity to 44 BCE is not far to seek, with Caesar's semi-regal outfit and golden throne, the humiliation of the senate, and the fears of *his* monarchy:[66] especially as the distant future has already so often been felt as a presence in *Romulus*.[67] Then Romulus too dies, mysteriously. One version, aired by Plutarch though left uncertain, is that he is killed by the hostile senators (*Rom.* 27.6). The people are certainly suspicious, and threaten those aristocrats whom they see as the murderers. And the appearance of Proculus Iulius, announcing he has seen the dead Romulus in a dream (*Rom.* 28.1–3), pre-enacts the role of Cinna the poet (*Caes.* 68), though it does not turn out so murderously.

If this is right, Plutarch is constructing his whole series to go together. Rome begins with kingship, with the dangers of regal mentality, and with all the suspicions and hostilities which that mentality and that showiness excite. It ends the same way. The founder-figure is seen as instituting not merely his nation's greatness, but also the perils that will bring it to its greatest crisis.[68] Neither Romulus' story nor Caesar's can now be told as if they are simply matters of the man alone. Both stories are now the story of Rome.

So let us see Plutarch as constructing his sequence not merely in pairs but also as a coherent whole: and that has a further implication as well. His whole project may now seem to be more in the style of Drumann–Groebe,[69] splitting up Rome's history (and in Plutarch's case Greek history as well) under the leading figures – doing in a sense, but in a more refined sense and in a more skilful way, a version of what Plutarch had already done for the principate in his *Lives of the Caesars*, though those seem to have been closer to 'history' in genre.[70] The underlying assumption will be that a way, perhaps even the best way, to approach history is to see it through the filters of its leading individuals.[71] We talked of Caesar's person turning history into biography; in a different sense, the whole project of Plutarch is to do the same. Yet we also saw ways in which Caesar did not fit the usual pattern, and was something of an exception in the themes Plutarch chooses to stress. Indeed, there is a sense in which Caesar himself resists that process precisely because he is *nothing but* a historical figure, lives only for power. Normally one can relate a man's historical role to other, more intimate aspects of the personality; with Caesar, at least with Plutarch's version of Caesar, this is no longer possible. If that is so, then one can better understand the distancing from Caesar's achievement which is the note on which Plutarch bids his great hero farewell.

That note is finally not one of crude denunciation, but of sadness, even of sympathy for the futility of so much achievement. Yet again the moralism of Plutarch is seen to be a good deal subtler than it has sometimes seemed.[72]

Notes

¹ Plut. *Caes.* 23.3.

² Suet. *Div. Iul.* 77. On what this phrase may mean, see the discussion of Morgan 1997, 35–7, preferring to take it as 'was not a scholar' and linking it with Caesar's preceding remark in Suetonius about the insubstantiality of the res publica: a better scholar than Sulla would have realized the questionable relation between word and reality. I am not convinced.

³ Cicero should know. He had received a similar response with his own ὑπόμνημα on his consulship, and may well even have been angling for that response. He sent this to Posidonius 'so that he might write with more adornment on the same theme'; but he was also proud to have used up 'Isocrates' entire perfume-cabinet' and 'some of Aristotle's cosmetics too' (Cic. *Att.* 2.1 [21].1–2). Not so 'unadorned', then: cf. Bömer 1953, 236–8, Marincola 1997, 54–5 and n. 81, 181–2. In that letter Cicero goes on to say that he has 'thrown into confusion the entire Greek people, so that those who were pestering me to give them something to work up have stopped causing me any trouble'. A stylish piece of Cicero's own was the best possible way to stop the 'pestering'. In that case there is no need to assume that Cicero failed to grasp the irony in Posidonius' reply to his request there, that he was 'altogether put off' from writing (so e.g. Bömer 237 and Kidd 1988, 27): both men would understand the polite game they were playing. Cf. Pelling 2006, 16–18.

⁴ Which is not to deny Velleius' interest in personality, and use of personalities to control his narrative, even before that stage: cf. Woodman 1977, 41, pointing to Pompey's domination of the narrative from 29.2–5 onwards. Caesar still seems to mark a new departure. His introduction and back-story (41–3) are much more elaborate than Pompey's, and he dominates the narrative more decisively: contrast the emphasis on Cicero at 34 and Cato at 35, both intruding on Pompey's narrative.

⁵ Thus the titles of Woodman's commentaries: *Velleius Paterculus: the Tiberian Narrative* (1977); *Velleius Paterculus: the Caesarian and Augustan Narrative* (1983). Woodman's own treatment of genre is rather different from the one presented here: 1977, 28–56.

⁶ Quint 1993, 9.

⁷ Comber (forthcoming).

⁸ This is a very simplified way of putting the general thesis argued subtly by Conte 1986, 141–84.

⁹ Rosenmeyer 1985.

¹⁰ Pelling 1999a; cf. also Marincola 1999 in the same volume.

¹¹ The same may already be true for Nepos, *Pelopidas* 1 ('...quod vereor, si res explicare incipiam, ne non vitam eius enarrare, sed historiam videar scribere'): but that passage is more easily reconcilable with the suggestion that Nepos is groping towards and introducing a generic distinction rather than taking one over. Cf. Geiger 1985, 115, '...the apology is added because of the novelty of the material and the newly discovered danger of the biographer of slipping into a different literary genre'. I am not sure that Geiger is wholly right about this 'novelty', but he may be. Desideri 1995, 17–19 has some further good comments on the differences between the Plutarch and the Nepos formulations.

¹² 'On-the-whole' expectations: Pelling 1999a, 328–30, citing Dubrow 1982, Burridge 2004, and Fowler 1991, esp. Fowler 34 on pigeon-holes and pigeons. There are problems, though, in applying Fowler's approach straightforwardly to some ancient genres: cf.

Hinds 2000, esp. 222–3, on the way in which Roman epic tends to essentialize and reify a conception of its own genre, even though real epic poems time after time had qualified and renuanced those expectations in practice. There the pigeon-hole survived in a shape which the pigeons had failed to fit – and new pigeons revelled in it.

[13] That is already true of Herodotus: see the interesting remarks of Boedeker 2000, especially the way in which Herodotus constructs constraints that he then 'has to' follow.

[14] Conte 1986, 100–29, 141–84.

[15] Marincola 1999, 318–20.

[16] Pelling 1997a.

[17] On this see especially Questa 1957; Swan 1987; Pelling 1997a.

[18] As I unpleasingly called it in Pelling 1997a.

[19] Catiline conspiracy: 37.29–42. Other cases in the fifties which could have been more focused around one or other great man: Caesar's consulship, 38.1–12; Cicero's return, which could have been more controlled around either Cicero or Pompey, 39.6–11; the Ptolemy issue, which could have been more Pompey-directed 39.12–16. Caesar's campaigns and space given to lieutenants: esp. 39.40–3, 40.5, 40.8, 40.31, 40.44.

[20] 'Dio beginnt die Geschichte Oktavians bereits im Stile der Kaisergeschichte', Manuwald 1979, 28. Cf. Millar 1964, 46; Gowing 1992, 60.

[21] And the narrative goes on to trace the origins of other imperial practices, 43.44.3, 46.5–6, (48.4 – a failed precedent, for this 'never happened again'), 49.1–2, 50.5, 51.3.

[22] Thus Dio painted events there with much more furtiveness and concealment than in the other accounts (esp. 37.58.1, 38.5.5), and also with a more elaborate version of Caesar's own role, first securing the support of Crassus and Pompey independently, then later reconciling the two (37.54–6).

[23] Early examples are 36.43, 37.22.1, 37.37.3, 37.44.2–3, 37.56.1: cf. Rich 1989: 93.

[24] Before, only 36.1a, where the mention of Cicero is simply to make a point about Hortensius' rhetorical skill.

[25] Below, p. 261; cf. 37.44.2 too.

[26] Cf. esp. 37.23.

[27] Millar 1964, 49 not unreasonably sums up Dio's Cicero as 'vain, self-seeking, cowardly, and, in a word, contemptible'; cf. also Lintott 1997, 2514–7, esp. 2515–6 for scepticism about Dio's version of the Milo trial.

[28] Including some good qualities, for instance his refusal to read the secret letters which he found in Pompey's camp, 41.63.5–6: that allowed Brutus to survive. For the crucial mistakes in the final phases note esp. 43.41–3 and 44.3 ff.; Pelling 2006, 11–12. For Rich 1989, 96, once he becomes dictator Dio's Caesar is 'the exemplar of the good ruler': I think not.

[29] Cf. Rich 1989, 92–4. Dio's portrayal of the triumviral period similarly stresses the similar motives of all the major players, and the similar consequences which would have attended any victory: cf. Gowing 1992, 35, Reinhold–Swan 1990, 158–9, and for some ruminations on this characterizing reductionism Pelling 1997a, 143–4.

[30] The issues here are discussed by Bucher 2000, 418–29, who argues that Appian's writing plans grew firmer and clearer between the time of writing this general *Proem* and that to *B.C.* Some difference between the two proems is also noticed by Magnino 1993, 523–4.

[31] Woodman 2003 now suggests that the 'consulship of Metellus' of Hor. *Odes* 2.1.1 refers to the consulship of Metellus Numidicus in 109 BCE rather than that of Q. Caecilius Metellus in 60: Pollio, he thinks, may have included his own version of

a *pentecontaetia* to illuminate the fuller background to the war. I am not convinced. Much of Woodman's argument rests on his thesis that the 'first triumvirate' was formed not in 60 but in 59, where Vell. 2.44.1 puts it. The issue is a complicated one, but Cic. *Att.* 2.3 (23).3, which Woodman 2003, 206 says 'virtually proves that the Triumvirate was not formed until 59', shows even more clearly that Caesar had a close link with Pompey by late 60. That is so even if the inclusion of Crassus was still to come. If Pollio followed, perhaps even quoted, Cato's view that 'it was not the rift of Caesar and Pompey that brought about the civil wars, it was rather their friendship' (Plut. *Caes.* 13.5, cf. *Pomp.* 47.4), the year 60 was still the place to start.

[32] Gabba 1956, 119 observes the thematic link of the Catilinarian episode with Spartacus, and the lack of any strong connection between this sequence and the next episode in Book 2, Caesar in Spain.

[33] For Catiline as Sulla's στασιώτη ('ally in *stasis*') cf. 2.2.4; in Sallust, cf. *B.C.* 5.6, 11.4–8, 28.4, 37.9.

[34] In particular, the echoes of 'it is men which make a city', ἄνδρες γὰρ πόλις (Thuc. 7.77.7) at 37.146–7 and 50.205. That was admittedly a commonplace even before Thucydides, and one which was current at the time of the events themselves (Cic. *Att.* 7.11[134].3, cf. Shackleton Bailey ad loc. and Gabba 1956: 123–4). But 2.58.240 is more immediate a pointer to Nicias, where Pompey over-reacts to the loss of two scouts as something 'not auspicious' (οὐκ αἴσιον) and observers are impatient with him: cf. Nicias and the eclipse at 7.50.4. Thucydides is also in the air at 39.152–8 (Epidamnus), and is named at 39.158. All this suggests that the ἄνδρες γὰρ πόλις echoes would be felt as distinctively Thucydidean too.

[35] Curio: esp. 27.102–6, 28.110–11, 29.113, 30.119. Antony: esp. 32.130–2.

[36] Luke Pitcher points out to me the frequency with which Appian uses προ-compounds of Caesar: προεπιχειρεῖν, 34.136, προὔπεμψεν, 35.136, ἀεὶ προλαμβάνων, 42.169, προεξελεῖν, 64.125, προεπιβουλεύων, 110.459. Caesar is someone who gets his retaliation in first. There again may be hints of Thucydides here, especially 3.82.5.

[37] Cf. 2.38.151–2, 49.200–1, 55.230, 61.254–5.

[38] In each case Dio's narrative is much less colourful: 41.4.1, 41.46. Plutarch is much more similar to Appian, *Caes.* 32 and 38; that is relevant to the question how much derives from Pollio, below pp. 264–5 and nn. 42–6.

[39] Dio again makes much less of the Dyrrhachium reverses, 41.50.2–4. This demonic strand on the Caesarian side is mirrored by a divinely-driven destruction of wits (θεοβλάβεια) on the Pompeian: on this see esp, Goldmann 1988, 33–4; Gowing 1992, 16; Sion-Jenkis 2000, 182, 191; and, for the return of the theme at and after Philippi, Gowing 1992, 174, 176, 201, 204.

[40] Elsewhere the closest parallels are *Celt.* frs. 1.3 and 1.9 (both interestingly of the Gauls: is there a hint that Caesar's men had learnt from their eight-year enemy?), *Lib.* 124.590, and *Iber.* 92.420. I am again grateful to Luke Pitcher here.

[41] When Brutus is later 'hunted down', the same imagery recurs: 4.129.545. Lucilius there gives himself up pretending to be Brutus, and reveals his trick when brought to Antony: 'οὐ μείονά μοι τήνδε ἄγραν,' εἶπεν, 'ἀλλὰ ἀμείνονα ἧς ἐνομίζετε ἐθηρεύσατε, ὅσῳ κρείττων ἐχθροῦ φίλος.' ('This catch you have brought me,' said Antony, 'is no less, but greater than you thought, just as a friend is greater than an enemy...').

[42] This is not the place to make the case that Appian and Plutarch both derive much of their narrative from Pollio: it seems to me as strong now as it did in 1979 (Pelling 1979 = 2002a chap. 1 = Scardigli 1995, 265–318). To be cautious we should perhaps talk in

terms of a 'Pollio-source', as I did in 1979, leaving open the possibility that an intermediate writer may have transmitted the material to both; but that is not particularly likely, and I have been less cautious here. An especially sharp contribution since then is Hahn 1982, finding good reasons to think that Appian would follow a favoured source (usually one contemporary with the events) closely in terms of substance, but could still fit that material skilfully into his own interpretative schemes. See also the thoughtful discussion of Gowing 1992, 39–50.

[43] Pelling 1980, 133–5 = 2002a, 99–102 = Scardigli 1995, 138–42; also Pelling, forthcoming. There are times when Appian takes that even further than Plutarch; both contrast with Dio, who is more inclined to make Pompey an initiator (above, p. 261), sometimes a cunning one. Thus at App. 2.27.103 it is Marcellus who is behind the proposal to designate Caesar's successor; in Plut. *Caes.* it is Pompey himself, acting 'through himself and his friends' (δι' ἑαυτοῦ καὶ τῶν φίλων, 29.4). Plut. *Pomp.* has a more elaborate version again, but still highlights Pompey's own machinations (56.1–3). But Dio at the end of Book 40 makes Pompey a much subtler and more effective operator, calling the shots himself ('making' people consul and tribune, for instance: 40.59.4).

[44] Again there is a contrast with Dio, who makes it Pompey himself who is so sure that he has as good as won, 41.52.1, 42.1–2. So Dio does not develop that analysis of the over-confident grandees, though he clearly knows of it: cf. 42.1.3, where the possibility that Pompey's hand was 'forced by his co-leaders' is mentioned, but not really favoured, in a list of alternative explanations for the battle; but all Dio's emphasis there, as earlier, centres on miscalculations of Pompey's own. Then Pompey's obituary at 42.5.5, 'even though he had once been called "Agamemnon"', shows knowledge of the same tradition (~ *Pomp.* 67.5, *Caes.* 41.2, App. 2.67.278).

[45] There may also be a hint of the same image-system in Dio, who, just after Caesar's death, makes 'Cicero' conclude a litany of the Republic's ills by saying that their life has been reduced to 'that of wild beasts', 44.30.8. Earlier Caesar's mutinous troops at Vesontio had also grumbled that they had been reduced to 'wild beasts', 38.35.2. This is much less developed than in Appian, but Dio probably knew the Pollio-tradition too; this may be a faint echo, conscious or not. – We may also be able to trace other image-motifs from Pollio coming through in Appian and Plutarch: especially a flower-pelting system, with some patterning to link Curio and Pompey. At *Pomp.* 57.3 people throw flowers for Pompey on his return to Rome after his illness (ἀνθοβολούμενον); at 58.9 they do the same for Curio (ἀνθοβολοῦντες, 'as if he were an athlete') after he has made his senatorial stance for Caesar. At App. 2.27.106 we again have the flower-throwing for Curio, in contrast with his later humiliation when his body lies *decapitated* in *Africa* (2.45.187) – and that looks like another implied comparison with Pompey, this time with his terrible end (2.86.361 ~ *Pomp.* 80). So neither Appian nor Plutarch has the full complement of elements here: Appian does not have Pompey's return after illness and Plutarch does not have Curio's end. That makes it look as if each is taking elements from the complete system in Pollio's original.

[46] This Pollio is brought out best by Syndikus 1958, 1–11, esp. 4–5; it too is visible in Morgan 2000, esp. 57, and see Nisbet–Hubbard 1978, 9. Cf. also Pelling 1988, 27–8.

[47] Sulla's death and funeral are near to the end of Book 1, Caesar's to the end of Book 2; but the sequels are very different. After Sulla's, the consuls begin disputing, citizens take sides, the senate steps in (1.107.501–3); the book ends with the *dēmos* acting not to initiate *stasis*, as at the beginning of Book 1, but to conciliate and calm it (1.121.562–3). That is all different from the end of Book 2, when the senate and *dēmos* are reduced to

a more passive role.

[48] Cf. Hose 1994, 290–4 on Appian's unenthusiastic portrayal of the senate here.

[49] Goldmann 1988, 27 and nn. 19, 21; Swain 1996, 250–1 n. 43. For the introduction of the theme in late Book 2 cf. 109.454, 124.520, 130.543–4, 131.550–1, 137.573, 138.575–6, 139.578, 154.469 etc. For Antony the assassins are 'the accursed ones', οἱ ἐναγεῖς, 133.556. For the later tracing of vengeance cf. 3.1.1, 26.101, 98.408–9, 4.1.1, 134.568: Gabba 1956, 143–4.

[50] Thus Antony already has monarchical power at 3.7.22 (cf. Gowing 1992, 104); Octavian slily speaks of the liberators' fears that Antony might be Caesar's successor in tyranny, 3.15.53; Antony replies in kind at 3.18.66–7; the tribune Cannutius scaremongers about Antony at 3.41.167; Piso indignantly replies to such calumnies from Cicero at 3.56.233 ff.; by 3.62.254 Antony is calling Cicero himself a truer tyrant than Caesar; the threat of a new tyranny is firmly there by the end of book, 3.90.371–2. The theme was already there within days of the Ides: cf. 2.124.518 with Gowing 1992, 119, 124.

[51] A theme which is important in *Mithridatica*, where the image of 'Alexander's heir' is contested. Mithridates too lays claim to it (20.76, cf. 89.407), but in the final triumph it is Pompey who has Alexander's cloak ('if anyone can believe it', *Mith.* 117.577, an interesting qualification which perhaps invests the whole theme with an air of unreality or uncertainty). There may be earlier Alexander-hints for Pompey at *Mith.* 104.489, *proskynēsis*, and 94.433, king of kings, a description which comes back to haunt him at *B.C.* 2.67.278. Alexander is in the air for Lucullus too at 83.374. *Mith.* is earlier than *B.C.* (*B.C.* 1.55.241), and it is possible that memories of that Alexander–Pompey theme are still in play in the Alexander–Caesar *synkrisis*; but, if so, it is only in the distant background. (I am grateful to Luke Pitcher for help on all this.)

[52] So also Bucher 2000, 437, 453; Prandi 2000, 377–8 n. 9 is more sceptical. – Some have believed that the Alexander–Caesar *synkrisis* too goes back to Pollio: cf. Kornemann 1896, esp. 569 f.; Haller 1967, 136; and, more doubtful, Weippert 1972, 154 n. 1.

[53] Not that the passage is quite in Plutarch's manner, in fact. His epilogues, for good reasons, tend to stress the differences, with the similarities pointed out in a pair's proem or more subtly insinuated in the narrative itself. Appian has not been able to do that, and so his *synkrisis* dwells on the similarities rather than the differences.

[54] For recent close analysis of the wording, see Duff 1999, 14–22: cf. also Pelling 2002b and 2004.

[55] See now Beneker 2002–3, and also my own remarks in Pelling 1980, 136–7 (= 2002, 103–5 = Scardigli 1995, 145–8), and in Pelling forthcoming (b).

[56] Above, n. 55.

[57] On this theme cf. Pelling 1997b: 219–20, 225.

[58] And hence I took it as the paradigm of a 'historical' *Life* in Pelling 1980 = 2002a chap. 4: cf. Duff 1999, 20–1.

[59] Pelling 1997b.

[60] Notice for instance how Caesar's physical appearance and sickness, including his epilepsy, is treated in *Caes.* 17.1–3: '...he never made his physical weakness an excuse for slacking, preferring to use campaigning as a way to strengthen his physique: his way of fighting against his illness and keeping his body fit was a prescription of long marches, simple diet, nights in the open air, and constant hard work...' So even a feature which does not seem to fit, his physical frailty, is made to play a part in the picture of his formidable generalship: it illustrates the drive with which he fought against it. Contrast Suet. *Div. Iul.* 45.1, who treats the physical appearance and the epilepsy as self-standing

points, without the same concern to 'integrate' them tightly with his other traits.

[61] It does however have something in common with the way in which Ronald Syme planned to sum up Caesar in the biography which he left unfinished at his death (I am most grateful to Mark Toher for drawing my attention to this manuscript, and to Fergus Millar for permission to quote from it): 'the heroic and tragic figure of ambition, failure, and disillusionment'. Syme had earlier criticized Gelzer for producing a 'depersonalized' Caesar, a man whose story was simply one of power (Syme 1944, 92 = 1979, 150). In their different ways both Gelzer and Syme reflect, were perhaps even unconsciously responding to, Plutarch's emphases.

[62] Pelling 1997c = 2002a chap. 17. Duff 1999, 253–5 gives me a hearing, but is unconvinced.

[63] Thus Mossman 1992 cautiously but convincingly suggests that the *Lives* of the period of the Successors, *Demetrius, Eumenes*, and *Pyrrhus*, are to be read not merely with a general knowledge of Alexander, but specifically with the *Life of Alexander* in mind. See also now Beneker 2005.

[64] Above, p. 259.

[65] Cross-references seem to suggest that *Thes.–Rom.* falls in a group with *Lyc.–Numa* and *Them.–Cam.*: *Thes.* 1.4 quotes *Numa, Numa* 9.8 and 12.7 quote *Cam.*, and *Cam.* 33.10 cites *Rom.* The intricate argument of Jones 1966 seems to put this *Thes.–Rom.* group in positions VI–IX: cf. also Piccirilli 1980, van der Valk 1982, 303–7. (For some reservations about this type of argument cf. Geiger 1979, 61 n. 47 and Pelling 1979, 80–1 = 2002a, 7–10 = Scardigli 279–81, but this part of the reconstruction seems reasonably solid.) *Dion–Brut.* belongs in position XII (*Dion* 2.7), and *Brutus* seems to be part of a group of late Roman *Lives* prepared as a single project (*Caes., Pomp., Crass., C.Min., Ant., Brut.*): Pelling 1979 = 2002a chap. 1.

[66] Especially in the Lupercalia affair: see *Caes.* 61 and *Ant.* 12, with Pelling 1988, 144–7, esp. 145–6 on the Romulean elements. Fears of Caesar's monarchy: esp. *Caes.* 60.1, 'lust for kingship' (ὁ τῆς βασιλείας ἔρως). Humiliation of the senate: esp. *Caes.* 60.3–8, 'as if the senate's humiliation formed an insult to the whole city' (ὡς ἐν τῇ βουλῇ καὶ τῆς πόλεως προπηλακιζομένης· cf. *Rom.* 27.3, (Romulus)...'seemed to be inflicting total humiliation on the senate' (ἔδοξε κομιδῇ τὴν γερουσίαν προπηλακίζειν).

[67] Rome's general glory, esp. *Thes.* 1.5, *Rom.* 1.1, 8.9. The *Life* is full of aetiologies of customs and places which 'still today' survive: esp. 1.3, 4.5, 5.4–5, 8.7, 9.5, 13.6, 15, 18.1, 18.6, 18.9, 19.8, 20.2, 21.2, 24.2, 25.7, 27.4. Particular later crises: Celtic conflict, 22.1; Hannibalic War: 22.5. Other big names of the future: Augustus, 17.3; 'Gaius Caesar' (i.e. Caligula), 20.8; Scipio Africanus, 27.5; 'times of Varro', 12.3–6. Hints of Caesar himself are more elusive, but notice that the calendar at 21.1 and the Lupercalia at 21.4–10 introduce themes which will occur in the same order at *Caes.* 59 and 61; and in the context of Romulus' disappearance, 27.4 notes – *apparently* incidentally – the renaming of the fifth month as 'July'.

[68] Similar points can be made about *Theseus*, and suggestions there of Pericles and the great crisis of Athens during the Peloponnesian War: Pelling 2002a, 181–5, elaborating Pelling 1999b.

[69] Drumann–Groebe 1899–1929.

[70] On the 'generic' closeness of those *Lives* to history cf. now Duff 1999, 19–20; Pelling 1997a, 127–8; and especially Ash 1997, 190–1, for sensible caution about drawing conclusions about the whole series from *Galba* and *Otho*.

[71] If this is right, then it is of course most interesting in terms of 2nd-century CE

historical *mentalité*, but this is not the place to pursue this implication.

⁷² This chapter was delivered as a paper to the Langford Seminar on Caesar at Florida State University, Tallahassee, in March 2001: my thanks to Elaine Fantham for that invitation. It has also been inflicted on audiences in the University of Virginia at Charlottesville, Duke University, New York University, London, Durham, Birmingham, and Oxford, and I am grateful to all those audiences for valuable and stimulating discussion. Luke Pitcher has also made very helpful comments on a written version, and Philip Stadter, Tony Woodman, John Marincola, and Christina Kraus have as usual shared in some fascinating discussion. My greatest thanks are due to Judith Mossman, not merely for organizing the Dublin conference but for the original suggestion that Caesar as boundary-breaker might be mirrored in generic deviation. That idea is hers.

Bibliography

Ash, R.
  1997 'Severed heads: individual portraits and irrational forces in Plutarch's *Galba* and *Otho*', in Mossman (ed.) *Plutarch and his Intellectual World*, 189–214.
Beneker, J.
  2002–3 'No time for love: Plutarch's chaste Caesar', *GRBS* 43, 13–30.
  2005 'Thematic correspondences in Plutarch's *Lives* of Caesar, Pompey and Crassus', in L. de Blois, J. Bons, T. Kessels and D.M. Schenkeveld (eds.) *The Statesman in Plutarch's Works* ii, Leiden and Boston, 315–25.
Boedeker, D.
  2000 'Herodotus' genre(s)', in M. Depew and D. Obbink, *Matrixes of Genre: Authors, canons, and society*, Harvard, 97–114.
Bömer, F.
  1953 'Der Commentarius: zur Vorgeschichte und literarischen Form der Schriften Caesars', *Hermes* 81, 210–50.
Braund, D.C. and Gill, C.
  2003 *Myth, History, and Culture in Republican Rome: Studies in honour of T.P. Wiseman*, Exeter.
Bucher, G.S.
  2000 'The origins, program, and composition of Appian's *Roman History*', *TAPA* 130, 411–58.
Burridge, R.A.
  1992 *What are the Gospels? A comparison with Graeco-Roman biography*, 1st edn Cambridge, 2nd edn Michigan and Cambridge 2004. .
Cameron, A. (ed.)
  1989 *History as Text: The writing of ancient history*, London.
Comber, M.
  Forthcoming 'Spaghetti epic: Lucan's *De Bello Civili* and the western films of Sergio Leone'.
Conte, G.B.
  1986 *The Rhetoric of Imitation: Genre and poetic memory in Virgil and other Latin poets*, Cornell; Italian original 1991.
Depew, M. and Obbink, D.
  2000 *Matrixes of Genre: Authors, canons, and society*, Harvard.

Desideri, P.
1995 ' "Non scriviamo storie, ma vite", Plut. *Alex.* 1.2: la formula biografica di Plutarco', in Gabba, Desideri and Cipriani, *Testis Temporum*, 15–25.

Drumann, W., rev. Groebe, P.
1899–1929 *Geschichte Roms in seinem Übergange der republikanischen zur monarchischen Verfassung* i–vi, Berlin and Leipzig.

Dubrow, H.
1982 *Genre*, London.

Duff, T.
1999 *Plutarch's Lives: Exploring virtue and vice*, Oxford.

Edwards, M. and Swain, S. (eds.)
1997 *Portraits: Biographical representation in the Greek and Latin literature of the Roman Empire*, Oxford.

Erbse, H.
1956 'Die Bedeutung der Synkrisis in den Parallelbiographien Plutarchs', *Hermes* 84, 378–424.

Fontana, M.J., Piarino, M.T. and Rizzo, F.P.
1980 *Miscellanea di Studi Classici in onore di Eugenio Manni* i–vi, Rome.

Fowler, A.
1991 *Kinds of Literature: An introduction to the theory of genres and modes*, Oxford.

Gabba, E.
1956 *Appiano e la storia delle guerre civili*, Florence.

Gabba, E., Desideri, P. and Cipriani, G.
1995 *Testis Temporum: Aspetti e problemi della storiografia antica,* (*Incontri del Dipartimento di Scienze dell'Antichità dell'Università di Pavia*), Como.

Geiger, J.
1979 'Munatius Rufus and Thrasea Paetus on Cato the Younger', *Ath.* 57, 48–72.
1985 *Cornelius Nepos and Ancient Political Biography,* (*Historia* Einzelschriften 47), Stuttgart.

Gelzer, M.
1941 *Caesar der Politiker und Staatsmann*, Munich. English transl. by P. Needham, Oxford 1969.

Goldmann, B.
1988 *Einheitlichkeit und Eigenständigkeit der Historia Romana des Appian*, Hildesheim.

Gowing, A.M.
1992 *The Triumviral Narratives of Appian and Cassius Dio*, Michigan.

Hahn, I.
1982 'Appian und seine Quellen', in G. Wirth (ed.) *Romanitas–Christianitas: Untersuchungen zur Geschichte und Literatur der römischen Kaiserzeit Johannes Straub zum 70. Geburtstag am 18. Oktober 1982 gewidmet*, Berlin and New York, 251–76.

Haller, B.
1967 *C. Asinius Pollio als Politiker und zeitkritischer Historiker*, Diss. Münster.

Hinds, S.
2000 'Essential epic: genre and gender from Macer to Statius', in Depew and Obbink, *Matrixes of Genre*, 21–44.

Hose, M.
1994   *Erneuerung der Vergangenheit: die Historiker im Imperium Romanum von Florus bis Cassius Dio*, Stuttgart and Leipzig.

Jones, C.P.
1966   'Towards a chronology of Plutarch's works', *JRS* 56, 61–74, repr. in B. Scardigli (ed.) *Essays on Plutarch's Lives*, Oxford, 95–123.

Kidd, I.G.
1988   *Posidonius: Vol. II: The Commentary*, Cambridge.

Kornemann, E.
1896   'Die historische Schriftstellerei des C. Asinius Pollio', *Jb.f. class. Phil*, Suppl. 22, 555–692.

Kraus, C.S. (ed.)
1999   *The Limits of Historiography: Genre and narrative in ancient historical texts*, Leiden, Boston and Cologne.

Lintott. A.W.,
1997   'Cassius Dio and the history of the late Republic', *ANRW* ii.34.3, 2497–523.

Magnino, D.
1993   'Le "Guerre Civili" di Appiano', *ANRW* ii.34.1, 523–54.

Manuwald, B.
1979   *Cassius Dio und Augustus*, Wiesbaden.

Marincola, J.
1997   *Authority and Tradition in Ancient Historiography*, Cambridge.
1999   'Genre, convention, and innovation in Greco-Roman historiography', in Kraus (ed.) *The Limits of Historiography*, 281–324.

Millar, F.
1964   *A Study of Cassius Dio*, Oxford 1964.

Morgan, L.
1997   'Levi quidem de reö: Julius Caesar as tyrant and pedant', *JRS* 87, 23–40.
2000   'The autopsy of C. Asinius Pollio', *JRS* 90, 51–69.

Mossman, J.M.
1992   'Plutarch, Pyrrhus, and Alexander', in Stadter (ed.) *Plutarch and the Historical Tradition*, London and New York, 90–108.

Mossman, J.M. (ed.)
1997   *Plutarch and his Intellectual World*, London.

Nisbet, R.G.M., and Hubbard, M.
1978   *A Commentary on Horace* Odes *Book II*, Oxford.

Pelling, C.B.R.,
1979   'Plutarch's method of work in the Roman Lives', *JHS* 99, 1, 74–96, repr. with a Postscript in Scardigli (ed.) *Essays on Plutarch's Lives*, 265–318 and with revisions in Pelling, *Plutarch and History*, 1–44.
1980   'Plutarch's adaptation of his source-material', *JHS* 100, 127–40, repr. in Scardigli (ed.) *Essays on Plutarch's Lives*, 125–54 and with revisions in Pelling, *Plutarch and History*, 91–115.
1988   *Plutarch: Life of Antony*, Cambridge.
1997a   'Biographical history: Cassius Dio on the early Principate', in Edwards and Swain (eds.) *Portraits*, 117–44.
1997b   'Plutarch on Caesar's fall', in Mossman (ed.) *Plutarch and his Intellectual*

World, 215–31.

1997c 'Is death the end? Closure in Plutarch's *Lives*', in Roberts, Dunn, and Fowler (eds.) *Classical Closure*, 228–50, repr. with revisions in Pelling, *Plutarch and History*, 365–86.

1999a 'Epilogue', in Kraus (ed.) *The Limits of Historiography*, 325–60.

1999b ' "Making myth look like history": Plato in Plutarch's *Theseus–Romulus*', in Pérez Jiménez, García López and Aguilar (eds.) *Plutarco, Platón, y Aristoteles*, 431–43; expanded version in Pelling, *Plutarch and History*, 171–95.

2002a *Plutarch and History*, Swansea.

2002b 'Plutarch's *Caesar*: a *Caesar* for the Caesars?', in Stadter and van der Stockt (eds.) *Sage and Emperor*, 213–26; also in Pelling, *Plutarch and History*, 253–65.

2004 'Plutarch's *Lives*', in I.J.F. de Jong, R. Nünlist, A. Bowie (eds.) *Narrators, Narratees, and Narratives in Ancient Greek Literature: Studies in ancient Greek narrative* i, Leiden and Boston, 403–21; also under the title ' "You for me and me for you": narrators and narratees in Plutarch's *Lives*', in Pelling, *Plutarch and History*, 267–82.

2006 'Judging Julius Caesar', in Wyke (ed.) *Julius Caesar in Western Culture*, 3–26.

Forthcoming 'Cashing in politically: Plutarch on the late Republic', in Zadorojnyi and Livingstone (eds.) *Purse and Paideia*.

Pérez Jiménez, A., García López.J., Aguilar, R.M. (eds.)

1999 *Plutarco, Platón, y Aristoteles. Actas del V Congreso Internacional de la I.P.S. Madrid–Cuenca, 4–7 de Mayo de 1999*, Madrid.

Piccirilli, L.

1980 'Cronologia relativa e fonti della Vitae Lycurgi et Numae di Plutarco', in Fontana, Piarino, and Rizzo, *Miscellanea di Studi Classici in onore di Eugenio Manni*, v. 1751–64.

Prandi, L.

2000 'L'Alessandro di Plutarco: Riflessioni su *de Al. Magn. Fort.* e su *Alex.*', in Van der Stockt (ed.) *Rhetorical Theory and Praxis in Plutarch (Collection d'Études Classiques* 11), 375–86.

Questa, C.

1957 'Tecnica biografica e tecnica annalistica nei ll. LIII–LXIII di Cassio Dione', *Studi Urbinati* 31 N.S. B 1–2, 37–53.

Quint, D.

1993 *Epic and Empire: Politics and generic form from Virgil to Milton*, Princeton.

Raaflaub, K.A. and Toher, M. (eds.)

1990 *Between Republic and Empire: Interpretations of Augustus and his principate*, Berkeley, Los Angeles and Oxford.

Reinhold, M. and Swan, P.M.

1990 'Cassius Dio's assessment of Augustus', in Raaflaub and Toher (eds.) *Between Republic and Empire*, 155–73.

Rich, J.W.

1989 'Cassius Dio on Augustus', in Cameron (ed.) *History as Text*, 87–110.

Roberts, D., Dunn, F. and Fowler, D. (eds.)

1997 *Classical Closure: Endings in ancient literature*, Princeton.

Rosenmeyer, T.G.
  1985   'Ancient literary genres: a mirage?', *Yearbook of Comparative and General Literature* 34, 74–84.
Scardigli, B. (ed.)
  1995   *Essays on Plutarch's* Lives, Oxford.
Sion-Jenkis, K.
  2000   *Von der Republik zum Prinzipat: Ursachen für den Verfassungswandel in Rom im historischen Denken der Antike,* (*Palingenesia* 69), Stuttgart.
Stadter, P.A. (ed.)
  1992   *Plutarch and the Historical Tradition*, London and New York.
Stadter, P.A. and van der Stockt, L. (eds.)
  Forthcoming   *Sage and Emperor: Plutarch and Trajan*, Louvain.
Swain, S.
  1996   *Hellenism and Empire: Language, classicism, and power in the Greek world, AD 50–250*, Oxford.
Swan, P.W.
  1987   'Cassius Dio on Augustus: a poverty of annalistic sources?', *Phoenix* 41, 272–91.
Syme, R.
  1944   Review of Gelzer 1941, *JRS* 34, 92–103, repr. in Syme, *Roman Papers* i, 49–71.
  1979   *Roman Papers* i, Oxford.
Syndikus, H.P.
  1958   *Lucans Gedicht vom Bürgerkrieg*, Diss. München.
Van der Stockt, L. (ed.)
  2000   *Rhetorical Theory and Praxis in Plutarch,* (*Collection d'Études Classiques* 11), Louvain and Namur 2000.
Van der Valk, M.
  1982   'Notes on the biographies of Plutarch', in *Studi in onore di Aristide Colonna*, Perugia, 301–37.
Weippert, O.
  1972   *Alexander-imitatio und römische Politik in republikanischer Zeit*, Augsburg.
Wirth, G. (ed.)
  1982   *Romanitas–Christianitas: Untersuchungen zur Geschichte und Literatur der römischen Kaiserzeit Johannes Straub zum 70. Geburtstag am 18. Oktober 1982 gewidmet*, Berlin and New York.
Woodman, A.J.
  1977   *Velleius Paterculus: The Tiberian narrative, (2.94–131)*, Cambridge.
  1983   *Velleius Paterculus: The Caesarian and Augustan narrative, (2.41–93)*, Cambridge.
  2003   'Poems to historians: Catullus 1 and Horace, *Odes* 2.1', in Braund and Gill, *Myth, History, and Culture in Republican Rome*, 191–216.
Wyke, M. (ed.)
  2006   *Julius Caesar in Western Culture*, Malden, Oxford and Carlton.
Zadorojnyi, A.V. and Livingstone, N. (eds.)
  Forthcoming   *Purse and Paideia*, Leiden.

16

TRAVEL WRITING, HISTORY, AND BIOGRAPHY

Judith Mossman

A momentous but until then overlooked fact was making its first appearance: that I had inadvertently brought myself with me to the island.[1]

Travel as a literary theme, and travel writing of every kind, have been the focus of much scholarly attention in recent years across a wide variety of disciplines. This is welcome, as the subject has been shown to be a fertile one from all sorts of points of view: travel writing is obviously important to ethnography and contiguous fields and by describing the Other can reveal much about the Self.[2] The description of travel also provides a ready-made structure for a narrative; and travel can also become a powerful metaphor for the development of the narrative's subject.[3] Hence a fictional journey has since the *Odyssey* proved a highly sophisticated literary device to explore character and create character-development within a narrative.[4] In this essay I want to examine (from one perspective only, and that one limited by space) the way in which Plutarch uses the theme of travel to delineate character by exploring the relations between the traveller and the people he encounters on his journeys. I also want to ask whether it can be shown that this theme is used differently in biography from the way it is used in history – whether different kinds of travel anecdotes are necessary to different types of narrative. It is not hard to see some significant differences in the use of travel anecdotes in the *Lives* from their use in the non-biographical writings of Plutarch (and I will discuss those briefly at the end), but, in this as in other matters, it is much less easy to clarify the difference between biography and the kind of history which is organized around individuals.[5]

Such anecdotes about travel, after all, share with travel writing proper the capacity to reveal essential facets of the subject's ethnicity, his difference from those around him, and this is a matter of interest common to biography and history.[6] Sometimes in Plutarch and elsewhere a form of cultural tourism is involved in the subject's journey (whatever its basic purpose),[7] when the subject of the *Life* takes time during his progress to visit some *Sehenswürdigkeiten* which lie in his way. Lying behind this form of tourism there lurks an element of appropriation, actual or attempted, of the culture which is viewed, again a theme which is at least as important to history as to biography: I will return to that in a moment.

I

Let us begin with some non-Plutarchan examples of characterization through this type of cultural tourism, and see whether they suggest any ways of proceeding. Take for example two very different accounts of the same incident: Augustus viewing the body of Alexander. Suetonius says (*Life of Augustus*, 18):

> Per idem tempus conditorium et corpus Magni Alexandri, cum prolatum e penetrali subiecisset oculis, corona aurea imposita ac floribus aspersis veneratus est consultusque, num et Ptolemaeum inspicere vellet, regem se voluisse ait videre, non mortuos.[8]

Dio, however, completely changes this dignified picture (51.16.3):

> καὶ μετὰ ταῦτα τὸ μὲν τοῦ Ἀλεξάνδρου σῶμα εἶδε, καὶ αὐτοῦ καὶ προσήψατο, ὥστε τι τῆς ῥινός, ὥς φασι, θραυσθῆναι·[9]

It has been suggested that Augustus deliberately broke off part of the nose (as well as stealing Alexander's signet, which also happens in Suetonius) in order to appropriate his strength in some mystical way: be that as it may, the historian still suggests a far more aggressive type of appropriation than the assumption of likeness skilfully projected by Augustus' remark in Suetonius.

Even so, this seems less a difference of genre than of authorial attitude: Dio's greater cynicism is part of his constant interest in the contrast between appearance and reality in relation to Augustus,[10] while Suetonius' more dignified portrayal is in keeping with the general pattern of the *Lives of the Caesars*, which must establish Augustus as a standard against which his successors can be measured, and therefore cannot afford to undermine him.

Tacitus *Annals* 2.53–5 provides a good illustration of how to use a contrast in tourist attitudes to fill out characters: when he visits Greece Germanicus, perfect as always, does the right thing; Piso the lager lout, on the other hand, insults the locals.[11] Perhaps one would be less likely to find such a developed comparison in a biography? But one might easily find such a passage in any of Plutarch's longer and more developed *Lives*: the implicit comparison between Octavia and Cleopatra in *Antony*, for instance. So far there doesn't seem to be any way of classifying these anecdotes by genre, though one can see differences between authors: it seems plausible to say that Plutarch uses these stories more subtly than Suetonius, at least.

282

Antony 23.2–4 illustrates this nicely:

τοῖς μὲν οὖν Ἕλλησιν οὐκ ἄτοπος οὐδὲ φορτικὸς συνηνέχθη τό γε πρῶτον,
ἀλλὰ καὶ τὸ παῖζον αὐτοῦ πρὸς ἀκροάσεις φιλολόγων καὶ θέας ἀγώνων καὶ
μυήσεις ἔτρεπε, καὶ τὰς κρίσεις ἦν ἐπιεικής, καὶ φιλέλλην ἀκούων ἔχαιρεν,
ἔτι δὲ μᾶλλον φιλαθήναιος προσαγορευόμενος, καὶ τῇ πόλει πλείστας δωρεὰς
ἔδωκε. βουλομένων δέ τι καὶ Μεγαρέων καλὸν ἀντεπιδείξασθαι ταῖς Ἀθήναις
καὶ τὸ βουλευτήριον ἰδεῖν αὐτὸν ἀξιωσάντων, ἀναβὰς καὶ θεασάμενος, ὡς
ἐπυνθάνοντο τί δοκοίη, Μικρὸν μέν, ἔφη, σαπρὸν δέ. πρὸς δὲ καὶ τὸν τοῦ
Πυθίου νεὼν κατεμέτρησεν ὡς συντελέσων· τοῦτο γὰρ ὑπέσχετο πρὸς τὴν
σύγκλητον.[12]

This passage not only foreshadows the change in Antony's attitude to Greece
as he becomes more desperate and more enslaved to Cleopatra, it also is
highly indicative of some of the tensions in his character: basically genial
and kindly, in some ways wanting to do the proper thing (though not really
carrying it through, we note), but also a bit crude, not quite as cultured as he
would like to pretend.

Another, rather different, example from the *Sertorius* also illustrates the
use of travel to characterize a Plutarchan subject: in chapters 8–9, as a result
of a storm, Sertorius breaks a significant geographical boundary by sailing
out through the straits of Gibraltar and landing on the Atlantic coast of
Spain.[13] There he meets sailors who have returned from the Atlantic Isles,
which Plutarch describes in idyllic terms and connects with the Homeric Isles
of the Blest. Sertorius, he says, ἔρωτα θαυμαστὸν ἔσχεν οἰκῆσαι τὰς νήσους καὶ
ζῆν ἐν ἡσυχίᾳ, τυραννίδος ἀπαλλαγεὶς καὶ πολέμων ἀπαύστων.[14] Antony can
be epitomized by his rather laddish reaction to old buildings; this breaking
of boundaries and whimsical desire for far-off semi-mythical islands also
brings out an important strand in Sertorius' character: ever the rebel, he is
nonetheless often curiously detached from his surroundings and companions
(this emerges particularly strongly in his death-scene at 26.9). His desire
for the unattainable islands is again a very subtle touch of characterization.
Sertorius is perhaps too close to his Hispanic barbarians ever to be a tourist
– too ambivalent in his Self ever to enjoy the observation of the Other – but
he does desire to be an explorer, a traveller. It is no less typical of him that his
desire is condemned to be unfulfilled.[15]

II

Back to cultural appropriation. All travellers want a souvenir, but 'souvenir' is
also the time-honoured euphemism for what soldiers bring back from wars:
loot, in fact. Once again, the kind of appropriation the traveller indulges in
can also be used to show what sort of person he is (and, again, Plutarch can
use this very subtly); Herodotus uses a Babylonian statue to show that Xerxes

is mad and bad, even more so than Darius, in an aside in Book I;[16] in Plutarch, Sulla doesn't even bother to go to Delphi, but still steals the dedications there and keeps one as a battle mascot;[17] his complex relation to the ideal of Athens reveals his contradictory character: 'Perhaps it was some spirit of envious emulation which drove him to fight as it were with the shadow of the city's former greatness'; but then he tells ambassadors 'Rome did not send me to Athens to study ancient history. My task is to subdue rebels'; when he takes the city he says 'I forgive a few for the sake of the many, the living for the sake of the dead', but then burns the Piraeus, including the famous arsenal of Philo.[18] But not all cultural appropriation, for Plutarch, at least, is worthy of condemnation: Marcellus' spoils from Sicily might also have been described as straightforward loot, but as Simon Swain has pointed out, in fact Plutarch makes Marcellus' 'souvenirs' seem more a necessary education than a theft.[19]

III

Some appropriation, of course, is purely intellectual (and I will return to this at the end). A passage of Cicero's *De Finibus* (5.1.2) furnishes a nice contrast with Marcellus and Sulla, and also with Cicero's more acquisitive letter to Atticus (I.6.2).[20] Cicero describes his philosophical cultural tourism in Athens:

> Itaque ad tempus ad Pisonem omnes. Inde vario sermone sex illa a Dipylo stadia confecimus. Cum autem venissemus in Academiae non sine causa nobilitata spatia, solitudo erat ea quam volueramus. Tum Piso: 'Naturane nobis hoc,' inquit, 'datum dicam an errore quodam, ut, eam ea loca videamus in quibus memoria dignos viros acceperimus multum esse versatos, magis moveamur quam si quando eorum ipsorum aut facta audiamus aut scriptum aliquod legamus? Velut ego nunc moveor. Venit enim mihi Platonis in mentem, quem accepimus primum hic disputare solitum, cuius etiam illi propinqui hortuli non memoriam solum mihi afferunt sed ipsum videntur in conspectu meo ponere. Hic Speusippus, hic Xenocrates, hic eius auditor Polemo...[21]

Here Cicero describes a reaction which is only appropriation in so far as the speaker clearly feels himself in tune with the past and culturally part of it (dare one say, perhaps more part of it than his contemporary Athenians). This is a tone very familiar from the writings of much later visitors to Greece, as Alcock and Eisner have shown:[22] it has something in common with Germanicus' reactions to his sightseeing, though, significantly, it is not philosophy which excites Germanicus' most sympathetic imaginings, but history, and Roman history – indeed, family history – at that: it is Actium and Troy (2.53.3, 54.3 *namque ei, ut memoravi, avunculus Augustus, avus Antonius erant, magnaque illic imago tristium laetorumque...igitur adito Ilio quaeque ibi varietate fortunae et nostri origine veneranda, relegit Asiam*).[23] In these examples, again, it seems impossible to suggest a meaningful contrast between biography and history: both the biographer and the historian are interested in the internal effects of the cultural appropriation on the appropriator, and the differences in the nature of those effects are more explicable in terms of the cultural background of the author and the nature of his subject than in terms of genre. The philosophical passage is the one which seems qualitatively different. It has something important in common with the phenomenon of pilgrimage, in that, to adapt Rutherford's distinction between pilgrimage and tourism, this visit is made not for its own sake but for reasons of a form of piety and quasi-religious celebration.[24]

IV

Some travellers, then, feel at one with their surroundings and more or less aggressively appropriate them; others often feel hopelessly alienated from them, even frightened of being absorbed by them.[25] In Plutarch this usually happens to armies, collectively, and the character of the general is then revealed by his reaction to the situation: one thinks of the nightmare experiences of Crassus and Antony in Parthia, where the terrain, as well as the encircling Parthians, seems to be actively hostile to them: but the *locus classicus* for this is surely Germanicus and his men coming upon the bones of Varus' troops in the Teutoburger forest and reliving their predecessors' torment in imagination: Roman history again stirring Roman travellers.[26] Note again the *ecphrasis*-style account, in structure not unlike Cicero's: the reader arrives with the troops and sees what they see:[27]

> *primo* Vari castra lato ambitu et dimensis principiis trium legionum manus ostentabant; *dein* semiruto vallo, humili fossa accisae iam reliquiae consedisse intellegebantur: *medio campi* albentia ossa, ut fugerant, ut resisterant, disiecta vel aggerata. *adiacebant* fragmina telorum equorumque artus, simul truncis arborum antefixa ora. *lucis propinquis* barbarae arae, apud quas tribunos ac primorum ordinum centuriones mactaverant.[28]   (61.3)

The scene is provided with grim tour guides in the form of survivors of the massacre, and these take over from the narrator the 'gee syndrome' survey of horrors:

> referebant *hic* cecidisse legatos, *illic* raptas aquilas; primum *ubi* vulnus Varo adactum, *ubi* infelici dextera et suo ictu mortem invenerit; *quo tribunali* contionatus Arminius, quot patibula captivis, quae scrobes, utque signis et aquilis per superbiam inluserit'[29]   (61.6)

As Woodman and Pelling have pointed out, the impact of all this is the greater because in the next chapters there is a strong fear that history may repeat itself and that this army may go the same way as their fallen comrades;

this indeed is likely to have dictated the crafting of the whole episode. If so, it is a testimony to the power of this narrative theme.

Absorption by a hostile environment is also a scenario very typical of the post-colonial novel, where the traveller who wants to be in control of his surroundings and believes that he is, is suddenly confronted with the reality that he is not, and indeed that these surroundings are very hostile indeed; or else he is revealed by the narrative to have grotesquely misunderstood the situation and to be taking refuge in various mental strategies to comfort himself. So Susan Barton in *Foe* makes endless plans for the improvement of life on Cruso's island which never come to anything (and indeed Cruso's simple hut and precious fire are overwhelmed by a storm); Mr Rochester (in *Wide Sargasso Sea*) gets lost in the impossibly green shades of the West Indian island where he is spending his doomed honeymoon; Kipling's Morrowbie Jukes falls into the horrific Village of the Dead and narrowly escapes losing his identity; and Mrs Moore and Adela Quested react in their own very different, but equally alienated, ways on the trip to the Marabar Caves in E.M. Forster.[30]

These fictional strategies are designed to explore ' "contact zones", social spaces where disparate cultures meet, clash, and grapple with each other, often in highly asymmetrical relations of domination and subordination – like colonialism, slavery, or their aftermaths.'[31] (Perhaps one could even see travel writing, and travel anecdotes, as forming a sort of literary 'contact zone' between genres – not just history and biography, but philosophy and geography as well.)[32] Just as travel writing has proved a fruitful way of exploring more modern colonial and post-colonial relationships, it seems to me that such ancient travel writing may be helpful in considering the colonial relationship between Greece and Rome, especially as these anecdotes do undoubtedly reflect a historical reality.[33]

'Contact zones' do not only occur between Greeks and Romans, of course. Contact zones of various kinds (physical and imaginary) between Greeks and barbarians in classical times have been much discussed. However, less work has been done on Greeks and barbarians (not Romans) in the imperial period, and it seems to me that more could be said here.[34] Any Greek writer of the second century AD who writes about the Greeks as colonizers is, I would argue, not writing entirely for a Greek audience, but for Romans as well, and is emphasizing for both Greek and Roman readers that the Greeks have been conquerors as well as conquered. So when Plutarch writes about Greeks and barbarians, many textual 'contact zones' are created: Roman readers, for example, might be encouraged to compare their own empire with the actions of the Greek conquerors. Greek readers might not only look back with nostalgia for past achievements, but also might be encouraged to reflect on their experience as a people colonized by Rome. It might be important for these Greek readers to remember that this was an extraordinarily complex experience, given their paradoxical cultural ascendancy over their conquerors (as Horace put it, *Graecia capta ferum victorem cepit*).[35]

I would therefore like to focus on one life where Plutarch is able to explore colonizing travel from the perspective of a Greek traveller, not a Roman one: the *Life of Alexander*. This is also a *Life* whose form is particularly intriguing, as it is here (1.2) that Plutarch makes his clearest overt distinction between biography and history, but seems not to carry it through in the body of the *Life* or its pair.[36] Alexander himself is the iconic figure par excellence, but Plutarch succeeds in individualizing him and posing complex questions about his mission, its validity, and its effect on him. In another essay[37] I suggested that Alexander is characterized as a highly ambivalent and complex personality through the use of epic and tragic colouring, but that is clearly not the only strand in this very complex text; Alexander's travels and his reaction to cultural artefacts are also used to portray his character, naturally enough given that those travels were one of the aspects of his achievement which most fascinated later writers (this can be seen particularly clearly in the *Alexander Romance*).[38]

V

Significantly, immediately after Alexander crosses the Hellespont, Plutarch shows him sightseeing at Troy (θεᾶσθαι: *Alex.* 15.4–5):

ἀναβὰς δὲ εἰς Ἴλιον ἔθυσε τῇ Ἀθηνᾷ καὶ τοῖς ἥρωσιν ἔσπεισε. τὴν δὲ Ἀχιλλέως στήλην ἀλειψάμενος λίπα καὶ μετὰ τῶν ἑταίρων συναναδραμὼν γυμνός, ὥσπερ ἔθος ἐστίν, ἐστεφάνωσε, μακαρίσας αὐτὸν ὅτι καὶ ζῶν φίλου πιστοῦ καὶ τελευτήσας μεγάλου κήρυκος ἔτυχεν. ἐν δὲ τῷ περιϊέναι καὶ θεᾶσθαι τὰ κατὰ τὴν πόλιν ἐρομένου τινὸς αὐτὸν εἰ βούλεται τὴν Ἀλεξάνδρου λύραν ἰδεῖν, ἐλάχιστα φροντίζειν ἐκείνης ἔφη, τὴν δ'Ἀχιλλέως ζητεῖν, ᾗ τὰ κλέα καὶ τὰς πράξεις ὕμνει τῶν ἀγαθῶν ἀνδρῶν ἐκεῖνος.[39]

This has been called 'a declaration of Alexander's heroic intentions',[40] but that simple formula should be refined. Clearly Alexander is determinedly associating himself with Achilles rather than Paris, and in most respects that can be seen as praiseworthy.[41] The passages in Homer which relate to this passage impact strongly on its interpretation if they are specifically recalled by the reader. *Iliad* 3.54 is Hector upbraiding Paris for showing fear before Menelaus, '…the man whose blossoming wife you have taken. The lyre would not help you then, nor the favours of Aphrodite, nor your locks…', so the lyre seems to be associated with the seduction of Helen. In *Iliad* 9, on the other hand, Achilles is singing the 'glorious deeds of men' (κλέα ἀνδρῶν) to the accompaniment of the lyre. But that lyre, we are told, was part of the spoils from the city of Eetion, the father of Andromache, whom Achilles killed along with his entire family (*Il.* 6.414–24). The lyre is booty, and booty from an Asian city. Perhaps, then, there is rather more edge to this anecdote than at first meets the eye, and this is confirmed when one compares the way it is presented in the essay *On the Fortune or Virtue of Alexander*, which in general presents a much less ambivalent view of Alexander.[42] One interesting detail is that in the *Moralia* version the lyre is 'of Paris' (Πάριδος) (twice); in the life it is 'of Alexander' (Ἀλεξάνδρου), prompting one to wonder whether the 'someone' who offered him a sight of this lyre was being wholly ingenuous? Was he actually trying to belittle the youthful Alexander? In the *Life* Alexander has very specifically honoured Achilles just before this offer is made: the anonymous attempt to identify him not with the great hero but with the gigolo who assassinated Achilles in a cowardly fashion is brusquely brushed aside. The form of the anecdote about Augustus in Suetonius (discussed above) is very similar, and there is a similar urgency and arrogance in the self-definition of the would-be world conquerors (Augustus has just conquered Egypt: the next sentence in Suetonius begins 'when he had reduced Egypt to a province...'). One might wish to contrast with Alexander's aggressiveness in the *Life* his more cerebral portrayal in the essay: Alexander pictures heroic deeds (ἀνατυπούμενος)[43] to himself, very like Germanicus at Actium; the lyre of Paris is not only to be shown him, but given him, yet he turns it down because he actually already owns (as opposed to would like to see) the lyre of Achilles – the implication being that he already possesses his qualities rather than aspires to them (at 331b he has been described, significantly, as 'most swift-footed', ποδωκέστατος, which reinforces that impression). The decadence of Paris is made very explicit, and so Alexander's refusal to be associated with it can call forth the final comment from Plutarch that this incident shows a philosophical turn of mind. That would be an unexpected comment on the incident as related in the *Life*, I think: the rebuff there seems more prompted by ambition than by philosophic discretion. One might wish to contrast with Alexander's and Augustus' haughtiness the rather puppylike attitude of Germanicus in the Black Sea (*Annals* 2.54.2): he wants to see everything 'cupidine...noscendi' ('in his enthusiasm for knowledge'), and bounds around enjoying it all. But there is also a further significant contrast to be made: Alexander is aggressively defining himself not only as a Homeric-style hero, but as a Hellenic hero (Paris is one of the more oriental characters in the *Iliad*, with his penchant for leopard skins: 3.17); Augustus, on the other hand, is seeking to legitimize his presence in Egypt by appropriating the authority of a previous conquest; Alexander does something similar in appropriating the cultural authority of Midas when he cuts the Gordian knot.[44]

What does an Alexander historian make of these events? Arrian is the best test-case, as the part of Curtius which might have dealt with the Trojan material is lost and Diodorus omits the Gordian knot. Arrian's treatment in both cases is very interesting, though whether it is possible to argue that his account differs from Plutarch's for reasons of genre is another matter: clearly in fact it is not. He deals at some length with Alexander's Trojan activities, including an earlier sacrifice to Protesilaus at Elaeus, but there is no mention of the lyre: instead Arrian elaborates on the remark that Achilles was lucky to have Homer and uses it to introduce his long programmatic statement, the climax of which runs: 'and that is why I venture to claim the first place in Greek literature, since Alexander, about whom I write, held first place in the profession of arms'. Arrian assimilates himself and his work to his subject: Alexander's journey has just truly begun, so Arrian's literary journey is given a second, more impressive, and very Homeric start (compare the second invocation to the Muse in *Iliad* 2).[45] Plutarch's image of the painter in 1.3 conveys the opposite impression of his method: an air of detachment, of looking from outside, which is borne out by the subtle and ambivalent use of anecdote we have observed.[46]

On the Gordian knot, Arrian, in rather Herodotean mode, has a much fuller account of the traditions which lay behind the story of this local conundrum, shaped in the manner of folk-tales to give the impression that Alexander has much in common with Gordius and Midas (the marriage of whose parents is attended by miracles, and who is adopted onto the throne and puts an end to civil strife) and is indeed the one who will be chosen to be lord of Asia. The more detailed and reverential treatment again seems to minimize Arrian's objectivity. Once again, there may be differences in approach between authors, but not observably between genres.

Let us return to Plutarch, and to Greeks and barbarians. After Alexander's firm self-characterization as Hellene in 15, the whole of the rest of the *Life* actually shows him trying to negotiate his identity and preserve his moral status in a shifting series of contact zones. (Not even this, though, can be called uniquely the province of biography: Arrian may strike different notes from Plutarch, but he is just as concerned with Alexander's moral status.) Is he a straightforward conqueror, with a conqueror's style of travel and cultural appropriation, or a more Herodotean traveller, aware of the power of *nomos*?[47] Is his Hellenism aggressive, or of the idealistic kind attributed to him in *Mor.* 329c–d? Whitmarsh argues that he is less and less successful in this attempt as he goes further and further East (2002, 186–92), but I am unconvinced that the *Life* presents a straightforward linear decline of that kind, partly because it seems to me that the text of the *Life* is so constructed as to allow the reader a genuinely ambivalent attitude to the policy of transculturation

289

which he attributes to Alexander (unhistorically, of course).[48] In chapter 45, where Alexander first puts on Persian dress, Plutarch, significantly, suggests two possible motivations, one creditable (and this is put first), one not. He says Alexander put it on: 'either from a desire to adapt himself (συνοικειοῦν) to the native customs, believing that community of race and custom goes far towards softening the hearts of men; or else this was an attempt to introduce the *proskynēsis* among the Macedonians, by accustoming them little by little to put up with changes and alterations in his mode of life.' This is very different from 28, where Alexander treats Greeks and barbarians differently, stressing his supposed divine origin to barbarians, but less so to his fellow Greeks. 'Alexander himself was not foolishly affected or puffed up by the belief in his divinity, but used it for the subjugation of others (καταδουλούμενος)'. These two passages present multiple ambiguities: does treating Greeks and barbarians differently and then seeking to treat them the same represent a decline or a growth in moral wisdom? Is it good or bad to assume the customs of those you have conquered?

A complex passage encapsulates this metaphorically (*Alex.* 35.1–2 and 7–8). Alexander, the distinguished visitor, has the extraordinary properties of naphtha demonstrated to him by the locals (rather like Lucius Memmius' visit to the crocodiles); in a very off-key little sequel a naive young singer volunteers to experiment with the stuff himself and suffers terrible burns – the land, it seems, is actively hostile to one Greek at least. Sansone and Whitmarsh have argued plausibly that this passage looks back to the description of Alexander's fiery nature at 4.2–4, and that, to quote Whitmarsh, 'the heat of the East is inflaming Alexander, whose nature is already highly flammable'.[49]

Both rightly associate the next anecdote with the same train of thought: in Harpalus' garden all Greek plants will grow save ivy. This passage is indeed very important – and it is very strategically placed, introducing the important and recurrent theme of the problems Alexander's men have adapting to life in Asia: but I would question Whitmarsh's conclusion that Alexander's moral status is thereby *necessarily* compromised. Alexander certainly seems to have a natural affinity with this fiery land, and the other Greeks do not, in fact Stephanus is all but destroyed by the naphtha, and Plutarch identifies that substance with the poison Medea used to destroy the Corinthian princess Glauce. But in 4.2–4 the fiery nature of Alexander's make up not only makes him ποτικὸν καὶ θυμοειδῆ ('prone to drink and hot-tempered') it also accounts for the natural εὐωδία ('sweet fragrance') which hangs about him, and that is also associated with the spice-bearing lands which he is to conquer. In other words, Alexander's affinity with the East is intrinsically potentially both destructive and creative: it makes him far more complicated than his

Macedonian companions and leads him into tragic conflicts with those, like Cleitus, who do not share it, but it is also part of his achievement.[50]

There is more to be said about the Harpalus passage, too. It is placed just before Alexander takes possession of Susa and its treasures, which include water brought from the Nile and the Danube and stored 'as a sort of confirmation of the greatness of their empire and the universality of their sway' (36). Harpalus' planting is a parallel attempt at control over the physical substance of the conquered territory (earth and water are tokens of surrender); he tries however to Hellenify what cannot be wholly Hellenified, and this could be read as being as futile an attempt at colonialization as the Persians' captured-water-collection or Coetzee's Cruso obsessively terracing his island, even though he has no seed to plant.

Confirmation that Hellenism is not always to be equated with morality may be found in the next episode: the taking of Persis and the burning of Persepolis in ch. 38, a great act of cultural vandalism which Alexander instantly regrets. Whitmarsh claims that here 'Oriental values are seen to triumph over Greek' and calls Thais 'a barbarizing woman',[51] but the text suggests otherwise: Thais is an Athenian,[52] and her suggestion that the palace should be burned – in revenge for the burning of Athens – is described as being τῷ μὲν τῆς πατρίδος ἤθει πρέποντα, befitting the character of her native country. Alexander's followers join in the 'drunken procession' (κῶμος) which she leads (a Greek concept, κῶμος) because they think it means Alexander wants to go home 'and did not intend to dwell among barbarians'.

Alexander's negotiation of his identity, then, may be an intolerably, impossibly complex task. There is always, in the *Life* and indeed in some modern post-colonial fiction, particularly Kipling (the Strickland stories and *Kim*), the danger that in trying to create a new, transcultural, identity, one may lose one's own.[53]

Alexander's reactions to two landmarks may show a progression in his character, if not (I would suggest) a deterioration.[54] In 37, at Persis, Alexander communes with the fallen statue of Xerxes, but fails to raise it, presumably because his Hellenism ultimately will not allow it, despite his consciousness of Xerxes' 'great-heartedness and virtue' (μεγαλοφροσύνην καὶ ἀρετὴν) (as far as I know, this story does not occur elsewhere). In 69 he puts to death a Macedonian for robbing the tomb of Cyrus, has the inscription on it translated, and muses on the uncertainty of the human condition. The basic story here stems from Aristoboulos and Onesicritus and is also found in both Arrian (6.29.4–30) and Curtius (10.1.22 ff.) as well as Strabo (15.3.7), but those writers are not interested in what Alexander thought on the occasion, but rather in who was responsible and what Alexander did about it, and in any case the significance of the episode is different when it is made the second of a pair of anecdotes. So there is something distinctively Plutarchan about this, if not distinctively biographical.

It seems fair to say that Alexander's reaction in the latter passage is less nationalistically Hellenic and more philosophically Greek than in 37. But at the same time, he is identifying more with the founder of the Persian empire than with a man from Pella: is that not exactly what people like Cleitus and Callisthenes were afraid of (this is not long before he falls out with his veterans over the thirty thousand Persian boys he has had trained)? And if he is a wiser Alexander here than he was, he is also sadder: this is a melancholy part of the *Life*, and the chapter ends with Calanus foretelling Alexander's death before immolating himself. This section is dominated by tombs: Cyrus', the tomb of the Indian, a tourist attraction at Athens (δείκνυται), Hephaestion's in 72. Travel has certainly broadened Alexander's mind, but perhaps something important has also been lost along the way.

VI

So in this biography travel is very carefully used to suggest the tensions in Alexander's character, and in his use of that last pair of passages we can perhaps see something that, if not a defining characteristic of biography, is at least particularly at home there, namely the creation of patterns in the events of a life which can suggest a journey of the soul: for Alexander a morally problematic one, but not for everyone. The moral status of the traveller is not always parlous, though the autocrat is always more morally at risk than the anthropologist. The prototype is epic: Odysseus' original reasons for and mode of travel may have been conquest and booty, and his first action on leaving Troy was to sack another city (*Od.* 9.39–40) but, as Rutherford has shown, he learns wisdom and better ways of interaction with the people he meets as the journey progresses.[55] This was a particularly popular interpretation of the *Odyssey* throughout the imperial period – hence Lucian's parody of it in the *True History*.[56] Herodotus' account of Solon's travels 'on the excuse of seeing the world' (κατὰ θεωρίης πρόφασιν) represents Solon as giving to his host Croesus far more than he gains: and Plutarch's retelling of the story in the *Solon* if anything stresses that aspect.[57] As I have already hinted, despite Plutarch's professed but rhetorical dislike of Herodotus, it seems plausible that he would have approved of Herodotus' own travels (whether or not they actually took place, Plutarch will have assumed they did), and the desire to learn from all sorts and conditions of men which Herodotus evinces.[58]

Plutarch himself was sometimes a cultural tourist: rather surprisingly, he says that he witnessed the violent rituals at Artemis Orthia, and he was also taken to see the battlefield of Bedriacum by Mestrius Florus.[59] And *De Pythiae Oraculis*, it seems to me, provides a very good indicator of what 'proper' sightseeing, according to Plutarch, might be, and also seems to confirm this reading of the anecdote about Alexander and Cyrus' tomb: it is the reaction to what is seen, and the discussion of it in a thoughtfully philosophical manner, especially when what is seen is a site or object which is somehow sacred, that makes for the right kind of travel.

It is interesting to compare this with the activities of Apollonius of Tyana in book iv of the *Life* of that worthy, since one might expect that the biography of a holy man might in this resemble a philosophical work more than an ordinary biography. Elsner has shown how important the presentation of his visits to sanctuaries and temples is in '[constructing] not only those whom Apollonius confronts within the text, but also the author and the reader as potential disciples of the holy man whom the text presents as becoming a god.'[60] There are actually some resonances with Alexander's biography: the sanctuaries Apollonius visits are often those of Homeric heroes, and he goes one better than Alexander in two respects in relation to these Homeric sites: he actually raises a fallen statue (of Palamedes, iv.13) and he conducts an actual conversation in Odyssean mode with Achilles (iv.16) – no messing about with mere possessions, he communes with the man himself.[61] In each case the focus is not as much on Apollonius' reactions to what he sees, as on the reactions of the local inhabitants to him, and indeed in the end he himself becomes the object of pilgrimage.[62] Although we hear a good deal about what Apollonius does and says, the religious instruction he passes on and the reforms he carries out, there is much less decription of his own feelings on seeing these sights than there is in the *Alexander*, let alone in *De Pythiae Oraculis*. The sites he visits still structure the narrative, still help to construct a character for Apollonius, but from an almost entirely external perspective.

On the contrary, perhaps what is most striking about *De Pythiae Oraculis* is that, having taken the trouble to set up the touristic framework for the dialogue, Plutarch then allows the setting to fade out almost completely, as in some Platonic dialogues, once the question of verse oracles comes to the fore (this is foreshadowed right from the start of the dialogue). The characters in the dialogue sit down on the temple steps and completely forget, apparently, where they are, in their absorption in the conversation. They could be anywhere – though that they have arrived at the official centre of the world is clearly relevant – it is discussing philosophy which is important. This is wholly unlike the examples from biography and history we have discussed, where the artefact, even if it is not described (though Cyrus' tomb is actually thoroughly described by Arrian), is essential, not only the hook on which the philosophy hangs, but also the motive power for the narrative. But it is also wholly unlike *De Finibus* 5.1.2 – perhaps a confirmation of Greg Woolf's point that the Greeks define themselves much less in terms of their material culture and much more in terms of their language.[63] The guides in this dialogue function (as one can still sometimes feel they do) as a distraction from the real point of proper sightseeing, namely this philosophical contemplation inspired, not always terribly directly, by the travellers' surroundings. *Sehenswürdigkeiten* become rather *Denkenswürdigkeiten*.

In the *Pericles* (chap. 2)[64] Plutarch takes the same principle further not in an actual account of travel but in an extended metaphor: the visitor's gaze is only valuable if it is the first step towards virtuous action, and for that to be achieved the spectator must not only look, but inquire into the meaning of what he sees. In this context travel is genuinely seen to broaden the mind and enrich the experience, but the traveller must already have the receptivity and the philosophical background to allow his mind to be broadened.[65] Otherwise, like Nancy Mitford's Uncle Matthew, he will only conclude that 'abroad is unutterably bloody and foreigners are fiends'. Uncle Matthew had his reasons, since his only travel abroad had been to the trenches of the First World War; but Plutarch would have thought it better to travel more hopefully, and, above all, more philosophically.

Acknowledgements

A very different first version of this paper was delivered at the 'Greek Romans, Roman Greeks' conference in Lund in June 1998. My perception of the whole topic was greatly enhanced by attending the conference on 'Realities and representations of travel in ancient Greece and the eastern Mediterranean' held at Nottingham in April 2002. I am greatly indebted to the organizers of those conferences and to the audiences in Lund and Dublin for helpful discussion. I am also most grateful (as always) to Chris Pelling and also to Brian McGing, Stuart Murray and Colin Adams.

Notes

[1] De Botton 2002, 20.

[2] On travel writing see e.g. Greenblatt 1991, Pratt 1992, Eisner 1993 (on classical lands), Ghose 1998 and 1998a (specifically on women travel writers), Elsner 2001, esp. 123–4, and Wolff 2003. In classical studies this tendency is perhaps revealed most clearly in the recent upsurge of interest in Pausanias, whose description of Greece, as Elsner has shown, 'combines a representation of the Other (in this case of Greece by a Greek-speaking foreigner, a native of Asia Minor) with the self-accreditation of the text as witness for the Other (in that authentically Greek histories and myths are made to "speak" through and for the Greek monuments...' (Elsner in Alcock, Cherry and Elsner 2001, 5). It might be added that Pausanias is also simultaneously 'Other' in that he is describing the past and interpreting it for his contemporaries, and 'Self' in that he is culturally shaped by that past and emotionally committed to it (as in L.P. Hartley's aphorism from *The Go Between* 'The past is a foreign country: they do things differently

there'). Further on Pausanias see Habicht 1985, Elsner 1992, Arafat 1996, and Alcock, Cherry, and Elsner 2001.

³ For an interesting example of travel creating narrative structure and simultaneously developing the subject (though this phenomenon is almost too obvious and frequent to illustrate: it runs from early epic to the road movie) see Heinrich Heine's *Deutschland. Ein Wintermärchen* (1844), where the experience of travelling through Germany prompts the narrator to reflect on his life and his attitude to Germany and its past, experiencing at different times both sentiment and alienation. Heine's poem shares with Pausanias' accounts the placing of the reader 'in the phenomenological position of traveller' (Elsner in Alcock, Cherry and Elsner 2001, 5).

⁴ Or even earlier: on this motif in the *Epic of Gilgamesh* see van Nortwick 1996, 8–38. For an imaginative and stimulating treatment of travel and its significance in the *Odyssey*, see Dougherty 2001, esp. 3–7 on travel and its association with knowledge in Greek thought.

⁵ That is, history which employs 'biostructure': on this in Cassius Dio see Pelling 1997, 117–44, esp. 118 n. 6, and the introduction to this volume, p. xii with n. 19. The advantages of travel as a theme in a somewhat different type of ancient biography are succinctly put by Elsner 1997, 22–37, esp. 22.

⁶ Travel writing involves a narrator describing what is seen and experienced, travel anecdotes a narrative subject seeing and experiencing, but these are no more different than novels in the first person are from novels in the third person.

⁷ 'Gab es damals Touristen?' asked Regenbogen in his review of Legrand (Regenbogen 1941, 491, quoted in Fehling 1971, 4 n. 17). I think one can say that there were, though the concept requires some investigation. What is a tourist? The *OED* defines it as 'One who makes a tour or tours; *esp.* one who does this for recreation; one who travels for pleasure or culture, visiting a number of places for their objects of interest, scenery, or the like.' An early usage quoted is '*c.* 1800 PEGGE *Anecd. Eng. Lang.* (1814) 313 A Traveller is now-a-days called a Tour-*ist*', which seems to reflect the development of travel for pleasure from necessary travel. This definition points to the main difference between ancient and modern tourism: most ancient tourism is undertaken as part of a journey originally made for other reasons. Redfield (2002, 25) cites three reasons to travel in the ancient world: 'commerce, war, and seeing the sights' – the last being *theōria*, which includes attendance at festivals and games but also what we would consider tourism. Karl-Wilhelm Weeber in his *Neue Pauly* article (10.854–67) includes tourism in his category of educational travel, and also identifies a category which unites attendance at festivals and pilgrimage (Festspieltourismus und Wallfahrten). Rutherford puts his finger on an important point when he stresses that ancient pilgrimage and tourism are very hard to distinguish (Rutherford 2001, 40–52, esp. 41). It is not hard to see that journeys of all kinds can have a touristic component, in both the ancient and modern worlds (how many academics have been to conferences and incidentally also taken a day to be a tourist?). The other striking contrast between ancient and modern tourism suggested by this definition is that in the ancient world scenery *per se* is never the object of *theōria*.

⁸ 'About this time he had the sarcophagus and body of Alexander the Great brought forth from its shrine, and after gazing on it, showed his respect by placing upon it a golden crown and strewing it with flowers; and being then asked whether he wished to see the tomb of the Ptolemies as well, he replied, "My wish was to see a king, not

corpses"' (tr. J.C. Rolfe).

[9] 'After this he viewed the body of Alexander and actually touched it, whereupon, it is said, a piece of the nose was broken off.' (tr. E. Cary).

[10] In particular the gulf between the appearance of his rule as a continuation of the republic in contrast to its true nature as a monarchy: see e.g. Rich 1990, 13–14: Dio seeks 'to expose the gap between appearance and reality and lay bare the true springs of men's actions'.

[11] On this passage see Pelling 1993, esp. 74–6; Woolf 1994, 121 and n. 29.

[12] 'In his dealings with the Greeks, Antony's behaviour was moderate and courteous enough, at least in the beginning, and for his entertainment he was content to attend games and religious ceremonies and listen to the discussions of scholars. He was lenient in his administration of justice, and took pleasure in being addressed as a lover of Greece, and still more as a lover of Athens, where he showered gifts upon the city. But when the people of Megara wanted to show him something to rival the beauty of Athens and invited him to see their senate-house, he duly travelled there and looked it over. Then they asked him to tell him what he thought of it, to which he replied, "Of course it is not very large, but then it is very rotten!" He also had the temple of the Pythian Apollo surveyed so as to complete it: at least he promised the senate that he would do this.' (tr. Scott-Kilvert, adapted).

[13] On the Pillars of Hercules as a vital psychological boundary see Clarke 2001, 95–8 and also 1999, 38–9, 113.

[14] '...was seized with an amazing desire to settle in the islands and live in peace, finished with tyranny and endless wars.' (*Sertorius* 9.1, tr. Scott-Kilvert).

[15] On Sertorius as a misfit and his relationship with barbarians see Mossman, forthcoming. Redfield 2002, 27, acutely remarks: 'The tourist makes no attempt to fit in; he rather accepts a specific social role: that of foreigner. In so doing he shows himself comfortable with his own culture, which is strong enough to sustain him even in his temporary position as outsider... Tourism is thus both a proof and a source of cultural morale.'

[16] Hdt. 1.183: it was coveted by Darius, but then removed forcibly by Xerxes. See Mossman 1991, 103.

[17] *Sulla* 12, cf. 29.

[18] *Sulla* 13–14: fine words but destructive deeds. In the *synkrisis*, however (5.4), his treatment of Athens overall becomes a point in his favour in comparison to Lysander's treatment of the city.

[19] *Marcellus* 21: see Swain 1995, 239–40.

[20] Cicero *Att.* I.6.2 (67 BC): 'Tu velim, si qua ornamenta γυμνασιώδη reperire poteris, quae loci sint eius, quem tu non ignoras, ne praetermittas.' 'If you succeed in finding any *objets d'art* suitable for a lecture hall, which would do for you know where, I hope you won't let them slip.' (tr. Shackleton Bailey). See also I.9.2.

[21] 'And so we all went to Piso's at the appointed time. From there we beguiled with conversation on various subjects the six stades from the Dipylon Gate. When we reached the walks of the Academy, which are so deservedly famous, we had them entirely to ourselves, as we had hoped. Thereupon Piso remarked: "Whether it is a natural instinct or a mere illusion I can't say; but one's emotions are more strongly aroused by seeing the places that tradition records to have been the favourite resort of men of note in former days, than by hearing about their deeds or reading their writings. My own feelings at the

present moment are a case in point. I am reminded of Plato, the first philosopher, so we are told, that made a practice of holding discussions in this place; and indeed the garden close at hand over there not only recalls his memory but seems to bring the actual man before my eyes. This was the haunt of Speusippus, of Xenocrates, and of Xenocrates' pupil Polemo...' This physical visualization, akin to *ecphrasis* but with the same techniques applied to topography, seems to be a very Roman thing (called by Christopher Pelling 'the "gee" syndrome' in undergraduate lectures), also met with in *Aeneid* 2 and 8 and (off-key) in Propertius 4.1.

[22] Alcock 1993, esp. 224–30, Eisner 1993, esp. 101, where he cites Trelawney's account of Shelley's encounter with some Greek seamen: the poet who wrote 'We are all Greeks' in the preface to *Hellas* was unimpressed by the real thing, and strongly felt his own connection with 'the ancient Greek fire' was stronger than theirs. Conversely, see de Botton 2002, 16: 'Des Esseintes ended up in the paradoxical position of feeling more *in* Holland – that is, more intensely in contact with the elements he loved in Dutch culture – when looking at selected images of Holland in a museum than when travelling with sixteen pieces of luggage and two servants through the country itself.'

[23] 'for, as I have pointed out, he was the great-nephew of Augustus and the grandson of Antony, and there his imagination could re-enact mighty triumphs and tragedies...and so, when he had inspected Troy and whatever was venerable there for the vicissitudes of fortune and our origins, he again coasted along Asia' (tr. Grant, adapted). See Goodyear 1981 ad loc. for useful comment on this passage. I agree with him that Germanicus is not emulating Alexander here.

[24] Rutherford 2001, 41.

[25] Strategies for controlling alien space must therefore be evolved: for cartography as a means of appropriating, controlling, and thus defusing the dangers of, alien territory through the exercise of one's knowledge of it, see Ryan 1994. This is perhaps why the earliest known maps are attempts to make sense of the universe as a whole rather than detailed local maps. Whether or not Alexander's bematists employed maps *per se*, their activities too represent an aspiration of control as well as a practical purpose, and as such are forerunners of Agrippa's world map. See *OCD*[3] s.v. maps (Nicholas Purcell).

[26] Tacitus, *Annals* I. 60–2, on which see Woodman 1998, 70–85 and 1988, 168–79 and Pelling 2002, 159–60.

[27] 'Cinematographical' is Woodman's term: 1998, 70, n. 2, with further bibliography.

[28] '*First* there was Varus' camp, testifying to the strength of three legions with its wide area and its headquarters marked out; *then* a half-ruined rampart and a low ditch where the last stricken remnant had obviously gathered. *In the open ground in the middle* there were whitening bones, scattered where they had fled, heaped up where they had fought back. Fragments of weapons and horses' limbs *lay around*, and also skulls fixed to the trunks of the trees. *In the groves nearby* there were barbarian altars at which they had butchered the tribunes and the first-rank centurions.'

[29] 'they recalled that *here* the legates had fallen, that *there* the eagles had been snatched up; *where* Varus had received his first wound, *where* he had found death at the blow of his own unhappy right hand; *on what platform* Arminius had addressed his men, how many gibbets there were for the prisoners, what pits, and how in his pride he had mocked the standards and the eagles.' The emphasis on showing and topography gradually alters in the second half of the sentence, by means of a change in the nature of the indirect questions, to an account of events which left no visible traces and depend on the guides'

memories alone: an impressive effect.

[30] J.M. Coetzee, *Foe* (1986) and Jean Rhys, *Wide Sargasso Sea* (1966); (more melodramatically) Rudyard Kipling, 'The strange ride of Morrowbie Jukes', first pub. in *Quartette* (1885); E.M. Forster, *A Passage to India* (1924).

[31] Pratt 1992, 4.

[32] See Clarke 1999 *passim* on ancient geography and its power to bust genres.

[33] This must be done with care, and the many differences between the ancient and modern imperial experiences borne in mind (see also Mossman, 2005). But though the registers of ancient biography and post-colonial fiction are very different, I still feel that it may be illuminating to create an analogy between the two. As to the historical reality of ancient cultural tourism, the evidence of papyri and *proskynēmata* gives us an insight into this phenomenon at work in Roman Egypt: a papyrus from Tebtunis (P. Tebt. I 33/P. Select. 416) is particularly revealing. It concerns the visit of an important Roman, Lucius Memmius, who is to be given gifts and who will make the publicity gesture of feeding the sacred crocodiles, and be shown the sights. Both Memmius and his hosts apparently benefit from this exercise in terms (at least) of prestige. On travel and tourism in Egypt see Adams 2001, 138–66 and Foertmayer 1989: the *proskynēmeta* from the 'Tomb of Memnon' give an insight into the feelings of those who visited it (see Bernand and Bernand 1960). The 'itinerant temples' discussed by Alcock (1993, 191–8 and see Plut. *Aem. Paull.* 28) are even more remarkable: the temple of Ares, probably originally in Acharnai, was dismantled and reerected in the Agora. Fifth-century architectural elements were privileged over other periods (a practice familiar until comparatively recently in Greek archaeology), and Alcock has argued plausibly that these moving monuments were being dismantled and appropriated in order to place the imperial cult literally in the centre of Athenian life and to give it the legitimacy of the most glorious period of Athens' past.

[34] See Schmidt 1999, esp. 1–9 on the state of the question; Bowie 1991 suggests that Plutarch is more complex than his contemporaries; see also e.g. Swain 1996, 350–1 and Whitmarsh 2001, 20–6. See also Mossman, 2005. On Greek and Roman readers see Pelling 2002 chap. 12, esp. 215; Swain 1996, 139–45; on Roman readers see Stadter 2002, 123–35; Duff 1999 rightly stresses Plutarch's multivocal qualities and his refusal to take sides, or to be simplistic, at e.g. 302–3 and 309.

[35] 'Captive Greece took her savage conqueror captive': Horace, *Ep.* 2.1.156.

[36] See Duff 1999, 14–22.

[37] Mossman 1988.

[38] On this see Romm 1992, 82–120, Spencer 2002, esp. 138–63 and 205–18, and Aerts 1994, 30–8.

[39] 'Then, going up to Ilium, he sacrificed to Athena and poured libations to the heroes. Furthermore, he anointed the gravestone of Achilles with oil, ran a race by it with his companions naked, as is the custom, and then crowned it with garlands, pronouncing the hero happy in having, while he lived, a faithful friend, and after death, a great herald of his fame. As he was going about and viewing the sights of the city, someone asked him if he wished to see the lyre of Paris (Alexandros). "For that lyre", said Alexander, "I care very little; but I would gladly see that of Achilles, to which he used to sing the glorious deeds of brave men."' (tr. Perrin, slightly adapted).

[40] Mossman 1988, 87.

[41] Perhaps, indeed, necessary, at least for a Roman readership: see Spencer 2002, 4:

'The ultimate joke in all this must be that the "original" Alexander is not Alexander the Great, but *Paris of Troy,* wife-stealer and anti-hero *par excellence.* So the first "Alexander" who *did* accomplish a westward smash-and-grab raid lurks, ever-contemporary, behind all successive models.'

[42] Plutarch, *Moralia* 331d–e; and see Hamilton 1969, xxiii–xxxiii, Schmidt 1999, 272–99, Hartog 2001, 150–60, esp. 153–4, and Whitmarsh 2002, 176 and 179–80.

[43] This rare word, which implies a strongly visual mental picture, strikingly occurs twice in the space of a few chapters in this essay, here and at 329b6, where Zeno is said to foreshadow the idea of a world community which is then realized by Alexander. In the earlier passage combining the verb with the phrase ὄναρ ἤ εἴδωλον ('a dream or image') brings out the pictorialism of the verb even more strongly. See also Dio Chrysostom 12.26, where the pictorial element is also strong, even though the sense of the word is slightly different.

[44] Plut. *Alex.* 18.2.

[45] On this passage see Moles 1985, 162–8, Marincola 1989, 186–9. On second prefaces in general see Conte 1992, 147–59: the stress on the increased greatness of the theme is typical. Pelling (forthcoming) argues convincingly that Plut. *Caesar* 15–17 can be seen as a second preface: again, no formal difference between biography and historiography in this respect.

[46] 'Accordingly, just as painters get the likenesses in their portraits from the face and the expression of the eyes, in which the character shows itself, but take very little account of the other parts of the body, so I must be permitted to devote myself rather to the signs of the soul in men, and by means of these to portray the life of each, leaving to others the description of their great contests.' On this important passage see Duff 1999, 14–22 and Pelling 2002, 112 n. 37, 259–60, 276–7 and elsewhere in this volume. Contrast Arrian's emphasis on deeds in 1.12.2–4.

[47] Redfield 2002, 26–7, 29, 39, 47–9.

[48] See especially Badian 1958 and Bosworth 1980, esp. 3–4, with further bibliography.

[49] Sansone 1980, 63–74 and Whitmarsh 2002, 189–90. (The quotation is on p. 190).

[50] Sansone 1980, 69–70 and 73, also stresses the power of naphtha, and of Alexander, for good or ill, but argues that only self-control allows Alexander to turn his fiery nature to good account. While this is a good Plutarchan message, and consistent with the theme of the education of Alexander and the presentation of him earlier in the *Life* in anecdotes such as the taming of Bucephalas (on which see Stadter 1996 and Whitmarsh 2002, 180–1), it seems to me that there is a less straightforwardly moralistic aspect which is worth stressing as well.

[51] Whitmarsh 2002, 187. Sansone 1980, 69–70, sees this incident as illustrating 'the extraordinary effort required of "cholerics" to keep their fiery natures under control.'

[52] Sansone 1980, 69 notes that the man Athenophanes, who suggests the experiment with naphtha, is also said to be Athenian.

[53] See e.g. Saïd 1987, 40–1.

[54] Plutarch, *Life of Alexander* 37.3, 69. 2–3 (see also Mossman 1988, 92–3 and 1991, 116–7 but both are inadequate); and cf. 'the Indian's Tomb' at 69.4.

[55] Homer, *Odyssey* 1.3; Rutherford 1986, 145–62.

[56] Rutherford 1986, 145, with further bibliography; on Lucian see Georgiadou and

Larmour 1998, 5–22.

[57] Herodotus 1.29–30 (Solon); Plutarch, *Life of Solon* 25.4–28.4.

[58] On the reality or otherwise of Herodotus' travels see Fehling 1971; Plutarch's attack on him (*Mor.* 854e ff.) is based on other grounds. On Herodotus' travels and their links with Solon's see Redfield 2002, 30: 'Solon, I would suggest, appears in Herodotus' narrative as a kind of *alter ego* of the narrator himself.'

[59] Plutarch's own sightseeing: *Lycurgus* 18. 2 (the rituals at Artemis Orthia); *Otho* 14 (the battlefield at Bedriacum).

[60] Elsner 1997, 25–8 (the quotation is on p. 28).

[61] He also goes even further East than Alexander does: on this see Elsner 1997, 28–32, esp. 30 n.49.

[62] Elsner 1997, 27.

[63] Woolf 1994, 127–30.

[64] On this passage see Duff 1999, 34–45. It is no accident that the objects viewed are the Zeus at Olympia and the Hera of Argos, that is images of divinity which can give only a poor impression of the reality in Platonic, and also Plutarchan, terms.

[65] It is not impossible that Plutarch, influential in Enlightment education, lies behind some of the issues canvassed in 18th century debates about the value or otherwise of the Grand Tour. This passage, for example, from Martin Sherlock's *New Letters from an English Traveller* (1781, 147–9) has a Plutarchan ring to it: 'Nothing is so useful as travelling to those who know how to profit by it. Nature is seen in all her shades, and in all her extremes. If the mind of the traveller be virtuous, it will be confirmed in the love of virtue, and in abhorrence of vice... The traveller has, besides, the advantage of making continual comparisons, which strengthen his judgement extremely...' (quoted from Black 1992, 292).

Bibliography

Adams, C.

    2001   '"There and back again": getting around in Roman Egypt', in C. Adams and R. Laurence (eds.) *Travel and Geography in the Roman Empire*, London, 138–66.

Aerts, W.J.

    1994   'Alexander the Great and ancient travel stories', in Z. von Martels (ed.) *Travel Fact and Travel Fiction: Studies on fiction, literary tradition, scholarly discovery and observation in travel writing*, Leiden, 30–8.

Alcock, S.E.

    1993   *Graecia Capta: The landscapes of Roman Greece*, Cambridge.

Alcock, S.E., Cherry, J.F. and Elsner, J. (eds.)

    2001   *Pausanias: Travel and memory in Roman Greece*, Oxford.

Arafat, K.W.

    1996   *Pausanias' Greece: Ancient artists and Roman rulers*, Cambridge.

Badian, E.

    1958   'Alexander the Great and the unity of mankind', *Historia* 7, 425–44.

Bernand, A. and Bernand, E.

    1960   *Les inscriptions grecques et latines du Colosse de Memnon*, Cairo.

Black, J.
1992   *The Grand Tour in the Eighteenth Century*, Stroud.
Bosworth, A.B.
1980   'Alexander and the Iranians', *JHS* 100, 1–21.
Botton, A. de
2002   *The Art of Travel*, London.
Bowie, E.L.
1991   'Hellenes and Hellenism in writers of the early Second Sophistic', in S. Saïd (ed.) Ἑλληνισμός. *Actes du Colloque de Strasbourg 25–27 oct. 1989*, Leiden, 183–204.
Clarke, K.
1999   *Between Geography and History: Hellenistic constructions of the Roman world*, Oxford.
2001   'An island nation: re-reading Tacitus' *Agricola*', *JRS* 91, 94–112.
Conte, G.B.
1992   'Proems in the middle', *YCS* 29, 147–59.
Dougherty, C.
2001   *The Raft of Odysseus: The ethnographic imagination of Homer's* Odyssey, Oxford.
Duff, T.
1999   *Plutarch's Lives: Exploring virtue and vice*, Oxford.
Eisner, R.
1993   *Travelers to an Antique Land: The history and literature of travel to Greece*, Michigan.
Elsner, J.
1992   'Pausanias: A Greek pilgrim in the Roman world', *Past and Present* 135, 3–29.
1997   'Hagiographic geography: travel and allegory in the *Life of Apollonius of Tyana*', *JHS* 117, 22–37.
2001   'Describing self in the language of the Other: Pseudo(?)-Lucian at the temple of Hierapolis', in S. Goldhill (ed.) *Being Greek Under Rome: Cultural identity, the Second Sophistic and the development of empire*, Cambridge, 123–53.
Fehling, D.
1971   *Die Quellenangaben bei Herodot*, Berlin.
Foertmeyer, V.A.
1989   *Tourism in Graeco-Roman Egypt*, PhD thesis, University of Princeton.
Georgiadou, A. and Larmour, D.H.J.
1998   *Lucian's Science Fiction Novel* True Histories: *Interpretation and commentary*, Leiden.
Ghose, I.
1998   *Women Travellers in Colonial India*, Delhi.
Ghose, I. (ed.)
1998a   *Memsahibs Abroad: Writings by women travellers in nineteenth-century India*, Delhi.
Goodyear, F.R.D. (ed.)
1981   *Tacitus*: Annals, (II): *Annals 1. 55–81 and Annals 2*, Cambridge.

Greenblatt, S.
 1991   *Marvellous Possessions: The wonder of the New World*, Oxford.
Habicht, C.
 1985   *Pausanias' Guide to Ancient Greece*, Berkeley.
Hamilton, J.R. (ed.)
 1969   *Plutarch:* Alexander, Oxford.
Hartog, F.
 2001   *Memories of Odysseus: Frontier tales from ancient Greece*, Edinburgh.
Hutchinson, J. and Smith A.D. (eds.)
 1996   *Ethnicity*, Oxford.
Marincola, J.M.
 1989   'Some suggestions on the proem and "second preface" of Arrian's *Anabasis*',
         JHS 109, 186–9.
Moles, J.L.
 1985   'The interpretation of the "second preface" in Arrian's *Anabasis*', *JHS* 105,
         62–8.
Mossman, J.M.
 1988   'Tragedy and epic in Plutarch's *Alexander*', *JHS* 108, 83–93, repr. in B. Scar-
         digli (ed.) *Essays on Plutarch's 'Lives'*, Oxford, 209–28.
 1991   'Plutarch's use of statues', in M.A. Flower and M. Toher (eds.) *Georgica: Greek
         studies in honour of George Cawkwell*, BICS Supplement 58, 98–119.
 2005   '*Taxis ou barbaros*: Greek and Roman in Plutarch's *Pyrrhus*', *CQ* 55.2,
         498–517.
 Forthcoming   'The misfits: *Paideia* and society in *Sertorius-Eumenes*'.
Nortwick, T. van
 1996   *Somewhere I Have Never Travelled: The hero's journey*, Oxford.
Pelling, C.
 1993   'Tacitus and Germanicus', in T.J. Luce and A.J. Woodman (eds.) *Tacitus and
         the Tacitean Tradition*, Princeton, 59–85.
 1997   'Biographical history? Cassius Dio on the early Principate', in M.J. Edwards
         and S. Swain (eds.) *Portraits: Biographical representation in the Greek and
         Latin literature of the Roman Empire*, Oxford, 117–44.
 2002   *Plutarch and History*, Swansea.
Pelling, C. (ed.)
 1988   *Plutarch:* Life of Antony, Cambridge.
 Forthcoming   *Plutarch:* Life of Caesar.
Pratt, M.L.
 1992   *Imperial Eyes: Travel writing and transculturation*, London.
Redfield, J.
 2002   'Herodotus the tourist', in T. Harrison (ed.) *Greeks and Barbarians*,
         Edinburgh, 24–49.
Regenbogen, O.
 1941   Review of Ph.-E. Legrand, *Hérodote. Introduction et I*, *Gnomon* 17, 486–
         520.
Rich, J.W. (ed.)
 1990   *Cassius Dio: The Augustan settlement, (Roman History 53–55.9)*, Warminster.

Romm, J.S.
    1992   *The Edges of the Earth in Ancient Thought*, Princeton.

Rutherford, I.
    2001   'Tourism and the sacred: Pausanias and the traditions of Greek pilgrimage', in Alcock, Cherry, and Elsner (eds.) *Pausanias*, 40–52.

Rutherford, R.B.
    1986   'The philosophy of the *Odyssey*', *JHS* 106, 145–62.

Ryan, S.
    1994   'Inscribing the emptiness: cartography, exploration and the construction of Australia', in C. Tiffin and A. Lawson (eds.) *De-Scribing Empire: Post-colonialism and textuality*, London.

Said, E.W.
    1987   *Introduction to 'Kim'*, London.

Sansone, D.
    1980   'Plutarch, Alexander, and the discovery of Naphtha', *GRBS* 21.1, 63–74.

Schmidt, T.S.
    1999   *Plutarque et les barbares: la rhétorique d'une image*, Leuven.

Stadter, P.A.
    1996   'Anecdotes and the thematic structure of Plutarchean biography', in J.A. Fernandez Delgado and F. Pordomingo Pardo (eds.) *Estudios sobre Plutarco: aspectos formales*, Salamanca, 291–6.
    2002   'Plutarch's Lives and their Roman readers', in E.N. Ostenfeld (ed.) *Greek Romans and Roman Greeks*, Aarhus.

Spencer, D.
    2002   *The Roman Alexander: Reading a cultural myth*, Exeter.

Swain, S.
    1990   'Hellenic culture and the Roman heroes of Plutarch', *JHS* 110, 126–45, repr. in B. Scardigli (ed.) *Essays on Plutarch's 'Lives'*, Oxford, 229–64.
    1996   *Hellenism and Empire: Language, classicism and power in the Greek world*, AD 50–250, Oxford.

Whitmarsh, T.
    2002   'Alexander's Hellenism and Plutarch's textualism', *CQ* 52.1, 174–92.

Wolff, A.
    2003   *How Many Miles to Babylon?: Travels and adventures to Egypt and beyond, from 1300 to 1640*, Liverpool.

Woodman, A.J.
    1988   *Rhetoric in Classical Historiography: Four studies*, London.
    1998   'Self-imitation and the substance of history: Tacitus, *Annals* 1.61–5 and *Histories* 2. 70, 5.14–5', in *Tacitus Reviewed*, Oxford.

Woolf, G.
    1994   'Becoming Roman, staying Greek: Culture, identity, and the civilizing process in the Roman East', *PCPS* 40, 116–43.

17

'THIS IN-BETWEEN BOOK':
LANGUAGE, POLITICS AND GENRE
IN THE *AGRICOLA*

Tim Whitmarsh

Tacitus' *Agricola* remains a bamboozling text. For the most recent commentator, 'the *Agricola* is full of paradox and ambiguity',[1] and it is hard to disagree. Not only is there a puzzle about its genre, but also – and more congenially to the temper of recent scholarship – its political positioning is difficult to gauge. If nothing else, the sheer range of ideological 'messages' that scholars have claimed to disencrypt, from a fawningly pro-Trajanic celebration of conformism to a powerfully anti-imperial stance, demonstrates the intensity of the problem. How do we read this challenging text? What does is stand for? What does it mean? *How* does it mean?

The architecture of the text is eloquent. The *Agricola* begins with a preface, which proclaims the aim of the work to be the commemoration of the deeds and character of Tacitus' father-in-law; such an enterprise was impossible under Domitian (when imperial jealously meant that eulogists risked death), but is now possible under the benign Trajan (1–3). The major portion is devoted to the life of Agricola, narrated chronologically, including detailed description of Britain and the governor's exploits there, culminating with the victorious battle of Mons Graupius and Domitian's recognition of his success; his peaceful death is briefly narrated (4–43). The *exordium* (44–6) returns to the eulogistic mode, again contrasting Domitian's viciousness with Trajan's beneficence, and hoping for eternal remembrance of his father-in-law.

The structure is, then, ring-cyclical, the description of Britain flanked on either side by Roman matters, commemoration of the virtuous, and the Trajan-Domitian polarity. Two critical positions on the macro-structure of the *Agricola* are now widely accepted. First, the narrative of Agricola's life vicariously explores Tacitus' own public profile: in flagging up the virtuous life of one who succeeded under the Flavians, the author is also defending himself against the dangerous charge of collaboration with the now-damned regime of Domitian.[2] The policy of strategic adoption of quietism and leisure (*quies et otium*), of 'loyalty and the middle path' (*obsequium ac modestia*), which allows one to maintain integrity without self-sacrifice, is throughout implicitly contrasted with the ostentation and vanity of oppositional martyrs such as Thrasea Paetus and Helvidius Priscus.[3] Second, the British episodes are thematically unified with the framing Roman episodes. The rebellious but unsuccessful Britons – and in particular the Caledonian chief Calgacus, who is accorded a thundering oration before the battle of Mons Graupius (30–2) – are subtly associated with Thrasea and Helvidius.[4] Both camps speak out against oppression; both stand for *libertas* (*libertatem senatus*, 2.2; *initium libertatis toti Britanniae fore*, 30.1; cf. 30.4, 32.4).[5] Calgacus opposes *servitus* (30.1, 31.2 [*bis*]),[6] the word Tacitus uses to describe the condition under Domitian (3.3). Most intriguingly of all, Calgacus argues against the quietist policy emblematized by Domitian and Tacitus: 'in vain will you try to escape their arrogance through obsequiousness and moderation' (*quorum superbiam frustra per obsequium ac modestiam effugias*, 30.4).

It is possible to read the *Agricola* as a manifesto for political quietism, dramatizing the art of survival amid oppressive conditions under the light of the Trajanic ideology of *obsequium*.[7] But this reading involves simplification of the critical issues. In particular, if we accept *both* the two critical positions characterized above, Agricola emerges as a dissonant figure: at Rome he is subjected to imperial power, which he negotiates through quietism; in Britain, on the other hand, he is the *agent* of that power, and it is upon the subject Britons that quietism is urged. There is, for sure, nothing inherently problematic about a provincial governor reproducing the symbolic authority of the emperor: provinces can easily be viewed as synecdochic of the empire as a whole, and the governor as a surrogate *princeps*. But in the context of a moralizing biography that explores the ethics of power, the correlation of Agricola with *Domitian*, the tyrant *par excellence*, is profoundly troubling. This crux, I suggest, condenses the central critical problems raised by the *Agricola*.

This chapter will approach the problem as one of discourse. Insufficient attention has been given to the politicization of language itself in the *Agricola*. Like all of Tacitus' works, the *Agricola* focuses closely and carefully upon the role of veiled language, irony and insinuation;[8] indeed, while the affinities with the ethnographic *Germania* and the historiographical *Annals* and *Histories* are often commented upon, there has been little awareness of the links with the *Dialogus*, with its interrogation of the relationship between the quality of expressive language and political conditions. How – this will be my central question – do we interpret a text that seems at once ideologically committed and rhetorically ambiguous?

I am aware that terms such as 'ambiguity' raise hackles. Virgil's *Aeneid* is (still) the central focus for vigorous debates between 'optimists', who see it as necessarily pro-Augustan, and 'pessimists', who perceive a subjacent layer of ideological resistance, indexed by tensions and lacunae at the 'surface-level' semantic and thematic level.[9] Underlying this *querelle* is a profound mistrust of alternative critical positions: on one side a suspicion of the modish quest for indeterminacy and subversion; on the other, resentment of a too-swift recourse to (what is arbitrarily constructed as) 'historical structure' as a means of closing off interpretative avenues. I do not propose to intervene here in general debates about the relationship between language and political structure. Certainly, my argument depends upon a view of the principate that can accommodate the possibility of subversive language, or at least subversive interpretations of potentially subversive language. But the reading I propose is specific to the *Agricola*; and more than that, it seeks to offer a coherent interpretation of the *work* performed by ambiguity within this text.

Genre

What kind of text is the *Agricola*? What interpretative framework does it presuppose in the reader? An older generation of scholars worried themselves about its apparent liberties with genre: this is a *vita* sloping into encomium via funeral oration, but also integrating lengthy episodes that replicate the generic features of Tacitus' other works (the ethnography of the *Germania*, the historical narrative of the *Histories* and *Annals*).[10] Even the title is uncertain: most MSS have *De Vita Iulii Agricolae*, one has *De Vita et Moribus Iulii Agricolae*. If this question has largely been bracketed by recent criticism, it is largely because we are now, in general, less mechanistic about genre. As Conte puts it, 'genres are to be conceived <of> not as recipes but as strategies; they act in texts not *ante rem* or *post rem* but *in re*'.[11] Perceived hybridity in a text is now less a problem to be resolved than the marker of powerful authorial inventiveness.

But despite the fluidity and dynamism of genre in sophisticated formulations like Conte's, it remains (as indeed Conte argues) a crucial communicative device. Certainly, genre is not a Platonic form: there is no final constitutive analysis of 'biography', any more than 'elegy' or 'epic'; still, texts depend for their legibility – or, depending upon the 'openness' of the text, their *legibilities* – upon their ability to manipulate interpretative frameworks received by their readers.[12] What matters is less whether an inert description of the *Agricola* resembles (for example) that of a Nepotian or Sallustian *vita*, and more how the text evokes, and strategically manipulates, its readers' awareness of precedents.

The text begins as follows: 'The transmitting of the deeds and character of conspicuous men to posterity...' (*clarorum virorum facta moresque posteris tradere...*), a comforting statement of generic positionality, every word a burnished husk of tralatitious piety. The allusion to the beginning of Cato's *Origines* further underlines the generic trajectory towards high-minded moralism.[13] But this is a booby-trapped clause; and the detonation follows instantly. The sentence is completed with parsimonious mock-generosity: '...not even in our time has the age, indifferent though it be towards its own, neglected...' (*ne nostris quidem temporibus quamquam incuriosa suorum aetas omisit*, 1.1). The pleasing language of tradition and continuity (*posteris tradere*), of the immanence of Roman virile ethics, is immediately and brutally undercut by the emphasis on the fragility of that tradition. 'Our time' demands (and, sure enough, gets) a contrast with 'the age of our forebears' (*apud priores*), when virtue was encouraged and appreciated.

The question of generic identification is raised in the first sentence, only to be strategically frustrated. We (think we) know what a text recording the *clarorum virorum facta moresque* would look like;[14] but do we know what it would look like if written in and for 'an age so hostile to virtue' (*tam saeva et infesta virtutibus tempora*, 1.4)? The strain placed upon biographical form here is, then, carefully tied to issues of political and cultural decline.

As paradigms of biographical form, Tacitus presents the case of the *vitae* of those men of integrity and principle who opposed imperial despotism:

> legimus, cum Aruleno Rustico Paetus Thrasea, Herennio Senecioni Priscus Helvidius laudati essent, capitale fuisse, neque in ipsos modo auctores, sed in libros quoque eorum saevitum.

> We read [or: we have read] that when Thrasea Paetus was praised by Rusticus Arulenus and Helvidius Priscus by Senecio Herennius, it was a capital offence, and fury pursued not only the authors, but even their books too.   (2.1)

This sentence further elaborates the text's metagenerics. The reading *legimus* has been suspected, but Turner's recent defence (on palaeographical and other grounds) is convincing: 'we read' immediately cues a self-reflexive twist, so that Tacitus is referring not solely to Thrasea and Helvidius (another father-in-law / son-in-law pair, interestingly) as comparators for Agricola, but also to Rusticus and Senecio as comparators for his own literary project...and also, in a seemingly infinite proliferation of dangerous discourse, to writers about Rusticus and Senecio.[15] Comparison (*synkrisis*) is central to ancient biography, and though the *Agricola* lacks any formal articulation of the principle, Tacitus does (as McGing argues) construct a strong implicit opposition between the first-century 'martyrs' and their biographers, on the one hand, and himself and his subject, on the other.[16] Tacitus and Agricola are survivors, who know how to surf the waves of imperial politics. Agricola will prove to be a canny (*gnarus*) reader of life in Nero's reign, for example, when 'inaction was a form of wisdom' (*inertia pro sapientia fuit*, 6.3, specifically under Nero);[17] he has mastered the strategic deployment of quietism (*quies*) and leisure (*otium*).[18] Tacitus is implied, by analogy, to understand the art of tactical discourse. Unlike Rusticus and Senecio.

Near the end of the text, Tacitus states that 'it is possible for great men to exist even under bad emperors' (*posse etiam sub malis principibus magnos viros esse*), contrasting Agricola's life and death with those who 'have won fame offering no service to the state except by their self-seeking death' (*in nullum rei publicae usum nisi ambitiosa morte inclaruerunt*, 42.5).[19] This implicit ethical contrast between Agricola and empty oppositionalists – Thrasea and Helvidius are again strongly hinted at – can be shown to intersect, *prima facie*, with a broader critique of empty theatricality in Tacitus' works. In *Annals* 15, Seneca's showy death (15.60–2) is offset by the quietly virtuous exit of the unnamed soldier (15.67).[20] And indeed, Thrasea's public exit from the senate in *Annals* 14 is presented as more ostentatious than efficacious: he brought danger upon himself, but 'did not bring about the beginning of liberty for others' (*ceteris libertatis initium non praebuit*, 14.12.1). From this perspective, the *synkrisis* that begins the *Agricola* is quickly deciphered into a qualitatively loaded polarity between dutiful integrity and 'a code of conduct which is admirably, but wastefully, courageous'.[21]

Synkrisis, however, presents more complex interpretative challenges than this reading suggests.[22] The pattern across Tacitus' works suggests that Thrasea and Helvidius are not straightforwardly negative; rather they are controversial figures who inspire different judgements in different audiences, and in conspicuous places the narrator sides with them against imperial oppression.[23] The author's practice in other works is not, for sure, an authoritative guide to his practice in this one; but his generous, albeit in places equivocal, treatment of Thrasea and Helvidius elsewhere should at least give us pause before we assume that they necessarily occupy the negative pole in the *Agricola*'s syncritical structure. More particularly, it poses the question of whether they can be read as richer, more complex and provocative figures.

Like much biography, the *Agricola* repeatedly refers to the 'praise' (*laus*: 42.5, 46.2; *laudare*: 2.1, 3.3) of its subject. Encomium invites polar thought: the praise-blame axis suggests an interpretative template, a fixed, schematic distribution of subjects into good and bad. But it also, of necessity, draws attention to the 'constructedness' of this distribution, and to this extent every encomium exposes its own arbitrariness. If our earlier argument is right, and the *Agricola* begins by dramatizing its own inability to serve as a 'proper' biography, then we may begin to question the text's own rhetorical polarities. What authorizes the view that Agricola and Tacitus occupy the unequivocally positive pole in this contrast? Indeed, should we be thinking at all in terms of a crude opposition between 'good' and 'bad'? Does Tacitus the 'hidden author' subvert the surface-level position of Tacitus the narrator?[24]

Commentators have often been troubled by the *synkrisis*. Turner alludes to 'Tacitus' apparent self-criticism for failing to live up to the examples provided in real life by Rusticus and Senecio';[25] McGing, downplaying the interpretative problems with cautious understatement, to his 'slightly ambiguous' attitude towards Thrasea and Helvidius, in that 'he admires their courage, but is critical of their "political extremism"'.[26] By alluding so early on to the lives of Thrasea and Helvidius (which are also subtly invoked later in the text, as we shall see), the *Agricola* powerfully magnifies its own narrative palimpsests. The heroic resistance to tyranny is the tale that the *Agricola* never tells – or, rather, repeatedly tells us that it is not telling. Indeed, this is arguably a tale of the sordid complicity and collaboration undertaken by quietists. In a passage near the end, Tacitus writes that it was 'our hands' (*nostrae manus*) that imprisoned the younger Helvidius (the equally obstreperous son of the earlier mentioned), 'we' (*nos*) who separated Mauricus and Rusticus,[27] 'us' (*nos*) whom Senecio spattered with his innocent blood (45.1).[28] The first-person plurals are given particular emphasis by proleptic positioning in the sentences, and by the tricolonic polyptoton. Can the text be read as a self-subverting critique of Tacitus' and Agricola's complaisance? And as a sad indictment of its own inability to live up to anything that we – the implied readership familiar with established paradigms of senatorial virtue – might call a *vita*?

Addressing Trajan

The contrast between Tacitus and his rival biographers is, in the first instance, one of historical circumstance. Rusticus, Thrasea, Senecio and Helvidius, and the authors of their *vitae*, lived in the bad old days of imperial depravity; Tacitus in the Trajanic 'new age'. This ideologically charged opposition, I suggest, is played out through a self-reflexive examination of the politics of the voice. When is it right to speak out?[29] Is silence ever justified in the face of evil? Agricola, as we have seen, operates a policy of tactical *quies* (6.3, 42.2), and there is a calculated analogy here with the previous silence of the author. Under Domitian, there could be no voice: those who burned the biographies of Thrasea and Helvidius 'perhaps thought that the voice of the Roman was being destroyed in that fire' (*scilicet illo igne* vocem *populi Romani...aboleri arbitrantur*, 2.2);[30] 'even traffic in speaking and listening was banned, thanks to the informers' (*adempto per inquisitiones etiam loquendi audiendique commercio*, 2.3); 'we should have lost our very memory too with our voice, had it been as much in our power to forget as to be silent' (*memoriam quoque ipsam cum* voce *perdidissemus, si tam in nostra potestate esset oblivisci quam tacere*, 2.4).[31] It is this final word of the last-cited sentence, *tacere*, that activates the pun. Tacitus is the 'silent man', the one who kept silent throughout all those years.

Under Trajan, however, it is possible, finally, to speak. Trajanic rhetoric proclaims the dawning of a 'new age' of tolerance and openness,[32] and Tacitus' narrator concurs:

> Nunc demum redit animus; sed quamquam primo statim beatissimi saeculi ortu Nerva Caesar res olim dissociabilis miscuerit, principatum et libertatem, augeatque quotidie felicitatem temporum Nerva Traianus, nec spem modo ac votum securitas publica, sed ipsius voti fiduciam ac robur adsumpserit, natura tamen infirmitatis humanae tardiora sunt remedia quam mala; et ut corpora nostra lente augescunt, cito extinguuntur, sic ingenia studiaque oppresseris facilius quam revocaveris.

> Now, at last, the spirit returns. But although immediately, in the first rising of the blessed age, Nerva Caesar has mixed things once unmixable, namely the principate and liberty, and Nerva Trajan increases daily the happiness of the times, and public safety has introduced not only hopes and prayers, but the robust confidence in those prayers, nevertheless, in the nature of human weakness, cures come more sluggishly than ills. Just as our bodies grow slowly, but die suddenly, so you will oppress genius and talent more easily than you will call it back again. (3.1)

Nunc demum redit animus ties together the breaking of Tacitus' silence, the return to health of the biographical genre, and the dawning of a *novum saeculum* of imperial tolerance and liberty: the *animus* belongs simultaneously to him, to literature, and to Rome. Everything suggests a sudden and radical break with the past. The novelty of the Nervan and Trajanic renaissance is pleonastically marked (*primo statim...ortu*),[33] and sharply distinguished from the indeterminate *olim* that preceded it. But like all imperial accessions, Trajan's innovation must be at once a return to the same:[34] *redit animus*. The new age is – paradoxically – also a return to a previous age, even if the parameters of that earlier age are left (necessarily?) ambiguous: the Augustan period? The republic? The pre-Gracchan republic?

The *Agricola*, then, mimics Trajanic propagandistic idiom. The sudden, total contrast between Flavian and post-Flavian, advocated across a range of texts in the period (most notably Pliny's *Panegyricus*),[35] commits to the vision of the *novum saeculum* as a new phase of imperial openness, when – to anticipate the words Tacitus will later write in the preface to the *Histories* – 'you can think what you like and say what you think' (*sentire quae velis et quae sentias dicere licet*, 1.1.4). But the rhetoric of a sudden, clean break with Flavianic excess is also specifically problematized. Old habits die hard: the sudden, total change suggested by 'now at last' (*nunc demum*) is qualified by the sluggishness of the remedies (*tardiora...remedia*) for maleficence. How different *is* the Trajanic *nunc* from its predecessors? Earlier in the prologue, Tacitus has referred to the present as *nunc* ('now as I prepare to narrate', nunc *narraturo mihi*, 1.4), but has glossed it in Sallustian fashion as 'a time so savage and hostile to virtue' (*tam saeva et infesta virtutibus tempora*, 1.4). No hint *there* of any ethical differentiation between the rules of Trajan and his predecessor.[36] It is of course arguable that the distinction should be drawn between the general tenor of the times (*saeva et infesta virtutibus*) and imperial morality – but this is not a necessary conclusion, nor is it one that Tacitus follows elsewhere.[37] Indeed, the apophthegmatic four-worder, *nunc demum redit animus*, is sprung upon the reader with almost indecent haste, as though correcting a faux-pas.[38]

What is more, the *nunc* that marks the long-awaited appearance of a positive imperial ethics is immediately qualified by the following words. The reference to the *beatissimum saeculum* is carefully sited in a protracted concessive clause ('although...'), which suspends the punch – the 'nevertheless' (*tamen*) clause – for an agonizing length. The effect is reinforced by the syntax, which devolves the simplistic, celebratory four-worder into a complex, periodic sentence. Like a promise that immediately rescinds itself (*sed...*), ramifying with a raft of qualifications. And what is more, the rhetoric of the new age is itself old hat. Any accession can parrot the language of *felicitas*, *beatitas*, *securitas publica* and the *novum saeculum* – even Nero's.[39] As Syme (who nevertheless cleaves to the belief that Trajan represented a firm break) states, this new age was only the latest in a series of attempts to make a break with besmirched imperial pasts:

> The dawn of a new era in the Roman Commonwealth was no longer a novelty. Not only had three emperors, Augustus, Claudius and Domitian, celebrated and exploited the *Ludi Saeculares*, reckoning centuries by the computation that happened to suit their convenience. Any reign could use the language of the golden years. With the growth of monarchy each ruler tended to annex the age and call it his own... Bright hopes had been blasted before, and conventional enthusiasm discredited, when the annunciation of a new era of felicity followed conspiracy or civil war, when the early promise of a principate faded, disclosing black despotism.[40]

Every new age is a cliché: its rhetoric of newness will be defused by awareness of the fundamental iterability of that rhetoric. So how real is the Trajanic revolution? How meaningful? And how real is Tacitus' supposed bursting into free speech? Is this perhaps, rather, the master of survival up to his old tricks again, mimicking imperial dogma to save his skin? After all, there are different ways of playing the quiet man: *tacitus* means not only 'silent', but also 'tacit', 'subtle', 'allusive'.

At the conclusion of the preface, Tacitus returns to the contrast between

Trajan and Domitian. After alluding to the latter's *saevitia*, the deaths and the *silentium*, he closes the introductory part of the text with the following, tantalizing litotes:

> Non tamen pigebit vel incondita ac rudi voce memoriam prioris servitutis ac testimonium praesentium bonorum composuisse. hic interim liber honori Agricolae soceri mei destinatus, professione pietatis aut laudatus erit aut excusatus.

> I shall not, however, be displeased to have composed a record of our former slavery and testament to our present boons, albeit with unrefined and immature voice. This in-between book, devoted to my father-in-law, will either be praised or excused for its profession of piety. (3.3)

The reference to his 'unrefined and immature voice' (*incondita ac rudi voce*, 3.3) can be taken simply as a topical *captatio benevolentiae*,[41] or (albeit over-literally) as a reference to the author's inexperience in the sphere of literature.[42] Following on from the reference to Domitianic *silentium*, however, it also suggests that the author's literary inexperience is linked to the youthfulness of the Trajanic new age. This interpretation has implications for *interim liber* in the next sentence.[43] This phrase is usually taken as proleptic of his 'mature' works of history: the *Agricola* is 'in-between' in the sense that it serves as a bridge between his career as a mature politician and his career as a mature writer. But in the context of the politicized reading of *incondita ac rudi voce*, it takes on new meaning: the book is also liminal because Trajan's new age is liminal, inchoate. Uncertain, even.

The *synkrisis* between Trajan and Domitian recurs at the end of the text, where Tacitus announces the compensation for Agricola: if he did not live to see 'this light of the most beautiful era and Trajan as emperor' (*hanc beatissimi saeculi lucem ac principem Traianum*), still he did not see the worst of Domitian's reign (44.5). It is clear that the polarity of the two is designed as a major structuring principle in the text. But as we have also seen, much of the work of structuring is left to the reader. Domitian is certainly to be read as an unmitigated evil; but what are we to make of Trajan? How committed is Tacitus to the ideology of the new age? Can we tell for sure? As Solon might have said, call no emperor good until he is dead. *Synkrisis* is a rhetorical provocation, not an interpretative solution.

Early years

The narrative of Agricola's early life further foregrounds the difficulty of interpreting inward intentions, and the concealing effects of social protocol. It begins with one small section of education and early years (4), before proceeding straight into the 'rudiments of military life' (*prima castrorum rudimenta*, 5.1) in Britain. His hyperaccelerated upbringing perhaps bespeaks his good parts: he is impelled into adulthood by a 'good, wholesome nature' (*bonam integramque naturam*) and a wholly complementary upbringing. But it also strategically focuses attention away from Agricola's inner psychology – and in doing so, draws attention to this diversion strategy. He is pointedly distanced from the destructive forces that hamper other men: he is molly-coddled and embosomed by his mother (*in…sinu indulgentiaque*, 4.2), and protected from the perversities of sinners (*arcebat eum ab inlecebris peccantium…*, 4.3). This narrative of seclusion and protection also positions the *Agricola* generically: this *vita* will be light on psychology, heavy on militarism. But it also prefigures a notable feature of the narrative: this will be a text of surfaces, of actions, of social codes rather than psychic depths. We never get underneath Agricola's skin – no one does. The biographical subject is emblematic of the text as a whole: with neither Agricola nor *Agricola* is it possible to read the real character underlying.

Yet he does have one weakness, an overindulgence in philosophy:

> Memoria teneo solitum ipsum narrare se prima in iuventa studium philosophiae acrius, ultra quam concessum Romano ac senatori, hausisse, ni prudentia matris incensum ac flagrantem animum coercuisset. scilicet sublime et erectum ingenium pulchritudinem ac speciem magnae excelsaeque gloriae vehementius quam caute adpetebat. mox mitigavit ratio et aetas, retinuitque, quod est difficillimum, ex sapientia modum.

> I remember how he himself used to recount that in his first youth he had drunk too keenly of enthusiasm for philosophy, beyond what is permitted to a Roman – and a senator too – had his mother's prudence not held back his enflamed, blazing spirit. No doubt his lofty, upright character sought after the beautiful vision of great and exalted glory with more ardour than common sense. Soon reason and maturity softened him, and (the most difficult thing of all) he retained a sense of moderation in his wisdom. (4.4–5)

The danger of adolescence – that *lubrica aetas* – is a topos of Roman biography;[44] and that Agricola's temptation is limited to philosophical zeal marks the intensity of the encomiastic operation. But the passage does not simply function at the 'realist' level of biographical narrative. It also serves as another self-reflexive generic signpost, a loop back to the now-carbonized *vitae* of philosophical martyrs mentioned at 2.1, and (I have argued) ever-present countertexts offsetting the narrative of the *Agricola*. 'Wisdom' (*sapientia*; cf. 2.2, *expulsis…sapientiae professoribus*) and the desire for glory: these qualities trammel the subject towards the biographical paradigm of a Helvidius Priscus or Thrasea Paetus, 'blazing' like their books. It is, however, Agricola's fate (the recurrent motif of the *vita*) always to turn back before reaching the logical limit of senatorial virtue. The references to what is 'permitted' to a Roman senator, to the 'moderation' of ambitions, hint at the glass ceiling that prevents Agricola from being what he could have been, and the *Agricola* from being the *vita* it would (should?) have been. *Cautio*, 'common sense', the survival instinct, both reins in the idealism of Agricola's youth, and censors his son-in-law's text. Neither says what it wants to say. But in dramatizing the process of erasure, Tacitus also signals the presence of lacunae in his own discourse.

Thinking of Britain

And so on to Britain. Tacitus now sidelines psychoprofiling and recasts the *vita* as constitutively defined by military acts. Again, it is conspicuous just what kind of biography this is *not*. Alexander, Pompey, Caesar...all had the power of self-determination, and hence the power of self-magnification.[45] But under the principate, icons of conquest are monopolized by the emperor; Trajan, in particular, laid claim to Alexander.[46] Britain represents Agricola's opportunity to make something of his *vita*; but also the ultimate test to his strategic self-fashioning under the jealous eye of the emperor.

Britain is, as we are reminded throughout the *Agricola*, the *terminus* of the world, the *finis*, the *ne plus ultra* (although, as Katherine Clarke reminds us, it is ambiguously placed, sited both within and beyond the Ocean that marks the frontier of the empire).[47] Yet Britain does not simply represent the 'other': it is also a space for exploring issues that cut to the heart of Romanness.[48] The Britons are the last survivors against luxury, 'like men whom long peace has not yet softened' (*ut quos nondum longa pax emollierit*, 11.5).[49] An equivocal sentiment: their resistance to luxury may be admirable, but it is doomed to submission by a natural entelechy (marked by *nondum*).[50] Two different, irreconcilable temporal modalities are at work here: Romanization represents linear time, the unstoppable march of progress; primitive time, on the other hand, is defined by cycles of repetition (the conceit that, as in the *Germania*, allows for the representation of an ethnos as changeless, immune to history).[51] Progress is simultaneously empowering and destructive.

Equally equivocal is the Britons' distinctive *ferocia*.[52] At one level, this supports the close equation of this people with bestiality and nature.[53] At the battle of Mons Graupius, the Britons' destruction is compared to the hunting of animals, both by Agricola (33.4, 34.2) and the narrator (37.4). Fighting the Britons, Agricola states, involves fighting 'against the very natural order' (*adversus ipsam rerum naturam*, 33.2).[54] Against this 'fierceness', civilized technologies and organizational prowess invariably win out.[55] But the language of *ferocia*, as so often in Tacitus,[56] mixes positive evaluation in with the negative. As a counterpoint to the enervating luxuries instilled by Romanization (esp. 21, on which see below), *ferocia* also represents the primal, rugged manliness that is destroyed by civilization and progress. (Though it can be recaptured in circumstances: in warfare, Roman soldiers can show *ferocia*, cf. 27.1 and 37.6.)

Perhaps the most famous section of the *Agricola* is the scintillating critique, placed in the mouth of the Caledonian chief Calgacus as he addresses his troops at Mons Graupius (30–2), of the imperialist policy practised by the Roman 'pirates of the earth' (*raptores orbis*, 30.5). 'Words of a concentrated power which I find without equal', Raymond Williams once said.[57] Calgacus' speech, as observed at the start of this chapter, powerfully promotes *libertas* over *servitium*, decrying the policy of *obsequium ac modestiam* (30.5) – which, of course, characterizes Agricola's approach to Domitian. At issue in this conflict is not simply British freedom or servitude, but also two different, indeed exclusive, models of relating to oppressive power: the submissive *obsequium* practised by Agricola, and the feisty resistance shared by Thrasea and Helvidius, on the one hand, and Calgacus on the other. Calgacus is not simply a barbarian, but also a reminder of the ethics once possessed by Romans: '[o]ld Roman values are located at the edge of the earth…and as far from Rome as one can imagine'.[58]

Calgacus is, however, an equivocal figure, exemplifying simultaneously the heroism of the resistant and the military and organizational inferiority of the barbarian. Indeed, in the context of the rigorously progressivist construction of Romanizing time, British primitivism is fundamentally ambiguous: both a lack, an absence of the values of civilization and technologies of militarism,[59] and a plenitude, an integrity that will be shattered by the inevitable defeat. From this perspective, it has been tempting to some to view him as a necessary, if in a sense attractive, victim of war, who offsets but in no sense challenges Agricola's policy. There are, for sure, many parallels for the doomed but romanticized barbarian: Tacitus commonly puts heroic, republican-sounding rhetoric (in particular the opposition between *libertas* and *servitium*) into the mouths of marginal figures, only to allow the Roman military machine to crush them;[60] and, indeed, earlier writers too gave barbarians anti-Roman speeches similar to Calgacus' charge against the *raptores orbis*.[61] But the existence of parallels in no sense neutralizes the interpretative challenge. Tacitus has carefully presented the case from both sides. Indeed, Calgacus is given a much longer and more refined performance than any of Tacitus' other idealized barbarian orators; and this specific speech, unusually, is reported in direct speech.[62]

Calgacus' address is balanced by Agricola's, which is shorter, more sober, and more straightforwardly protreptic (33.2–34).[63] The dyad, evoking the rhetorical exercise (established since at least Antiphon's *Tetralogies*) of 'speaking on both sides of the case' (*in utramque partem disserere*), constitutes another challenging *synkrisis*:[64] Agricola is militarily dominant, but who wins the ethical battle? The agonistic structure invites the reader to judge for herself or himself, and many have indeed been tempted to offer judgements. Classicists are not, in general, keen to cast themselves as romantics; the dominant trend in recent years has been to view Agricola as the victor in the debate. The primary evidence is the stated response of the two camps to the two speeches. The Britons 'received the oration eagerly, as is the way with barbarians, with wailing and singing and discordant shouts' (*excepere orationem alacres, ut barbaris moris, cantu fremituque et clamoribus dissonis*, 33.1). In the case of the Romans, on the other hand, 'the soldiers' ardour burst out while he was still speaking, a great eagerness attended the end of his oration, and immediately they rushed to arms' (*adloquente adhuc Agricola militum ardor eminebat, et finem orationis ingens alacritas consecuta est, statimque ad arma discursum*, 35.1). Two ways of expressing 'eagerness' (*alacritas*), one disorderly and explicitly marked as barbarian, the other idealized and typically Roman. 'Where the modern reader may find Calgacus exciting and Agricola dull', writes Braund, 'the moralistic Roman reader would probably consider Calgacus rash and Agricola sound...in Tacitean terms, if not our own, it is Agricola who wins the duel'.[65] But 'probably' bespeaks the problem with an argument based upon hypothetical constructs of implied readerships. What of the non-'moralistic' Roman reader – that is to say, one who opposes the tyranny of order, discipline and power? Can we imagine such a figure? And – more seriously – does not the dyadic structure invite the reader to ponder *both* sides? The Stoicizing contrast between order and disorder, for sure, presents *one* interpretative paradigm; but this stands (as we shall see presently) in troubling tension with other, more disruptive paradigms.

In terms of the content of the speeches, another recent critic has attempted to find implicit authorial condemnation:

> Calgacus' speech evokes the values of the Roman republic, but these, shown up by Tacitus as generally undesirable in certain contexts, do not lead one necessarily to admiration of Calgacus; instead they lead to a destabilized reading that calls into question a defiant republicanism as opposed to a compliant *obsequium* under the principate.[66]

The second proposition does not follow from the first. It is true enough that the reader is not *necessarily* led to admiration of Calgacus (though '*generally* undesirable *in certain contexts*', my emphasis, seems self-contradictory); but it does not follow that we are led to condemn him. Despite the rhetoric of indeterminacy ('destabilized', 'calls into question'), this is a decidedly closed reading of a genuine interpretative dilemma. Which is not to say Rutledge's reading is wrong (i.e. discounted by textual indications), but that in privileging only the 'imperialist' perspective, and hence imposing a tactical closure, it remains, of necessity, only a partial account. Indeed, the argument that the *Agricola* is fully committed to the ideology of *obsequium* periodically implodes, incapable of bearing the weight that is placed upon it. Rutledge notes the 'inconsistency in Tacitus' text where Calgacus is simultaneously idealized and disparaged';[67] but then he downplays the 'idealization', to the extent that the inconsistency evaporates and Calgacus becomes a figure marked, 'in the final analysis',[68] as unequivocally negative.

Raymond Williams, whom I have already cited, rather self-consciously favours the romantic Calgacus.[69] And indeed, evidence for authorial validation can be found. The latter's celebrated claim 'where the Romans make desolation, they call it peace' (*ubi solitudinem faciunt, pacem appellant*, 30.6) seems to be born out in the narrator's ecphrastic description of the aftermath of battle: 'a vast silence everywhere, lonely hills, buildings smoking in the distance, no one to meet the scouts' (*vastum ubique silentium, secreti colles, fumantia procul tecta, nemo exploratoribus obvius*, 38.2).[70] That the silence is 'vast' (*vastum*) implies both the panoramic totality of the ecphrastic sweep and the horrific de*vast*ation.[71] Arguably, the *silentium* created by Agricola's devastation is a horrific metastasis of his policy of tactical *quies* (cf. 21.1, where he attempts to accustom the Britons to *quieti et otio*); more chillingly, it evokes the *silentium* imposed by Domitian at Rome.[72] From this perspective, Calgacus' speech represents humanity inveighing righteously against the *raptores orbis*, a category that incorporates Domitian and Agricola alike.

It is, moreover, possible to recoup Calgacus even as a surrogate for the authorial persona. Calgacus is one of only two figures in the *Agricola* who penetrates surfaces, who perceives the mismatch between rhetoric and 'reality' (the other being Domitian, as we shall see presently): 'they use false names: stealing, butchering, pillaging they call *imperium*, and where they make desolation, they call it peace' (*auferre trucidare rapere falsis nominibus imperium, atque ubi solitudinem faciunt, pacem appellant*, 30.7). The identification and exposure of catachrestic signification, of *falsa nomina*, is a classic Tacitean strategy.[73] In addition, the awareness of twin names, one Roman and one native, is constructed in the *Germania* and *Agricola* alike as a prerogative of the ethnographer (though the case cited above is, for sure, anomalous: it is a question not of different languages, but of different perspectives accommodated within the same language).[74]

In the *Agricola*, the predominant example of narratorial identification in misnaming comes in the summation of an earlier ethnographic digression: 'this [Romanization] was called *humanitas* among the inexperienced, when it was part of their slavery' (*idque apud inperitos humanitas vocabatur, cum pars servitutis esset*, 21.3). This statement has also been much discussed: is Tacitus critiquing Roman imperial strategy?[75] Or mocking British naïveté?[76] In the light of our discussion so far, however, it is questionable whether we should be thinking in terms of a single target, and (in contingency) a static, pellucid distinction between praise and blame. For sure, the cultural inferiority of the Britons is identified. Arguably even, it is their inability to negotiate servitude in a cultured way that is decried: the 'inexperienced' (*inperitos*) Britons might be contrasted with Agricola, '*experienced* in obsequiousness, learned in mixing pragmatism with honour' (*peritus obsequi, eruditusque utilia honestis miscere*, 8.1). But read closely, the latter sentence is not unequivocal praise: the knowing remoulding of Horace's famous apophthegm (*omne tulit punctum, qui miscuit utile dulci, Ars Poet.* 343) serves to illustrate the linguistic (and hence political) warping whereby Horatian literary artfulness (which the reader must share, in order to identify the allusion) has been transfigured into Tacitean obsequiousness. Moreover, the *servitus* imposed by Agricolan policy is itself problematic, correlating as it does the imperialist strategy of Agricola with that of Domitian (2.3, 3.3). The means may be subtler, but the end result is the same.

The ethical clash between Roman and British is not open to resolution either way. No reader can locate a comfortable ethical position in the rhetorical *agon* between Calgacus and Agricola: to side with the former is to oppose Rome and civilization, to side with the latter is to collaborate with the Domitianic cause and its violent extirpation of heroic values.

We might note in conclusion that, although the *Agricola* is primarily a commemoration of military triumph, the final triumph is not achieved, and the general's conquests are impermanent.[77] After the notable success of Mons Graupius, he returns to Rome, leaving the highlands of Caledonia still unstable. *We* know this – how much Tacitus' contemporaries would have known about the immediate abandonment of the Roman frontier in northern Scotland, we can only guess.[78] One thing is clear, though: Hibernia remains unconquered (24). Tacitus claims to have heard his father-in-law imagining its conquest: 'if Roman arms were ubiquitous, and freedom were, as it were, removed from view...' (*si Romana ubique arma et velut e conspectu libertas tolleretur*, 24.3). But despite the assertion that it would be an easy feat, Hibernia's shores are not broached. The empire is not complete; and the rhetorical construction of Agricola as the conqueror of the world's limits is, or can be read as, provocatively subverted. Even in the sphere of militarism, Agricola arguably comes up short, hoisted with the petard of encomiastically overstated underachievement.

Silence and repute

Agricola is, as we have noted repeatedly, characterized by quietism: *quies et otium* constitute his tactical response to imperial jealousy (6.3, 42.1; cf. *otium*, 40.4); *quies et otium* is what he seeks to foist upon the conquered Britons (21.2; cf. *otium*, 11.5). Elsewhere in Tacitus, these qualities are far from positive virtues. *otium* is (as indeed at *Agr.* 16.4) usually destructive of order, discipline and moral values.[79] *quies* (the word and cognates occur some 94 times in Tacitus) generally refers to the absence of war, sometimes in the positive sense of calm and order,[80] but often with the implication of the pacification of disorderly subject peoples.[81] Read in conjunction with Maternus' speech that closes the *Dialogus*, indeed, Agricola's policy of *quies et otium* looks decidedly unflattering. 'The long peace of the present period and the continual leisure of the people...had also tamed eloquence itself, just as they had everything else' (*longa temporum* quies *et continuum populi* otium...*ipsam quoque eloquentiam sicut omnia alia pacaverat*, *Dial.* 38.2). Rhetoric is not a 'leisurely and quiet matter (otiosa *et* quieta *re*, 40.2; cf. 36.2, rhetoric can not exist in a *quieta* state); it is a product of licence (*licentia*), which the foolish call freedom (*libertas*), stirring up the masses without any compliance (*sine obsequio*, 40.2).[82] There are no good orators, only those 'experienced in obsequiousness before the ruler' (*in obsequium regentis paratos*, 41.3). It is impossible to enjoy at once great fame and great quiet (*magnam famam et magnam quietem*, 41.5). Though it remains difficult to determine whether the *Dialogus* or the *Agricola* is the prior text, it is an attractive proposition to read Maternus' speech – with its apparently close textual echoes – as a critique of the ethics of the *Agricola*.[83] Both Agricola and Tacitus would, by this token, be rhetorically ennervated.

The *Dialogus* does not straightforwardly validate Maternus' argument (it concludes without explicit resolution of the debate); and, indeed, this later speech famously presents an apparent clash with the same speaker's earlier performance, which is *prima facie* supportive of the emperor.[84] Moreover, Maternus' critique of the etiolating effects of *otium* are already subverted by Aper's observation that attacks on *otium* are motivated more by 'the innate malice of humans' (*humana malignitas*) than by accurate perception (18.5). Nevertheless, whatever its problematic status within the *Dialogus*, this second argument of Maternus' dramatizes a position that directly opposes Agricola's, and that of the narrator of the *Agricola*.

But the intertextuality works equally well in the opposite direction.[85] Unlike the submissive lethargy practised by those attacked by Maternus, and exceptionally within the Tacitean corpus, Agricola's *quies et otium* is self-delib-erated, tactical and provisional. Furthermore – and this is the most striking case of the *Agricola* 'correcting' Maternus – the claim that it is impossible to enjoy at once great fame and great quiet (*magnam famam et magnam quietem*, *Dial.* 41.5) is specifically subverted. After Mons Graupius, Agricola turns to 'tranquillity and leisure' (*tranquillitatem atque otium*, 40.4), but the times are 'such as not to allow there to be silence about Agricola' (*tempora quae sileri Agricolam non sinerent*, 41.2). A striking paradox: the general's tactical *quies* results not in *silentium* but in a proliferation of discourse.

The fame of Agricola's deeds (*fama rerum*, 46.4) is a central concern in this text, which presents itself as one (the most important) of many machineries of commemoration – as a result of which, 'Agricola, narrated and transmitted to posterity, will survive' (*Agricola posteritati narratus et traditus superstes erit*, 46.4). But Agricola's *fama* is throughout subject to the paradox described in the previous paragraph: he becomes talked about because he keeps his quiet. Under Nero, at any rate, 'there is no less danger from good *fama* than from bad' (5.4); Agricola understands the system, artfully succeeding in gaining fame, though 'not even fame...did he seek by displaying his virtue, or by art' (*ne famam quidem...ostendanda virtute aut per artem quaesivit*, 9.5). Even after his first stint in the province, Agricola shows an impressive ability to leave the laurels to others:

> nec Agricola umquam in suam famam gestis exultavit; ad auctorem ac ducem ut minister fortunam referebat. ita virtute in obsequendo, verecundia in prae-dicando extra invidiam nec extra gloriam erat.

> Nor did Agricola ever exult in the fame earned by his deeds; he referred them to the author and leader fortune, like a subordinate. And so by virtuous compli-ance and humility in self-promotion he lacked envy without lacking glory.
>
> (8.3)

The paradox is signposted by careful use of balance and antithesis (*virtute in obsequendo* :: *verecundia in praedicando* // *extra invidiam* :: *extra gloriam*): arresting style is a medium for insinuating the cultural-political perversity of the times.[86] 'Deeds' – *gesta* – are of central issue in the *Agricola*, which (as we have noted) presents the *vita* as an aggregate of actions, not as the workings of a psyche. But the memorialization of *gesta* brings us into potential conflict with the representational factory pumping out imperial *res gestae*. By referring his *gesta* to fortune as the 'author and leader', Agricola defers to a powerful authority figure – a *dux* with *auctoritas* – who is not the emperor, but shares his attributes.[87] What sort of a gesture is this? It depends on how you translate *ut*: does Agricola refer his *gesta* to fortune, 'in that he is' (*ut*) a subordinate?[88] Or does he knowingly, artfully, assume a pose 'like' (*ut*) a subordinate? The way we answer this question has implications for the way we construe Agricola (and Tacitus too), as craven lackey or virtuoso survivor.

And again after the subjugation of Anglesey, a parallel passage:

> nec Agricola prosperitate rerum in vanitatem usus, expeditionem aut victoriam vocabat victos continuisse; ne laureatis quidem gesta prosecutus est, sed ipsa

dissimulatione famae famam auxit, aestimantibus quanta futuri spe tam magna tacuisset.

> Nor did Agricola use this pattern of success for self-exultation, proclaiming his expedition, his victory, or that he had kept in hand those already subjected; nor did he even follow up his deeds with letters adorned with laurels. But thanks to this concealment of fame he increased his fame, for those who reckoned how great his hopes for the future were when he had been silent about such great things. (18.7)

This allusion to the *fama* achieved by Agricola's *gesta* operates, certainly, at the narrative level; but as so often in Tacitus' later writings, the response of an internal audience constitutes a metadiscursive prompt, a cue to think about our own act of reading. In this specific context, the reader is nudged to read these early successes as anticipating (*futuri spe*) greater later; but also, to read the *fama* begun here as anticipating the climactic commemoration in which we are participating now, as reader. At one higher level of abstraction, the passage also serves as an invitation to consider Agricola as a self-reflexive figuring of the author. Self-restraint speaks louder than ostentation; Tacitus' own *dissimulatio* speaks louder than more showy imperial critiques. This subtext is indexed by the use of the neon verb *tacere*, laced with innuendo (as we have seen) from the very start of the *Agricola*.

Certainly, Agricola's *dissimulatio famae*, or Tacitus' commemoration of it, can be interpreted as a critique of imperial *gesta*. 'Agricola never avidly intercepted deeds effected through others' agency' (*nec Agricola umquam per alios gesta avidus intercepit*, 22.4) – an oblique snipe at the emperor's standard appropriation of military success? Nor does the subversion latent in Agricola's broadcast quietism escape Domitian, who proposes a sharply political reading of the *vita*. The emperor's reaction to his devastating victory over the Caledonians at Mons Graupius serves to bring about a personal interpretation – albeit by a marked, not to say problematic, figure – of Agricola's significance as a political icon:

> Hunc rerum cursus, quamquam nulla verborum iactantia epistulis Agricolae auctum, ut erat Domitiano moris, fronte laetus, pectore anxius excepit. inerat conscientia derisui fuisse nuper falsum e Germania triumphum, emptis per commercia, quorum habitus et crines in captivorum speciem formarentur: at nunc veram magnamque victoriam tot militibus hostium caesis ingenti fama celebrari. id sibi maxime formidolosum, privati hominis nomen supra principem attolli: frustra studia fori et civilium artium decus in silentium acta, si militarem gloriam alius occuparet.

> This course of affairs, though exaggerated by no boasting words in letters from Agricola, as usual with Domitian, was received with joyous countenance but anxious heart. He was conscious that his recent false triumph from Germany

had been mocked, given that he had purchased some slaves on the market then done up their clothes and hair to resemble vanquished prisoners. But now, he reflected, a real victory was being famously celebrated, and a great one too, with so many thousands of foes slaughtered. This was a source of great fear to him, that the name of a private citizen should be raised above the emperor; in vain would public speaking and the glory of peaceful arts have been silenced, he thought, if another should usurp military glory. (39.1–3)

If Domitian is indeed a *lector in fabula*, then he is no doubt a shrewd and accomplished one, honed as his skills are by the same hypersensitive paranoia that all experts bring to bear. What is particularly gripping about this passage, however, is its narratological anomalousness, which leads the reader into new and uncomfortable territory. Tacitus here introduces a new distinction, between external presentation (*fronte laetus*) and inner thoughts (*pectore anxius*).[89] The *Agricola*, as we have said, is largely a text of surfaces, and this is particularly true in narratological terms. There is little or no pause for character-bound focalization.[90] Here, however, we have a rare depiction of cognition in action, and certainly unparalleled in its detail and length. Although the mode of reading proposed here is certainly problematized, anchored as it is to the unsavoury character of Domitian (and syntactically held at a distance, by the use of indirect speech, signalled in the translation by 'he reflected...he thought'), it also offers instruction in a certain way of reading, intellectual guidance toward the real political bite of the text. Agricola's achievements (and Tacitus' commemoration of them) are not to be read simply as triumphant; they also have powerful implications for the emperor's monopolization of encomiastic capital.

The 'wrong' reading of Agricola's modest *vita* is also dramatized, in a passage that follows hard on the heels of that just cited:

ceterum uti militare nomen, grave inter otiosos, aliis virtutibus temperaret, tranquillitatem atque otium penitus hausit, cultu modicus, sermone facilis, uno aut altero amicorum comitatus, adeo uti plerique, quibus magnos viros per ambitionem aestimare mos est, viso aspectoque Agricola quaererent famam, pauci interpretarentur.

But so that he might moderate his reputation (which leisured civilians found troubling) for soldiery with other virtues, [Agricola] drank deep of tranquillity and leisure: he was modest in dress, easy in conversation, accompanied by only one friend or another, to the extent that most people (who tend to evaluate great men by the criterion of ambition), when they saw and scrutinized him, wondered how he had acquired his fame, and few interpreted the situation. (40.4)

Drawing back, characteristically, from the extreme, Agricola seeks to 'moderate' his name/fame; once again the paradox, the self-conscious attempt to control public image through the evasion of reputation. But the heavily-loaded contrast between the receptions by *plerique* and *pauci* ups the stakes, constructing a model of (social, political, intellectual) distinction in the reading of Agricola. The majority wonder about his *fama* (or, at the level of metaliterary: why is Tacitus bothering to commit *this* to posterity?); the few *interpret*, realizing that (for Agricola and Tacitus alike) discreet self-fashioning is now an integral part of the art of life. This passage also, of course, constitutes a challenge to the reader: how do *you* take Agricola? And while the surface-level narrative steers us towards the 'proper' reading, the subtextual insinuation always points to alternative – albeit vulgar – interpretative avenues.[91]

In these passages that deal with Agricola's fame, the syncritical contrast between quietism and ostentation is still powerfully operative. Agricola's fame, staged as subtler but more permanent, stands in contrast to the immediate fame of Helvidius and Thrasea, massive celebrities in their lifetimes but denied perpetual remembrance by the destruction of their commemorative machinery. But as we have stressed throughout, *synkrisis* does not simply establish inert poles of contrast; it also points up – and thus exposes, even interrogates – the processes that manufacture difference. In laying bare the rhetorical premises for the arrogation of fame to Agricola (one kind of reader prefers this kind of celebrity, another prefers another), he also reveals the arbitrariness of the phenomenon.

Conclusion

The *Agricola* is an ambiguous text. It dramatizes a position of quietist *obsequium*, enacts a rhetoric of compliance; but in doing so, it points up the array of choices, exposes the roads not taken. For Agricola and Tacitus alike, 'the selection of a particular kind of conduct implied the deliberate rejection of another kind'.[92] The quietist policy is continually energized by its dynamic, syncritical polar opposite, the aggressive confrontation with the despot. The two positions are reciprocally constitutive: 'moderation' could not exist without 'excess', 'heroic resistance' could not signify without 'collaboration'. The *Agricola* does not simply promote one particular perspective on imperial power; it continually, repeatedly, defines and redefines that perspective in (tense, complex, embattled) relationship with its dyadic partner.

The political ambiguities of the *Agricola* do not, I have argued, spring from any 'figured speech' or 'doublespeak'. 'Figured speech', as Ahl presents it, presents two different messages, one superficial and one deeper and truer;[93] 'doublespeak', as Bartsch presents it, 'carries different meanings according to the nature of its audience'.[94] Both imply that there is a fixed, secure, finally identifiable meaning that is appropriate to the audience in question. I have argued that *Agricola*, at any rate, confronts all readers with difficult and unsettling choices. It is a discomforting, challenging read; a text that seems to promise a guide to virtuous life under the principate, but stages instead the disturbing compromises involved in pursuing such a life. It is, as I have said, not a counterideological text, in the sense of offering an underlying critique of the dominant ideology; but nor is it a straightforwardly pro-ideological text, in the sense of unqualified propagandizing for the regime. Galinsky has suggested that 'the real power of propaganda now is considered to lie in "its capacity to conceal itself"';[95] the *Agricola*, on the other hand, repeatedly exposes, defamiliarizes, denaturalizes the ideology of *obsequium* by pointing up the lurid seductions of oppositionalism and the complaisance of collaboration. The relationship between the *Agricola* and the dominant ideology is, I think, best expressed by adapting Althusser's words on Balzac and Tolstoy:

> The fact that the content of the work of Balzac and Tolstoy is 'detached' from their political ideology and in some way makes us 'see' it from the *outside*, makes us 'perceive' it by a distantiation inside that ideology, *presupposes that ideology itself.*[96]

The effect of struggle within the text, of ambiguity, tension and ideological warfare, is a result of the author's ideological commitment. The *Agricola* is not a commentary from without upon alien institutions or practices, but itself a significant move in the intensely fought struggle for ideological self-representation. At the same time, however – and by virtue, primarily, of its sheer quality as a composition – it also represents the tensions that lie at the heart of the ideology of quietism. And, hence, the tensions underlying an encomiastic biography of a quietist. As Agricola strives for, but fails to reach, the final frontiers of the world; so the *Agricola* attacks the ultimate limits of biographical superhero narrative only to turn back upon itself, assessing its own adequacy for the task, and hence gesturing towards its own (brilliant) generic failures.

Notes

[1] Clarke 2001, 109.

[2] Bastomsky 1985, 393: Agricola is 'a type of *alter ego*' of the author; Petersmann 1991, 1805–6 on 'die Vernetzung von Autor und Figur des Werkes'.

[3] Cf. 6.3 (*quiete et otio*), 21.1 (*quieti et otio*), 42.1 (*quietem et otium*); 8.1 (*peritus obsequi*), *moderatione* (42,4), *obsequium ac modestiam* (42.5; cf. 30.3); *obsequium* also at 8.3, 30.3, 42.4; *moderatio* at 5.1, 7.3, 42.3. Thrasea and Helvidius are named at 2.1; and there is a heavy allusion to them near the end, when Tacitus contrasts Agricola's virtuous but compliant life and death under the principate with the 'self-seeking death' (*ambitiosa morte*) that gains fame in the eyes of the masses (42.5).

⁴ Esp. Liebeschuetz 1966, 135–6; McGing 1982, 22–3; Rutledge 2000, 87–8; Clarke 2001, 105–6.

⁵ On the changing meaning of *libertas*, see esp. Wirszubski 1950. Kennedy 1992 argues that the word is radically indeterminate; cf. however the historicist response (arguably overhastily dismissive) by Galinsky 1994, 304–5 (and implicitly at Galinsky 1996, 54–7).

⁶ Cf. *servientium*, 30.3, 32.5, *servituri*, 31.1, *servorum*, 31.1, *servorum…conservis* (31.3).

⁷ So already Syme 1958, 125: 'The treatise…is concerned with much more than the life and laudation of Tacitus' father-in-law. It is a document of Roman political literature, a manifesto for the Emperor Trajan and the new imperial aristocracy'.

⁸ See most prominently Henderson 1998; O'Gorman 2000.

⁹ For a survey, see Harrison 1990; and for more recent contributions, Perkell 1994, Galinsky 1994, Kallendorff 1999, Thomas 2000. Kennedy 1992 and Martindale 1993 present the case for a reception-based approach, whereby all such ascriptions are the function of the reader's agenda.

¹⁰ The issues are sharply summarized by Liebeschuetz 1966, 126; see further Petersmann 1991, 1786–94.

¹¹ Conte 1994, 112.

¹² See especially the classic discussion at Culler 1974, 131–60.

¹³ 'The thoughts of famous and great men should stand out no less in leisure than in work' (clarorum hominum *atque magnorum non minus otii quam negotii rationem exstare opportere*, fr. 2 Chassignet = Cic. *Planc.* 66).

¹⁴ A proemial cliché, of course: cf. Livy 1 *praef* 9: *quae vita, qui mores fuerint, per quos viros quibusque artibus…et partum et auctum imperium sit*; Val. Max. 1.1: *facta simul ac dicta memoratu digna*.

¹⁵ Turner 1997.

¹⁶ McGing 1982. See further Focke 1923 for the centrality of *synkrisis* to a range of literary and rhetorical practices.

¹⁷ Bastomsky 1985, 389 perceives a playful ambiguity in *pro*: was *inertia* 'a form of' wisdom, or 'a substitute' for it (i.e. Agricola is being criticized for his lack of *sapientia*)? The suggestion misses the point. Nothing in the *Agricola* suggests that it would be particularly *sapiens* as such to confront despotic emperors. Rather this is (what will become in his later writing) a familiar Tacitean strategy: traditional language (*sapientia*) is being warped to accommodate new political perversions. See further O'Gorman 2000, 14–15 for the Thucydidean trope of 'words losing their meaning' in the *Annals*.

¹⁸ *Agr.* 6.3, 42.2.

¹⁹ Reading *nisi* with Furneaux.

²⁰ Woodman 1993, 117–19.

²¹ McGing 1982, 22–3.

²² On Plutarchan *synkrisis*, see Pelling 1986, Duff 1999, 252–87.

²³ For Helvidius, see *Hist.* 2.91.3 (Helvidius' brave, self-righteous intervention: 'many' laugh at him, 'others' are pleased); 4.5–4.6.2 (positive, although he did seem to 'some' *adpetentior famae*, 4.6.1). Thrasea in the *Annals* is again a figure who provokes differing reactions, though here the narrator is generally prejudiced against his assailants. His first intervention, criticizing lavish gladiatorial shows in Syracuse, gives his 'critics' (*obtrectatoribus*) the opportunity to inveigh (13.49.1). His proposal that Antistius' death penalty

should be commuted is passed, and his *libertas* is said to free the other senators from their *servitium*, 'with a few exceptions' (*paucis exemptis*, 14.49.1), who are classed as flatterers. The *Annals* closes, at least in the form we have it, with the trial and death of Thrasea, Barea Soranus and Servilia, and the exile of Helvidius and others. The Tacitean narrator here presents them in much more uniformly positive light: the murder of Thrasea is that of 'virtue herself' (*virtutem ipsam*, 16.21.1), and his qualities of *spiritus et libertatem* (16.24.2) are opposed to the perverse fearfulness of the emperor and his entourage. Still, the senators' response is ambiguous: they feel no sadness (*maestitia*), owing to the frequency of such events, but a *novus et altior pavor* (16.29.1). Cf. 15.20, 23 for Thrasea's free-speaking integrity, again postively appraised. See further Syme 1958, 555–62.

[24] Conte 1996 for an interpretation of Petronius along these lines.

[25] Turner 1997, 592.

[26] McGing 1982, 22–3.

[27] Reading *divisimus*, but the text is difficult.

[28] 'mox nostrae duxere Helvidium in carcerem manus; nos Mauricum Rusticum divisimus, nos innocenti sanguine senecio perfudit?'

[29] 'Free-speaking' becomes a central issue in philosophical ethics under the principate, particularly in the Greek texts that deal with parrhsiva. See e.g. Gallo 1988 on Plutarch, Glad 1996 on Philodemus, and generally Fitzgerald ed. 1996; Konstan 1997, 108–13.

[30] For book-burning as a strategy of imperial control, see also *Ann.* 4.35.4, Cass. Dio 56.27.1; and further Moles 1998; O'Gorman 2000, 177–8.

[31] Cf. *senes prope ad ipsos exactae aetatis terminus per* silentium *venimus* (3.3); *studia fori et civilium artium decus in* silentium *acta* (39.3).

[32] See, briefly, Jones 1978, 118–19; on the image of Trajan heeding the senate, see Bennett 1997, 65–6; and for the *LIBERTAS* coinage, see also Syme 1958, 250, curiously unheeded by Bennett 1997, 71–3.

[33] See Heubner 1984, 11 for this 'dreifache Abundanz'.

[34] Compare esp. Velleius: '"restoration" is the key note of Velleius Paterculus' panegyric to Tiberius' (Woodman 1975, 290). See also Galinsky 1996, 58–77 on the nuances of the restoration trope under Augustus.

[35] Esp. Bartsch 1994, 148–87.

[36] Liebeschuetz 1966, 133: 'The age which is hostile to virtue and is unfavourably contrasted with an earlier, better age of necessity includes the time when Nerva and Trajan are reigning and Tacitus is writing'. Contrast Ogilvie and Richmond 1967, 136, who take *nunc* in 'a narrower sense than in c. 1.4'.

[37] Cf. *Ann.* 3.55, where *obsequium…in principem et aemulandi amor* are said to raise the standard of popular morality under Vespasian.

[38] The structure – narrating decline, then a sudden reversal – does, however, suggest the established pattern of a rhetorical encomium. That is also, broadly, the shape of the preface to Dionysius of Halicarnassus' *On the ancient orators*, where the final rescue of oratory from its poor state is credited to Rome (2, esp. 3.1).

[39] Cf. Seneca's *Apocolocyntosis*: *initio saeculi felicissimi* (1.1), *felicia lassis saecula praestabit* [sc. Nero] (4.1.23–4), *aurea saecula* (4.1.9) suspended from a *felici manu* 4.1.6). Also – if the poem is indeed Neronian – Calp. Sic. 4.6–7 (*aurea saecula*), 137–40. For further references, see Ogilvie and Richmond 1967 ad loc.

[40] Syme 1958, 217.

[41] Ogilvie and Richmond 1967, 139; Murgia 1980, 103.

[42] Syme 1957, 671; Ogilvie, Saddington and Keppie 1991, 1718.

[43] Perhaps alluding to Virg. *Georg.* 3.40: *interea Dryadum silvas sequamur.* The Virgilian passage, a promise to turn to write about Octavian in the future, may also be alluded to in the preface to the *Histories*: see Whitmarsh (forthcoming).

[44] Gill 1983, 476.

[45] Borzsák 1982, 40: 'In einer enkomiastischen Biographie...mußte der so wenig Alexander-ähnlich Agricola die Rolle Alexanders übernehmen'. Cf. also Clarke 2001, 98.

[46] Moles 1990, 299–300.

[47] Cf. 27.1: *Britanniae* terminum; 30.1: *nullae* ultra *terrae*; 30.3: *in ipsis* penetralibus; 30.4: *terrarum ac libertatis* extremos recessus...*nunc* terminus *Britanniae patet*; 33.3: *ergo egressi, ego veterum legatorum, vos priorum exercituum* terminos, finem *Britanniae non fama nec rumore, sed castris et armis tenemus: inventa Britannia et subacta.* Cf. Clarke (2001), 98: 'Where are we to locate Britain – within or without the boundary that conventionally delimits Roman imperial aspirations?'

[48] See most recently and most fully Clarke 2001, 106–9.

[49] A recurrent Tacitean motif: cf. *Germ.* 14.2, *Dial.* 38.2.

[50] Cf. *Annals* 14.34: *libertas* still (*etiam tum*) blazed among the Britons, given that they were not yet (*nondum)* aware of the power of freedmen.

[51] For the role of time in progressive acculturation, cf. 21.3: *paulatimque discessum ad delenimenta vitiorum.* For the absence of history among the Britons, see Rutledge 2000; O'Gorman 1993, 139–40 observes that the description of battles in the ethnographic portions of the *Germania* lack 'temporal underpinning'.

[52] Britain is a *feroci provincia*, 8.1; the Britons excel the Gauls in *ferocia*, 11.5; cf. the description of Calgacus' claim of *virtus...ac ferocia*, 31.4.

[53] Cf. e.g. Mela, *Chor.* 3.50 (Britain is *fecunda, verum iis quae pecora quam homines benignius alant*); cf. 3.52 for Britons as *inculti omnes*. Isidore *Orig.* 9.2.102 preserves the etymology deriving *Britanni* (via *Brittones*) from *bruti* (Maltby 1990, 85).

[54] Borca 1996.

[55] Rutledge 2000, 87–9.

[56] Traub 1953.

[57] Williams 1989, 49 (from a Classical Association address delivered in 1984).

[58] Clarke 2001, 106.

[59] Rutledge 2000, *passim* e.g. 76 on Britain as 'negative space'; cf. O'Gorman 1993, 135 on the *Germania* as 'an exploration of a country (Germany) in search of the ideological (Roman) self'.

[60] Cf. the speeches of Civilis (*Hist.* 4.14.2–4, 4.32.2–3), Arminius (*Ann.* 1.59.2–6), Flavus and Arminius (*Ann.* 2.9.3–2.10), Tacfarinas (*Ann.* 4.24.1), Caratacus (*Ann.* 12.34), Prasutagas (*Ann.* 14.31.2). *Libertas* is at issue in all of these speeches. With Agricola's military discipline (*compositos firmis ordinibus*, 37.5) compare e.g. 4.25.2 (*confertus pedes, dispositae turmae, cuncta proelio provisa*); and see further Ash 1999 on the importance of military order, in the *Histories* at any rate.

[61] Sall. *Epist. Mithr.* 22 (where Mithridates refers to them as *latrones gentium*) and Vell. Pat. 2.27.2 (Telesinus: *raptores Italicae libertatis lupos*).

[62] Of the examples in n. 60, only Civilis' brief speech at *Hist.* 4.32.2–3 is reported in direct speech.

[63] See Ogilvie and Richmond 1967, 265 on the multiple allusions here to Scipio's and

Hannibal's speeches at Liv. 21.40–4.

[64] McGing 1982, 22–3.

[65] Braund 1996, 169. Laird 1999, 121–6 distinguishes between the modes of presentation of the two speeches: Calgacus is introduced with the phrase 'is held to have said' (*locutus fertur*, 29.4), Agricola with 'he discoursed' (*disseruit*, 33.1). According to Laird, *locutus fertur* implies 'that the reported words...are of...doubtful reliability – either in their content or their provenance'. 'Unreliability', however, implies too much ethical judgement, and the conflation of unreliable 'content' with unreliable 'provenance' is too swift. It is preferable, in my view, to take the narratorial distance implied in *locutus fertur* as a self-conscious indication that this speech is a rhetorically expedient fiction – which does not necessitate a negative judgement upon the content.

[66] Rutledge 2000, 87.

[67] Rutledge 2000, 87. Similarly, Braund 1996, 165 acknowledges 'ambivalence' and 'outright criticism of the spread of Romanization', but does not regard these as interfering with the laudatory aims of the text.

[68] Rutledge 2000, 89: the echo of *obsequium ac modestiam* 'cannot be accidental, and, in the final analysis, reflects negatively on Calgacus'.

[69] Williams 1989.

[70] *vastum...silentium* alludes to Livy 10.34.6 and the description of the Samnite town of Feritrum (*solitudo* is also used there, at 10.34.8). The phrase is also used by Tacitus at *Hist.* 3.13.2 and *Ann.* 4.50.2.

[71] For this semantic node, see e.g. Evans 1999, 56.

[72] For references, see above, n. 30.

[73] Cf., in a different connection, Braund 1996, 163: 'Inappropriate naming, a sure sign of warped thinking, is a familiar concern of the historian concerned with setting forth his version of the truth and claiming to expose the truth of others'; see further Plass 1988, 42; Henderson 1998, 260–5; O'Gorman 2000, 23–45. For Tacitean examples, see e.g. *Hist.* 4.5.1 (*nomine magnifico segne otium velaret*), *Ann.* 4.19.2 (*proprium id Tiberio fuit, scelera nuper reperta priscis verbis obtegere*).

[74] O'Gorman 1993, 142–4.

[75] e.g. Ogilvie and Richmond 1967, 228: 'The attitude of Tacitus, himself an administrator, towards the policy of conquest by assimilation is remarkable'.

[76] Braund 1996, 163 writes that 'the target of [these] remarks is not Agricola, but the Britons: his salutary planning is contrasted with their misidentification of the nature of civilization'.

[77] Clarke 2001, 108: Agricola 'is not allowed to complete his campaign'. Cf. O'Gorman 1993, 146 on the representation of precarious military conquest as a destabilizing tactic in the *Germania*. In connection with other campaigns, Tacitus represents Britain as impermanently conquered: cf. *Agr.* 5.2 (*in ambiguo Britannia fuit*); *Hist.* 1.2.1 (*perdomita Britannia et statim missa*).

[78] The Agricolan forts in Scotland were never completed, and the newest coins found at the site have been (apparently newly minted) Domitianic *dupondii* and *asses*. See Hobley 1989.

[79] Cf., most explicitly, *Germ.* 14.2, *Dial.* 18.5, 38.2, *Ann.* 1.16.2, 12.12.1. I have found no example in Tacitus of the idealized *otium* of the ethnographic tradition, though *Ann.* 4.67.3 (Tiberius' *luxus et malum otium* at Capri) may play upon that tradition. See Thomas 1982, 52.

[80] e.g. *Germ.* 40.3 (*pax et quies* only known to Germans during festal times) *Hist.* 4.1.3 (*pax et quies bonis artibus indigent*), *Ann.* 12.54.4 (*quies provinciae reddita*).

[81] e.g. *Hist.* 2.15.1 (*nec Vitelliani quamquam victi quievere*), 2.97.1 (*numquam satis quieta Britannia*), *Ann.* 13.53.1 (*quietae ad id tempus res in Germania fuerant*). Cf. *Agr.* 40.3 (*provinciam quietam tutamque*).

[82] For the reworking of Cic. *Brut.* 45, see Bartsch 1994, 110, with 251 n.22 for further bibliography.

[83] For an analogous example of intertextuality within the Tacitean corpus, see Woodman 1979.

[84] Bartsch 1994, 98–125.

[85] Murgia 1980 argues that the *Agricola* necessarily postdates the *Dialogus*. I am still agnostic.

[86] Plass 1988, 40–1.

[87] Galinsky 1996, 10–41.

[88] Ogilvie and Richmond 1967, 158 are overhasty in enforcing this reading: '*ut minister* must mean "as a subordinate should" (which he was)'.

[89] Plass 1988, 43; and for the similar separation between Tiberius' thoughts and self-presentation in the *Annals*, see O'Gorman 2000, 78–105.

[90] Thought processes are occasionally narrated: e.g. Agricola is *ceterum animorum provinciae* prudens (19.1); the army is conscientia *ac fama ferox* (27.1); the Britons' perceive that they have been beaten *non virtute...sed occasione et arte* (27.3). Character-bound focalization as such (i.e. where the narratorial voice adopts the perspective of a character: see e.g. Bal 1999, 142–9), however, is all but absent elsewhere, notwithstanding the odd ambiguous case (e.g. 29.1: *in luctu bellum inter remedia erat*).

[91] Cf. the use of rumours in the *Annals* (Shatzman 1974): at e.g. *Ann.* 4.10–11 the salacious rumour (*vulgo iactata*, 11.1) about the death of Drusus is high-handedly dismissed, but nevertheless offered up for the reader's pleasure.

[92] 'By denigrating an alternative course of conduct involving "defiance", a "parade of freedom", "precipitous paths", and "ostentatious death", and in continually criticizing men who admired such "forbidden conduct", Tacitus suggests that his biography has a controversial as well as a laudatory aim. He implies that the selection of a particular kind of conduct implied the deliberate rejection of another kind' (Liebeschutz 1966, 127–8).

[93] Ahl 1984.

[94] Bartsch 1994, 109–10.

[95] Galinsky 1996, 40.

[96] Althusser 1984, 177.

Bibliography

Ahl, F.
    1984   'The art of safe criticism in Greece and Rome', *AJP* 105, 174–208.
    1989   'Homer, Vergil and complex narrative structures in Latin epic', *ICS* 14, 1–31.
Althusser, L.
    1984   'A letter on art in reply to André Daspre', in *Essays on Ideology*, London, 173–9.

Ash, R.
1999   *Ordering Anarchy: Armies and leaders in Tacitus'* Histories, London.
Bal, M.
1999   *Narratology: An introduction to the study of narrative*, 2nd edn, Buffalo.
Bartsch, S.
1994   *Actors in the Audience: Theatricality and double-speak from Nero to Hadrian*, Cambridge, Mass.
Bastomsky, S.J.
1985   'The not-so-perfect man: some ambiguities in Tacitus' picture of Agricola', *Latomus* 44, 388–93.
Borca, F.
1996   '*Adversus ipsam rerum naturam*: note on Tacitus, *Agricola* 33', *Britannia* 27, 337–40.
Borszák, I.
1982   'Alexander der Große als Muster taciteischer Heldendarstellung', *Gymnasium* 89, 37–56.
Clarke, K.
2001   'An island nation: re-reading Tacitus' *Agricola*', *JRS* 91, 94–112.
Classen, C.J.
1988   'Tacitus: historian between republic and principate', *Mnemosyne* 41, 93–116.
Conte, G.B.
1994   *Genres and Readers*, Baltimore.
1996   *The Hidden Author: An interpretation of Petronius'* Satyricon, Berkeley.
Culler, J.
1974   *Structuralist Poetics: Structuralism, linguistics and the study of literature*, London.
Duff, T.E.
1999   *Plutarch's Lives: Exploring virtue and vice*, Oxford.
Evans, R.
1999   'Ethnography's freak show: the grotesque at the edges of the Roman earth', *Ramus* 28, 54–73.
Focke, F.
1923   '*Synkrisis*', *Hermes* 58, 327–68.
Furneaux, H.
1922   *Cornelius Tacitus*, De vita Agricolae, 2nd edn, rev. J.G.C. Anderson and F. Haverfield, Oxford.
Galinsky, K.
1994   'Roman poetry in the 1990s', *CJ* 89, 297–309.
1996   *Augustan Culture: An interpretive introduction*, Princeton.
Gallo, I.
1988   'La *parrhesia* epicurea e il trattato *De adulatore et amico* di Plutarco: qualche reflessione', in I. Gallo (ed.) *Aspetti dello stoicismo e dell' epicureismo in Plutarco*, Ferrara, 119–28.
Gill, C.J.
1983   'The question of character development: Plutarch and Tacitus', *CQ* 33, 469–87.

Glad, C.E.

1996   'Frank speech, flattery and friendship in Philodemus', in J. Fitzgerald (ed.) *Friendship, Flattery, and Freedom of Speech: Studies on friendship in the New Testament world*, Leiden, 21–59.

Hammond, M.

1963   '*Res olim dissociabiles: principatus ac libertas*', *HSCP* 67, 93–113.

Henderson, J.

1998   'Tacitus: the world in pieces', in *Fighting for Rome*, Cambridge, 257–300; revised from *Ramus* 18, 167–210.

Hobley, A.S.

1989   'The numismatic evidence for the post-Agricolan abandonment of the Roman frontier in northern Scotland', *Britannia* 20, 69–74.

Jones, C.P.

1978   *The Roman World of Dio Chrysostom*, Cambridge, Mass.

Kallendorff, C.

1999   'Historicizing the "Harvard School": pessimistic readings of the *Aeneid* in Italian renaissance scholarship', *HSCP* 99, 391–403.

Kennedy, D.F.

1992   ' "Augustan" and "anti-Augustan": reflections on terms of reference', in A. Powell (ed.) *Roman Poetry and Propaganda in the Age of Augustus*, Bristol, 26–58.

Konstan, D.

1997   *Friendship in the Classical World*, Cambridge.

McGing, B.C.

1982   'Synkrisis in Tacitus' *Agricola*', *Hermathena* 133, 15–25.

Maltby, R.

1990   *A Lexicon of Ancient Latin Etymologies*, Leeds.

Martindale, C.

1993   'Descent into hell: reading ambiguity, of Virgil and the critics', *PVS* 21, 111–50.

1996   'Introduction: the classic of all Europe', in *id.* (ed.) *The Cambridge Companion to Virgil*, Cambridge, 1–18.

Moles, J.L.

1990   'The *Kingship Orations* of Dio Chrysostom', *PLLS* 6, 297–375.

1998   'Cry freedom: Tacitus, *Annals* 4.32–5', *Histos* 2.

Murgia, C.

1982   'The date of Tacitus' *Dialogus*', *HSCP* 84, 99–125.

O'Gorman, E.

1993   'No place like Rome: identity and difference in the *Germania* of Tacitus', *Ramus* 22, 135–54.

2000   *Irony and Misreading in the Annals of Tacitus*, Cambridge.

Ogilvie, R. and Richmond, I.

1967   *Tacitus, Agricola*, Oxford.

Ogilvie, R., Saddington, D.B. and Keppie, L.J.F.

1991   'An interim report on Tacitus' *Agricola*', *ANRW* 2.33.3, 1714–40.

Pelling, C.B.R.

1986   '*Synkrisis* in Plutarch's *Lives*', in F. Brenk et al. (eds.) *Miscellanea Plutarchea:*

atti del I convegno di studi su Plutarco, Ferrara, 83–96.

Perkell, C.
1994   'Ambiguity and irony: the last resort?', *Helios* 21, 63–74.

Petersmannn, G.
1991   'Die Agricola-Biographie: Versuch einer Deutung', *ANRW* 2.33.3, 1785–806.

Plass, P.
1988   *Wit and the Writing of History: The rhetoric of historiography in imperial Rome*, Madison.

Roller, M.B.
2001   *Constructing Autocracy: Aristocrats and emperors in Julio-Claudian Rome*, Princeton.

Shatzman, I.
1974   'Tacitean rumours', *Latomus* 33, 549–78.

Thomas, R.
1982   *Lands and People in Roman Poetry: The ethnographical tradition*, *PCPS* supplement vol. 7, Cambridge.
2000   'A trope by any other name: "polysemy", ambiguity, and *significatio* in Virgil', *HSCP* 100, 381–407.

Traub, H.W.
1953   'Tacitus' use of *ferocia*', *TAPA* 84, 250–61.

Turner, A.J.
1997   'Approaches to Tacitus' *Agricola*', *Latomus* 56, 582–93.

Whitmarsh, T.
Forthcoming   ' "Say what you like"...Trajan, Tacitus and the troublesome preface to the *Histories*'.

Williams, R.
1989   'Writing, speech and the "classical" ', in *What I Came to Say*, London, 44–56.

Wirszubski, C.
1950   Libertas *as a Political Idea at Rome during the Late Republic and early Principate*, Cambridge.

Woodman, A.J.
1975   'Questions of date, genre, and style in Velleius: some literary answers', *CQ* 25, 272–306.
1979   'Self-imitation and the substance of history: Tacitus *Annals* 1.61–6 and *Histories* 2.70, 5.14–15', in A.J. Woodman and D. West (eds.) *Creative Imitation in Latin Literature*, Cambridge, 143–55.
1993   'Amateur dramatics at the court of Nero: *Annals* 15.48–74', in T.J. Luce and A.J. Woodman (eds.) *Tacitus and the Tacitean Tradition*, Princeton, 104–28.

18

BIOGRAPHY IN LETTERS;
BIOGRAPHY AND LETTERS

Michael Trapp

Augustus to Tiberius:
My dear Tiberius, do not be carried away by your youthful vehemence in this matter, or take it too much to heart that someone should speak ill of me; it is enough of an achievement if we can prevent anyone *doing* us evil.

Agesilaus to Hidrieus:
If Nicias is not guilty, acquit him. If he is guilty, acquit him for my sake. In any case, acquit him.

Apollonius to Iarchas and his fellow sages:
Greetings. I came to you on foot, and you have made me a present of the sea; but by sharing with me the wisdom which is yours, you have bestowed on me also the gift of travelling through the heavens. This I shall report to the Hellenes; and I shall share my discourses with you as if we were in one another's presence, unless it was to no purpose that I have drunk from the cup of Tantalus. Farewell, good philosophers.

As the last of the trio makes fully explicit, these are all quotations from letters, made in biographies (Suetonius *Augustus* 51; Plutarch, *Agesilaus* 13; Philostratus *Apollonius* 3.51). In each case, the point of the quotation is not so much to document an event in the subject's career, as to illustrate a facet of his character: Augustus' restraint; Agesilaus' willingness to bend the requirements of strict justice for a friend, Apollonius' thirst for enlightenment, gracious gratitude to those who can satisfy it, and readiness to acknowledge his debts. Each time, that is to say, the quoting biographer implicitly makes use of what ancient critical theory recognized as a salient characteristic of epistolary form, its special effectiveness in embodying and displaying character. 'The letter', in the words of Demetrius *De Elocutione* 227, '...should abound in glimpses of character (πλεῖστον…ἐχέτω τὸ ἠθικόν). It may be said that everybody reveals his own soul in his letters. While it is possible to discern the writer's character in every other kind of composition too, in none does this happen so clearly as in the epistolary.' The letter's perceived primary function as a surrogate for intimate conversation, between friends who have nothing to hide from each other,[1] makes it also extremely valuable to the biographer, eavesdropping on the 'conversation' from a later point in time and perhaps, in addition to the simple information content, catching glimpses of his subject of a kind that the grander, more formal record does not preserve.

However, although letters can be used in this way in ancient biography, and can be valued for this characteristic,[2] it is perhaps surprising that we do not hear more of a noise being made of it by the biographers themselves; both the valuation, and the sense of letters as bearers of character, seem to remain implicit, rather than being overtly articulated. And yet Plutarch, at least, drawing his celebrated contrast between *historiai* and *bioi*, declares that for the latter, with their overriding concern with moral character, trivial episodes are as telling as great deeds.[3] Some such context as this would seem to be ideal for acknowledging the special value of letters; but, as far as I am aware, no such acknowledgement is ever forthcoming.

Moreover, quotation for the purposes of illuminating character is only one among several guises in which letters appear in biography. They feature also as events: the writing, sending, receiving, reading, and subsequent manipulation of letters are regular punctuating occurrences in biographical narrative, just as they are in historical narrative more generally – sometimes with implications for character, sometimes as foreground episode, sometimes as insignificant cog in the causal machinery. When Archias in Plutarch's *Pelopidas* drunkenly places a letter betraying a plot against him unread under his pillow with the words 'serious business tomorrow', the episode both explains a well-known saying and testifies to a defect in his character (10). When Demosthenes commits suicide, he does so – in one of several rival versions – by drinking poison concealed in his pen; what he is writing as cover for the taking of the poison is a letter, which is found after his death to consist of the salutation – to his Macedonian enemy Antipater – at the head of an otherwise blank page (Plut. *Dem.* 29–30). This again both characterizes the protagonist, and adds symbolic richness to the narrative: like the empty radar screen, or the flat line on the oscilloscope, the blank page images death in the absence of what ought normally to be there. At the same time, of course, letters are also regularly appealed to, directly or indirectly, as evidence, to confirm or refute this or that claim or version of events; that is to say, they feature as part of the argument for the narrative as well as part of the narrative itself. So Philostratus appeals to letters to prove Apollonius' ownership of a certain *bon mot* (7.31), or the reality of the story of his encounter with a satyr (6.27);[4] Suetonius for Augustus' dietary habits (*Aug.*

76.1–2); and Plutarch for Cicero's concern over his son's tutors in philosophy and rhetoric (*Cic.* 24.5–6).[5]

What is most interestingly debatable, however, is what collective status in ancient biographical writing all this allows us to attribute to letters. I have already registered my sense of a spark that didn't quite jump in connection with the idea of letters as windows on character. I have something of the same feeling overall. Letters are indeed exploited in a number of different ways by ancient biographers, and thus implicitly valued by them, but always as just one strand among others, without any strong sense of letters being in any way a special, privileged category of material for their project. A good test case, I think, is provided by Plutarch's *Cicero*.

Here, if at all, the modern scholar is tempted to think, letters ought to bulk large. We know very well how much of *our* sense of Cicero the man, and of the feel of his career, depends on them; we know too that collections of Cicero's were published, made available to the wider world in ordered form, close to his lifetime.[6] Plutarch certainly knows about Cicero's letters and uses them, and there is a good chance that some of this use is direct. In chap. 29.6, dealing with the prosecution of Clodius over the Bona Dea scandal, we find two close paraphrases of *Ad Att.* 1.16 (1.16.5 and 1.16.10) side by side (and in the same order as they appear in their original context); and in chap. 36.5, Cicero's famous excuse to Caelius about panthers is reproduced from *Fam.* 2.11, immediately following a reference to the campaign against the bandits, which is the subject of *Fam.* 2.10. Both times, what Plutarch produces is expanded paraphrase, clarifying for the sake of the reader who does not have the full text of the letter before his eyes; but the original Latin wording is rendered closely enough into Greek to suggest direct acquaintance. Chaps. 36.6 to 37.1 also seem to echo the wording of *Fam.* 16.11. And there are further references to letters, both surviving and no longer extant (though without quotation or paraphrase from them) in chaps. 24, 37, 40, 43 and 45. But, in the context of the *Life* as a whole, these are relatively isolated episodes. The bulk of the narrative seems to be built from the great speeches (perhaps with the aid of a commentary), Cicero's own περὶ ὑπατείας and *De Consiliis Suis*, and the biography by Tiro (which may indeed already have processed much of the material from speeches and letters alike that comes through in Plutarch).[7]

Also intriguing is the case of Suetonius, in both his *Caesars* and his *Men of Distinction*. A first impression could well be that letters are heavily exploited in both works; but closer examination shows that the use made of epistolary material is at least a little more restricted than that. The *Life of Julius* quotes from Cicero's correspondence, and refers to Julius' and Augustus' without quotation; the *Life of Augustus* quotes and discusses letters of Augustus, Mark Antony and Cassius Patavinus, and refers to Cicero; the *Life of Tiberius* quotes Augustus' and Tiberius'; the *Lives of Gaius* and *Claudius* quote again from Augustus; the *Life of Domitian* mentions a compromising letter of the young Domitian preserved by Claudius Pollio.[8] In connection with Suetonius' grammarians and rhetoricians, there are quotations from Cicero again and Messalla Corvinus.[9] The *Life of Horace*, finally, quotes letters of Augustus to Maecenas and to Horace himself, and refers to a letter of Horace to Maecenas, which however on stylistic grounds Suetonius is inclined to believe a forgery. Suetonius thus knows that there is useful material in letters, and uses it when he can, both to establish factual points and to illuminate character; but the overall range of material is not huge, and it is unevenly distributed through his work. One way of making the point is to observe that if you subtract the letters of Cicero and Augustus, you are left with very little epistolary material indeed; another would be to point out that six of the twelve lives of the Caesars mention letters only as events within the narrative, or not at all.[10]

Plausible explanations of this state of affairs are not far to seek. Ancient biographers value letters, and certainly use them especially to illuminate private detail, and traits of character. They do not, however, use them more than modestly, or acknowledge them explicitly as a special category of source-material, for a combination of two converging reasons. In the first place, letters were always hard to come by in any quantity or with any reliability. Unlike the modern biographer, the ancient scholar did not have the resources either to travel to archives of private papers, or indeed to discover that they existed in the first place. What he could use was what private material he might know about in his own vicinity, and what had in some sense been formally published. Suetonius and Plutarch both can know of and use Cicero's correspondence, which had gone into circulation in collected editions; but Suetonius seems to owe the extent and detail of his access to the correspondence of Augustus to the happy individual accident of being an Imperial secretary.[11]

But it may also be, secondly, that considerations of genre and propriety weighed too. Sensitivities about the dignity of history, and the need to control carefully the quantity of 'low' material admitted into historical narrative, are well known: a good example is provided by Cassius Dio's several justifications for his inclusion of mundane but telling detail in his *History*.[12] Something of the same feeling may have operated so as to restrict recourse to letters, above all private letters, which are in their very nature informal, and in both subject and style liable to fall beneath the more elevated standards of biography.[13] The point is not that letters may thus have been felt wholly inappropriate. Clearly they were not: biography, with its heightened interest in moral character, did not work to precisely the same standards as history, and even a historian could openly quote and refer to correspondence on occasion. It will have been more a question of degree and balance: too much epistolary matter, too frequent quotation, might bring the level down too far, both stylistically and in terms of the subjects referred to; but with judicious restraint there was much to be gained from admitting it. In this way, too, the incentive to search out letters when the materials for biographical composition were being assembled, though certainly not removed entirely, will have been blunted.

All of this, however, is to look at the issue of letters and biography from the vantage-point of just one set of interested parties among several. For letters are not only passive biographical data, requiring to be made into such by the questing biographer. They are also more actively biographical, both as individual items in primary circulation, as participants in a live epistolary transaction, and (perhaps still more markedly) when collected and re-released *en masse* for a broader readership. Either first writer or compiler, or both, may have what we might want to call biographical aims, and either an individual letter or a collection can exercise a biographical effect on the reader.

As already acknowledged, an individual letter can be directly biographical on at least two – maybe three – levels. In its style, turns of thought, and also explicit declarations of taste, resolutions and plans, it can be read as representing the personality of its sender to the recipient, not analytically or descriptively, but by direct embodiment. Or it can constitute a fragment or an element of narrative biography, by retelling events from the writer's recent or not so recent experience: this can stretch all the way from small exercises in autobiography proper, to the kind of miscellaneous snatches of recent news that are the common currency of so much letter-writing.[14] Or, thirdly, the focus can be not on the writer him- or herself, but on some third party, in which case the evocation of character or the tracing of the career is normally more direct and descriptive: central cases of this would be the obituary letter (e.g. Pliny 7.24 on Ummidia Quadratilla or Jerome 23 on the saintly Leah)[15] and (often but not always) the letter of recommendation.[16]

But to talk about these possibilities in the individual letter as straight-forwardly biographical is to occlude another important factor: that this parading of personal detail, of career or character or both, is seldom if ever done for neutrally, disinterestedly descriptive purposes – just to get the record right. On the contrary, there are almost always (should we say just 'always'?) ulterior motives and special projects in play; the addressee (or a subsequent reader already envisaged) is in some way being worked on. The game may be to further the writer's own status and prestige, in the content of what is said or the way it is said, or to secure some more specific change of belief or attitude on the part of the recipient, whether or not this is to lead to corresponding action. Cicero reporting back to Caelius about his doings in Cilicia (successfully suppressing bandits and unsuccessfully questing for panthers) is not just sending dispatches; by sending *that* news to *that* recipient, he is seeking to maintain an important social and political alliance; and the same purpose is served by the distinctive tone of the letters, which presents an urbane Cicero not always on parade to every correspondent. Cicero thus narrates his own past doings, *and* embodies in the letter the character he wishes to impress upon his correspondent of the moment; and he does so in pursuit of some pretty transparent further goals. Or again, to give a second example, Ovid, writing from exile, recalls his own past life in happier times and displays his current beliefs and attitudes (to friends, to misfortune, to others' luck), not for the sake of the record, but to win sympathy and, ideally, active helpers to secure his recall. So in *Tristia* 5.13, gently reproaching a friend for his failure to write more frequently, Ovid both recalls their shared past, in good times and in bad, and makes great efforts to paint himself as generous and forgiving, where another might say harsher things.[17] Some letters invite this kind of reading of their biographical elements more readily than others, but few if any are entirely immune to it.

A special case of the display of personal detail (narrative or ethical) for affective purposes is constituted by the didactic letter. Perhaps the most obvious examples in this category come from philosophical epistolography, where the deeds and character of the instructing writer are regularly appealed to in order to clarify the lesson or to lend it persuasive force. Think of Plato (whether it is really Plato or not) describing his own career in Sicily as a model for philosophical engagement with politics in the *Seventh Letter*. Think of Epicurus describing his own happiness in adversity as pattern and exhortation for his addressees;[18] or of Seneca's and Horace's self-presentations, likewise aimed at the guidance and persuasion of their initial addressees, and then of their wider readership.[19]

However, the example which it seems specially appropriate to highlight in this volume is that of the Epistles of Paul. Most often read over nearly two thousand years for their doctrine, or more recently for the historical light they shed on the growth and circumstances of primitive Christianity, they are also documents in which persuasive intent licences repeated display of the writer's character and career, and the writer accordingly, designedly or not, constructs himself for posterity.

Individual Pauline epistles make regular reference to facts about Paul's past activities, present desires and attitudes to his correspondents, and future hopes and plans, as part of his didactic venture. Paul urges his past efforts and concern as proof of his present seriousness, and as a means of exerting moral pressure for an appropriate, practical response. Often these notes are struck towards the beginning and the end of the message, where, in normal epistolary practice, closeness to the formulae of salutation make personal reference and comment on the relationship between writer and addressee most comfortable.[20] So 1 Corinthians begins (chaps. 1–3.3) with reminiscence of Paul's previous visit and its reception, and ends (chaps. 15–16) with the story of his conversion and his plans for the journey that will include his next visit. But this is by no means a rigid rule. The extended account of Paul's experiences in Macedonia comes in the middle of the first component of 2 Corinthians (chaps. 7–9); and the whole of the second component of that same letter is heavily personal, with a calculated outburst of self-stigmatized 'raving' and 'boasting' at its centre (11.16–12.10). The persuasive, rhetorical nature of Paul's 'autobiographical' interludes is particularly evident in this last passage, with its insistence that it is the Corinthians, in their deafness and stubbornness, who have forced him into it (12.11).

> And what I do I will continue to do, in order to undermine the claim of those who would like to claim that in their boasted mission they work on the same terms as we do. For such men are false apostles, deceitful workmen, disguising themselves as apostles of Christ... I repeat, let no one think me foolish; but even if you do, accept me as a fool, so that I may boast a little... [W]hatever any one dares to boast of – I am speaking as a fool – I also dare to boast of that... Are they servants of Christ? I am a better one – I am talking like a madman – with far greater labours, far more imprisonments, with countless beatings, and often near death. Five times I have received at the hands of the Jews the forty lashes less one. Three times I have been beaten with rods; once I was stoned. Three times I have been shipwrecked; a night and a day I have been adrift at sea; on frequent journeys, in danger from rivers, danger from robbers, danger from my own people, danger from the Gentiles, danger in the city, danger in the wilderness, danger at sea, danger from false brethren; in toil and hardship, through many a sleepless night, in hunger and thirst, often without food, in cold and exposure... At Damascus, the governor under King Aretas guarded the city of Damascus in order to seize me, but I was let down in a basket through a window in the wall, and escaped his hands... I have been a fool! You forced me to it, for I ought to have been commended by you.[21]

In their initial context, and for their first addressees, personal details like these in any didactic epistle are not primarily descriptive; they have a job of persuasion to do. However, when the separate epistles are gathered up and can be read together, new possibilities open up. Read end-to-end, their individual passages offer themselves up to be made, precisely, into a biography of their writer, separable from their original persuasive aim.

So it is with Paul's Epistles. Piecing them together and re-ordering them, the reader can look back to Paul's early upbringing and his conversion, on to his cat's-cradle of routes across the Mediterranean world and his episodes of imprisonment, and forward to the threat of his martyrdom. This is the Paul of Acts, but seen dynamically, from a more vivid first-person vantage-point. The division of his story into separate episodes, seen from different points in time, and with uncertain chronological relations between them, calls forth a more actively biographical response from the reader, the very incompleteness and uncertainty prompting more intimate engagement.[22] (I note in passing that it has indeed been suggested that we see this very biographical response at work within the Pauline corpus itself: that the Pastoral Epistles [to Timothy and Titus], not genuinely Pauline, should be seen as a kind of 'epistolary novel' about Paul, added so as to flesh out and extend the biography extractable from the city letters.[23])

But this is not just a point about the effect of collection on didactic epistles; it holds for any epistolary collection in which personal material deployed for local, tactical purposes in the individual items can be aggregated in a reading of the whole set. Cicero's correspondence is at least as good an example of a 'real', utilitarian correspondence in which we can see both the overt and latent biography of individual letters, and the cumulative effect of the whole. Cicero paints himself at the time of writing, and recent fragments of his life, as he wishes them to be seen, at that particular time and for that particular correspondent. But when this correspondence then comes to be collected, the net result is almost a biography in the larger sense, in which the subject's self-presentation, the organizing work of the compiler, and the questioning of the reader all intertwine. Cicero can now be seen as the sum of all his local, tactical self-presentations, which may or may not be felt to be consistent with each other; the reader, in quest of the character of the man, can both attend to the self-portrayal, and reflects on what else the very volume of them, and the effort put into them, also betrays. At the same time, the juxtaposition of so many individual pieces of communication sets their author at the centre of his own multifarious social network, and thus also (given the necessary contextual knowledge on the part of the reader) into a particular position in a known historical period. In terms of narrative, even as large a collection as this falls far short of a full and connected account of the career; but, partly because the individual letters constantly intersect with other bodies of surviving evidence, and partly because of their very incompleteness, they call forth a biographical – narrative biographical – response from the reader. As with the Pauline epistles, both the gaps between individual letters (chronological or causal, or both), and each letter's own context-bound allusiveness, cry out for supplement and exegesis, and the end towards which this exegesis tends is a complete narrative of the writer's life.[24]

How many interested parties share in the biographical venture varies from case to case. Cicero may have entertained the idea of publishing his own collected correspondence, as another means of ensuring his continuing fame, both as leading citizen and as worker in words; but what we now possess and can read seems to reflect the efforts, and the commemorative aims, of another party.[25] In the case of the younger Pliny, however, there is no such gap; original writer and subsequent compiler are one, and there is correspondingly a much more marked (and not necessarily more amiable) sense of the building of a monument. Indeed there is a still stronger sense of conscious and calculating (auto)biography, as Pliny sets out to display his social connections, his taste and learning, and all the most creditable facets of his career and character, from sensitive (and much loved) husband to efficient administrator and confidant of the Emperor.[26] A nice instance is *Epistles* 6.7, to his wife. Expressing his appreciation for the yearning love with which she says she receives and cherishes his letters from abroad, yet insisting on his own still greater pain at their separation, Pliny simultaneously displays himself to the wider world and to posterity as (in his own estimation) deeply lovable, deeply fortunate, and deeply sensitive:[27]

> Caius Plinius to his dear Calpurnia, good health. You write that you are feeling my absence very much and that your only consolation when you don't have me is to hold my books and frequently even place them in my imprint beside you on the bed. I am happy to know that you miss me and happy too that you can ease the pain with this sort of medication. I for my part read and reread your letters and return to them again and again as if they had just arrived. But this only fans the flames of my longing for you: if there is such pleasure in reading what you write, think what joy it is to talk with you! Do write as often as you can, even though it will torture me as much as it delights me.

Collection, and the kind of reading that collection makes possible, can thus conjure large-scale biography – both biographical narrative, and sustained consideration of an individual – out of elements that may originally have been biographical in only a weaker, more atomistic sense. The case is different again if we move on to one last category of epistolography, which I have mentioned but not so far focused on at any length: the pseudepigraphic letter, above all as produced not as an individual item, but as part of a planned set. Here there is no question of collection changing the nature of the items collected, or the possible responses to them, for collection, and the collective impression of the whole set, is part of the plan from the outset. And here epistolography and biography come together in a particularly straightforward way.

Each surviving set of pseudepigraphic letters, attributed to one or another famous figure of the past – Diogenes and the Cynics, Socrates and the Socratics, Plato, Hippocrates, Demosthenes, Themistocles, Phalaris – has its own particular identity. A number of different aims and anticipated ways of reading seem to be in play, bearing on epistolary form and style as well as on content.[28] But biographical interest, the presentation of a historical personality or that personality's deeds, is nonetheless a consistent ingredient. So, for instance, in the *Letters* of Phalaris, although there is no consistent chronological thread, and much of the point of the collection seems to be to provide a handbook of model letters, there are intermittent sub-narratives (such as that concerning Stesichorus and his daughters), and the personality of the purported writer is constantly in view. Intriguingly, though, Phalaris' character seems to be in view as a teasing question, rather than as a wholly agreed quantity. This set of letters gives an impression of consciously and calculatingly playing with two divergent impressions of the man: as cruel, scheming, devious tyrant on the one hand; and as enlightened statesman, wearily aware of his reputation, yet determined to act as right dictates, on the other.[29]

In other sets of pseudepigraphic letters, the narrative thread can be stronger, as for instance those of Hippocrates, with the story of the great doctor's dealings with the people of Abdera, and the supposedly mad Democritus (*Ep. Hippoc.* 10–18).[30] But there is one collection in particular which stands out for the way in which a single narrative line is sustained throughout a lengthy sequence, and which combines this single narrative line with the presentation, through his own words, of a single, exemplary character.

The 17 letters of Chion of Heraclea were supposedly written and sent over a period of over five years in the first half of the fourth century BC.[31] They unfold in his own words the story of a young aristocrat from the Black Sea, and in particular the road that led him from carefree youth to heroic tyrannicide, via a philosophical commitment acquired from contact with the pupils of Socrates – the practical example of Xenophon, encountered en route in Byzantium, and the theoretical teaching of Plato in Athens.[32] This is a history, an adventure story, a conversion story, and a lesson in personal ethics and political theory rolled into one. But it courts consideration as a biography too: because centred so firmly on a single individual (the supposed author of the letters); because unfolding at length the narrative of the crucial, defining phase of his life; and because so clearly concerned to highlight his character, above all his moral character – his principles, his moral choices, and his virtues. Non-committally entitled 'The Letters of Chion', Χίωνος ἐπιστολαί, this collection turns out to have not only a narrative cohesion, but also a depth and intensity of focus on the character and personal experiences of the alleged author, not by any means automatically to be expected of an epistolographic text. One ends up feeling that a title similar to that given to Philostratus' account of Apollonius, or Chariton's of Chaireas and Callirhoe, τὰ εἰς (or τὰ περὶ) τὸν Χίωνα, *Chion's Story*, might be as appropriate.

The work begins *in mediis rebus*, with Chion in Byzantium, apparently already on a voyage from his home town of Heraclea on the Black Sea to Athens. Letters 1 to 3 are addressed to his father Matris, back in Heraclea, from Byzantium, where Chion is detained by contrary winds. The third tells of a crucial, revelatory encounter with Xenophon, himself freshly arrived in Byzantium from his adventure with the Ten Thousand. Seeing him at close quarters, Chion affirms, has changed his outlook, and specifically his view of philosophy, sweeping away his adolescent scorn for philosophical commitment as incapable of forming a man of active virtue too. And at the same time, it has changed his purposes in sailing to Athens; he now has a new and higher project – to study with Socrates' other pupil, Plato, so as to get as close as he can to the truths and the teaching that inspired the great Xenophon. Letter 4, again to Chion's father, comes from Chios, a stage further on in what has now become Chion's pilgrimage, and describes a perilous encounter with some marauding Thracians at Perinthus. With letters 5 to 13 we have reached Athens, and the stay of over five years in which Chion studies with Plato; most are once more to Chion's father, but one (Letter 9) is to an old, but now estranged friend, with whom Chion wishes to effect a reconciliation. The last of these Athenian letters are darkened by the news from home of the rise to power of the vicious tyrant Clearchus, and by Chion's decision that, much as he would like to spend another five years with Plato, his homeland needs him. Letters 14 to 16 come from Byzantium, as Chion makes his way homewards and lays his plans. 14 and 15 explain his strategy and his thoughts on tyrannicide to his father; 16 is a carefully crafted pack of lies, to the tyrant himself, intended to allay his suspicions and to convince him of Chion's harmlessness. The final letter, 17, from back home in Heraclea, is Chion's farewell to his teacher Plato, written on the very eve of the assassination attempt (which history records was partly successful, but fatal for Chion himself) – the last, noble words of a philosophical and a political martyr, going open-eyed and glad to his heroic doom:

2. I am well aware that I shall lose my life, but if I can only bring off the assassination successfully, then I positively pray for such a fate. If I can only have destroyed the tyrant's power when I depart from the world of men, then I will take my leave with a hymn of praise and a victor's crown. All portents and auguries – in a word, all forms of prophecy – indicate that I will succeed in my venture and die. I myself had a vision more compellingly vivid than any dream. I seemed to see a woman, a miracle of beauty and stature, crowning me with an olive-wreath and ribbons, and then after a brief interval showing me a marvellously beautiful tomb and saying to me, 'You are weary, Chion; come then to this tomb and take your rest.' As a result of this dream, I have high hopes of dying a noble death, as I am convinced that the soul never prophesies falsely, since you too are of this opinion. 3. And if the prediction proves true, then

I consider that I will be a most fortunate man, more so than if I were granted a life lasting into old age after the tyrannicide. I reckon it a fine thing that on completion of a great deed I should depart from the world of men before any benefit should accrue to me with the passage of time; whatever I manage to achieve will be considered far greater than anything I may suffer, and I myself will stand higher in honour than those I have benefited, if my gift of freedom to them is bought at the cost of my own life. Beneficiaries feel that they have been done a greater service if the agent himself does not share in it. Such is my eager confidence in the face of the prophecy of death. Keep well, Plato, and may you enjoy good fortune to a ripe old age. I am convinced that this is the last time I will address you.

As my summary has tried to show, there is a strong and carefully-controlled narrative line to this set of letters. But along with this goes also a consistently strong focus on Chion's character, in its development from unreflective decency to full philosophical virtue. From the outset, we are informed that Chion is someone special: the very first letter has him draw a pointed contrast between the attitudes of ordinary people and his own. As the story develops, we are brought to see more and more fully how this good native disposition grows into something still more admirable (or, alternatively, how someone who initially might seem a rather callow and priggish young man comes good). Perhaps most obviously, the initial, instinctive bravery and capacity for quick action Chion shows in Byzantium and Perinthus (testified to also by his immediate admiration for Xenophon) grows into the reasoning, reflective courage he shows in thinking through both the justification and the mechanics of the plot against Clearchus, and in facing up to the risk of his own death. But one can point too to the way Chion's initial instincts of hospitality and friendliness (2) also grow into the more reflective capacity for friendship shown in his dealings both with Plato and with his estranged friend Bion (6, 7, 10); the way his aristocratic scorn for tradesmen (2) flowers into a maturely philosophical attitude to wealth and material possessions (6, 10); and, finally, how his juvenile candour paves the way for the care he takes to limit and justify the lies he later has to tell for the greater good (7, 12, 13, 15).

Chion's *Epistles* have often been described as an 'epistolary novel' – even, indeed, the sole surviving ancient work fully to deserve that label; more recently, they have also been styled a 'philosophical novel in letters'.[33] This is fair enough if one looks mainly to the narrative line, which shares many kinds of episode with novel plots, and first-person delivery with at least one; or if one looks solely to the moral and political content; but it is arguable that neither label really takes enough account of the focus on the moral character of the protagonist, which goes way beyond anything to be found in the standard novel. For this reason, I would suggest that 'epistolary biography' is at least as good and revealing a label.

Letters thus emerge as interestingly poised on the margins of biography. Not all letters are in any strong sense (auto)biographical, or obvious material for the biographer, particularly if one keeps the Plutarchan, character-oriented understanding of biography in mind; little of the individual, or of individual personality, comes through from the mounds of business and formulaic social correspondence preserved on papyrus. But the letter form has none the less obvious biographical potential, which tends to be more fully realized in the more literate (and literary) correspondence that survives in the major published collections, 'real' or fictitious. This potential is created above all by the highly personalized kind of communication constituted by a letter, from named sender X to named recipient Y, and the fact of spatial separation of X from Y (also definitive of the epistolary situation) which places on X the obligation to spell out the self-representation that can be dispensed with face-to-face. At the same time, letters have a clear attraction for the biographer, on the lookout for both narrative detail, and the revelation of individual character, even if the attraction is tempered by problems of access, and concerns for integrity of style and tone. The welcoming but cautious exploitation of letters that results seems to match the position of the letter form itself, always potentially but never obligatorily (auto)biographical.

Notes

¹ Demetrius *De Eloc.* 224–5, 231; Koskenniemi 1956, 35–7; Trapp 2003, 40–2.

² See for instance Plutarch, *Brut.* 2.5–8, *Eum.* 11, *Alex.* 7 and 28.

³ *Alex.* 1.2; the same principle is more briefly stated at *Cato Min.* 24.1 and 37.10.

⁴ And Philostratus is careful to refer to the letters in *Vit. Ap.* 1.2, when listing the sources that give authority to his biography.

⁵ Further examples, where the letters in question are not those of the principal subject: Plutarch's use of Plato's *Epistles* in *Dion*, and of Cicero's in *Pompey* 42.

⁶ Note for comparison Nepos' verdict in *Atticus* 16.3: Cicero's letters constitute an almost complete history of the times in which they were written (*quae [sc. volumina epistularum] qui legat, non multum desideret historiam contextam eorum temporum*), as well as testifying to Cicero's uncanny prescience (*non enim Cicero ea solum quae vivo se acciderunt futura praedixit, sed etiam quae nunc usu veniunt cecinit ut vates*).

⁷ Tiro's biography is explicitly cited at 41 and 49, but seems also to be behind the description in 20 of Terentia's hold on Cicero. Moles 1988, 28–31 gives a full analysis of Plutarch's sources.

⁸ *Julius* 9, 26, 49, 55, 56; *Aug.* 3, 4, 7, 50, 51, 69, 71, 76, 86, 87; *Tib.* 21, 26, 67; *Gaius* 8; *Claud.* 4; *Domit.* 1.

⁹ *Gram.* 4, 14; *Rhet.* 2.

¹⁰ The *Life* in which letters are not used or mentioned at all is that of Vitellius. For a more detailed analysis of Suetonius' use of letters, broadly in agreement with that given here, see Wallace-Hadrill 1983, 91–5.

¹¹ As Wallace-Hadrill 1983, 93–5 points out, a scatter of references by Quintilian,

Tacitus and the elder Pliny show that some knowledge of Augustus' correspondence was diffused before Suetonius' time, but not so much as to force the conclusion that a full-scale edition, like that of Cicero's correspondence, had been published and was generally available. See also Wallace-Hadrill 1983, 87–9, on Suetonius' professional interest in the details of Augustus' letters.

[12] 64.6.5, 65.9.4, 65.14.1, on which see Millar 1964, 43–4.

[13] For this perception of the (especially stylistic) informality of the letter, see for instance Demetrius *De Eloc.* 223–31.

[14] Compare for instance the first category in Cicero's informal typology of letter-writing in *Ad Fam.* 2.4(=48 SB).1: *unum illud [sc. genus] certissimum, cuius causa inventa res ipsa est, ut certiores faceremus absentis si quid esset quod eos scire aut nostra aut ipsorum interesset* ('that one indubitable kind, for the sake of which the whole business was thought up in the first place, so as to enable us to inform those not present of anything it was important to us or them that they should know').

[15] On Jerome's obituary of Leah, see Trapp 2003, 110–13, 263–5.

[16] For letters of recommendation, see above all Cicero, *Ad Familiares* Book 13; also Trapp 2003, 86–95, 236–45.

[17] For a commentary on this letter, with special reference to its use of epistolary convention, see Trapp 2003, 210–13.

[18] Frs. 138, 177 Usener.

[19] On Seneca and his didactic technique, see Russell 1974 and Hadot 1969; on Horace, Macleod 1979.

[20] See Koskenniemi 1956, 64–87 and 145–8; White 1989, 198–202; Trapp 2003, 35–6.

[21] 2 Cor. 11.12–12.11, RSV translation.

[22] Murphy-O'Connor 1996 is a recent large-scale attempt to base a biography of Paul primarily on his correspondence, reversing the usual practice of fitting the data of the letters into the framework provided by Acts. I owe this reference to Justin Taylor.

[23] R. Pervo, 'Romancing an oft-neglected stone', *JHC* 1, 1994, 25–47 (and on the web at http://www.depts.drew.edu/jhc/pervope.html). This is however a difficult and controversial area (it may be for instance that the Pastoral Epistles do not make a homogeneous set, and that one of them may be genuinely Pauline).

[24] See again Nepos' assessment, noted in n. 6 above.

[25] For the details, see *Ad Att.* 16.5 (=410 SB).5, *Ad Fam.* 16.17. (=126 SB)1, Nepos, *Att.* 16.2–4, with Shackleton Bailey 1965, 59–76 and 1977, 23–4.

[26] See in general Radicke 1997 and Rudd 1992.

[27] For commentary, see Trapp 2003, 221–2; cf. also Shelton 1990.

[28] See in general Rosenmeyer 2001, 193–233.

[29] See Russell 1988, Rosenmeyer 2001, 224–31, Hinz 2001, 19–126, and Trapp 2003, 28–9, with items 11–12, 25, 38, 51, 60 and 70.

[30] See Rosenmeyer 2001, 217–21, with further bibliography. Costa 2001, 96–107 and 176–9 gives text and translation of *Ep.* 17, with commentary.

[31] But there is a chronological problem: historically, the last letter must date from about 353, and the encounter with Xenophon, related in the third, to 401/400; yet the internal chronology of the letters allows fewer than ten years between these two points.

[32] For Chion's letters, see Düring 1951; Konstan and Mitsis 1990; Costa 2001, xviii–xix,

108–123 and 179–186; Rosenmeyer 2001, 234–52; Trapp 2003, 30–1, 70–3, 217–19.
[33] Düring 1951 and Konstan and Mitsis 1990.

Bibliography

Costa, C.D.N. (ed.)
2001   *Greek Fictional Letters*, Oxford.

Düring, I. (ed. and transl.)
1951   *Chion of Heraclea. A novel in letters*, Göteborg, repr. New York.

Hadot, I.
1969   *Seneca und die griechish-römische Tradition der Seelenleitung*, Berlin.

Hinz, V.
2001   *Nunc Phalaris doctum protulit ecce caput. Antike Phalarislegende und Nachleben der Phalarisbriefe*, Beiträge zur Altertumskunde 148, Munich and Leipzig.

Konstan, D. and Mitsis, P.
1990   'Chion of Heraclea: a philosophical novel in letters', *Apeiron* 23, 257–79.

Koskenniemi, H.
1956   *Studien zur Idee und Phraseologie des griechischen Briefes bis 400 N.Chr.*, Helsinki.

Macleod, C.W.
1979   'The poetry of ethics: Horace, *Epistles* I', *JRS* 69, 16–27, repr. in id., *Collected Essays*, Oxford 1983, 280–91.

Millar, F.G.B.
1964   *A Study of Cassius Dio*, Oxford.

Moles, J.L. (ed.)
1988   *Plutarch. The Life of Cicero*, Warminster.

Murphy-O'Connor, J.
1996   *Paul. A critical life*, Oxford.

Radicke, J.
1997   'Die Selbstdarstellung des Plinius in seinen Briefen', *Hermes* 125, 447–69.

Rosenmeyer, P.A.
2001   *Ancient epistolary fictions. The letter in Greek literature*, Cambridge.

Rudd, N.
1992   'Strategies of vanity: Cicero *Ad Familiares* 5.12 and Pliny's letters', in A.J. Woodman and J.G.F. Powell (eds.) *Author and audience in Latin literature*, Cambridge, 18–32.

Russell, D.A.
1974   'Letters to Lucilius,' in Costa (ed.) *Seneca*, London, 70–95.
1988   'The ass in the lion's skin: thoughts on the *Letters* of Phalaris', *JHS* 108, 94–106.

Shackleton Bailey, D.R. (ed.)
1965   *Cicero's letters to Atticus*, vol. I, Cambridge.
1977   *Cicero: Epistulae ad familiares*, Cambridge.

Shelton, J.-A.
1990   'Pliny the Younger and the ideal wife', *CM* 41, 163–86.

Trapp, M.B. (ed.)
  2003   *Greek and Latin Letters. An anthology*, Cambridge.
Wallace-Hadrill, A.
  1983   *Suetonius*, London.
White, J.L.
  1986   *Light from Ancient Letters*, Philadelphia.

19

LORDS OF THE FLIES:
LITERACY AND TYRANNY IN
IMPERIAL BIOGRAPHY

Alexei V. Zadorojnyi

– Mais il faudra écrire!
– Oh! oui. C'est indispensable. Deux mots de la main de Votre Majesté et votre
cachet particulier.
– Mais ces deux mots, c'est ma condamnation, c'est le divorce, l'exil!

Alexandre Dumas, *Les Trois Mousquetaires*, chap. xvii

'*C'est par mon ordre et pour le bien de l'État*
que le porteur du présent a fait ce qu'il a fait. Richelieu'

Ibid., chaps. xlv, xlvii, and lxvii

Me, poor man, my library / Was dukedom large enough.

Shakespeare, *The Tempest*, i.2.109–10

I

Among the bad press given to the emperor Domitian in antiquity,[1] one
curiously intimate close-up episode is found. Never a sociable person,
Domitian spent much time alone. During these periods of seclusion he had
a habit of impaling flies upon his writing stylus. When someone asked, 'Who
is in with Domitian?', a court wit replied, 'Not even a fly!'

The story is contextualized differently in different sources. Suetonius
(*Dom.* 3.1) and Cassius Dio (66.9.4–5) place it well before Domitian's
accession. Sidelined by his father and brother, the depressive prince kills
flies and time as the darkness in his character is biding and brewing. In the
account of Cassius Dio the focus is on the absurdity of Domitian's behaviour.
Fly-stabbing was a pathetic prank of his feigned madness (66.9.4 μωρίαν ἔστιν
ὅτε προσεποιεῖτο…ἄλλα τε πολλὰ καὶ γελοῖα ἔπραττε). Yet with hindsight it
is easy to guess where this will lead. The episode is emphatically brought
forward as a relevant detail for understanding Domitian:

unworthy as this incident is of the dignity of history (τοῦ τῆς ἱστορίας ὄγκου),
yet because it is a good indicator of his personality (ἱκανῶς τὸν τρόπον αὐτοῦ

351

ἐνδείκνυται) and especially because he continued to do this after he became emperor, I felt obliged to write about it.   (Cass. Dio 66.9.4)

In Aurelius Victor (*De Caes.* 11.5, cf. epitom. 11.6–8) Domitian is a fully developed bloodthirsty tyrant in power. He kills flies when he is not busy executing Roman elite citizens (*boni*). Again, the leisure lacks any dignity (*segnisque ridicule*). The story also snipes at the emperor's sex life, a sad combination of lewdness and declining potency:[2]

> From now on he was terrible for his slaughter of honourable men and absurdly idle. He would shut everyone out and chase swarms of flies, when he had less energy for sex, a shameful exercise which he called, in Greek, 'bed-wrestling'. This was the origin of many jokes. For when someone enquired about who actually was in the palace, the reply was, 'Not even a fly, except maybe in the wrestling room.'

> dehinc atrox caedibus bonorum segnisque ridicule remotis procul omnibus muscarum agmina persequebatur, postquam ad libidinem minus virium erat, cuius foedum exercitium Graecorum lingua κλινοπάλην vocabat. Hincque iocorum pleraque: nam percontanti cuidam, quis iamne in palatio esset, responsum: ne musca quidem, nisi forte apud palaestram.   (*De Caes.* 11.5)

Young or mature, this is very much Domitian as we expect him to be.[3] The anecdote, with its unmistakable Hollywood-thriller touch, confirms him in his pre-programmed part of a disgusting, psychotic, if slightly boring, villain. To stab a fly would require a lot of patience and quite deadly precision.[4] So the parallel is neat. Domitian's treatment of the flies mirrors or foretells cruelty (*saevitia*) towards people – his cat-and-mouse-style, ever dissembling and delaying the strike against his victims, was notorious.[5] Tacitus' vision of Domitian practically killing the whole state 'with a single stab' (*Agr.* 44.5 *continuo et velut uno ictu rem publicam exhausit*) becomes a flashback. Ancient readers might have recalled that bit of popular wisdom about human life being worth less than that of a fly (*minoris quam muscae sumus*: Petron. *Sat.* 42.4).[6]

In this case the pessimism would have been coloured by more specific resentment. Our position is made increasingly fly-like under despotism. From the ancient perspective Domitian's pathology is to be read politically, since he is not just any person, he is one of the more extreme examples of a bad ruler. The story is unique and paradigmatic at the same time. It helps to signal the tyrannical cruelty along with such traditional themes as isolation of the tyrant and, perhaps, the unreliable, slippery flattery of his entourage as represented here by the cynical joker.[7]

According to Suetonius and Cassius Dio, Domitian used a peculiar weapon to stab his poor flies: a stylus. How important is this stylus as the preferred instrument of killing? What does it tell us about Domitian? Few modern commentators have paid attention to the presence of the stylus. More recently John Penwill interpreted the fly-stabbing scene as evidence of writer's block while working on the (otherwise attested) epics about the Capitoline and Jerusalem Wars: dead flies *were* Domitian's poetry.[8] This reading, however, is too narrow. The fact that Domitian handles a stylus in an episode of symbolic significance for his image as a tyrant must be linked with the broader pattern of authoritarian government in ancient political and biographical writing. Domitian's stylus is a feature of tyrannical power as well as (as we shall see) the tyrant's vulnerability. It can serve as a starting-point to explore the persistent yet varied model of despotism as regime strongly associated with literacy in Graeco-Roman thought.

II

Claude Lévi-Strauss famously formulated the idea about the alliance of literacy and political and economic control when he studied the impact of colonialism on the indigenous cultures of Brazil:

> The only phenomenon with which writing has always been concomitant is the creation of cities and empires, that is the integration of large numbers of individuals into a political system and their grading into castes and classes...it seems to have favoured the exploitation of human beings rather than their enlightenment...the primary function of written communication is to facilitate slavery... Through gaining access to the knowledge stored in libraries, these peoples have also become vulnerable to the still greater proportion of lies propagated in printed documents.[9]

The academic value of Lévi-Strauss' speculation has been questioned. Like every Big Theory, it fails most practical tests.[10] But the importance of his insight lies elsewhere. Behind the objection to the progressivist (and eurocentric) view of literacy as the path of civilization, technological improvement, liberation of reason, and ultimately the good life[11] there is a sense of anxiety affecting liberal Western intelligentsia in the wake of political events of the first half of the twentieth century. Nightmares of contemporary history created a climate where literacy was identified with the oppressive bureaucracy of the state that invaded and destroyed individual freedom. (Franz Kafka in his 1914 tale *In der Strafkolonie* prefigured this negative experience of literacy as a sophisticated torture machine that would physically write the statutes on the offender's body.) Literacy mistrusted and feared as means of unwished-for integration, literacy appropriated by the sinister forces of the government, turned into a mechanism for policing and brainwashing by colonialists and fascists: these are the assumptions in Lévi-Strauss' analysis that make it a manifesto of crisis, pessimism, and dissent.[12] While deploring the fate of traditional oral societies that are subjugated through writing, the passage cited above is an expression of anti-literacy rhetoric that originates from *within* the literate culture – indeed, among the educated class to which Lévi-Strauss, Kafka, and their readers all belong. Such critique of literacy can only take place in a highly advanced literate domain as a kind of anti-power power game.[13] The playground is busy, with the Lévi-Straussian argument presenting just one possible line of attack on literacy. I shall hereafter refer to it as the 'slavery' objection in order to distinguish it from other approaches, such as 'philosophical' objection(s) to written discourse (as in Plato), the 'occupational' objection to literacy as an activity that is socially and economically unrewarding, insufficiently heroic, etc. ('warriors *vs.* bookworms'), the 'grassroots' objection that rejects literate culture as irrelevant for the good ordinary folks (as in late Tolstoy), or the 'lazy' reductionist argument that complains about the quantity and quality of literary mass production ('too much rubbish is being published').[14]

In this paper I shall examine a selection of Graeco-Roman texts, concentrating on texts that contain biographical information on Roman emperors,[15] for evidence of broadly Lévi-Straussian concerns about the closeness of literacy and power. None of these texts articulates the 'slavery' objection to literacy explicitly. Furthermore, the concepts of literacy, bureaucracy, or imperialism did not exist in the ancient world. On the other hand, bureaucrats and empires did exist, as did the reflecting literati. In the literature they produced there is a large amount of descriptive, that is to say narrative and anecdotal, material that allows to believe that similar apprehensions about literacy were held and experimented with throughout antiquity[16] and had a part in the ideological (mis)construction of autocratic power[17] by the politically active class.

III

Writing first appears in Homer in the form of 'baneful signs' (σήματα λυγρά) on the tablet carried by Bellerophon (*Il.* 6.168–9).[18] In the age of pre-literacy and early literacy written communication is a suspected novelty, a code. Codes mean ciphers, and ciphers mean deception. In Herodotus' *Histories* letters transmitted in exotic ways (tattooed on a slave's head, sewn into a hare), are a recurrent motif cropping up in situations of secrecy, treason, and clandestine intrigue.[19] The sneaky manner of transmission reflects the hazardous contents, and vice versa. The medium and the message overlap.

There is another dimension to the portrayal of writing in Herotodus' narrative. Deborah Steiner, following François Hartog,[20] has shown that in the *Histories* writing and, generally, inscribing and numbering tend to be a characteristic of authoritarian as well as manipulative policy. Writing is (ab)used to stir up conspiracies (1.123.4, 5.35.3), to initiate military expansion (5.14), to herd the army (4.87.1; 7.100.1–2; 8.90.4), to assert completed conquest (2.102.4–5; 2.106.1–4; 7.30.2; 4.91.1), to trigger assassination by remote control: Oroetes' bodyguards are forced into killing their master by letters sealed with the royal seal that are read out to them (3.128.2–5). Through tomb inscriptions the wise queen Nitocris extends her own authority beyond death and scores a point over Darius (1.187). Effectively Herodotus sets up a no-win dilemma. If hidden, written discourse is subversive; if public, dictatorial. Whichever route is taken, there will be transgression involved.

It was argued by Hartog and Steiner that Herodotus presents literacy as a trademark of oriental despotism. Acts of writing in the *Histories* are associated primarily with Asian, notably Persian, monarchs; accidentally the alphabet is an Eastern invention, too (5.58). Considerably fewer instances of writing occur on the Greek side. When they do occur, they are of a rather different kind.[21] Greek individuals who resort to written messages are typically tyrants and plotting politicians exposed to alien influence through their contact with the Persians (Aristagoras: 5.35.5; Demaratus: 7.239.3–4; Themistocles: 8.22). 'Noble savages' communicate orally or by gestures and symbols (2.30.4; 3.21.2–3; 4.131–2): this befits their narrative role, which is to defy imperialist centralization.

Literacy thus contributes to the 'Greek *vs.* the barbarian Other' polarity[22] in Herodotus. Greek tyrants and eastern kings are clearly on opposite sides of this cultural fence. Yet beyond a certain point they also merge as sub-species of a universal model commensurate with the 'rise-and-decline' principle introduced as a blanket pattern of political history (1.5.3–4). The fact that the term 'tyranny' is occasionally applied to oriental regimes (1.6.1, 1.7.2, 1.14.1, 1.15, 1.73.3, 1.77.2, 1.96.1, 1.100.1, 1.109.4, 3.80.4, 7.52.2), and that, reversedly, a Greek tyrant can be called *basileus* (3.42.2, 3.52.4, 5.35.1, 5.92 ε2, 5.113.2, 7.161.1), suggests that Herodotus is again thinking globally. There is a generic across-the-board sameness to local brands of one-man rule, especially when it goes astray;[23] the East-West dichotomy gets blurred. The wrongs of hubristic monocracy, as summed up by Otanes during the Constitutional Debate (3.80.5), are illustrated both in the Greek and non-Greek sections of the narrative.[24]

I argue that the motif of writing in the *Histories* is related to this generalized notion of (abusive) despotism and, in fact, helps to create this unified notion. Literacy is, for Herodotus, a concomitant of autocracy in its variable guises.[25] Political positioning is primary, nationality secondary. The Herodotean attitude to literacy, as I read it, is anti-tyrannical rather than anti-Persian. It will be referred to hereafter as the 'tyranny' argument.

355

Herodotus' stories about writing are so crucial in the history of ancient reception of literacy because they are archetypal, but also because his work marks the transitional stage in the development of Greek literacy. It stands on the cusp between pre-literacy and texts, between storytelling as performance and complex literary œuvre aimed at elite readership.[26] Calculating the exact percentage of orality and literacy in the *Histories* is a desperate task. Does Herodotus mistrust writing because he is still not used to it? Or is he inventing the fear of literacy from a literate's perspective?[27] The latter is likely to be the case, making the Herodotean 'tyranny' argument analogous to the Lévi-Straussian 'slavery' argument discussed above. The two arguments visibly differ in context and motivation. The modern argument is, at the end of the day, counter-hegemonic as it seeks to promote the interests of the underprivileged many, whereas the ancient argument is worried about tyranny infringing the rights of the elite.[28] But this should not blind us to the fundamental similarity between them, namely that utilization of literacy under oppressive government is denounced, explicitly or implicitly, by highly literate intellectuals engaging in polemical dialogue with power. It takes a literate mind to discover the evil of literacy in politics.

The Herodotean 'tyranny' argument against literacy encapsulates a lasting tendency in Greek and then Graeco-Roman thought. As a tendency it is seriously fuzzy and certainly not exclusive, even in Herodotus.[29] In the classical period it was evidently understood that both good regimes and tyrannical regimes made use of writing. Thus, a community may commemorate its heroic dead or its benefactors with an inscription (e.g., Hdt. 7.228, Dem. 20.64); written records protect the state from embezzlers (e.g., Plut. *Lys.* 16.2–4). In a democracy, the axial role of writing is to be a durable, trustworthy medium for the constitutional statutes.[30] No surprise that written laws get praised as the basis of justice (Gorg. *Palam.* fr. 11a.30; Eur. *Suppl.* 433–4); in the more elitist Platonic model, the best form of government is monarchy 'yoked' by written rules (*Pol.* 302e10–12) whereas at the opposite end of the scale is the hubristic tyrant who breaks all laws, including written ones (301b10–c5). Yet there is also the insistence that written legislation is hollow unless supported by a superior political force, such as the people's will to actually uphold it (Dem. 21.224–5), living examples of civic virtue (Pl. *Leg.* 822e4–823a6), or the τέχνη of knowledge-based statesmanship (Pl. *Pol.* 299d6–e4, 300c10–d2; Ar. *Pol.* 1286a9–16).[31] Worse, the link between tyranny and the material actuality of written discourse could be perceived as straightforward:

> ...a city's writing on legal topics should turn out, on being opened (διαπτυττόμενα), to be the finest and best of all... So what *is* the style in which a state's laws ought to be written, in our opinion? Should the regulations appear

as a loving and prudent father and mother (ἐν πατρός τε καὶ μητρὸς σχήμασι)? Or should they act the tyrant and despot, posting their orders and threats on walls and leaving it at that? (ἢ κατὰ τύραννον καὶ δεσπότην τάξαντα καὶ ἀπειλήσαντα γράψαντα ἐν τοίχοις ἀπηλλάχθαι;)

(Plato, *Laws* 858e–859a, transl. T.J. Saunders, modified)

For if we were tyrants in charge of cities, it would truly be in our power (ἐφ᾽ ἡμῖν ἂν ἦν) to summon the courts and to take counsel for public affairs so that, whenever we wrote speeches, we could then call the other citizens to listen to them. But since it is others who are in control of these things...

(Alcidamas, *Against Writers of Speeches*, 11, transl. J.V. Muir)[32]

Bad laws rely primarily (or solely) on their written form instead of persuasion. This is what makes them resemble tyrants. The blunt visibility of tyrannical public writing ('on walls') cancels all chance of debate, as does the coercion of a tyrant's recital from a text. Written statements hijack obedience by the sheer fact of being written; the text usurps power in the same brutal way as the tyrant himself.

Fast-forwarding several centuries into the Imperial era, one finds that 'tyranny' very much survives among bywords of political discourse: bad emperors are persistently categorized as tyrants.[33] Nor is the alliance between evil despotisim and literacy ever forgotten. Herodian (3.11.9) adopts a pointedly timeless tone when dwelling on one of tyranny's hallmarks:

The tyrants have a habit, when they order someone to be killed without trial, of instructing about this in writing so that the action is not unconfirmed.

ἔθος γὰρ τοῦτο τυραννικόν, εἴ τινα ἐκπέμποιεν ἐπὶ φόνον ἄκριτον, ἐντέλλεσθαι τοῦτο διὰ γραμμάτων, ἵνα μὴ γινόμενον ἦ ἀκατασήμαντον. (Herodian 3.11.9)

The tyrannical writing 'on the wall' crops up, too: Caligula tests the limits of the topos when he apparently pioneers the practice of small print. The people demand that the already happening tax-increases are confirmed by a bill. Caligula then posts up regulations, written out in tiny letters, either in a narrow place or too high to be read and copied (Suet. *Cal.* 41.1; Cass. Dio 59.28.11). Display of unreadable and inaccessible law adds to the tyrant's hubris against the community; the people are mocked in their helplessness, while Caligula is counting on penalties and fines as a result of regulatory confusion (Cass. Dio 59.28.11).[34] A story like this does not merely evince the readiness of the Imperial narratives to typecast political experience and the behaviour of leaders by way of evoking classical clichés: it is also a reminder that the attitude towards literacy (vis-à-vis power) in these texts is honeycombed with such allusiveness – something to be kept in mind throughout the next sections of this paper.

IV

At any period of Graeco-Roman history advanced bookish literacy was confined to a privileged minority standing out in the sea of restricted semi-literacy. Literary education in the Hellenistic and Imperial age became a paramount factor of prestige and social status. The educated elite defined itself in terms of *paideia* as much as of power.[35] The immanent assumption is that culture facilitates one's political progress (e.g. Val. Max. 8.11.1; Fronto *Ad Am.* 1.4.1; Cass Dio 71.35.1). Encomiasts are advised to take stock in the truism that well-educated people are 'most worthy of power' ([D. Hal.] *Ars Rhet.* 5.3 p. 274, 22–4 Us.-Rad. οἱ πεπαιδευμένοι μάλιστα ἄξιοι ἀρχῆς καὶ τοιαύτης ἡγεμονίας). 'Who reigns better than a littérateur?' Roman senators allegedly exclaimed in October of AD 275 as they tried to talk Tacitus into rule (*SHA Tac.* 3.4 *ecquis melius quam litteratus imperat?*).[36] True greatness cannot be ensured without education:

> They [sc. Galerius and Constantius I] were so remarkable for their natural abilities that if those abilities emanated from cultivated minds and did not give offence because of their lack of taste, without doubt they would be considered exceptional. For it is indisputable that learning, refinement, and courtesy are essential, particularly in emperors, since without these qualities natural talents are despised as if they are unfinished or even crude, yet those very qualities prepared everlasting glory for Cyrus, king of the Persians.
>
> adeo miri naturae beneficiis, ut ea si a doctis pectoribus proficiscerentur neque insulsitate offenderent, haud dubie praecipua haberentur. Quare compertum est eruditionem elegantiam comitatem praesertim principibus necessarias esse, cum sine his naturae bona quasi incompta aut etiam horrida despectui sint, contraque ea Persarum regi Cyro aeternam gloriam paraverint.
> (Aurel. Vict. *De Caes.* 40.12–13, transl. H.W. Bird, modified).[37]

The rule of thumb, then, is that a good statesman would be lettered. Securing a reputation for culture justifies the expense of buying a big library (*SHA Gord.* 18.2), and it is a shame when an emperor who read Plato, Aristotle, Cicero, and Virgil, comes to a sticky end (*SHA Gord.* 7.1). In such a cultur-ally anxious environment the exterior of one's literary habits pans out into an ethico-political diagnosis. A provincial governor could be dismissed because of a spelling mistake (Suet. *Aug.* 88; Cass. Dio bk. 56 fr. 3); a sensual emperor keeps Ovid's erotic poems handy on his couch (*SHA Hel.* 5.9 *Ovidii libros amorum semper in lecto habuisse*); a deluxe edition of Homer may be jumped upon as *omen imperii* (*SHA Max.* 30.4).

It is hardly surprising that biography and historiography, both high-end genres of elite literary discourse, are interested in the cultural profile of their elite protagonists. Power and culture are played off against each other in evaluating personalities of statesmen, with the emperor's figure attracting most attention and flak – Suetonian *Lives* have a dedicated section on *paideia*, whereas most authors seem to favour the smörgåsboard-approach.[38] Augustus' spelling was scrutinized (Quint. 1.7.2; Suet. *Aug.* 87.3–88); Domitian is condemned by Suetonius for not bothering with even the 'necessary' style[39] and reading only Tiberius' memoirs and enactments (*Dom.* 20); bad emperors, such as Commodus or Caracalla, hate and despise *paideia* in others (Herodian 1.13.8; Cass. Dio 72.7.3, 77.11.2). In late antiquity, the downhill trend of literary culture amongst emperors is increasingly deplored. This, Aurelius Victor chides the *Soldatkaiser* Maximinus and Vetranio calling them 'nigh-illiterate' boors (*De Caes.* 25.1, 41.26), and the 'Anonymous Valesianus' (14/79) gloats over the extreme illiteracy of Theoderic who in ten years did not learn to sign the documents with the formula *LEGI* and so had to use a golden stencil (*lamina*).[40]

A deficit of culture in a ruler is clearly bad. On the other hand, an emperor's political faults can be partially offset by his cultural achievements. Aurelius Victor, a self-made *pepaideumenos* (*De Caes.* 20.5), is prepared, while recognizing the primacy of morals (*De Caes.* 19.3, 20.8), to make big concessions on the grounds of culture: if the vices of Tiberius, Caligula, Claudius, and Nero were not so notorious, they might have got away with them because they were so well-versed in literature and eloquence (*De Caes.* 8.7 = epitom. 8.6 *tantae artes professo texissent modica flagitia*).[41] Even more outspoken are Victor's comments on the posthumous reputation of Didius (Salvius?) Julianus,[42] the short-lived emperor of AD 193:

> Septimius Severus commanded the name of Salvius and his writings and achievements to be erased, but this was the one thing he could not carry out. So great is the prestige of the learned arts that not even a violent character can harm the writer's image. Moreover, death of this kind glorifies them but makes the agents of the deed detestable, since all men, especially later generations, consider that those talented individuals could not have been suppressed except through public banditry and madness.

> Septimius...Salvii nomen atque eius scripta factave aboleri iubet; quod unum effici nequivit. Tantum gratia doctarum artium valet, ut scriptoribus ne saevi mores quidem ad memoriam officiant. Quin etiam mors huiusquemodi ipsis gloriae, exsecrationi actoribus est, cum omnes, praecipueque posteri, sic habent illa ingenia nisi publico latrocinio ac per dementiam opprimi non potuisse.
> (*De Caes.* 20.1–4, transl. H.W. Bird, modified)

'More culture!' is generally one of the overarching slogans of Graeco-Roman discourse. For statesmen, however, there is the additional imperative to balance their paideutic pursuits against the decorum and pressures of political leadership. Public stature and career would be expected to have priority over education and to delimit its quota in one's life.[43] Cultural professionalism is best avoided. The emperor must not turn into a poet or an orator – his position requires quite different qualities (*SHA Gall.* 11.9). Trajan, the best *princeps*, appreciated and promoted *paideia* without claiming it for himself (Philostr. *VS* 488; Cass. Dio 68.7.4). Often the emperors fail to draw the line correctly: Claudius and Nero are the most obvious of examples, but even a nice(ish) guy like Hadrian can be marked down for being 'over-addicted' to literature (*SHA Hadr.* 14.8 *poematum et litterarum nimium studiosissimus*).[44]

So the balance grows out of tension. Lack of *paideia* at the top is a menace, and yet its counterpoint is the fear that the autocrat might be distracted and corrupted by overexposure to culture. This sets in relief the extant evidence that the elite class occasionally resented and resisted the autocrat interfering with *paideia*. We are told that Tiberius, who was generally rigorous about purity of Latin in political idiom,[45] used a Greek word in an edict. He apologized to the senate for this one-off linguistic lapse. A flattering senator (Ateius Capito) said that the word so graced by the emperor should be added to classical vocabulary straightaway (ἐς τὰ ἀρχαῖα καταριθμήσομεν). But one Marcellus objected: 'You, Caesar, can confer Roman citizenship upon people, but not upon words' (Cass. Dio 57.17.2; cf. Suet. *Tib.* 71). Suetonius mentions the story about Augustus cashiering a governor for having written *ixi* instead of *ipsi*, but rejects it as untrue because Augustus also misspelled a lot: misspelling, Suetonius concludes in a tongue-in-cheek way, is a common failure of humanity (*Aug.* 88 *communis hominum error est*). The sophist Dionysius of Miletus snapped at Avidius Heliodorus, Hadrian's secretary *ab epistulis*: 'Caesar can give you money and office, but he cannot make you an orator!' (Cass. Dio 69.3.5) Anecdotes such as these show how the Graeco-Roman elite can be over-protective about literate culture as their field of group solidarity.[46] The autocrat is momentarily tipped that here he is a player on the same level as others: he is not lord over words, he should not (if he wants to rule with justice, that is) punish others for spelling mistakes which he makes himself.

At the same time there is the pervasive realization that under empire the autocrat's literacy has an exceptional status. 'It is difficult to write against him who can proscribe you', warns the cheerless pun by the Augustan historian, poet, and politician Asinius Pollio (ap. Macrob. 2.4.21: *non facile est in eum scribere qui potest proscribere*). From the early days of the principate, the emperor is construed as a privileged reader of the past: thus Livy, mulling over the true rank of a fifth-century republican nobleman (4.20.5–11), cagily accepts Augustus' version – because Augustus said he had seen with his own eyes the relevant inscription on a temple-kept artefact (4.20.7 *ego cum Augustum Caesarem...se ipsum in thorace linteo scriptum legisse audissem*).[47]

In relation to the present, the emperor's literacy is clearly the most potent of all literacies.[48] Favorinus' excuse for having ceded to Hadrian in a philological dispute is that '...the man who commands thirty legions must be more learned than all men' (*SHA Hadr.* 15.12–13).

As the emperor embodies power, so his written word, processed through the administrative machine,[49] embodies his will and authority. It is taken for granted that after a missive from Rome compliance will ensue (Cass. Dio 69.23.2; Ael. Arist. *In Rom.* 33–207). The sentiment is epitomized in the story about riots in Alexandria, quelled by a single letter from Hadrian:

the emperor's word carries more strength than weapons

πλέον ἰσχύει αὐτοκράτορος λόγος τῶν ὅπλων   (Cass. Dio 69.8.1a)

Dio's phrase derives from the rhetoric of allegorizing discourse as a weapon, usually a sword.[50] Significantly, under the Empire the trope regularly brings out the death-dealing side of despotism. Sword-blade (*acies*) is a metaphor of autocratic power (Sen. *Clem.* 1.11.2 *hebetare aciem imperii sui*), but this power, extending over life and death, really sits on the tip of the autocrat's tongue (*acies linguae*: Amm. Marc. 18.3.7, 29.1.19). Caligula ominously refers to his own speech as 'the weapon of his vigil' (Suet. *Cal.* 53.3 *stricturum se lucubrationis suae telum minabatur*); Tigellinus' henchman whose job it is to fabricate charges against the holy sage Apollonius (Philostr. *V. Ap.* 4.44) brandishes his pamphlet (γραμματεῖον) like a sword (ὥσπερ ξίφος ἀνασείων).[51]

Despite the fact that ancient biography and historiography were composed for elite literates by elite literates, in several cases by career apparatchiks (Suetonius, Aurelius Victor) the Herodotean misgivings about literacy as a medium of despotism are widely reflected in these texts. ('Lévi-Straussier and Lévi-Straussier!' Alice might have said.) An explanation, if there has to be one, should probably be sought in the symbiosis of small-scale innovation and overall traditionalism in Graeco-Roman political and historical thought. An ancient study of power and the person in power is seldom able to disengage from the old stereotypes of virtuous, just leader and cruel, unjust tyrant (e.g. Dio Chr. 1.67–8, 3.43–4). Julius Caesar in Cassius Dio confronts the dilemma head-on, declaring to the senate that his aim is 'to be a champion and a leader, not despot and tyrant' (43.17.2 οὐ δεσποτίζειν ἀλλὰ προστατεῖν, οὐ τυραννεύειν ἀλλὰ ἡγεμονεύειν). While each emperor is different (and while the same emperor may not be exactly the same in different texts), the vices and virtues that individualize him are weighed against the canonical 'good king *vs.* tyrant' polarity. Elements of characterization develop and re-mix in a potentially infinite number of ways as variations on a theme, but nonetheless crystallize into habitual clauses of praise or censure.[52] Carefully manipulated shadings of detail resolve into the pre-programmed primary colour; Imperial history necessarily breaks down into goodies and baddies. *Tyrannus* is the verdict on Tiberius, Nero, Commodus, Caracalla, and many late emperors (Suet. *Tib.* 75.3; Cass. Dio 61.10.2, Tac. *Hist.* 4.42; Herodian 2.2.4–5, 6.1.2; *SHA Macr.* 1.1 *vitae illorum principum seu tyrannorum sive Caesarum*); young Caligula was an all-right *princeps* when he was young, but then became a monster (Suet. *Cal.* 22.1 *hactenus quasi de principe, reliqua ut de monstro narranda*); just one act – actually a non-act – of Heliogabalus was that of a 'good autocrator', otherwise his reign was dictatorship and scandal (Cass. Dio 80.3.2).

In the rest of this paper I shall examine the following literacy-related aspects in the negative portrayal of Roman autocracy: preference for written communication, control of the written word, and instances of bureaucratic literacy backfiring on the rulers. I shall attempt a structured survey of diverse anecdotal material, arguing that: (a) it is when imperial power shows signs of degenerating into scheming and bloody tyranny of the broadly Herodotean kind that the sinister political semantics of writing is switched on by biographers and historians, and (b) that it is therefore not accidental that literacy is often presented as the immediate cause of the tyrants' demise.

V

Autocrats rely on records and letters. One archetypal story is found, once again, in Herodotus: Deioces the Mede consolidates his power over the people by isolating himself in a palace and communicating only through written messages (1.99–100).[53] Hellanicus of Lesbos reports that the Persian queen Atossa, a masculinized female, was the first person ever to 'give responses through letters', as well to wear tiara (and trousers) and to employ eunuchs:[54] literacy is part of the combined inversion of the 'normal' political and gender paradigms. Xerxes, another despot-figure of timeless significance, is accompanied by note-taking scribes (Hdt. 7.100.1–2; 8.90.4; Plut. *Them.* 13.1), and even sends threatening letters to Mount Athos (Plut. *De Coh. Ira* 455D–E).[55]

With tyrannical emperors, record-keeping could similarly escalate as a vehicle, or rather a focal point, of state-run terror. The soldiers guarding Agrippina and Nero keep a diary of all their visits (Tac. *Ann.* 4.67); Nero tries to extenuate some of his worst crimes, namely Agrippina's murder and suppression of the Pisonian conspiracy, by publication of dossiers (Tac. *Ann.* 14.10–11, 15.73); under Domitian, Tacitus laments, 'our every breath was being logged' (*Agr.* 45.2 *cum suspiria nostra subscriberentur*); the officer Ursicinus conducting cruel trials for Gallus Caesar is surrounded by scribes (*notarii*) who immediately report the interrogation-minutes to the prince himself (Amm. Marc. 14.9.3 *assistebant hinc inde notarii, quid quaesitum esset quidve responsum, cursim ad Caesarem perferentes*). It is salient, if slightly amusing, that in late antiquity the supernatural, too, gets bureaucratized: daemons are called 'servants and secretaries' of the gods (Plut. *De Def.* 417A ὑπηρέταις καὶ γραμματεῦσι), and the Parcae are no longer spinning, but writing and maintaining the gods' archive (Mart. Cap. 1.64 *librariae superum archivique custodes*)![56]

One route for criticism of excessive monocracy in the Graeco-Roman world is thus to zero in on its excessive use of literacy. Reliance on written documents and unusual efficiency in dealing with them can be interpreted as symptoms of tyranny. Julius Caesar is the perfect litmus test. Caesar was exceptionally good with paperwork – reading, listening, dictating, and writing at the same time, on the move (Pliny *NH* 7.91: *scribere aut legere, simul dictare et audire solitum*, Plut. *Caes.* 17.4, 7). Too busy to meet his friends in person, he thought of a 'new arrangement' of writing notes to them instead (Plut. *Caes.* 17.8 πρῶτον μηχανήσασθαι). He 'invented' a new format of communication with the senate (Suet. *Caes.* 56.6); he wrote in cipher (Suet. *Caes.* 56.6; Gell. 17.9.1–5; Cass. Dio 40.9.3) This is impressive but not entirely innocent, and μηχανήσασθαι remains an ambiguous word: given his tyrannical ambition,[57] Caesar is the sort of man to be all-too-clever with writing – and not to be trusted. Asinius Pollio, cited by Suetonius (*Caes.* 56.4), points out that Caesar's war memoirs contain much unreliable information (*parum diligenter parumque integra veritate compositos...vel consulto vel etiam memoria lapsus*). Surely these errors would have been corrected, Pollio adds, if Caesar had the time for revision... In one of the several arrogant quips by Caesar-the-dictator literacy aptly metaphorizes the authoritarian approach to politics: in his opinion, Sulla 'did not know his ABC when he gave up the dictatorship' (Suet. *Caes.* 77 *nescisse litteras qui dictaturam deposuerit*).

Why is writing a tyrannical thing? The answer must stem from the instinct that writing negates face-to-face communication, creating a remote authority while taking away the immediacy and freedom of oral exchange. Written dispatches segregate the tyrant (Deioces, Caesar) from the community. Any dialogue, any objection is precluded by the dominance of the text. Tyrannical hubris, unchallenged, flourishes in writing – and so could be picked on specifically by texts that pass sentence on the tyrant. Domitian, for example, insisted on being addressed as 'god and master' not only in conversation, but also in writing (Cass. Dio 67.5.7 οὐ μόνον ἐλέγετο, ἀλλὰ καὶ ἐγράφετο). Indeed, he personally introduced (Suet. *Dom.* 13.2 *pari arrogantia*)[58] the title when dictating a formula of official rescript (*formalem epistulam*) for his procurators. Commodus' insolence and ambition are patent in his titles used in a letter to the senate which Cassius Dio takes the trouble to quote in full (72.15.5):

> The Emperor Caesar Lucius Aelius Aurelius Commodus Augustus Pius Felix Sarmaticus Germanicus Maximus Britannicus, Pacifier of the Universe, Invincible, the Roman Hercules, Pontifex Maximus, Holder of the Tribunician Authority for the eighth time, Consul for the seventh time, Father of his Country, to consuls, praetors, tribunes, and the fortunate Commodian senate, greeting.

Macrinus in his letters to the senate assumed titles that had not yet been voted for (Cass. Dio 78.16.2–3). Constantius II uses the title 'My Eternity' when dictating letters; in those he writes personally he calls himself master of the whole world (Amm. Marc. 15. 1.3). By contrast Caligula on his accession, when he was still 'very democratic' (δημοκρατικώτατος), sent out no letters, took up no titles (Cass. Dio 59.3.1). When he lapsed into tyranny, he 'dared' to refer to Livia as of low birth in a letter to the senate (Suet. *Cal.* 23.2 *arguere ausus est*). Nero varies the paradigm as a decadent artistic tyrant: he never addressed the soldiers in person for the sake of saving his voice (Suet. *Nero* 25.3 *conservandae vocis gratia*, cf. Cass. Dio 63.26.1). Caracalla chooses to write to the senate that he is now the official reincarnation of Alexander the Great (Cass. Dio 77.7.2).

Tiberius is a more interesting case of tyrannical arrogance assisted by literacy. From the outset of his rule, behind his literary restraint, there are marks of a tight grip in exercising power: his first edict to the senate after Augustus' death is very moderate in wording and contents (*verba pauca...et sensu permodesto*), yet to the army he already writes as *princeps* (Tac. *Ann.* 1.7). The Rhodian magistrates who omitted the complimentary formula (*sine subscriptione*) in public letters addressed to himself he summons to Rome, tells them to correct the omission, and sends them away without harm (Suet. *Tib.* 32.2). The later Tiberius, however, replays the Deioces-model with a grim twist. His withdrawal to Capri, whence he communicates by mischievously opaque letters,[59] coincides with the build-up of his *saevitia* and sexual transgression. Tiberius' tyranny is on the increase hand-in-hand with his writing; in his most memorable letter the distinction between bitter misanthropy[60] and despotic churlishness is problematic:

> If I know, senators, what I should write to you, or how to write it, or what not to write at all for the present – may gods and goddesses destroy me in a worse way than I feel myself being destroyed daily!

> Quid scribam vobis, p.c., aut quo modo scribam, aut quid omnino non scribam hoc tempore, dii me deaeque peius perdant quam cotidie perire sentio, si scio.
> (Suet. *Tib.* 67.1, cf. Tac. *Ann.* 6.6)

According to Tacitus, it was Seianus who encouraged Tiberius to leave Rome. The plan of the villainous prefect was to benefit from the emperor's absence as would be in control of the imperial correspondence (Tac. *Ann.* 4.41). Ironically, Tiberius causes Seianus' arrest and execution by indirect orders in a letter which Seianus assumed to enclose rewards for himself (Cass. Dio 58.9.5, 58.10.1–7, Suet. *Tib.* 65.1) – his confidence almost brings Bellerophon to mind...

The fate of Seianus reflects another, related aspect of tyrannical writing: it is not only hubristic, it is also exploitable and deceptive. The text, signature, and seal of the remote autocrat carry power detachable from his person;[61] in Herodotus, Oroetes' bodyguards cut down their own master obeying letters with the royal seal (3.128). Hence messages, signatures, and seals can be manipulated to create authority that is impossible to verify on the spot. As Suetonius nonchalantly mentions, Augustus trained his grandsons to imitate his own handwriting (Suet. *Aug.* 64); Titus prided himself on being good at forging handwritings (Suet. *Tit.* 3.2);[62] Carinus' roguish secretary signed in his master's hand (*SHA Carin.* 16.8). Associates and heirs of Roman rulers sign and stamp documents for them – with permission, as Agrippa and Maecenas do for Augustus (Cass. Dio 51.3.6–7), and Mucianus and Titus for Vespasian (Cass. Dio 66.2.1–2, Suet. *Tit.* 6.1), or in the setting of intrigue after the emperor's death, as Otho for Nero (Plut. *Oth.* 3.2; Suet. *Oth.* 7.1), and Plotina for Trajan (Cass. Dio 69.1.4). Tiberius on his sickbed clung to his signet while the courtiers, urged by Caligula, tried to remove it (Suet. *Tib.* 73.2; *Cal.* 12.2). The last thing Petronius did before expiring was to smash his own signet so that it would not be used for evil (Tac. *Ann.* 16.19 *fregitque anulum ne mox usui esset ad facienda pericula*).

Apprehensions about manipulative nature of imperial literacy chime in with the elite's resentment of secrecy in political decision-making under the principate.[63] In the constitutional debate between Agrippa and Maecenas before Octavian (dramatized in Cassius Dio), Maecenas' strategic vision of monarchy includes the following procedure for important decisions and trials: opinions of councillors (senators?) should be collected via a secret ballot (ἐς γραμματεῖα), then read by the emperor alone, and subsequently destroyed (Cass. Dio 52.33.3–4). This is pretty much how Nero behaves in Suetonius' *Life* (15.1):

> When judging a case he would defer his judgement until the next day, and then respond in writing after consideration. ... Withdrawing to consider, he never openly consulted his advisers, but made each of them write his opinion which he then read silently in private; whatever he decided, he stated as if it were the view of the majority.

> in iuris dictione postulatoribus nisi sequenti die ac per libellos non temere respondit...quotiens autem ad consultandum secederet, neque in commune quicquam neque propalam deliberabat, sed et conscriptas ab uno quoque sententias tacitus ac secreto legens, quod ipsi libuisset perinde atque pluribus idem videretur pronuntiabat.

Written communication provides many opportunities for deception and spin. Trying to dupe the Roman public about their failed military campaigns Caligula and Domitian use letters: Caligula blatantly lies (Suet. *Cal.* 44.2 *magnificas Romam litteras misit*), whereas Domitian fakes a letter from the 'defeated' Dacian king (Cass. Dio 67.7.3). Caracalla similarly exaggerated his military success in letters to the senate (Herodian 4.11.8–9). Even good emperors view correspondence as an exercise in rigging publicity: Vespasian's letters to the senate towards the end of the civil war soft-pedal his *de facto* established control (Tac. *Hist.* 4.3 *ea prima specie forma*); Julian's secret letters to Constantius II are intoned very differently from the 'official' epistle (Amm. Marc. 20.8.4–17 *vs.* 20.8.18 *secretiores alias...obiurgatorias et mordaces*).

Deceptive letters can spell death. Thus the Cappadocian king Archelaus is lured to Rome by Tiberius' friendly letter, only to die in obscure circumstances (Tac. *Ann.* 2.42); Commodus' letter leads the son of the praetorian prefect Perennis into the trap (Herodian 1.9.8–9); Constantius II banks on 'gentle' letters (*mollioribus scriptis*) to ensnare and destroy Gallus Caesar (Amm. Marc. 14.11.1–10, 16); Valens makes use of both 'friendly' and secret letters to engineer assassination of the Armenian king (Amm. Marc. 30.1. 18–19, 22–23). As in the Herodotean Oroetes-episode (Hdt. 3.128.2–5), the exact moment of delivering letters could be chosen for the assassins' strike. Gordianus' men, posing as Maximinus' couriers, murder the praetorian prefect Vitalianus (Herodian 7.6.5–8; *SHA Gord.* 10.6–8); a similar plot by Septimius Severus to assassinate Clodius Albinus falls short by an inch (Herodian 2.15.3–4, 3.5.4, 3.5.7–8). The murder of Agrippa Postumus is probably the most illustrative episode of the convergence of tyranny, secrecy, and literacy. Agrippa was killed by a centurion acting on the basis of a written order, but it remained unclear who was behind that document – the late Augustus, Livia, or Tiberius who, of course, denied it (Tac. *Ann.* 1.6; Suet. *Tib.* 22. 1).

Literacy, then, tends to be cast as a tool of arrogant and plotting autocrats. By contrast, good-natured rulers would make an effort to communicate face-to-face. The Spartan king Cleomenes responded to petitioners directly, not through scribes (Plut. *Ag.–Cleom.* 34(13).3). Vespasian and Marcus Aurelius did their best to attend the senate meetings in person (Cass. Dio 66.10.5–6, *SHA M. Aurel.* 10.7); the former, when his health deteriorated, made his sons represent him (Suet. *Tit.* 6.1, Cass. Dio 66.10.5–6).[64]

It seems that Imperial biographies would routinely try to enhance the orality-aspect in portraits of good emperors while exaggerating the literacy-aspect in bad emperors. Alexander Severus is an example of a praiseworthy emperor deeply involved with paperwork which, therefore, has to be mitigated, moved away from the tyrannical paradigm. In the presentation of *Historia Augusta* Severus' literacy is not just efficient but also collegially shared, fair, and humane. Severus brings all secretaries of state together to work on documents;[65] they are allowed to sit if they are not well (*nonnunquam etiam, si stare per valetudinem non possent, sederent*); the emperor amends documents in his own hand yet does not ascribe ideas to himself (*sua manu adderet, si quid esset addendum, sed ex eius sententia qui disertior habebatur*); having dealt with letters, he holds conversations with his 'friends', again as a group, with exception for the prefect Ulpianus whom he sees alone (*SHA Alex. Sev.* 31.1–2). Severus also has excellent knowledge of his military, applying it in personal communication with them (*SHA Alex. Sev.* 21.6–8). He avoids the charge of establishing a framework of despotic bureaucracy. In particular, his responsibility and taking a personal interest in documents contrast with off-handed carelessness of tyrannical emperors who abandon paperwork to the misuse of administrators:

> Commodus himself was slow and heedless about signing state-papers; he would sign different documents with the same formula; in most letters he would merely write 'Farewell'. Everything was processed by others who reportedly turned condemnations into profit.

> ipse Commodus in subscribendo tardus et neglegens, ita ut libellis una forma multis subscriberet, in epistulis autem plurimis 'VALE' tantum scriberet. agebanturque omnia per alios qui etiam condemnationes in sinum vertisse dicuntur. (*SHA Commod.* 13.7–8)

> [Carinus] had such reluctance for paperwork that he appointed to the task of signing some filthy fellow with whom he had fun every afternoon; he scolded him a lot, too, for being [so] good at imitating his own handwriting.

> Fastidium subscribendi tantum habuit, ut inpurum quondam, cum quo semper meridie iocabatur, ad subscribendum poneret, quem obiurgabat plerumque, quod bene suam imitaretur manum. (*SHA Carin.* 16.8)

Moreover, in narratives about bad emperors the delivery of an address in person could be impaired by a detail associated with literacy and despotism. Objects of literary materiality, such as bookrolls, are poignantly mentioned; their physical presence as it were diminishes the orality of communication and throws its sincerity into doubt. Tiberius informs the senate about Augustus' death, but fails to finish due to a suspicious fit of grief, so his son Drusus reads the rest of the speech from a scroll (*perlegendum librum tradidit*), then a freedman reads Augustus' will (Suet. *Tib.* 23). Claudius rarely read out in the senate himself; when he did, he read seated (Cass. Dio 60.2.2). Nero reads addresses composed for him by Seneca; his senatorial speech is subsequently inscribed upon a silver tablet for the future consuls to read at the start of their term of office (Tac. *Ann.* 13.3; Cass. Dio 61.3.1). The boorish Maximinus reads out texts written for him by his friends (Herodian 7.8.3 ἐπιφερόμενος τὸ βιβλίον ὅπερ ἦσαν αὐτῷ συντάξαντές τινες τῶν φίλων, ἐξ ἀναγνώσεως ἔλεξε τοιάδε).

Augustus comes across as a uniquely curious case of an emperor's relationship with literacy. Augustus' political persona is wrapped in ambivalence since he deliberately placed himself in between monarchy and republican freedom;[66] he famously forbade the appellation 'master' (Suet. *Aug.* 53.1, Cass. Dio 55.12.2). His actions display a suitably fluid ratio of 'democratic' orality and authoritarian writing. On the one hand, Augustus has deep-running associations with manipulative and prescribing literacy. He used a cipher (Suet. *Aug.* 88; Cass. Dio 51.3.7). As already noted, Agrippa and Maecenas were given the authority to (re)write and seal his letters in his name (Cass. Dio 51.3.5–6); his grandsons were specially taught to imitate his handwriting (Suet. *Aug.* 64). He mobilized written texts for his propaganda – getting hold of Antony's will and reading it to the senate (Cass. Dio 50.3.3–4), copying out edifying passages from literature to generals and governors as well as reading whole books, such as Q. Metellus' oration *On Procreating Children*, to the senators (Suet. *Aug.* 89.2 *etiam libros totos et senatui recitavit et populo notos per edictum saepe fecit*; Livy *perioch.* 59 *recitavit...velut in haec tempora scriptam*). Trying to control senatorial absenteeism from meetings, he had all the senators' names listed on a tablet (Cass. Dio 55.3.2–3). He dated each letter to the exact hour (Suet. *Aug.* 50). The peculiar ailment of his right-hand thumb sometimes barely allowed him to write (Suet. *Aug.* 80). His frequent letters to Atticus inquired 'what Atticus was doing, especially what he was reading' (*in primis quid legeret*: Nep. *Att.* 20.1). His imminent death is foretold by the omen of the letter C falling off an inscription on his statue (Suet. *Aug.* 97.2; Cass. Dio 56.29.4).[67] He leaves behind a comprehensive set of texts: instructions about his own funeral, an account of his deeds, a record of the state of military and financial affairs of the empire as well as injunctions for Tiberius and the Roman people (Suet. *Aug.* 101; Cass. Dio 56.33.1–3). The evolution of Augustus' seal is laden with symbolism for understanding his career (Suet. *Aug.* 50; Pliny *NH* 37.10; Cass. Dio 51.3.6–7).[68] As Octavian, he sealed with the image of a sphinx. This seal existed in duplicate and was used by Augustus and Maecenas alike; uncertainty about the letters' authorship was added to the traditional ambiguity of the creature.[69] At some stage, presumably around the victory at Actium, he changed his seal to the image of Alexander the Great (Pliny *NH* 37.10 *non inficeto lepore accipientium, aenigmata adferre eam sphingem...postea ad devitanda convicia sphingis Alexandri Magni imagine signavit*; Cass. Dio 51.3.6). Finally, as Augustus, he sealed with the image of himself, which remained the imperial seal until Galba (Cass. Dio 51.3.7).

But Augustus is not a remote dictating tyrant: he is Father of the Fatherland – crucially, the title is conferred upon him in a scene of solemn dialogue in the senate (Suet. *Aug.* 58). Not just literacy for Augustus, then. It is as if he attempts to marry orality and literacy as two models of communicating from position of leadership. Laying siege to Alexandria, he boldly rebuts Antony's propaganda leaflets (Cass. Dio 51.10.2–3 ὁ γὰρ Καῖσαρ αὐτὸς τὰ βιβλία ἐθελοντὴς τοῖς στρατιώταις ἀνέγνω). He posts up laws on tablets in the curia for senatorial discussion (Cass. Dio 55.4.1), publishes his speeches in booklet form (App. *BC* 5.130/539), wants to recite his record of achievement to the senate – but cannot because of a sore throat, so the text (βιβλίον) has to be read out by a quaestor (Cass. Dio 54.25.5). Even in private conversation Augustus reads from a script:

> He avoided the risk of forgetting, and the waste of time in memorizing, his words: he decided to read everything out. Important conversations with single individuals, even with his wife Livia, he held only after having them written out and read from a notebook...

> ac ne periculum memoriae adiret aut in ediscendo tempus absumeret, instituit recitare omnia. Sermones quoque cum singulis atque etiam cum Livia sua graviores non nisi scriptos et e libello habebat...   (Suet. *Aug.* 84.2)

He adopts a friendly attitude when receiving written requests and teases a shy petitioner for hesitating to hand in his scroll, 'One might think you are offering a penny to an elephant!' (Suet. *Aug.* 53.2 *quasi elephanto stipem*). Augustus thus wants to be seen as a ruler surrounded by bureaucracy yet not a tyrannical monster, an elephant and non-elephant at the same time. In his case the princeps' literacy is not despotic, but admits accountability, restraint, and *parrhēsia*, as demonstrated through a cluster of unrelated anecdotes. It is important that at least a portion of Augustus' political will was written in his own hand (Suet. *Aug.* 101.1; Tac. *Ann.* 1.11). One Junius Novatus, who in the name of Agrippa the Younger puts into circulation a 'most scathing letter' about Augustus (*asperrimam de se epistulam in vulgus edidisset*), receives a fairly mild punishment (Suet. *Aug.* 51.1). Pseudo-Plutarch and Aurelius Victor's epitomator report that in order to calm down Augustus was advised to repeat the Greek alphabet silently ([Plut.] *Reg. et imp. apophth.* 207C; epitom. 48. 15). Cassius Dio (55.7.2) tells a more dramatic story of Maecenas who, on seeing Augustus passing judgement too severely, wrote on a tablet

'Stand up, executioner!' and threw it into the emperor's lap;[70] Augustus took the hint. Just as his model of the principate, Augustan manner of imperial literacy aims at a compromise between autocracy and responsibility.

It should be apparent from the preceding discussion that in Graeco-Roman texts the evaluation of literacy vis-à-vis political regime is never explicitly discursive, but operates on the level of anecdote and symbolic detail instead. Much of the time it is the emphatic presence of an artefact, a piece of stationery, that marks out the theme of literacy as an instrument of despotism. Domitian's fly-stabbing stylus and Augustus' duplicate seal are both cues for reflection on, respectively, violence and manipulation by men in power. Domitian is branded as tyrant, whereas for Augustus the suspicion is tentatively introduced only to be tentatively retracted. Writing as such may not even feature directly, but the notion of the 'tyrant's writ' is unmistakably there. One of Caligula's atrocities was to have a senator stabbed with styluses and eventually torn to pieces:

> When he wished that a certain senator should be torn to pieces, men were fitted out who attacked him, calling him public enemy as he entered the senate, pierced him with their styluses, then handed him over to others for mangling...

> cum discerpi senatorem concupisset, subornavit qui ingredientem curiam repente hostem publicum appellantes invaderent, graphisque confossum lacerandum ceteris traderent...
>
> (Suet. *Cal.* 28)

Here the tyrant takes advantage of implements of literacy for staging a quasi-trial coupled with a gory execution. Even more emblematic of the conflict between tyrannical literacy and the oral voice of oppressed *paideia* are the two stories about Nero's visit to Greece as told in the dialogue *Nero*, 9–10 by either Lucian or one of the Philostrati clan.[71] The narrator is the exiled Stoic Musonius Rufus. First comes the gruesome episode at the Isthmian games. A Greek performer dared to rival the emperor in a singing competition and stubbornly refused to concede:

> ...an Epirote with an excellent voice, which was praised and admired, was showing off, more flamboyantly than was normal, that he passionately desired the crown of victory and would not give it up unless Nero gave him ten talents as the price of victory. Nero was enraged and furious... As the Greeks shouted in applause of the Epirote, Nero sent his secretary with the order that the singer must yield to him. But the man raised his voice and competed in a democratic fashion. So Nero sent onto the platform his own actors, as if they belonged to the act. For they held in front of them writing tablets of ivory (double ones too†) like daggers. They stood the Epirote against the nearest column and smashed his throat with their tablets.

> ὁ δ' Ἠπειρώτης ἄριστα φωνῆς ἔχων, εὐδοκιμῶν δ' ἐπ' αὐτῇ καὶ θαυμαζόμενος λαμπροτέρᾳ τοῦ εἰωθότος ἐπλάττετο καὶ τοῦ στεφάνου ἐρᾶν καὶ μηδ' ἀνήσειν

πρότερον ἢ δέκα τάλαντα δοῦναί οἱ Νέρωνα ὑπὲρ τῆς νίκης, ὁ δ' ἠγρίαινέ τε
καὶ μανικῶς εἶχε...βοώντων τε τῶν Ἑλλήνων ἐπὶ τῷ Ἠπειρώτῃ πέμπει τὸν
γραμματέα κελεύων ὑφεῖναι ἑαυτῷ τούτου, τοῦ δὲ ὑπεραίροντος τὸ φθέγμα καὶ
δημοτικῶς ἐρίζοντος ἐσέπεμπε Νέρων ἐπ' ὀκριβάντων τοὺς ἑαυτοῦ ὑποκριτὰς
οἷον προσήκοντάς τι τῷ πράγματι, καὶ γὰρ δὴ καὶ δέλτους ἐλεφαντίνας (ἔχοντες
καὶ) διθύρους*** προβεβλημένοι αὐτάς, ὥσπερ ἐγχειρίδια καὶ τὸν Ἠπειρώτην
ἀναστήσαντες πρὸς τὸν ἀγχοῦ κίονα κατέαξαν αὐτοῦ φάρυγγα παίοντες ὀρθαῖς
ταῖς δέλτοις.   (*Nero* 9)[72]

Next, Nero cordons off the Pythia's cave, so that 'Apollo, too, would be
voiceless' (*Nero* 10 τὸ Πυθικὸν στόμιον...ἀποφράττειν ὥρμησεν ὡς μηδὲ τῷ
Ἀπόλλωνι φωνὴ εἴη). Both Greek song and Greek divinity are silenced – in
the former case, shut down by a violently physical application of literacy's
paraphernalia.

When the tyrannical stylus and tablets – Caligula's, Nero's, Domitian's,
and so on – are used to kill in the physical sense, we might remember that
more often they kill metaphorically through death-sentences.[73] Signing the
execution list on a regular basis Caligula joked, 'I'm clearing my accounts'
(Suet. *Cal.* 29.2 *rationem se purgare*); his notebooks containing death-lists
were titled 'Sword' and 'Dagger' (Suet. *Cal.* 49.3; Cass. Dio 59.26.1). Under
despotism, trials go, literally, as the despot's pen wishes (Suet. *Cal.* 53.2 *prout
stylus cesserat*).

Literacy is presented as pivotal to the operation of regimes constructed
by our narrative sources in terms of tyranny. This biased perception appears
to be matched by a certain nostalgic longing for orality in politics. The elite
class under Empire still view oral communication as a guarantee of sincerity
and an alternative to tyrannical arrogance. The nostalgia is, at best, limited:
running an Empire orally is impractical. It would be more pertinent to ask,
are there, for ancient biographers and historians, other literacies that can be
opposed to the tyrant's literacy?

VI

Probably the most bizarre among Domitian's victims was the senator Mettius
Pompusianus (*PIR*[2] M570). His crimes included propitious omens at his
birth, naming two of his slaves Mago and Hannibal, parading an interest in
speeches of kings and commanders in Livy's *History*, and possessing a map of
the world – either on parchment (Suet. *Dom.* 10.3 *depictum orbem terrae in
membrana contionesque regum et ducum ex Tito Livio circumferret*), or painted
on the walls of his bedroom (Cass. Dio 67.12.2 τὴν οἰκουμένην ἐν τοῖς τοῦ
κοιτῶνος τοίχοις εἶχεν ἐγγεγραμμένην). Why was Domitian provoked by
this? It is possible that a mappemond and excerpts from Livy could be interpreted as signs of an ambitious personality planning a coup d'état.[74] On the

other hand, Pompusianus' map must have been too general for any practical military use, and Livian exhortations were not that different from material traditionally used in rhetorical education. It seems that Mettius Pompusianus was only dangerous in so far as he was (on the face of it) mentally unstable. I believe the solution relates to the materiality of the documents he was so ostentatiously displaying – 'carrying around' (*circumferret*), as Suetonius puts it – rather than to his intentions. To show off a world map and selections from Rome's official history the way Pompusianus did was inappropriate, an act of trespassing on the imperial cartography and, broadly, literacy. As a tyrant, Domitian does not allow other people to get involved with texts and images that are commensurate in sway and scope with his own position as master of the world; no individual other than the emperor should be able to claim such authority for his writing.[75] Here the medium is manifestly the message – or rather, sends the wrong message. In effect, Mettius Pompusianus was punished for the outlook of his literacy. His fate illustrates, from an eccentric slant, the need of Roman autocracy to control and intervene in literate activities among the elite class. Simply writing at the wrong moment could attract the autocrat's suspicion: Octavian orders a Roman knight to be killed on the spot for taking some sort of notes during Octavian's speech (Suet. *Aug.* 27.3 *subscribere quaedam animadvertisset*).

Essentially, Imperial control over literacy can take two forms: ban and destruction or promotion and preservation. Politically motivated book-burning and repressions of the literati under the principate attract a lot of attention both in ancient texts and modern scholarship.[76] The link between book-burning and tyranny is point-blank: the worse the tyranny, the more thorough and ruthless chastisement befalls the offending text, its author, and other people connected with it. Domitian not only puts Hermogenes of Tarsus to death because of his history, but also makes sure all copyists are crucified (Suet. *Dom.* 10.1). Caligula, who during his early days in power had actually lifted prohibition on a few books, including Cremutius Cordus' (Suet. *Cal.* 16.1), later becomes tyrannical to the point of burning a comic poet alive right in the amphitheatre (Suet. *Cal.* 27.4). Commodus, in his turn, sentenced a man to death for reading Suetonius' *Life of Caligula* (*SHA Commod.* 10.2)

There are, however, other texts which tyrants normally would not burn but instead draw upon in their *saevitia*: incriminating letters.[77] Caligula uses his sisters' letters 'acquired by lies and seduction' as evidence (Suet. *Cal.* 24.3 *chirographa...requisita fraude ac stupro*); Septimius Severus, having seized the late Clodius Albinus' archive, treats Albinus' sympathizing correspondents as enemies (Herodian 3.8.6; *SHA Sept. Sev.* 10.2); Aurelian executes the philosopher Longinus because Zenobia's haughty letter was credited to him

(*SHA Aurel.* 30.3).[78] It is a noble gesture to burn an archive, typically that of a defeated opponent, so that its evidence could do no harm to anybody. This is the approach of Pompey (Plut. *Sert.* 27.4–5, *Pomp.* 20.7–8), Otho (Cass. Dio 64.15.1), Marcus Aurelius (Cass. Dio 71.28.4, 71.29.1–2; Amm. Marc. 21.16.11), and a few others (Plut. *Eum.* 16.4; Cass. Dio 67.11.1–2). A tyrant would take the opposite course: Caligula pretends to have burned documents incriminating family enemies, but in fact he keeps them, even makes additional copies, and uses them to prosecute people (Suet. *Cal.* 15.4, 30.2; Cass. Dio 59.4.3–4; 59.10.8; 59.16.2–3, 60.4.5). Caesar does indeed burn all the letters found in Pompey's and Scipio's baggage (Cass. Dio 41.63.5–6, 43.13.2), but equally does not fail to make a point of his non-tyrannical magnanimity in propaganda (Cass. Dio 43.17.4, 44.47.5–6). Augustus, as always, does not go all the way in either direction: he only destroys some letters (Cass. Dio 52.42.8; App. *BC* 5.132/548).

Libraries, in particular the major libraries at Rome, constitute another channel for the autocrats wishing to control and set trends for elite literacy.[79] A special role was reserved for the imperial Palatine library. It was a privileged storehouse of texts that could be tapped into or taken out of circulation. Thus, Augustus forbade publication (*vetuit...publicari*) of Caesar's juvenilia in a 'very short and simple' letter (*brevem admodum ac simplicem*) to the imperial librarian Pompeius Macer (Suet. *Caes.* 56.7 *cui ordinandas bibliothecas delegaverat*) – 'publication' here probably means a properly edited copy made available in the library. But the primary function of the Palatine Library was political, not scholarly. The stocks and interior trappings of the emperor's library[80] (that also served as state chambers: Suet. *Aug.* 29.3; Tac. *Ann.* 2.37; *P.Oxy.* 2435, lines 31–3), were to send out a message about the regime's cultural policy – to be a benchmark for other public and possibly private libraries to follow. The emperor's interference in library holdings may be either positive or censuring.[81] We hear about books and authors that were personally promoted by emperors – Greek erotic poetry by Tiberius (Suet. *Tib.* 70.2), Antimachus by Hadrian (Cass. Dio 69.4.6), one Marcellus' medical text by Hadrian and Antoninus Pius (*Ant. Gr.* 7.158), Tacitus' historical works by his namesake (*SHA Tac.* 10.5). This is tantamount to public endorsement. To be specifically denied a place on the imperial shelves was a serious reproach and effectively a milder form of ban; the exiled Ovid laments the non-admittance of his poetry into two most important Roman libraries – the Palatine Library and the Atrium Libertatis (*Trist.* 3.1.59–72). The library policy of an insane tyrant such as Caligula is predictably outrageous: he considered total elimination of the Homeric poems and nearly succeeded in removing the works and portraits of Virgil and Livy from all libraries (Suet. *Cal.* 34.2 *scripta et imagines paulum afuit quin ex omnibus bibliothecis amoveret*).

Yet on the whole there are few anecdotes in the ancient texts that might read as evidence of Graeco-Roman literati scowling at libraries as institutions by which autocracy reinforces itself. Ancient intelligentsia seems to have appreciated the cultural assets accommodated in libraries (cf. Plut. *Dem.* 2.1, *Luc.* 42.1) too strongly to be critical about them. There is a lurking memory that some of the earliest Greek libraries were founded by tyrants (Athen. 1.3a; Gell. 7. 17. 1; Isid. 6.6.1; Phot. *Bibl.* cod. 224 p. 222b). This may raise questions about the interest emperors such as Caesar and Domitian take in improving the state of Roman libraries (Suet. *Caes.* 44.2; Isid. 6.5.1; Suet. *Dom.* 20): is it supposed to underscore a genuine concern for *paideia* or to activate the tyrannical stereotypes? Names and locations of several Roman libraries could suggest that their organizers wanted to dispel from the public mind any association of their libraries with tyranny. The first public library in the city was founded by Asinius Pollio in the Atrium Libertatis; the same site was chosen by Trajan for the Bibliotheca Ulpia; Vespasian set up a library in the Templum Pacis. Freedom, peace, and books – a charm offensive on the collective unconscious, perhaps?

An area ancient writers could have explored more critically is the connection between Roman libraries and Roman imperialism. Originally, victorious Roman generals brought back book-collections as trophies from the East. It is remarkable that more often than not a positive spin is put on their plundering activities, even by Greek authors.[82] Thus Plutarch commends Aemilius Paullus and Pompey for picking out books as their share of booty (*Aem.* 28.11, *Pomp.* 4.2) and enthuses over Lucullus making his home library accessible to visiting Greek intellectuals (*Luc.* 42.1–3), although he must have known where Lucullus' books came from (cf. Isid. 6.5.1 *e Pontica praeda*).[83] Pliny the Elder praises Pompey for arranging publication of Latin translation of medical works seized from Mithridates – it was as great a benefit to humankind as the victory itself was for Rome (Pliny *NH* 25.7 *vitaeque ita profuit non minus quam reipublicae victoria illa*). Sulla is a more controversial case, yet moving Aristotle's library to Italy certainly rescued the books from decay and made them available to the literati (cf. Plut. *Sull.* 28.1–3; Strabo 13.1.54; Cic. *Ad Att.* 4.10.1).[84] As we move into the Imperial age, there is a shift: barbarian loot now supplies not books, but financial resources for construction of splendid new libraries at Rome. Asinius Pollio's library was 'the first library in the world to be set up from spoils' (Pliny *NH* 7.11.5 *in bibliotheca quae prima in orbe ex manubiis publicata Romae est*, cf. Isid. 6.5.2 *additis auctorum imaginibus in atrio, quod de manubiis magnificentissimum instruxerat*); the Augustan library in the Porticus Octaviae was financed out of Dalmatian booty (Cass. Dio 49.43.8 τάς τε στοὰς ἀπὸ τῶν λαφύρων αὐτῶν καὶ τὰς ἀποθήκας τῶν βιβλίων τὰς Ὀκταουιανὰς ἐπὶ τῆς ἀδελφῆς αὐτοῦ κληθείσας κατεσκεύασεν.) Conquest means ever more books and more libraries; Roman imperialism translates war into culture. Lévi-Strauss would have been unhappy, yet Graeco-Roman intellectuals are glad to be at the consuming end of the process.

VII

Autocracy employs and controls literacy for its own ends. Tyrannical regimes tend to do it in a more heavy-handed manner. Maybe the argument itself should be reversed: heavy dependence on bureaucracy and cruel intervention in elite literacy contribute towards a regime's being labelled a tyranny. But is literacy also utilized to resist tyranny?

In the case of prohibited texts, such as Cremutius Cordus' *History*, their written format made possible the survival of hidden copies (Tac. *Ann.* 4.35; Cass. Dio 57.2.4). It can also ricochet disguised as a metaphor: Cordus wrote his work as if with his own blood (Sen. *Ad Marc.* 1.3). In a mood of defiance, the historian Timagenes burned his own books that covered the deeds of Augustus – yet this was probably driven by spite rather than political protest; the emperor did not take umbrage (Sen. *De Ira* 3.23.4–7). The evidence that dissident writers under the principate[85] were consciously developing the theme of anti-tyrannical literacy *qua* literacy is scarce. For that matter, there are no good reasons to suppose that Cremutius Cordus, Helvidius Priscus, Hermogenes of Tarsus, and other martyrs were any more systematically outspoken compared to Tacitus, Suetonius or Cassius Dio – simply less lucky. The burned and banned books might have contained criticism of despotic literacy in the broadly Lévi-Straussian-Herodotean spirit, but they hardly articulated a theory of liberating literacy as in the case, for example, of Paulo Freire.

There are, however, in Graeco-Roman biography and historiography several recurrent motifs linking literacy with resistance, once again, on the descriptive anecdotal level. Firstly, subversive pamphlets (*libelli*) and graffiti regularly get mentioned.[86] Although the sophistication of some of these texts (e.g. Suet. *Nero* 39.2) as well as the sites of distribution (the curia: Suet. *Aug.* 55) indicate that they originated among the elite class, they are largely anonymous and so more likely intended to represent the voice of the people. To what extent are the elite authors and readers prepared to identify with that voice? Only to a degree, I think. Dislike of despotism would be counterbalanced by fear of violent commotion among the masses. Graffiti signpost a route of resistance that the *pepaideumenoi* are usually wary of. Notably, Plutarch as a guru of practical ethics for the elite class instructs his audience to avoid reading even harmless graffiti on walls: 'nothing useful or pleasant' there (*De Curios.* 520D–E). The most thought-provoking story about inscription used to defeat an autocrat is told by Lucian towards the end of *How History Should be Written*. The architect of the Pharos Lighthouse, Sostratus of Cnidus, inscribed his own name on the edifice, then plastered it over (ἐπιχρίσας δὲ τιτάνῳ καὶ ἐπικαλύψας), and wrote the name of the current king on the surface – rightly expecting the truth to be revealed as gypsum peels off with time (*Hist. Scr.* 62). Lucian treats the anecdote as a parable of historical narrative that should supply posterity with a true picture of events without necessarily putting the author at risk in the present. Textual literacy and epigraphic literacy team up to create an idiolect of resistance, but any resistance here is intellectual rather than political as well as emphatically discreet.

Ancient biography and history appear much more fascinated with the possibility of a tyrant being somehow let down and destroyed by the literacy that envelops him, outmanoeuvred at his own game, as it were. One topos is that of a tyrant ignoring a letter that warns about the imminent conspiracy. Archias the Theban became proverbial for carelessly failing to read such a letter (Plut. *De Gen. Socr.* 596 E–F, *Pel.* 10.7–10; *Quaes. Conv.* 619D–E). With Julius Caesar the scenario is replayed with greater subtlety. On the Ides of March Caesar wants to read Artemidorus' letter, but the bustling crowd makes that impossible (Plus. *Caes.* 65.3 δεξάμενος οὖν ὁ Καῖσαρ, ἀναγνῶναι μὲν ὑπὸ πλήθους τῶν ἐντυγχανόντων ἐκωλύθη, καίπερ ὁρμήσας πολλάκις).[87] This is another way of representing Caesar's demise as caused by those around him.[88]

Literacy itself did Caesar a bad turn. According to Nicolaus of Damascus (*FGrHist* 90 fr. 130.78–9), Caesar aroused (ἤγειρε) great hatred of potential conspirators by failing to pay attention to a congratulatory procession led by 'the best of Romans' (οἱ Ῥωμαίων ἄριστοι) because he was absorbed in papers pertaining to reconstruction of the Forum. Only after someone told him, 'Look who is before you!' he put down his notebooks and turned around (ἀποθέμενος τὰ γραμματίδια ἐπεστράφη). Neglecting citizens for the sake of documents was interpreted as tyrannical insolence.[89] So it is fit that on the Ides of March the assassins took advantage of Caesar's involvement with paperwork, hiding their daggers in pen-cases (Cass. Dio 44.16.1 καὶ σφίσιν εὐπορίαν ἀσφαλῆ ξιφῶν ἐν κιβωτίοις ἀντὶ γραμματείων τινῶν ἐσκομισθέντων ὑπάρξειν), and that Caesar unsuccessfully defended himself with his stylus (Suet. *Caes.* 82.2). Augustus was anxious not to repeat Caesar's mistakes. He does not offend the people by writing and reading during public shows (Suet. *Aug.* 45.1 *seu vitandi rumoris causa, quo patrem Caesarem vulgo reprehensum commemorabat, quod inter spectandum epistulis libellisque legendis aut rescribendis vacaret*).[90] With stationery, he also prefers to err on the side of safety: suspecting that a praetor who held writing-tablets under his robe (*tabellas duplices veste tectas tenentem*) during the imperial *salutatio* might be hiding a sword, he orders the man to be arrested, tortured, and executed (Suet. *Aug.* 27.4).[91]

Literacy empowers tyrannical hubris, but coincidentally generates hostility towards tyrants. Tyrants may be betrayed by documents they are used to relying upon. A letter to Caracalla, advising him to get rid of Macrinus, gets intercepted by Macrinus himself (Herodian 4.12.4–8). The tale of Domitian's assassination in Suetonius gives a new turn to the 'warning letter' motif: the emperor is stabbed at the very moment he is reading the alleged warning letter, by the very man who brought it in (*Dom.* 17.1 *legenti traditum a se libellum et attonito suffodit inguina*).

Domitian also starts the series of emperors whose assassination was precipitated by a leaked death-list. In the version of Cassius Dio (67.15.3–4), Domitian does receive a proper letter informing him of the names of the conspirators. He puts it under his pillow, but a pet-boy (*deliciae*) takes it by chance and brings it to the empress who is involved in the conspiracy and immediately hastens the others to act. The end of Commodus is almost identical. Commodus writes down names of planned victims, then, again, a *deliciae*-boy inadvertently brings the document to the emperor's wife (Herodian 1.17.1–6; *SHA Commod.* 9.3). Next, Gallienus. The story of his assassination, as told (exclusively) by Aurelius Victor (*De Caes.* 33.20), is built around death-lists faked by the rebel Aureolus when besieged in Milan. These death-lists with names of Gallienus' officers are deliberately dropped from the city walls to be discovered by the people mentioned in them; the survival instinct of Gallienus' *duces* and tribunes takes care of the rest. Finally, Aurelian. On him several stock motifs of tyrannical literacy converge. There is the wicked secretary Mnest(h)eus who has reasons to fear the emperor's wrath. Imitating Aurelian's hand, he forges a death-list (includes his own name, too) and 'generously' shows it to the people on it. As might be expected, they decide to strike first (*SHA Aurel.* 35.5–36.6; Aurel. Vict. *De Caes.* 35.8; epitom. 35.8).[92]

The nemesis of literacy turning on its master: a crisis of tyrannical literacy, maybe? Do Suetonius and Cassius Dio antedate Lévi-Strauss? When facing a plethora of anecdotes, it is important to resist the temptation to over-generalize. While broadly Lévi-Straussian perceptions about literacy and power float about, with surprising persistency, from Herodotus right down to Aurelius Victor, the absence of theoretical articulation is a serious problem. Ancient criticism of oppressive state literacy is at best oblique and fragmented into narrative details. It is 'safe' criticism[93] – still a criticism and a 'hidden transcript' of resistance operating at the level of 'infrapolitics'.[94] A unified overview of stories about Roman rulers writing, reading, dictating, handling stationery, and so forth, may seem unsatisfactorily varied in the end. The anecdotal approach to the past is non-committal and slippery. On the plus side, it is flexible and therefore useful for dealing with hard-to-pigeonhole figures (Augustus, Hadrian) as well as for interacting with the traditional ideological templates. Anecdotes, including the literacy-related anecdotes, enable political biography under the Empire to straddle sameness and novelty. In a culture nucleated around embedded social stereotypes and discursive codes, autocracy is a tricky topic for writers: to spell out too much could be unwise both politically and rhetorically.

Acknowledgements

This article was prepared in parallel with Zadorojnyi 2005; I have tried to keep overlaps to a minimum. I am grateful to the audiences at Liverpool, Leeds, and the Nijmegen Congress for their comments. Special thanks are due to Robin Seager.

Notes

[1] See, generally, Waters 1964; Jones 1992; Southern 1997.

[2] Cf. Suet. *Dom.* 22; Tac. *Hist.* 4.2; Jones and Milns 2002, 127.

[3] On the static, pre-given concept of character in ancient historiography and biography, see Gill 1983, with Pelling 2002a; Averintsev 2002, 25–6, 35.

[4] Suet. *Dom.* 3.1 *muscas* captare *ac stilo praeacuto* configere – that is, the flies were first caught and then put to death like prisoners; cf. Cizek 1977, 41. I am puzzled by the suggestion of Jones 1996, 29, that Domitian's true motive was 'obsession with cleanlinesss'(!).

[5] Suet. *Dom.* 11, esp. 11.1: *erat autem non solum magnae, sed etiam callidae inopinataeque saevitiae*; Tac. *Agr.* 39.1, Pliny *Pan.* 66.3; Cass. Dio 67.1.1, 3. Jones 1996, 97. Note also Domitian's uncanny skill at archery: Suet. *Dom.* 19.

[6] It may not be totally gratuitous to mention fly-stabbing in Shakespeare's *Titus Andronicus*, 3.2.53–78; also *King Lear* 4.1.36–7.

[7] Whom Suetonius identifies as Vibius Crispus: cf. Juv. 4.81–93; Quint. 5.13.48, 8.5.15; Mooney 1930, 517; Jones 1992, 57–8.

[8] Penwill 2000, 63, 75, 77 (ignoring the version of Aurelius Victor). For Domitian's literary activity, cf. Mart. 5.5.7; Val. Fl. 1.12–14; Quintil. 10.1.91; generally, Coleman 1986, 3088–91.

[9] Lévi-Strauss 1973, 299–300; cf. Goody 1986, 87–126; Hopkins 1991, 135–44.

[10] Harbsmeier 1989, 197–204; Larsen 1988; Woolf 1994, 98; Baines 1988; Clanchy 1979; Pattison 1982, 61–85; Harris 1989, 36–40, 206–18, 334–5; Thomas 1992, 128–32, 144–50; various contributions in Schousboe and Larsen 1989, Bowman and Woolf 1994, Street 1995b; and, from a different perspective, Derrida 1976, 101–40.

[11] This view at least as old as D.Hal. 12.13. Cf. Sir Edward Millis in his foreword to Diringer 1947, xi: 'the invention of writing…may fairly be taken as the step leading directly to full civilization'; Cohen 1958, 1–9; Oxenham 1980. More nuanced argumentation offered by Havelock 1963, 1976, 1982; Goody and Watt 1968; Goody 1977,

1986; Solomon 1986; particularly Ong 1982 and Olson 1994, who highlight cognitive and psychological effects of literacy while moving away from social determinism. The 'social' and the 'cognitive' variants of the progressivist view are equally opposed by the New Literacy school: Street 1984, 1995a, esp. 16–45, 153–9, 1995b; Scribner and Cole 1981; Pattison 1982, 40–60, 118–55; Graff 1986, 1987; Shousboe and Larsen 1989; Harris 1989, 40–2; Thomas 1989, 21–34, 1992, 16–28.

[12] Cf. Goody and Watt 1968, 56–63; Lévi-Strauss in Charbonnier 1969, 21 and 30.

[13] The next move is to demand educational reform that would produce a new model of literacy to empower the oppressed masses: Freire 1985; Freire and Macedo 1987; Bee 1980; Archer and Costello 1990. This is pure politics of course.

[14] More on the 'occupational' and the 'philosophical' objections to literacy in Zadorojnyi 2005 and (forthcoming) respectively.

[15] The nature of the topic requires using the term 'biography' in the broadest possible sense of testimonies about and reception of person X – what Pelling 1997c, 117–25 calls 'biostructuring'; see also Swain 1997, 1–2, 23–7; Cooper 2004, esp. 45–6, Späth 2005, 28–30, 40–2. The handful of authors who constitute the surviving genre of ancient biography remain, naturally, my main focus. However, many snippets of precious personal information are scattered outside the generic boundaries in historical, rhetorical, and philosophical texts. I do not claim to have an explanation of their relationship to 'proper' biography either *en masse* or in each particular case, but it might be helpful to think of ancient biographical tradition as a syncretic intertextual phenomenon based on that woolly principle of λέγεται, *dicitur* and *sunt qui putent*; see Pauw 1980; Cook 2002.

[16] *Pace* Thomas 1992, 130.

[17] Roller 2001, 6.

[18] The standard view is that Bellerophon's tablet is a reminiscence of Linear B: Kirk 1990, 181–2. More enthusiastic is Bellamy 1989, 289–95, arguing that the episode implies Homeric awareness of Near-Eastern royal records. Powell 1997, 27–8 is soberly reserved. On the thematic importance of Bellerophon's message, see Rosenmeyer 2001, 40–4, 344.

[19] Hdt. 1.123.4; 5.35.3; 7.239.3–4; 8.22 (with 9.98.2–99.1); 8.128.1–3.

[20] Steiner 1994, esp. 127–85; Hartog 1988, 277–81; Thompson 1996, 81–2; Rosenmeyer 2001, 47–54.

[21] e.g., the land-census at Miletus (5.29): it is decided upon communally, carried out by a third party, and, most importantly, it brings an end to *stasis* in the city.

[22] For its complexities, see Cartledge 1990; Pelling 1997a.

[23] *Contra* Waters 1971, Ferrill 1978, Gray 1996: see Alföldi 1955; Gammie 1986; Lateiner 1989, 165–86; McGlew 1993, 34; Barceló 1993, 149–82, Parker 1998, 161–4; Cartledge 2000, 21. Dewland 2003, 26–40, 47–9. Classical reception of tyranny: Dem. 6.25; [Dem.] 17.3; Aristoph. *Vesp.* 464–70; Seager 1967, 6–7; Rosivach 1988; Barceló 1993, 129–202; McGlew 1993; Parker 1998, 149–67; Raaflaub 2003, esp. 71–2, 82–3; Seaford 2003; on the link between tyranny and the Orient, see Ar. *Pol.* 1313a27–b10; Fadinger 1993.

[24] Otanes' list includes: subversion of ancestral customs, rape of women, and killing people without trial (3.80.5 νόμαιά τε κινέει πάτρια καὶ βιᾶται γυναῖκας κτείνει τε ἀκρίτους). Themes of murder and assault on women are key to the criticism of tyranny during the corresponding Greek debate (5.92 ε2–η4); the death of Cambyses' sister

(3.31–2) is echoed by the death of Periander's wife (3.50.1); Masistes' family is destroyed by tyrannical passions of Xerxes and Amestris (9.108–13). See further, Gammie 1986.

[25] The medieval Arab historian Ibn-Khaldoun (quoted in Harbsmeier 1989, 198) constructs a more structured typology of power: the violent stage of the 'sword' is followed by the administrative stage of the 'pen'. In Herodotus sword and pen act together, as in the Oroetes-episode (3.128.2–5).

[26] See Murray 2001a, 2001b; Flory 1980; Thomas 1993; Johnson 1994; Fowler 1996, 2001, esp. 107–10.

[27] On 'literacy' and 'illiteracy' as ideological and often patronizing constructions by literates, see Harbsmeier 1988, 1989; Street 1995a, 74–96.

[28] Harbsmeier 1989, 204: 'Herodotus and Ibn-Khaldoun saw the pen and the sword, the oral and the written, as distinct but interdependent... Lévi-Strauss discovered the sword in the pen by postulating a new world characterized by the absence of both.' On the ancient reaction to autocracy, see perceptive remarks by Wallace-Hadrill 1982, 33–5, 45–7.

[29] Tyrants communicate by symbolic gestures, too: Hdt. 5.92 ζ2–η1.

[30] For fuller discussion, see Thomas 1989, 34–94, 1992, 67–71; Robb 1994, 84–156; Sickinger 2002; Gagarin 2003, esp. 67–8; Cohen 2003.

[31] In Plato's *Statesman*, 300a1–301e5 the route of written legislation is recommended as the second-best choice for communities lacking in true political knowledge, while individuals equipped with such knowledge are allowed to operate without the trammels of written laws.

[32] For contextualization of Alcidamas' text, see Friemann 1990; Ford 2002, 233–5.

[33] Raaflaub 1987, 30, 37–8; also n. 52 below.

[34] Cf. Suet. *Cal.* 41.1 *cum per ignorantiam scripturae multa commissa fierent.* On avarice as a tyrannical feature, see Kloft 1970, 153–5; Tabacco 1985, 116–18.

[35] Harris 1989, 248–52, Hopkins 1991, 142–4; Lendon 1997, 38; generally, Bowersock 1969; Saller 1982, 183, 190; Kaster 1988, 22–30; Millar 1992, 2; Fein 1994, 221–82; Swain 1996; Schmitz 1997, 44–55, 61–6, 94–6, 133–5, 230–1; T. Morgan 1998; Habinek 1998, 103–21; Whitmarsh 2001, 90–130, 189; Connolly 2001; Nellen 1981. On restricted literacy, see Harvey 1966; Thomas 1992; esp. Harris 1989, with critical responses in Humphrey 1991.

[36] See, further, Rösger 1978, 9–18.

[37] On the passage, see Bird 1984, 75–6. Cf. Cass. Dio 71.5.3, on Bassaeus Rufus, Amm. Marc. 14.6.1 on Orfitus.

[38] Suetonius: Wallace-Hadrill 1983, 66–72, 83–5; Baldwin 1983, 129–31, 362–8. Plutarch: Pelling 1989; Swain 1990; Van der Stockt 1995. Aurelius Victor: Bird 1974, 71–80. *Historia Augusta*: Rösger 1978. Generally, Fein 1994, 19; Lendon 1997, 117–18 n. 57; Roller 2001, 285.

[39] *numquam...operam ullam aut stilo vel necessarii dedit.* The possibility of a pun, with *stilus necessarius* referring back to the fly-stabbing scene (3.1), cannot be excluded.

[40] Moorhead 1992, 104–5 is sceptical about the anecdote's historicity, citing a rather similar account of the emperor Justin's illiteracy in the *Secret History* by Procopius (6.11–16). Note Procopius' barbed remark that such a thing never happened in the Roman Empire before (6.11 οὐ γεγονὸς ἔν γε Ῥωμαίοις πρότερον τοῦτό [γε]).

[41] Tac. *Ann.* 13.3 is more reserved on the same issue.

[42] Apparently confused with his grandfather or uncle: Bird 1994, 100, 102–3.

[43] e.g. Tac. *Agr.* 4.3, *Hist.* 4.5; Dio Chr. 2.26–7; Aurel. Vict. *De Caes.* 42.23 *litterarum ad elegantiam prudens*; Amm. Marc. 16.7.5 *litteris quantum tali fortunae satis esse poterat eruditus.*

[44] See Fein 1994, 31–2; Rösger, 21–9. Cf. Tiberius' 'ridiculous' interest in philology (Suet. *Tib.* 70.3 *usque ad ineptias atque derisum*). For Greek examples, cf. Plut. *Tim.* 31.1 (Mamercus), Luc. *Ign. Bibl.* 15 (Dionysius the Elder).

[45] See Rochette 1997, 101; Best 1979; Dubuisson 1986.

[46] 'Solidarity' with a caveat: both Roman *mores* and Greek *paideia* were ideals that yielded to much adaptation and focalization(s): Edwards 1993; Whitmarsh 2001; C. Jones 2004; Bowie 2004.

[47] On this passage, see White 1993, 142–5.

[48] And the dearest, too. Augustus' secretary Thallus betrayed the contents of one of the emperor's letters for 500 denarii; when this was found out, his legs were broken (Suet. *Aug.* 67.2).

[49] On the role of written documents in imperial administration, see Millar 1992, 213–28, 240–68, 537–49.

[50] e.g. *P. Bour* 1; Cic. *Pro Cluent.* 123; Hor. *Sat.* 2.1.39–41; Apul. *Flor.* 17.8; Amm. Marc. 30.5.10.

[51] Miraculously, in court his γραμματεῖον turns out to be blank. It is more common for the words or thoughts of *delatores* and litigants to be likened to assassins' weapons: Juv. *Sat.* 4.109–10 'cutting throats with a soft whisper' (*tenui iugulos aperire susurro*), and Amm. Marc. 30.4.9 'drawing the dagger of their talent' (*sicam ingenii destringentes*).

[52] On conventional characterization in Suetonius and Aurelius Victor, see Cizek 1977, 5, 137, and 107–55, esp. 154–5; Baldwin 1983, 156–8, 213, 324–78; Wallace-Hadrill 1983, 142–74; Bird 1984, 28–9; Bradley 1991, 3713–29. Generally Béranger 1953, 63–7, 243, 249–51, 262–5, 272–4; Charlesworth 1979; Wickert 1979, esp. 353; Tabacco 1985, 89–116; Roller 2001, 213, 241–62. Plutarch is a somewhat different case, since he does not always write about autocrats; on Plutarchan moral framework, see Bucher-Isler 1972; Duff 1999, 72–98.

[53] On the importance of the story and the underlying assimilation of Deioces to Greek tyrants, see Flory 1987, 122–8; Barceló 1993, 165–9, 238; Winton 2000, 107–8; Gagarin 2003, 63–4; Dewland 2003, 27–8.

[54] *FGrHist* 4 fr. 178a καὶ διὰ βίβλων τὰς ἀποκρίσεις ποιεῖσθαι, cf. 178b ἐπιστολάς συντάσσειν. See Rosenmeyer 2001, 25. Cf. also Hdt 8.98, on the super-efficient Persian royal mail.

[55] It falls outside the scope of this paper to discuss links between presentation of oriental despotism and the Roman Empire.

[56] See further Birt 1907, 70. For the notion of the Book of Life, cf. St John Rev. 5, 20.12, St Paul Ep. Phil. 4.3, but also Artemid. 2.45, and, more loosely, *Anth. Pal.* 11.41.1–2, Plut. *Cons. Ux.* 611A.

[57] On Caesar's presentation as tyrant, see Allen 1953, Béranger 1975; Pelling 1997b, 2002b; Duff 1999, 303.

[58] For the motif of Domitian's arrogance, see Jones 1996, 109.

[59] Tac. *Ann.* 4.70, 5.2–3, 6.5–6, 6.27, 6.29, 6.40, Cass. Dio 58.1.1, 58.6.3 πολλὰ καὶ ποικίλα…συνεχῶς ἐπέστελλε.

[60] So Seager 1972, 226 with n. 2. Levick 1976, 201–2 and 290 discerns an allusion to the idiolect of Roman comedy.

[61] Trajan's *omen imperii* was a dream of being stamped with a seal (σφραγίς) on the neck by an old senator (Cass. Dio 68.5.1). Maecenas' seal bearing the image of a frog caused fear because his letters often contained requests for financial contributions (Pliny *NH* 37.10 *quippe etiam Maecenatis rana per collationes pecuniarum in magno terrore erat.*) On Augustus' seal, see below text to nn. 68–9.

[62] Murphy 1991, 3786, misses Suetonius' point ('an odd detail to bring out').

[63] Esp. Cass. Dio 53.19.2–4; Tac. *Hist.* 1.1.1 *inscitia rei publicae ut alienae*, cf. 1.4 *imperii arcano*.

[64] To write in one's own hand (αὐτοχειρίᾳ, *sua manu*) rather than dictating to a secretary was the second best option, a gesture of goodwill – although it is attested not only for good lords such as Marcus Aurelius (Cass. Dio 71.36.2), but also for dubious characters such as Marcus Antony (Nep. *Att.* 10.4) or Constantius II (Amm. Marc. 16.5.3), and for the outright bad characters such as Commodus (*SHA Clod. Alb.* 2.2). It could be reserved for important moments: both Nerva, confirming to Trajan his adoption as heir to the throne (Cass. Dio 68.5.2), and Trajan, promising to the senate that nobody would be killed or disfranchised under his regime (Cass. Dio 68.3.4), did it by letters written in their own hand.

[65] See Millar 1992, 240–59.

[66] Tac. *Ann.* 1.9–10, 3.56; Cass. Dio 52.1.1, 53.1.3, 53.8.5, 53.11.5, 53.12.1, 53.17.1–2, 53.18.2, 56.43.4. Meier 1990, 66–70; Yavetz 1990, 30–41; Roller 2001, 253–5, 258. Broader picture sketched in Wallace-Hadrill 1982.

[67] Similarly, Septimius Severus in Cass. Dio 76.11.

[68] Baldwin 1983, 128; generally, Instinsky 1962, 10, 23–36.

[69] *Pace* Zanker 1988, 270–1, describing the sphinx as 'a symbol of hope', and 'a symbol of new age', and Eder 1990, 108, who considers that trusting your mates to write and sign letters in your name is a 'republican' trait. Instinsky 1962, 27–9 inclines to interpret the symbolism of the sphinx as Sibylla's heraldic beast (*Wappentier*).

[70] On the episode, see Bauman 1982.

[71] Philostratean authorship is preferred: Solmsen 1940, 569–70; Korver 1950.

[72] Whitmarsh 2001, 154, describes the episode as 'the collision between the tyrant and the native Greek…thematized as a bloody conflict between writing, emblematized by Nero's servile bureaucrats, and the "voice" of Greece, which is brilliant, democratic, and free.' This is too generous towards the Epirote singer whose profile in the passage is not entirely commendable – he is highfalutin (ἐπλάττετο) and trading victory for money. The key phrase δημοτικῶς ἐρίζοντος is equivocal: 'competing democratically' or 'squabbling vulgarly'? For Nero's competitiveness, cf. Suet. *Nero* 23.2–3. For silencing as a tyrannical act, cf. Suet. *Dom.* 13.1, contrast Hadrian in Cass. Dio 69.6.1–2.

[73] 'I wish I was illiterate!' young Nero hypocritically exclaims when asked to sign a death warrant (Suet. *Nero* 10.2 *quam vellem nescire litteras*). Pliny the Younger is thrilled about his own narrow escape: a *libellus* with charges against him was found in Domitian's papers (*Ep.* 7.27.14).

[74] So Jones 1992, 186 = 1996, 90: 'a map outlining possible conquests or weak points most susceptible to attack, speeches at hand to urge his warriors and their leaders'; generally, Arnaud 1983.

[75] Similarly, the downfall of Cornelius Gallus in 27/26 BC was partly caused by the overambitious format of his political statements: he put up statues of himself 'all over Egypt' and inscribed his own deeds (ἔργα) on the pyramids (Cass. Dio 53.23.6); cf. Gibson 1997.

[76] Cf. Sen. Ma. *Contr.* 10 *praef.* 5, 8; Tac. *Agr.* 2.1–2, *Ann.* 1.72, 4.34–5, 14.50; Pliny *Ep.* 7.19.5–6; Suet. *Aug.* 31.1, *Tib.* 61.3, *Dom.* 10.1; Sen. *Ad Marc.* 1.2–3; Quint. 10.1.104; Cass. Dio 56.27.1, 57.24.2–4, 77.7.3 (book-burning planned); Amm. Marc. 28.1.26, 29.1.41. Speyer 1981 is fundamental; also Cramer 1945, 165–77; Rawson 1986; Blanck 1992, 131–2.

[77] Private letters are regularly used to denounce people: cf. Amm. Marc. 14.9.7, 18.3.2–4, 28.1.20–1, 28.1.32–3, 28.6.26–7, 29.2.25.

[78] A singular case of self-incrimination by letter is the story of Julius Montanus: having been assaulted by Nero's street-gang, he sends a letter of apology to the emperor. This proved to be a most ill-advised move, as Nero could not publically admit his hooliganism. Montanus had to commit suicide as a result (Cass. Dio 61.9.4).

[79] Brief recent survey of imperial libraries: Blanck 1992, 152–222. On ancient libraries as a stake in the power-game, see Jacob 1996, 50; Neudecker 2004, 293–4; for stimulating general discussion of libraries' influence, see Freire and Macebo 1987, 37–46; Latour 1996.

[80] Furniture and décor mattered: for example, a bust of the orator Hortensius (Tac. *Ann.* 2.37) would indicate loyalty to ancestral civic values and, perhaps, hint at toying with the republican tradition.

[81] Marshall 1976, 261–3; Speyer 1981, 61; Horsfall 1993, esp. 60–1; Canfora 1996, 261–3.

[82] There is, exceptionally, a vestigial possibility of criticism in Gellius' passage on the fate of Pisitratus' library in Athens which Xerxes took away to Persia during the invasion (7.17.1–2 *abstulit asportavitque in Persas*); Xerxes' actions are a flashback of the Roman practice; Lucullus, for one, was nicknamed 'Xerxes in a toga' (Vell. Pat. 2.33.4).

[83] On Lucullus' library, see Blanck 1992, 154–5; Keith Dix 2000.

[84] Gottschalk 1987, 1083–7; Blanck 1992, 153–4; Lindsay 1997; Barnes 1997.

[85] See, generally, McMullen 1967, 19–45; Timpe 1987.

[86] Pamphlets: e.g., Suet. *Caes.* 20.2, 80.2; *Aug.* 55; *Tib.* 66; *Nero* 39.2; *Dom.* 14.2; Tac. *Ann.* 1.72; Cass. Dio 44.12.1, 56.27.1, 66.11.1; Amm. Marc. 20.4.10. Graffiti: e.g., Plut. *Caes.* 62.7, *Brut.* 9.5–7; Suet. *Caes.* 80.3; *Aug.* 70.2; *Nero* 45.2; *Dom.* 13.2; Cass. Dio 44.12.3, 61.16.2–2b.

[87] Cf. Suet. *Caes.* 81.4; Nic. Dam. *FGrHist* 90 fr. 130.66; Vell. Pat. 2.57.2 *et libelli coniurationem nuntiantes dati neque protinus ab eo lecti erant*; Cass. Dio 44.18.3.

[88] See, generally, Pelling 1997b.

[89] In Suet. *Caes.* 78.1 notebooks do not appear.

[90] Yavetz 1969, 55, 100–1; Millar 1992, 370–1. Marcus Aurelius worked with documents during circus performances and was ridiculed by the crowd (*SHA M. Aurel.* 15.1).

[91] The dangers posed by ancient stationery in surprise short-range attack should not be underestimated: a Roman knight, angry with the verdict he received from Claudius, wildly threw his stylus and tablets (*graphium et libellos*) in the emperor's face and badly gashed his cheek (Suet. *Claud.* 15.4).

[92] For more (and different) versions of Aurelian's assassination see Watson 1999, 104–5. Ammianus Marcellinus tells a similar story about the noble general Silvanus who was forced into rebellion against the emperor after incriminating letters under his name had been faked by one Dynamius (15.5.3–14, 19.12.13).

[93] Seminal discussion by Ahl 1984.

[94] See Scott 1990.

Bibliography

Ahl, F.
1984   'The art of safe criticism in Greece and Rome', *AJPh*, 105, 174–208.

Alföldi, A.
1955   'Gewaltherrscher und Theaterkönig', in K. Weitzmann (ed.) *Late Classical and Mediaeval Studies in Honor of A.M. Friend Jr*, Princeton, 15–55.

Allen, W. Jr
1953   'Caesar's Regnum (Suet. *Iul.* 9.2)', *TAPhA* 84, 227–36.

Archer, D. and Costello, P.
1990   *Literacy and Power: The Latin American battleground*, London.

Arnaud, P.
1983   'L'affaire Mettius Pompusianus ou le crime de cartographie', *MEFR* 95, 677–99.

Avertintsev, S.S.
2002   'From biography to hagiography: some stable patterns in the Greek and Latin tradition of *Lives*, including *Lives* of the Saints', in P. France and W. St Clair (eds.) *Mapping Lives: The uses of biography*, Oxford, 19–36.

Baines, J.
1988   'Literacy, social organization, and the archaeological record: the case of early Egypt', in Gledhill, Bender and Larsen (eds.) *State and Society*, 192–214.

Baldwin, B.
1983   *Suetonius*, Amsterdam.

Baratin, M. and Jacob, C. (eds.)
1996   *Le pouvoir des bibliothèques: la mémoire des livres en Occident*, Paris.

Barceló, P.
1993   *Basileia, monarchia, tyrannis. Untersuchungen zu Entwicklung und Beurteilung von Alleinherrschaft im vorhellenistischen Griechenland*, Stuttgart.

Barnes, J.
1997   'Roman Aristotle', in J. Barnes and M. Griffin (eds.) *Philosophia Togata II: Plato and Aristotle at Rome*, Oxford, 1–69.

Bauman, R.A.
1982   ' "Hangman, call a halt!" ', *Hermes* 110, 102–10.

Bee, B.
1980   'The politics of literacy', in R. Mackie (ed.) *Literacy and Revolution: The pedagogy of Paulo Freire*, London, 39–56.

Bellamy, R.
1989   'Bellerophon's tablet', *CJ* 84, 289–307.

Béranger, J.
1953   *Recherches sur l'aspect idéologique du Principat*, Basel.
1975   'Tyrannus. Notes sur la notion de tyrannie chez les Romains, particulièrement à l'époque de César et de Cicéron', in *Principatus: Études de notions et d'histoire politiques dans l'Antiquité gréco-romaine*, Gent, 51–60.

Best, E.G.
1979   'Suetonius: The use of Greek among the Julio-Claudian dynasty', *CB* 53, 9–45.

Bird, H.W.
1984   *Sextus Aurelius Victor: A historiographical study*, Liverpool.

1994   *Liber De Caesaribus of Sextus Aurelius Victor*, Liverpool.

Birt, T.

1907   *Die Buchrolle in der Kunst: archäologisch-antiquarische Untersuchungen zum antiken Buchwesen*, Leipzig.

Blanck, H.

1992   *Das Buch in der Antike*, Munich.

Borg, B.E. (ed.)

2004   *Paideia: The world of the Second Sophistic*, Berlin and New York.

Bowersock, G.

1969   *Greek Sophists in the Roman Empire*, Oxford.

Bowie, E.

2004   'The geography of the Second Sophistic: cultural variations', in Borg (ed.) *Paideia*, 65–83.

Bowman, A.K. and Woolf, G. (eds.)

1994   *Literacy and Power in the Ancient World*, Cambridge.

Bradley, K.R.

1991   'The imperial ideal in Suetonius' "Caesares"', *ANRW* 2.33.5, 3701–32.

Bucher-Isler, B.

1972   *Norm und Individualität in den Biographien Plutarchs*, Bern and Stuttgart.

Canfora, L.

1996   'Les bibliothèques anciennes et l'histoire des textes', in Baratin and Jacob (eds.) *Le pouvoir des bibliothèques*, 261–72.

Cartledge, P.

1990   'Herodotus and "The Other": A meditation on Empire', *EMC/CV* 34, 27–40.

2000   'Greek political thought: the historical context', in Rowe and Schofield (eds.) *The Cambridge History of Greek and Roman Political Thought*, 11–22.

Charbonnier, G.

1969   *Conversations with Claude Lévi-Strauss*, London, transl. J. and D. Weightman, French orig. Paris.

Charlesworth, M.P.

1979   'Die Tugenden eines römischen Herrschers: Propaganda und die Schaffung von Glaubwürdigkeit', in Kloft (ed.) *Ideologie und Herrschaft in der Antike*, 361–87. First published in 1937 as 'The virtues of a Roman emperor. Propaganda and the creation of belief', *Proc. Brit. Acad.* 23, 105–33.

Cizek, E.

1977   *Structures et idéologie dans* Les vies des douze Césars *de Suétone*, Paris.

Clanchy, M.T.

1979   *From Memory to Written Record*, London.

Cohen, D.

2003   'Writing, law, and legal practice in the Athenian courts', in Yunis, *Written Texts and the Rise of Literate Culture in Ancient Greece*, Cambridge, 78–96.

Cohen, M.

1958   *La grande invention de l'écriture et son évolution*, vol. 1, Paris.

Coleman, K.M.

1986   'The Emperor Domitian and literature', *ANRW*, 2.32.5, 3087–115.

Connolly, J.
  2001   'Problems of the past in imperial Greek education', in Y.L. Too (ed.)
          Education in Greek and Roman Antiquity, Leiden 339–72.
Cook, B.L.
  2002   'Plutarch's use of λέγεται: narrative design and source in *Alexander*', *GRBS*
          42, 329–60.
Cooper, C.
  2004   '"The appearance of history": making some sense of Plutarch', in R.B.
          Egan and M.A. Joyal (eds.) *Daimonopylai. Essays in classics and the classical
          tradition presented to Edmund G. Berry*, Winnipeg, 33–55.
Cramer, F.H.
  1945   'Bookburning and censorship in ancient Rome. A chapter from the history
          of freedom of speech', *JHI* 6, 157–196.
Derrida, J.
  1976   *Of Grammatology*, transl. G.C. Spivak, Baltimore and London; French orig.
          Paris 1967.
Dewald, C.
  2003   'Form and content: the question of tyranny in Herodotus', in Morgan (ed.)
          Popular Tyranny, Austin, 25–58.
Diringer, D.
  1947   *The Alphabet: A key to the history of mankind*, London.
Dubuisson, M.
  1986   'Purisme et politique: Suétone, Tibère et le grec au Sénat', in *Mélanges
          J. Veremans*, Brussels, 109–17.
Duff, T.
  1999   *Plutarch's Lives: Exploring virtue and vice*, Oxford.
Eder, W.
  1990   'Augustus and the power of tradition: The Augustan principate as binding link
          between Republic and Empire', in Raaflaub and Toher (eds.) *Between Republic
          and Empire*, 71–122.
Edwards, C.
  1993   *The Politics of Immorality in Ancient Rome*, Cambridge.
Edwards, M.J. and Swain, S. (eds.)
  1997   *Portraits: Biographical representation in the Greek and Latin literature of the
          Roman Empire*, Oxford.
Fadinger, V.
  1993   'Griechische Tyrannis und Alter Orient', in K. Raaflaub (ed.) *Anfänge
          politischen Denkens in der Antike*, Munich, 263–316.
Fein, S.
  1994   *Die Beziehungen der Kaiser Trajan und Hadrian zu den Litterati*, Stuttgart.
Ferrill, A.
  1978   'Herodotus on tyranny', *Historia* 27, 385–98.
Flory, S.
  1980   'Who read Herodotus' *Histories*?', *AJPh* 101, 12–28.
  1987   *The Archaic Smile of Herodotus*, Detroit.
Ford, A.
  2002   *The Origins of Criticism. Literary culture and poetic theory in classcial Greece*,

Princeton and Oxford.

Fowler, R.L.
1996   'Herodotus and his contemporaries', *JHS* 116, 62–87.
2001   'Early *Historiê* and literacy', in Luraghi, *The Historian's Craft in the Age of Herodotus*, 95–115.

Freire, P.
1985   *The Politics of Education: Culture, power and liberation*, transl. D. Macedo, Basingstoke and London.

Freire, P. and Macedo, D.
1987   *Literacy: Reading the world and the world*, London.

Friemann, S.
1990   'Überlegungen zu Alkidamas' Rede Über die Sophisten', in W. Kullman and M. Reichel (eds.) *Der Übergang von der Mündlichkeit zur Literatur bei den Griechen*, Tübingen, 301–15.

Gagarin, M.
2003   'Letters of the law: written texts in archaic Greek law', in Yunis, *Written Texts and the Rise of Literate Culture in Ancient Greece*, 59–77.

Gammie, J.
1986   'Herodotus on kings and tyrants: objective historiography or conventional portraiture?', *JNES* 45, 171–95.

Gibson, B.J.
1997   'Horace *Carm.* 3.30.1–5', *CQ* 47, 312–14.

Gill, C.
1983   'The question of character-development: Plutarch and Tacitus', *CQ* 33, 469–87.

Giovannini, A. (ed.)
1987   *Opposition et résistances à l'Empire d'Auguste à Trajan*, Vandœuvres and Genève = *Entr. Hardt*, 33.

Gledhill, J., Bender, B. and Larsen, M.T. (eds.)
1988   *State and Society. The emergence of social hierarchy and political centralization*, London.

Goody, J.
1977   *The Domestication of the Savage Mind*, Cambridge.
1986   *The Logic of Writing and the Organization of Society*, Cambridge.

Goody, J. and Watt, I.
1968   'The consequences of literacy', in J. Goody (ed.) *Literacy in Traditional Societies*, Cambridge, 27–68.

Gottschalk, H.B.
1987   'Aristotelian philosophy in the Roman world from the time of Cicero to the end of the second century AD', *ANRW* 2.36.2, 1079–174.

Graff, H.
1986   'The legacies of literacy: continuities and contradictions in western society and culture', in S. de Castell, A. Luke and K. Egan (eds.) *Literacy, Society and Schooling: A reader*, Cambridge, 61–86.
1987   *The Legacies of Literacy: Continuities and contradictions in western society and culture*, Bloomington and Indianapolis.

Gray, V.
1996   'Herodotus and images of tyranny: the tyrants of Corinth', *AJPh* 117, 361–89.

Habinek, T.
1998   *The Politics of Latin Literature: Writing, identity, and empire in ancient Rome*, Princeton.

Harbsmeier, M.
1988   'Inventions of writing', in Gledhill, Bender and Larsen (eds.) *State and Society*, 253–76.
1989   'Writing and the Other: traveller's literacy or towards an archaeology of orality', in Schousboe and Larsen (eds.) *Literacy and Society*, 197–228.

Harris, W.V.
1989   *Ancient Literacy*, Cambridge, Mass. and London.

Hartog, F.
1988   *The Mirror of Herodotus. The representation of the Other in the writing of history*, Berkeley, Los Angeles and London, transl. J. Lloyd; French orig. Paris 1980.

Harvey, F.D.,
1966   'Literacy in the Athenian democracy', *REG* 79, 585–635.

Havelock, E.A.
1963   *Preface to Plato*, Cambridge, Mass.
1976   *The Origins of Western Literacy*, Toronto.
1982   *The Literate Revolution in Greece and its Cultural Consequences*, Princeton.
1986   *The Muse Learns to Write: Reflections on orality and literacy from antiquity to the present*, New Haven and London.

Hopkins, K.
1991   'Conquest by book', in Humphrey (ed.) *Literacy in the Roman World*, 133–58.

Horsfall, N.
1993   'Empty shelves on the Palatine', *G&R* 42, 58–67.

Humphrey, J.H. (ed.)
1991   *Literacy in the Roman World*, Ann Arbor = *JRA* Suppl. 3.

Jacob, C.
1996   'Lire pour écrire: navigations alexandrines', in M. Baratin and C. Jacob (eds.) *Le pouvoir des bibliothèques: la mémoire des livres en Occident*, Paris, 47–83.

Johnson, W.A.
1994   'Oral performance and the composition of Herodotus' *Histories*', *GRBS* 35, 229–54.

Instinsky, H.
1962   *Die Siegel des Kaisers Augustus (Ein Kapitel zur Geschichte und Symbolik des antiken Herrschersiegels)*, Baden-Baden.

Jones, B.W.
1992   *The Emperor Domitian*, London and New York.

Jones, B.W. (ed.)
1996   *Suetonius: Domitian*, Bristol.

Jones, B.W. and Milns, R.D. (eds.)
2002   *Suetonius:* The Flavian Emperors. *A Historical Commentary*, Bristol.

Jones, C.P.
2004   'Multiple identities in the age of the Second Sophistic', in Borg (ed.) *Paideia*, 13–21.
Kaster, R.A.
1988   *Guardians of Language: The grammarian and society in late antiquity*, Berkeley, Los Angeles and London.
Keith Dix, T.
2000   'The library of Lucullus', *Athenaeum* 88, 441–64.
Kirk, G.S.
1990   *The* Iliad*: A commentary*, vol. 2, Cambridge.
Kloft, H.
1970   *Liberalitas principis*, Cologne.
Kloft, H. (ed.)
1979   *Ideologie und Herrschaft in der Antike*, Darmstadt.
Korver, J.
1950   'Néron et Musonius', *Mnemosyne* 3, 319–29.
Larsen, M.T.
1988   'Introduction: literacy and social complexity', in Gledhill, Bender and Larsen (eds.) *State and Society*, 173–91.
Lateiner, D.
1989   *The Historical Methods of Herodotus*, Toronto.
Latour, B.
        'Ces réseaux que la raison ignore: laboratoires, bibliothèques, collections', in Baratin and Jacob (eds.) *Le pouvoir des bibliothèques*, 23–46.
Lendon, J.E.
1997   *Empire of Honour: The art of government in the Roman world*, Oxford.
Levick, B.M.
1976   *Tiberius the Politician*, London.
Lévi-Strauss, C.
1973   *Tristes Tropiques*, transl. J. and D. Weightman, New York. French orig. Paris 1955.
Lindsay, H.
1997   'Strabo on Apellicon's Library', *RhM* 140, 290–8.
Luraghi, N.(ed.)
2001   *The Historian's Craft in the Age of Herodotus*, Oxford.
Marshall, A.J.
1976   'Library resources and creative writing at Rome', *Phoenix* 30, 252–64.
McGlew, J.F.
1993   *Tyranny and Political Culture in Ancient Greece*, Ithaca.
McMullen, R.
1967   *Enemies of the Roman Order: Treason, unrest and alienation in the Empire*, Cambridge, Mass.
Meier, C.
1990   'C. Caesar Divi Filius and the formation of the alternative in Rome', in Raaflaub and Toher (eds.) *Between Republic and Empire*, 54–70.
Millar, F.G.B.
1992   *The Emperor in the Roman World*, 2nd edn, London.

Mooney, G.W. (ed.)
1930   *C. Suetoni Tranquilli* De vita Caesarum *libri VII–VIII, with Introduction, Translation, and Commentary*, London. Repr. New York 1979.

Moorhead, J.
1992   *Theoderic in Italy*, Oxford.

Morgan, K.A. (ed.)
2003   *Popular Tyranny*, Austin.

Morgan, T.
1998   *Literary Education in the Hellenistic and Roman Worlds*, Cambridge.

Murphy, J.P.
1991   'The anecdote in Suetonius' Flavian "Lives"', *ANRW* 2.33.5, 3780–93.

Murray, O.
2001a   'Herodotus and oral history', in Luraghi (ed.) *The Historian's Craft in the Age of Herodotus*, 16–44. Orig. publ. in H.W.A.M. Sancisi-Weerdenburg and A. Kuhrt (eds.) *Achaemenid History II: The Greek sources*, Leiden 1987, 93–115.
2001b   'Herodotus and oral history reconsidered', in Luraghi (ed.) *The Historian's Craft in the Age of Herodotus*, 314–25.

Nellen, D.
1981   *Viri litterati. Gebildetes Beamtentum und spätrömisches Reich in Westen zwischen 284 und 395 nach Christus*, 2nd edn, Bochum.

Neudecker, R.
2004   'Aspekte öffentlicher Bibliotheken in der Kaiserzeit', in Borg (ed.) *Paideia*, 293–313.

Olson, D.R.
1994   *The World on Paper: The conceptual and cognitive implications of writing and reading*, Cambridge.

Ong, W.
1982   *Orality and Literacy. The technologizing of the word*, London and New York.

Oxenham, J.
1980   *Literacy: Writing, reading and social dynamization*, London.

Parker, V.
1998   'Τύραννος. The semantics of a political concept from Archilochus to Aristotle', *Hermes* 126, 145–72.

Pattison, R.
1982   *On Literacy. The politics of the word from Homer to the age of rock*, New York and Oxford.

Pauw, D.
1980   'Impersonal expressions and unidentified spokesmen in Greek and Roman historiography and biography', *AClass* 23, 83–95.

Pelling, C.
1989   'Plutarch: Roman heroes and Greek culture', in M. Griffin and J. Barnes (eds.) *Philosophia Togata. Essays on philosophy and Roman society*, Oxford, 199–232.
1997a   'East is east and west is west – or are they? National stereotypes in Herodotus', *Histos* 1, www.dur.ac.uk/Classics/histos/1997/pelling.html.
1997b   'Plutarch on Caesar's fall', in J. Mossman (ed.) *Plutarch and His Intellectual*

World, London, 215–32.

1997c   'Biographical history? Cassius Dio on the early Principate', in Edwards and Swain (eds.) *Portraits*, 117–44.

2002a   'Childhood and personality in Greek biography', in *Plutarch and History: Eighteen studies*, London, 301–38; first version published in C. Pelling (ed.) *Characterization and Individuality in Greek Literature*, Oxford 1990, 213–44.

2002b   'Plutarch's *Caesar*: A *Caesar* for the Caesars?', in *Plutarch and History: Eighteen studies*, London, 253–65.

Penwill, J.L.

2000   'Quintilian, Statius and the lost epic of Domitian', *Ramus* 29, 60–83.

Powell, B.

1997   'Homer and writing', in I. Morris and B. Powell (eds.) *A New Companion to Homer*, Leiden, 3–32.

Raaflaub, K.A.

1987   'Grundzüge, Ziele und Ideen der Opposition gegen die Kaiser im 1. Jhr.n. Chr.: Versuch einer Standortsbestimmung', in Giovannini (ed.) *Opposition et résistances à l'Empire d'Auguste à Trajan = Entr. Hardt* 33, 1–55.

2003   'Stick and glue: the function of tyranny in fifth-century Athenian democracy', in Morgan (ed.) *Popular Tyranny*, 59–93.

Raaflaub, K.A. and Toher, M. (eds.)

1990   *Between Republic and Empire: Interpretations of Augustus and his Principate*, Berkeley, Los Angeles and Oxford.

Rawson, E.

1986   'Cassius and Brutus: the memory of the liberators', in I.S. Moxon, J.D. Smart and A.J. Woodman (eds.) *Past Perspectives: Studies in Greek and Roman historical writing*, Cambridge, 101–19.

Robb, K.

1994   *Literacy and Paideia in Ancient Greece*, New York and Oxford.

Rochette, B.

1997   *Le Latin dans le monde grec. Recherches sur la diffusion de la langue et des lettres latines dans les provinces hellénophones de l'Empire romain*, Brussels.

Roller, M.B.

2001   *Constructing Autocracy: Aristocrats and emperors in Julio-Claudian Rome*, Princeton and Oxford.

Rosenmeyer, P.A.

2001   *Ancient Epistolary Fictions. The letters in Greek literature*, Cambridge.

Rösger, A.

1978   *Herrschererziehung in der Historia Augusta*, Bonn.

Rosivach, V.J.

1988   'The tyrant in Athenian democracy', *QUCC* 30, 43–57.

Rowe, C. and Schofield, M. (eds.)

2000   *The Cambridge History of Greek and Roman Political Thought*, Cambridge.

Saller, R.P.

1982   *Personal Patronage under the Empire*, Cambridge.

Schmitz, T.

1997   *Bildung und Macht: zur sozialen und politischen Funktion der zweiten*

Sophistik in der griechischen Welt der Kaiserzeit, Munich.

Schousboe, K. and Larsen, M.T. (eds.)
1989   *Literacy and Society*, Copenhagen.

Scott, J.C.
1990   *Domination and the Arts of Resistance: Hidden transcripts*, New Haven and London.

Scribner, S. and Cole, M.
1981   *The Psychology of Literacy*, Cambridge, Mass. and London.

Seaford, R.
2003   'Tragic tyranny', in Morgan (ed.) *Popular Tyranny*, 95–115.

Seager, R.J.
1967   'Alcibiades and the charge of aiming at tyranny', *Historia* 16, 6–18.
1972   *Tiberius*, London.

Sickinger, J.P.
2002   'Literacy, orality, and legislative procedure in classical Athens', in I. Worthington and J.M. Foley (eds.) *Epea and Grammata. Oral and written communication in ancient Greece*, Leiden, 147–69.

Solmsen, F.
1940   'Some works of Philostratus the Elder', *TAPhA*, 71, 556–72.

Solomon, R.C.
1986   'Literacy and the education of the emotions', in S. de Castell, A. Luke and K. Egan (eds.) *Literacy, Society and Schooling: A reader*, Cambridge, 37–58.

Southern, O.
1997   *Domitian: Tragic tyrant*, London and New York.

Späth, T.
2005   'Das Politise und der Einzelne: Figurenkonstruktion in Biographie und Geschichtschreibung', in L. de Blois, J. Bons, T. Kessels and D.M. Schenkeveld (eds.) *The Statesman in Plutarch's Works*, vol. ii, Leiden and Boston, 27–42.

Speyer, W.
1981   *Büchervernichtung und Zensur des Geistes bei Heiden, Juden und Christen*, Stuttgart.

Steiner, D.T.
1994   *The Tyrant's Writ. Myths and images of writing in ancient Greece*, Princeton.

Street, B.V.
1984   *Literacy in Theory and Practice*, Cambridge.
1995a   *Social Literacies. Critical approaches to literacy in development, ethnography and education*, London and New York.

Street, B.V. (ed.)
1995b   *Cross-Cultural Approaches to Literacy*, Cambridge.

Swain, S.
1990   'Hellenic culture and the Roman heroes of Plutarch', *JHS* 110, 126–45.
1996   *Hellenism and Empire: Language, classicism, and power in the Greek world AD 50–250*, Oxford.
1997   'Biography and biographic in the literature of the Roman Empire', in Edwards and Swain (eds.) *Portraits*, 1–37.

Tabacco, R.
1985   'Il tiranno nelle declamazioni de scuola in lingua latina', *Memorie*

dell'*Accademia delle Scienze di Torino, Classe di Scienze morali, storiche e filologiche*, 9, 1–141.

Thomas, R.
1989 *Oral Tradition and Written Record in Classical Athens*, Cambridge.
1992 *Literacy and Orality in Ancient Greece*, Cambridge.
1993 'Performance and written publication in Herodotus and the Sophistic generation', in W. Kullmann and J. Althoff (eds.) *Vermittlung und Tradierung von Wissen in der griechischen Kultur*, Tübingen, 225–44.

Thompson, N.
1996 *Herodotus and the Origins of the Political Community. Arion's leap*, New Haven and London.

Timpe, D.
1987 'Geschichtsschreibung und Prinzipat-Opposition', in Giovannini (ed.) *Opposition et résistances à l'Empire d'Auguste à Trajan = Entr. Hardt* 33, 65–102.

Van der Stockt, L.
1995 'L'homme d'état et les beaux arts selon Plutarque', in I. Gallo and B. Scardigli (eds.) *Teoria e prassi politica nelle opere di Plutarco*, Naples, 457–65.

Wallace-Hadrill, A.
1982 'Civilis Princeps: Between citizen and king', *JRS* 72, 32–48.
1983 *Suetonius. The scholar and his Caesars*, London.

Waters, K.H.
1964 'The character of Domitian', *Phoenix* 18, 49–77.
1971 *Herodotus on Tyrants and Despots: A study in objectivity*, Wiesbaden.

Watson, A.
1999 *Aurelian and the Third Century*, London and New York.

White, P.
1993 *Promised Verse. Poets in the society of Augustan Rome*, Cambridge, Mass. and London.

Whitmarsh, T.
2001 *Greek Literature and the Roman Empire: The politics of imitation*, Oxford.

Wickert, L.
1979 'Entstehung und Entwicklung des römischen Herrscherideals', in Kloft (ed.) *Ideologie und Herrschaft in der Antike*, 339–60.

Winton, R.
2000 'Herodotus, Thucydides and the Sophists', in Rowe and Schofield (eds.) *The Cambridge History of Greek and Roman Political Thought*, 89–121.

Woolf, G.
1994 'Power and the spread of writing in the West', in Bowman and Woolf (eds.) *Literacy and Power in the Ancient World*, 84–98.

Yavetz, Z.
1969 *Plebs and Princeps*, Oxford.
1990 'The personality of Augustus: reflections on Syme's *Roman Revolution*', in Raaflaub and Toher (eds.) *Between Republic and Empire*, 21–41.

Yunis, J.
2003 *Written Texts and the Rise of Literate Culture in Ancient Greece*, Cambridge.

Zadorojnyi, A.V.
2005 '"Stabbed with large pens": trajectories of literacy in Plutarch's Lives', in

L. deBlois, J.A.E. Bons, T. Kessels, D.M. Schenkeveld (eds.) *The Statesman in Plutarch's Works*, vol. ii, Leiden and Boston, 113–37.

Forthcoming   'Cato's suicide in Plutarch'.

Zanker, P.

1988   *The Power of Images in the Age of Augustus*, transl. A. Shapiro, Ann Arbor.

20

BEYOND THE LIMITS OF GREEK BIOGRAPHY: GALEN FROM ALEXANDRIA TO THE ARABS

Simon Swain

This chapter has two aims. The first (Section 1) is to reconsider the role played in the transmission of biographical data about Galen of Pergamum by the problematical late Greek author known to Arabic writers as 'John the Grammarian'. I shall suggest that the existence of John should not be doubted, that the work on the history of medicine ascribed to him was genuine, and crucially that John drew for this work on already existing biographical traditions about Galen. It is argued that these traditions show there was a widespread interest in Galen as a biographical figure in late antiquity which in some ways foreshadows the interest taken in him by later Arabic (and Syriac) writers. The second aim (Sections 2–3) is to study cultural aspects of the uses of Galen's biography in authors of the classical period of Islam (*c.* 9th–14th centuries CE) and specifically the fictionalizing of biographical details about him and his insertion into the cultural life of the elite. I shall pay particular attention to the two best known Arabic biographies of him. I shall not here go into the technical medical or philosophical Galen.

The story traced below is part of the story of the transmission of Greek culture to Islam, an event of fundamental importance. If this provisional study raises the profile of this movement among classicists, it has done its job.[1]

1. From Alexandria to the Arabs

Although the names of a great many medical practitioners are known from Graeco-Roman antiquity, we know very little about their lives. The only person we know to have written a work called 'lives of doctors' is Soranus of Ephesus, the early second-century author of the famous *Gynaecology*. This is lost, but we do have a short biography of Hippocrates attributed to Soranus.[2] Apart from this there are the several biographies of doctors in the *Lives of the Sophists and Philosophers* by Eunapius at the end of the fourth century. Eunapius' inclusion of this group tells us much about the development of medicine after Soranus. They owe their place to their skill in rhetoric in which they followed their teacher, Zeno of Cyprus. Rhetoric and persuasion

had always held an important place in Greek medicine. But the 'philosophizing' of rhetoric in the High Roman Empire on the one hand,[3] and the
Galenic legacy of philosophized medicine on the other, reinforced an old
attraction. Other than these lives, there is silence. Some biblio-biographical
information circulated of course – presumably in the medical schools – and
we see its legacy in the brief notices of physicians in the tenth-century
Byzantine schoolroom encyclopedia called the Suda. But proper biographies
are lacking. Why?

(Ps.-)Soranus' Life of Hippocrates and the Eunapian lives are biographies
only. They contain no list of writings. Works such as Galen's lost *Authentic
and Inauthentic Works of Hippocrates* were the place to go for this type of
information. Galen himself introduced a new sort of biography for the
professional intellectual (drawing on the traditions of the grammarians)
by writing two biblio-biographical works, *On His Own Books* (the *Pinax*)
and *On the Order of his Own Books*. Here the scholar was identified and
defined by his books which were linked to various stages of his life.[4] But this
experiment was apparently not repeated till Augustine's *Retractationes*. We
may contrast the very different situation with philosophers. Philosophical
biography began with the early Aristotelians and continued with many
notable examples throughout the Roman period. The ancient philosophers
at all times had a sense of tribal belonging that kept stories of their founders
and leading figures alive. Furthermore enough members of the elite aspired to
be philosophers to create a market for philosophical biography, which should
be seen as part of the broad category of what is called 'political biography'.
Doctors on the other hand were perhaps too individualist and too technical
to become cultural models. There is certainly evidence of medical sectarianism in the Hellenistic period and later (especially among the Empiricists
and Methodists) and doxographies were produced. But Galen's insistence
on Cos versus Cnidos and on the Empiricists, Dogmatists (which comprises
a rag bag of different physicians), and Methodists as quite distinct groups is
suspicious. It was part of his 'philosophizing' of medicine to package doctors
(frequently rivals) like philosophers who followed erroneous theories or
contradicted fellow-sectarians. After Galen we hear little of independent
value on the sects.[5] The contrast with the philosophers, then, is striking.
Although interest in medicine was widespread among the ancient elite,
doctors themselves did not generate a biographical literature.

Only one doctor, Hippocrates, was sufficiently important to need more
than a short biography. During the Hellenistic period and after there arose
– no doubt by accretion – a lengthy correspondence dealing with Hippocrates' opinions and travels and focusing on his philhellenism (he refused
to treat Persians) and his meeting with the great scientist and philosopher,

Democritus.[6] This correspondence would certainly have appealed to the Greeks' consciousness of their past in the Second Sophistic period and their desire to confirm the classical credentials of their intellectual heroes. It has a popular flavour too, and that may be why there is no direct mention of it in Galen. We can, however, assume that Galen knew of the biographical traditions about Hippocrates – he affirms that he was a contemporary of Democritus, and that he refused to treat Artaxerxes (and was cautious about Perdiccas of Macedon), but he mentions nothing else.[7] For him, what was important was the intellectual inheritance of Hippocrates, whose 'road (of healing)' he had completed and whose views he had reformed to promote himself.[8]

Galen was the other medical superstar of antiquity. Yet no ancient biography of him is known. We may wonder if his biblio-biographical works and the autobiographical information that is spread throughout his writings made one unnecessary. Maybe; but it should also be remembered that the dominance of Galenic medicine (and hence the greatness of Galen) was only achieved slowly. Thus Oribasius in the mid-fourth century made a (lost) collection of excerpts from Galen, but his great synthetic works drew from many earlier doctors as well, even if they point the way to the dominant Galenic future.[9] In other words, for much of the Roman period Galen may not have been important enough to merit a biographical treatment comparable to that of the classical Hippocrates. In late antique Alexandria, however, Galen in conjunction with (his) Hippocrates became the focus of a very active medical school which adopted the commentary traditions of Neoplatonism to raise the self-confidence of the subject and the standards of its teaching.[10] Men like Stephanus and Palladius lectured on both of them in the sixth and seventh century. Paul of Aegina (who worked at Alexandria) uses Galen extensively in his extant *Epitome of Medicine* from the same epoch. Stephanus' lectures to students apparently formed part of a curriculum of twelve Hippocratic and sixteen Galenic works which (according to most Arabic sources) were students' required reading before they proceeded further.[11] We may assume that these students were naturally keen to learn more about the men who wrote these works and that they wanted bibliographical and biographical information about them. This demand explains the fragmentary Latin life of Hippocrates which was almost certainly written first in Greek after 500 and contains detailed lists of Hippocrates' works.[12] For Galen one would expect something similar.

In what follows I shall argue that the indirect evidence of the extensive Arabic tradition about Galen (Arabic *Jālīnūs*) allows us to assume that there were Graeco-Roman biographical traditions about him on various levels. These did not amount to a biography as such; but they do show that Galen had a biographical persona at the end of antiquity. I shall begin with the mysterious Alexandrian Greek author whom the Arabs called 'John the Grammarian' (Yaḥyā al-Naḥwī) and with his use of apparently popular traditions about the 'Christian' Galen to assist his own partisan vision of medical history.

According to the Arabic sources, John the Grammarian was an Alexandrian who was active at the time of the invasion of Egypt by the Arabs under 'Amr b. al-'Āṣ. There are three main tellings of the story of his life by authors whose names will be mentioned often below: in the famous *Fihrist* of the Baghdadian bookseller, Ibn al-Nadīm (henceforth Ibn al-Nadim; written 987/8), in the *Information for the Learned about the Accounts of the Wise* by al-Qifṭī (henceforth Qifti; surviving abridgement written 1249), and in the *Sources of Information on the Generations of Physicians* by Ibn abī Uṣaybi'a (henceforth Ibn abi Usaybi'a; written 1268). The *Fihrist* is a biblio(-bio)graphical list of books known to Ibn al-Nadim at the time of writing. Ibn al-Nadim gives his readers background information on material outside the Arabic tradition.[13] Qifti's book is an alphabetic biographical dictionary (a genre that is common in classical Arabic literature) which deals mainly with philosophers and physicians; he appends (partial) bibliographies of his subjects.[14] Ibn abi Usaybi'a's work is an encyclopedia of physicians (including many with other interests) arranged in the loosely chronological form of *ṭabaqāt* or 'generations' (lit. 'layers'), a sub-genre of Arabic biographical literature that was suited especially to professional groups with an interest in demonstrating the ancientness of their discipline.[15] It 'abounds in information regarding the teaching and practice of medicine'.[16] All three works include non-Muslim authors, especially Greek ones.

The Arabic sources report that John was a bishop who fell foul of other bishops in Egypt because of his view on the Trinity,[17] and that he was pleased when the Arabs invaded in 640/1.[18] Qifti adds the story of his unintentional involvement in the Arabs' destruction of the Library of Alexandria. The sources give John's works as a number of commentaries (*tafsīr*, pl. *tafāsīr*) on Aristotle and a number on Galen.[19] Ibn abi Usaybi'a makes it plain that he was useful as a major authority on the history of Greek medicine. It is pretty clear that he quotes him in this regard through the short *History* [or *Chronicle*][20] *of Physicians* by Isḥāq b. Ḥunayn (d. 911; henceforth Ishaq), son of the most famous translator of Greek medical science and philosophy, Ḥunayn b. Isḥāq (d. 873; henceforth Hunayn). Curiously John's own historical work (which we may call his *History*) is not listed among the works ascribed to him by Arabic sources in their lists, and it has been surmised that it formed part of another treatise or commentary.[21] Perhaps the omission indicates rather that it was never translated apart from the extract in Ishaq. Before considering the character and authenticity of the *History*, we must pay attention to an unfortunate mistake made by the Arabic sources. In calling John 'John the Grammarian' they were clearly identifying him with John Philoponus, the heretical Christian and famous Aristotelian commentator who lived at Alexandria and died in 570, for Philoponus was known to Arabic authors precisely as 'John the Grammarian' (a name he had in fact been called in his own lifetime). Philoponus was never a bishop; and no one much accepts that he wrote commentaries on any of Galen's works philosophical or otherwise (cf. below n. 27). Thus the medical historian Max Meyerhof pronounced the medical *History* of 'John the Grammarian' a forgery.[22]

There is no reason to foist the thoroughly unhistorical information in this *History* upon Philoponus. At the same time, the Galenic commentaries plainly existed in Arabic and the strong belief that they and information in the *History* about Galen and others went back to *a* John must not be discarded. To add to the confusion, some late Alexandrian commentaries are in fact attributed to John Philoponus in the MSS, but it is certain that they should be ascribed rather to 'John the Alexandrian' who is a known commentator from this era with works surviving in Greek and Latin translation.[23] Nothing is known about the life of this John the Alexandrian. But since he commented *inter alia* on Galen's *De Sectis* and since Arabic sources ascribe a commentary on this work to John the Grammarian, there is no disadvantage in identifying the two, though detailed work is needed before there can be any certainty.[24]

According to Ibn abi Usaybi'a (the medical) John the Grammarian wrote commentaries on most of the Sixteen used (so the Arabic sources maintained) as introductory works by the Alexandrians.[25] He also wrote summaries (*jawāmi'*) of (an) *On Theriac* and *On Venesection*. Additionally he is credited with his own *Treatise on the Pulse*. No doubt some, perhaps most, of this output is supposititious. John was a known 'name' from the great period of Alexandrian medicine and it is highly likely that his name was borrowed to give authority to works produced in Arabic but which claim to have been translated. In this category of Arabic works claiming Greek ancestry may well fall much of the literature known as the 'Summaries of the Alexandrians', which is a series of epitomes of Galen's works (both the Sixteen and others). There is no clear proof that these translated already existing Greek epitomes from late antiquity.[26] But with regard to John, extant manuscripts name him as the author of an 'epitome' (*ikhtiṣār*) of the introductory works which is indeed likely to be a translation, and of a 'summary' of *De Usu Partium*; though our bio-bibliographies do not associate him with summaries other than those mentioned above.[27]

In short, total scepticism about John is as unwarranted as total belief, and he may be accepted as a representative of the late Alexandrian school of medicine in its final phase under Byzantine control.

Practically all we know of John's *History* is contained in Ishaq's *History* (text and translation in Rosenthal 1954).[28] John and Ishaq outline a Christianized historical scheme for the development of medicine based on Galen's identification of three groups of Empiricists, Dogmatists (or 'Analogists', as they were known to the Arabs), and Methodists. Ishaq begins by discussing whether medicine was human or god-given.[29] He then proceeds to chronology and quotes a long passage from John directly. We are given a scheme of eight major physicians: Asclepius (I), Ghūrūs, Mīnus, Parmenides, Plato (the Physician), Asclepius (II), Hippocrates, and Galen. For each of the eight John gives the years when they were children and students and the years when they were scholars and teachers, as well as some other information. For example, for Hippocrates and Galen he writes, 'Hippocrates 95 years, 16 as a child and student, and 79 as a scholar and teacher. Galen lived 87 years, 17 as a child and student, and 70 as a scholar and teacher' (66 text = 76 transl.). I shall return to Galen's figures in due course.

What is the aim of the scheme of the Eight?[30] At least two (and maybe four) philosophers have been introduced among the doctors – (?Anaxa-)goras, (?Anaxi-)menes, Parmenides, Plato. The role of the philosophers in 'philosophizing' medicine was no doubt appreciated by the Alexandrians, though in fact Parmenides at least was held in antiquity to have founded a real medical sect.[31] What of the physicians? John says that until Hippocrates experience and 'analogy'[32] prevailed in medicine. After Hippocrates, Methodism reared its ugly head. Then Galen 'appeared' (i.e. flourished), disproved the intruder's credentials, and burnt all books about it. Galen himself lived in a golden age along with Dioscorides. He benefited from the learning of many other doctors including a woman 'from whom he derived his knowledge of many drugs and various treatments, especially in matters concerning women' (69 text = 79 transl.). A later source, the *Cabinet of Wisdom*, ascribed to the tenth-century Baghdad philosopher al-Sijistānī (henceforth Sijistani), draws heavily from John the Grammarian and preserves the woman's name in this context as 'Cleopatra'.[33] It is certain that Cleopatra the lover of Mark Antony is meant, for Galen quotes extensively (via Statilius Crito) from her pseudonymous treatise on cosmetics in *De Compositione Medicamentorum Secundum Locos*, and purveyors of biographical fiction were on cue to make more of what could easily pass for a direct relationship.

Cleopatra's association with Galen's knowledge of female medicine is something I shall return to shortly. For now I want to consider the implications of the erroneous synchronicity of Galen and the queen for the historicity and purpose of John's text. We are already in the medieval age and we should not be entirely surprised to find as a consequence examples of quite shocking ignorance of the classical period and blatant fictions. But if John was a Galen expert (as is clear), his historical outline could not have been due to ignorance. It must have had a purpose. Fritz Zimmermann pointed out some years ago that his text claimed two fundamental correspondences, the contemporaneity of Adam and Asclepius the founder of medicine on the one hand, and on the other the contemporaneity of Galen and Jesus Christ. Ishaq slightly obscured John's original intention by changing some of his chronology, probably because he used different dates of the life of Jesus; but the original aim is beyond any doubt.[34] Both Ishaq and John shared one clear purpose in making Asclepius coincide with the first man. Before he quotes John directly, Ishaq airs the possibility that medicine began with the Egyptians, Indians, and others. He then goes directly to John for the proof that Asclepius was in fact the first doctor. The dismissal of competing wisdoms should be seen as a part of an old debate in early Christianity about the priority of knowledge. Christian apologists and chronographers worked with the Torah to produce a chronology that put Pythagoras and Plato firmly in their arriviste places. In the heyday of Hellenism, in the Second Sophistic, Greeks were happy enough to dispute these claims and argue that theirs was the oldest culture. Thus Diogenes Laertius' *Lives of the Philosophers* in the early third century opens with a powerful statement of the Greek case at a time when members of the educated elite were converting to Christianity. Galen himself was interested in the problem of the antiquity of wisdom and it is clear from the Arabic fragments of his *Commentary on the Hippocratic Oath* that he argued that God had created medicine and had made Asclepius its first practitioner.[35] As I have noted, these arguments were used by John with the crucial addition that he 'christianized' the story by making Asclepius coincide with Adam.

The erroneous synchronicity of Galen and Cleopatra is thus part of a much deeper and well-established ideological performance. Zimmermann tentatively suggested that the 'combination of religious, national and professional *ta'assub* [party zeal]' shown in all this pointed to an origin of around 800 AD in the milieu of the Nestorian Christians, the group to which Ishaq himself belonged. These 'stood to gain vicarious prestige from upholding the priority of the Greeks' (over the Egyptians, etc.) in the eyes of Muslims who were now becoming seriously interested in Greek science. But Zimmermann also referred to Walzer's allusion to Byzantine refutations of the idea that Galen was a coeval of Christ.[36] The Byzantine discussions surely do go back to a *Greek* biographical tradition about Galen. For although it is possible that the story was introduced by Arab visitors to Constantinople or translations of Arabic texts,[37] it is said by one source who reports it (Michael Glycas) to be 'among the masses' (see below). In a word, if the Nestorians had 'vicarious prestige' (Zimmermann) to gain by asserting the age of Greek medicine, then Christian Greeks of antiquity had direct prestige to gain. It is not surprising that an originally pagan chauvinism was put at the disposal of Greek Christianity. As a Christian, a Greek, and a doctor, John was well motivated to make Greek medical science as old as the Christian world. On this line of argument, then, John could, as Zimmermann alternatively suggested, be a 'pre-Islamic Greek-speaking citizen (of Alexandria, the then home of Galenic studies)'. Or, to be more precise, a citizen of Alexandria at the very coming of Islam.

As to the synchronization of Galen and Jesus, it is clear that this could only be asserted by someone ignorant or by someone whose desire for religious-professional propaganda and polemic was greater than his regard for historical dates. For John, Galen was the 'Seal of the Physicians' (65 text = 75 transl. 'last of the physicians' is weak) who assured the future of medicine by defeating the Methodist evil.[38] What could be more satisfactory than to make his life-span overlap with the other great healer, Jesus, who also brought about a new order? It may be suggested that the cue for this rewriting of history was offered by Galen's own respectful references to Christians (and Jews) and to Moses and Christ. Galen disagrees with them, but goes as far as to state in a surviving Arabic extract from his summary of the *Republic* that the Christians were in some ways not inferior to genuine philosophers.[39] To someone of the mid-seventh century whose grasp of classical history was likely to be hazy and who was determined to map an arbitrary scheme of eight major physicians onto a Christian chronology, his hero Galen's awareness of Christianity was a very powerful hint. John may partly have been led to exploit the hint by the existence of a semi-popular tradition which made Galen a pupil of Cleopatra.

On one level the relationship of the queen and the doctor must have had a scholarly origin, since it ultimately reflects reading of Galen. Yet it must also be seen as part of a wider, semi-popular fictional tradition in Greek and Arabic which makes Cleopatra a teacher of alchemy who is often featured in discussions with her pupils. Ullmann has placed one such Arabic dialogue surviving in a Dublin manuscript against the background of Cleopatra literature, especially alchemical texts, in Greek and in Arabic.[40] The Dublin text is probably an Arabic composition rather than a translation; but it has clear Greek elements, and in general the Arabic sources for Cleopatra follow Greek ones closely. There is every reason to think that Cleopatra's instruction of Galen is also part of a Greek tradition from the period of the later Roman Empire. This story would have helped a Christian reader to associate Galen chronologically with Jesus (for the disparity in time was not too great). Moreover, it is also likely enough that the two great healers were directly associated in popular storytelling. The evidence surfaces in twelfth-century

Byzantium. Here Galen discusses the scientific basis of Jesus' healing powers with Mary Magdalen, who had told him of his healing of the blind man at John 9.1–12. The age of this story cannot be known. But its popular nature (φημίζεται παρὰ τοῖς πολλοῖς) strongly suggests, as I have noted above, that it is part of a Greek tradition rather than an import from Arabic sources.[41] On this basis John's synchronization of Galen and Jesus seems to represent a Christian partisan's intellectualization of a popular story assisted by Galen's own references to Christianity and by the semi-popular tradition making him a pupil of Cleopatra.

I want to move on now from John himself to related biographical reports about Galen's death and the location of his tomb which are found in Arabic and Syriac, for one strand of the Arabic tradition has Galen die in Sicily on his way to seek out Jesus' Apostles. This too may go back to ancient times. The information is found in the Andalusian pharmacologist Ibn Juljul of Cordova (d. 1009), whose *Generations of Physicians and Sages* is probably the oldest such collection of medical biographies.[42] His work is quoted by Qifti,[43] and the story of the tomb itself was followed by Andalusian geographical writers like al-Bakrī (henceforth Bakri; d. 1094), whose *Book of Routes and Realms* was written in 1067, and the less well known al-Harawī, who visited Sicily about 1178/9 (henceforth Harawi). The latter even manages directions.[44]

What is the source of the tale of Galen dying in Sicily on his way to visit the companions of Jesus? Ibn Juljul's brief biography of Galen begins with a citation of Isidore of Seville (41§2 Sayyid).[45] This is the only occasion when he cites Isidore and Sayyid observes that we do not know whether he read him in an Arabic translation (for which there is no evidence) or in Latin (but there is no evidence Ibn Juljul knew Latin).[46] It may well be that he got the reference at second hand, of course, for the passage, which states that Pergamum housed an imperial prison, is not identifiable in Isidore's works and may simply have been attributed to him. When shortly after this (p. 42§2) Ibn Juljul reports the story of Galen's death, he says he left Rome for Jerusalem and 'wandered to Sicily which in those days was called Sicania'.[47] This etymological information is very Isidorean. Indeed, Isidore records that 'Sicilia a Sicano rege Sicania cognominata est, deinde...Sicilia' (*Etym.* 14.6.32). Thus the story of Galen's death in Sicily *en route* to visit the Apostles is mixed up with material apparently drawn from Isidore. Isidore himself would hardly have accepted it: his *Chronicon* places Galen firmly in the reign of Antoninus Pius (83: 1044 Migne). Ibn Juljul introduces the story of Galen's death with the statement that 'the Christian religion had appeared in his days' (42§1). Could this also go back to (garbled) Isidorean material? The information that Jesus lived 'in the furthest part of the nation of Caesar Octavian in the Holy City' is interesting.[48] First, the geographical perspective is western (or at least not eastern). Second, it is odd to place the birth of Jesus under Octavian rather than Augustus. Isidore does this both in his *Chronicon* and in his later *magnum opus*, the *Etymologies* (83: 1038 M. 'Octavius Augustus...Christus...nascitur'; 5. 39. 25 Lindsay 'Octavianus...Christus nascitur'). It appears again that Ibn Juljul's information reflects a western, Isidorean tradition.

A further important point can be made: Ibn Juljul does not know of John the Grammarian and the scheme of the Eight Physicians, but uses his own arrangement of 'generations' with different medical personnel. This serves to corroborate the suggestion above that the synchronization of Galen and Jesus did not come from Arabic sources but developed a Graeco-Roman tradition. As to the origin of the story, it is possible that the specific information about the location of Galen's tomb in Harawi reveals local, oral information of the sort that was mixed up by someone (if not Ibn Juljul himself) with the material from Isidore. Again, if we look at the account in Bakri, the Galen notice plainly comes from Ibn Juljul, but is placed immediately after mention of the island's capital *Balarma*. The normal Arabic form of Palermo is *Balarm*. Amari noted that the form used here indicates 'l'origine cristiana, o almeno siciliana, della notizia'.[49] It looks as if Bakri was like Harawi drawing on a living local tradition. If we want an informant for Ibn Juljul himself, we can find one in Abū 'Abdallāh 'the Sicilian', who was part of a group of physicians and pharmacologists working in Greek at Cordova in the 950s and 960s to improve the Arabic text of Dioscorides on the basis of an illustrated Greek manuscript gifted by the Byzantine emperor. The emperor had sent a Latin and Greek speaking monk called Nicholas to supervise the work. 'These men,' says Ibn Juljul, 'formed a team with Nicholas. I was involved with them and with him.'[50]

Two main accounts of Galen's death circulated in the East. The first (in Arabic) seems to have no origin in antiquity. The great geographer, Istakhrī (d. 961), in his own *Routes and Realms* mentions that al-Farāmā (ancient Pelusium) was the site of Galen's tomb.[51] More information about Galen's reasons for being here is given by Mubashshir (cf. n. 33 and section 3.i below). It is not really possible, as Nutton has suggested, that Faramā represents confusion with Ferghāmus *vel sim.*, the Arabic for Greek 'Pergamon',[52] since the letter forms are sufficiently distinct and confusion is certainly not present in Mubashshir or Ibn abi Usaybi'a. Mubashshir (289 Badawi = Rosenthal 1975, 34) says Galen died there while he was on his way home from a drug-collecting expedition in Egypt. He does not name his sources here or elsewhere, so we cannot say whether he made the tale up. It is clear, however, that Galen's death 'on Egypt's furthest border' is quite distinct from the alleged visit to the Apostles.[53]

The second story is much more significant. In the tenth-century lexicon of the Syriac author Bar Bahlūl, a contemporary of Ibn Juljul, we are told in the article on Luke that 'some say Luke was Galen's pupil, others the son of his sister. When they heard news of our Lord...he and his master Galen were in doubt as to the truth of the story...so they set off for Judaea to find out the truth. On the way Galen died, Luke came to the Lord'.[54] Since in a preceding part of the article Bar Bahlul names his sources for Luke, we may assume that this story was not literary but popular, oral information circulating among Syriac-speaking Christians (it does not appear in Arabic authors). This story complements Ibn Juljul very well except here Galen goes to see Jesus himself and there is no mention of Sicily. It also squares with the tradition of Galen and Cleopatra. A Galen who was young enough to be a pupil of the queen – one strand of the classical tradition, as I have suggested – was in this fairytale chronology about the right age to be the instructor of the physician-evangelist.

Perhaps to be related to this story is the curious information in the Persian biographical writer al-Bayhaqī (henceforth Bayhaqi; d. 1169/1170), who wrote (in Arabic) a *Supplement* to the *Cabinet of Wisdom*. According to Bayhaqi,[55] the Christian Baghdadian philosopher Ibn al-Ṭayyib (the Abul-pharagius Abdalla Benattibus of the Latin Middle Ages) said he was the descendant of St Paul and that Paul was the son of Galen's sister. Galen in fact sent Paul to Jesus when he heard about him, excusing his own infirmity. Ibn al-Ṭayyib (d. 1043) wrote or translated commentaries on Galen and according to Bayhaqi knew and taught both Latin and Greek.[56] We cannot say where he (or possibly Bayhaqi – an unreliable authority) got the idea of Galen and Paul from. But there may be an appropriation of the story of doctor Luke (who is after all associated with Paul at Col. 4.14).

Before I consider the uses of the fictional Galen in more detail, there remains one important matter left over concerning his death: how long did he live for? John the Grammarian claimed Galen lived for 87 years. This is the origin of similar information in writers following him (*Cabinet of Wisdom*, Mubashshir, Ibn abi Usaybi'a). John divided Galen's life into 17 years of childhood and student life and 70 years of professional activity. Vivian Nutton has reviewed the evidence for Galen's longevity in detail.[57] It is evident from the treatise *On Theriac, to Piso* that Galen lived after 204 since he refers to the Saecular Games of that year.[58] Further, since this work alludes to the joint reign of Septimius Severus and his son, it was finished before Septimius' death in 211. Scholars have till recently accepted the information in the Suda (γ 32) that Galen lived for 70 years. Since this means he died in 199, the Suda is obviously wrong. But is John's 87 years obviously correct? The answer must be 'no', for John's divisions of his doctors' lives into two parts is sheer fiction.

As Ibn abi Usaybi'a notes at the start of his life of Galen, 'we must realize that it is impossible to expect that firm information is confined to what [John] reports. Indeed, logic dictates that some of it is inconceivable and this includes his report that Galen was a youth and a student for seventeen years and a teacher and an instructor for seventy years' (110 R. = 71 M.). He goes on to quote from *On the Order of his Own Books* (19.59 K) the story of the dream of Galen's father which led him to make his son study medicine. This happened when Galen was in his 'seventeenth year'. Ibn abi Usaybi'a remarks, 'this is the passage and it is clear that there is a difference between what Galen says and what is recorded about him.' That is, Galen became a (medical) student at the age of 17, not a teacher as John claimed. It is still possible that John's 17 comes from this passage and that it was reinterpreted by him to mean adult, professional life. The same figure is picked up by Ibn Juljul: 'he excelled in medicine and philosophy and all the mathematical sciences when he was 17. He expounded (his learning) when he was 24' (41. 9–10 Sayyid). For Ibn Juljul the 17-year-old Galen knew it all too. As for Galen's lifespan, Ibn Juljul records 88 years.[59] This *could* be right. That is, the figure of 17 comes from Galen (however it was interpreted). John's round figure of 70 is suspicious. Ibn Juljul's 71 is less so – though, against this, if Galen had passed his 87th birthday, he died in his 88th year. Whatever the case, the alternative Byzantine tradition which has Galen die in the (sole) reign of Caracalla (211–17) is clearly correct.[60] But the exact date will never be known.

2. The fictional Galen: sex and wisdom

(i)

I want now to look at some more overtly fictional uses of Galen in Arabic authors. I begin by considering a double work which may well go back to a Greek source. There survive in Arabic two unpublished treatises entitled 'On the Secrets of Women' and 'On the Secrets of Men'.[61] These form one work. They are products of the medieval sex industry and offer pharmacological recipes for various sorts of sexual frustration and perversion. They are ascribed to Galen. Such was Galen's reputation in Islam that pseudonymous works are hardly surprising; but this one is unusual in the extent of the fictional background it provides. According to the conclusion of the text, it was 'copied by Isḥāq ibn Ḥunayn'.[62] Unfortunately the authors of the English translation (on which I am relying) confuse Ishaq here with his father, the great Hunayn. Nor are they clear in using the word 'copied'. They apparently mean 'translated', for they go on to say that the 'materia medica of the texts...would seem to indicate that the texts came from a Greek author and that the final paragraph [of the second treatise] is correct, i.e., that the treatise is a translation from the Greek'. Ishaq himself undertook a lot of translation, mostly of Greek philosophy (and mostly of Aristotle). If he says he was translating treatises ascribed to Galen, it is worth taking this seriously and entertaining the possibility that the treatises have an origin in Greek fictional biography about Galen. But we must also remember that the borrowing of a famous translator is a strategy for giving a text authority, one found for example in the ascription of the Galenic Summaries to Hunayn.[63]

The work begins with the story of Queen Fīlānus asking Galen to prepare a treatise 'on the secrets of women' to allow her to improve her body and to 'cause difficulty' for her rivals. There are many recipes for beauty. The text also gives 'drugs which make lesbianism so desirable to women that they would…passionately lust for it', 'drugs which excite the desire of women so that they go wandering around…looking for sexual satisfaction, throwing themselves before men', 'drugs which harden the hymen', 'drugs which soften the hymen'.[64] The story of 'Secrets of Men' is that a certain Qusṭās al-Qahramān once dropped by to greet Galen and discovered him at work on 'Secrets of Women'. Both were embarrassed, since the book was supposed to be a secret. They resolved the problem by an exchange of gifts: an estate for Galen and for al-Qahramān a book on the same lines about men which should be for 'his private use'.[65] The contents include drugs for and against sodomy, masturbation, pederasty, sex with women or not with women.[66] It is perhaps not so astonishing after all that Ishaq was prepared to accept these tracts as authentic if we recall his readiness to build on the fictions of John the Grammarian, different though these were.

Ibn abi Usaybiʿa also records the double work at the end of his biography of Galen in a section on works omitted by Hunayn in his *Letter* (149 R. = 102 M.). But here the queen is named Fīlāfūs, a simple swop of the letters *nūn* [فيلانوس] and *fāʾ* [فيلافوس], which would be quite possible in hasty writing or copying. Meyerhof noted that by placing two dots above the *fāʾ* one gets the letter *qāf* and that 'Fīlāqūs' was 'vielleicht das griechische παλλακίς'.[67] He also suggested less convincingly a corruption of φιλαδελφός, an allusion to the wife of Ptolemy Philadelphus. Both of these ideas concur with the notion of a Greek origin of the text or at least of its framing story. Another suggestion may be made. Greek sex manuals were habitually ascribed to a certain Φιλαινίς.[68] This name is very close to the form given in Ishaq's version of the tract on women, Fīlānus, though there is nothing in the legends about Philainis to connect her with royalty. Perhaps what we have, in what may well be a Greek tale in origin, is a conflation of the famous author of erotic handbooks with the famous erotic queen of Egypt from whom Galen 'derived his knowledge of many drugs and various treatments, especially in matters concerning women' according to John the Grammarian.[69]

(ii)

The combination of fiction and pharmacology points to the involvement of intellectuals. In this context I want to return to the *Cabinet of Wisdom*. Bayhaqi, the author of the *Supplement* to the *Cabinet*, was confused by seeing the name of Sijistani in the work and made the mistake of ascribing it to this prominent Persian intellectual who was a pupil of the great philosopher al-Fārābī at one remove.[70] But the *Cabinet* certainly comes from the 'school' of Sijistani and may be dated with confidence to about 1000.[71] The published long epitome and the unpublished short epitome show that the original contained biographies of both Greek and Muslim scholars of varying lengths and qualities. The key section in each of these is the sayings of the man in question, and this is the 'wisdom' (*ḥikma*) of the book's title.[72] For the history of medicine, which is found in the introduction, Sijistani used John the Grammarian and (as has been noted) had access to a version that is fuller than the text recovered by Rosenthal in Ishaq (Rosenthal 1954). Here Galen was presented as the last great physician in accordance with John's scheme. When it comes to Galen's own entry in the *Cabinet*, we get a rather different story. It is in two parts.[73] The first (ll. 2200–340 Dunlop) contains a fabulous tale of Galen's relations with two kings, Nīfās and Bāz. The second (ll. 2341–98 Dunlop) is a list of his sayings.[74]

According to the author of the *Cabinet*, Galen lived in a town called 'Macedonia' in Egypt where he was the favourite doctor of the good king Nīfās. Nasty king Bāz lives in the Magrib. The good king is obliged to send his favourite when Bāz threatens war if Galen does not come to cure one of his girls who has signs of leprosy on her face. Galen arrives and finds a 'tyrant, full of excess'.[75] Various stories follow. The tyrant cannot bear the thought that Galen will have to look at the girl, so Galen cleverly uses a mirror. Galen refuses to eat the tyrant's unhealthy food. He writes him a 'register' (*dustūr*) which will be kept in the royal storerooms to remind the king that Galen had predicted he would suffer from leprosy, and a 'treatise' (*maqāla*) on the prognosis of epidemic diseases. The tyrant fails to heed Galen's dietary advice and suffers accordingly: his hair thins, his eyelids lose shape, his nails shrink. Now Galen escapes disguised as a black man. Bāz, ill, follows him and pretends to enroll as a pupil. Galen recognizes him. After a year in Galen's company, the tyrant is reformed and returns with a Greek, civilized view of the world. Further stories are told: Galen's reconciliation with Nīfās (whom he has been avoiding), how the three men become pen-pals, how Nīfās and Galen visit Bāz when he becomes ill again, how Bāz presents Galen with his son Glaucon, who then becomes his star pupil and Nīfās' heir. The second part of the biography (if one can use this word) contains nineteen sayings of Galen (including an extract from *De Moribus*;

see below). It is followed by one further piece of biographical information: 'Abū al-Nafīs said, "Galen suffered from a speech impediment/could not pronounce his r's" ' (l. 2398).[76]

Galen's opinions were not treated uncritically once the Islamic sciences came of age. Our anonymous author may have been influenced by this development. But his story about Galen, the king, and the tyrant is sheer fun with clear irreverential elements, rather than a serious critique like Rhazes' (d. 925/932) *Doubts about Galen* and similar texts. There are some garbled facts of Galenic biography in our account which add to the entertainment. Glaucon is the man to whom Galen dedicated two books of *On Healing* which were part of the introductory course for medical students. The storing of the register in the royal storehouse recalls Galen's description of the loss of his works during the fire in the royal depositories of the Temple of Peace (Forum of Vespasian) at Rome which is well known in the biographical tradition (Mubashshir, Ibn abi Usaybiʻa).[77] As to the names and rival characters of the kings, it is *just* possible that we have a deliberate perversion of Galen's characterization of the good Marcus Aurelius and the (by implication) not so good Lucius Verus at *On his Own Books* 19.18 K. (98 Mueller). The name Nīfās *could* just be an alteration of 'Nīnūs' (i.e. Antoninus);[78] Bāz *could* just be an alteration of 'Bār' (i.e. Verus).[79] A further sign of irreverence is Galen's escape in the guise of a black man, since classical Arabic culture was at least ambiguous towards blacks.[80] And the last words of the biography offer a tantalizing remark about Galen's inability to pronounce his r's. To cap the sayings – the core of the wisdom – with such a remark can only undermine the sayer. The statement about Galen looks as if it should have introduced an anecdote that has been cut off by the epitomizer. There are in fact extant examples of irreverent lipogrammatic texts in Arabic,[81] and one would love to believe that the *Cabinet* included some r-less Galenic *sententia* at this point. Whether it did or not, the remark shows well enough the tone of this whole biography.[82]

What is going on? Rosenthal has well remarked that 'the scholars around as-Sijistānī...can be suspected of not having been above...falsification'. The context of this remark is invented elements in the biography of Diogenes the Cynic, a favourite in Arabic philosophical biography, and specifically the information that he was the teacher of the 'Greek *shaykh* [elder/teacher]'. This figure is first so named in the *Cabinet*. It has long been realized that material under his name is in fact by Plotinus, but had become detached from its author. Obviously Diogenes was not the teacher of Plotinus.[83] Rosenthal's remark about Sijistani and his followers comes in a study of such Plotinian material in an Oxford manuscript containing an unpublished collection which is very similar in form and content to the *Cabinet* and for various reasons can be ascribed to a scholar who knew that work and admired members of the circle it came from.[84] The anecdotes and wise sayings (*ḥikam*) found in such collections reflect the courtly, intellectual society of their age when possession of *adab* or high culture and the figure of the cultured man, the *adīb*, are central to elite self-definition.[85] There are many comparisons to be made here with *paideia* and the *pepaideumenos* or *philologos* of the Greek culture of the High Roman period. The comparability of these two cultural movements is clearly a factor in the interest Arabic culture took in Greek men of wisdom.

As regards Galen specifically, the folktale of Nīfās and Bāz is a precious example of the sort of stories told in the salons (*majlis*; pl *majālis*) by these cultural stakeholders. We might compare the (at first sight) surprising degree of fiction in the first Arabic collection of Greek wisdom, Ḥunayn's *Anecdotes of the Philosophers and Sages and Examples of the Culture [ādāb] of the Teachers of Old*, which survives in an epitome.[86] In book 1 (Hebrew order), for example, Ḥunayn includes numerous stories of what philosophers said when they were 'gathered together in a certain golden palace', and so on. Sometimes they are named, sometimes not. The aim is explicitly given at the start of the book as entertainment ('word games' and 'conundrums') *and* 'moral instruction'.[87] The need to display this culture actively is summed up in the section (45–6 B.; I.v.11) on what famous thinkers (including Galen) had inscribed on their seal rings. A tenth-century text of courtly behaviour includes such inscriptions in a long series of suggestions about displaying one's culture in words appropriate to various media.[88] More relevant here is Ḥunayn's story of Plato, king Rūfasṭanīs (Dinfastanis in the Hebrew[89]), the king's son Niṭāfūras, and Aristotle (his future tutor) at 51–3 B. (I.ix). Clearly this is 'based' on Plato, Philip, Alexander, and Aristotle. Although it is perfectly reasonable to hold that Ḥunayn would have supposed that Plato lived under a monarchy, *everybody* knew that Alexander had been the pupil of Aristotle, not 'Niṭāfūras'. The story is clearly an enjoyable fiction.[90] It is the same with the story of Galen and Nīfās in the *Cabinet*. Entertainment of this kind, very loosely based on what Galen said himself, gave a man something to say in the salons of the great, and this ensured respect for his own *ḥikma*. Thus we should not classify the Galen story as a sort of debased biography. We must see it for what it was in its own context. It may be suggested that Ibn al-Ṭayyib's claims (if actually his own) about Galen and Paul should be viewed in the same light. As we shall see, the *Cabinet* gets serious in one long passage drawn from Galen's *De Moribus* which is cited (with notes) to tell us something about Galen. Genuine learning of this type goes closely with the entertainment of the rest of the piece.

3. The definitive Galen: from Mubashshir to Ibn abi Usaybi'a

(i)

In 1084 (or 1089) prince Mubashshir b. Fātik was writing the Galen section of his *Choicest Maxims and Best Sayings*.[91] Mubashshir was a man of many parts and his book, which was written when he was about thirty years of age, proved highly successful.[92] It consists almost entirely of biographies of Greek thinkers and writers including two Church Fathers who had a career in the Greek and Arabic gnomologies, Basil and Gregory. These biographies are divided into a section of biography proper (*akhbār*, 'information') and a section of sayings and wisdom (*ḥikam, ādāb*). Mubashshir enjoyed a medical training with the great Cairene doctor Ibn Riḍwān and Galen was therefore of major interest to him.[93] The account begins with the scheme of the Eight Physicians followed by a categorical chronological statement which ignores questions of Galen's links with early Christians. A section on education to death is followed by information on Galen's attitude to learning, details of his teachers and philosophical contacts, his journeys, material relevant to the fire at Rome in which he lost his books, and finally a section of praise for the 'Greek kings' of Galen's time who were ever ready to support intellectuals with payments for pharmacological work, and a description of Galen's appearance and deportment. This description is the only original part of Mubashshir's account; his interest in this aspect of his subjects has been noted.[94]

Overall, one has the impression of a very neat biographical creation with no room for extraneous material (like a catalogue of works) or ambiguities. This is in accordance with Mubashshir's Preface where he stresses the moral and quasi-religious utility of his book and says he has not been deflected from his purpose by historical niceties.[95] Is there any classical material here other than that drawn from Galen's own works? One is tempted to say 'none'. But Rosenthal's study of Mubashshir's Zeno, Solon, and Pythagoras proves that a lot of material came his way – via an intermediary – from Porphyry's *History of Philosophy*.[96] This work went only as far as Plato, and with later figures like Galen we do not know; but the possibility should be left open.

What of Galen's 'culture and maxims', i.e. the gnomological material?[97] In the Preface Mubashshir lays the greatest emphasis on this. Ibn abi Usaybi'a takes over (with acknowledgement) all but one of his sayings; whereas he shares little of the sayings material in the *Cabinet*, and then with differences that make it clear he did not use this source. There is only one example of overlap between sayings material in Mubashshir and in the *Cabinet* and this is also discrepant (I return to it shortly). Some of the sayings in Ibn abi Usaybi'a and Mubashshir do not coincide exactly. These are sayings Ibn abi Usaybi'a drew with acknowledgement from Hunayn's *Anecdotes*. Rosenthal has observed that 'al-Mubashshir's dependence upon Hunayn's [*Anecdotes*] is a minor one'.[98] Yet we see from Ibn abi Usaybiʿa's own quotations from Hunayn's collection that Mubashshir also drew on it, albeit with less care (or, put better, with more editing, since he is clearly a 'hands-on' author). Thus Ibn abi Usaybiʿa quotes the apophthegm, 'Sorrow [*ghamm*] is about something that happened; worry [*hamm*] about something that will happen'. Mubashshir quotes it with the terms 'sorrow' and 'worry' reversed.[99] But Ibn abi Usaybiʿa's version is the second of three related quotations, the second and third having the same order of 'sorrow' and 'worry'. He is in any case very accurate when quoting his sources.[100] Another example shows Mubashshir abbreviating from a longer passage on love and lovers.[101]

In his study of the diffusion of Platonic lore in Islam, Rosenthal focuses on Mubashshir's Socrates.[102] Socrates and Plato form Mubashshir's longest lives by far. Many of the sayings in these sections do have a Platonic colour. Most are certainly apocryphal: Rosenthal remarks that Muslims used them 'to get new food for their own thoughts, new rules for their own ethical conduct.' Some of the maxims adapt parts of Plato's surviving works. To account for the changes in the Arabic in these Rosenthal suggests that 'Arabic writers must have used a paraphrase or a similar work'.[103] But there is no need to make such a rule, if we remember the ethical purpose, and we see that Arabic writers were quite capable of modifying or inventing material to suit them. Exactly the same issues are raised by Hunayn's *Anecdotes*. Editors (Loewenthal, Badawi) have again wanted to believe in a Greek origin for the material, albeit one with an 'eastern', 'Byzantine' complexion.[104] Yet for most of this, *Quellenforschung* will yield no results. We may believe that there *was* comparable, perhaps identical, material extant in antiquity; but we do not know. Only in the case of a collection like the *Sententia (Monosticha) Menandri* do we have both the Greek and the Arabic (and a known translator).[105]

As to the Galenic material in Mubashshir and Hunayn, it certainly *looks* Galenic; but it was unguarded of Loewenthal to suggest that the sayings were 'highly likely to be excerpts from Hunayn's translations of Galen'.[106] Two of the Galenic sayings in Mubashshir (followed by Ibn abi Usaybiʿa) are indeed based on material in *Exhortation to the Arts*, the first (the looser one) concerning the ignorant rich (who become 'kings' in the Arabic), the second (the closer) concerning Galen's contempt for the ability of the athlete Milo (not named in the Arabic) to lift a sacrificed bull (again, 'kings' are added in the Arabic).[107] There is not much else.[108] What we have here is 'sub-Galenic' material, based on a loose understanding/recollection of his works (cf. above on the *Cabinet*). So in the passage on love already mentioned (n. 101) there is nothing in Galen's surviving works that exactly corresponds to the discussion of the three faculties of the brain, imagination (*takhayyul*), intellect (*fikr*), memory (*dhikr*); and though the recently discovered missing section of *De Libr. Propr.* reveals that Galen wrote an (unknown) work on precisely these 'faculties of the rational soul', only a brave man would expect to find the passage if this work turned up.[109] Again, the material in Ibn abi Usaybiʿa drawn from Hunayn on Galen's experiment to determine the effect of worry on the heart (130.24–131.2 R. = 88.17–19 M.; Hunayn 122 B. = II.x.2) recalls experiments on the brain in *Anatomical Procedures* book 9 and various remarks here and there (e.g. *Opinions of Hippocrates and Plato* 3. 5. 45) about *lupē* and *phobos* and the condition of the heart. But the fact that Hunayn ascribes an identical experiment to Alexander the Great shows the essential popularity of this story (87 B. = II.v).[110]

We might pursue the matter by looking at the use made by Mubashshir, Ibn abi Usaybiʿa, and the *Cabinet* of Galen's *De Moribus*. The work was translated by Hunayn into Arabic under the title *Book of Character Traits*.[111] Only an epitome of this survives.[112] *De Moribus* develops the argument that character is an innate irrational disposition of the soul. The result is one of Galen's most sententious essays. It is not surprising that it was mined for maxims. Ibn abi Usaybiʿa (131.5–7 R. = 88.21–3 M.) drew one passage directly from Hunayn's *Anecdotes* on the parallelism between disorders of the soul and the body.[113] From Mubashshir he drew three or four passages from or based on *De Moribus*. First are the two maxims on accustoming oneself to a virtuous life from one's youth (132.7–9, 10–12 R. = 89.14–17, 17–19 M. [maxims 21–22]; Mubashshir 295.1–4, 5–7 [maxims 14–15]), the second of which is not in the Epitome of *De Moribus* (cf. 28.8–11 Kr.; 238§3M.), but was in the original (in a much expanded form as we shall see). Of the two following sayings in Mubashshir (295.8, 9–13 [maxims 16–17]), which Ibn abi Usaybiʿa also uses, the first on embarrassment may belong to *De Moribus* and the second on self-love certainly does.[114]

As has been remarked, there is little cross-over between sayings material in the *Cabinet* and in Mubashshir and Ibn abi Usaybiʿa. The two maxims in Mubashshir (nos. 14–15) on accustoming oneself to a virtuous life from one's youth appear in the *Cabinet* as part of a long extract that seems to offer a reasonably faithful version of Hunayn's translation (*Cabinet* ll. 2366–89 D.; maxim 17). The extract begins with material that is very similar to Epitome 27.19–28.6 Kr. (238§2M.) on the analogy between control by the rational soul over the irrational and control by the master or the hunter over his dog or horse.[115] Then there is a short quotation of Plato on the tripartite soul and comments from Galen (ll. 2374–80 D.), all of which is omitted from the Epitome.[116] Third, we have a section developing this from which Mubashshir (followed by Ibn abi Usaybiʿa) has drawn his maxim 14 on accustoming oneself from youth to a life of virtue (2380–89). The *Cabinet* finishes (ll. 2389–95) by appending remarks about the policy of the 'ancient philoso-phers' in investigating the character of children and the use of education (*adab = paideia*) in improving the soul, which accord loosely with the lines of argument in the succeeding sections of the Epitome. On this Mubashshir has based his maxim 15.[117]

The tone of this passage in the *Cabinet* contrasts with the ludic quality of much of the rest of the Galen section there. As I have noted, we should not find this disparity awkward. Both the genuine and the fictional Galen had their role in allowing Muslims to manufacture myths for their own times. But there is more to say. Kraus, Stern, and Zonta have traced quotations of Hunayn's text of *De Moribus* in Arabic, Hebrew, and Syriac authors.[118] It is clear that the work was widely used, and Kraus observes that Yaḥyā b. ʿAdī and Miskawayh were 'particularly influenced' by it.[119] These two intellectuals were closely associated with the circle of Sijistani in Baghdad. Major works of theirs and their admirers show how philosophy was integrated into the posh *adab/majlis* culture of the time.[120] The particular passage copied out in the *Cabinet* was evidently well liked for its ethical content, its literary quality, and its divisibility. It well exemplifies Galen's place as an honorary member of Muslim elite culture.

(ii)

Ibn abi Usaybiʿa's *Sources of Information on the Generations of Physicians* is a huge work. The section on Galen (excluding the bibliographical catalogue) would amount to nearly 15,000 words in English, and the whole work would be something like 440,000. The vastness of Arabic literature itself has led to a neglect of this great achievement by western scholars after its first publication by Müller in 1882.[121] There has been recent interest in Arabic scholarship including the first volume of a scholarly edition which has some account of the manuscripts,[122] and three chapters of a conference proceedings held in Aleppo in 1984. The most useful of these examines Ibn abi Usaybiʿa's methods, laying great stress on his scientific and linguistic *diqqa* ('accuracy'), his love of detail and analysis, his scrupulous presentation of rival viewpoints, and his care over quotations.[123] Much of the bulk of the *Sources* is indeed due to the extensive quotations which Ibn abi Usaybiʿa uses to establish his version of this or that physician. The long lists of works, genuine and attributed, are part of this.

Ibn abi Usaybiʿa (b. after 1194; d. 1270), a practising physician who spent most of his life in Damascus, finished his first edition in 1242.[124] Soon after this he discovered Qifti's biographical work, and a good deal of Qifti was incorporated into the second edition of 1268. Qifti's work has been mentioned already and I shall say something more about it here to bring out the distinctive qualities of Ibn abi Usaybi'a. The original was written about 1234/5 and survives in the epitome made one year after Qifti's death (1248) by al-Zawzani. Most of the chapter on Galen is drawn from Ibn Juljul and Ibn al-Nadim. Qifti begins (123–5 L.) with Ibn Juljul (named), copying most of what he says and including two anecdotes from Galen's works and a passage on his travels to Cyprus. He then uses Ibn al-Nadim (not named) for chronology and in particular takes his citation of a passage in *De Moribus* which Galen dates to 'year 514 of Alexander' (AD 183), including Ibn al-Nadim's comment that this is the 'truest' thing recorded about Galen's 'time and his place in time'.[125] He also draws from Ibn al-Nadim an alternative chronology which blends material from John the Grammarian/Ishaq with erroneous information about the king of the Parthians in Galen's time, ending with the synchronicity of Galen and Jesus (125 L.).[126] Qifti clearly passes implicit judgement on these chronologies, or at least on the synchronicity of Galen and Jesus, for he goes on to quote from the physician 'Ubaydallah b. Bakhtishu' (d. 1058) a discussion of whether Galen was a contemporary of the Messiah. 'Ubaydallah wrote *inter alia* a *Garden of Medicine* on the medical philosophical ideas of the ancients and a discussion of the somatic and psychic origins of love.[127] As a member of a famous family of physicians and a friend of the doctor Ibn Butlan,[128] he was naturally interested in Galen. Qifti actually quotes only a little of 'Ubaydallah's text and especially part of his proof that Galen was born in the tenth year of the reign of Trajan. In the course of this he quotes 'Ubaydallah's citation of Ishaq/John that Galen lived till 87 without noting the discrepancy from Ibn Juljul's 88.[129] The rest of his account (128–32 L.) is a list of the works of Galen forming the Sixteen and a list of some of the other works.

Although Qifti only survives in an abridgement, it is clear the text was not as polished as it might be. By contrast, Ibn abi Usaybi'a is a far more organized and impressive author. His most visible technique is quotation to back up his own views. Indeed, about 40 per cent of the narrative section of his Galen chapter (109–30 R. = 71–88 M.) is quotation from Galen, some of it embedded in other authors. This figure would rise considerably if one included the huge quotations from 'Ubaydallah on the dating of Galen, with its own ample quotation from Galen (over 25 per cent of the narrative), and Yusuf b. al-Daya on Galen's house (some 15 per cent of the narrative section). The Galenic quotations have particular functions (e.g. Galen's dates). But they must also be seen as complementing the sayings section which follows the narrative (130–4 R. = 88–90 M.). They help to establish Galen's character. The accuracy of the quotations can be seen plainly from the extensive use of *On Examinations By Which the Best Physicians are Recognized*, for Ibn abi Usaybi'a is an important witness to the manuscript tradition.[130]

Ibn abi Usaybiʿa promises

a complete discussion of the evidence for Galen and his activities... What is known about Galen – and is indeed knowledge that is attested in its particulars and generalities in many nations – is that he was the 'Seal' of the great master doctors and eighth of them. No one came near to him in the Art of Medicine let alone was his equal. Moreover, when he came on the scene he found the Art of Medicine was dominated by the teaching of the iatrosophists and that its good qualities were being effaced. He took this matter in hand and showed their views were useless. He championed and built up the language and doctrines of Hippocrates and his Successors. These prevailed because of his own abilities. He composed many treatises on them and in these he clarified many of the obscurities of the Art and eloquently expressed its truths... None of the doctors who lived after him was his superior or learned without him.

This beginning (109 R. = 71 M.) is a paraphrase of the tradition going back to John the Grammarian. Ibn abi Usaybiʿa quotes John's words about Galen's lifespan. Then (let us call this section 1) he identifies the problems of this 'learned information' (109–17 R. = 71–7 M.). As we have seen, he dismisses John's division of Galen's life into seventeen years of education and seventy of teaching: 'following a report of someone like Galen about himself is superior to following the words of another about him.' Next he calculates from Ishaq b. Hunayn that Galen 'was fifty-nine years after the time of the Messiah on the dating of Ishaq. As for the suggestion of the man who claims he was his contemporary and went to visit him and believed in him, this is without truth.' He singles out Bayhaqi for criticism here and cites the story that Paul was Galen's nephew.[131] From Ibn al-Nadim he cites Galen's mention of an event in 'in year 514 of Alexander'. To reinforce this he deploys ʿUbaydallah. Ibn abi Usaybiʿa quotes ʿUbaydallah quite independently of Qifti and includes his own lengthy quotation from the Christian chronographer, Hārūn the Monk.[132] The satisfaction he evidently derives from him is doubtless connected with the fact that both share a love of quoting, for ʿUbaydallah also bases his argument firmly on Galen.[133] The section ends with three of Galen's testimonies about Moses and the Messiah cited from Ibn al-Mutrān, the teacher of one of his own teachers.

The importance accorded to chronology should be seen both against the various competing traditions we have been looking at and the basic chronological focus of *ṭabaqāt* literature. With this problem out of the way, Ibn abi Usaybiʿa turns to provenance (let us call this section 2). Ibn Juljul provides the information that Galen was born at Pergamum. He then quotes a long passage from a comparatively early (and obscure) historian, Yūsuf b. al-Dāya, on Galen's 'abode' (117–121 R. = 77–80 M.). Yūsuf b. al-Dāya 'the Calculator' (d. 878) became a client of Ibrāhīm b. al-Mahdī (d. 839), the playboy son of the caliph al-Mahdī and half-brother of the caliph Hārūn al-Rashīd. The story relates to one of Harun's incursions into Byzantine territory, perhaps that of 798.[134] It consists of a question from Ibrahim to Jibrā'īl b. Bakhtīshū' on the location of Galen's home. Jibra'il (Jibrīl) (d. 828) was the third member of the prominent Christian family of physicians to tend the Abbasid court. He is mentioned several times by Hunayn in his *Letter* (cf. n. 29) as a patron during his youth, and not always favourably. It was he who had made a bad Syriac version of the commentary on the *Aphorisms* (of Hippocrates) far worse (40. 7–8 = p. 33 transl. Bergsträsser), and who had spent much effort with little result in searching for the Greek text of *De Demonstratione* (no. 115).[135] In his biography of Jibra'il (187–201 R. = 127–38 M.) Ibn abi Usaybi'a records from Yusuf several other questions put to him by Ibrahim. In the life of Galen Jibra'il is cited as recording a visit to the house of Galen in a village two parasangs from Smyrna (118 R. = 78 M.).[136] In several passages Galen recalls that he studied in Smyrna as a young man. These were perhaps enough to generate the story that a village near Smyrna, and not Pergamum, was Galen's birthplace and home. It is not impossible that a house of Galen *was* pointed out near Smyrna in antiquity and after, and that Jibra'il had got to hear of this.[137] The main point of the quotation for Ibn abi Usaybi'a and his audience no doubt lay in the following (to us) somewhat tedious discussion of the status (*sharaf*) of Galen relative to the Roman emperor and whether or not this was greater than that of Jibra'il relative to the caliph.

In the next section (3) Ibn abi Usaybi'a begins by invoking Ibn Juljul to introduce Galen's conquest of Rome. He then quotes extensively from *On Examinations By Which the Best Physicians are Recognized* (121–3 R. = 80–1 M.), and caps the section by citing from Ibn Juljul (unnamed[138]) a passage with a similar import (Galen exposes a charlatan at Rome) from the lost *On Diseases Which are Difficult to Cure* and a passage from *On the Composition of Drugs by Type* which is not in our Greek text.[139] Next (section 4) Ibn abi Usaybi'a moves on briefly to consider Galen's travels and death (Mubashshir, Mas'ūdī, and 'someone else', i.e. Ibn Juljul). He finishes with an unattributed story of how Galen dealt with his pupils when he knew death was near by making ice in the summertime. The anecdote is straight from the salons: 'this story is, I reckon, fabricated' (124.13 R. = 82.30 M.).

A bare summary like this obscures the belletristic nature of the *Sources of Information on the Generations of Physicians*. Here the fictional tale of the ice allows Ibn abi Usaybi'a to pause, for he inserts a recipe of how to make ice at home.[140] The next section (5) starts with Mubashshir and his anecdote about Galen's frivolous schoolmates. Typically Ibn abi Usaybi'a goes back to Galen. A long passage is taken from *On Good and Bad Juices* (6.755–6 K.) on the best upbringing Galen the best of sons received from the best of fathers. The start of *On Anatomical Procedures* is cited for information on Galen's teachers and *On his Own Books* and the lost *On Getting Rid of Sorrow* for early works of Galen. The section finishes with Mubashshir again on Galen's loss of his early books in the fire at Rome. Ibn abi Usaybiʿa now pauses.

> Overall there is countless information about Galen and stories useful to any who can examine them and snippets and anecdotes scattered throughout his books and in the course of tales transmitted about him, and many narratives of the things that happened to him during his treatment of the sick and in his demonstrations of his ability and skill in the art of medicine. It does not seem right to recall all this at this point.'

Instead, he promises a single book on this material, 'God willing'. The book was never written.

For now Ibn abi Usaybiʿa pursues the theme of Galen's prowess in medicine with a short quotation from *On Prognosis* and a lengthy one from *On Examinations By Which the Best Physicians are Recognized* (127–9 R. = 85–6 M.). The narrative part ends with Mubashshir's description of Galen's appearance, a discussion of the meaning and pronunciation of Galen's name, and some lines in praise of Galen and Hippocrates by the celebrated tenth-century poet, Maʿarrī. This transition to the second (Galen's sayings) and third (Galen's writings) parts shows again Ibn abi Usaybiʿa's literary intentions.[141]

4. Final remarks: the Arabic Galen

'Galen was present in the minds of the whole erudite class of Muslim society...we may expect to find quotations from his works anywhere in the vast scholarly Arabic literature of the Middle Ages'.[142] And, one may add, not only quotations: the belletrist historian Yaʿqūbī (d. *c.* 900), for example, includes a list of some thirty Galenic titles in his *History* which men of culture might like to know about.[143] On the surface the Muslim Galen was twofold. First, there was the Galen of the physicians, the technical, medical-philosophical Galen. Second, there was the gnomological and philosophical Galen, the Galen whose wisdom was esteemed in the salons and courts as a key representative of the learning of the ancients. Yet such a division is false of course, for medicine pervaded the lives and minds of the Muslim elite, just as it had the elites of Rome. The Arabic biographers treat Galen as one of a series of 'sages' (*ḥakīm*, pl. *ḥukamāʾ*), a term which had come to mean specifically 'doctor' or 'philosopher'. In assembling their information about him they naturally relied on his own works. Otherwise they recorded popular and semi-popular traditions and variant chronologies. It is only Ibn abi

Usaybiʿa (of surviving sources) who seeks to control this material. The huge length of his Galen biography actually makes it rather less attractive to read than that of Mubashshir; while his determination to be accurate loses him some of the spontaneity of the brief Ibn Juljul. This extensive biographical literature often tempts modern scholars to look for sources. But that is not what is interesting about the Arabic Galen. From the *Cabinet of Wisdom* and related texts we are able to peek into the world of the salon and of the 'study circle' (*ḥalqa*) of the 'erudite class of Muslim society' and see the real and fictionalized Galens providing entertainment and moral edification through anecdotes and sententious comments that show the educated at play with knowledge. This cultural pattern will be familiar to students of the Roman period. I have suggested that some of the popular traditions recorded in Arabic (and Syriac) about Galen and Cleopatra(?-Philainis), Jesus and his followers, and Sicily, surely originate from Graeco-Roman antiquity. I have argued that John the Grammarian should be accepted as a Galenic scholar working in mid-seventh-century Alexandria and that his sectarian chronology of the Eight Physicians built in the case of Galen on these semi-popular traditions. It seems clear at any rate that John's sectarianism left a most important legacy. For by elevating the association of Galen and Christ into an intellectual context he upgraded the physician himself. The Arabic biographical machine (where there was always a very strong focus on the world of religion) embraced this development. All in all, the absence of Galen from the Greek collections of wisdom is a sign that interest in him in the West remained restricted in a way that is not true of Muslim society.[144] This is not simply due to the absence of a literary genre of 'lives of doctors' in antiquity. Fortunately, through the western European translations of the stylish biographies of Mubashshir the Arabic Galen was brought to life for the Western late Middle Ages and Renaissance.[145]

Acknowledgements

I should like to thank Vivian Nutton, Peter Pormann, Emilie Savage-Smith, and especially Fritz Zimmermann for their help and advice.

Notes

Macrons have usually been left off Arabic names and terms after their first occurrence.

[1] For a sensitive and authoritative history of the translation of Greek culture into Islam and the reasons for it, see Gutas 1998. For a brief overview, Hoyland 2006. There is much interesting discussion of possible literary echoes of Greek poetry and prose in Arabic literature by ʿAbbas 1993.

[2] Ed. Ilberg CMG 4, 175–8 (mentioning *inter alia* a work *On Medical Genealogy* by

the Hellenistic doctor Andreas of Carystus). Lives: Suda σ 852.

³ Kennedy 1983.

⁴ Esp. in *De Libr. Prop.* Cf. the end of *Ars Medica*, 1.406–12 K. *De Prop. Plac.* (ed. Nutton, CMG V. 3. 2 [1999]) has much in common with these works. Autobiographical accounts without a bibliographical element occur frequently in Galen, of course: esp. *De Opt. Med. Cogn.* (Iskandar 1988), *De Praecognitione* (ed. Nutton, CMG V. 8. 1 [1979]), the lost *On Slander* (19.46 K. = 122 Mueller).

⁵ Note the neat sectarian doxographies at the start of the *Introductio seu Medicus* (14, 674–797 K.) which is contemporary with Galen. Cf. Nutton 2004, chap. 13 on Methodism, Walzer and Frede 1985 for key Galenic texts.

⁶ Rosenmeyer 2001, 217–21, Rütten 1992. Text: Littré vol. 9, 312–428; translation Wesley Smith, Leiden 1990.

⁷ *Institutio logica* 13. 7 Kalbfleish; *Quod opt. med. sit quoque phil.* 1. 58 K. = 5 Mueller; *Commentary on the Hippocratic Oath* fr. 3 a–e in Rosenthal 1956.

⁸ *De Methodo Medendi* 10.633. 10 ff. See esp. *De Placitis Hippocratis et Platonis* for Galen's intellectual heroes and their unanimity.

⁹ De Lucia 1999.

¹⁰ On the physicians' development of Neoplatonism, see Manetti 1992, Gundert 1998, 139.

¹¹ The list of books in Arabic varies to some extent and cannot be examined here: see Temkin 1932, 75–9 (doubts); Iskandar 1976, (optimistic faith in the description of the curriculum by Ibn Riḍwān, on whom see n. 93); Lieber 1981; Duffy 1984; Savage-Smith 2002, 126–7. The classic list of the Sixteen can be found in Ibn al-Nadim 255 Flügel = 2, 682–3 Dodge (on whom more below). For the work of Stephanus and Palladius see Gundert 1998, 93–4 with notes; Garofalo 2000, 148.

¹² Schöne 1903.

¹³ Text: Flügel 1871; translation: Dodge 1970 (not always accurate). For the genesis of the material on Galen, see Zimmermann 1976, 270–3.

¹⁴ Text: Lippert 1903.

¹⁵ Guidance on the huge Muslim biographical literature: Auchterlonie 1987; Young 1990; Robinson 2003, 55–79. Both types developed from the *rijāl* ('persons') books of Hadith scholarship.

¹⁶ Young 1990, 174. Ibn abi Usaybiʻa is cited by Müller 1884a, vol. 1 (unless stated) and Rida 1965.

¹⁷ Ibn al-Nadim 254 F. = 2, 612–13 D.; Qifti 354–7 L.; Ibn abi Usaybiʻa 151–3 R. = 104–5 M.

¹⁸ Cf. John of Nikiu (late 7th cent.) on the Egyptians' hostility to the Byzantine government at this time because of religious differences: Hoyland 1997, 154.

¹⁹ The fullest list occurs only in Ibn abi Usaybiʻa: see below.

²⁰ The Arabic word *taʼrīkh* really means 'chronicle'.

²¹ Rosenthal 1954; cf. Rosenthal 1961a for additional MSS. As Rosenthal noted (56), John's *History* is quoted by the 10th cent. historian Agapius (Maḥbūb) al-Manbijī (*CSCO, Script. Ar.*, Ser. 3, vol. 5 [Beirut 1912] 289 [ed. Cheikho]); but the passage actually refers to 'Yaḥyā b. ʻAdī the Grammarian'; it apparently (cf. Vasiliev's doubts about the translation at *Patr. Or.* 7.4 [1911] 562) gives a quotation in John's *History* (so named) from 'Qusṭanṭūs' (?Constantine) on the length of Adam's and Seth's reigns. There is clearly confusion with Agapius' contemporary, the Christian philosopher Yaḥyā

b. 'Adī of Baghdad (d. 974; cf. n. 120), possibly stemming from marginalia by him (cf. Zimmermann 1987, 124–5; he was *inter alia* a professional copyist). In any case the passage cannot prove that the *History* handled non-medical material.

22 Meyerhof 1932. Similar doubts in Temkin 1932, 51–71. On confusion between John the Grammarian (Philoponus) and another John (Yaḥyā b. 'Adī), see Zimmermann *loc. cit.*

23 Braeutigam 1908, 48–51. On John the Alexandrian see Pritchet 1975, p. vii, 1982, p. vii; Garofalo 1999, 190–2; cf. Nutton 1991. Two Latin versions of the *De Sectis* commentary and a Latin version of the Epidemics commentary survive; there is also an unpublished Greek commentary on Hippocrates' *De Nat. Pueri* under his name.

24 See Garofalo 1999, 187–93 for a positive but ultimately cautious view of the identity of the Greek-Latin John the Alexandrian and the Arabic John the Grammarian. Pormann 2003 tends in the same direction. See also the discussion by Savage-Smith (1969) 17–29.

25 Except for *De Differentiis Febrium, De Crisibus, De Criticis Diebus* (though these are treated in the epitome preserved in BL MS Arundel Or. 17, below n. 27). He is also credited with a commentary on *De Usu Partium* (below n. 27). The full list of John's commentaries on the Sixteen in Ibn abi Usaybi'a is: *Book of Sects, Small Book of the Art, Small Book of the Pulse* (preserved: Garofalo 1999), *Book of Glaucon, Book of Elements* (preserved: cf. Garofalo 2000, 136), *Book of Mixtures* (preserved: ib.), *Book of the Natural Faculties, Small Book of Anatomy, Book of Causes and Symptoms, Book on Knowing the Diseases of the Internal Parts, Big Book of the Pulse, Book of the Method of Healing, Book of Procedures for the Healthy, Book on the Uses of the Parts* (153–4 R. = 105 M.). Cf. the table of the Alexandrian works as classified by Hunayn and others in Lieber 1981, 173; and the helpful overview in Garofalo 2003, 203–8.

26 The schematic outlines of introductory Galenic works studied by Gundert 1998 in codex Vindob. med. gr. 16 (cf. Garofalo 2003, 208–13) share some notable didactic characteristics with the preserved Arabic summaries, but they are clearly not the *basis* of these; cf. Savage-Smith 2002, 125 noting the problem of dating these texts.

27 See Sezgin 1970, 140–50, 157–60 for information on MSS (he suggests it is not clear whether the commentaries are on the Summaries or the original Galenic works); Ullmann 1970, 90; Manetti 1992, 216; esp. Garofalo 2000 for the epitome contained in BL MS Arundel Or. 17 (139 'non è un compendio servile...vuole offrire un manuale di Galenismo', 143 John's epitome of *De Puls.* is on the basis of his own commentary on Galen); Savage-Smith 2002, 127 for the commentary on *De Usu Partium* (Bk. 11 only) translated into Arabic by Ibn Zur'a (Gotha, Landesbibliothek, arab. 1906, fols. 1–86), 127 and 130 for the fragment of the 'summary' of *De Usu Partium* (with references). Strohmaier 2004 argues that the aforementioned commentary on *De Usu Partium* must be by John Philoponus because it mentions philosophers not in Galen's text; but these household names (Epicurus, Anaxagoras, Democritus, Pythagoras, Plato) prove nothing; on Philoponus and medicine cf. Schiano 2003.

28 See also n. 21. A 'tolerably accurate' (Rosenthal 1954, 59) and in some ways fuller version was incorporated in the *Cabinet of Wisdom* (cf. n. 33): text in Dunlop 1979, ll. 265–397.

29 This material goes back to Galen's *Commentary on the Hippocratic Oath* (unknown in Greek; Arabic fragments in Rosenthal 1956, 53–9; see also Ullmann 1970, 62 no. 111), which Ishaq's father had translated; no doubt Ishaq drew also on John's account which

must again have rested on Galen. It is worth noting that there is no cause to dispute the authenticity of Galen's *Commentary*, which Hunayn accepted without hesitation in his famous *Letter* (*Risāla*) detailing his translations of Galen (Bergsträsser 1925 no. 87).

[30] Useful basic discussion in Dunlop 1979, xviii–xx.

[31] Musitelli 1985, 275–6; Nutton 2004, 46 for references.

[32] 'Analogy' (*qiyās*), i.e. dogmatic, logical reasoning (cf. Ullmann 2002 s.v. *dogmatikos*). In classical Islamic thought the fundamental idea of *qiyās* was originally defined in Islamic law by the great legist Shāfiʿī (d. 820), and was then taken up to mean 'syllogism' and more loosely logical thought. Ishaq's use of the term to translate John shows him trying to adapt the Greek tradition for his Muslim patron. Cf. below n. 38.

[33] Dunlop 1979, p. 23, l. 364 (corrected on the basis of Ibn abi Usaybiʿa); see also the 11th-century life of Galen in Mubashshir b. Fātik, *Choicest Maxims and Best Sayings* 289 Badawi = Rosenthal 1975, 34. The *Cabinet* contains many names which Ishaq omitted in his own quotations from John's *History* (Dunlop 1979, xxi–xx).

[34] Zimmermann 1974, 326.

[35] Rosenthal 1956, 53–76.

[36] Walzer 1949, 95 on Tzetzes against those who assert that Galen was ἰσόχρονος with Christ. His contemporary, Michael Glycas, exposes as lies a popular story that Galen met Mary Magdalen and discussed the story of the man blind from birth who was cured by Christ (John 9): *Annals* 430. 11–431. 5 Bekker. Gero 1990, 396 n. 75 adds a letter of Tzetzes to the superintendent of the Pantocrator hospital who believed in the meeting.

[37] So Gero 1990, 396–7 n. 75 (referring *inter alia* to the late 11th-century translations by Constantinus Africanus).

[38] 'Seal' is actually modelled on the Koranically inspired title of Muhammad, 'Seal of the Prophets', and is another example of Ishaq adapting John's text (which presumably had something comparable) to the religion of his patron; cf. n. 32.

[39] References: Walzer 1949; Gero 1990, esp. 402–11. *Republic*: Walzer 15–16, 89–96. Gero prefers the testimony of Barhebraeus that the remarks came in Galen's summary of the *Phaedo* (see n. 59 for the reference).

[40] Ullmann 1972.

[41] Glycas: nn. 36–7.

[42] Sayyid 1955 (with a summary of the Arabic introduction in French).

[43] 123.15 ff. L. for the section on Christians.

[44] The sources are translated in Amari 1880, 1, 346 Ibn Shabbāt (drawing on Bakri), 1889, 3 with 1880, 1, p. xxix Harawi; Sourdel-Thomine 1957, 25 (Harawi). Texts can be found in Amari 1857, 209–13, (1875–87) *Sec. App.* 1–2 (Harawi); Hajji 1968, 215 (Bakri). I have not seen Sourdel-Thomine's text of Harawi.

[45] *bashir al-Ishbīlī al-mutrān*, 'Bashir of Seville the Bishop'. Ibn abi Usaybiʿa 117 R. = 78 M. has *Lashīdhar al-Ishbīlī*. The unique manuscript of Ibn Juljul used by Sayyid is lacunose and quotations from Ibn abi Usaybiʿa and others have manuscript authority. This makes the identification of Isidore certain (*Lashīdhar* represents a hasty reading of initial *lām–shīn* for *alif–shīn*), لش for اش.

[46] Sayyid 1955, p. 35 of the introduction.

[47] Qifti and Ibn abi Usaybiʿa both bowdlerize the name 'Sicania' when they use this passage to 'Sulṭania' *vel sim.*

[48] Sayyid 42 n. 23 'Octavian' (اكتبيان); cf. Müller 1884a, 14 for variants in Ibn abi Usaybiʿa.

[49] Amari 1880, 1, 346 n. 1. Cf. Amari 1857, index: this is the only occurrence of *Balarma* in all his Arabic texts on Sicily (though *Balārma* occurs a few times). Note that *Balarma* is based on a correction of the pointing of the Arabic MS (Hajji 1968, 213); this is not suspicious. Away from this context Bakri uses the regular *Balarm* (with a similar repointing), Hajji 1968, 221.

[50] Ibn abi Usaybiʿa 494 R. = 2, 47–8 M. Ibn Juljul's surviving additions to Dioscorides and treatise on theriac (which Nicholas introduced to Andalusia) both attest the involvement. He begins the latter (Garijo 1992) by mentioning Galen's 'letter/treatise [*risāla*] to Antonius Caesar and Tiberius Caesar the joint kings in the City of Rome' (8 text = 22 trans.). 'Antonius' is perhaps for Antoninus = Marcus Aurelius (a form Galen does use e.g. in *De Antidotis*); but Tiberius can only mean Tiberius (one of two examples in Galen occurs *ibidem*), and a Galen alive under Tiberius is a contemporary of Christ. Note that the meagre reference to 'the voyage via Sicily' in Galen's *On Prognosis* (14. 648.13 K.) is surely not enough to have sparked the idea of Galen stopping off there.

[51] Ed. de Goeje vol. 1, p. 54.

[52] Respectively مارف and سماغرف. Nutton 2001, 31 n. 73. On the Arabic forms of Pergamum cf. Sayyid 1955, 44 n. 2.

[53] The great 15th-century historian of Egypt and its topography, Maqrīzī, still mentions the tomb in his *Khiṭaṭ* (*Districts*) (ed. G. Wiet vol. 4, p. 28 with n. 11). But the reference could well be traditional, as the list of sources makes clear.

[54] Hassan Bar Bahlūl ed. Duval 1901, 2, 958.3–11; transl. E. Castell, *Lexicon heptaglotton* 1669, 2, 1893 f. s.v. *l-w-q*. I owe these references to Fritz Zimmermann who wishes to acknowledge the help of Prof. Otto Kurz.

[55] Shafiʿ 1935, 1, 30–1.

[56] Shafiʿ 1935, 1, 28. Commentaries: cf. Garofalo 2000, 143 n. 28.

[57] Nutton 1995.

[58] Swain 1996, 430–2.

[59] 42.8 Sayyid; followed by Qifti 123.10 L. (but later Qifti gives 87, p. 127 L., in his report of ʿUbaydallāh b. Bakhtīshūʿ drawing on Ishaq/John the Grammarian; on ʿUbaydallāh see n. 127), Barhebraeus (Ibn al-ʿIbrī), *Taʾrīkh mukhtaṣar al-duwal* ed. A. Salihani (Beirut 1890) 123. Cf. Sayyid 1955, 45 n. 26.

[60] Nutton 1995, 27–8.

[61] Cf. Ullmann 1970, 60–1 nos. 104–5 (but *Secrets of Women* is not restricted to cosmetics).

[62] Levey and Souryal 1968, 218.

[63] Cf. Savage-Smith 2002, 126; Sezgin 2001 for summaria ascribed to Hunayn.

[64] Levey and Souryal 1968, 209–14. The translators note that the recipes are all paired in positive and negative reactions.

[65] For the idea of the 'hidden' (sexual) disease, see Rosenthal 1978.

[66] Levey and Souryal 1968, 214–18.

[67] Meyerhof 1928, 13 n. 2.

[68] Parker 1992, 93–4.

[69] Rosenthal 1975, 79. Cf. Strohmaier 2002, 116 for the romanticizing of a tale from *On Prognosis* in an 11th-century text.

[70] On Sijistani see Badawi 1974, introduction; Dunlop 1979, introduction; Netton 1992, 63–72.

[71] Al-Qāḍī 1981, 117–18.

[72] The plural (*ḥikam*) of the Arabic word regularly means 'wise sayings', 'maxims'.

[73] I refer to the Dunlop text only unless stated.

[74] See Badawi 1974, 26–30 for a summary of the short epitome by al-Sāwī: the section on Galen took up less than one side of a folio in the manuscript Badawi refers to.

[75] l. 2242 *jabbāran, mutafarṭasan*. There is apparently a double entendre in the latter word: cf. Kazimirski, *Dictionnaire*, vol. 2, 1860, p. 577 s.v. فرطس 'allonger (se dit, *p. ex.* du cochon qui allonge le groin *ou* d'un autre animal dont le pénis est en érection).' Badawi 265§2 l. 1 prints *mufriṭ* 'excessive', a reading not recorded in Dunlop's apparatus.

[76] The key word is *althagh* (see n. 82). For Abū al-Nafīs cf. *Cabinet* 3555 'the most careful of men about the stories of the philosophers'.

[77] Galen refers to it often: *On his Own Books* 19. 19, 41 K. = 99, 117 Mueller; *De Antidotis* 14. 66 K.; *De Comp. Med. Per Gen.* 13. 362 K.

[78] For the swop of *nūn* and *fāʾ* cf. above on Fīlānūs/Fīlāfūs.

[79] In Arabic the letters for *r* and *z* are distinguished only by a dot (which is easily omitted): باز and بار (though the vocalization is odd).

[80] Cf. recently Ullmann 1998 for the range of references in poetry. But note also the fascinating *Praise of the Blacks against the Whites* by the irrepressible 9th cent. littérateur, Jāḥiẓ.

[81] Cf. Zimmermann 1991 on the theologian Wāṣil ibn ʿAṭāʾ (d. 748).

[82] It also shows an awareness of Galen's discussions of the problem he calls *traulizein* (esp. *In Hipp. Aph. comm.* 18a. 51 K.): Wollock 1997, 191–2, 283–5 (but Galen does not actually use *traulismos*). It is very likely that *althagh* (n. 76) translates *traulos* in this context: Ullmann 2002, 681, id., *Wörterbuch d. klass. arab. Spr.* vol. 2 p. 191. The detailed entry in *WKAS* confirms that *l-th-gh* was used about the r-lessness of Wāṣil (n. 81) by Jāḥiẓ (cf. n. 80) and others, though the Arabic and Greek terms vary in their application in particular authors.

[83] Rosenthal 1952, 473; the study continues in vols. 22 and 24 of the same journal. 'Greek *shaykh*' essentially = 'Anonymus Graecus'. For a comparable abbreviation, cf. Robinson 2003, 182.

[84] For example, he quotes from the philosopher ʿĀmirī and the historian and littérateur Miskawayh. His date is 11th or 12th century. 'The manuscript [Bodl. Or. Marsh 539]...occupies itself mostly with rendering views ascribed to Greek authors' (Rosenthal 1940, 396). It needs to be re-examined for its Galen material.

[85] For an excellent study of the cultural use of knowledge in the later classical period see Chamberlain 1994.

[86] Badawi 1985 for the Arabic with introduction (cited by Badawi page). Loewenthal 1896 offers a German translation of the Hebrew translation of the epitome (cited by book, chapter, section and/or Loewenthal page); see Badawi 1985, 10 ff. on the Hebrew's rearrangement of the material.

[87] I.i 'Buch der Wortspiele der Philosophen, ihrer Rätselfragen und Sittenlehren' p. 49 L. (cf. 37 B.), I.ii = 43–4 B.

[88] Ibn al-Washshā, *Das Buch des buntbestickten Kleids* (transl. D. Bellmann) (Bremen 1984) vol. 3.

[89] The variation is presumably due to the formal proximity of Hebrew *resh* and *daleth*.

[90] Badawi 1985, 51 n. 1 'to extract the moral [*ʿibra*]'. On the question of the 'Greek' origin of such stories in the *Anecdotes* see below p. 412.

⁹¹ Date: Rosenthal 1961b, 133; 1975, 33.

⁹² For the later history of the work in Europe, see Rosenthal 1961b, 132–3 (*inter alia* an English translation from the French resting on a Latin version of the Spanish original translation; the Spanish dates from before 1257; the English became 'the first book in the English language to be printed in England'), 149–58; Crombach 1971, introduction. The existence of the Spanish undermines the suggestion of Musitelli (1985) that Latin lives of Hippocrates and Galen by Giovanni da Procida (d. 1299) reflect knowledge of the Arabic sources; indeed, these texts reinforce the old idea that Giovanni translated into Latin the Spanish (which had parted company with Mubashshir's name).

⁹³ Mubashshir: Badawi 1958, text and introduction (to be supplemented by Rosenthal 1961b; Crombach 1971, XII–XVII). Galen: 288–93 B. life = translation in Rosenthal 1975, 33–6; 293–6 B. sayings (untranslated). For Ibn Riḍwān and his obsession with Greek learning, see Schacht and Meyerhof 1937.

⁹⁴ Mourad 1939, 65–6 (French trans. of various passages), 81–2 (texts).

⁹⁵ Mubashshir 2–3, 3.4 B. not put off by *taqādum 'ahdihim*, 'progression of their ages' (with apposite citation of Koran 39. 19).

⁹⁶ Rosenthal 1937.

⁹⁷ Comparable material from Mubashshir in English translation can be found in Rosenthal 1975 124–44 (296–322 B.).

⁹⁸ Rosenthal 1961b, 135.

⁹⁹ Ibn abi Usaybi'a 130.14 R. = 88.8 M.; Mubashshir 293.11 B.

¹⁰⁰ It is easy to see what has happened in Mubashshir: he has the first quotation 'Worry is decay of the heart while sorrow is a disease of the heart' (293.10 B.), and has kept this order in his next quotation, 'Worry is about something that happened; sorrow about something that will happen' (= the second in Ibn abi Usaybi'a).

¹⁰¹ Mubashshir 294.3–7 B.; Ibn abi Usaybi'a 131.12–18 R. = 88.27–33 M. Interest in Galen's view of love is shown by Ibn Bakhtīshū' on love ed. Klein-Franke 1977. See further n. 109.

¹⁰² Rosenthal 1940, 389–91; Mubashshir 82–126 B. (Socrates), 126–78 B. (Plato).

¹⁰³ Rosenthal 1940, 396.

¹⁰⁴ Both are, however, happy to posit an Arabic origin for the extensive Alexander material (organized as Bk. III in the Hebrew).

¹⁰⁵ Ullmann 1961. Contrast Rosenthal 1937, pt II on the sayings material of Zeno, which is not classical. On Graeco-Arabic gnomological material see esp. Gutas 1975.

¹⁰⁶ Loewenthal 1896, 19.

¹⁰⁷ (i) Mubashshir 294.8–12 B. = Ibn abi Usaybi'a 131.25–28 R. = 89.4–8 M. from *Adhortatio* 6 (1. 9 K.; 108–9 Marquardt); (ii) Mubashshir 296.6–8 B. = Ibn abi Usaybi'a 132.28–133.2 R. = 89.31–90.2 M. from *Adhortatio* 13 (1. 34 K.; 126 Marquardt).

¹⁰⁸ Galen does not in fact appear in the Greek gnomological/paroemiographical collections (cf. Strohmaier 2002, 116). It is worth noting that some of the Greek pseudo-Galen contains sententious material: cf. *Introductio seu Medicus* (14.674 ff. K.), *Definitiones Medicae* (19.346 ff. K.); but this is thin pickings. There is virtually no 'biography' in these works (cf. *De Succedaneis*, 19. 721 ff. K., *ad init.*; works addressed to acquaintances, *De Optima Secta ad Thrasybulum*, 1. 106 ff. K., *De Remediis Parabilibus*, 14. 311 ff. K., *De Theriaca ad Pamphilianum*, 14. 295 K., *De Pulsibus ad Antonium*, 19. 629 ff. K.).

¹⁰⁹ Boudon 2002, 18. This work is 'not so far identified'. The next work mentioned in the new section is a treatise on the faculties which are the 'foundation of the body', i.e. *De*

Plac. Hipp. et Plat.; and for the relationship of love to brain, heart, and liver in the Arabic gnomological material one may cf. and contrast *De Plac. Hipp. et Plat.* 6.8.79–80 (cf. Ibn Bakhtīshūʿ 83/50 Klein-Franke), further on love (*aphrodisia*), memory (*anamnēsis*), and imagination (*phantasia*), a passage like *De Locis Affectis* 8. 450–1 K.

[110] If we had Galen's Περὶ ἀλυπίας (cf. Nutton 2002, 166) we might know more. For some fragments and echoes of this work, esp. in the 13th cent. Jewish philosopher Ibn Falaquera, see Zonta 1995, 18–20, 113–23.

[111] *akhlāq* (perhaps 'ethics', 'moral qualities'). Hunayn's translation: Bergsträsser 1925, no. 119.

[112] Text: Kraus 1937. Translation: Mattock 1972. I refer to both in what follows. There are of course fragments, notably in the Jewish philosophers Ibn Falaquera and Ibn ʿAqnīn: Zonta 1995, 29–80.

[113] 122.18–123.2 B. = II.x.5. The passage does not come from Hunayn's translation of *De Moribus* because it is part of a longer section taken from his *Anecdotes* (122–3 B. = II. x); it does of course preserve the full text, not that of the Epitome.

[114] Epitome 46.17–47.7 Kr. = 254§2 M. offers a loose correspondence, but Ibn Falaquera presents a fairly full version of the sentiment: Zonta 1995, 66–8 no. 36. As Zonta notes, Mubashshir has pruned hard but kept the sense. Cf. also interesting comparable material in Galen's lost synopsis of Plato's *Laws* in Gutas 1997, 114 ff.

[115] There are minor differences of order and some additional material in the Epitome, perhaps from the editor. This was a well remembered analogy: Stern 1956, 91–3, Zonta 1995, 41–3 no. 8 for Ibn Falaquera.

[116] Zonta 1995, 43–4 no. 9 for Ibn Falaquera and Ibn ʿAqnīn. Zonta suggests *Timaeus* 89e-90a; but Galen's summary is perhaps a better bet.

[117] Zonta 1995, 46 no. 12 for the accurate quotation in Ibn Falaquera and Ibn ʿAqnīn.

[118] Kraus 1937, 18–23 for longer passages with addenda in Stern 1956; Zonta 1992, 20–3; 1995, 29–80.

[119] Kraus 1937, 24 n. 4 (cf. 37 n. 1).

[120] Yaḥyā, *Reform of Moral Qualities* (transl. S.H. Griffith, Provo, Utah, 2002), cf. 97.16–19 the Complete Human Being must be characterized by *adab* and associate with scholars to discuss knowledge and political kingship, 'stories about sages and their moral qualities', and biographies of kings; Miskawayh, *Reform of Moral Qualities* (trans. C. Zurayk, Beirut 1968); Tawḥīdī (pupil of Sijistani, circle of Yaḥyā), *Muqābasāt* (*Table Talk*).

[121] See Müller 1884b, a general lecture. Otherwise there is only the short article in the *Encyclopedia of Islam*², 3:693–4 (Vernet).

[122] Najjar 1996. The Galen section is covered. There is, however, no *apparatus criticus* and one must still depend on Müller 1884a.

[123] Himsi 1984, esp. 59–63.

[124] Note again Chamberlain 1994 for the cultural negotiations of Ibn abi Usaybiʿa's contemporaries.

[125] On the meaning of the 'era of Alexander' in *De Moribus*, see Kraus 1937, 14.

[126] 289 F. = 2, 682 Dodge.

[127] See Graf 1947, 111–12, Klein-Franke 1977.

[128] Cf. Schacht and Meyerhof 1937.

[129] Cf. n. 59. Though note (a) the form of Qifti's work is not chronological, and

(b) provision of alternative dates without specific comment is a feature of Muslim historiography.

[130] *De Opt. Med. Cogn.*: Iskandar 1988, 15–16; note Meyerhof 1929 for translations of many of the quotations (superseded for *De Opt. Med. Cogn.* by Iskandar).

[131] Ibn abi Usaybiʻa does not refer to Ibn al-Ṭayyib.

[132] Graf 1947, 112.

[133] e.g. 'These passages, and others we have not cited in the interests of brevity, show...' (114.17 R. = 74.27–8 M.), ' I find it strange how something like this has gone on despite the clarity of the Galenic passages we have argued from and the texts of the accurate chronographers. I find it strange how no one's attention was drawn to the paragraph of the *Book of Ethics*...' (116.9–10 R. = 76.14–16 M.).

[134] The raid on Ephesus in this year is the closest report in the historical sources: Tabari 3.646–7 transl. Williams. The presence in the story of the commander Ibrāhīm b. ʻUthmān b. Nahīk makes the date earlier than 803 (cf. Tabari 3, 699–701).

[135] Hunayn's restraint is commendable, for Jibra'il's son, Bakhtīshūʻ, became his great enemy: Ibn abi Usaybiʻa 264 R. = 190 M.

[136] Not Pergamum, as Strohmaier 1981, 187 reports; cf. Nutton 2004, 324 n. 77.

[137] Galen and Smyrna: e.g. *De Anat. Admin.* 2. 217 K., *In Hipp. Aphorism. Comm.* 18a. 29 K., *De Humero iis Modis Prolapso...* 18a. 347 K., *De Libr. Prop.* 19. 16–17 K. = 97–8 M. A House of Galen was still being shown at Pergamum in the mid-thirteenth century when the sight of it cheered up the Byzantine dynast Theodore Lascaris II (*Epistulae* ed. N. Festa p. 108). When Ibn Battūta, the greatest of the Muslim travellers, visited Pergamum about 1331/2 he reported that the house of 'Plato the sage' is 'known by his name to the present day' (trans. H. Gibb, vol. 2, p. 449): evidently the name of the 'sage' had been forgotten in the confusion of the Turkish conquest and Plato substituted for Galen.

[138] The text of both anecdotes accords with Qiftī, not Ibn Juljul; but given the problems of his text (cf. n. 45), Ibn abi Usaybiʻa may still have been quoting directly.

[139] Vivian Nutton suggests to me that the passage (which ends with 'and he was not content with knowledge of subjects based on tradition aside from practice') partly echoes *De Comp. Med. Per Gen.* 13.459 K. on book knowledge *vs.* real training.

[140] The source, Ibn Bakhtawayh, was a mid-11th cent. author of a *Treasury of Physicians* (brief life in Ibn abi Usaybiʻa, 340 R. = 253 M.). Since he was devoted to the 'writings of the ancients', it is possible the anecdote about Galen also comes from him. Cf. Sezgin 1970, 335.

[141] Ibn abi Usaybiʻa was himself a poet and a good deal of verse is included in the *Sources of Information on the Generations of Physicians*, including his own lines on contemporaries.

[142] Strohmaier 2002, 114.

[143] Ed. Houtsma 1883, 1, 130–3.

[144] A footnote to this is the tradition found in a work of the Jewish physician-philosopher-mystic, Dūnash b. Tāmīm (d. *c.* 960), that Galen was in fact a Jew of impeccable ancestry, Rabbi Gamaliel: Vajda 1955. Vajda pp. 650–1 rightly considers the report a 'Jewish rejoinder' to the legend of Galen the Christian, but holds it is an interpolation since Dūnash knew his Galen too well; on this point we may again compare John the Grammarian, and also Ibn Juljul.

[145] See n. 92.

Bibliography

'Abbas, I.

1993   *Malāmiḥ yūnāniyya fī l-adab al-ʿarabī*[2], Beirut.

Amari, M.

1857   *Biblioteca arabo-sicula*, Leipzig, texts.

1880   *Biblioteca arabo-sicula* vols. 1–2, Turin and Rome, translations.

1875–87   *Biblioteca arabo-sicula*, Appendice and Seconda Appendice, Leipzig 1875–87, texts.

1889   *Biblioteca arabo-sicula*, Appendice, Florence and Rome, translations.

Auchterlonie, P.

1987   *Arabic Biographical Dictionaries. A summary guide and bibliography*, Durham.

Badawī, ʿA.

1958   *Abū-l-wafā' al-Mubassir ibn Fātik, Les Bocados de Oro (Mujtār al-Ḥikam)*, Madrid. Repr. Beirut, 1980, Arabic.

1974   *Abū Sulaymān al-Sijistānī. Muntakhab Ṣiwān al-Ḥikmah et Trois Traités*, Tehran.

1985   *Ḥunain ibn Isḥāq, Ādāb al-falāsifa, (Sentences des philosophes)*, Kuwait

Bergsträsser, G.

1925   *Ḥunain ibn Isḥāq Über die syrischen und arabischen Galen-Übersetzungen*, Leipzig.

1932   *Neue Materialien zu Ḥunain ibn Isḥāq's Galen-Bibliographie*, Leipzig.

Boudon, V.

2002   'Galen's *On My Own Books*. New material from Meshed, Rida, tibb. 5223', in Nutton (ed.) *The Unknown Galen*, BICS Suppl. 77, London, 9–18.

Braeutigam, W.

1908   *De Hippocratis Epidemiarum libri sexti Commentatoribus*, Diss. Königsberg.

Chamberlain, M.

1994   *Knowledge and Social Practice in Medieval Damascus, 1190–1350*, Cambridge.

Crombach, M.

1971   *Bocados de oro. Kritische Ausgabe des altspanischen Textes*, Bonn.

De Lucia, R.

1999   'Doxographical hints in Oribasius' *Collectiones Medicae*', in P.J. van der Eijk (ed.) *Ancient Histories of Medicine*, Leiden, 474–89.

Dodge, B. (transl.)

1970   *The Fihrist of al-Nadim*, vols. 1–2, New York.

Duffy, J.

1984   'Byzantine medicine in the sixth and seventh centuries: aspects of teaching and practice', in J. Scarborough (ed.) *Symposium on Byzantine Medicine*, = DOP 38, Washington, 21–7.

Dunlop, D.M. (ed.)

1979   *The 'Muntakhab Ṣiwān al-Ḥikmah' of Abū Sulaimān as-Sijistānī*, The Hague.

Flügel, G.

1871   *Ibn al Nadīm, Kitāb al Fihrist* vol. 1 [text], Leipzig.

Garijo, I.
1992   *Ibn Yulyul, Tratado sobre los medicamentos de la tríaca*, Cordova.

Garofalo, I.
1999   'La traduzione araba del commento di Ioannnes grammatikos al *De Pulsibus* di Galeno', in A. Garzya and J. Jouanna (eds.) *I testi medici greci. Traduzione e ecdotica*, Naples, 185–218.
2000   'II sunto di Ioannes 'Grammatikos' delle opere del canone di Galeno', in D. Manetti (ed.) *Studi su Galeno*, Florence, 135–51.
2003   'I sommari degli Alessandrini', in Garofalo and Roselli (eds.) *Galenismo e medicina tardoantica*, 203–27.

Garofalo, I. and Roselli, A. (eds.)
2003   *Galenismo e medicina tardoantica. Fonti greche, latine e arabe*, Atti del seminario intern. di Siena, 9–10 Sept., Naples.

Gero, S.
1990   'Galen on the Christians. A reappraisal of the Arabic evidence', *Or. Chr. period.* 56, 371–411.

Graf, G.
1947   *Geschichte der christlichen arabischen Literatur*, vol. 2 *Die Schriftsteller bis zur Mitte des 15. Jahrhunderts*, Vatican.

Gundert, B.
1998   'Die Tabulae Vindobonenses als Zeugnis alexandrinischer Lehrtätigkeit um 600 n.Chr.', in K.-D. Fischer, D. Nickel and P. Potter (eds.) *Text and Tradition. Studies in ancient medicine and its transmission, presented to J. Kollesch*, Leiden, 91–144.

Gutas, D.
1975   *Greek Wisdom Literature in Arabic Translation. A study of the Graeco-Arabic Gnomologia*, New Haven.
1997   'Galen's synopsis of Plato's *Laws* and Fārābī's *Talhīṣ*', in G. Endress and R. Kruk (eds.) *The Ancient Tradition in Christian and Islamic Hellenism*, Leiden, 101–19.
1998   *Greek Thought, Arabic Culture. The Graeco-Arabic translation movement in Baghdad and early 'Abbasid society (2nd–4th/8th–10th centuries)*, London.

Hajjī, 'A. 'Alī al-, [Al-Bakrī,]
1968   *The Geography of Al-Andalus and Europe from the Book 'Al Masālik wa-l-Mamālik*, Beirut.

Ḥimṣī, H.
1984   'Manhaj al-Baḥth al-'ilmī 'inda Ibn abī Usaybi'a' ('The research methodology of Ibn abi Usaybi'a'), in *Abḥāth al-Mu'tamar al-sanawī al-thāmin al-mun'aqid fī Jāmi'at Hialab, 25–26 Nisan (April) 1984*, Aleppo, 39–68.

Hoyland, R.G.
1997   *Seeing Islam as Others Saw It*, Princeton.
2006   'The Islamic background to Polemon's Treatise', in S. Swain (ed.) *Seeing the Face, Seeing the Soul: Polemon's* Physiognomy *from Classical Antiquity to Medieval Islam*, Oxford.

Iskandar, I.Z.
1976   'An attempted reconstruction of the late Alexandrian medical curriculum', *Medical History* 20, 235–58.

1988   *Galen. On Examinations By Which the Best Physicians are Recognized*, CMG Suppl. Orient. IV, Berlin.

Kennedy, G.

1983   *Greek Rhetoric under Christian Emperors*, Princeton.

Klein-Franke, F.

1977   [Ibn Bakhtīshūʿ,] Über die Heilung der Krankheiten der Seele und des Körpers, Beirut.

Kraus, P.

1937   'The *Book of Ethics* by Galen', *Bull. Fac. Arts Univ. Egypt* 5.1, (Arabic Section): 1–51, [Arabic text and introduction].

Levey, M. and Souryal, S.S.

1968   'Galen's *On the Secrets of Women* and *On the Secrets of Men*. A contribution to the history of Arabic pharmacology', *Janus* 55, 208–19.

Lieber, E.

1981   'Galen in Hebrew: the transmission of Galen's works in the mediaeval Islamic world', in Nutton (ed.) *Galen*, 167–86.

Lippert, J.

1903   *Ibn al-Qifṭī's taʾrīh l-ḥukamāʾ*, Leipzig.

Loewenthal, A.

1896   *Honein ibn Ishāk, Sinnsprüche der Philosophen. Nach der hebräischen Uebersetzung Charisi's*, Berlin.

Manetti, D.

        'P. Berol. 11739A e i commenti tardoantichi a Galeno', in A. Garzya (ed.) *Tradizione e ecdotica dei testi medici tardoantichi e bizantini, (Atti del convegno inter. Anacapri, 29–31 Ottobre 1990)*, Naples, 211–35.

Mattock, J.N.

1972   'A translation of the Arabic epitome of Galen's book Περὶ ἠθῶν', in S.M. Stern, A. Hourani and V. Brown (eds.) *Islamic Philosophy and the Classical Tradition. Essays presented…to Richard Walzer…*, Oxford, 235–60.

Meyerhof, M.

1928   'Über echte und unechte Schriften Galens nach arabischen Quellen', *Sitzungsb.d. deutsch. Akad.d. Wissen., phil.-hist. Kl.*, 1–18.

1929   'Autobiographische Bruchstücke Galens aus arabischen Quellen', *Sud. Arch.* 22, 72–86.

1932   'Joannes Grammatikos (Philoponos) von Alexandrien und die arabische Medizin', *Mit. Deutsch. Instit.f. ägypt. Altertums. in Kairo* 2, 1–21.

Mourad, Y.

1939   *La physiognomonie arabe et le Kitāb al-Firāsa de Fakhr al-Dīn al-Rāzī*, Paris.

Müller, A.

1884a   *Ibn abi Useibia, Kitāb 'Uyūn al-anbāʾ fī ṭabaqāt al-aṭibbāʾ*, vols. 1–2 (printed as one vol.) revised edn Konigsberg [original Cairo 1882]).

1884b   'Ueber Ibn Abi Oçeibiʾa und seine Geschichte der Aerzte', *Travaux de la 6 session du Congrès international des Orientalistes à Leide*, Leiden [separately printed extract].

Musitelli, S.

1985   'Da Parmenide a Galeno. Tradizioni classiche e interpretazioni medievali nelle biografie dei grandi medici antichi', *Mem. Acc. Linc.* 28, 213–76.

Najjār, ʿĀ. al-,
1996   *Ibn abī Usaybiʿa, Kitāb ʿUyūn al-anbāʾ fī ṭabaqāt al-aṭibbāʾ*, vol. 1, Cairo.

Netton, I.R.
1992   *Al-Fārābī and his School*, London.

Nutton, V.
1984   'Galen in the eyes of his contemporaries', *Bull. Hist. Med.* 68, 315–24 = id.,
       From Democedes to Harvey III, London.
1991   'John of Alexandria again: Greek medical philosophy in Latin translation',
       CQ 41, 509–19.
1995   'Galen "ad multos annos"', *Dynamis* (Acta Hisp. Med. Sci. Hist. Illus.) 15,
       25–39.
2001   'God, Galen and the depaganisation of ancient medicine', in P. Biller and
       J. Ziegler (eds.) *Religion and Medicine in the Middle Ages*, York, 15–32.
2004   *Ancient Medicine*, London.

Nutton, V. (ed.)
1981   *Galen: Problems and prospects*, London.
2002   *The Unknown Galen*, BICS Suppl. 77, London.

Parker, H.N.
1992   'Love's body anatomized: the ancient erotic handbooks and the rhetoric of
       sexuality', in A. Richlin (ed.) *Pornography and Representation in Greece and
       Rome*, New York, 90–111.

Pormann, P.
2003   'Jean le grammarian et le "De sectis" dans la littérature médicale d'Alexandrie',
       in Garofalo and Roselli (eds.) *Galenismo e medicina tardoantica*, 233–63.

Pritchet, C.D.
1975   *Iohannis Alexandrini commentaria in sextum librum Hippocratis Epidemi-
       arum*, Leiden.
1982   *Iohannis Alexandrini commentaria in librum De Sectis Galeni*, Leiden.

al-Qāḍī, W.
1981   'Kitāb Ṣiwān al-Ḥikma', *Der Islam* 58, 87–124.

Riḍā, N.
1965   *Ibn abī Uṣaybiʿa, Kitāb ʿUyūn al-anbāʾ fī ṭabaqāt al-aṭibbāʾ*, Beirut.

Robinson, C.F.
2003   *Islamic Historiography*, Cambridge.

Rosenmeyer, P.A.
2001   *Ancient Epistolary Fictions. The letter in Greek literature*, Cambridge.

Rosenthal, F.
1937   'Arabische Nachrichten über Zenon den Eleaten', *Orientalia* 6, 21–67 = id.,
       Greek Philosophy in the Arab World III, Aldershot 1990.
1940   'On the knowledge of Plato's philosophy in the Islamic world', *Islamic Culture*
       14, 387–422 = id., *Greek Philosophy in the Arab World* II, Aldershot 1990.
1952   'As-Sayh al-Yūnānī and the Arabic Plotinus Source', *Orientalia* 21, 461–92 =
       id., *Greek Philosophy in the Arab World* III, Aldershot 1990.
1954   'Isḥāq b. Ḥunayn's "taʾrīh al-aṭibbā"', *Oriens* 7, 55–80 = id., *Science and
       Medicine in Islam* II, Aldershot 1990.
1956   'An ancient commentary on the Hippocratic Oath', *Bull. Hist. Med.* 30,

52–87 = id., *Science and Medicine in Islam* III, Aldershot 1990.

1961a   'From Arabic books and manuscripts. VII: Some Graeco-Arabica in Istanbul', *JAOS* 81, 7–12.

1961b   'Al-Mubashshir ibn Fatik. Prolegomena to an abortive edition', *Oriens* 13–14, 132–58.

1975   *The Classical Heritage in Islam*, transl. E. and J. Marmorstein, London.

1978   'ar-Rāzī on the hidden illness', *Bull. Hist. Med.* 52, 45–60 = id., *Science and Medicine in Islam* IX, Aldershot 1990.

Rütten, T.
1992   *Demokrit, lachender Philosoph und sanguinischer Melancholiker: eine pseudo-hippokratische Geschichte*, Leiden.

Savage-Smith, E.
1969   'Galen on Nerves, Veins and Arteries: A critical edition and translation from the Arabic, with notes, glossary and an introductory essay', PhD diss., University of Wisconsin-Madison.

2002   'Galen's lost ophthalmology and the "Summaria Alexandrinorum"', in Nutton (ed.) *The Unknown Galen*, 121–38.

Sayyid, F. (ed.)
1955   *Les générations des médecins et des sages ... par ... Ibn Gulgul al-Andalusī*, Cairo, (Arabic).

Schacht, J. and Meyerhof, M.
1937   *The Medico-Philosophical Controversy between Ibn Buṭlan of Baghdad and Ibn Riḍwan of Cairo. A contribution to the history of Greek learning among the Arabs*, Cairo.

Schiano, C.
2003   'Il trattato inedito "Sulle febbri" attribuito a Giovanni Filopono: contenuto, modelli e struttura testuale', in Garofalo and Roselli (eds.) *Galenismo e medicina tardoantica*, 75–100.

Schöne, H.
1903   'Bruchstücke einer neuen Hippokratesvita', *RhM* 58, 56–66.

Sezgin, F.
1970   *Geschichte des arabischen Schrifttums*, vol. 3, Leiden.

2001   *The Alexandrian Compendium of Galen's Work. Jawāmi ʿal-Iskandarāniyyīn translated by Ḥiunayn ibn Isḥāq, (d. 260/873)* vols. 1–2, Frankfurt.

Shafī, M.
1935   *Kitāb Tatimmat Ṣiwān al-ḥikmah*, vols. 1–2, Lahore.

Sourdel-Thomine, J. [al-Harawī,]
1957   *Guide des lieux de pèlerinage*, Damascus.

Stern, S.M.
1956   'Some fragments of Galen's *On Dispositions* (Περὶ ἠθῶν) in Arabic', *CQ* 6, 91–101 = id., *Medieval Arabic and Hebrew Thought* III, London 1983.

Strohmaier, G.
1981   'Galen in Arabic. Prospects and projects', in Nutton (ed.) *Galen: Problems and prospects*, 187–96.

2002   'The uses of Galen in Arabic literature', in Nutton (ed.) *The Unknown Galen*, 112–20.

2004   'Der Kommentar des Johannes Grammaticus zu Galen, "De Usu Partium",

(Buch 11), in einer unikalen Gothaer Handschrift', in id., *Hellas im Islam*, Wiesbaden, 109–12.

Swain, S.
1996   *Hellenism and Empire*, Oxford.

Temkin, O.
1932   'Geschichte des Hippokratismus im ausgehenden Altertum', *Kyklos* 4, 1–80.

Ullmann, M.
1961   *Die Arabische Überlieferung der sogenannten Menandersentenzen*, *AKM* 34.1, Wiesbaden.

1970   *Die Medizin im Islam*, Leiden and Cologne.

1972   'Kleopatra in einer arabischen alchemistischen Disputation', *Wiener Zeitschr. f.d. Kunde des Morgenlandes* 63–4, 158–75.

1998   *Der Neger in der Bildersprache der arabischen Dichter*, Wiesbaden.

2002   *Wörterbuch zu den griechisch-arabischen Übersetzungen des 9. Jahrhunderts*, Wiesbaden.

Vajda, G.
1955   'Galien-Gamaliel', *Mélanges Isidore Lévy, Ann. de l'Inst. de Phil. et d'Hist. orient. et slaves* 13 [1953], Brussels, 641–52.

Walzer, R.
1949   *Galen on Jews and Christians*, Oxford.

Walzer, R. and Frede, M.
1985   *Galen: Three treatises on the nature of science*, Indianapolis.

Wollock, J.
1997   *The Noblest Animate Motion. Speech, physiology and medicine in PreCartesian linguistic thought*, Amsterdam.

Young, M.J.L.
1990   'Arabic biographical writing', in id., J.D. Latham and R.B. Serjeant (eds.) *The Cambridge History of Arabic Literature. Religion, learning and science in the 'Abbasid Period*, Cambridge, 168–87.

Zimmermann, F.W.
1974   'The chronology of Isḥāq b. Ḥunayn's "ta'rīh al-aṭibbā'"', *Arabica* 21, 324–30.

1976   'On the supposed shorter version of Ibn an Nadīm's "Fihrist" and its date', *Der Islam* 53, 267–73.

1987   'Philoponus' impetus theory in the Arabic tradition', in R. Sorabji (ed.) *Philoponus and the Rejection of Aristotelian Science*, London, 121–9.

1991   Review of H. Daiber, 'Wāṣil ibn 'Aṭā' als Prediger und Theologe: ein neuer Text aus dem 8. Jahrhundert n.Chr.', in *Bull. Sch. Or. and Afr. St.* 54, 153–4.

Zonta, M.
1992   *Fonti greche e orientali dell' 'Economia' di Bar-Hebraeus nell'opera 'La crema della scienza'*, *AION* 52.1, Suppl. 70, Naples.

1995   *Un interprete ebreo della filosofia di Galeno. Gli scritti di Galeno nell'opera di Shem Tob ibn Falaquera*, Turin.

INDEX